PHYSICS for Scientists and Engineers 1

Third Edition

W. Bauer
G. D. Westfall
Michigan State University

Boston Burr Ridge, IL Dubuque, IA New York San Francisco St. Louis
Bangkok Bogotá Caracas Lisbon London Madrid
Mexico City Milan New Delhi Seoul Singapore Sydney Taipei Toronto

The McGraw·Hill Companies

Physics for Scientists and Engineers 1
Third Edition

1 2 3 4 5 6 7 8 9 0 DIG DIG 0 9 8 7

ISBN 13: 978-0-07-723149-1
ISBN-10: 0-07-723149-X

Custom Publishing Specialist: James Doepke
Production Editor: Susan Culbertson
Printer/Binder: Digital Impressions

Table of Contents

The Big Picture: Modern Physics Frontiers

Throughout this book we will attempt to give you insight into the astounding recent progress made in all fields of physics, and to give you examples from these advanced areas that are accessible even with the knowledge available at the introductory level. At many top research universities freshmen and sophomores are already intimately involved in cutting-edge physics research. Often, this participation requires nothing more than the tools developed in the course of this book, a few days or weeks of additional reading, and the necessary curiosity and willingness to learn new facts and skills.

In the following couple of pages we will introduce you to some of the amazing new cutting-edge physics research that is going on at present and the results that have been obtained during the last few years. This introduction is held at a qualitative level, skipping all mathematical and other technical details. It is meant to wet your appetite for things to come, and we will return to most or all of these advanced topics periodically throughout the book, for a more in-depth exploration.

The year 2005 marked the 100th anniversary of Albert Einstein's landmark papers on Brownian motion (proving that atoms are real, see chapters 13 for an overview and then 38 for an in-depth discussion), on the theory of relativity (which we will cover in chapter 35 of this book) and on the photoelectric effect (which we will cover in chapter 36). Quantum physics is a product of the 20th century and has for example led to the invention of lasers, which are now routinely used in CD and DVD players, as well as for eye surgery, among many other applications. It also has given us a more fundamental understanding of chemistry; physicists are now using ultra-short laser pulses of less than 10^{-15} s duration to gain an understanding of the time development of chemical bonds. The quantum revolution has given us exotic discoveries like antimatter. And there is still no end in sight: only during the last decade Bose-Einstein condensates of atoms confined to electromagnetic traps have been formed; this has opened an entire new realm of research in atomic and quantum physics.

Physics innovation has been driving the modern high-tech industry. Only slightly more than 50 years ago the first transistor was invented at Bell Labs, ushering in the electronic age. Now the typical home computer or laptop contains more than 100 million transistor elements in its central processing unit. The rise of computers and their incredible growth in power has been made possible by the research in condensed matter physics during the last few decades. Gordon Moore, co-founder of Intel, famously stated that computer processing power doubles every 18 months. And this tendency is predicted to continue for at least another decade or more. Computer storage capacity, i.e. memory, grows even faster, with a doubling cycle of 12 months. Network capacity even doubles every nine months. And so you can now go to almost every country on Earth and find wireless access points, from which you can connect your laptop to the Internet; yet it is only slightly more than one decade after the initial conception of the World Wide Web by Tim Berners-Lee, who was then working at the European particle physics laboratory CERN in Switzerland.

Cell phones and other new and ever-more powerful communication devices have found their way into just about everybody's hands. Modern physics research enables a continuous miniaturization of consumer electronics devices. This drives a digital convergence, making it possible to equip cell phones with digital cameras, video recorders, email capability, web browsers, and global positioning system receivers. More functionality is added continuously, while prices continue to fall. Less than 40 years after the first Moon landing, advanced cell phone devices are now packing more computing power than the Apollo space ships had.

And physics is by no means done pushing the limits of computing. At present, many physics groups are investigating ideas to build a quantum computer. Theoretically, a quantum computer consisting of N processors should be able to execute 2^N instructions simultaneously, whereas a conventional computer consisting of N processors can only execute N instructions at the same time. Thus the perfect quantum computer consisting of 100 processors would outperform the combined computing power of all present day supercomputers in the world. To be sure, many deep problems have to be solved before this vision can become reality, but then again 50 years ago it also seemed utterly impossible to pack 100 million transistors onto a computer chip the size of a thumbnail.

But the interaction between physics and computers works both ways. Traditionally, physics investigations were either experimental or theoretical in nature. Necessarily, a textbook favors the theoretical side, as it develops the main conceptual ideas and formulas of physics. On the other hand much research originates on the experimental side, where new phenomena first seem to defy a theoretical description. However, with the arrival of computers a third branch of physics has become possible: computational physics. Most physicists now rely on the computer to process data, to visualize data, to process large sets of coupled equations, or to study systems for which simple analytical formulations are not known. The emerging science of chaos and non-linear dynamics is the prime example for the latter. Arguably MIT atmospheric physicist Edward Lorenz found the first example for chaotic behavior with the aid of a computer in 1963, when he solved three coupled equations for a simple model of weather and detected a sensitive dependence on the initial conditions. Solutions that were initially very close to each other ran away from each other exponentially in time. This is now sometimes called the "butterfly effect", because a butterfly flapping its wings in China could change the weather in the USA a few days or weeks later. This implies that long-term deterministic weather prediction is impossible.

Systems of many constituents can often exhibit very complex behavior, even if the individual constituents follow very simply rules or chaotic dynamics. Physicists have started to address complexity in many systems, including simple sand piles, traffic jams, the stock market, biological evolution, fractals, and self-assembly of molecules and nanostructures. The science of complexity is again a field of research that was only discovered during the last decade and experiences rapid growth.

We will return to chaos and non-linear dynamics soon, in chapter 7 on momentum and in chapter 14 on oscillations. Often the models encountered are quite straightforward, and even first-year physics students can make valuable contributions, but their solution requires some computer programming skills. We recommend that you acquire some programming expertise as soon as possible; this will enable you to contribute to many advanced physics research projects right away.

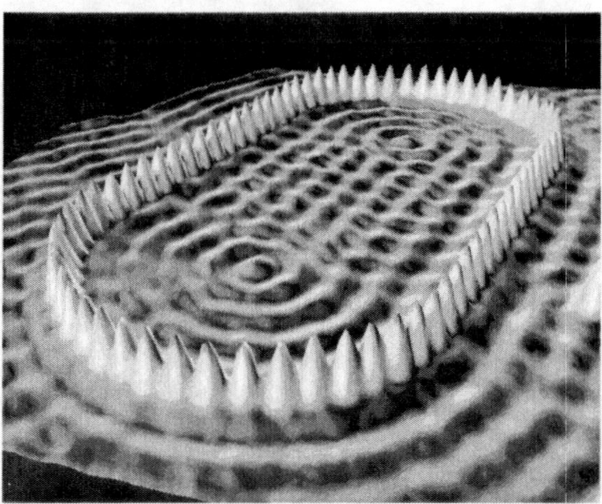

Figure 1: Individual iron atoms, arranged in the shape of a stadium on a copper surface. The ripples inside the stadium show the electron density. This arrangement was created by using a scanning tunneling microscope.

Physicists are beginning to acquire the knowledge and skills to manipulate matter one atom at a time. During the last two decades the scanning, tunneling, and atomic force microscopes were invented and now enable us to see individual atoms, as in Figure 1. In some special cases we can even begin to move atoms around in controlled ways. Nanoscience and nanotechnology are devoted to these types of problems and carry the promise for great technological advances, from even more miniaturized and thus more powerful electronics, to the design of new drugs, or even the manipulation of DNA to cure some diseases.

Just as physicists moved into the domain of chemists during the 20th century, the 21st century will see a rapid interdisciplinary convergence of physics and molecular biology. Already now we are able to use laser tweezers, covered in our chapter 34 on wave optics, to move individual bio-molecules. X-ray crystallography, also introduced in chapter 34, has become sophisticated enough that we can obtain pictures of very complicated proteins and their three-dimensional structures. And theoretical biophysics is beginning to be successful in predicting the spatial structure and the associated functionality of these molecules from their coding as a sequence of amino acids.

We will return to some of these recent biophysics advances later in this book, but Figure 2 can give us a taste of what is currently possible. Shown is a model calculation of the spatial structure of the RNA Polymerase II protein, with the color-coding representing the charge distribution (blue: positive, red: negative) at the surface of this bio-molecule. (Chapter 23 is on the subject of electrostatic potentials and will give us an understanding of the methods needed to calculate charge distributions and their potentials, albeit for much simpler arrangements.) Shown also is a segment of the DNA molecule (yellow spiral structure in the center), giving us a microscopic understanding of how RNA Polymerase II attaches to DNA and functions as a cleaver.

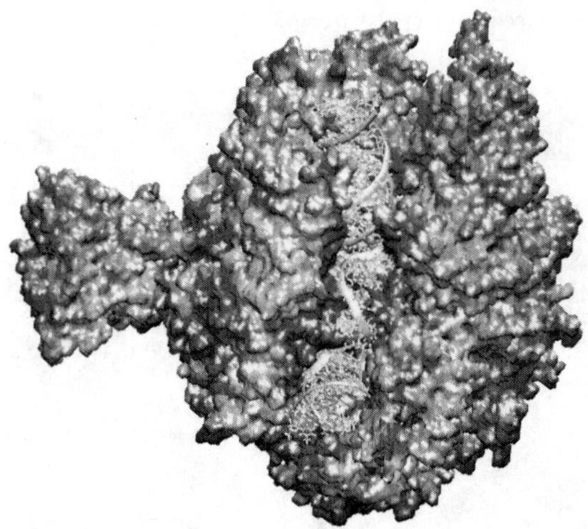

Figure 2: Model calculation of the RNA Polymerase II protein.

Sixty years ago, nuclear physicist Hans Bethe and his colleagues figured out that nuclear fusion in our Sun produces the light that makes life on Earth possible. Now nuclear physicists are working to utilize nuclear fusion energy, with the promise of nearly limitless energy production. In chapter 5 we will discuss the concept of energy and return to it numerous times throughout this book. The international thermonuclear fusion reactor (see chapter 40), which will be constructed soon in a collaboration of many industrialized countries, will go a long way toward answering many of the important experimental and theoretical questions that need to be solved before fusion energy is technically feasible and commercially viable.

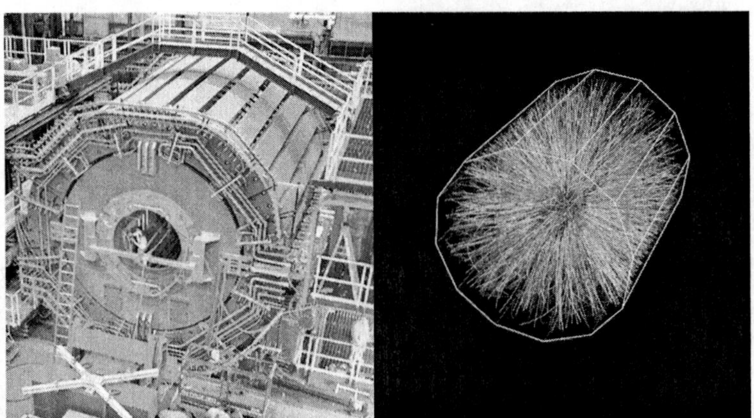

Figure 3: Left side: photograph of the STAR detector at RHIC during its construction; right side: electronically reconstructed tracks of more than 5,000 subatomic charged particles produced inside the STAR detector as a result of a central collision of two gold nuclei.

Nuclear and particle physicists are also probing deeper and deeper into the smallest constituents of matter. Most of chapters 39 and 40 is devoted to letting you experience this quest. At Brookhaven National Laboratory, Brookhaven, Long Island, for example, the Relativistic Heavy Ion Collider (RHIC) smashes two gold nuclei into each other in order to re-create the state of the Universe only a small fraction of a second after its beginning, called the Big Bang. Figure 3a is a photo of STAR, a RHIC detector, while Figure 3b shows a computer analysis of the tracks left in the STAR detector by the more than 5,000 subatomic particles produced in such a collision. In chapters 27 and 28 on magnetism and magnetic field we will explain how to analyze these tracks in order to find the properties of the particles that produced the tracks.

An even bigger instrument for particle physics research is under construction at the European CERN accelerator laboratory in Geneva, Switzerland. The Large Hadron Collider (LHC) is located in a circular underground tunnel of 27 km (16.8 miles) circumference, indicated by the red circle in Figure 4. Starting in 2008, particle physicists will use this facility to try to find out what causes different elementary particles to have different masses.

Figure 4: Aerial view of Geneva, Switzerland, with the underground tunnel of the Large Hadron Collider ring indicated in red.

While particle physics has a standard model of all particles and their interactions (see chapter 39), we still do not understand why this model works so well and what the underlying structure is. String theory is currently thought to be the most likely candidate for a framework that will eventually provide this explanation. Sometimes string theory is hubristically called the "theory of everything", and many theoretical physicists are currently working on fleshing it out.

Physics and astronomy have strong interdisciplinary overlap when it comes to investigating the history of the early universe, or to modeling the evolution of stars, or to studying the origin of gravitational waves or cosmic rays of the highest energies. Ever-more precise and sophisticated observatories, like for example the Very Large Array (VLA) radio telescope in New Mexico (Figure 5), have been built to study these questions.

Figure 5: Some of the 27 individual radio telescopes that are part of the Very Large Array.

Astrophysicists continue to make astounding discoveries and continue to reshape our understanding of the universe. Only during the last few years have we begun to appreciate that most of the matter in the universe is not contained in stars. This "dark matter" is still unknown in its composition; see our chapter 12 on gravitation. But we can see the effects of dark matter through "gravitational lensing", as shown in Figure 6 by the arcs observed in the galaxy cluster Abell 2218. These arcs are images of very distant galaxies, distorted by the presence of large quantities of dark matter. We will return to this phenomenon in our chapter 35 on relativity.

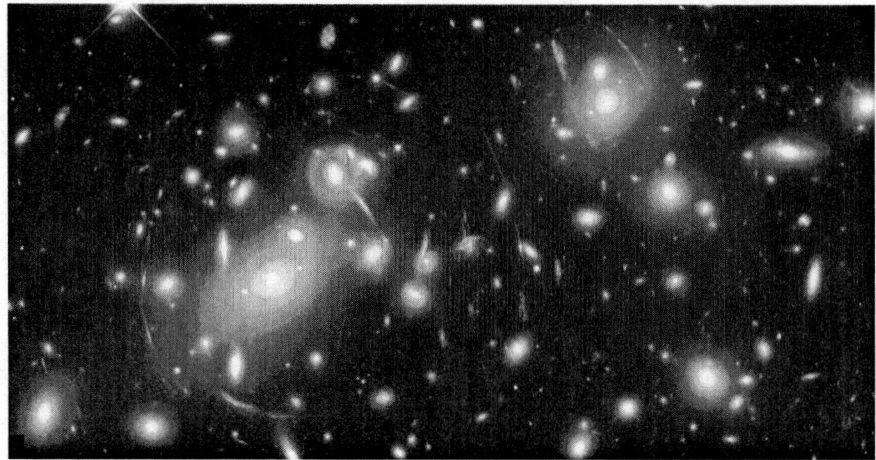

Figure 6: Galaxy cluster Abell 2218, with the arcs that are created by gravitational lensing from dark matter.

From the smallest sub-atomic particles and strings to the universe at large, physical laws govern all of the structure and dynamics. We have discovered a lot, but each new discovery opens more unknown territory. Physicists continue to construct theories to help us understand the world around us. What guides the development of these theories is of course the ability to match experimental facts. But in addition, we also hold the conviction that symmetry, simplicity, and elegance are the design principles of any good theory. The fact that laws of nature can be formulated in often very simple mathematical equations ($F = ma$, $E = mc^2$, and many other, less famous ones) nevertheless is stunning.

In this section we have tried to convey a little bit of the flavor of modern physics research at the frontiers. Hopefully, our introductory textbook will help you build the foundation to appreciate, understand, and perhaps even participate in this vibrant research enterprise that continues to refine and in many cases even to reshape our understanding of the world around us.

Chapter 1: Overview

What we will learn:

- To appreciate studying physics and reading this book are good ideas.
- To use scientific notation and the appropriate number of significant figures.
- To utilize the international unit system and to learn the definitions of the base units.
- To use the incredible range of length, mass, and time scales available to establish reference points for grasping the vast diversity of systems in physics.
- To apply several problem-solving strategies that will be useful in fulfilling job qualifications in many sectors of our economy.
- To work with vectors: addition, subtraction, multiplication with scalars, unit vectors, length and direction of vectors.

1.1. Why Study Physics?

So, why study physics? Perhaps your initial answer to this question will be: "Because it is required for my major!" While this is certainly a worthy motivation, let us try to point out a few additional benefits.

First, physics is the science upon which all other natural and engineering sciences are built on. All of our technological advances, from laser surgery to television, from computers to refrigerators, from cars to airplanes, directly trace back to basic physics. A good grasp of the essential physics concepts ensures a solid foundation on which to construct advanced knowledge in all sciences. The conservation laws and symmetry principles you will learn invariably will also hold true in all other aspects of science and life in general.

The study of physics serves to help us grasp the scales and orders of magnitude in our world, from the smallest constituents inside the nuclei of atoms, to the galaxies that make up our universe. All of them follow the same basic laws of physics, thus providing a unifying concept.

Physics is intimately connected with mathematics. It brings the abstract concepts of mathematics, such as the ones used in trigonometry, algebra, or calculus, to life. Analytical thinking and general techniques for problem solving are practiced here and will remain useful for the rest of your life.

Science, and in particular physics, is the way to remove irrationality from our models of explanation for the world around us. Pre-scientific thinking was forced to resort to mythology to explain natural phenomena. For example, the old Germanic tribes believed thunder to be caused by the god Thor using his hammer. You may smile when you read this, knowing that thunder and lightning come from electric discharges in the atmosphere. However, if you read the daily news, you will see that even in the 21st century some misconceptions and examples from pre-scientific thinking still persist. But by and large the scientific progress over the last millennium has accomplished a more rational explanation for the natural world surrounding us. The study of physics will enable you to benefit from this progress.

Through consistent theories and well-designed experiments, physics has helped us obtain a deeper understanding of our surroundings, and has given us greater ability to control them. You may not find the answer to the meaning of life in this course, but at the very least you will come away with some of the intellectual tools that enable you to weed out inconsistent, logically-flawed theories that are in contradiction to experimentally verifiable facts. In order to accomplish this you need to acquire scientific literacy, an essential tool for a citizen in our technology-driven society.

One cannot become scientifically literate without command of the necessary elementary tools, just like it is impossible to make music without the ability to play an instrument. This command is the main purpose of this introductory text: to properly equip you so that you can start to make sound contributions to the important discussions of our time. You will emerge from reading and working with this text with a deeper appreciation for the fundamental laws that govern our universe and for the tools that mankind has developed to uncover them, tools that transcend cultures and historic eras.

1.2. Working with Numbers

Scientists have established rules to communicate quantitative information to each other. If you want to report the result of a measurement, for example the distance between two cities, your own weight, or the length of a lecture, then you have to specify this result in multiples of a unit. So your answer will be the product of a number and a unit.

At first sight, there is not much to writing down numbers. But we need to deal with two complications, one is how to deal with very big or very small numbers, and the other is how to specify precision.

Scientific Notation

If a number we want to quote gets to be really big, it becomes tedious to write it out. For example, there are approximately 7,000,000,000,000,000,000,000,000,000 atoms in the human body. If you use this number often, you surely would like to have a more compact notation for it. This is exactly what scientific notation accomplishes. In it, we represent numbers as the product of a simple number (called the mantissa) and a power (or exponent) of ten.

$$\text{number} = \text{mantissa} \cdot 10^{\text{exponent}} \tag{1.1}$$

The number of atoms in the human body can then be written as $7 \cdot 10^{27}$, nice and compact, where 7 is the mantissa and 27 is the exponent.

What is even better is the ease with which we can multiply and divide large numbers in this scientific notation. In order to multiply to numbers in scientific notation, we multiply their mantissas and then add their exponents. If we had the urge, for example, to find out approximately how many atoms are contained in the bodies of all people on Earth, we could do this rather easily. Earth hosts approximately 7 billion ($= 7 \cdot 10^9$) humans (We will reach this number in the year 2012!). All we have to do to find our answer is to multiply $7 \cdot 10^{27}$ by $7 \cdot 10^9$. We do this task by multiplying the two mantissas and adding the exponents:

$$(7 \cdot 10^{27}) \cdot (7 \cdot 10^9) = (7 \cdot 7) \cdot 10^{27+9} = 49 \cdot 10^{36} = 4.9 \cdot 10^{37} \tag{1.2}$$

In the last step, we follow the common convention that we keep only one digit in front of the decimal point of the mantissa, and adjust the exponent accordingly. (But please be advised that we will have to adjust our answer a little in the end – read on!)

Division is equally straightforward: If we want to calculate A / B, we divide the mantissa of A by that of B and multiply this by 10 to the power of (the exponent of A minus the exponent of B).

In-class exercise:
The surface of Earth, including area covered by the oceans, is $A = 4\pi R^2 = 4\pi (6370\text{ km})^2 = 5.099 \cdot 10^{14}\text{ m}^2$. Assuming that there are 7.0 billion humans on the planet, what is the area per person that is available?
a) $7.3 \cdot 10^4\text{ m}^2$
b) $7.3 \cdot 10^{24}\text{ m}^2$
c) $3.6 \cdot 10^{24}\text{ m}^2$
d) $3.6 \cdot 10^4\text{ m}^2$

Significant Figures

When we just specified the number of atoms in the human body as $7 \cdot 10^{27}$, we meant to indicate that we know that it is at least 6.5 10^{27} and smaller than 7.5 10^{27}. But if we had written $7.0 \cdot 10^{27}$ instead, we would have implied that we know that the real answer is somewhere between 6.95 10^{27} and 7.05 10^{27}. This statement is much more precise and thus stronger than the one we made in the last section.

As a general rule, the number of digits you write down in the mantissa specifies how precisely you claim you know it. The more digits specified, the more precision is implied. We also call this number of digits we write down the number of "significant figures".

Here are some rules and examples:

- The number 1.62 has 3 significant digits; 1.6 has 2 significant digits.
- If you give a number as an integer, then you specify it with infinite precision. Example: If someone says that he or she has 3 children, this really means absolutely exactly 3, no less, no more.
- Leading zeros do not count for our significant digits. 1.62 has the same number of significant digits as 0.00162. It is 3 in both cases. We only start counting from the left at the first non-zero digit.
- Trailing zeros, on the other hand, do count. 1.620 has 4 significant digits. Writing down a trailing zero implies a greater precision!
- Numbers in scientific notation have as many significant digits as their mantissa. Example: the number $9.11 \cdot 10^{-31}$ has 3 significant digits because that's what the mantissa (9.11) specifies. The size of the exponent has no influence.
- You can never have more significant figures than you start with in any of the factors of a multiplication or division. Example: 1.23 / 3.4461 is not equal to 0.3569252. Your calculator may give you that answer, but the number of significant figures displayed by the calculator is not correct. Instead, 1.23 / 3.4461 = 0.357. Rounding to the proper number of significant digits is required.
- You can only add or subtract when there are significant figures for that place in every number. Example: 1.23 + 3.4461 = 4.68, and not 4.6761 as you may think. This rule, in particular, requires some getting used to.

So let us return to the problem of the number of atoms in the human race. We started with two quantities that were only given to one significant figure. So the result of our multiplication needs to be properly rounded to one significant digit. The combined number of atoms in all bodies of humankind is thus $5 \cdot 10^{37}$.

In-class exercise:
How many significant digits are in the following numbers?
a) 2.150
b) 0.000215
c) 215.00
d) 0.215000
e) 0.215 + 0.21

1.3. SI Unit System

In high school you may have been introduced to the international system of units and may have had it compared to the old British system of units that is in use in the United States. Or you may have driven on a freeway on which the distances are posted both in miles and in kilometers (a practice common in Canada).

Table 1.1: Unit names and abbreviations for the base units of physical quantities described by the SI system of units.

Unit	Abbreviation	Base unit for
meter	m	length
kilogram	kg	mass
second	s	time
Ampere	A	current
Kelvin	K	temperature
mole	mol	amount of a substance
candela	cd	luminous intensity

The international system of units is often abbreviated as SI units (Système International). Sometimes you will also find the expression “metric units”. The base units for the SI system are given in Table 1.1.

Figure 1.1: Photograph of Earth. Originally, the meter was defined as one ten-millionth of the length of the meridian through Paris from the North Pole to the Equator.

From the first letters of the first four base units derives another commonly used name for the SI system, the "MKSA" system. We will use the first three units (meter, kilogram, and second) for the entire first part of the book and all of mechanics. The definitions of these base units are:

- 1 meter is the distance that a light beam in vacuum travels in 1/299,792,458 of a second. The symbol for the meter is m. Previously the meter was related to the size of the Earth, as indicated in Figure 1.1.
- 1 kilogram of mass is defined as the mass of the international prototype of the kilogram. This prototype, shown in its elaborate storage container in Figure 1.2, is located outside Paris, France, under carefully controlled environmental conditions. The symbol for the kilogram is kg.
- 1 second is the time interval during which 9,192,631,770 oscillations of the wave that corresponds to the transition between the two specific states of the cesium-133 atom take place. Up until 1967 the standard for the second was 1/86,400 of a mean solar day. But now we use the previously mentioned atomic definition because it is more precise and more easily reproducible. The symbol for the second is s.

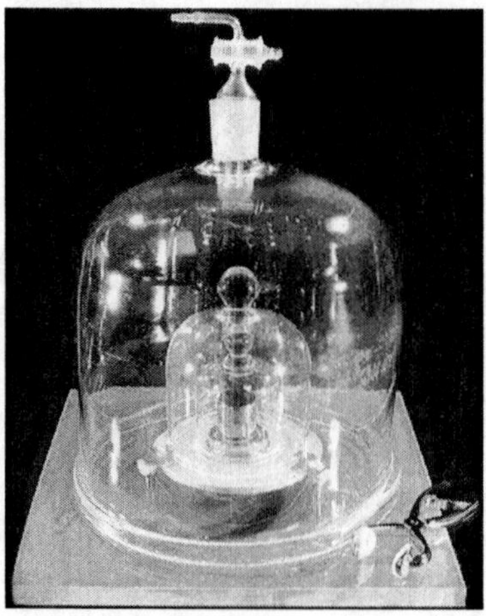

Figure 1.2: Prototype of the kilogram, stored in Paris, France.

Notation Convention: It is common practice to use roman letters for the units and italic letters for the physical quantities. We will always follow this convention in this book. For example "m" stands for the unit "meter", while "*m*" is use for the physical quantity "mass". So the expression "m = 17.2 kg" specifies that the mass of an object is 17.2 kilogram.

Table 1.2: SI derived units that have received their own names.

Derived Quantity	Name	Symbol	Expressions	
Absorbed dose	gray	Gy	J/kg	$m^2\ s^{-2}$
Activity	becquerel	Bq	-	s^{-1}
Angle	radian	rad	-	-
Capacitance	farad	F	C/V	$m^{-2}\ kg^{-1}\ s^4\ A^2$
Catalytic activity	katal	kat	-	s^{-1} mol
Dose equivalent	sievert	Sv	J/kg	$m^2\ s^{-2}$
Electric charge	coulomb	C	-	s A
Electric conductance	siemens	S	A/V	$m^{-2}\ kg^{-1}\ s^3\ A^2$
Electric potential	volt	V	W/A	m^2 kg $s^{-3}\ A^{-1}$
Electric resistance	ohm	Ω	V/A	m^2 kg $s^{-3}\ A^{-2}$
Energy	joule	J	N m	m^2 kg s^{-2}
Force	newton	N	-	m kg s^{-2}
Frequency	hertz	Hz	-	s^{-1}
Illuminance	lux	lx	lm/m^2	m^{-2} cd
Inductance	henry	H	Wb/A	m^2 kg $s^{-2}\ A^{-2}$
Luminous flux	lumen	lm	cd sr	cd
Magnetic flux	weber	Wb	V s	m^2 kg $s^{-2}\ A^{-1}$
Magnetic flux density	tesla	T	Wb/m^2	kg $s^{-2}A^{-1}$
Power	watt	W	J/s	m^2 kg s^{-3}
Pressure	pascal	Pa	N/m^2	m^{-1} kg s^{-2}
Solid angle	steradian	sr	-	-
Temperature	degree Celsius	°C	-	K

All other units for all physical quantities can be derived from the seven base units of Table 1.1. The unit for area, for example, is m^2. The units for volume and mass density are m^3 and kg/m^3, respectively. The units for velocity and acceleration are m/s and m/s^2, respectively. Some of the physical quantities have been deemed so important that it was convenient to give them their own name and symbol. Often the name is that of a famous physicist. Table 1.2 lists those 22 derived SI units. In the two Expressions columns, the named unit is listed in terms of other named units and then in terms of SI base units. Included in this table also are the radian and steradian, the dimensionless units of angle and solid angle, respectively.

One can obtain valid SI-recognized multiples of the base units by multiplication with various factors of 10. These factors have universal letter abbreviations as shown in Table 1.3. It is thus easy to determine, for example, how many centimeters (cm) are in a kilometer (km):

$$1 \text{ km} = 10^3 \text{ m} = 10^3 \text{ m} \cdot (10^2 \text{ cm/m}) = 10^5 \text{ cm} \quad (1.3)$$

Compare this to how tedious it is to figure out how many inches are in a mile:

$$\begin{aligned} 1 \text{ mile} &= 1{,}760 \text{ yards} \\ &= 1{,}760 \text{ yards} \cdot (3 \text{ feet/yard}) \\ &= 5{,}280 \text{ feet} \cdot (12 \text{ inches/foot}) \\ &= 63{,}360 \text{ inches} \end{aligned} \quad (1.4)$$

As you can see, not only do you have to memorize more odd conversion factors, but your calculations also become vastly more complicated. In the SI system you only have to know the standard letter prefixes shown in Table 1.3, and how to add or subtract integers in the power of 10.

Table 1.3: SI standard prefixes.

Factor	Name	Symbol	Factor	Name	Symbol
10^{24}	yotta	Y	10^{-24}	yocto	y
10^{21}	zetta	Z	10^{-21}	zepto	z
10^{18}	exa	E	10^{-18}	atto	a
10^{15}	peta	P	10^{-15}	femto	f
10^{12}	tera	T	10^{-12}	pico	p
10^{9}	giga	G	10^{-9}	nano	n
10^{6}	mega	M	10^{-6}	micro	μ
10^{3}	kilo	k	10^{-3}	milli	m
10^{2}	hecto	h	10^{-2}	centi	c
10^{1}	deka	da	10^{-1}	deci	d

This international system of units has been with us since 1792 and is now used in almost all countries of the world, the one notable exception being the United States. Of course we agree that the international system has incredible computational advantages. But we also realize that at the end of the day we buy milk and gasoline in gallons, not in liters. Our cars show speed in miles per hour, not meters per second. And when we go to the lumberyard, we also get our two-by-fours (1.5 inches by 3.5 inches actually, but this is a different story). So it is clear that we use British units in our daily lives. And in this book we will use British units where appropriate, to establish the connections with our everyday experiences. But we will provide the conversions to SI units as well. And of course we will essentially always use the SI unit system in our calculations, because we do not want to have to remember all of the British unit conversion factors. We hope that this establishes a happy compromise until that day when the US decides to convert as well.

Figure 1.3: Artist Rendition of the Mars Climate Orbiter, a victim of faulty unit conversion.

The use of British units can be costly. This cost can range from a small expense like the necessity for car mechanics to purchase two sets of wrench socket sets, one metric and one British, to the following incident that could be blamed on the use of British units. This event was the crash-landing of the Mars Climate Orbiter spacecraft (Figure 1.3) in September 1999, where one of the engineering teams used British units, while the other one operated in SI units.

The use of the powers of 10 is not even completely consistent within the SI system itself. The only, but very notable, exception is the use of time units that are not factors of 10 times the base unit second:

- 365 days form a year,
- a day has 24 hours,
- an hour contains 60 minutes,
- and a minute consists of 60 seconds.

The early metric pioneers tried to establish a completely consistent metric time unit system, but these attempts met catastrophic failure. And the not-exactly-metric use of time units also extends to some of the derived units. So your European sedan's speedometer will not show speeds in meters per second, but kilometers per hour.

Metrology - Research on Measures and Standards

Our knowledge of the standards for the base units of the SI system is by no means complete. There is a large research enterprise devoted to refining measurement technologies and pushing them to ever-greater precision. This field of research is called *metrology*. In the US, the laboratory that has the primary responsibility for this process is the National Institute for Standards and Technology (NIST). NIST works in collaboration with similar institutes in other countries to provide accepted standards for the SI base units.

One of the current research projects is to find a definition of the kilogram that is based on invariant quantities in nature. This is needed to replace the current definition of the kilogram, which is simply based on the mass of a standard object kept in Paris, as we have seen. The most promising candidate seems to be Project Avogadro, which attempts to define the kilogram with highly purified silicon crystals.

Research on keeping time ever more precisely is at the center of the work of NIST and similar institutions. Figure 1.4 shows the currently most accurate clock at NIST in Boulder, Colorado, the NIST-F1 cesium fountain atomic clock. It is accurate to plus-minus one second in 30 million years! However, NIST researchers are already working on a new optical clock that promises an accuracy of up to 1000 higher than that of the NIST-F1.

More and more precision in time-keeping is needed for many applications in our information society, where signals can travel around the world in less than two tenths of a second. The Global Positioning System is one example of a technology that would be impossible to realize without the precision of atomic clocks and the physics research that enters into their construction.

Figure 1.4: Cesium Fountain Atomic Clock at NIST

1.4. The Scales of our World

The most amazing fact about physics is that its laws govern every object, from the smallest to the largest. The scales of the systems for which physics holds predictive power span many orders of magnitude (powers of 10).

But before we go into this subject in the next three subsections, please keep the following in mind. The numbers quoted here are primarily meant to give you an idea of the scales. Your professor will probably not require you to memorize them; they will typically not be on an exam.

Nomenclature: In the next three sections you will read "on the order of" several times. This phrase means "within a factor of 2 or 3".

Length Scales

In Figure 1.5 you can see length scales that span over 40 orders of magnitude and find some of the physical systems and their characteristic length scales.

Let's start with ourselves. On average, an American women is 5'4" (=1.62 m) tall, and a man measures 5'9" (1.75 m). So the human size is on the order of a meter.

If you reduce the length scale of a human body by a factor of a million, you arrive at the scale of a micrometer, the typical size of a cell in your body, of bacteria, or of microbes.

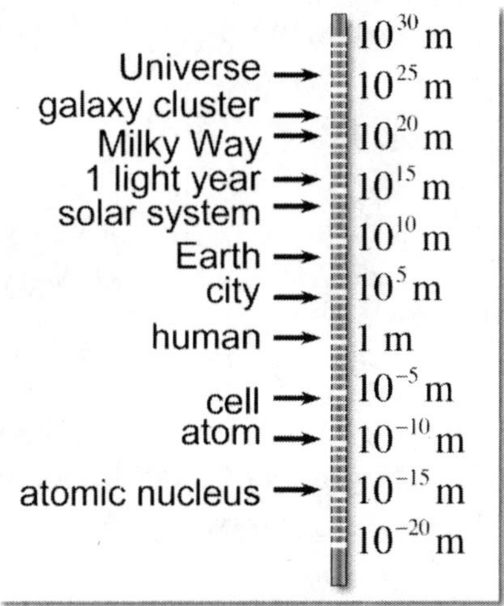

Figure 1.5: Range of length scales of physical systems.

If you reduce the size of your measuring stick by another factor of 10,000, you are at dimensions of 10^{-10} m, the typical size of an individual atom. This dimension is the smallest size that we can resolve with the aide of the most advanced microscopes.

Inside the atom, with a diameter of about a factor of 10,000 less than that of an atom, is the nucleus of the atom, with a size on the order of 10^{-14} m. The individual protons and neutrons that make up the atomic nucleus have a diameter of approximately 10^{-15} m = 1 fm, a femtometer.

If we consider objects larger than ourselves, then we can look at the size of a typical city. It is on the order of kilometers. The diameter of our planet Earth is just a little bigger than 10,000 km. As discussed earlier, the definition of the meter is now stated in terms of the speed of light. However, the meter was originally defined as one ten-millionth of the length of the meridian through Paris from the North Pole to the equator. If a quarter circle has the arc length of ten million meters (= 10,000 km), then the circumference of the entire circle would have been exactly 40,000 km. Using the modern definition of the meter, the circumference of the Earth is a little larger than 40,000 km.

The distance from the Earth to the Moon is 384,000 km, and the distance from the Earth to the Sun is a factor of approximately 500 bigger, 150 million km. Sometimes this distance is called an "astronomical unit" and has the symbol au:

$$1 \text{ au} = 1.495\,98 \cdot 10^{11} \text{ m} \tag{1.5}$$

The size of our solar system is approximately 10^{13} m or 70 au.

We have already remarked that light travels at a speed of approximately 300,000 km/s. So the distance between Earth and Moon is covered by light in just over 1 second, and light from the Sun takes approximately 8 minutes to arrive on Earth. In order to cover distance scales outside our solar system, astronomers have introduced the (non-SI, but handy) unit of the light year, the distance that light can travel in one year:

$$1 \text{ light year} = 9.46 \cdot 10^{15} \text{ m} \tag{1.6}$$

The nearest star to our own Sun is a distance of 4 light years away from us. The Andromeda Nebula, the sister galaxy of our own Milky Way, is about 2 million light years $= 2 \cdot 10^{22}$ m away.

And finally, the radius of the entire Universe is approximately 15 billion light years $= 1.5 \cdot 10^{26}$ m. There are therefore 41 orders of magnitude between the size of an individual proton and that of the entire Universe.

Mass Scales

When you consider the range of the masses of physical objects, you obtain an even more awesome span of orders of magnitudes as illustrated in Figure 1.6.

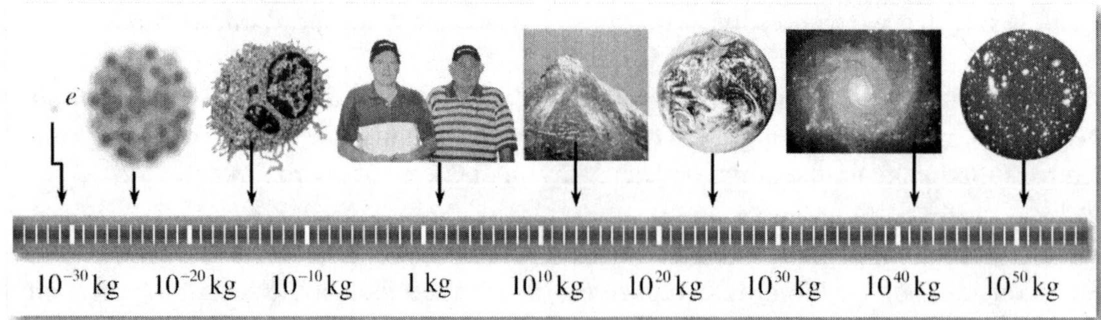

Figure 1.6: Range of mass scales for physical systems.

Atoms and their parts have incredibly small masses. That of an electron is only $9.1 \cdot 10^{-31}$ kg. A proton's mass is $1.67 \cdot 10^{-27}$ kg, roughly a factor of 2,000 more than that of an electron. An individual atom of lead has a mass of $3.4 \cdot 10^{-25}$ kg.

The mass of a single cell in the human body is on the order of 10^{-15} kg to 10^{-14} kg. Even a fly has more than ten billion times the mass of a cell at approximately 10^{-4} kg.
A car's mass is on the order of 10^{3} kg, and that of a passenger plane is on the order of 10^{5} kg.

A typical mountain has a mass of 10^{12} kg to 10^{14} kg, and we estimate the combined mass of all the water in all of the Earth's oceans to be of the order of 10^{19} kg to 10^{20} kg.

The mass of the entire Earth can be specified fairly precisely to be $6.0 \cdot 10^{24}$ kg, and the Sun has a mass of $2.0 \cdot 10^{30}$ kg, 300,000 times the mass of the Earth. Our entire galaxy, the Milky Way, is estimated to have 100 billion stars in it and thus have a mass of $3 \cdot 10^{41}$ kg. Finally, the entire Universe contains billions of galaxies. Depending on the assumptions about dark matter, a currently hot research topic, the mass of the Universe as a whole is roughly 10^{51} kg. But please understand that the latter number is just an estimate and can be up to a factor of 100 off.

Interestingly, there are objects without any mass. For example photons, the "particles" that light is made of, have exactly zero mass.

Time Scales

We can also go through a similar listing of time scales. The human time scales lie in the range of second, the typical duration of a human heartbeat, to a century, the typical lifespan on a person now. Incidentally, the human life expectancy is increasing and increasing at an ever faster rate. During the times of the Roman Empire, 2000 years ago, a person could expect to live only 25 years. Actuary tables listed the mean lifetime of a human as 39 years in 1850. Now that number is 80 years. So it took almost 2000 years to add 50% to the life expectancy, and in the last 150 years the life expectancy has doubled. Science has an ever-increasing role in this process, and this is perhaps the most direct evidence that science has direct benefits for all of us. Physics contributes to this progress with ever more sophisticated imaging and treatment equipment, and what constitutes basic and fundamental research today will enter clinical practice tomorrow. Laser surgery, cancer radiation therapy, magnetic resonance imaging, and positron emission tomography are a few examples.

In their research, the authors study ultra-relativistic heavy ion collisions. These collisions occur during time intervals of the order of 10^{-22} s, more than a million times shorter than the time intervals we can measure directly. During this introductory course of physics we will learn that the time scale for the oscillation of visible light is 10^{-15} s, and that of audible sound 10^{-3} s.

The longest time span we can make a statement about is the age of the universe. Current research puts this number at 13.7 billion years, but there is an uncertainty of up to 1 billion years.

We cannot leave this topic, though, without giving one interesting fact to ponder during your next lecture. These lectures typically last 50 minutes at most universities. A century, by comparison, has $100 \cdot 365 \cdot 24 \cdot 60 \approx 50{,}000{,}000$ minutes. So a lecture lasts about one millionth of a century leading to a handy (non-SI) time unit of the micro-century = duration of a lecture.

1.5. General Problem Solving Strategies

There is more to physics than problem solving. But it is a big part of it. And at times, while you are laboring over your homework assignments, it may seem to you that that's all you do.

A basketball player has to practice the fundamentals of free throw shooting. Many repetitions of the same action enable a good player to become very reliable at this task. We have to develop the same philosophy towards solving mathematics and physics problems. We have to practice good fundamental problem solving techniques. And this will pay huge dividends, not just during the remainder of your physics courses, not just during exams, not even just during the remainder of your college education and in your other science classes, but also in your job later in life.

So what constitutes good problem solving fundamentals? Everybody develops his or her own routines, his or her own procedures, and his or her own shortcuts. However, here is a general blueprint that should get you started:

1. THINK: Read the problem carefully. Ask yourself what quantities are known, what quantities are unknown, and what quantities are asked for in the solution. Write down these quantities and represent them with their commonly used symbolic letters. Convert into SI units, if needed.
2. SKETCH: Make yourself a sketch of the physical situation. This action will help you visualize the problem. For many learning styles, a visual or graphical representation is essential.
3. RESEARCH: Write down the physical principles that apply to this problem. Use formulas that represent these principles to connect the known and the unknown quantities to each other. In some cases you will be able to find an equation that has only the quantities that you know and the one unknown that you are supposed to calculate in it, and nothing else. In general you may have to do a bit of "deriving", i.e. combining two or more known equations into the one that you are looking for. This requires some experience, more than any other of the steps listed here. And to the beginner the task of deriving a new equation may look daunting. But we can guarantee that you will get better at it the more you practice your skills.

4. **SIMPLIFY:** Do not plug in numbers yet! Instead, simplify your result algebraically as much as possible. For example, if your result is expressed as a ratio, cancel out common factors in the numerator and the denominator.
5. **CALCULATE:** Put in the numbers with units and get to work with the pocket calculator. Typically, you will obtain the product of a number and a physical unit as your answer.
6. **ROUND:** Look at the number of significant figures that you want to quote for your result. As a rule of thumb, your result obtained by multiplying or dividing should be rounded to the same number of significant figures as the input quantity given with the least number of significant figures. You should not round in intermediate steps, as rounding too early might give you a wrong solution. Include the proper units in your answer.
7. **DOUBLE-CHECK:** Step back and look at the result. Judge for yourself if the answer (both the number and the units) seems realistic. Often you can prevent handing in a wrong solution by making this final test. Sometimes the units are simply wrong, and you know you must have made an error. Or sometimes the orders of magnitude come out totally wrong. For example, if your task is to calculate the mass of our Sun (we will do this later in this book), and your answer comes out in the range of a few thousand tons, then you know that you made a mistake somewhere.

Let's put this strategy to work in the following example:

Solved Problem

Solved Problem 1.1: Volume of a cylinder

Question:
What is the volume of a cylinder of height $4\frac{13}{16}$ inches and circumference $8\frac{3}{16}$ inches?

Answer:
In order to practice good problem solving skills, we will go through each of the steps above in detail.

THINK: When you read the question above, you will notice that the height of the cylinder is given as:

$$\begin{aligned} h &= 4\tfrac{13}{16}\text{inch} = 4.8125 \text{ inch} \\ &= (4.8125 \text{ inch})\cdot(2.54 \text{ cm/inch}) \\ &= 12.22375 \text{ cm} \end{aligned}$$

Also, the circumference of the cylinder is specified as:

$$\begin{aligned} c &= 8\tfrac{3}{16}\text{inch} = 8.1875 \text{ inch} \\ &= (8.1875 \text{ inch})\cdot(2.54 \text{ cm/inch}) \\ &= 20.79625 \text{ cm} \end{aligned}$$

Obviously, the sizes given were rounded to the nearest 16th of an inch. So it makes no sense to pretend that we can specify 5 digits after the decimal point for our sizes in cm, as the output of our pocket calculator seemed to suggest. A more realistic way to specify the given quantities is thus: $h = 12.2$ cm and $c = 20.8$ cm.

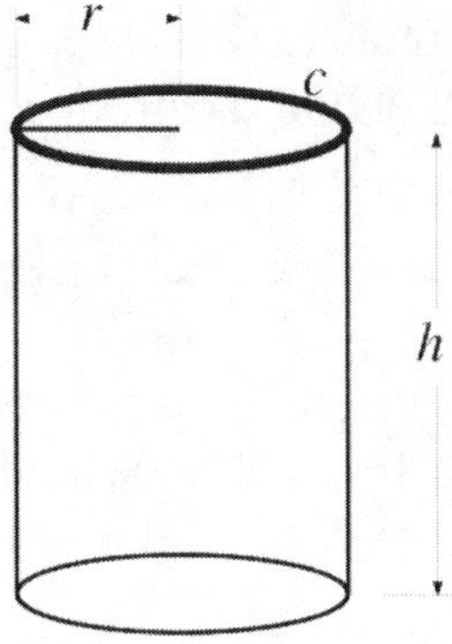

Figure 1.7: Sketch of right cylinder.

SKETCH: Next we produce a sketch. Our sketch could look something like Figure 1.7. Please note that the important given quantities are drawn in with their symbolic representations, not with their numerical values. The circumference is represented by the thicker circular (oval, actually, in this projection) line.

RESEARCH: Now we have to find the volume of the cylinder in terms of its height and its circumference. This is not something commonly listed in formula collections. Instead what you will find is the volume as a product of its base area and height,

$$V = \pi r^2 h \tag{1.7}$$

We have to find a way to connect the radius to the circumference, and we are halfway home. The top and bottom area of a cylinder are circles, and for a circle we know:

$$c = 2\pi r \tag{1.8}$$

SIMPLIFY: Remember: Do not plug in numbers yet! Here is what we can do to simplify our numerical task. We solve the second equation for r and insert this result into the first equation:

$$\begin{aligned} c = 2\pi r \Rightarrow r = \frac{c}{2\pi} \\ V = \pi r^2 h = \pi \left(\frac{c}{2\pi} \right)^2 h = \frac{c^2 h}{4\pi} \end{aligned} \tag{1.9}$$

CALCULATE: Now it is time to get out the pocket calculator and put in the numbers:

$$\begin{aligned} V &= \frac{c^2 h}{4\pi} \\ &= \frac{(20.8 \text{ cm})^2 \cdot (12.2 \text{ cm})}{4\pi} \\ &= 420.026447 \text{ cm}^3 \end{aligned}$$

Solved Problem

Solved Problem

ROUND: The output of our pocket calculator has again made our result look much too precise relative to what we can claim realistically. We need to round. Since the input quantities are only given to 3 significant figures, our result also needs to be rounded to three significant figures. So our final answer would be: $V = 420.\ \text{cm}^3$.

DOUBLE-CHECK: Last step: check if this is reasonable. First we just look at the units that our result came out in. Cubic centimeters are certainly a unit for volume. So our result passes its first test. Now let's look at the magnitude of our result. You might recognize that the height and circumference of the cylinder correspond pretty closely to the corresponding dimensions of a soda can. If you look on a can of your favorite soft drink, it will list its contents as 12 fluid ounces and give you also the information that this is 355 ml. Since $1\ \text{ml} = 1\ \text{cm}^3$, our answer is reasonably close to what the can label tells us. Note that this does *not* tell us that our calculation is correct, but at least it shows us that we are not way off.

Ratios

There is another very common class of problems that physicists like to pose. It asks what happens to a quantity that is dependent on a certain parameter, if you change that parameter by a certain factor. Your physics professor tends to think that this problem is quite easy to solve, and that it will take almost no time to do so. And this is true in general, ***if*** two conditions are met: First, you have to know what formula to use, and second somebody has to have told you once how to solve this class of problems in general. But that is a big "***if***". We will assume that it is up to your studying to equip your memory with the correct formula, but this still leaves the skill of solving problems of this class in general.

Here is the trick: You write down the formula that connects the dependent quantity to the parameter you have to change. You write it down twice, once with index 1, and once with index 2. Then you divide the two equations by each other. You do this by dividing the right-hand sides by each other, and the left-hand sides by each other. Then you insert the factor of change for the parameter and do the calculation to find the factor of change for the dependent quantity.

If this sounds too vague, here is an example problem that shows how to do it:

Example

Example 1.1: Change in volume

Question:
If you increase the radius of a cylinder by a factor of 2.73, by what factor does the volume change? Assume that the height of the cylinder stays the same.

Answer:
The formula that connects the volume of a cylinder, V, to its radius, r, is:

Example

$$V = \pi\, r^2 h \tag{1.10}$$

The way the question is phrased, V is the dependent quantity, and r is the parameter it depends on. The height of the cylinder, h, also appears in the equation. It stays constant, because the problem says so.

According to the general solution process, we write down the equation twice, once with index 1 and once with index 2 attached:

$$\begin{aligned} V_1 &= \pi\, r_1^2 h \\ V_2 &= \pi\, r_2^2 h \end{aligned} \tag{1.11}$$

Now we divide the lower equation by the upper and obtain:

$$\frac{V_2}{V_1} = \frac{\pi\, r_2^2 h}{\pi\, r_1^2 h} = \left(\frac{r_2}{r_1}\right)^2 \tag{1.12}$$

As you can see, h did not receive an index, because it stayed constant in the process and was cancelled out in the division process.

The question states that the change in radius is given by:

$$r_2 = 2.73\, r_1$$

We insert this into our ratio and get:

$$\frac{V_2}{V_1} = \left(\frac{r_2}{r_1}\right)^2 = \left(\frac{2.73\, r_1}{r_1}\right)^2 = 2.73^2 = 7.4529$$

or:

$$V_2 = 7.45\, V_1$$

where we have taken the liberty to round the solution to the same 3 significant digit accuracy that the problem specified. So the answer is that the volume of the cylinder increases by a factor of 7.45 when you increase its radius by a factor of 2.73.

1.6. Vectors

Vectors are quantities that have both magnitude and direction. Vectors occupy an important place in physics and in all of science. Before we can start our study of physics, we therefore need to provide an introduction into the vector concept.

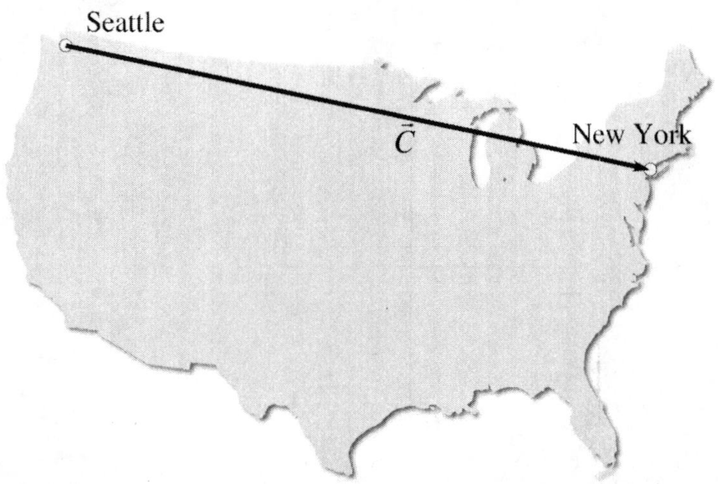

Figure 1.8: Flight from Seattle to New York as an example for a vector.

Vectors have a beginning and an endpoint. For example, consider a flight from Seattle to New York. To represent the change of the plane's position for this flight, you can draw an arrow from the departure of the flight to the destination. (Note: real flight paths are not exactly straight lines due to airspace restrictions and air traffic regulations, but for the present purpose a straight line is a reasonable approximation.) This arrow represents a position vector, which will always go from somewhere to somewhere else. Any vector quantity has a magnitude and a direction. If the vector represents a physical quantity, such as velocity, it will also have a physical unit. A quantity that can be represented without giving a direction is called a scalar. So a scalar quantity has a magnitude and possibly a physical unit. Examples for scalar quantities are time and temperature.

In this book we will always denote a vector quantity by a letter with a small horizontal arrow pointing to the right drawn above it. In our drawing of the trip from Seattle to New York, we have given this trip vector the symbol $\vec{C}$. In the following we will learn how to work with vectors, how to add them, subtract them, and how to multiply them with scalars. In order to perform these operations, it is very useful to introduce a coordinate system in which to represent vectors.

Cartesian Coordinate System

A Cartesian coordinate system is defined as a system of two or more axes with angles of 90 degrees between each pair. These axes are then orthogonal to each other. In a two-dimensional space, the coordinate axes are typically labeled x and y. We can then uniquely specify any point P in a two-dimensional plane by giving its components P_x and P_y along the two coordinate axes as shown. We will use the notation (P_x, P_y) to specify a point in terms of its coordinates. In Figure 1.9, for example, the point P shown has the value (3.3,3.8), because its x-component has a value of 3.3, and its y-component has a value of 3.8. Note that each component is a real number and can have positive or negative values, or be zero.

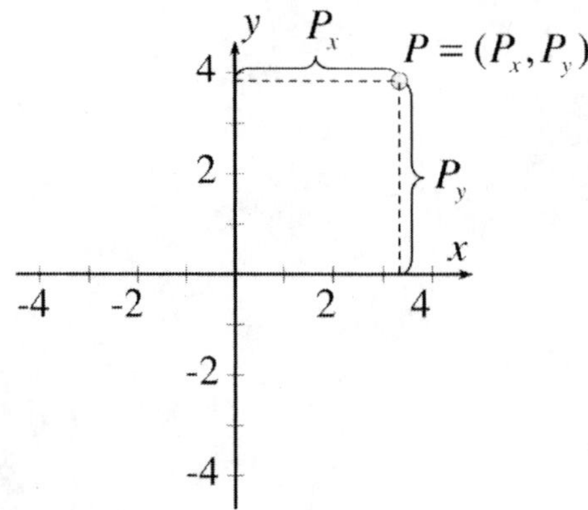

Figure 1.9: Representation of a point *P* in two-dimensional space in terms of its Cartesian coordinates.

One can also define a one-dimensional Cartesian coordinate system, for which any point is located on a single straight line, conventionally called the x-axis. Any point in this one-dimensional space is then uniquely defined by specifying one number, the value of the x-component, which again can be negative, zero, or positive, see Figure 1.10. The point P in this case has an x-component of $P_x = -2.5$ cm .

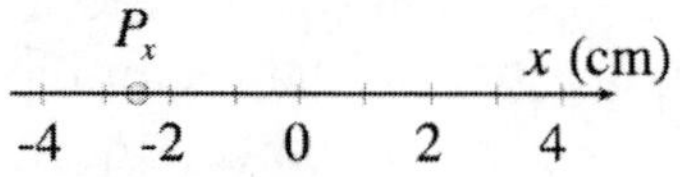

Figure 1.10: Representation of a point P in a one-dimensional Cartesian coordinate system.

Obviously, one- and two-dimensional coordinate systems are easiest to draw, because the surface of the paper has two dimensions. In a true-three-dimensional coordinate system the third coordinate axis would have to be perpendicular to the other two that are in the plane of the page, and would thus have to stick straight out of the surface. In order to draw a three-dimensional coordinate system, one has to rely on conventions that make use of the techniques for perspective drawings. We then represent the third axis by a line that is at a 45-degree angle with the other two, as shown in Figure 1.11.

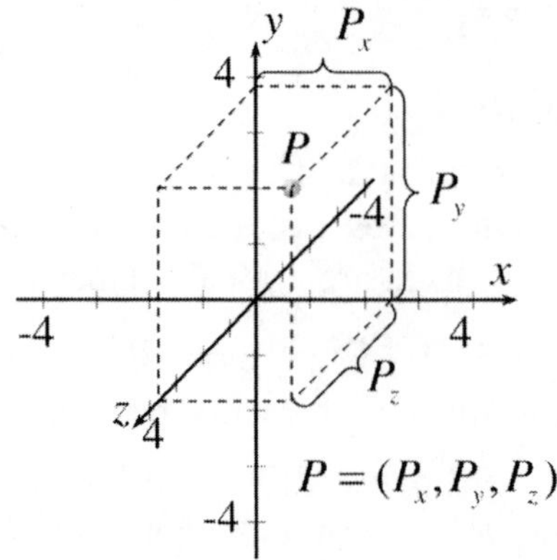

Figure 1.11: Representation of a point P in a three-dimensional space in terms of its Cartesian coordinates.

In a three-dimensional space we have to specify three numbers to uniquely determine the coordinates of a point, and we use the notation $P=(P_x,P_y,P_z)$ to accomplish this. While almost impossible to visualize, we can also construct Cartesian coordinate systems with more than three orthogonal axes. Modern string theories, for example, are constructed in 10-dimensional spaces. However, for the purpose of the present book and for almost all of physics, three dimensions are sufficient. As a matter of fact, for most applications, the essential mathematical and physical understanding can even be obtained from two-dimensional representations.

Cartesian Representation of Vectors

In our example of the flight from Seattle to New York we have already established that vectors are characterized by two points, start and finish, or the tail and tip of an arrow respectively. Since we have just introduced the Cartesian representation of points, we can then define the Cartesian representation of a position vector as the difference in the coordinates of the end point and the starting point. Since only the difference of the two endpoints matters for a vector, we can shift the vector around in space as much as we like. As long as we do not change the length and direction of the arrow, mathematically the vector remains the same. Consider the two vectors in Figure 1.12.

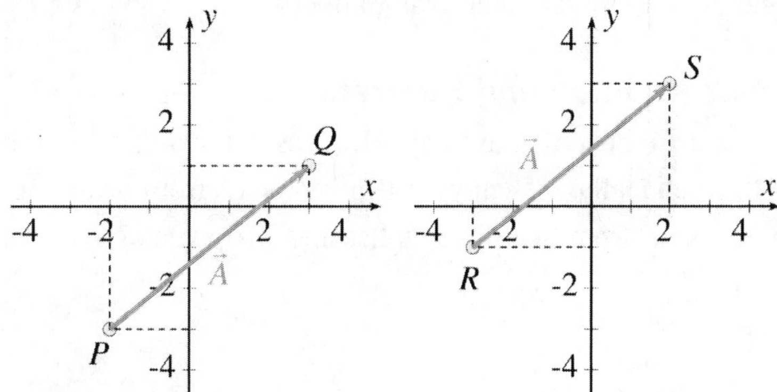

Figure 1.12: Cartesian representation of a vector.

On the left side of Figure 1.12 we show the position vector $\vec{A}$ that points from point $P=(-2,-3)$ to point $Q=(3,1)$. With the definition just introduced, the components of the vector $\vec{A}$ are the components of the point Q minus those of the point P, $\vec{A}=(3-(-2),1-(-3))=(5,4)$. On the right side of this figure we show another vector from point $R=(-3,-1)$ to point $S=(2,3)$. The resulting difference is $(2-(-3),3-(-1)=(5,4)$, which is the same as the vector $\vec{A}$ pointing from P to Q.

For simplicity we can thus shift the beginning of the vector to the origin of the coordinate system, and the components of the vector will be the same as that of its endpoint, see Figure 1.13.

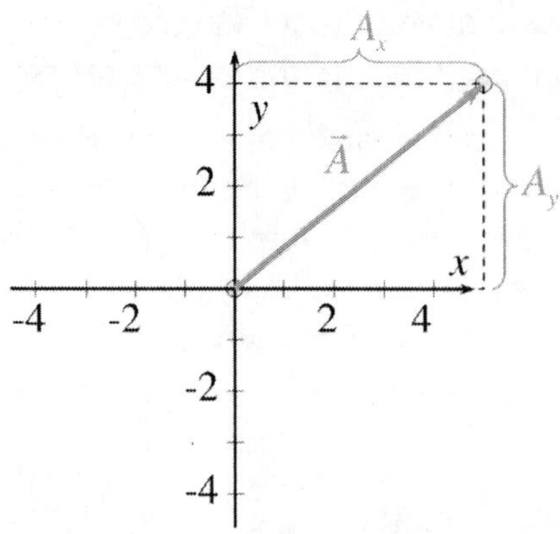

Figure 1.13: Cartesian components of a vector in two dimensions.

As a result, we see that we can represent a vector in Cartesian coordinates via

$$\vec{A} = (A_x, A_y) \text{ in a two-dimensional space} \tag{1.13}$$

$$\vec{A} = (A_x, A_y, A_z) \text{ in a three-dimensional space} \tag{1.14}$$

where A_x, A_y, and A_z are conventional real numbers.

Graphical Vector Addition and Subtraction

Suppose that the direct flight shown in Figure 1.8 was not available, but that you had to use a connection through Dallas. Then your trip vector $\vec{C}$ from Seattle to New York is the sum of a trip vector $\vec{A}$ from Seattle to Dallas and a trip vector $\vec{B}$ from Dallas to New York,

$$\vec{C} = \vec{A} + \vec{B} \tag{1.15}$$

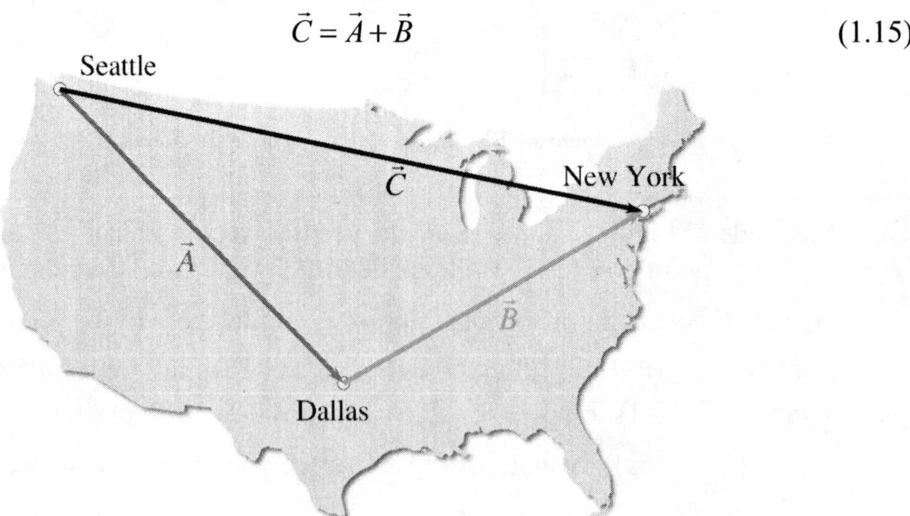

Figure 1.14: Direct flight versus connection flight as an example of vector addition.

This example shows us the general procedure for vector addition in a graphical way: Move the beginning of the second vector to the end of the first vector, and the vector from the beginning of the first vector to the end of the second vector is the sum vector of the two.

If you add two real numbers, the order does not matter. $3+5=5+3$. Everybody would say that this is obvious. This property that the order of summation does not matter is called commutative. Vector addition also is commutative,

$$\vec{A}+\vec{B}=\vec{B}+\vec{A} \tag{1.16}$$

We demonstrate this commutative property of vector addition graphically in Figure 1.15, where we show the same vector addition as in Figure 1.14, but then also move the beginning of vector $\vec{A}$ to the tip of vector $\vec{B}$ (dashed arrows), and find that the resulting sum vector is the same as before.

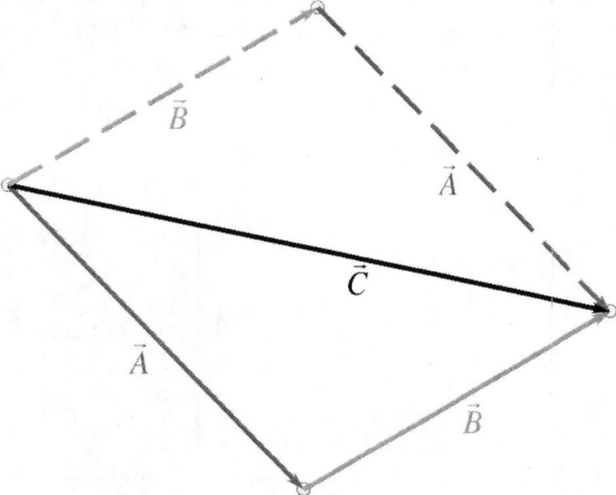

Figure 1.15: Commutative property of vector addition.

Next, we introduce the inverse (or "reverse" or also "negative") vector, $-\vec{C}$, to the vector $\vec{C}$ as a vector with the same length as $\vec{C}$, but pointing in opposite direction.

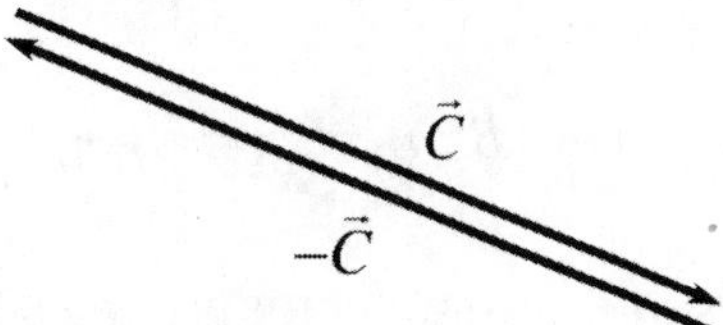

Figure 1.16: Inverse vector.

In our example of flying across the country, the inverse vector is the return trip. Clearly, once you add $\vec{C}$ and its inverse vector $-\vec{C}$, you end up at the same point you started from. So we find that

$$\vec{C}+(-\vec{C})=\vec{C}-\vec{C}=0 \tag{1.17}$$

This seemingly simple identity shows that we can treat vector subtraction just the same way as vector addition, by simply adding the inverse vector. For example, the vector $\vec{B}$ in Figure 1.14 can be obtained as $\vec{B} = \vec{C} - \vec{A}$. So vector addition and subtraction using vector components follow exactly the same rules as the addition and subtraction of real numbers.

Vector Addition in Components

Graphical vector addition is a useful illustration of the concepts, but for practical purposes the component method for addition is much more useful. (This is because calculators are easier to use than rulers and graph paper.) In the following we show the equations for three-dimensional vectors. The equations for two-dimensional vectors are special cases that follow by setting all z-components to 0. And the one-dimensional equation can be obtained by setting all y- and all z-components to 0.

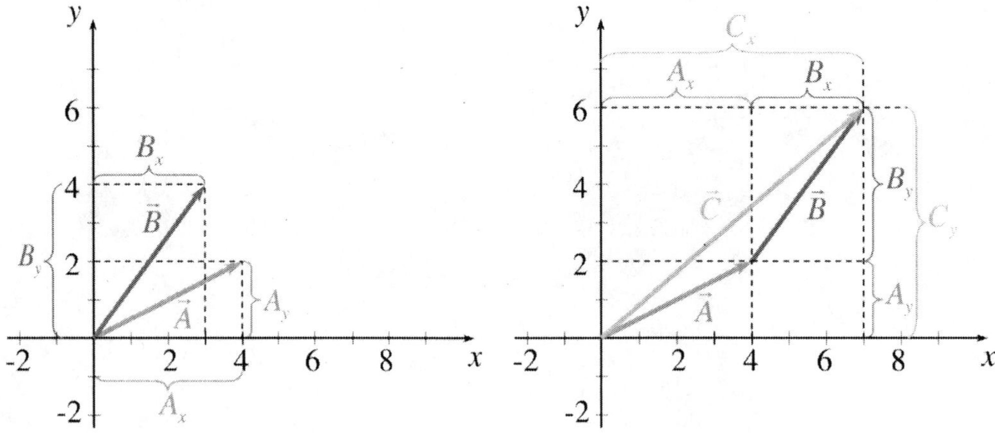

Figure 1.17: Vector addition in components.

If you want to add two vectors $\vec{A} = (A_x, A_y, A_z)$ and $\vec{B} = (B_x, B_y, B_z)$, then the resulting vector is:

$$\vec{C} = \vec{A} + \vec{B} = (A_x, A_y, A_z) + (B_x, B_y, B_z) = (A_x + B_x, A_y + B_y, A_z + B_z) \qquad (1.18)$$

In other words, the components of the sum vector are the sum of the components of the individual vectors,

$$\begin{aligned} C_x &= A_x + B_x \\ C_y &= A_y + B_y \\ C_z &= A_z + B_z \end{aligned} \qquad (1.19)$$

We have illustrated the relationship between graphical and component methods in Figure 1.17. On the left side we show two vectors $\vec{A} = (4,2)$ and $\vec{B} = (3,4)$ in two-dimensional space, and on the right side their sum vector $\vec{C} = (4+3, 2+4) = (7,6)$ is displayed. The right diagram clearly shows that $C_x = A_x + B_x$, since the whole is equal to the sum of its parts.

In the same way we can take the difference $\vec{D} = \vec{A} - \vec{B}$, and the Cartesian components of the difference vector are given by

$$\begin{aligned} D_x &= A_x - B_x \\ D_y &= A_y - B_y \\ D_z &= A_z - B_z \end{aligned} \tag{1.20}$$

Multiplication of a Vector with a Scalar

What is $\vec{A} + \vec{A} + \vec{A}$? If your answer to this question is $3\vec{A}$, you have already understood all there is to multiplying a vector with a scalar. The vector that results from multiplication of the vector $\vec{A}$ with the scalar 3 is a vector that points in the same direction as the original vector $\vec{A}$, but that is 3 times as long.

Multiplication of a vector with an arbitrary positive scalar, i.e. a positive number, results in another vector that is pointing in the same direction, but has a length that is the product of the length of the original vector times the value of the scalar. Multiplication of a vector by a negative scalar results in a vector pointing in the opposite direction to the original with a length that is the product of the length of the original vector times the magnitude of the scalar.

Again, it is useful to involve the component notation. For the multiplication of a vector $\vec{A}$ with a scalar s we obtain:

$$\vec{E} = s\vec{A} = s(A_x, A_y, A_z) = (sA_x, sA_y, sA_z) \tag{1.21}$$

In other words, the length of each component of the vector $\vec{A}$ is multiplied by the scalar in order to arrive at the product vector,

$$\begin{aligned} E_x &= sA_x \\ E_y &= sA_y \\ E_z &= sA_z \end{aligned} \tag{1.22}$$

Unit Vectors

We can introduce special vectors that will make much of the math associated with vectors easier. These are dimensionless vectors of length 1 and directed along the main coordinate axes of the coordinate system. In two dimensions, these are the vectors of length 1 that point in positive x-direction and in positive y-direction. In three dimensions, we add the vector of length 1 in positive z -direction. In order to distinguish these as special vectors, we give them the symbols $\hat{x}$, $\hat{y}$, and $\hat{z}$. Their component representation is

$$\begin{aligned}\hat{x} &= (1,0,0)\\ \hat{y} &= (0,1,0)\\ \hat{z} &= (0,0,1)\end{aligned} \tag{1.23}$$

In Figure 1.18 the unit vectors are shown in two dimensions (left side) and three dimensions (right side).

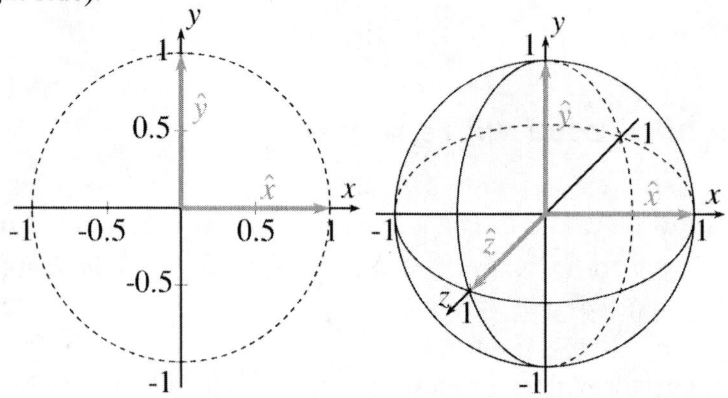

Figure 1.18: Cartesian unit vectors in two (left) and three (right) dimensions.

What is the advantage of introducing unit vectors? Using these unit vectors, we can write any other vector as a sum of these unit vectors, with each unit vector multiplied by the corresponding Cartesian component of the vector, as shown in (1.24).

$$\begin{aligned}\vec{A} &= (A_x, A_y, A_z)\\ &= (A_x,0,0)+(0,A_y,0)+(0,0,A_z)\\ &= A_x(1,0,0)+A_y(0,1,0)+A_z(0,0,1)\\ &= A_x\hat{x}+A_y\hat{y}+A_z\hat{z}\end{aligned} \tag{1.24}$$

or, in two dimensions,

$$\vec{A} = A_x\hat{x}+A_y\hat{y} \tag{1.25}$$

This unit vector representation of a vector will be of value later in the book when we learn to multiply two vectors together.

Vector Length and Direction

Provided we know the component representation of a vector, how can we find out the length of this vector and the direction it is pointing in? Here we answer this question for the most important case, the case of a vector in two dimensions. In two dimensions, a vector $\vec{A}$ can be specified uniquely by giving the two Cartesian components A_x and A_y. We can also uniquely specify the same vector by giving two other numbers, its length A and its angle θ with respect to the positive x-axis.

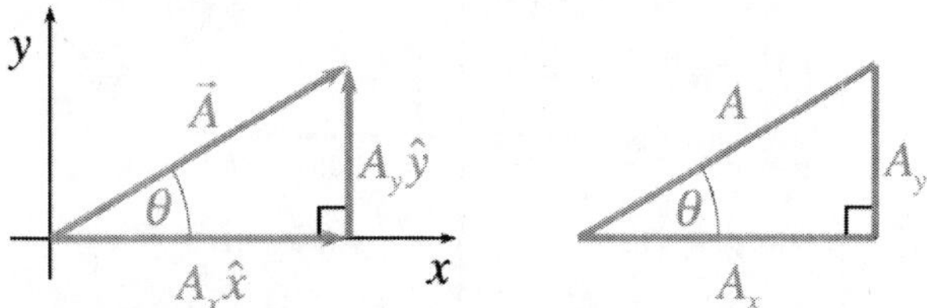

Figure 1.19: Length and direction of a vector.

Please take a look at Figure 1.19 to see how A and θ can be determined from A_x and A_y. On the left side, we show the result of equation (1.25) in graphical representation. The vector $\vec{A}$ is the sum of the vectors $A_x\hat{x}$ and $A_y\hat{y}$. And since the unit vectors $\hat{x}$ and $\hat{y}$ are by definition orthogonal to each other, these vectors form a 90-degree angle. So the three vectors $\vec{A}$, $A_x\hat{x}$, and $A_y\hat{y}$ form a right triangle with side lengths A, A_x, A_y, as shown on the left-hand side of Figure 1.19.

Now we can employ basic trigonometry to find θ and A. Using the Pythagorean theorem results in

$$A = \sqrt{A_x^2 + A_y^2}\,, \tag{1.26}$$

while we can find the angle θ from the definition of the tangent function

$$\theta = \tan^{-1}\frac{A_y}{A_x} \tag{1.27}$$

In equation 1.27 you must be careful that θ is in the correct quadrant. Of course, we can also invert the equations (1.26) and (1.27) to obtain the Cartesian components of a vector of given length and direction,

$$A_x = A\cos\theta \tag{1.28}$$
$$A_y = A\sin\theta \tag{1.29}$$

We will encounter the same trigonometric relations again and again throughout the introductory physics sequence. If you need to re-familiarize yourself with trigonometry, please consult the mathematics primer that we have provided in the appendix.

In-class exercise:
Into which quadrant do the following vectors point?

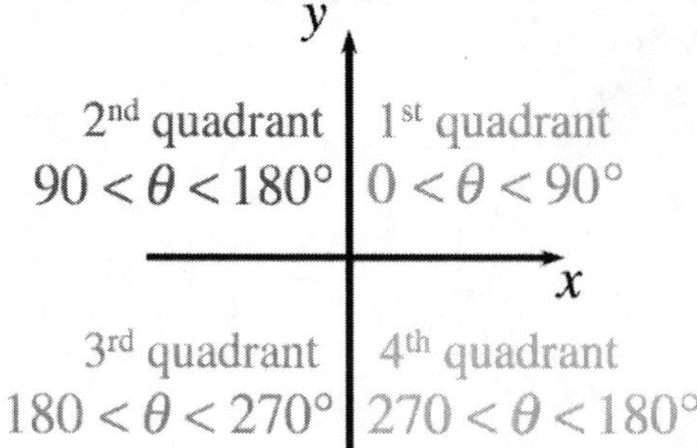

a) $A = (A_x, A_y)$ with $A_x = 1.5$ cm, $A_y = -1.0$ cm
b) A vector of length 2.3 cm and angle of 131 degrees
c) The inverse vector to vector $B = (0.5 \text{ cm}, 1.0 \text{ cm})$
d) The sum of the unit vectors in x and y directions

What we have learned/Exam Study Guide:

- Large and small numbers can be represented using scientific notation consisting of a mantissa and an exponent of ten.
- Physical systems are described by the SI system of units. These units are based on reproducible standards and provide convenient methods of scaling and calculation. The base units of the SI system are meter (m), kilogram (kg), second (s), and Ampere (A). Other units can be obtained from the base units by simple multiplication or division of the base units and powers of 10.
- These physical systems have widely varying sizes, masses, and time scales, but the same physical laws govern all of them.
- A number (with a specific number of significant digits) combined with a unit is used to describe physical quantities.
- Vectors in three dimensions can be specified by their three Cartesian components, $\vec{A} = (A_x, A_y, A_z)$. Each of these Cartesian components is a real number.
- Vector can be added and subtracted. In Cartesian components, $\vec{C} = \vec{A} + \vec{B} = (A_x, A_y, A_z) + (B_x, B_y, B_z) = (A_x + B_x, A_y + B_y, A_z + B_z)$.
- Multiplication of a vector with a scalar results in another vector, $\vec{E} = s\vec{A} = s(A_x, A_y, A_z) = (sA_x, sA_y, sA_z)$.
- Unit vectors are vectors of length 1. The unit vectors in Cartesian coordinate systems are denoted by $\hat{x}$, $\hat{y}$, and $\hat{z}$.
- The length and direction of a two-dimensional vector can be determined from its Cartesian components as $A = \sqrt{A_x^2 + A_y^2}$ and $\theta = \tan^{-1}(A_y / A_x)$.

- The Cartesian components of a two-dimensional vector are calculated from the length and angle with respect to the x-axis via $A_x = A\cos\theta$ and $A_y = A\sin\theta$

Additional Solved Problems

Problem 1.2: Hiking

Question:

If you hike in the Florida Everglades and leave your base camp, head Southwest for 1.72 km, then make a 90 degree right turn and hike another 3.12 km, how far away are you then from your base camp?

Answer:

THINK: If we are hiking, we are moving in a two-dimensional plane, the surface of Earth (which is locally flat, because altitude changes in the Everglades are negligible). Thus we can use two-dimensional vectors to characterize the motion of the hiker. Making one straight-line hike, then performing a turn, followed by another straight-line hike amounts to a problem of vector addition. Phrased in terms of a vector addition problem, our question asks us for the length of the sum vector.

SKETCH:

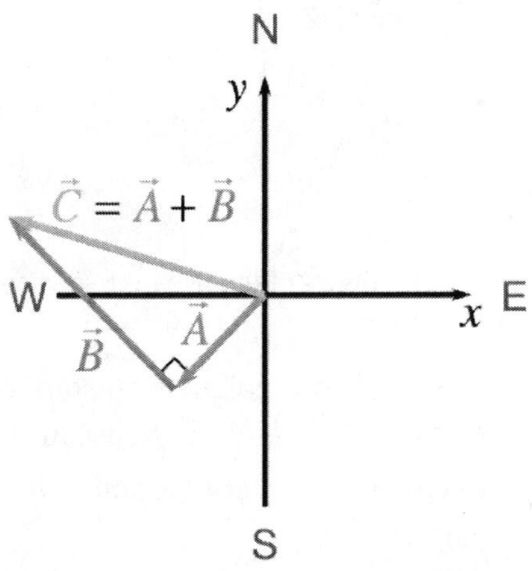

Figure 1.20: Hike with a 90-degree turn.

Here we have introduced a coordinate system for which the y-axis points North and the x-axis points East, as is conventional. The first portion of the hike, in the Southwestern direction, is indicated by the vector $\vec{A}$, and the second portion by the vector $\vec{B}$. And we have also drawn the sum vector $\vec{C} = \vec{A} + \vec{B}$, for which we want to determine the length.

RESEARCH:

If you have drawn the sketch with sufficient accuracy, scaling the length of the vectors in your drawing proportional to the length of the segments of the hike (as was done in

Figure 1.20), then you can measure the length of the vector $\vec{C}$ to determine the distance that you are away from your base camp. But the input data are specified to three significant digits, so we should also produce an answer that is accurate to three significant digits. Thus we need to go beyond the graphical method and use the component method of vector addition.

In order to calculate the components of the vectors, we need to know their angles relative to the positive x-axis. For the vector $\vec{A}$, which points in Southwestern direction, this angle is $\theta_A = 225°$, as shown in Figure 1.21. The vector $\vec{B}$ has an angle of 90 degrees relative to $\vec{A}$ and thus an angle of $\theta_B = 135°$ relative to the positive x-axis. To make this point more obvious we have moved the starting point of $\vec{B}$ into the origin of the coordinate system. (Remember: we can move vectors around at will. As long as we leave the direction and length of the vector the same, the vector remains unchanged.)

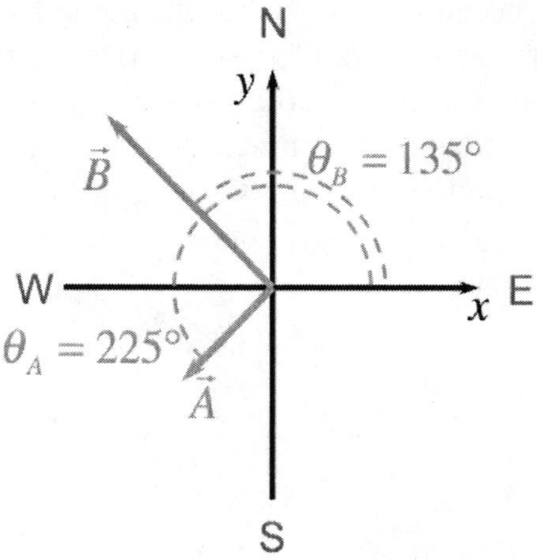

Figure 1.21: Angles of the two hike segments.

Now we have everything in place to get our calculation started. We have the lengths and directions of both vectors, allowing us to calculate their Cartesian components. Then we need to add their components to calculate the components of the vector $\vec{C}$, from which we can calculate the length of this vector.

SIMPLIFY:

The components of the vector $\vec{C}$ are:

$$\begin{aligned} C_x &= A_x + B_x = A\cos\theta_A + B\cos\theta_B \\ C_y &= A_y + B_y = A\sin\theta_A + B\sin\theta_B \end{aligned} \tag{1.30}$$

Thus the length of the vector $\vec{C}$ is (compare (1.26)

$$C = \sqrt{C_x^2 + C_y^2} = \sqrt{(A_x + B_x)^2 + (A_y + B_y)^2}$$
$$= \sqrt{(A\cos\theta_A + B\cos\theta_B)^2 + (A\sin\theta_A + B\sin\theta_B)^2} \quad (1.31)$$

CALCULATE:

Now all that is left is to put in the numbers to obtain the vector length

$$C = \sqrt{((1.72\text{ km})\cos 225° + (3.12\text{ km})\cos 135°)^2 + ((1.72\text{ km})\sin 225° + (3.12\text{ km})\sin 135°)^2}$$
$$= \sqrt{\left(1.72\cdot(-\sqrt{1/2}) + 3.12\cdot(-\sqrt{1/2})\right)^2 + \left((1.72\cdot(-\sqrt{1/2}) + 3.12\cdot\sqrt{1/2}\right)^2}\text{ km}$$

Entering these numbers into your pocket calculator, you obtain:

$$C = 3.562695609\text{ km}$$

ROUND:

Since the initial data were given to three significant figures, our final answer should also be (at most) to the same precision. Rounding our result to three significant figures then yields our final answer

$$C = 3.56\text{ km}$$

DOUBLE-CHECK:

We wanted to practice vector concepts with this problem. However, if you forget for a moment that these vectors have arrows and only consider that they form a right triangle, then you can immediately calculate the length of side C from the Pythagorean theorem as

$$C = \sqrt{A^2 + B^2} = \sqrt{1.72^2 + 3.12^2}\text{ km} = 3.56\text{ km} \quad (1.32)$$

Here we also rounded our result to three significant figures; and we see that it agrees with the one obtained following the longer procedure of vector addition.

Solved Problem

Chapter 2: Motion in a Straight Line

What we will learn:

- To describe the motion of objects in a straight line or in one dimension.
- To understand the definitions of position, displacement, and distance.
- To calculate the position, velocity and acceleration of objects moving in a straight line.
- To describe motion with constant acceleration.
- To understand objects undergoing free-fall motion.

2.1. Introduction: Kinematics

The study of physics is divided into several large parts, one of which is mechanics. Mechanics is usually subdivided into smaller units. In this chapter and the following one we examine the kinematics aspect of mechanics. Kinematics is the study of the motion of objects. These objects can include cars, baseballs, people, planets, atoms, etc. For now, we will hold off on the question of what causes this motion. We will return to this question when we study forces.

We will also not yet consider rotations, and instead only concentrate on translational motion (motion without rotation). When we consider rotation, we are forced to look at objects as extended entities, for which we have to sum or integrate over their parts.

However, in order to get us started we can neglect all internal structure of a moving object. To this end we introduce the concept of a "point particle", or point-like object. In order to determine the equations of motion for an object, we can imagine it to be located at a single point at each time. What point do we choose to represent an extended object? Initially we simply will use the geometric center, the middle. In our chapter 8 on systems of particles and extended objects we will give a more precise definition for this point, which we will call the center of mass.

2.2. Position Vector, Displacement Vector, and Distance

The simplest motion we can investigate is that of an object moving in a straight line. Examples of this motion include a 100 m dash, a car driving on a straight segment of road, or a stone falling straight down off a cliff. In later chapters, we will consider motion that is not on a straight line but for now we will concentrate on motion in one dimension.

If an object is located on a particular point on a line, we can denote this point with its position vector. We will use the symbol x to denote the position vector, where we use the common convention to omit vector arrows above the letter symbols for vectors in one dimension. This convention allows us to make the formulas look like the familiar expressions from calculus when we take derivatives. One number, the x-coordinate or x-component of the vector and a corresponding unit, uniquely specifies the position vector in one-dimensional motion. The following are valid ways of writing a position vector: $x = 4.3$ m, $x = 7\frac{3}{8}$ inches, $x = -2.04$ km. Please note that a position vector's x-component can have a positive or a negative value, depending on the location of the point and the axis direction that we choose to be positive. These x values are, of course, also dependent on where we define the origin of our coordinate system, the zero of our straight line. The units "m" and "km" are valid SI units, while the unit "inch" is not. However, in the USA our everyday experiences are tied to the old British system of units (like "inch", "pound", "gallon", …), and so we will use them in our examples as well, being always careful to provide the conversion to the metric units.

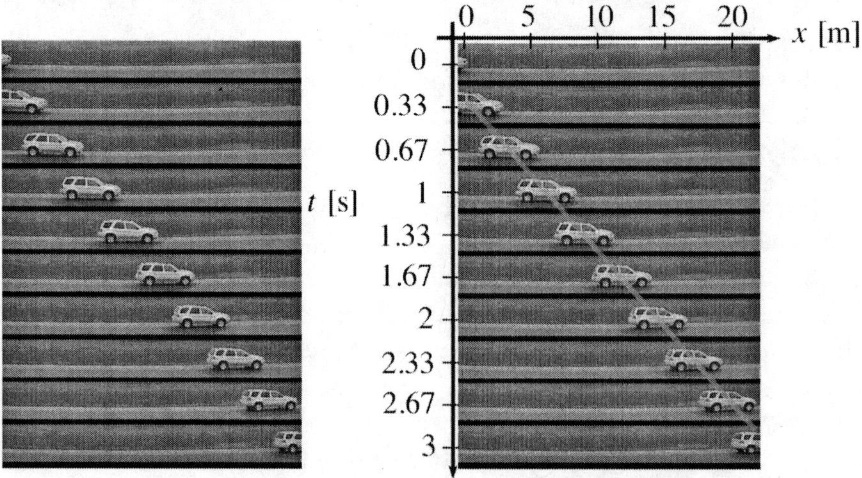

Figure 2.1: Left side: Series of video frames of a moving car, taken every 1/3 s; Right side: Same series, but now with a coordinate system overlaid, as well a red line connecting the centers of the car in each frame.

The position of an object can change as a function of time t; the object can move. We can therefore formally write the position vector in function notation, $x = x(t)$. If we want to specify the position vector at some specific time t_1, then we will use the functional notation $x_1 \equiv x(t_1)$.

Before we go any further, we will consider graphing the position as a function of time. In Figure 2.1 we illustrate the principle involved by showing several frames of a video of a car driving down a road. The video frames are taken in time intervals of 1/3 of a second. These frames are shown in the left part of Figure 2.1.

We are free to choose the origins of our time and of our coordinate system. In this case we choose the time of the first frame to be $t = 0$ and the position of the center of the car in the first frame as $x = 0$. We can now draw our coordinate axes and graph over the frames, as shown in the right panel of Figure 2.1. The position of the car as a function of time lies on a straight line. Again, keep in mind that we represent the car by a single point!

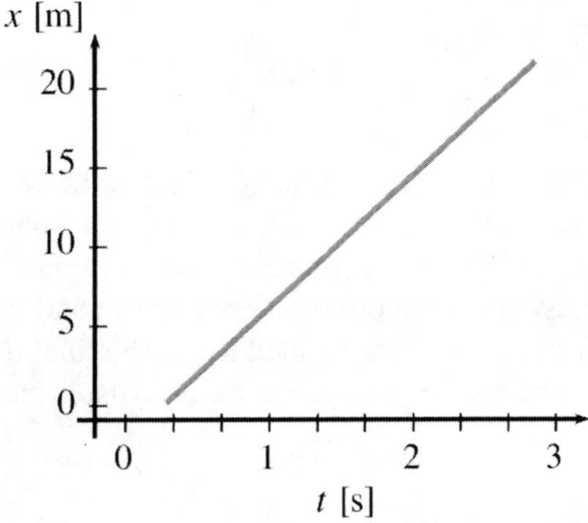

Figure 2.2: Same as the previous figure, but now rotated so that the time-axis is horizontal, and without the pictures of the car.

For graphs, it is customary to plot the independent variable - in this case the time t - on the horizontal axis. We plot x, which is called the dependent variable as it "depends" on the value of the time t, on the vertical axis. In order to arrive at this customary way of displaying the position as a function of time, we rotate the previous figure by 90 degrees in counter-clockwise direction. The result of this procedure is shown in Figure 2.2. Here we have also eliminated all pictures of the car, but only kept the red line showing the position of the car as a function of time.

Now that we have specified the position vector, let us go one step further and define displacement. Displacement is simply the difference between the final position, $x_2 \equiv x(t_2)$, at the end of a motion and the initial position, $x_1 \equiv x(t_1)$,

$$\Delta x = x_2 - x_1 \tag{2.1}$$

Here we have used the notation Δx for the displacement vector to indicate that it is a difference between two position vectors. Please note that the displacement vector is independent of the location of the origin of the coordinate system. Why? Any shift in the coordinate system will add to the position vector x_2 the same amount that it adds to the position vector x_1, and by taking the difference the effect of shifting the origin of the coordinate system cancels out.

Just like position vectors, displacement vectors can also be positive or negative. In particular, the displacement vector Δx_{ba} for going from point a to point b is exactly the negative of Δx_{ab} going from point b to point a:

$$\Delta x_{ba} = x_b - x_a = -(x_a - x_b) = -\Delta x_{ab} \tag{2.2}$$

Distance

We now introduce the distance, ℓ, as the absolute value of the displacement:

$$\ell = |\Delta x| \tag{2.3}$$

The distance is always greater than or equal to zero and is measured in the same units as position and displacement. However, the distance is a scalar quantity, not a vector. If the displacement is not in a straight line or if it is not unidirectional, the displacement must be broken up into segments that are approximately straight and unidirectional and then the distances for the various segments are added to get the total distance. The following example illustrates the difference between distance and displacement.

Solved Problem

Solved Problem 2.1: Trip segments

The distance between Des Moines, Iowa, and Iowa City, is 106.0 miles, and as you can see from the map (Figure 2.3), it is a straight line along Interstate 80 to a good approximation. Approximately halfway in between the two cities, where I80 crosses highway US63 is the city of Malcom, 54.0 miles km from Des Moines.

Figure 2.3: Roundtrip between Des Moines and Iowa City

Question:

If we take a trip Malcom – Des Moines – Iowa City, what is the total distance and displacement for this trip?

Solved Problem

Answer:

THINK:

Distance and displacement are not identical. If the trip only consisted of one segment in one direction, the distance would just be the absolute value of the displacement, according to (2.3). However, this trip is broken up into segments, and so we need to be careful. Let us treat each segment individually, and then add up the segments in the end.

SKETCH:

Since I80 is almost a straight line, it is sufficient to just draw one straight horizontal line and make this our coordinate axis. We enter the positions of the three cities as x_I (Iowa City), x_M (Malcom), and x_D (Des Moines). Since we always have the freedom to define the origin of our coordinate system, we elect to put it into Des Moines, thus setting $x_D = 0$. As is conventional, we define the positive direction to the right, in the direction East.

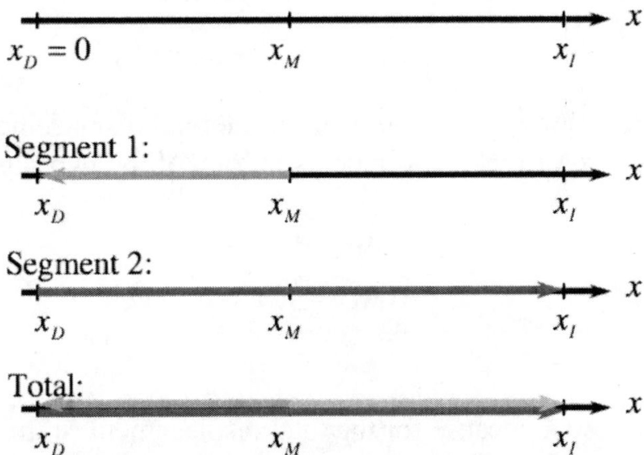

Figure 2.4: Definition of coordinate system and trip segments for the Malcom, Des Moines, Iowa City trip.

We also draw arrows for the displacements in each of the two segments of the trip. We represent segment 1 from Malcom to Des Moines by the red arrow, and segment 2 from Des Moines to Iowa City is shown in blue. Finally, we draw a diagram for the total trip as the sum of the two trips.

RESEARCH:

With our assignment of $x_D = 0$, Des Moines is put in the origin of the coordinate system. According to the problem, Malcom is then at $x_M = +54.0 \text{ miles} = +89.9 \text{ km}$ and Iowa City is at $x_I = +106.0 \text{ miles} = +170.5 \text{ km}$. Please note that we have written a plus sign in front of the numbers for x_M and x_I to remind us that these are components of position vectors and can have positive or negative values. Also, we have converted the miles into kilometers, which are valid SI units.

Solved Problem

For the first segment, the displacement is given by:

$$\Delta x_1 = x_D - x_M$$

and thus the distance driven for this segment is:

$$\ell_1 = |\Delta x_1| = |x_D - x_M|$$

In the same way, the displacement and distance for the second trip segment are:

$$\Delta x_2 = x_I - x_D$$

$$\ell_2 = |\Delta x_2| = |x_I - x_D|$$

For the sum of the two segments, the total trip, we then obtain by simple addition for the displacement:

$$\Delta x_{total} = \Delta x_1 + \Delta x_2 \,,$$

and for the total distance:

$$\ell_{total} = \ell_1 + \ell_2 .$$

SIMPLIFY:

Please note that we can simplify the equation for the total displacement a little bit by inserting the expressions for the displacements in each of the two segments.

$$\begin{aligned}\Delta x_{total} &= \Delta x_1 + \Delta x_2 \\ &= (x_D - x_M) + (x_I - x_D) \\ &= x_I - x_M\end{aligned}$$

This is an interesting result, because for the total displacement of the entire trip it does not matter at all that our driver had a visit to Des Moines. All that matters is where the trip started and where it ended. The total displacement is a result of a one-dimensional vector addition, as indicated in the bottom part of our sketch in Figure 2.4 by the purple arrow.

CALCULATE:

Now it is time to insert the numbers for the positions of the three cities in our coordinate system. We then obtain for the net displacement in our trip

$$\Delta x_{total} = x_I - x_M = (+170.5 \text{ km}) - (+89.9 \text{ km}) = +80.6 \text{ km}$$

And for the total distance driven we get

$$\ell_{total} = |89.9 \text{ km}| + |170.5 \text{ km}| = 260.4 \text{ km}$$

(Remember, the distances between Des Moines and Malcom (=Δx_1) and between Des

Solved Problem

Monies and Iowa City (= Δx_2) were given in the problem; so we do not have to calculate them again from the differences in the position vectors of the cities.)

ROUND:

The initial numbers for the distances were given to a tenth of a mile, which is also the precision we kept when we converted our data to kilometers. Since our entire calculation only amounted to adding or subtracting these numbers, it is not surprising that with end up with numbers that are also accurate to one tenth of a kilometer. No further rounding is needed.

DOUBLE-CHECK:

At first sight it may be a surprise that the net displacement for the trip is only 80.6 km and thus much smaller than the total distance. This is a good time to remind us that the relationship between the absolute value of the displacement and the distance (2.3) is only valid as long as we do not change direction between the beginning and the end, as was the case in this example.

This discrepancy is even more apparent for a round trip. Then the total distance driven is twice the distance between the two cities, but the total displacement is 0, because the starting point and end point of the trip are identical.

This result is a general one: If the initial and final positions are the same, the total displacement is 0. As straightforward as this seems in the present example, it still provides a potential pitfall in many exam questions. You need to be aware that the net displacement is a vector, whereas the distance is a positive scalar.

Self-Test Opportunity:
Suppose you had chosen to put the origin of the coordinate system into Malcom instead on Des Moines. Would the final result of your calculation change? If yes, how? If no, why not?

2.3. Velocity Vector, Average Velocity, Speed

We now define v_x , the x-component of the velocity vector, as the change in position (i.e. the displacement) in a given time interval divided by the time interval, $\Delta x / \Delta t$. Velocity can change from moment to moment. The velocity that we have calculated by taking the ratio of displacement per time interval is the average of the velocity over this time interval. We will use this concept as our definition of the average velocity, $\bar{v}_x$

$$\bar{v}_x = \frac{\Delta x}{\Delta t} \tag{2.4}$$

Please note that we are using the bar above the symbol as the notation for averaging over a finite time interval.

In calculus, one arrives at the definition of the time derivative by demanding that the time interval approaches zero. We will use the same definition here to define the velocity as the time derivative of the displacement vector:

$$v_x = \lim_{\Delta t \to 0} \bar{v}_x = \lim_{\Delta t \to 0} \frac{\Delta x}{\Delta t} \equiv \frac{dx}{dt} \tag{2.5}$$

This relationship between displacement, time interval, average velocity, and velocity as the limit of the average velocity for vanishing time interval is illustrated in Figure 2.5. Here the position of an object as a function of time, $x(t)$, is shown by the black curve. At a certain instant in time (red dot) the velocity is the tangent line to this path (red dashed lines). The approximations of the average velocities for ever-smaller time intervals are shown by the blue, purple, and magenta dashed lines. As one can see, the sequence of slopes of these lines converges rapidly to that of the red line.

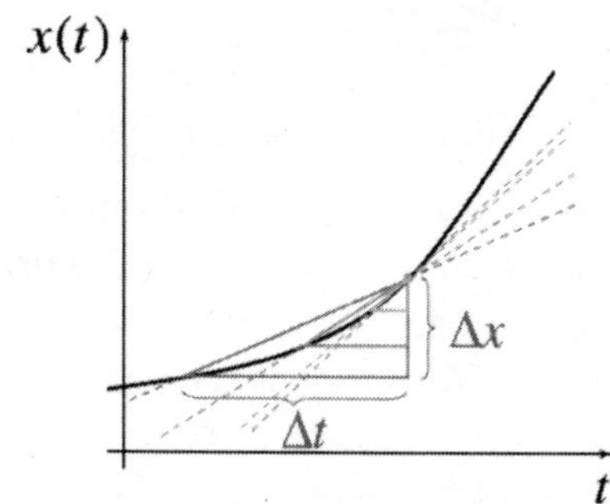

Figure 2.5: Instantaneous velocity as the limit of the ratio of displacement per time interval.

The expression "instantaneous velocity" is sometimes used for the velocity to indicate that it is the result in the limit $\Delta t \to 0$. Note that the velocity is a vector, which is pointing in the same direction as the vector of the infinitesimal displacement, dx. Because the position $x(t)$ and the displacement $\Delta x(t)$ are functions of time, so is the velocity. Because the velocity is defined as the time derivative of the displacement vector, all of our usual rules of differentiation introduced in calculus hold. If you need a refresher, then you can consult Appendix A.

Example

Example 2.1: Time dependence of the velocity

Question:
During the time interval from 0.0 to 10.0 seconds, the position vector of a car on a road is given by $x(t) = a + bt + ct^2$ with $a = 17.2$ m, $b = -10.1$ m/s, and $c = 1.10$ m/s^2. What is its velocity as a function of time? What is the average velocity during this interval?

Example

Answer:
According to our definition in equation (2.5) for the velocity, we simply have to take the time derivative of the function for the position vector to arrive at our solution:

$$v_x = \frac{dx}{dt} = \frac{d}{dt}(a + bt + ct^2) = b + 2ct = -10.1 \text{ m/s} + 2 \cdot (1.10 \text{ m/s}^2)t$$

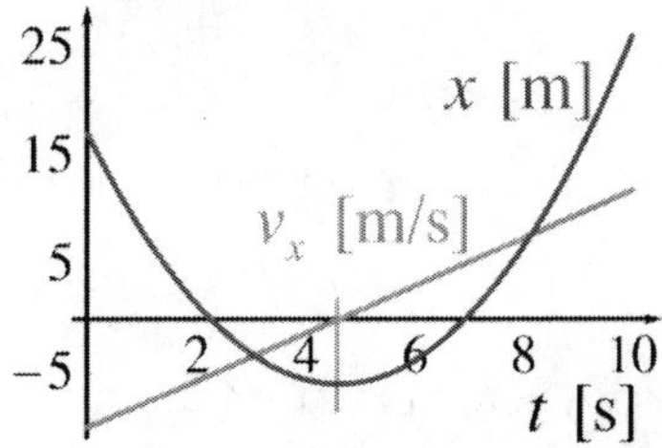

Figure 2.6: Graph of the position x and velocity v_x as a function of the time t.

It is instructive to graph this solution. In Figure 2.6 the position as a function of time is shown in dark blue, and the velocity as a function of time is shown in red. Initially, the velocity has a value of -10.1 m/s, and at $t = 10$ s the velocity has a value of $+11.9$ m/s.

Note that the velocity is initially negative, is zero at 4.59 seconds Indicated by the vertical gray line in Figure 2.6), and then is positive after 4.59 seconds. At 4.59 seconds the position graph $x(t)$ shows an extremum (a minimum in this case), just like expected from calculus since

$$\frac{dx}{dt} = b + 2ct_0 = 0 \Rightarrow t_0 = -\frac{b}{c} = -\frac{-10.1 \text{ m/s}}{2.20 \text{ m/s}^2} = 4.59 \text{ s}$$

From the definition of average velocity, we know that to determine the average velocity during a time interval we need to subtract the position at the beginning of the interval from the position at the end of the interval. By inserting $t = 0$ and $t = 10$ s into the equation for the position vector as a function of time, we obtain: $x(t = 0) = 17.2$ m and $x(t = 10 \text{ s}) = 26.2$ m. So $\Delta x = x(t = 10) - x(t = 0) = 26.2 \text{ m} - 17.2 \text{ m} = 9.0 \text{ m}$. We then obtain for the average velocity over this time interval:

$$\bar{v}_x = \frac{\Delta x}{\Delta t} = \frac{9.0 \text{ m}}{10 \text{ s}} = 0.90 \text{ m/s}$$

Figure 2.7: Measuring the speed of passing cars.

Speed

The absolute value of the velocity vector is called the speed. For a moving object, speed is always positive. Speed and velocity are used interchangeably in common language, but in physical terms they are very different. Velocity is a vector, which has a direction. For our one-dimensional motion, the velocity can point either in the positive or negative direction, i.e. it can have either sign. Speed is the absolute magnitude of the velocity vector and thus a scalar quantity.

$$\text{speed} \equiv v = |v_x| \tag{2.6}$$

In our everyday experience we clearly accept that speeds can never be negative; speed limits are always posted as positive numbers, and the radar used to measure the speed of passing cars also always quotes a positive number (see Figure 2.7).

Previously we introduced the distance as the absolute value of the displacement for each segment in which the movement does not reverse direction (see our discussion below equation (2.3)). The average speed when a distance ℓ is traveled during a time interval Δt is:

$$\text{average speed} \equiv \overline{v} = \frac{\ell}{\Delta t} \tag{2.7}$$

Example 2.2: Speed and Velocity

Suppose a swimmer swims the first 50 m of the 100 m freestyle in 38.2 seconds. Once she reaches the far side of the pool, she turns around and swims back to the start in 42.5 seconds.

Question:
What is the average velocity and average speed for the leg from start to the far side of the pool, for the return leg, and for the total trip?

Example

Answer:

Figure 2.8: Definition of the x-axis in the swimming pool.

We start by defining our coordinate system, as shown in Figure 2.8. The positive x-axis points to the bottom of the page.

First leg of the swim:
Our swimmer starts at $x_1 = 0$ and swims to $x_2 = 50$ m. It takes her $\Delta t = 38.2$ s to accomplish this task. Her velocity is then, according to our definition:

$$\bar{v}_{x,\text{leg 1}} = \frac{x_2 - x_1}{\Delta t} = \frac{50\text{ m} - 0\text{ m}}{38.2\text{ s}} = \frac{50}{38.2}\text{ m/s} = 1.31\text{ m/s}$$

Her average speed is distance/time interval which, in this case, is the same as the absolute value of her average velocity, or $\left|\bar{v}_{x,\text{leg 1}}\right| = 1.31$ m/s.

Second leg of the swim:
We still use the same coordinate system as for leg 1. This choice means that now she starts at $x_1 = 50$ m, finishes at $x_2 = 0$, and takes $\Delta t = 42.5$ s to do so. Her average velocity is then:

$$\bar{v}_{x,\text{leg 2}} = \frac{x_2 - x_1}{\Delta t} = \frac{0\text{ m} - 50\text{ m}}{42.5\text{ s}} = \frac{-50}{42.5}\text{ m/s} = -1.18\text{ m/s}$$

Note the negative sign for the velocity in this case. The average speed again turns out to be the absolute magnitude of the velocity and thus $\left|\bar{v}_{x,\text{leg 2}}\right| = \left|-1.18\text{ m/s}\right| = 1.18$ m/s.

The entire lap:
We can calculate the average velocity in two ways, showing that they result in the same answer. First we notice that because we started at $x_1 = 0$ and finished at $x_2 = 0$, the difference is 0. Thus the net displacement is 0, and consequently the average velocity is also 0.

We can also find the average velocity for the whole lap by taking the time-weighted sum

Example

of the average velocities of the individual legs:

$$\bar{v}_x = \frac{\bar{v}_{x,\text{leg }1} \cdot \Delta t_1 + \bar{v}_{x,\text{leg }2} \cdot \Delta t_2}{\Delta t_1 + \Delta t_2} = \frac{(1.31 \text{ m/s})(38.2 \text{ s}) + (-1.18 \text{ m/s})(42.5 \text{ s})}{(38.2 \text{ s}) + (42.5 \text{ s})} = 0$$

What do we find for the average speed? The average speed, according to our definition, is the total distance divided by the total time. The total distance is 100 m, and the total time is 38.2 s plus 42.5 s, equaling 80.7 s. Thus:

$$\bar{v} = \frac{\ell}{\Delta t} = \frac{100 \text{ m}}{80.7 \text{ s}} = 1.24 \text{ m/s}$$

We can also use the time-weighted sum of the average speeds, leading to the same result. Note that the average speed for the entire lap is between that of leg 1 and that of leg 2. It is not exactly halfway between these two values and is closer to the lower value of leg 2 because the swimmer spent more time on leg 2 with its lower speed, lowering the average.

2.4. Acceleration Vector

Just as the average velocity is defined as the displacement per time interval, we can define the average acceleration as the velocity change per time interval:

$$\bar{a}_x = \frac{\Delta v_x}{\Delta t} \tag{2.8}$$

Similarly, the instantaneous acceleration is defined as the limit of the time interval approaching 0,

$$a_x = \lim_{\Delta t \to 0} \bar{a}_x = \lim_{\Delta t \to 0} \frac{\Delta v_x}{\Delta t} \equiv \frac{dv_x}{dt} \tag{2.9}$$

Because the acceleration is the time derivative of the velocity, and the velocity is the time derivative of the displacement, the acceleration is the second derivative of the displacement.

$$a_x = \frac{d}{dt} v_x = \frac{d}{dt}\left(\frac{d}{dt} x\right) = \frac{d^2}{dt^2} x \tag{2.10}$$

Unlike speed or distance, there is no special name for the absolute value of the acceleration in our everyday language.

In the one-dimensional case presented in this chapter an acceleration, which is a change in the velocity, necessarily entails a change in the magnitude of the velocity, the speed.

However, in the following chapter we will treat motion in more than one spatial dimension. Then the velocity vector can also change its direction, and not just its magnitude. In particular, in chapter 9 on circular motion in a two-dimensional plane we will see that motion in a circle is possible with constant speed. In that case there is a constant acceleration that forces the object on a circular path, but leaves the speed constant.

Computer Solutions and Difference Formulas

We can also deal with situations in which the acceleration changes as a function of time, but where the exact functional form is not know beforehand. Furthermore, we can extract this information approximately even in cases where the position is only known at certain points in time. The following example illustrates this procedure.

Example 2.3: World-Championship 100m Dash

t [s]	x [m]	$\bar{v}_x$ [m/s]	$\bar{a}_x$ [m/s^2]
0.00	0		2.83
		5.32	
1.88	10		2.66
		9.26	
2.96	20		1.61
		10.87	
3.88	30		0.40
		11.24	
4.77	40		0.77
		11.90	
5.61	50		-0.17
		11.76	
6.46	60		0.17
		11.90	
7.30	70		0.17
		12.05	
8.13	80		-0.65
		11.49	
9.00	90		0.00
		11.49	
9.87	100		

Figure 2.9: Time, position, velocity, and acceleration during Carl Lewis' World record 100 m dash.

In the 1991 Track and Field World Championships in Tokyo, Japan, Carl Lewis (USA) set a new world record in the 100 m dash. Figure 2.9 lists the times at which he arrived at the 10 m mark, the 20 m mark, and so on. We can then use our formulas for the average velocity and average acceleration to calculate these observables for his race. From Figure 2.9 it is clear that after about 3 seconds, Mr. Lewis has reached an approximately constant velocity of 11 to 12 m/s.

In Figure 2.9 we also indicate how one arrives at the values for the velocity and acceleration displayed. Take, for example, the upper two green boxes. They contain the

Example

times and positions for two measurements. We can then get $\Delta t = 2.96\ \text{s} - 1.88\ \text{s} = 1.08\ \text{s}$ and $\Delta x = 20\ \text{m} - 10\ \text{m} = 10\ \text{m}$. The average velocity in this time interval is then $\bar{v} = \Delta x / \Delta t = 10\ \text{m} / 1.08\ \text{s} = 9.26\ \text{m/s}$. We have rounded this result to three significant digits, because the times were given to that accuracy. The accuracy for the distances can be assumed to be even better, because these data were extracted from video analysis by observing at which times the athlete crossed marks on the ground. In Figure 2.9 we have written the velocity halfway between the lines, indicating that the average velocity extracted is a good approximation for the instantaneous velocity in the middle of the time interval.

In the same way, we can obtain the average velocities for other time intervals. If you use the second and third green box in the table above, you obtain an average velocity of 10.87 m/s for the time interval from 2.96 s to 3.88 s. Now that we have two velocity values, we can take our difference formula for the acceleration and calculate the average acceleration. Here we will assume that the instantaneous velocity at a time corresponding to a time in the middle of the first two green boxes (2.42 s) is equal to the average velocity during the interval between the first two green boxes or 9.26 m/s. Similarly, we take the velocity at 3.42 s (midway between the second and third boxes) to be 10.87 m/s. Then the average acceleration between 2.42 s and 3.42 s is

$$\bar{a}_x = \Delta v_x / \Delta t = (10.87\ \text{m/s} - 9.26\ \text{m/s})/(3.42\ \text{s} - 2.42\ \text{s}) = 1.61\ \text{m/s}^2.$$

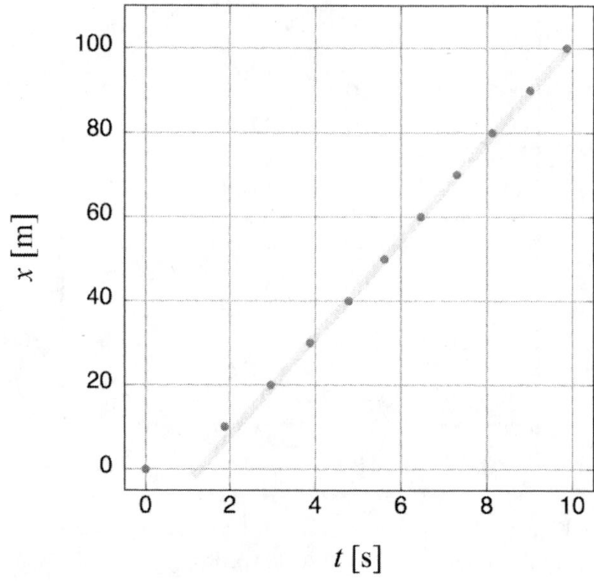

Figure 2.10: Graph of position versus time for Carl Lewis' 100 m dash in 1991.

From the entries in Figure 2.9 that we obtain in this way, we can see that Mr. Lewis initially accelerates until he reaches the 30 m mark, where he has reached his maximum velocity of 11 to 12 m/s, and then runs with that velocity until he reaches the finish line. This result becomes perhaps more apparent when we look at a graphical display of his position versus time during the race, as done in Figure 2.10. The red dots represent the data points from the table, while the green straight line represents a constant velocity of 11.58 m/s.

The type of numerical analysis used to extract average velocities and accelerations as approximations for the instantaneous values of these quantities is very common in all types of scientific and engineering applications. It is indispensable in cases where the precise functional dependencies on time are not known. In these cases one relies on numerical approximations for derivatives via the difference formulas that we have used. Most practical solutions of scientific and engineering problems obtained with the aid of modern computers make use of difference formulas like the ones introduced here.

The entire field of numerical analysis is devoted to finding better numerical approximations that enable more precise and faster computer calculations and simulations of natural processes. Difference formulas similar to the ones introduced here have at least equal importance for the everyday work of scientists and engineers that the calculus-based analytic expressions do. This importance is a consequence of the computer revolution in science and technology. However, this situation does not make the contents of the present textbook any less important. In order to devise a valid solution to an engineering or science problem, you still have to understand the basic underlying physical principles, no matter what calculation techniques you use. This fact is well recognized by cutting-edge movie animators and creators of special digital effects who have to take basic physics classes to ensure that the product of their computer simulations looks realistic to the audience in the movie theater.

2.5. Inverse Relationships

Integration is the inverse operation to differentiation. We can integrate to obtain the velocity and displacement from the acceleration. To do this, we integrate the above defining equations for velocity (2.5) and acceleration (2.10) over time. Let us start with the equation for the velocity (2.5):

$$v_x(t) = \frac{dx(t)}{dt} \Rightarrow$$

$$\int_{t_0}^{t} v_x(t')dt' = \int_{t_0}^{t} \frac{dx(t')}{dt'}dt' = x(t) - x(t_0) \Rightarrow$$

$$x(t) = x_0 + \int_{t_0}^{t} v(t')dt' \tag{2.11}$$

Here we have used the convention $x(t_0) = x_0$, the initial position. In the same way we can integrate the relationship between velocity and acceleration (2.10) to obtain:

$$a_x(t) = \frac{dv_x(t)}{dt} \Rightarrow$$

$$\int_{t_0}^{t} a_x(t')dt' = \int_{t_0}^{t} \frac{dv_x(t')}{dt'}dt' = v_x(t) - v_x(t_0) \Rightarrow$$

$$v_x(t) = v_{x0} + \int_{t_0}^{t} a_x(t')dt' \tag{2.12}$$

Here $v_x(t_0) = v_{x0}$ indicates the initial velocity.

This result means that for any given time dependence of the acceleration vector we are able to calculate the velocity vector, provided we are given the initial value of the velocity vector. And in the same way we can calculate the displacement vector, if we know its initial value and the time dependence of the velocity vector.

In calculus you probably learned that the geometrical interpretation of the definite integral is that of an area under a curve. This is also true for the two equations (2.11) and (2.12), where we can interpret the area under the curve of $v_x(t)$ between t_0 and t as the difference in the position between these two times, as indicated in the left side of Figure 2.11. The right side of Figure 2.11 shows that the area under the curve of $a_x(t)$ in the time interval between t_0 and t is the velocity difference between these two times.

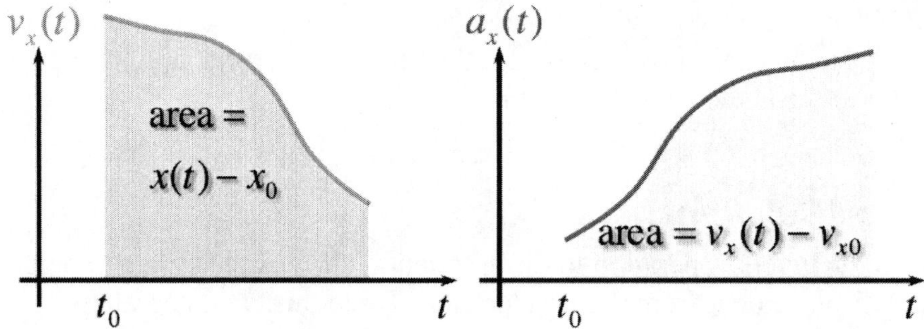

Figure 2.11: Geometrical interpretation of the integrals over velocity (left) and acceleration (right).

2.6. Motion with Constant Acceleration

There are many physical cases in which the acceleration experienced by an object is approximately or perhaps even exactly, constant. We can obtain useful equations for these special cases of motion with constant acceleration. If the acceleration, a_x, is a constant, then the time integral to obtain the velocity in equation (2.11) results in:

$$v_x(t) = v_{x0} + \int_{t_0}^{t} a_x dt' = v_{x0} + a_x \int_{t_0}^{t} dt' \Rightarrow$$

$$v_x(t) = v_{x0} + a_x t \tag{2.13}$$

This means that the velocity is a linear function of time. We can then insert this result into our time integration to obtain the position as a function of time:

$$x = x_0 + \int_0^t v_x(t')dt' = x_0 + \int_0^t (v_{x0} + a_x t')dt'$$
$$= x_0 + v_{x0}\int_0^t dt' + a_x \int_0^t t'dt' \Rightarrow$$
$$x(t) = x_0 + v_{x0}t + \tfrac{1}{2}a_x t^2 \tag{2.14}$$

Thus we find that for a constant acceleration the velocity is always a linear function of time, and the position is a quadratic function of time. Besides equations (2.13) and (2.14), we can derive three other useful equations using these equations as a starting point. We will first write them down and then provide their derivations.

First we'll obtain an expression for the average velocity in the time interval from 0 to t. It is the average of the velocities at the beginning and end of the time interval:

$$\bar{v}_x = \tfrac{1}{2}(v_{x0} + v_x) \tag{2.15}$$

With equation (2.15) for the average velocity, we will then find an alternative way to express the position as

$$x = x_0 + \bar{v}_x t \tag{2.16}$$

Finally we will get an equation for the square of the velocity that does not contain the time explicitly:

$$v_x^2 = v_{x0}^2 + 2a_x(x - x_0) \tag{2.17}$$

Derivation 2.1:
Mathematically, to obtain the time average of a quantity over a certain interval Δt, we have to integrate this quantity over the time interval and then divide by the time interval:

$$\begin{aligned}\bar{v}_x &= \frac{1}{t}\int_0^t v_x(t')dt' = \frac{1}{t}\int_0^t (v_{x0} + at')dt' \\ &= \frac{v_{x0}}{t}\int_0^t dt' + \frac{a}{t}\int_0^t t'dt' = v_{x0} + \tfrac{1}{2}at \\ &= \tfrac{1}{2}v_{x0} + \tfrac{1}{2}(v_{x0} + at) \\ &= \tfrac{1}{2}(v_{x0} + v_x)\end{aligned} \tag{2.18}$$

This averaging procedure is explained in graphical form in Figure 2.12. One can see that the area of the trapezoid formed by the red line representing $v(t)$ and the two vertical lines at t_0 and t is equal to the area of the square formed by the horizontal line to $\bar{v}$ and

Derivation

the two vertical lines. The base line for both areas is the horizontal t-axis. To make it more apparent that these two areas are equal, we have colored the triangular area above the square and below the red line marking the upper edge of the trapeze in orange. The area of the orange triangle is equal to the area marked in yellow. The trapezoid and the square share the blue area. Thus we have shown in graphical form that both areas are equal.

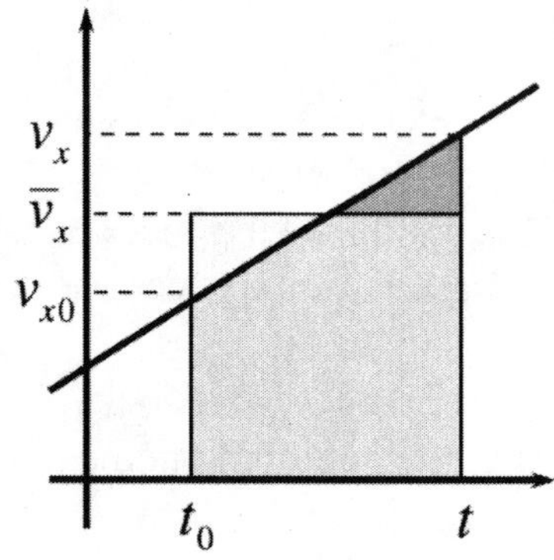

Figure 2.12: Graph of velocity versus time for motion with constant acceleration

To derive the equation for the position, let us use the second to last expression for the average velocity in (2.18) and multiply both sides by the time:

$$\begin{aligned}\bar{v}_x &= v_{x0} + \tfrac{1}{2}a_x t \\ \Rightarrow \bar{v}_x t &= v_{x0}t + \tfrac{1}{2}a_x t^2\end{aligned} \tag{2.19}$$

Now we compare this result to the expression that we had already obtained for x, equation (2.14), and find:

$$x = x_0 + v_{x0}t + \tfrac{1}{2}a_x t^2 = x_0 + \bar{v}_x t \tag{2.20}$$

For the derivation of (2.17) for the square of the velocity, we solve $v_x = v_{x0} + a_x t$ for the time and get $t = (v_x - v_{x0})/a_x$ and insert it into the expression for the position of equation (2.14):

$$\begin{aligned}x &= x_0 + v_{x0}t + \tfrac{1}{2}a_x t^2 \\ &= x_0 + v_{x0}\left(\frac{v_x - v_{x0}}{a_x}\right) + \tfrac{1}{2}a_x\left(\frac{v_x - v_{x0}}{a_x}\right)^2 \\ &= x_0 + \frac{v_x v_{x0} - v_{x0}^2}{a_x} + \tfrac{1}{2}\frac{v_x^2 + v_{x0}^2 - 2v_x v_{x0}}{a_x}\end{aligned} \tag{2.21}$$

Now we subtract x_0 from both sides of the equation and then multiply with a:

Derivation

$$\begin{aligned} &a_x(x-x_0)=v_xv_{x0}-v_{x0}^2+\tfrac{1}{2}(v_x^2+v_{x0}^2-2v_xv_{x0}) \\ &\Rightarrow a_x(x-x_0)=\tfrac{1}{2}v_x^2-\tfrac{1}{2}v_{x0}^2 \\ &\Rightarrow v_x^2=v_{x0}^2+2a_x(x-x_0) \end{aligned} \tag{2.22}$$

Let us finally collect the five kinematical equations we have obtained for the special case of constant acceleration in one location:

$$\begin{aligned} &(i) && x=x_0+v_{x0}t+\tfrac{1}{2}a_xt^2 \\ &(ii) && x=x_0+\bar{v}_xt \\ &(iii) && v_x=v_{x0}+a_xt \\ &(iv) && \bar{v}_x=\tfrac{1}{2}(v_x+v_{x0}) \\ &(v) && v_x^2=v_{x0}^2+2a_x(x-x_0) \end{aligned} \tag{2.23}$$

These five equations allow us to solve many kinds of problems for motion in one dimension with constant acceleration.

Many problems in real life involve motion along straight lines with constant acceleration. In these situations, the five equations in (2.23) provide the template for the solution of any question about the motion. In the following, we will solve several example problems for motion in one dimension. This will illustrate how useful the above equations are, and we will frequently refer back to them. However, let us keep in mind that physics is not really about finding an appropriate equation and plugging in numbers, but is instead about understanding concepts. Only if we understand the underlying ideas will we be able to extrapolate from specific examples to a more general problem-solving strategy.

Solved Problem 2.2: Airplane takeoff

As an airplane rolls down the runway to reach takeoff speed, its engines accelerate the plane. On one particular flight, one of the authors measured the acceleration produced by the jet engines. Figure 2.13 shows the result of this measurement.

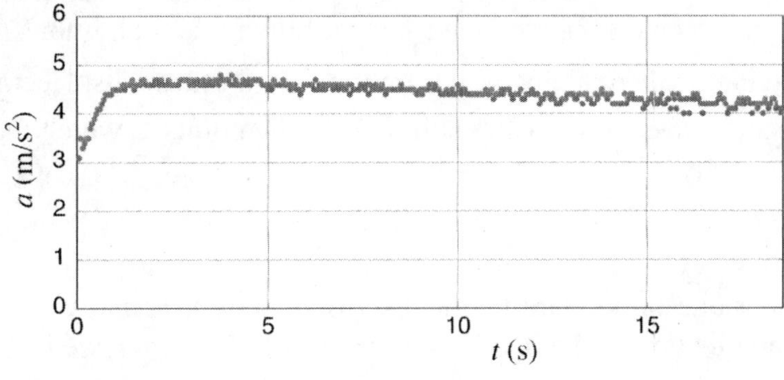

Figure 2.13: Data for the acceleration of a jet down the runway for takeoff.

We can see that the assumption of constant acceleration is not quite correct in this case. However using an average acceleration of $a_x = 4.3 \text{ m/s}^2$ for the 18.4 seconds (measured with a stop watch) it took the airplane to reach takeoff will provide a good approximation to the real situation.

Question:

Assuming a constant acceleration of $a_x = 4.3 \text{ m/s}^2$ starting from rest, what is the takeoff speed of the airplane reached after 18.4 seconds? And how far down the runway has this airplane moved by the time it takes off?

Answer:

THINK:

An airplane moving along a runway on the way to takeoff is a nearly perfect example for one-dimensional accelerated motion. Since we are supposed to assume constant acceleration, we know that the velocity increases linearly in time, and the displacement increases as the second power of time. Since the plane starts from rest, the initial value of the velocity is 0. And as usual we are able to define the origin of our coordinate system to any location; so it is convenient to locate it at the point of the standing start.

SKETCH:

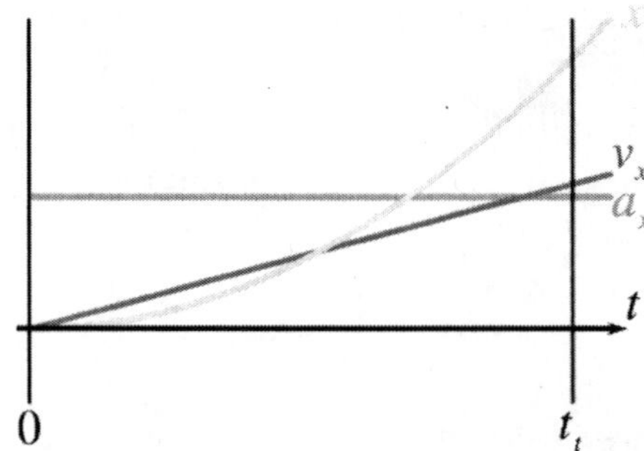

Figure 2.14: Sketch of the acceleration, velocity, and displacement of the airplane during takeoff.

In this sketch we indicate how we expect the velocity and displacement to increase for the case of constant acceleration, where we have set the initial conditions to $v_{x0} = 0$ and $x_0 = 0$. Please note that there are no scales on the axes, because displacement, velocity and acceleration are measured in different units. So the points at which the three curves intersect are completely arbitrary.

RESEARCH:

The first part of our question regarding the takeoff velocity is actually a rather straightforward application of the relationship (*ii*) of (2.23), which we just derived:

$$v_x = v_{x0} + a_x t$$

Similarly, the second question on how far down the runway the airplane travels before taking off can be obtained from relationship (i) of (2.23):

$$x = x_0 + v_{x0}t + \tfrac{1}{2}a_x t^2$$

Simplify:

The airplane accelerates from a standing start, so the initial velocity is $v_{x0} = 0$, and by our choice of coordinate system origin we have also set $x_0 = 0$. So our two answers simplify in this case to:

$$v_x = a_x t$$
$$x = \tfrac{1}{2}a_x t^2$$

Calculate:

The only thing left to do is to put in the numbers.

$$v_x = (4.3 \text{ m/s}^2)(18.4 \text{ s}) = 79.12 \text{ m/s}$$
$$x = \tfrac{1}{2}(4.3 \text{ m/s}^2)(18.4 \text{ s})^2 = 727.904 \text{ m}$$

Round:

The acceleration was specified to two significant digits, and the time to three. Multiplication of the two numbers then must result in an answer that can be quoted to two significant digits. So our final answers are:

$$v_x = 79. \text{ m/s}$$
$$x = 7.3 \cdot 10^2 \text{ m}$$

In passing we note that the takeoff time of 18.4 s was probably stated to a precision that has a too high claim of accuracy; if you have ever tried to determine the moment at which the plane starts to accelerate down the runway, you will have noticed that it is almost impossible to determine that point in time accurate to 1/10th of a second.

Double-check:

The most straightforward check of any answer to a physics problem is to make sure the units work out right. This is the case here, because we find our displacement in units of meters and our velocity in units of meters per second. In future solved problems we will almost always skip mentioning this little test; however, if you want to do a quick check for algebraic errors in your calculations this first step can be valuable.

Now let us see if we arrive at the appropriate order of magnitude for our results. A takeoff displacement of 730 m (~0.5 miles) is reasonable, because it is on the order of the length of an airport runway. And a takeoff speed of $v_x = 79.$ m/s translates into

$$79. \text{ m/s} = (79. \text{ m/s})(1 \text{ mile}/1609 \text{ m})(3600 \text{ s}/1 \text{ hour}) \sim 180 \text{ mph}$$

This answer also appears to be in the right ballpark.

Alternate Answer 2:

Many problems in kinematics can be solved in several ways, because there is often more than one relationship between the known and unknown quantities that we can utilize. In

Solved Problem

Solved Problem

this case, since we already have obtained an answer for the final velocity in part 1 of this example, we can also use this information and solve our fifth kinematical equation (2.23), $v_x^2 = v_{x0}^2 + 2a_x(x - x_0)$ for x. This results in:

$$v_x^2 = v_{x0}^2 + 2a_x(x - x_0) \Rightarrow$$
$$x = x_0 + \frac{v_x^2 - v_{x0}^2}{2a_x} = 0 + \frac{(79.\text{ m/s})^2}{2(4.3\text{ m/s}^2)} = 7.3 \cdot 10^2\text{ m}$$

So we arrived at the same answer in a different way, giving us additional confidence that our solution makes sense.

The solved problem that we have just worked was a fairly easy one; it actually amounted to little more than plugging in numbers. But nevertheless it shows that the kinematical equations that we derived can be applied to real-world situations and lead to answers that have physical meaning. Let us look at another short example, this time from motor sports. It addresses the same concepts of velocity and acceleration, but in a slightly different light.

Example

Example 2.4: Top Fuel Racing

Accelerating from rest, a top fuel racer (Figure 2.15) can reach 333.2 mph (= 148.9 m/s, record established in 2003) at the end of a quarter mile (= 402.3 m) run. For this example, we will assume constant acceleration.

Figure 2.15: Top-fuel NHRA race car

Question 1:
What is the value of this acceleration?

Answer 1:
Since the initial and final values of the velocity are given, and the distance is known, we are looking for a relationship between these three quantities and the acceleration, our unknown. So it is most convenient in this case to use the fifth kinematics equation (line

Example

(v) from equation(2.23)) and solve for the acceleration, a_x:

$$v_x^2 = v_{x0}^2 + 2a_x(x - x_0) \Rightarrow a_x = \frac{v_x^2 - v_{x0}^2}{2(x - x_0)} = \frac{(148.9 \text{ m/s})^2}{2(402.3 \text{ m})} = 27.6 \text{ m/s}^2 \tag{2.24}$$

Question 2:
How long does it take to complete quarter mile race from a standing start?

Answer 2:
Because the final velocity is 148.9 m/s, the average velocity is (line (*iv*) of equation (2.26)): $\bar{v}_x = \frac{1}{2}(148.9 \text{ m/s} + 0) = 74.45 \text{ m/s}$. Relating this average velocity to the displacement and time, we obtain:

$$x = x_0 + \bar{v}_x t \Rightarrow t = \frac{x - x_0}{\bar{v}_x} = \frac{402.3 \text{ m}}{74.45 \text{ m/s}} = 5.40 \text{ s}.$$

Please note that we could also have obtained the same result by using kinematics equation (*iii*) in (2.23), because we have already calculated the acceleration above.

If you are a fan of top fuel racing, however, you know that the real record time for the quarter mile is slightly lower than 4.5 seconds. Our assumption of constant acceleration was not quite satisfied. The acceleration at the beginning of the race is actually higher than the value we calculated above, while the actual acceleration is lower towards the end of the race.

2.7. Free-Fall

The acceleration due to the gravitational force is a constant, to a good approximation, near the surface of Earth. If this statement is true, then it must have observable consequences. What we would like to do here is to state this fact, then work out the consequences for motion of objects under the influence of a gravitational attraction to the Earth. Once we know what to expect, we can compare with experimental observations and see if a constant acceleration due to gravity makes sense.

The acceleration of gravity has the value $g = 9.81 \text{ m/s}^2$. If we call the vertical axis the y-axis and define the positive direction as up, then we can express the acceleration vector due to gravity as

$$a_y = -g \tag{2.25}$$

This situation is a specific application of motion with a constant acceleration, which we discussed in Section 2.6. We modify the equations shown in (2.23) by substituting our acceleration vector from (2.25). We also use y instead of x to indicate that the displacement takes place in y-direction. We then obtain:

$$
\begin{array}{ll}
(i) & y = y_0 + v_{y0}t - \tfrac{1}{2}gt^2 \\
(ii) & y = y_0 + \overline{v}_y t \\
(iii) & v_y = v_{y0} - gt \\
(iv) & \overline{v}_y = \tfrac{1}{2}(v_y + v_{y0}) \\
(v) & v_y^2 = v_{y0}^2 - 2g(y - y_0)
\end{array}
\qquad (2.26)
$$

Motion under the sole influence of the gravitational acceleration is called "free-fall" and the equations shown in (2.26) allow us to solve problems for objects in free fall.

Now let us confront the assumption of constant gravitational acceleration with experiment. To do this, we went to the top of a building of height 12.7 m and dropped a computer from rest ($v_{y0} = 0$). We filmed this drop and digitized the frames. Since the camera records at 30 frames per second, we know the time information. In Figure 2.16 we display 14 frames, equally spaced in time, from this experiment and mark the time after release for each frame on the horizontal time axis. The yellow curve that we overlay has the form

$$y = 12.7\text{ m} - \tfrac{1}{2}(9.81\text{ m/s}^2)t^2 ,$$

which is what we expect for initial conditions $y_0 = 12.7$ m, $v_{y0} = 0$ and the assumption of a constant acceleration of $a_y = -9.81\text{ m/s}^2$. As you can see, the computer's fall follows this parabola almost perfectly. This is, of course, not a conclusive proof, but it is a strong indication that the gravitational acceleration is constant near the surface of Earth, and that it has the stated value.

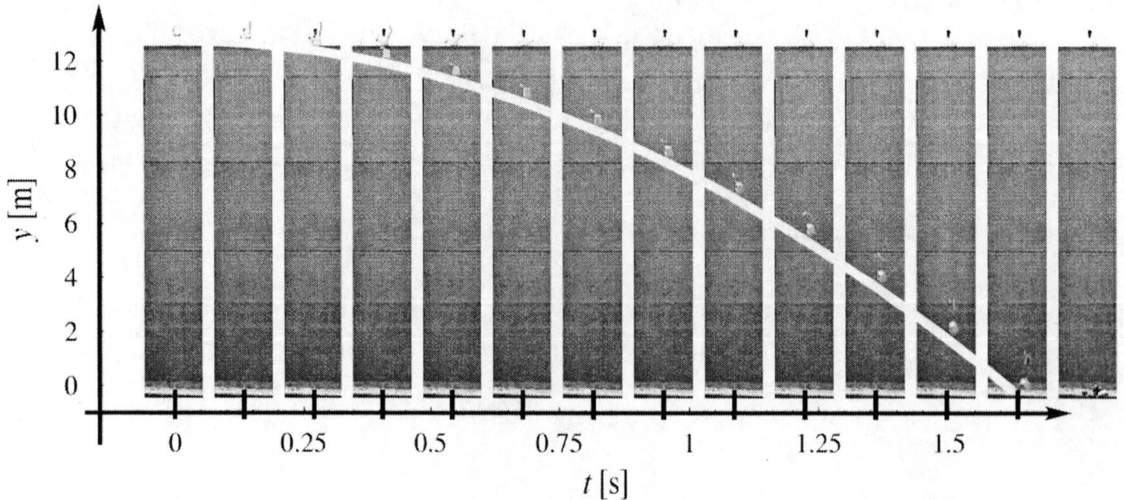

Figure 2.16: Free-fall experiment: dropping a computer off the top of a building.

Furthermore the value of this acceleration is the same for all objects. This is by no means a trivial statement. Objects of different size and weight, if released from the same height, should then hit the ground at the same time. Is this consistent with our everyday experience?

Well, not quite! In a common lecture demonstration one drops a feather and a coin from the same height. It is easy to observe that the coin reaches the floor first, while the feather slowly sails down. This difference is due to air resistance. If one repeats the same experiment in an evacuated glass tube, the coin and the feather fall at the same rate. We will return to air resistance later, but for now we can conclude that the gravitational acceleration near the surface of Earth is constant, has the absolute value of $g = 9.81 \text{ m/s}^2$, and is the same for all objects provided we can neglect air resistance. When we return to air resistance in chapter 4, we will discuss under which conditions the assumption of zero air resistance is justified.

In-class exercise:
If you throw a ball straight up into the air, this is a particular example of free-fall motion. At the instant that the ball reaches its maximum height, which of the following statements it true?
a) The ball's acceleration points down and its velocity points up.
b) The ball's acceleration is zero and its velocity points up.
c) The ball's acceleration points up and its velocity points up.
d) The ball's acceleration points down and its velocity is zero.
e) The ball's acceleration points up and its velocity is zero.
f) The ball's acceleration is zero and its velocity points down.

Example

Example 2.5: Reaction time
It takes a certain time for a person to react to external stimuli. For example, at the beginning of a 100 m dash competition in track and field, a gun is fired by the starter. Then there is a slight time delay before the runners come out of the starting blocks. This delay is due to the finite reaction time. In fact, it counts as a false start if a runner leaves the blocks less than 0.1 s after the gun is fired. Any shorter time would be evidence that the runner has "jumped the gun".

The following exercise is a simple test that you can perform to determine your reaction time. This test is shown in Figure 2.17. Your partner holds a meter stick, and you get ready to catch it when your partner releases it in the way shown (left frame). From the distance h the meter stick has fallen after it was released and you grab it (right frame), you can determine your reaction time.

Question:
If the meter stick falls 0.20 m before you catch it, what is your reaction time?

Answer:
This situation is a free-fall scenario. For these problems, invariably the solution comes back to one of the five basic formulas in Equation 2.25. The problem we need to solve

Example

now involves the time as an unknown. We are given the displacement, $h = y_0 - y$. We also know the initial velocity of the meter stick is zero because it is released from rest. We can use the first kinematical equation, $y = y_0 + v_{y0}t - \frac{1}{2}gt^2$ from equation (2.26), and get our answer. With $h = y_0 - y$ and $v_0 = 0$, this equation becomes:

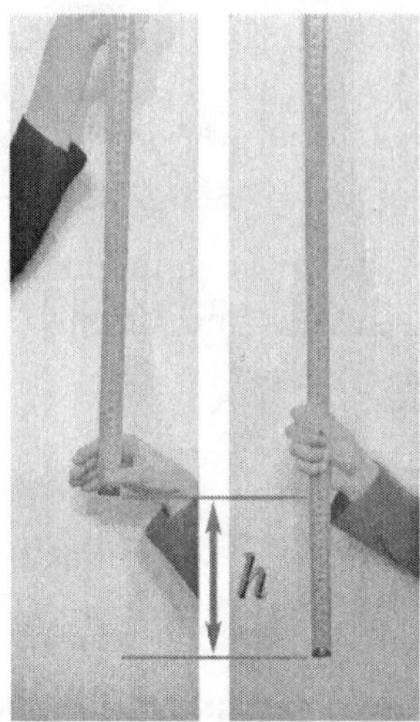

Figure 2.17: Simple experiment to measure reaction time.

$$\begin{aligned} y &= y_0 - \tfrac{1}{2}gt^2 \\ \Rightarrow h &= \tfrac{1}{2}gt^2 \\ \Rightarrow t &= \sqrt{\frac{2h}{g}} = \sqrt{\frac{2 \cdot 0.20\ \text{m}}{9.81\ \text{m/s}^2}} = 0.20\ \text{s} \end{aligned} \tag{2.27}$$

We find that in this case the reaction time was 0.20 s. This reaction time is typical. For comparison, when Tim Montgomery established a 100 m sprint world record of 9.78 s in September 2002, his reaction time was measured to be 0.104 s.

In-class exercise:
If the reaction time of person B is twice as long as that of person A, then the displacement h_B measured for person B relative to the displacement h_A of person A is …

a) $h_B = 2h_A$

b) $h_B = \frac{1}{2}h_A$

c) $h_B = \sqrt{2}h_A$

d) $h_B = 4h_A$ ✔

e) $h_B = \sqrt{\frac{1}{2}}h_A$

Self-Test Opportunity:
Can you sketch a graph of the reaction time as a function of the distances that the ruler drops? Discuss if this method is more precise for reaction times around 0.1 s or those around 0.3 s.

Let us consider one more free-fall scenario, this time with two moving objects.

Solved Problem 2.3: Melon Drop

Suppose you decide to drop a melon from rest on the first observation platform of the Eiffel Tower, as indicated in Figure 2.18. The initial height h from which the melon is released is 58.3 m above the head of your French friend Pierre, who standing on the ground is right below you. At the very same instant that you release the melon, Pierre shoots an arrow straight up with an initial velocity of 25.1 m/s.

Question:
How long after you dropped the melon will the arrow hit it? And at which height above the head of Pierre does this collision occur?

Answer:

THINK:
At first sight, this looks like a very complicated problem. We will solve it in full detail and then examine what shortcuts we could have taken. Obviously, for the melon we have a free-fall problem. But since the arrow is shot straight up, the arrow is also in free-fall, only with a different initial velocity.

SKETCH:
We set up our coordinate system with the y-axis pointing vertically up, as is conventional. And we locate the origin of the coordinate system at Pierre's head, as shown in Figure 2.18. So the arrow is released from an initial position of $y = 0$, and the melon from $y = h$.

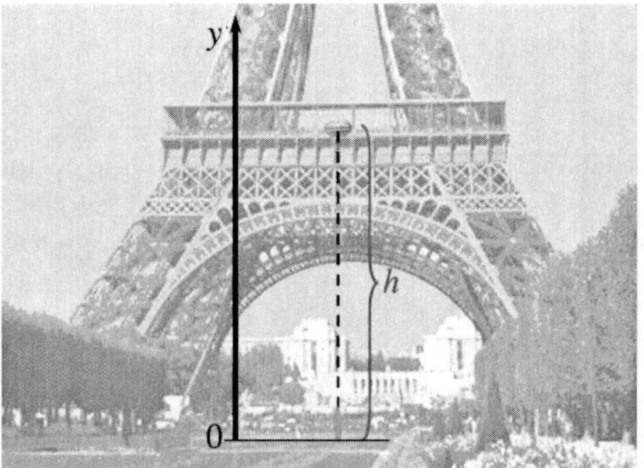

Figure 2.18: Sketch for the melon drop (melon is not drawn to scale!).

Solved Problem

RESEARCH:

We use the subscript m for the melon and a for the arrow. We start from the general free-fall equation, $y = y_0 + v_{y0}t - \frac{1}{2}gt^2$ and use the initial conditions given for the melon ($v_{y0} = 0,\ y_0 = h = 58.3$ m) and the arrow ($v_{y0} \equiv v_{a0} = 25.1$ m/s, $y_0 = 0$) to set up the two equations of motion:

$$y_m(t) = h - \tfrac{1}{2}gt^2$$
$$y_a(t) = v_{a0}t - \tfrac{1}{2}gt^2$$

The key insight is that at the moment t_c that the melon and arrow collide in the air, their coordinates are identical:

$$y_a(t_c) = y_m(t_c)$$

SIMPLIFY:

Inserting t_c into the two equations of motion and setting them equal results in:

$$h - \tfrac{1}{2}gt_c^2 = v_{a0}t_c - \tfrac{1}{2}gt_c^2 \Rightarrow$$
$$h = v_{a0}t_c \Rightarrow$$
$$t_c = \frac{h}{v_{a0}}$$

Once we have determined this value for the time of collision, we can insert it in either of the two free-fall equations for the arrow or the melon, and we obtain the height above Pierre's head, at which the collision occurs. We select the equation for the melon:

$$y_m(t_c) = h - \tfrac{1}{2}gt_c^2$$

CALCULATE:

All that is left to do is to insert the given numbers for the height of release of the melon and the initial velocity of the arrow. Typing this into our pocket calculator results in

$$t_c = \frac{58.3 \text{ m}}{25.1 \text{ m/s}} = 2.32271 \text{ s}$$

for the time of impact.

Having obtained this number for the time, we then find for the position at which the collision occurs:

$$y_m(t_c) = 58.3 \text{ m} - \tfrac{1}{2}(9.81 \text{ m/s}^2)(2.32271 \text{ s})^2 = 31.8376 \text{ m}$$

ROUND:

Since both initial conditions, release height and initial arrow velocity, were given to three significant digits, we also have to quote our final answer to three digits. So our answer is that the arrow will hit the melon after 2.32 seconds, and that this will occur at a position of 31.8 m above Pierre's head.

DOUBLE-CHECK:

Could we have obtained this answer in an easier way? Yes, if we realize that melon and arrow fall under the influence of the same gravitational acceleration, and thus the free-fall motion does not influence the distance between them. So the time it takes them to meet is simply their initial distance divided by their initial velocity difference. With this realization, we could have written $t = h / v_{a0}$ right away and would have been done. However, this way of thinking in terms of relative motion takes some practice, and we will return to it in more detail in the next chapter.

Figure 2.19 shows is the complete graph of the position of arrow and melon as a function of time. The dashed portions of both graphs indicate where the arrow and melon would have gone, had they not collided.

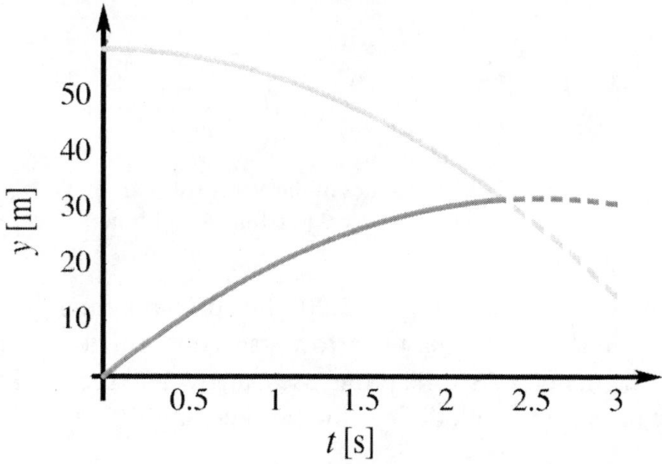

Figure 2.19: Position as a function of time for the arrow (red curve) and the melon (green curve).

Additional Question:
What are the velocities of melon and arrow at the moment of the collision?

Answer:
We obtain the velocity by taking the time derivative of the position. For arrow and melon this results in:

$$y_m(t) = h - \tfrac{1}{2} g t^2 \Rightarrow v_m(t) = \frac{dy_m(t)}{dt} = -gt$$

$$y_a(t) = v_{a0} t - \tfrac{1}{2} g t^2 \Rightarrow v_a(t) = \frac{dy_a(t)}{dt} = v_{a0} - gt$$

Now we have to insert the time of the collision, 2.34 s, and we get our answers. Note that, unlike the positions of the arrow and the melon, the velocities of the two objects are not the same right before contact!

Solved Problem

$$v_m(t_c) = -(9.81 \text{ m/s}^2)(2.32 \text{ s}) = -22.8 \text{ m/s}$$
$$v_a(t_c) = (25.1 \text{ m/s}) - (9.81 \text{ m/s}^2)(2.32 \text{ s}) = 2.34 \text{ m/s}$$

Further you should note that the difference between the two velocities is still 25 m/s, just as it was at the beginning of the trajectories.

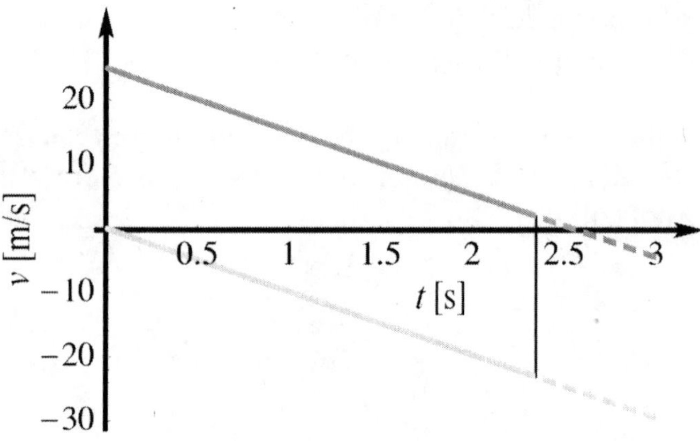

Figure 2.20: Velocities of the arrow (red curve) and melon (green curve) as a function of time.

We finish this example by plotting (Figure 2.20) the corresponding graph of the velocities as a function of time. You can see that the arrow starts out with a velocity that is 25.1 m/s greater than that of the melon. As time progresses, arrow and melon fall at the same rate under the influence of gravity, with their velocities keeping the same difference.

In-class exercise:
If the melon is thrown straight up with an initial velocity of 5 m/s at the same time that the arrow is shot, how long does it now take before the collision occurs?
a) 2.34 s
b) 2.92 s
c) 1.95 s
d) They do not collide before the melon hits the ground.

Self-Test Opportunity:
As you can see from the answer to our melon drop example, the velocity of the arrow is very small, only 2.34 m/s, when it hits the melon. This means that by the time the arrow hits the melon almost all of its initial velocity has been used up by its climb against gravity. Now suppose that the initial velocity of the arrow was smaller by 5.0 m/s! What would change in this problem? Would the arrow still hit the melon?

2.8. Motion in More than One Dimension

Motion in one spatial dimension is of course not the end. We can also investigate more general cases, in which objects move in more than one spatial dimension. We will do this in the next few chapters. However, there are some examples where the motion occurs in more than one dimension, but which can be reduced to one-dimensional motion. We will finish this chapter with a very interesting case of motion in two dimensions, for which each segment can be described by motion in a straight line.

Example 2.6: Aquathlon

The triathlon is a competition that was invented by the San Diego Track Club in the 1970s, is now already in the Olympic Games, and typically consists of a 1.5 km swim, followed by a 40 km bike race, and finished with a 10 km foot race. To be competitive, one needs to be able to swim the 1.5 km distance in less than 20 minutes, run the 10 km race in less than 35 minutes, and the do 40 km bike race in less than 70 minutes.

However, for the present example, let us consider a competition where thinking is rewarded in addition to athletic prowess. Our competition consists of only two legs, a swim followed by a run. (This competition is sometimes called "aquathlon"). Our athletes will start a distance of $b = 1.5$ km from shore, and the finish line is a distance of $a = 3$ km to the left along the shoreline, as shown in Figure 2.21. Suppose our athlete can swim with a speed of $v_1 = 3.5$ km/s , and can run across the sand with a speed of $v_2 = 14$ km/s .

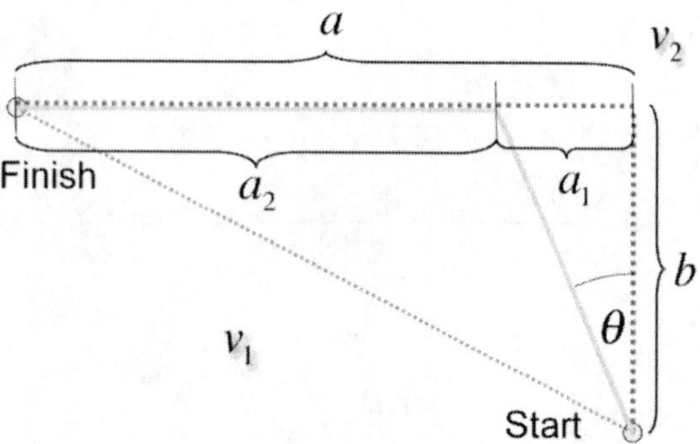

Figure 2.21: Aquathlon course geometry.

Question:
Which angle θ will result in the shortest finish time under these conditions?

Answer:
Clearly, the red dashed line marks the shortest distance between start and finish. This distance is $\sqrt{a^2+b^2} = \sqrt{1.5^2+3^2}$ km $= 3.354$ km . Since this entire path is in water, we find the time that is takes to complete the race in this way is

$$t_{red} = \sqrt{a^2+b^2}\,/\,v_1 = (3.354 \text{ km})/(3.5 \text{ km/h}) = 0.958 \text{ h}$$

Example

Since our athlete can run faster that he can swim, we can also try the approach indicated by the blue line. He can swim straight to shore and then run. This takes

$$t_{blue} = b/v_1 + a/v_2 = (1.5 \text{ km})/(3.5 \text{ km/h}) + (3 \text{ km})/(14 \text{ km/h}) = 0.643 \text{ h}$$

Right away we find that the blue course is better than the red one. But is it the best? To answer this question, we need to search the interval from 0 (blue path) to $\arctan(3/1.5) = 63.43°$ (red path). Let us set up the green path with an arbitrary angle θ with respect to the straight line to shore (=normal to the shoreline). On the green path we have to swim a distance of $\sqrt{a_1^2 + b^2}$ and then run a distance of a_2, as indicated in Figure 2.21. The total time that this approach takes is

$$\begin{aligned} t(\theta) &= \frac{\sqrt{a_1^2 + b^2}}{v_1} + \frac{a_2}{v_2} \\ &= \frac{\sqrt{(1+\tan^2\theta)b^2}}{v_1} + \frac{a - b\tan\theta}{v_2} \\ &= \frac{b}{v_1\cos\theta} + \frac{a - b\tan\theta}{v_2} \end{aligned} \tag{2.28}$$

To find the minimum time as a function of the angle, we have to first take the derivative with respect to the angle and then find the angle for which this derivative vanishes,

$$\begin{aligned} \frac{dt(\theta)}{d\theta} &= \frac{b\tan\theta}{v_1\cos\theta} - \frac{b}{v_2\cos^2\theta} \\ \frac{b\tan\theta_m}{v_1\cos\theta_m} &- \frac{b}{v_2\cos^2\theta_m} = 0 \Rightarrow \\ v_2\sin\theta_m &= v_1 \Rightarrow \\ \sin\theta_m &= \frac{v_1}{v_2} \end{aligned} \tag{2.29}$$

This is a very interesting result, because the distances a and b do not appear in it at all! Instead the sine of the optimum angle is simply given by the ratio of the speeds in water and on land. For the given values of the two speeds, this angle is

$$\theta_m = \arcsin(3.5/14) = 14.48°$$

Inserting this value of the angle into the above equation for the time as a function of the angle, we find a time of $t(\theta_m) = 0.629$ h. This is approximately 49 seconds faster than swimming straight to shore and then running (blue path).

Example

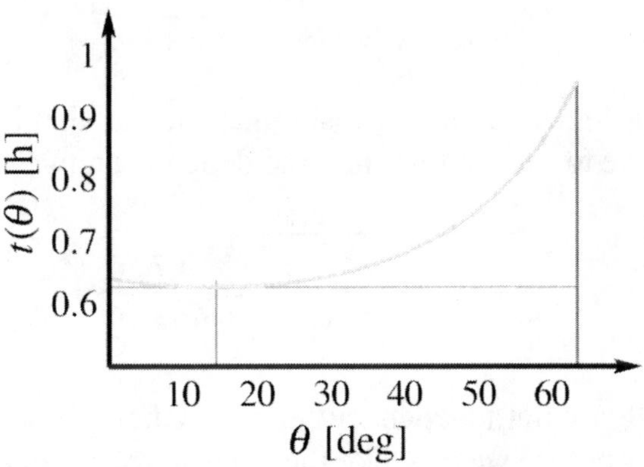

Figure 2.22: Duration of the race as a function of initial angle.

Strictly speaking we have not quite shown that this angle results in the minimum time. To accomplish this, we need to also show that the second derivative of the time with respect to the angle is larger than 0. But since we only found one extremum, and since its value is smaller than those of the boundaries, we already know that this extremum is a true minimum.

Finally, in Figure 2.22 we plot the time it takes, in hours, to complete the race for all angles between 0 degrees and 63.43 degrees. This is indicated by the green curve. We have used a vertical red line to mark the maximum angle that corresponds to a straight-line swim from start to finish. The vertical light blue line marks the optimum angle that we calculated, and the horizontal blue line marks the duration of the race for this angle.

After we have completed the previous example, we can address the next more complicated question: If the finish line is not at the shore, but a perpendicular distance b away from the shore, as in Figure 2.23, what are the angles θ_1 and θ_2 that a competitor needs to select for the minimum time? Going through the following derivation, we will arrive at Snell's Law, which is well-known from optics.

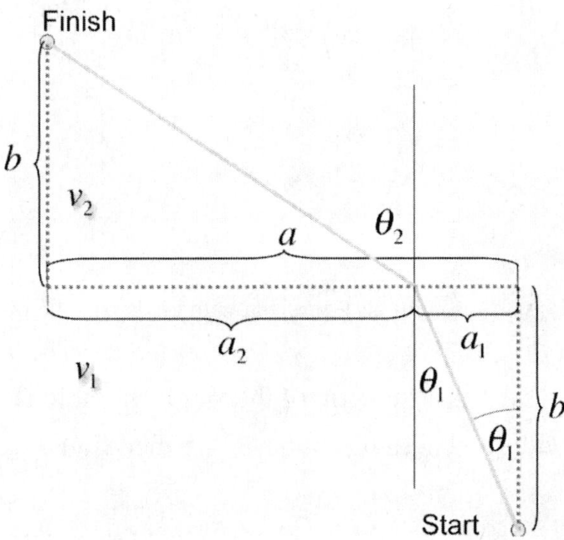

Figure 2.23: Modified aquathlon, with finish away from the coastline.

The discussion proceeds in a very similar fashion to the one that led us to our previous answer. But now we have to realize that the time depends on two angles

$$t(\theta_1,\theta_2)=\frac{\sqrt{a_1^2+b^2}}{v_1}+\frac{\sqrt{a_2^2+b^2}}{v_2}=\frac{b}{v_1\cos\theta_1}+\frac{b}{v_2\cos\theta_2} \tag{2.30}$$

The two angles θ_1 and θ_2 are not independent of each other. Thus we need to relate these two angles to each other before we can take the derivative in order to find the minimum as before. It is perhaps easiest to accomplish this by flipping up the lower triangle, as shown in Figure 2.24.

Now we see that the two right triangles a_1bc_1 and a_2bc_2 have a common side b, which helps us to relate the two angles to each other. Since we have

$$a_2=a-a_1=a-b\tan\theta_1,$$

just like before, we can insert this result in the equation for the time and obtain now

$$\begin{aligned} t(\theta_1)&=\frac{b}{v_1\cos\theta_1}+\frac{\sqrt{b^2+(a-a_1)^2}}{v_2} \\ &=\frac{b}{v_1\cos\theta_1}+\frac{\sqrt{b^2+(a-b\tan\theta_1)^2}}{v_2} \end{aligned} \tag{2.31}$$

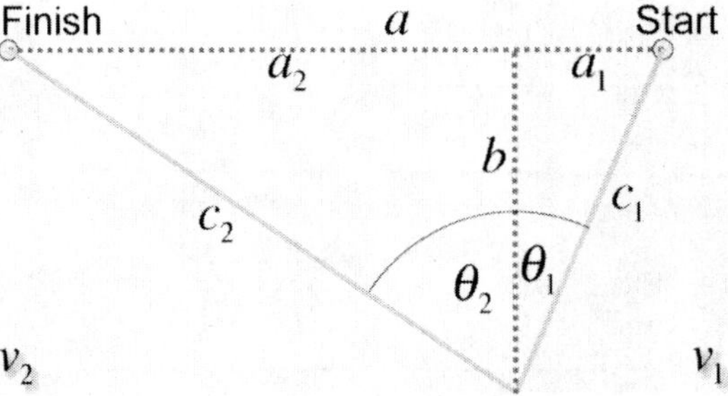

Figure 2.24: same as previous figure, but with lower triangle flipped over.

So the time is now expressed as a function of the single variable θ_1, and taking the derivative of the time with respect to the angle θ_1 we then find

$$\frac{dt(\theta_1)}{d\theta_1} = \frac{b\tan\theta_1}{v_1\cos\theta_1} - \frac{b(a-b\tan\theta_1)}{v_2\cos^2\theta_1\sqrt{b^2+(a-b\tan\theta_1)^2}} \tag{2.32}$$

Finding the root of this equation is again a necessary condition for the minimum and leads us to

$$\frac{b\tan\theta_1}{v_1\cos\theta_1} = \frac{b(a-b\tan\theta_1)}{v_2\cos^2\theta_1\sqrt{b^2+(a-b\tan\theta_1)^2}} \Rightarrow$$
$$\frac{\sin\theta_1}{v_1} = \frac{a-b\tan\theta_1}{v_2\sqrt{b^2+(a-b\tan\theta_1)^2}} \tag{2.33}$$

As a last step, we use again $a-b\tan\theta_1 = a_2$. Further we realize from Figure 2.24 that $\sqrt{b^2+(a-b\tan\theta_1)^2} = \sqrt{b^2+a_2^2} = c_2$, and that $a_2/c_2 = \sin\theta_2$. Combining this result with equation (2.33), we then find for our necessary condition to achieve the minimum time

$$\frac{\sin\theta_1}{v_1} = \frac{\sin\theta_2}{v_2} \tag{2.34}$$

We can now see that our previous result (2.29), where we forced the running to take place along the beach, is a special case of this more general result (2.34), with $\theta_2 = 90°$. Just like in the special case that we addressed before, we find that the relationship between the angles is not dependent on the values of the displacements a and b that were given, but depends only on the speeds with which the competitor can move in the water and on land. There is of course still the overall constraint that you have to get from the start to the finish that relates the angles to a and b, But the point is still that for the path of minimum time the change in direction at the border between water and land, as expressed by two angles θ_1 and θ_2, is determined exclusively by the ratio of the speeds v_1 and v_2.

As our initial condition we had demanded that the perpendicular distance b from the starting point to the land-water interface is the same as the perpendicular distance between this interface and the finish. This was done to keep our algebra relatively brief. However, in the final formula you see that there is no more reference to b; it has cancelled out. So the equation (2.34) is even valid in the case that the two perpendicular distances have different values. The ratio of angles for the path of minimum time is exclusively determined by the two speeds in the different media.

Interestingly, we will again encounter the same relationship between the two angles and two speeds for light changing direction at the interface between two media through which light moves with different speeds. We find that light also moves along the path of minimum time, and we will call the result obtained in (2.34) Snell's Law. We will learn more on this when we come to chapter 32 on geometric optics.

And, finally, we make an observation that may appear trivial: If we start at the point marked "Finish" in the drawing and want to end up at the point marked "Start", we have to take exactly the same path as the one we just calculated for the reverse direction. Snell's Law holds in both directions.

What we have learned/Exam Study Guide:

- x is the x-component of the displacement vector.
- Displacement is the change in position $\Delta x = x_2 - x_1$.
- Distance is the absolute value of displacement $\ell = |\Delta x|$ and is a positive scalar.
- The average velocity is given by $\bar{v}_x = \dfrac{\Delta x}{\Delta t}$.
- The (instantaneous) velocity vector is the derivative of the position vector as a function of time $v_x = \dfrac{dx}{dt}$.
- Speed is the absolute value of the velocity, $v = |v_x|$
- The acceleration vector is the change of the velocity vector as a function of time $a_x = \dfrac{dv_x}{dt}$.
- For constant accelerations, there are five kinematical equations describing motion in one dimension

  (*i*) $x = x_0 + v_{x0}t + \frac{1}{2}a_x t^2$

  (*ii*) $x = x_0 + \bar{v}_x t$

  (*iii*) $v_x = v_{x0} + a_x t$

  (*iv*) $\bar{v}_x = \frac{1}{2}(v_x + v_{x0})$

  (*v*) $v_x^2 = v_{x0}^2 + 2a_x(x - x_0)$

  where x_0 is the initial position and v_{x0} is the initial velocity.
- For situations involving free-fall (constant acceleration), we can replace the acceleration with $a = -g$ and x with y to obtain

  (*i*) $y = y_0 + v_{y0}t - \frac{1}{2}gt^2$

  (*ii*) $y = y_0 + \bar{v}_y t$

  (*iii*) $v_y = v_{y0} - gt$

  (*iv*) $\bar{v}_y = \frac{1}{2}(v_y + v_{y0})$

  (*v*) $v_y^2 = v_{y0}^2 - 2g(y - y_0)$

  where y_0 is the initial position, v_{y0} is the initial velocity, and the y-axis points up.

Additional Solved Problems

Solved Problem 2.4: Street Racing

Cheri has a new Dodge Charger with a Hemi engine and challenged Vince, who owns a tuned VW GTI, to a street race. Vince knows that the Cheri's Charger is rated to go from 0 to 60 mph in 5.3 seconds, whereas Vince's VW needs 7.0 seconds. So Vince wants a head start. Cheri agrees to give him exactly 1.0 second.

Question:
How far is Vince down the road before Cheri gets to start the race? At what time does Cheri catch Vince? And how far away from the start are they when this happens? (Assume constant acceleration for each car during the race!)

Answer:

THINK:

This street race is a good example of one-dimensional motion with constant acceleration. The temptation is to consult our set of five kinematical equations (2.23) and see which one we can apply. But we have to be a bit more careful here, because the time delay for the start of Cheri relative to the start of Vince adds an additional complication. So this problem requires some careful definition of the time coordinates for each racer.

SKETCH:

For our sketch we plot the time on the horizontal axis and position on the vertical axis. Both cars move with constant acceleration from a standing start. So we expect simple parabolas for their paths in this diagram.

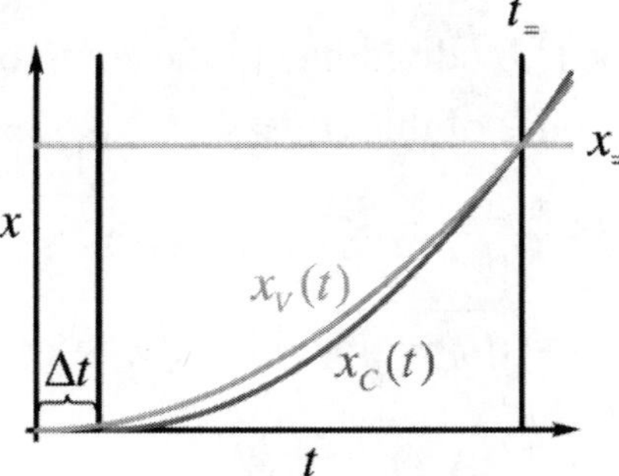

Figure 2.25: Sketch for the street race.

Since Cheri's car has the bigger acceleration, her parabola (blue curve in Figure 2.25) has the larger curvature and thus the steeper rise. So it is clear that Cheri will catch Vince at some point, but it is not clear yet where this is.

RESEARCH:

Now it is time to set up the problem quantitatively. Let us call the time delay before Cheri can start Δt, and let's use the index C for Cheri's Charger, and V for Vince's VW. We can put the coordinate system's origin at the starting line. Then both cars have initial positions of $x_C(t=0) = x_V(t=0) = 0$. Since both cars are at rest at the start, this implies zero initial velocities for both. So the equation of motion for Vince is

Solved Problem

$$x_V(t) = \tfrac{1}{2}a_V t^2$$

Here we use the symbol a_V for the acceleration generated by the VW. We can calculate its value from the 0 to 60 mph time quoted above, but we will postpone this step until it is time to put in the numbers.

To obtain the equation of motion for Cheri we have to be a little more careful, because she is forced to wait for Δt after Vince has taken off. We can write this fact as a shifted time: $t' = t - \Delta t$. Once t reaches the value of Δt, the time t' has the value 0 and then Cheri can take off. So her equation of motion is

$$x_C(t) = \tfrac{1}{2}a_C t'^2 = \tfrac{1}{2}a_C(t-\Delta t)^2 \qquad \text{for } t \ge \Delta t$$

Just like a_V, the constant acceleration a_C for Cheri's Charger will be evaluated below.

SIMPLIFY:

If and when Cheri catches Vince, their coordinates will have the same value. So we will call the time at which this happens $t_=$, and the coordinate where they are at that time $x_= \equiv x(t_=)$. If the two coordinates are the same, we have

$$x_= = \tfrac{1}{2}a_V t_=^2 = \tfrac{1}{2}a_C(t_= - \Delta t)^2$$

We can solve this equation for $t_=$ by dividing out the common factor of ½ and then taking the square root of both sides of this equation

$$\sqrt{a_V}\,t_= = \sqrt{a_C}\,(t_= - \Delta t) \Rightarrow$$
$$t_=\left(\sqrt{a_C} - \sqrt{a_V}\right) = \Delta t\sqrt{a_C} \Rightarrow$$
$$t_= = \frac{\Delta t\sqrt{a_C}}{\sqrt{a_C} - \sqrt{a_V}}$$

Why did we take the positive root and disregard the negative root here? Answer: the negative root would lead to unphysical solutions, because we are only interested in the time that the two cars meet *after* they have left the start, and not a negative time that would imply an instant before they left.

CALCULATE:

Now we can get a numerical answer for each of the questions that were asked. First, let's figure out the value for the acceleration constants for the two cars from the 0 to 60 mph specifications given. We use $a = (v_x - v_{x0})/t$ and get

Solved Problem

$$a_V = \frac{60 \text{ mph}}{7.0 \text{ s}} = \frac{26.8167 \text{ m/s}}{7.0 \text{ s}} = 3.83095 \text{ m/s}^2$$

$$a_C = \frac{60 \text{ mph}}{5.3 \text{ s}} = \frac{26.8167 \text{ m/s}}{5.3 \text{ s}} = 5.05975 \text{ m/s}^2$$

Again, we postpone rounding our results until we have completed all steps in our calculations. But with our values for the accelerations in hand we can immediately calculate how far Vince can drive during the time $\Delta t = 1.0$ s:

$$x_V(1.0 \text{ s}) = \tfrac{1}{2}(3.83095 \text{ m/s}^2)(1.0 \text{ s})^2 = 1.91548 \text{ m}$$

Now we can calculate the value of the time when Cheri catches Vince. It is

$$t_= = \frac{\Delta t\sqrt{a_C}}{\sqrt{a_C} - \sqrt{a_V}} = \frac{(1.0 \text{ s})\sqrt{5.05975 \text{ m/s}^2}}{\sqrt{5.05975 \text{ m/s}^2} - \sqrt{3.83095 \text{ m/s}^2}} = 7.70057 \text{ s}$$

At this time both cars have traveled to the same point. So we can insert $t_=$ into either equation of motion to find the position where this happens:

$$x_= = \tfrac{1}{2}a_V t_=^2 = \tfrac{1}{2}(3.83095 \text{ m/s}^2)(7.70057 \text{ s})^2 = 113.586 \text{ m}$$

ROUND:

Our initial data were specified only to a precision of two significant digits. Rounding our results to the same precision we finally arrive at our answers: Vince receives a head start of 1.9 m, and Cheri will catch him after 7.7 s. At that time they will be $1.1 \cdot 10^2$ m into their race.

DOUBLE-CHECK:

Let us end this problem with a plot of the equations of motion for both cars, this time with the proper units.

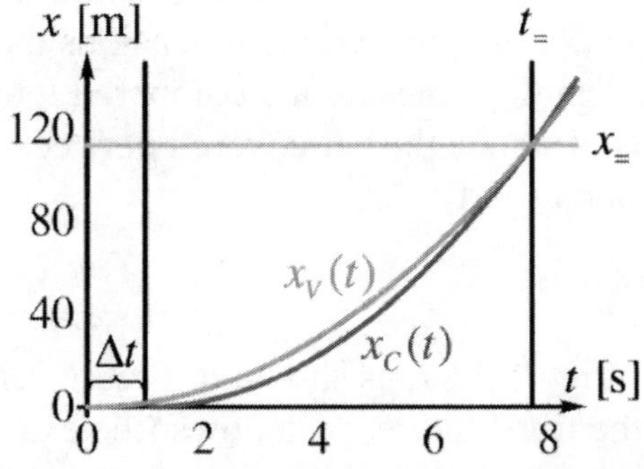

Figure 2.26: Plot of the street race parameters and equations of motion.

It may seem strange to you that Vince only was able to move 1.9 m, which is approximately half of the length of his car, during the first second. Have we done

Solved Problem

anything wrong in our calculation? The answer is no; from a standing start cars really move only a comparatively short distance during the first second of acceleration. The following solved problem actually contains visible proof for this statement.

Solved Problem 2.5: Accelerating Car

Figure 2.27: Video sequence of a car accelerating from a standing start.

Solved Problem

Question:

If you are given the image sequence shown in Figure 2.27, and you are told that there is a time interval of 0.333 seconds between each two frames, can you find out how fast this car (Ford Escape Hybrid, length 174.9 inches, height 69.7 inches, wheelbase 103.2 inches) was accelerating from rest? And can you give an estimate for the 0 to 60 mph time of this car?

Answer:

THINK:

Acceleration is measured in dimensions of length per time per time. To give a number for the value of the acceleration, we need to know the time and length scales in Figure 2.27. The time scale is actually straightforward, because we were given the information that 1/3 of a second has passed between each two frames that are shown. We can get the length scale from the information on the vehicle dimensions that were stated. For example, if we focus on the length of the car and compared it to the width of the overall picture, we can find out what distance the car covered between the first and the last time frame (which are 3.000 seconds apart).

SKETCH:

We draw vertical lines over Figure 2.27, as shown in Figure 2.28. We chose the center of the car at the line between the front and rear windows (the exact location is irrelevant, as long as we are consistent with our choice). Now we can use a ruler and measure the perpendicular distance between the two yellow lines, as indicated by the yellow double-arrow in the figure. We can also measure the length of the car, as indicated by the red double-arrow.

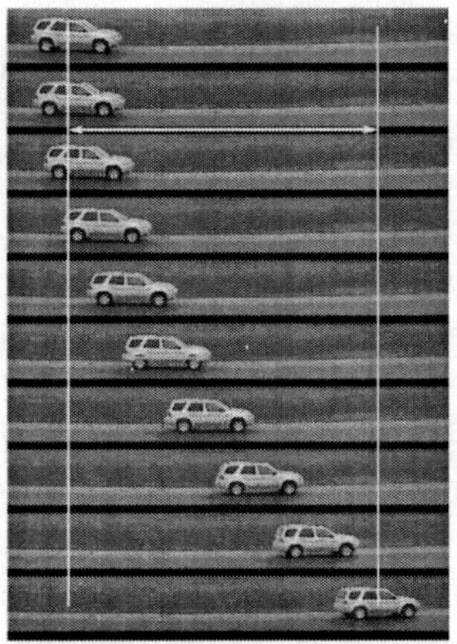

Figure 2.28: Determination of length scale.

RESEARCH:

By dividing the length of the yellow double-arrow by that of the red one, we find a ratio of 3.474 between the two lengths. Since the two vertical yellow lines mark the position of the center of the car at 0.000 s and 3.000 s, we thus know that the car covered a distance of 3.474 car lengths in this time interval. The car lengths was given as 174.9 inches = 4.442 m. So the total distance covered is $d = 3.474 \cdot \ell_{car} = 3.474 \cdot 4.442 \text{ m} = 15.4317 \text{ m}$ (Remember: we will only round to the proper number of significant digits in the end!).

SIMPLIFY:

Now we have two choices on how to proceed. The first one is the more complicated one in that we could measure the position of the car in each frame and then use difference formulas of the kind shown in Example 2.3. The other and much faster way to proceed is to assume constant acceleration and then only use the measurements of the positions of the car in the first and last frame. We use the second way, but in the end have to double-check that our assumption of constant acceleration is really justified.

Since we have a standing start, for a constant acceleration we then simply have

$$x = x_0 + \tfrac{1}{2}at^2 \Rightarrow$$

$$d = x - x_0 = \tfrac{1}{2}at^2 \Rightarrow$$

$$a = \frac{2d}{t^2}$$

This is the acceleration we want to find. Once we have the acceleration, we can give an estimate for the 0 to 60 mph time by using $v_x = v_{x0} + at \Rightarrow t = (v_x - v_{x0})/a$. A standing start means $v_{x0} = 0$, and so we find for the 0 to 60 mph time:

$$t(0-60 \text{ mph}) = \frac{60 \text{ mph}}{a}$$

CALCULATE:

We insert the numbers for the acceleration and find

Solved Problem

$$a=\frac{2d}{t^2}=\frac{2\cdot(15.4317\text{ m})}{(3.000\text{ s})^2}=3.42922\text{ m/s}^2$$

And for the 0 to 60 mph time:

$$t(0-60\text{ mph})=\frac{60\text{ mph}}{a}=\frac{(60\text{ mph})(1609\text{ m/mile})(1\text{ h/3600 s})}{3.42922\text{ m/s}^2}=7.82004\text{ s}$$

ROUND:

The length of the car set our length scale, and it was given to four significant digits. The time was given to three significant digits. But are we then entitled to quote our results to three significant digits? The answer is no, because we also performed measurements on the figure, which are probably only accurate to one percent at best. In addition, you can see field-of-vision and lens distortions in the image sequence: in the first frame you see a little bit of the front of the car, and in the last frame a little bit of the back. Taking this into account, our results should be quoted to two significant digits at best. So our final answer for the acceleration is:

$$a=3.4\text{ m/s}^2$$

And for the 0 to 60 mph time estimate we give:

$$t(0-60\text{ mph})=7.8\text{ s}$$

DOUBLE-CHECK:

The numbers that we have found for the acceleration and 0 to 60 mph time are fairly typical for cars or small SUVs; see also the previous solved problem. So we can have confidence that we are at least not off by orders of magnitude. What remains to double-check, however, is the assumption of constant acceleration. For constant acceleration with standing start, the points $x(t)$ should fall on a parabola $x(t)=\frac{1}{2}at^2$. So if we plot x horizontal and the time vertical, as done in Figure 2.27 the points $t(x)$ should follow a square-root dependence, $t(x)=\sqrt{2x/a}$. This functional dependence is overlaid in Figure 2.29 (red line). We can see that the same point of the car is hit by the line in every frame, giving us confidence that the assumption of constant acceleration is a reasonable one.

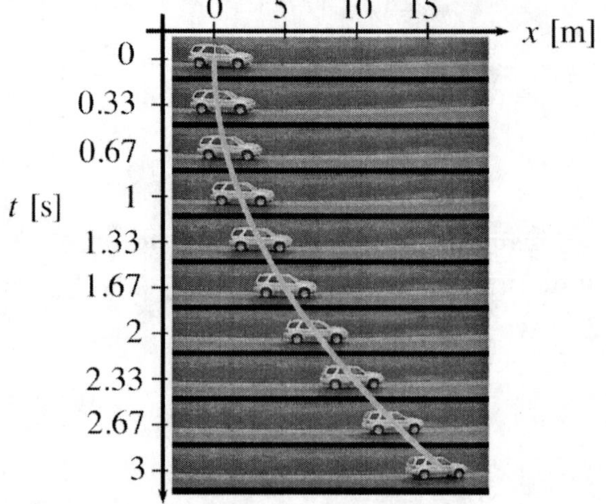

Figure 2.29: Graphical analysis of the accelerating car problem.

Chapter 3: Motion in 2 and 3 Dimensions

What we will learn:

- To handle motion in 2 and 3 dimension using methods developed for 1 dimensional motion.
- To determine the parabolic path of ideal projectile motion.
- To calculate the maximum height and maximum range of an ideal trajectory in terms of the initial velocity vector and the initial position.
- To describe the velocity vector of a projectile in flight at any time.
- To appreciate that realistic trajectories of real objects like baseballs are affected by air friction and spin and are not parabolas.
- To transform velocity vectors between different reference frames.

3.1. Working in Components

Having studied motion in 1 dimension, we will now tackle more complicated problems in 2 and 3 spatial dimensions. If we want to study, for example, the path that a thrown baseball takes in the air (red line in Figure 3.1) then we need to take into account that the baseball will land at a different point in the horizontal plane from the point where it was thrown, and that it will move up and then down in the vertical direction.

To describe this motion, we will work in Cartesian coordinates. We introduce a 3-dimensional Cartesian coordinate system, where we place the x- and y-axes in the horizontal plane, and the z-axis pointing vertically upward. This choice leads to three coordinate axes that are at 90 degrees (orthogonal) to each other, as required for a Cartesian coordinate system.

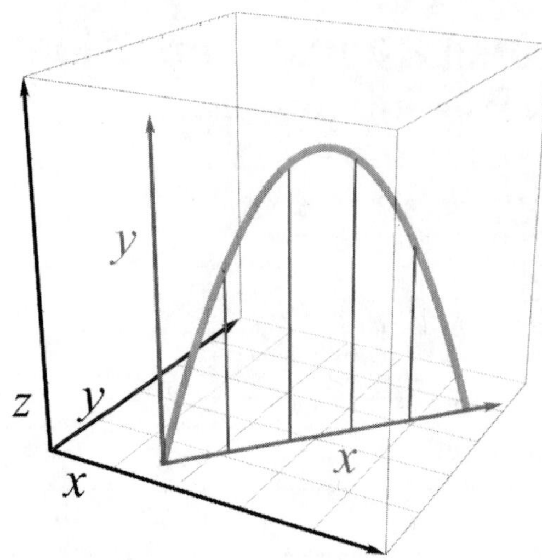

Figure 3.1: Trajectory in 3 dimensions reduced to a trajectory in 2 dimensions.

The convention that is followed without exception is that the coordinate system has to be "right-handed". This convention means that you can obtain the relative orientation of the three coordinate axes by using your right hand. To determine the positive direction of the three axes, hold your right hand with the thumb and index finger pointing straight out; they will naturally have a 90-degree angle relative to each other. Then stick out your middle finger so that it is at a right angle with the index finger and the thumb as shown in Figure 3.2. The three axes are assigned to the fingers as shown in the left panel of the figure: thumb- x , index finger- y , middle finger- z . You can rotate your right hand in any direction, but the relative orientation of the fingers stays the same. If you want, you can also cyclically exchange the letters on the fingers, as shown in the middle and right panels of the figure. But z has to always follow y , which always has to follow x . The three panels in Figure 3.2 show all possible combinations of the assignment of the axes to the fingers. You really only have to remember one of them, because your hand can always be rotated in three-dimensional space in such a way that for all three combinations shown in the figure the coordinate axes align with each other. In particular, you can see that the hand can be oriented to align with the coordinate axes in the schematic three-dimensional drawing shown in Figure 3.1.

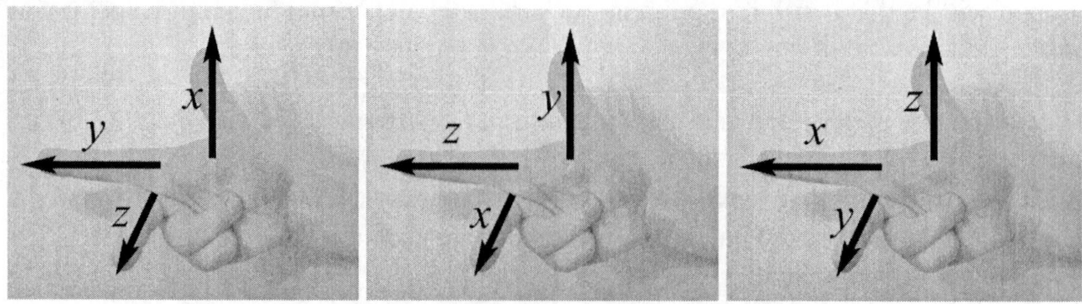

Figure 3.2: All three possible realizations of a right-handed Cartesian coordinate system.

The position vector can be written in Cartesian components as

$$\vec{r} = (x, y, z) = x\hat{x} + y\hat{y} + z\hat{z}\,, \tag{3.1}$$

and our velocity vector is

$$\vec{v} = (v_x, v_y, v_y) = v_x\hat{x} + v_y\hat{y} + v_z\hat{z} \tag{3.2}$$

For one-dimensional vectors we have learned that the time-derivative of the position vector defines the velocity vector. This is also the case for more than one dimension,

$$\vec{v} = \frac{d\vec{r}}{dt} = \frac{d}{dt}(x\hat{x} + y\hat{y} + z\hat{z}) = \frac{dx}{dt}\hat{x} + \frac{dy}{dt}\hat{y} + \frac{dz}{dt}\hat{z}\,. \tag{3.3}$$

In the last step of this equation, we have used the sum and product rules of differentiation, as well as the fact that the unit vectors are constants (fixed direction along the coordinate axes and constant magnitude 1). Comparing equations (3.2) and (3.3), we see that

$$\begin{aligned} v_x &= \frac{dx}{dt} \\ v_y &= \frac{dy}{dt} \\ v_z &= \frac{dz}{dt} \end{aligned} \tag{3.4}$$

The same procedure leads us from the velocity to the acceleration by taking another time derivative,

$$\vec{a} = \frac{d\vec{v}}{dt} = \frac{dv_x}{dt}\hat{x} + \frac{dv_y}{dt}\hat{y} + \frac{dv_z}{dt}\hat{z} \tag{3.5}$$

There are special cases of three-dimensional motion in which the horizontal projection of the trajectory is a straight line. This happens whenever the accelerations in the horizontal xy-plane are zero, and thus an object has constant velocity components in the horizontal plane. Such a case is shown in Figure 3.1 for the baseball toss. In this case, we can assign new coordinate axes in which the x-axis points along the horizontal projection of the trajectory, and the y-axis is now the vertical axis. In this special case, the motion in three dimensions can be described as an effective motion in two spatial dimensions. A large class of real life problems falls in this category, especially problems that involve ideal projectile motion.

3.2. Ideal Projectile Motion

An ideal projectile is any object that is released with some initial velocity vector and which then moves only under the influence of (constant, and in vertical downward direction) gravitational acceleration. A basketball free throw (Figure 3.3) is a good example of ideal projectile motion as is the flight of a bullet or the trajectory of a car that becomes airborne. Ideal projectile motion neglects air resistance and wind speed, spin of the projectile, and other effects influencing the flight of real life projectiles. For realistic situations of golf balls, tennis balls, or baseballs moving in air, the actual trajectory is not well described by ideal projectile motion and requires a more sophisticated analysis. We will discuss all of these effects in Section 3.4, but will not go into any quantitative detail.

We begin with ideal projectile motion, with no effects from air resistance. We work in two Cartesian components: x in the horizontal direction and y in the vertical (upward) direction. Therefore our coordinate vector for projectile motion is

$$\vec{r} = (x, y) = x\hat{x} + y\hat{y}\,, \tag{3.6}$$

and the velocity vector is

$$\vec{v} = (v_x, v_y) = v_x\hat{x} + v_x\hat{y} = \left(\frac{dx}{dt}, \frac{dy}{dt}\right) = \frac{dx}{dt}\hat{x} + \frac{dy}{dt}\hat{y} \tag{3.7}$$

With our choice of the coordinate system with a vertical y-axis, the acceleration due to gravity acts only downward, in the $-y$ direction; there is no acceleration in the horizontal direction,

$$\vec{a} = (0, -g) = -g\hat{y}\,. \tag{3.8}$$

Figure 3.3: Photograph of a free throw with a parabolic trajectory of the basketball superimposed

In this special case of a constant acceleration only in the y-direction and with zero acceleration in the x-direction, we are faced with the situation in which we have a free-fall problem for the vertical direction, and a motion with constant velocity in the horizontal direction. The kinematic equations for the x-direction are then those for an object moving with constant velocity:

$$x = x_0 + v_{x0}t \tag{3.9}$$

$$v_x = v_{x0} \tag{3.10}$$

Just like in the previous chapter, we use the notation $v_{x0} \equiv v_x(t=0)$ for the initial value of the x-component of the velocity. The kinematic equations for the y-direction are those for free-fall motion in one dimension:

$$y = y_0 + v_{y0}t - \tfrac{1}{2}gt^2 \tag{3.11}$$

$$y = y_0 + \bar{v}_y t \tag{3.12}$$

$$v_y = v_{y0} - gt \tag{3.13}$$

$$\bar{v}_y = \tfrac{1}{2}(v_y + v_{y0}) \tag{3.14}$$

$$v_y^2 = v_{y0}^2 - 2g(y - y_0) \tag{3.15}$$

For consistency we write $v_{y0} \equiv v_y(t=0)$. With these seven equations for the x- and y-components we can solve all ideal projectile problems.

Example

Example 3.1: Shoot the Monkey

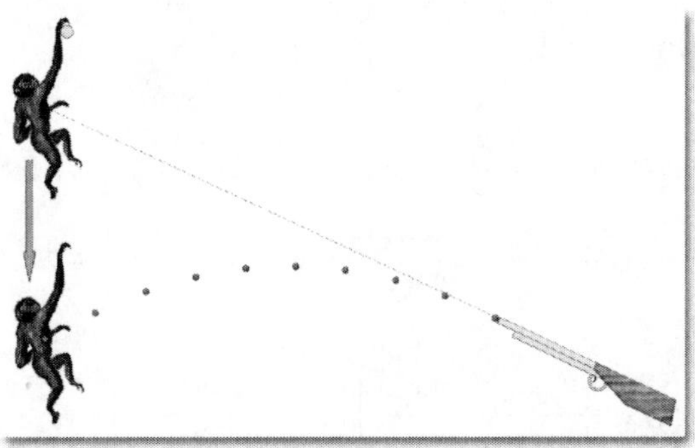

Figure 3.4: Illustration for the shoot-the-monkey lecture demonstration.

There are many demonstrations that one can perform to show that the motion in x- and y-direction are indeed independent of each other, as assumed in the derivation of the above 7 equations for projectile motion. One popular demonstration is "shoot the monkey, " shown in Figure 3.4.

Example

The demonstration is motivated with a story. A monkey has escaped from the zoo and has climbed a tree. The zookeeper wants to fire a tranquilizer dart at the monkey to recapture it. But she knows that the monkey will let go of the branch it is holding on to at the sight and sound of the firing of the gun. So the task is then to hit the monkey in the air as it is falling.

Question:
Where does the zookeeper need to aim to accomplish this feat?

Answer:
The zookeeper must aim directly at the monkey as show in Figure 3.4. As soon as the dart leaves the gun, it is in free fall, just like the monkey. Because both the monkey and the dart are in free fall, they fall with the same acceleration, independent of the motion in x-direction, and independent of the initial velocity vector. The dart and the monkey will meet at a point underneath the point from where the monkey originally dropped.

Discussion:
Any good marksman can tell you that, for a fixed target, you need to correct your gun sight for the free-fall motion of the projectile on the way to the target. Even a projectile fired from a high-powered rifle will not fly in a straight line, but will move under the influence of the gravitational acceleration. Only a scenario like shoot-the-monkey, where the target is in free fall as soon as the projectile leaves the muzzle, allows us to aim directly in a straight line at the target without making corrections for the free-fall motion of the projectile.

Flight Path

We now discuss the trajectory or the flight path of a projectile in 2 dimensions. To find y as a function of x, we solve the equation $x = x_0 + v_{x0}t$ for the time $t = (x - x_0)/v_{x0}$, and insert into the equation $y = y_0 + v_{y0}t - \frac{1}{2}gt^2$:

$$y = y_0 + v_{y0}t - \tfrac{1}{2}gt^2 \Rightarrow$$

$$y = y_0 + v_{y0}\frac{x - x_0}{v_{x0}} - \tfrac{1}{2}g\left(\frac{x - x_0}{v_{x0}}\right)^2 \Rightarrow$$

$$y = \left(y_0 - \frac{v_{y0}x_0}{v_{x0}} - \frac{gx_0^2}{2v_{x0}^2}\right) + \left(\frac{v_{y0}}{v_{x0}} + \frac{gx_0}{2v_{x0}^2}\right)x - \frac{g}{2v_{x0}^2}x^2 \tag{3.16}$$

We see that the flight path follows an equation of the general form $y = ax^2 + bx + c$, with constants a, b, c. This form is the equation for a parabola in the xy plane.

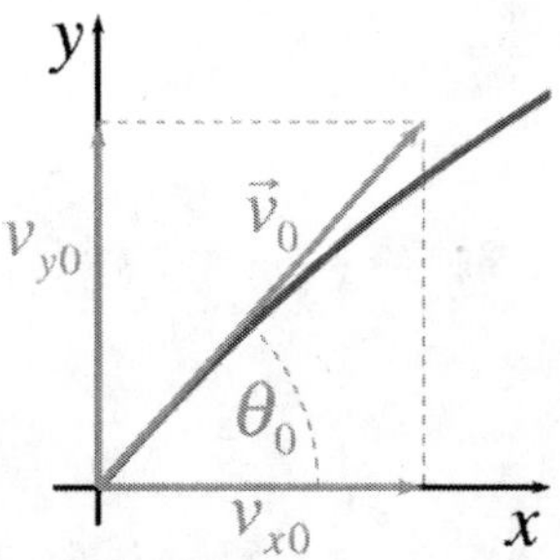

Figure 3.5: Initial velocity vector and its components.

It is customary to set the x-component of the initial point of the parabola to 0: $x_0 = 0$. In this case, our equation for the parabola becomes:

$$y = y_0 + \frac{v_{y0}}{v_{x0}}x - \frac{g}{2v_{x0}^2}x^2 \tag{3.17}$$

The trajectory of the projectile is completely determined by three input constants. These constants are the initial height of the release of the projectile, y_0, and the x- and y-components of the initial velocity vector.

One can also express the initial velocity vector $\vec{v}_0$ in terms of its magnitude, v_0, and direction, θ_0. Expressing $\vec{v}_0$ in this manner involves the transformation

$$\begin{aligned} v_0 &= \sqrt{v_{x0}^2 + v_{y0}^2} \\ \theta_0 &= \tan^{-1}\frac{v_{y0}}{v_{x0}} \end{aligned} \tag{3.18}$$

This transformation form Cartesian coordinates to length and angle of the vector was already discussed in chapter 1, as well as the inverse transformation:

$$\begin{aligned} v_{x0} &= v_0 \cos\theta_0 \\ v_{y0} &= v_0 \sin\theta_0 \end{aligned} \tag{3.19}$$

Expressed in terms of the magnitude and direction of the initial velocity vector, the equation for the path of the projectile then becomes:

$$y = y_0 + (\tan\theta_0)x - \frac{g}{2v_0^2\cos^2\theta_0}x^2 \tag{3.20}$$

Figure 3.6: Photograph of a water fountain with water following parabolic trajectories.

The fountain shown in Figure 3.6 is in the Detroit Metropolitan Wayne County (DTW) airport. This fountain gives confirmation to the claim of parabolic trajectories because one observes that water is shot out of many pipes and traces almost perfect parabolic trajectories.

Time Dependence of the Velocity Vector

From the kinematic equation (3.10), we know that the x-component of the velocity is constant in time, $v_x = v_{x0}$. This result means that a projectile will cover the same horizontal distance for each time interval of the same length. In particular, if we freeze frame a video of a projectile motion, as done in the picture of the basketball player shooting a free throw in Figure 3.2, then the horizontal displacement of the projectile from one frame of the video to the next will be a constant.

The y-component of the velocity vector changes according to kinematic equation (3.13), $v_y = v_{y0} - gt$, i.e. it falls steadily and at the same acceleration. Typically, for projectile motion, one starts with a positive value v_{y0}. The apex (= highest point) of the trajectory is then reached at the point where $v_y = 0$, and the projectile momentarily moves only in the horizontal direction. At the apex the y-component of the velocity is zero, and it is changing sign from positive to negative.

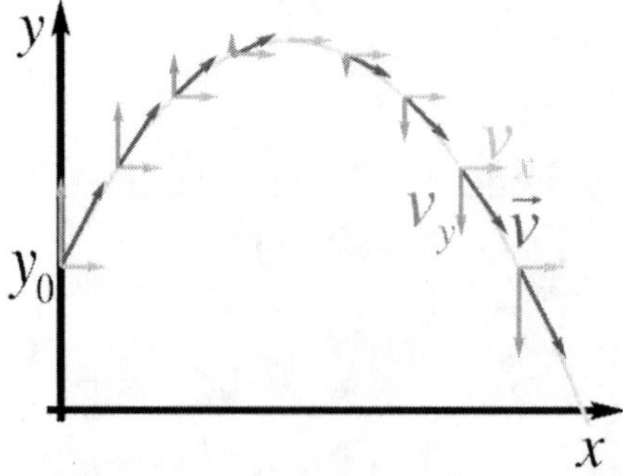

Figure 3.7: Graph of a parabolic trajectory with velocity vector and Cartesian components shown at constant time intervals.

We can indicate the instantaneous values of the x- and y-components of the velocity on a plot of y versus x for the flight path we just discussed. This plot is shown in Figure 3.7. The x-component, v_x, of the velocity vector is shown by the green arrows, and the y-component, v_y, by the red arrows. Note the identical lengths of the green arrows, demonstrating the fact that v_x remains constant. The blue arrows are the vector sum of the x- and y-velocity components and depict the instantaneous velocity vector along the path. Note that the direction of the velocity vector is always tangential to the flight path. This is because the slope of the velocity vector is

$$\frac{v_y}{v_x} = \frac{dy/dt}{dx/dt} = \frac{dy}{dx},$$

which is also the local slope of the flight path. At the top of the path, the green and blue arrows are identical, because the velocity vector only has an x-component, i.e. points in horizontal direction.

Although the vertical component of the velocity vector vanishes at the top of the trajectory, the gravitational acceleration is still the same constant as on any other part of the trajectory. Beware of the common misconception that the gravitational acceleration vanishes on the top. The gravitational acceleration has the same constant value everywhere along the trajectory.

What remains to explore is the functional dependence of the absolute value of the velocity vector on time and/or the y-coordinate. We start with how $|\vec{v}|$ depends on y. We use the fact that the absolute value of a vector is given as the square root of the sum of the squares of the components. Then we use kinematical equation (3.10) for the x-component, and kinematical equation (3.13) for the y-component. This analysis results in:

$$|\vec{v}| = \sqrt{v_x^2 + v_y^2} = \sqrt{v_{x0}^2 + v_{y0}^2 - 2g(y - y_0)} = \sqrt{v_0^2 - 2g(y - y_0)} \qquad (3.21)$$

Note that the initial launch angle does not appear in this formula. The absolute value of the velocity, the speed, depends only on the initial value of the speed and the difference between the y-coordinate and its initial value. So if a projectile is released from a certain height above ground, and we want to know the speed with which it hits the ground, it does not matter if the projectile is shot straight up, or horizontally, or straight down. In chapter 5 we will discuss the concept of kinetic energy, and then the reason for this strange fact will become more apparent.

We can also use kinematical equation (3.11) and insert it into the result we just obtained to determine the dependence of $|\vec{v}|$ on time. This substitution yields:

$$\begin{aligned}|\vec{v}| &= \sqrt{v_0^2 - 2g(v_{y0}t - \tfrac{1}{2}gt^2)} = \sqrt{v_0^2 - 2gv_{y0}t + g^2t^2} \\ &= \sqrt{v_0^2 - 2gtv_0\sin\theta_0 + g^2t^2}\end{aligned} \tag{3.22}$$

Self-Test Opportunity:
What is the dependence of $|\vec{v}|$ on the x-coordinate?

In-class exercise:
At the top of the trajectory of any projectile, which of the following statements, if any, are true?
a) The acceleration is zero.
b) The x-component of the acceleration is zero.
c) The y-component of the acceleration is zero.
d) The speed zero.
e) The x-component of the velocity is zero.
f) The y-component of the velocity is zero.

3.3. Maximum Height and Range of Projectiles

When launching a projectile, for example throwing a ball, we are often interested in how far it will travel before reaching its original vertical position, the range R, and what will be its maximum height (H) it will reach. These quantities R and H are indicated in Figure 3.8. We find that the maximum height reached by the projectile is:

$$H = y_0 + \frac{v_{y0}^2}{2g} \tag{3.23}$$

The distance the projectile will travel before it reaches the same height as the initial height from which it is released is called the range, and it is:

$$R = \frac{v_0^2}{g}\sin 2\theta_0 \tag{3.24}$$

where v_0 is the absolute value of the initial velocity, and θ_0 is the launch angle. The maximum range, for a given fixed value of v_0 is reached for $\theta_0 = 45$ degrees.

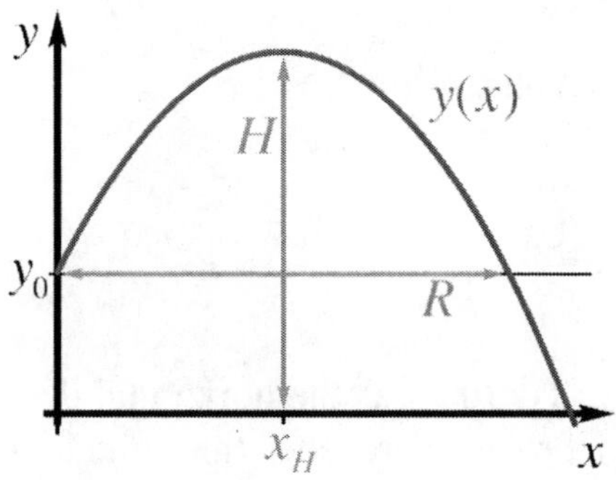

Figure 3.8: Definition of the maximum height and range

Derivation 3.1:
Let us investigate the maximum height first. To determine the maximum height, we will obtain an expression for the height, differentiate it, set the result equal to zero, and solve for the height. Suppose v_0 is the absolute value of the initial velocity, and θ_0 is the launch angle. We take the derivative of the path function $y(x)$ with respect to x:

$$\frac{dy}{dx}=\frac{d}{dx}\left(y_0+(\tan\theta_0)x-\frac{g}{2v_0^2\cos^2\theta_0}x^2\right)=\tan\theta_0-\frac{g}{v_0^2\cos^2\theta_0}x \quad (3.25)$$

Now we look for the point x_H where the derivative is 0:

$$\begin{aligned}0&=\tan\theta_0-\frac{g}{v_0^2\cos^2\theta_0}x_H\\ \Rightarrow x_H&=\frac{v_0^2\cos^2\theta_0\tan\theta_0}{g}=\frac{v_0^2}{g}\sin\theta_0\cos\theta_0=\frac{v_0^2}{2g}\sin 2\theta_0\end{aligned} \quad (3.26)$$

In the second line of (3.26) we have used the trigonometric identities $\tan\theta=\sin\theta/\cos\theta$ and $2\sin\theta\cos\theta=\sin 2\theta$. Now we insert this value for x into our equation for the path and obtain the maximum height, H:

$$\begin{aligned}H\equiv y(x_H)&=y_0+x_H\tan\theta_0-\frac{g}{2v_0^2\cos^2\theta_0}x_H^2\\ &=y_0+\frac{v_0^2}{2g}\sin 2\theta_0\tan\theta_0-\frac{g}{2v_0^2\cos^2\theta_0}\left(\frac{v_0^2}{2g}\sin 2\theta_0\right)^2\\ &=y_0+\frac{v_0^2}{g}\sin^2\theta_0-\frac{v_0^2}{2g}\sin^2\theta_0\\ &=y_0+\frac{v_0^2}{2g}\sin^2\theta_0\end{aligned} \quad (3.27)$$

Derivation

Because $v_{y0} = v_0 \sin\theta_0$, we can also write:

$$H = y_0 + \frac{v_{y0}^2}{2g} \tag{3.28}$$

The range, R, of a projectile is defined as the horizontal distance between the launching point and the point where the projectile reaches the same height from which it started, $y(R) = y_0$:

$$\begin{aligned} y_0 &= y_0 + R\tan\theta_0 - \frac{g}{2v_0^2\cos^2\theta_0}R^2 \\ \Rightarrow \tan\theta_0 &= \frac{g}{2v_0^2\cos^2\theta_0}R \\ \Rightarrow R &= \frac{2v_0^2}{g}\sin\theta_0\cos\theta_0 = \frac{v_0^2}{g}\sin 2\theta_0 \end{aligned} \tag{3.29}$$

Derivation

Note that the range, R, is twice as big as the x-coordinate, x_H, for which the trajectory reached its maximum height, $R = 2x_H$.

Finally, we can ask how we maximize the range of the projectile. One way to maximize the range is to maximize the initial velocity because the range grows as we increase the absolute value of the initial velocity, v_0. The question then is, given a specific initial speed, what is the dependence of the range on the launch angle θ_0. To answer this question, we take the derivative of the range with respect to the launch angle, which leads to another maximization problem.

$$\frac{dR}{d\theta_0} = \frac{d}{d\theta_0}\left(\frac{v_0^2}{g}\sin 2\theta_0\right) = 2\frac{v_0^2}{g}\cos 2\theta_0 \tag{3.30}$$

Then we set this derivative to 0 and find the angle for which the maximum is achieved. The angle between 0 and 90 degrees for which $\cos 2\theta_0 = 0$ is 45 degrees. So the maximum range of an ideal projectile is given by $R_{max} = v_0^2 / g$. One could have obtained this result from the formula for the range itself because the range is at a maximum when the sine function has its maximum value of 1, and it has this maximum where its argument is 90 degrees. So if $2\theta_0 = 90^0 \Rightarrow \theta_0 = 45^0$.

Self-Test Opportunity:
There is another way to arrive at the expression for the range. It uses the fact that it takes

just as much time to reach the top of the trajectory as it takes to come down, because of the symmetry of the parabolic trajectory. You can calculate the time to reach to top of the trajectory, where $v_{y0} = 0$, and then multiply this time by two times the horizontal velocity component to arrive at the range. Can you calculate the range in this way?

Obviously, most sports involving balls provide a great source for examples that we are now able to consider. We have picked a few examples here where the effects of air resistance and spin on the ball do not have an overpowering influence, and so the findings presented in these examples are reasonably close to what happens in reality.

Solved Problem 3.1: Baseball

When listening to a baseball broadcast on the radio, you can often hear the phrase "line drive" or "frozen rope" for a ball hit really hard and at a low angle with respect to the ground. Some even use the "frozen rope" expression for a particularly strong throw from second or third base to first base. This figure of speech implies movement on a straight line. But we have just convinced ourselves that the ball's actual trajectory is a parabola.

Question:
What is the maximum height that a baseball reaches if it is thrown from second or third base to first base, is released from a height of six feet, with a speed of 90 mph, and caught at the same height?

Answer:

THINK:

First we need to find the dimensions of a baseball diamond and then we need to perform a few unit conversions to the metric system. Six feet in height is equal to $y_0 = 6 \text{ ft} = 6 \cdot 0.348 \text{ m} = 1.83 \text{ m}$. A speed of 90 mph translates into $v_0 = 90 \text{ mph} = 90 \cdot 0.4469 \text{ m/s} = 40.2 \text{ m/s}$. The baseball infield is a square with sides 90 feet long. This distance is the distance between second and first base. So we get for this distance: $d_{12} = 90 \text{ ft} = 90 \cdot 0.3048 \text{ m} = 27.4 \text{ m}$. The distance from third to first is the diagonal of the infield square and thus: $d_{13} = d_{12}\sqrt{2} = 38.8 \text{ m}$. As with most trajectory problems, we have many ways to solve this problem. But here is the most straightforward way that follows from our considerations of range and maximum height: We can equate our base-to-base distances with the range of the projectile because the ball is thrown and caught at the same height.

SKETCH:

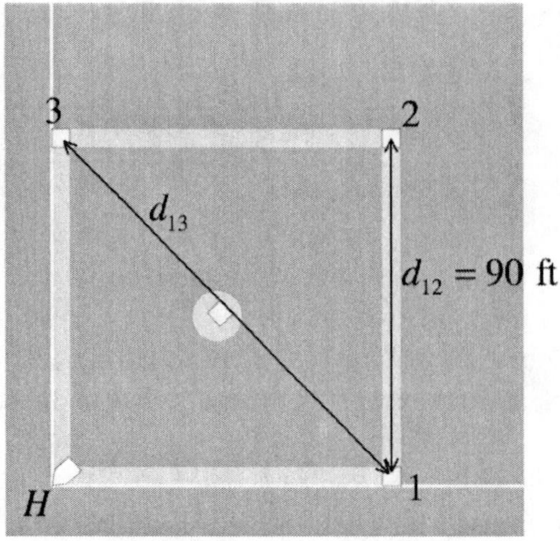

Figure 3.9: Baseball infield.

Solved Problem

RESEARCH:

In order to obtain the initial launch angle of the ball we thus use Equation (3.29), setting the range equal to the distance between first and second base:

$$d_{12} = \frac{v_0^2}{g}\sin 2\theta_0 \Rightarrow \theta_0 = \tfrac{1}{2}\sin^{-1}\left(\frac{d_{12}g}{v_0^2}\right) \tag{3.31}$$

Given this angle we then can use our formula for the height and obtain:

$$H = y_0 + \frac{v_0^2 \sin^2\theta_0}{2g} \tag{3.32}$$

SIMPLIFY:

Inserting (3.31) into (3.32) results in

$$H = y_0 + \frac{v_0^2 \sin^2\left(\tfrac{1}{2}\sin^{-1}\left(\frac{d_{12}g}{v_0^2}\right)\right)}{2g}$$

CALCULATE:

We are ready to insert numbers and find

$$H = 1.83\text{ m} + \frac{(40.2\text{ m/s})^2 \sin^2\left(\tfrac{1}{2}\sin^{-1}\left(\frac{(27.4\text{ m})(9.81\text{ m/s}^2)}{(40.2\text{ m/s})^2}\right)\right)}{2(9.81\text{ m/s}^2)} = 2.39315\text{ m}$$

ROUND:

The initial precision specified was at most three significant digits. So we round our final result to

$$H = 2.39 \text{ m}$$

This maximum height compares with the initial height of 1.83 m. We see that a 90 mph throw from second to first base is 56 cm, i.e. almost 2 ft, above a straight line at the middle of its trajectory.

DOUBLE-CHECK:

The numbers are even bigger for the throw from third to first base, where we need an initial angle of $6.81°$, and the ball reaches a maximum height of 2.99 m, 1.16 m (almost 4 ft) above the straight line connecting the points of release and catch.

Let us take one more look at baseball and calculate the trajectory of a batted ball.

Example

Example 3.2: Batting

During the flight of a batted baseball, in particular a home run ball, air resistance has a quite noticeable impact. For now, we want to neglect it, though. In the next section we will return to this question and include a discussion of the effect of air resistance.

Figure 3.10: Baseball hit

Question:

If the ball comes off your bat with a launch angle of 35 degrees and with an initial speed of 110 mph, how far will the ball fly? How long will it be in the air? What will be its speed at the top of its trajectory? What will be its speed when it lands?

Answer:

Again, we need to convert into SI units first: $v_0 = 110 \text{ mph} = 49.2 \text{ m/s}$. The first question

Example

asks for the range,

$$R = \frac{v_0^2}{g}\sin 2\theta_0 = \frac{(49.2 \text{ m/s})^2}{9.81 \text{ m/s}^2}\sin(70°) = 231.5 \text{ m} \tag{3.33}$$

This distance is a long 760 feet that would be a home run even in the biggest ballpark. However this distance does not take into account air resistance. If we take friction due to air resistance into account, the distance would be reduced to 400 feet (See our remarks in Section 3.4. Realistic Projectile Motion).

In order to find the time in the air, we can divide the range by the horizontal component of the velocity:

$$t = \frac{R}{v_0\cos\theta_0} = \frac{231.5 \text{ m}}{(49.2 \text{ m})\cos(35°)} = 5.74 \text{ s} \tag{3.34}$$

Now we will calculate the speeds at the top of the trajectory and at the landing. At the top of the trajectory, the velocity has only a horizontal component, which is $v_0\cos\theta_0 = 40.3$ m/s. When it lands, we can calculate its speed according to $|\vec{v}| = \sqrt{v_0^2 - 2g(y - y_0)}$, a result we had derived earlier. Because we assume here that the altitude at which it lands is the same as the one from which it was launched, we see that at the landing point our speed is the same as at the launching point, 49.2 m/s.

Real baseballs do not quite follow the trajectory calculated here. If instead we had launched a small steel ball bearing with the same parameters, it would have been a very good approximation to neglect air resistance, and the trajectory parameters just found would be verified in such an experiment. The reason why we can neglect air resistance much more safely for the steel ball bearing is that has a much higher mass density and smaller surface area so that drag effects (which depend on area) are small compared to gravitational effects.

Here is an example from football:

Solved Problem

Solved Problem 3.2: Hang Time

When a football team is forced to punt the ball away to their opponent, it is very important to kick the ball as far as possible, but also with a sufficiently long "hang-time", i.e. the time that the ball remains in the air before being caught, so that the punt-coverage team can tackle the receiver right after the catch without the chance of a long punt return.

Question:

What are the initial angle and speed with which a ball has to be punted so that its hang time is 4.41 s, and the punt has a length of 54.5 yards (= 49.8 m)?

Answer:

Solved Problem

THINK:

A punt is a special case of a projectile motion for which the initial and final values of the vertical coordinate are both zero. If we know the range of the projectile, then we can figure out the hang time from the fact that the horizontal component of the velocity vector remains at a constant value, and that then the hang time must simply be the ratio of the range divided by this horizontal component of the velocity vector. The hang time and range equations will give us two equations for the two unknown quantities v_0 and θ_0 that we are looking for.

SKETCH:

This is actually one of the few cases in which an additional sketch does not seem to provide additional information.

RESEARCH:

We have already figured out that the range of a projectile is given by (see (3.24))

$$R = \frac{v_0^2}{g}\sin 2\theta_0 .$$

As already discussed, the hang time can be most easily computed from realizing that the time between punt and catch is given by the range divided by the horizontal component of the velocity,

$$t = \frac{R}{v_0 \cos\theta_0} .$$

So we have two equations for two unknowns, v_0 and θ_0. (Remember, R and t were given in the question.)

SIMPLIFY:

We solve both equations for v_0^2 and set them equal:

$$\left.\begin{aligned} R = \frac{v_0^2}{g}\sin 2\theta_0 &\Rightarrow v_0^2 = \frac{gR}{\sin 2\theta_0} \\ t = \frac{R}{v_0\cos\theta_0} &\Rightarrow v_0^2 = \frac{R^2}{t^2\cos^2\theta_0} \end{aligned}\right\} \frac{gR}{\sin 2\theta_0} = \frac{R^2}{t^2\cos^2\theta_0}$$

Now we can solve for θ_0. Using $\sin 2\theta_0 = 2\sin\theta_0\cos\theta_0$, we find

$$\frac{g}{2\sin\theta_0\cos\theta_0} = \frac{R}{t^2\cos^2\theta_0} \Rightarrow$$

$$\tan\theta_0 = \frac{gt^2}{2R} \Rightarrow$$

$$\theta_0 = \tan^{-1}\frac{gt^2}{2R}$$

Now we can insert this result in either of our two equations we started with. We select the second one and solve for v_0:

$$t = \frac{R}{v_0\cos\theta_0} \Rightarrow v_0 = \frac{R}{t\cos\theta_0}$$

CALCULATE:

What remains is to insert our numbers into the equations that we have arrived at:

$$\theta_0 = \tan^{-1}\frac{(9.81\text{ m/s}^2)(4.41\text{ s})^2}{2(49.8\text{ m})} = 1.08966\text{ rad}$$

$$v_0 = \frac{49.8\text{ m}}{(4.41\text{ s})\cos 1.08966} = 24.4013\text{ m/s}$$

ROUND:

The range and hang time were specified to three significant digits. So we also state our final result to this precision

$$\theta_0 = 1.09\text{, or }\theta_0 = 62.4°$$

$$v_0 = 24.4\text{ m/s}$$

DOUBLE-CHECK:

We know that the maximum range is reached for a launch angle of 45 degrees. The punt here has an initial angle that is significantly steeper at 62.4 degrees. Thus the punt does not travel as far as it could go with the given value of the initial speed that we computed. Instead it travels higher and thus maximizes the hang time. If you watch good college or pro punters practice their skills during football games, you will see that they try to kick the ball off steeper than 45 degrees, in agreement with what we found in our calculations.

Solved Problem

In-class exercise:

The same range as in the previous problem could have been achieved with the same initial speed of 24.4 m/s, but with an angle different from 62.4 degrees. What is the value of this angle?

a) 12.4 degrees.
b) 27.6 degrees.
c) 45.0 degrees.
d) 58.4 degrees.

In-class exercise:
What is the hang time for this other angle that yields the same range?
a) 2.30 s.
b) 3.14 s.
c) 4.41 s.
d) 5.14 s.

3.4. Realistic Projectile Motion

If you are familiar with tennis or golf or baseball, you will know that our parabolic motion of a projectile is only a fairly crude approximation of the trajectory of the ball. The first effect that we need to take into account is air resistance. Typically, one can parameterize air resistance as a velocity dependent acceleration. The general treatment of this problem exceeds the scope of this book. However, the resulting trajectories are called ballistic curves.

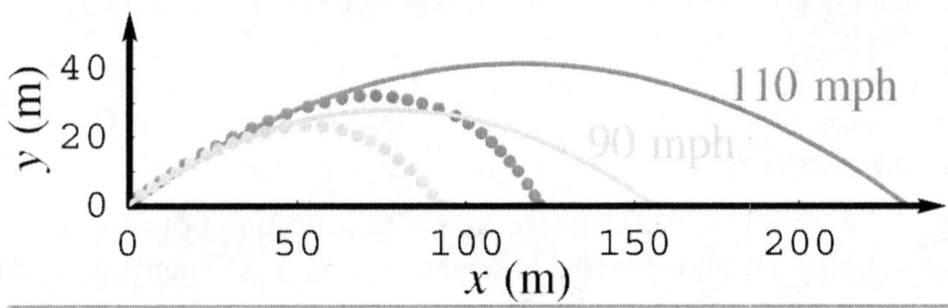

Figure 3.11: Trajectories of baseballs initially launched at an angle of 35 degrees from the horizontal at speeds of 90 and 110 mph. Solid lines: neglecting air resistance; dots: with air resistance.

Shown in Figure 3.11 are the trajectories of baseballs launched at an initial angle of 35 degrees with respect to the horizontal for initial speeds of 90 and 110 mph. Compare, for example, the trajectory shown for the launch speed of 110 mph with the result of our earlier calculation: The real range of this ball is only slightly more than 400 ft, whereas we had found 760 feet (equation (3.33) in Solved Problem 3.1) for the range when we neglected air resistance. Obviously, for a long fly ball the zero air resistance approximation is not valid.

Another important effect that we failed to include is the spin of the projectile as it moves through the air. When one throws a spiral in football, for example, the spin is important for the stability of the flight motion and prevents the ball from "going end-over-end." In tennis, a ball with topspin drops much faster than a ball without noticeable spin, given the same initial values of speed and launch angle. Conversely, a ball with under-spin "floats" deeper. In golf, under-spin, also called backspin, is desired, because it causes a steeper landing angle and thus helps the ball come to rest closer to the landing point than a ball hit without spin that lands at the same point. Depending on its sense of rotation, sidespin can cause draws and fades for good players, and hooks and slices for the rest of us.

In baseball, sidespin is the cause for curveballs. There is, by the way, no such thing as a "rising fastball" in baseball. However, balls thrown with severe backspin do not drop as fast as the batter expects and are thus sometimes perceived as rising – an optical illusion. In the graph of ballistic baseball trajectories, Figure 3.11, an initial backspin of 2,000 rpm was assumed.

Curveballs and practically all other effects of spin on the trajectory of moving balls are a result of the air molecules bouncing with higher speeds off the side of the ball that rotates in the direction of the flight motion (and thus has a higher velocity relative to the air molecules) than the one rotating against the flight direction. We will return to this topic in our chapter 13 on fluid motion.

The surface properties of projectiles have huge effects on the trajectories. Golf balls have dimples to make them fly farther. Otherwise identical golf balls with smooth surfaces result in drives of approximately half the length of balls with dimples. This effect is also the reason why sandpaper found in a pitcher's glove leads to ejection of that player, because a baseball that is roughed on parts of its surface moves differently from a smooth baseball.

3.5. Relative Motion

To study motion we have allowed ourselves to shift the origin of our coordinate system to a certain point by properly choosing the constants x_0 and y_0. In general, x_0 and y_0 are constants that can be chosen freely. If this choice is made intelligently, it can help make a problem more manageable. For example, when we calculated the path of the projectile, $y(x)$, we set $x_0 = 0$ to simplify our calculations. The freedom to select the constants x_0 and y_0 reflects our ability to describe any kind of motion that is not dependent on the selection of the location of the origin of the coordinate system.

So far we have considered physical problems where we have kept the origin of the coordinate system at a fixed location during the motion of the object we wanted to consider. However, there are physical situations in which it is impractical to choose a reference system with a fixed origin.

Consider, for example, an airplane landing on an aircraft carrier that is at the same time going forward under full steam. You want to describe the motion in the coordinate system that is fixed to the carrier, even though it is moving. The reason why this is important is that the aircraft needs to come to rest *relative* to the carrier on some fixed location on the deck.

Another example where we cannot neglect relative motion is a transatlantic flight from Detroit, MI, to Frankfurt, Germany, that is scheduled to take eight hours and ten minutes.

Using the exact same aircraft and going in the reverse direction, the flight is scheduled to take nine hours and ten minutes, a full hour longer. The primary reason for this difference is that the prevailing wind at high altitudes, the jet stream, tends to blow from West to East at high velocities. Even though the airplane's speed relative to the air around it is the same in both directions, that air is moving with its own speed. So the transformation from the coordinate system of the air inside the jet stream to the coordinate system in which the locations of Detroit and Frankfurt remain fixed is important in understanding the difference in flight times.

Figure 3.12: Man walking on a moving walkway, demonstrating reference frame transformations.

For an example of moving coordinate systems, we will consider motion on a moving walkway, typically found in airport terminals. This example is an example of 1 dimensional motion. Having solved this problem, we can generalize the result to 2 and 3 dimensions.

Let's suppose that the walkway surface moves with a certain velocity, v_{wt}, relative to the terminal. We use the indices *w* for walkway and *t* for terminal. Then a coordinate system that is fixed to the walkway surface has exactly this velocity v_{wt} relative to a coordinate system that is attached to the terminal. The man shown in Figure 3.12 is walking with a velocity v_{mw} as measured in a coordinate system on the walkway, and has a velocity $v_{mt} = v_{mw} + v_{wt}$ with respect to the terminal. The two velocities $v_{mw} + v_{wt}$ add as vectors since the corresponding displacements add as vectors. (We will show this explicitly when we generalize to three dimensions.) For example, if the walkway moves with v_{wt} of 1.5 m/s and the man moves with $v_{mw} = 2.0$ m/s, then he will progress through the terminal with a velocity of $v_{mt} = v_{mw} + v_{wt} = 2.0$ m/s + 1.5 m/s = 3.5 m/s.

It is common for children to walk in the opposite direction to the motion of the walkway. In particular, of course, one can achieve a state of no motion relative to the terminal, if one walks with velocity that is exactly the negative of the walkway velocity. So if a child were to walk with $v_{mw} = -1.5$ m/s on our walkway, her velocity would be 0 in the terminal.

It is essential for our consideration of relative motion that the two coordinate systems have a relative velocity to each other that is constant in time. If this is the case, then the accelerations measured in both coordinate systems are identical: If $v_{wt} = const. \Rightarrow dv_{wt} / dt = 0$. From $v_{mt} = v_{mw} + v_{wt}$ we then obtain:

$$\frac{dv_{mt}}{dt} = \frac{d(v_{mw} + v_{wt})}{dt} = \frac{dv_{mw}}{dt} + \frac{dv_{wt}}{dt} = \frac{dv_{mw}}{dt} + 0 \\ \Rightarrow a_t = a_w \tag{3.35}$$

So the accelerations measured in both coordinate systems are indeed the same. This type of velocity addition is also known as a Galilean transformation. Before we go on to the two- and three-dimension cases, note that this type of transformation is only valid for speeds that are small compared to the speed of light. Once we approach the speed of light we must use the Lorentz transformation, which we discuss in detail in our chapter 35 on the theory of relativity.

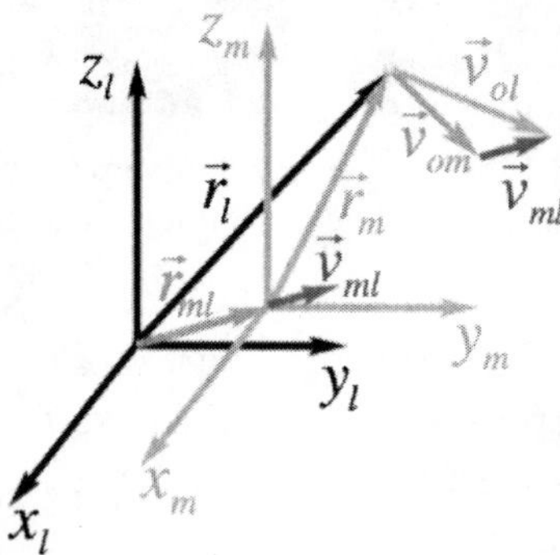

Figure 3.13: Reference frame transformation of a velocity vector and position vector at some particular time.

Now we generalize our considerations to more than one spatial dimension. We assume that we have two coordinate systems, x_l, y_l, z_l and x_m, y_m, z_m. (Here we use the subscripts l for the coordinate system that is at rest in the *l*aboratory, m for the one that is *m*oving). At time $t = 0$, the origins of both coordinate systems are located at the same point, with their axes exactly parallel to each other. As indicated in Figure 3.13 the origin of x_m, y_m, z_m moves with a constant translational velocity $\vec{v}_{ml}$ (blue arrow) relative to the origin of x_l, y_l, z_l. After a time t, the origin of x_m, y_m, z_m is thus located at the point $\vec{r}_{ml} = \vec{v}_{ml} t$. We can now describe the motion of any object in either coordinate system. If the object is located at coordinate $\vec{r}_l$ in coordinate system x_l, y_l, z_l, and at coordinate $\vec{r}_m$ in coordinate system x_m, y_m, z_m, then they are related to each other via simple vector addition (see Figure 3.13):

$$\vec{r}_l = \vec{r}_m + \vec{r}_{ml} = \vec{r}_m + \vec{v}_{ml} t \tag{3.36}$$

A similar relationship holds for the velocities of the object, as measured in the two coordinate systems. If the object has velocity $\vec{v}_{ol}$ in coordinate system x_l, y_l, z_l, and $\vec{v}_{om}$ in coordinate system x_m, y_m, z_m, then these two velocities are related via:

$$\vec{v}_{ol} = \vec{v}_{om} + \vec{v}_{ml} \tag{3.37}$$

This equation can be obtained by taking the time derivative of the previous equation, because $\vec{v}_{ml}$ is constant. Note that the two inner subscripts on the right hand side of this equation always match. This makes the equation understandable on an intuitive level, because it says that the velocity of the *o*bject in the *l*ab frame (subscripts *ol*) is equal to the sum of the velocity with which the *o*bject moves relative to the *m*oving frame (subscripts *om*) and the velocity with which the *m*oving frame moves relative to the *l*ab frame (subscript *ml*).

Another time derivative then leads us to the accelerations. Again, because $\vec{v}_{ml}$ is constant and thus has a zero derivative, we obtain just like in the one-dimensional case that

$$\vec{a}_l = \vec{a}_m \tag{3.38}$$

So the values of the acceleration for an object are the same in both coordinate systems.

Example

Solved Problem 3.3: Airplane in crosswind

Airplanes move relative to the air that surrounds them. Suppose a pilot points his airplane in NE direction. The airplane moves with a speed of 160. m/s relative to the wind. The wind is blowing at 32.0 m/s in a direction from E to W (relative to and instrument at a fixed point on the ground, which measures the wind speed).

Question:
What is the velocity vector – speed and direction – of the airplane relative to the ground? And how far off course does the wind blow this plane in 2.0 hours?

Answer:
A diagram of the velocities is shown in Figure 3.14. The airplane heads in direction NE, and the yellow arrow represents the velocity vector. The velocity vector of the wind is represented in orange and points due W. Graphical vector addition results in the light green vector arrow that represents the velocity of the plane relative to the ground. To solve this problem we will apply the basic transformation (3.37) as embodied in the following equation.

Example

$$\vec{v}_{pg} = \vec{v}_{pw} + \vec{v}_{wg}$$

Here $\vec{v}_{pw}$ is the velocity of the plane with respect to the wind and has components:

$$v_{pw,x} = v_{pw}\cos\theta = 160 \text{ m/s} \cdot \cos 45° = 113 \text{ m/s}$$

$$v_{pw,y} = v_{pw}\sin\theta = 160 \text{ m/s} \cdot \sin 45° = 113 \text{ m/s}$$

The velocity of the wind with respect to the ground, $\vec{v}_{wg}$, has components:

$$v_{wg,x} = -32 \text{ m/s}$$

$$v_{wg,y} = 0$$

So we obtain the velocity components of the airplane relative to a coordinate system fixed to the ground, $\vec{v}_{pg}$, as:

$$v_{pg,x} = v_{pw,x} + v_{wg,x} = 113 \text{ m/s} - 32 \text{ m/s} = 81 \text{ m/s}$$

$$v_{pg,y} = v_{pw,y} + v_{pw,y} = 113 \text{ m/s}$$

The absolute value of the velocity vector and its direction in the ground-base coordinate system are therefore:

$$v_{pg} = \sqrt{v_{pg,x}^2 + v_{pg,y}^2} = 139 \text{ m/s}$$

$$\theta = \arctan(v_{pg,y} / v_{pg,x}) = 54.4°$$

This result is the answer to the first question concerning the magnitude and direction of the velocity vector.

Figure 3.14: Flight direction of an airplane, the wind direction, and the track of the airplane along the ground

Now we consider the course correction due to the wind. To find this quantity, we can multiply the plane's velocity vectors in each coordinate system by a time of 2 hours = 7,200 s, then take the vector difference, and finally obtain the magnitude of the vector difference. The answer can be obtained more easily when we use Equation (3.37) multiplied by the time to realize that the course correction due to the wind is the wind velocity times 7,200 s:

$$|r_T| = |v_T|t = 32.0 \text{ m/s} \cdot 7200 \text{ s} = 230.4 \text{ km}$$

Discussion:
One may argue that the Earth itself moves a considerable amount in two hours, due to its own rotation and due to its motion around the Sun, and that one also has to take this motion into account in this example. That the Earth moves is true, but also irrelevant for the present example: The airplane, the air, and the ground all participate with the same common velocity in this rotation and orbiting motion, which is superimposed on the relative motion of the objects described in the problem setup. And so we can simply perform our calculations in a coordinate system, in which the Earth is at rest.

Another interesting consequence of relative motion is observing rain in a moving car. You may have wondered why the rain is almost always coming straight at you when you are driving in the rain. The following example answers this question.

Example

Example 3.3: Driving through rain
Let us look at a situation where rain is falling straight down from the sky. In Figure 3.15 you can see the rain falling down on the car, as indicated by the light blue lines. A stationary observer outside the car would be able to measure velocity vectors of the rain (blue) and driving car (red), as indicated in Figure 3.15.

Figure 3.15: The velocity vector of a moving car and the velocity vector of falling rain, as viewed by a stationary observed.

However if you are sitting inside the car, the outside world of the stationary observer just mentioned (including the street, and in particular also the rain) moves with a relative velocity of $\vec{v} = -\vec{v}_{car}$. The velocity of this relative motion has to be added to all outside events as observed from inside the car. The result is then a velocity vector $\vec{v}\,'_{rain}$ for the rain as observed from inside the car that is mathematically the vector sum $\vec{v}^{\,'}_{rain} = \vec{v}_{rain} - \vec{v}_{car}$, where $\vec{v}_{rain}$ and $\vec{v}_{car}$ are the velocity vectors of the rain and car as observed by the stationary observer as shown Figure 3.16.

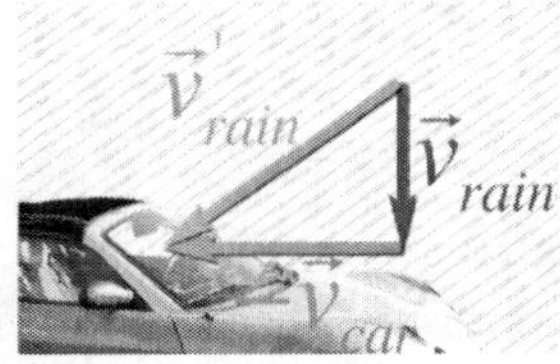

Figure 3.16: The velocity vector $\vec{v}^{\,'}_{rain}$ of rain, as observed from inside a moving car.

What we have learned/Exam Study Guide:

- Ideal projectile motion in 3 dimensions can be reduced to motion in 2 dimensions by choosing the proper coordinate system.
- In 2 dimensions the free-fall of an object can be separated into motion in the
  x-direction, described by the equations,
  (1) $x = x_0 + v_{x0}t$
  (2) $v_x = v_{x0}$
  and the y-direction, described by
  (3) $y = y_0 + v_{y0}t - \frac{1}{2}gt^2$
  (4) $y = y_0 + \bar{v}_y t$
  (5) $v_y = v_{y0} - gt$
  (6) $\bar{v}_y = \frac{1}{2}(v_y + v_{y0})$
  (7) $v_y^2 = v_{y0}^2 - 2g(y - y_0)$
- The relationship between the x- and y- coordinates for ideal projectile motion can be described by a parabola given by the formula
  $y = y_0 + (\tan\theta_0)x - \dfrac{g}{2v_0^2\cos^2\theta_0}x^2$, where
  y_0 is the initial vertical position, v_0 is the initial speed of the projectile, and θ_0 is the initial angle of the projectile with respect to the horizontal.
- The range R of a projectile is given by
  $R = \dfrac{v_0^2}{g}\sin 2\theta_0$.
- The maximum height H in ideal projectile motion is given by
  $H = y_0 + \dfrac{v_{y0}^2}{2g}$, where v_{y0} is the vertical component of the initial velocity.
- Projectile trajectories are not parabolas when air resistance is taken into account. In general the trajectories of realistic projectiles do not quite reach the same height as predicted by the parabolas, and have a significantly shorter range.
- A velocity $\vec{v}\,'$ as observed in a reference frame moving with velocity $\vec{v}_T$ can be calculated using a Galilean transformation of a velocity vector $\vec{v}$ in another reference frame as: $\vec{v}\,' = \vec{v} + \vec{v}_T$

Additional Solved Problems

Solved Problem 3.4: Time of Flight
You may have participated in the Science Olympiad competition during your middle school or high school days. There are many trajectory competitions. In one competition

the goal is to hit a target at a fixed distance that is decided by the judge with a golf ball that is launched by a trebuchet. The competing teams bring their own trebuchets. Our team has constructed a trebuchet that is able to launch a projectile with an initial speed of 17.2 m/s, according to extensive tests that they have performed before the competition.

Question:
How long will the golf ball be in the air before it hits the target, which is located at the same height as the one from which the golf ball is released and a horizontal distance of 22.42 m away.

Answer:

THINK:

Let us first eliminate what does not work: we cannot simply divide the distance between trebuchet and target by the initial speed, because this would imply that the initial velocity vector is in horizontal direction. Since the projectile is in free-fall in vertical direction during the shot, it would certainly miss the target. So we have to aim the golf ball with an angle larger than zero relative to the horizontal. But which angle?

If the golf ball, as stated, is released from the same height as the height of the target, then this shot is a simple range problem, where the horizontal distance between the trebuchet and the target is equal to the range. Since we also know the initial speed, we can then figure out the release angle. Knowing the release angle and the initial speed lets us determine the horizontal component of the velocity vector. This horizontal component does not change in time, and then the flight time is simply given by the Range divided by the horizontal component of the velocity.

SKETCH:

We can avoid a sketch here, because it is a simple repeat of a parabola that we find for all projectile motion. However, here we do not know the initial angle yet.

RESEARCH:

The range of a projectile is given by (see (3.24))

$$R = \frac{v_0^2}{g}\sin 2\theta_0 .$$

If we know the value of this range and the initial speed, then we can figure out the angle as

$$\sin 2\theta_0 = \frac{Rg}{v_0^2}$$

Once we have the angle, then we can use it to calculate the horizontal component of the initial velocity as

Solved Problem

$$v_{x0} = v_0 \cos\theta_0$$

And finally, as stated previously, we obtain the flight time as the ratio of the range and the horizontal component of the velocity

$$t = R / v_{x0}$$

SIMPLIFY:

If we solve the equation for the angle, we see that it has two solutions, one for an angle of less than 45 degrees, and one for an angle of more than 45 degrees. This is shown in Figure 3.17, where we plot the function $\sin 2\theta_0$ (in red) for all possible values of the initial angle and show where it crosses the value of gR / v_0^2 (blue horizontal line). The two solutions are called θ_a and θ_b.

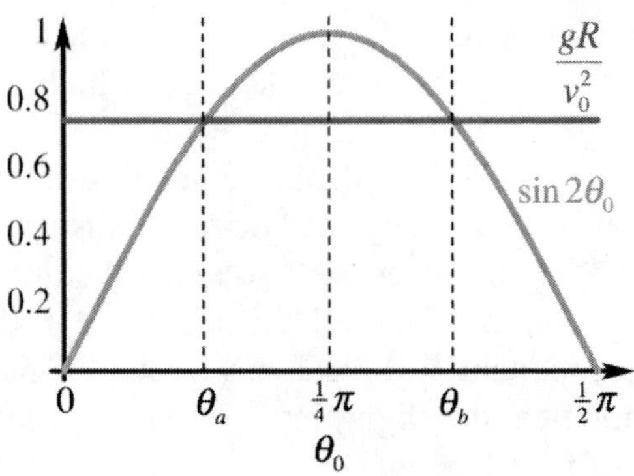

Figure 3.17: Two solutions for the initial angle.

Algebraically, the solutions are then given as

$$\theta_{a,b} = \tfrac{1}{2}\sin^{-1}\left(\frac{Rg}{v_0^2}\right)$$

Inserting this result into our formula for the horizontal velocity component above then results in

$$t = \frac{R}{v_{x0}} = \frac{R}{v_0 \cos\theta_0} = \frac{R}{v_0 \cos\left(\tfrac{1}{2}\sin^{-1}\left(\frac{Rg}{v_0^2}\right)\right)}$$

CALCULATE:

Inserting our numbers we find:

$$\theta_{a,b} = \tfrac{1}{2}\sin^{-1}\left(\frac{(22.42\text{ m})(9.81\text{ m/s}^2)}{(17.2\text{ m/s})^2}\right) = 24.0128° \text{ or } 65.9872°$$

Solved Problem

$$t_a = \frac{R}{v_0 \cos\theta_a} = \frac{22.42 \text{ m}}{(17.2 \text{ m/s})\cos(24.0128°)} = 1.42699 \text{ s}$$

$$t_b = \frac{R}{v_0 \cos\theta_b} = \frac{22.42 \text{ m}}{(17.2 \text{ m/s})\cos(65.9872°)} = 3.20314 \text{ s}$$

ROUND:

The range was specified to four significant digits, and the initial speed to three. So we also state our final result to three significant digits

$$t_a = 1.43 \text{ s}, \quad t_b = 3.20 \text{ s}$$

Please note that both solutions are valid in this case, and the team can select either one.

DOUBLE-CHECK:

Back to the answer that does not work: Simply take the distance from release to the target and divide it by the speed. This incorrect procedure leads to $t_{\min} = d / v_0 = 1.30 \text{ s}$. We write the symbol $t_{\min}$ for this case to indicate that this is some lower boundary that indicates the case in which the initial velocity vector points horizontally, and in which we neglect the free-fall motion of the projectile. So $t_{\min}$ serves as an absolute lower boundary, and it is reassuring to note that our result with the shorter time is still a little larger than this lowest possible, but physically unrealistic, value.

Solved Problem 3.5: Moving Deer

Our zookeeper who successfully captured the monkey in Example 3.1 is at it again. This time she has to capture a deer. Following our instructions, she had aimed directly at the monkey in that capture. She decides to again fire directly at her target, indicated by the bull's eye in Figure 3.18.

Figure 3.18: Moving deer. The velocity of the deer in zookeeper's reference frame is indicated

Question:

Where will the tranquilizer dart hit, if the deer is $d = 25.$ m away from her and runs from her right to her left with a speed of $v_d = 3.0$ m/s? The tranquilizer dart leaves her rifle horizontally with a speed of $v_0 = 90.$ m/s.

Answer:

THINK:

The deer is moving, and at the same time the dart is falling. This introduces two complications into our problem. It is easiest to think about this problem in the moving reference frame of the deer. In that frame the horizontal component of the motion of the dart is one with constant velocity of $-\vec{v}_d$. The vertical component of the motion is again a free-fall motion. The total displacement of the dart is then the vector sum of both of these displacements.

SKETCH:

We draw the two displacements in the reference frame of the deer, as indicated in Figure 3.19. The blue arrow is the free-fall motion, and the red arrow is the horizontal motion of the dart in the reference frame of the deer. The advantage of drawing our displacements in the frame of the deer is that the bull's eye is attached to the deer and thus is moving with it. So we can most easily calculate by how much we miss by working in this moving reference frame.

Figure 3.19: Displacement of the tranquilizer dart in the deer's reference frame.

RESEARCH:

First we need calculate the time it takes the tranquilizer dart to move the 25 m direct line of sight from the gun to the deer. Since the dart leaves the rifle in horizontal direction, the initial horizontal component of the dart's velocity vector is 90 m/s. For projectile motion the horizontal velocity component is constant. So we get for the time it take to cross the 25 m distance

$$t = \frac{d}{v_0}$$

During this time the dart falls under the influence of gravity, and this vertical displacement is

$$\Delta y = -\tfrac{1}{2}gt^2$$

Also, during this time the deer has moved a horizontal displacement in the reference frame of the zookeeper of $x = -v_d t$ (the deer moves to the left, hence the negative value of the horizontal velocity component). Therefore the displacement of the dart in the reference frame of the deer is (see Figure 3.19):

Solved Problem

$$\Delta x = v_d t$$

SIMPLIFY:

Inserting the expression for the time into the expressions for the two displacements results in

$$\Delta x = v_d \frac{d}{v_0} = \frac{v_d}{v_0} d$$

$$\Delta y = -\tfrac{1}{2} g t^2 = -\frac{d^2 g}{2 v_0^2}$$

CALCULATE:

We are now in the position to put in the numbers. This results in:

$$\Delta x = \frac{(3.0 \text{ m/s})}{(90. \text{ m/s})}(25 \text{ m}) = 0.8333333 \text{ m}$$

$$\Delta y = -\frac{(25 \text{ m})^2 (9.81 \text{ m/s}^2)}{2(90. \text{ m/s})^2} = -0.378472 \text{ m}$$

ROUND:

Rounding our results to two significant digits lets us state our final answer:

$$\Delta x = 0.83 \text{ m}$$

$$\Delta y = -0.38 \text{ m}$$

The net effect is the vector sum of the horizontal and vertical displacements, as indicated by the green diagonal arrow in Figure 3.19: the shot will miss below and behind the deer.

DOUBLE-CHECK:

Where should she aim?

If the zookeeper wants to hit the running deer, she has to aim approximately 0.38 m above and 0.83 m to the left of her intended target. This will hit the deer, but not in the center of the bull's eye. Why? Now that she aims higher the initial velocity vector does not point in horizontal direction any more. This lengthens the flight time, as we have just learned in the previous solved problem. A longer flight time translates into a larger displacement in both x - and y -directions. However, this correction is small, and one can calculate it. But for our purposes the algebra for this new problem is a bit too involved.

Chapter 4: Force

What we will learn:

- A force is a measure of how an object interacts with other objects.
- Forces have magnitudes and directions; they are vector quantities.
- Fundamental forces include gravitational attraction and electromagnetic attraction and repulsion. Other important forces include string tension, friction, and spring forces.
- Multiple forces acting on an object sum to a net force.
- Free-body diagrams are valuable aids in working problems.
- Newton's three laws govern the motion of objects under the influence of forces.
    a. The first law deals with objects for which external forces are balanced.

b. The second law is useful in those cases for which external forces are not balanced.
c. The third law addresses equal and opposite forces between two bodies.

- There are two types of masses, gravitational and inertial, and these two types of masses are equivalent.
- There are two kinds of friction, kinetic friction of objects in motion and static friction of objects at rest.
- Friction is important to the understanding of real world motion.
- Applications of Newton's Laws involve multiple objects, multiple forces, and friction.

4.1. Types of Forces

You are probably sitting on a chair as you are reading this. This chair is exerting a force on you, and you can feel this force from the chair on the underside of your legs and your backside. Conversely, you are also exerting a force on the chair.

If you pull on a string, you are exerting a force on the string, and that string in turn can also exert a force on something that is tied to it on the other end of the string. This situation, as well as the force from the chair on you just mentioned, is an example for a contact force, where one object has to be in contact with another to exert a force on it. If you push or pull on an object, you exert a force on it.

The friction force is another important contact force that we will study in more detail in this chapter. If you push a glass across the surface of a table, it will come to rest rather quickly. The force that causes this slowing down is the friction force, sometimes also simply called "friction". Interestingly, the exact nature and microscopic origin of the friction force is still under intense investigation. We will discuss some of the research issues in this chapter.

It takes a force to compress a spring as well as to extend a spring. This spring force has very special properties in that it depends linearly on the change in length of the spring. We will study spring forces in great detail in our chapter on oscillations, chapter 14.

There are also fundamental forces of nature that objects can exert on each other and that do not require direct contact, because they act at a distance. The gravitational force, sometimes also simply called gravity, is one example. If you hold an object in your hand and let go of it, it will obviously fall down. We know what causes this effect; it is the gravitational attraction between the Earth and the object. We have already introduced the value of the gravitational acceleration in the previous chapters, and now we will learn how it is related to the gravitational force. Gravity is also responsible for holding the moon in orbit around Earth and the Earth in orbit around the Sun. Isaac Newton famously was reported to have this insight in the 17th century, after sitting under an apple tree and being hit by an apple: It is the same gravitational force that acts between celestial objects and terrestrial objects.

Another fundamental long-range force that can act at a distance is the electromagnetic force. The most apparent manifestation of this force is the attraction or repulsion between two magnets, depending on their relative orientation, or the attraction of small metal particles to magnets. The entire Earth also acts as a huge magnet, which makes compass needles orient themselves towards the North Pole.

The other two fundamental forces act only on the length scales of atomic nuclei. These forces act at a distance by exchanging particles. We will return to this more advanced way of looking at forces between elementary particle in chapters 39 on particle and 40 on nuclear physics. In general we can define forces as the means for objects to influence each other.

4.2. Gravitational Force Vector, Weight, and Mass

Forces have a direction. For example, if you are holding a laptop computer in your hand, you can easily detect that the gravitational force acting on the computer points in the downward direction. This direction is then the direction of the vector of the gravitational force as shown in Figure 4.1. Again, to characterize a quantity as a vector quantity, we use a notation with a small arrow above the symbol throughout this book. Thus the force vector of the gravitational force acting on the book is denoted by $\vec{F}_g$ in the figure.

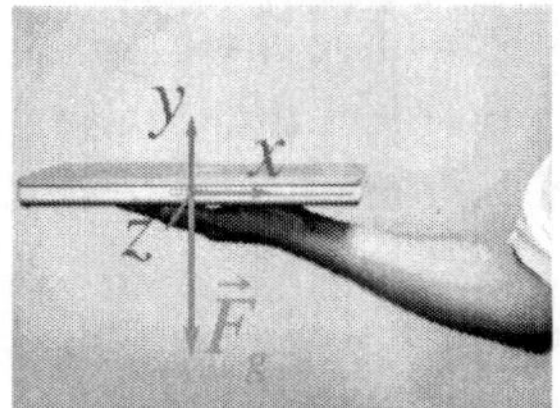

Figure 4.1: Force vector of gravity acting on a laptop computer together with the definition of a Cartesian coordinate system.

In the same figure we also show a convenient Cartesian coordinate system, where we follow the same convention in which vertically up is the y direction (and down the $-y$ direction) that we used in the previous chapter. The x and z directions then lie in the horizontal plane, as shown. As always, we use right-handed coordinate systems. And again we will restrict ourselves to two-dimensional coordinate systems with x and y axes wherever possible.

In our coordinate system just introduced, the force vector of the gravitational force acting on the book is then pointing in the negative y direction:

$$\vec{F}_g = -F_g \hat{y} \tag{4.1}$$

Here we have written the force vector as a product of its magnitude, F_g, and its direction, $-\hat{y}$. F_g is called the weight of an object.

Near the surface of the Earth (within a few hundred meters above ground) the magnitude of the gravitational force acting on an object is given by the product of the mass of the object, m, and the Earth's gravitation acceleration, g:

$$F_g = mg \tag{4.2}$$

We have already introduced the magnitude of the Earth's gravitational acceleration in the previous chapters. It has the value of $g = 9.81\ \mathrm{m/s^2}$. Note that this constant is valid only for heights of a few hundred meters above the ground, as we will see in Chapter 12. Also, it is worth pointing out one more time that we are denoting units by roman letters, whereas we denote the physical quantities by italic letters. So, consistent with chapter 1, the expression "$\mathrm{m/s^2}$" indicates the unit of the gravitational acceleration, g, meters per second per second. "m" is the unit for the physical quantity of length, meter, while "m" denotes the physical quantity of mass.

Before discussing forces in greater detail, it is necessary to have an understanding of the concept of mass.

Under the influence of gravity, objects have a weight that is proportional to their mass. This weight is a force that acts on an object due to the gravitational interaction with other objects. Near the surface of Earth the magnitude of this force is $F_g = mg$, as we just stated. The mass that enters this equation is also called the "gravitational mass", to indicate that it is responsible for the gravitational interaction. However, mass has a role in dynamics as well.

Newton's Laws, which we will introduce later in this chapter, deal with inertial mass. To understand the concept of inertial mass, consider the following examples. It is a lot easier to throw a tennis ball than a shot put. It is also easier to pull open a door made from lightweight materials like foam-core with wood veneer than one made from a heavy material like iron. The heavier objects seem to resist being put into motion more than the lighter ones do. This property of an object is referred as the inertial mass.

However, the gravitational mass and the inertial mass are identical, so we refer simply to the mass of an object.

For a laptop computer with mass $m = 3.00\ \mathrm{kg}$, for example, the magnitude of the gravitational force is then $F_g = mg = (3.00\ \mathrm{kg})(9.81\ \mathrm{m/s^2}) = 29.43\ \mathrm{kg\ m/s^2} = 29.43\ \mathrm{N}$, where we have used the general unit of the force, the Newton (N), as introduced in chapter 1:

$$\text{Force unit: } 1\ \mathrm{N} = 1\ \mathrm{kg\ m/s^2} \tag{4.3}$$

Now we can combine the two facts about the gravitational force that we know so far and write an equation for the force vector that contains both the magnitude and the direction of the gravitational force acting on the laptop computer (see Figure 4.1):

$$\vec{F}_g = -mg\hat{y} \tag{4.4}$$

To summarize, the mass of an object is measured in kg and the weight of an object is measured in N (or in pounds in the United States). They are related to each other by simply multiplying the mass (in units of kg) by the gravitational acceleration constant, $g = 9.81\ \mathrm{m/s^2}$, to arrive at the weight (in unit of N).

Higgs Particles

As far as our studies of physics are concerned, mass is an intrinsic, given, property of an object. The origin of the mass property is still under intense study in nuclear and particle physics. When one asks why different "elementary" particles have the mass that we observe them to have, one finds very interesting effects. In particle physics there is a search underway at the largest particle accelerators to find the "Higgs Particle", which is hypothesized to be responsible for the creation of the mass of all other particles. This Higgs Particle is believed to be one of the central missing pieces in the standard model of particle physics. However, the complete discussion of the origin of mass is beyond the scope of this book.

4.3. Net Force

So far we have only looked at the gravitational force acting on the laptop computer. There are other forces acting on it. Which ones?

Because forces are vectors, we must add them as vectors, using the methods developed in Chapter 1. We define the net force as the vector sum of all force vectors that act on an object.

$$\vec{F}_{net} = \sum_{i=1}^{n} \vec{F}_i = \vec{F}_1 + \vec{F}_2 + \ldots + \vec{F}_n \tag{4.5}$$

Following our considerations for the addition of vectors using components, the Cartesian components of the net force are then given by:

$$F_{net,x} = \sum_{i=1}^{n} F_{i,x} = F_{1,x} + F_{2,x} + \ldots + F_{n,x} \tag{4.6}$$

$$F_{net,y} = \sum_{i=1}^{n} F_{i,y} = F_{1,y} + F_{2,y} + \ldots + F_{n,y} \tag{4.7}$$

$$F_{net,z} = \sum_{i=1}^{n} F_{i,z} = F_{1,z} + F_{2,z} + \ldots + F_{n,z} \tag{4.8}$$

To explore the consequences of the concept of the net force, let us return again to the example of the laptop held up by a hand.

Normal Force

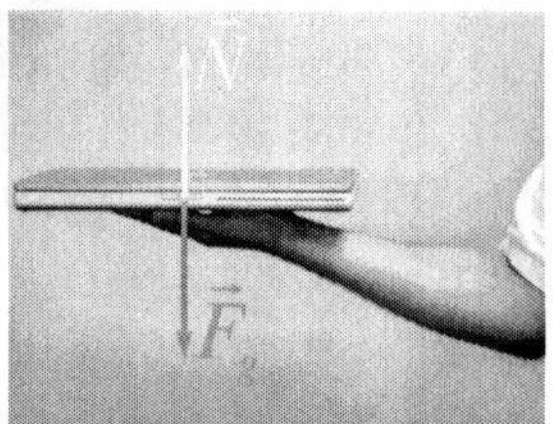

Figure 4.2: Force of gravity and normal force exerted by holding the laptop computer.

In Figure 4.2, we have drawn in the force exerted on the laptop computer by our hand, and we have assigned it the letter $\vec{N}$. (Careful: the normal force is represented by an italic letter N, whereas the force unit Newton is represented by a roman letter N.) Note that in the drawing the length of the vector $\vec{N}$ is exactly equal to that of the vector $\vec{F}_g$, and that the two vectors point in opposite directions, or $\vec{N} = -\vec{F}_g$. This result is not an accident. We will soon learn that there is no net force on an object at rest. If we calculate the net force acting on the laptop computer, we obtain:

$$\vec{F}_{net} = \sum_{i=1}^{n} \vec{F}_i = \vec{F}_g + \vec{N} = \vec{F}_g - \vec{F}_g = 0 . \tag{4.9}$$

In general, we can characterize the normal force $\vec{N}$ as a contact force that acts at the surface between two objects. The normal force is always directed perpendicular to the plane of the contact surface. (Hence the name: "normal" = perpendicular). The normal force is just large enough to prevent objects from penetrating through each other and is not necessarily equal to the force of gravity in all problems.

In the example of the hand holding the laptop computer, the contact surface between the hand and the computer is the bottom surface of the computer, which is aligned with the horizontal plane. So by definition the normal force has to point perpendicular to this plane, vertically upwards.

We will return to the significance of a vanishing net force later in this chapter when we discuss Newton's Laws. For now we just record our working hypothesis that an object can only stay at rest, if the net force acting on it is exactly zero. This will also turn out to be one of two necessary equilibrium conditions for all static equilibrium problems, which we will address in chapter 11.

We can put this zero net force condition to use to find the magnitude and direction of unknown forces in a problem. If we know that an object is at rest, then we can use the condition $\vec{F}_{net} = 0$ to solve for unknown forces. This method is how we knew how to construct the force $\vec{N}$ in the above example of the laptop computer being held at rest.

We can use this way of thinking as a general principle: If object 1 rests on object 2 (or in any other way is in contact with it), then the normal force $\vec{N}$ keeps object 1 at rest and therefore the net force on that object 0. If $\vec{N}$ would be larger, object 1 would have to lift off. If $\vec{N}$ were smaller, it would sink into object 2.

Before we move on, it is important to state that the equation $\vec{F}_{net} = 0$ as a condition for static equilibrium is really more than just one equation. Instead it represents one equation for each dimension of the coordinate space that we are considering. Thus, in three-dimensional space we really have three independent equilibrium conditions:

$$\begin{aligned} F_{net,x} &= \sum_{i=1}^{n} F_{i,x} = F_{1,x} + F_{2,x} + \ldots + F_{n,x} = 0 \\ F_{net,y} &= \sum_{i=1}^{n} F_{i,y} = F_{1,y} + F_{2,y} + \ldots + F_{n,y} = 0 \\ F_{net,z} &= \sum_{i=1}^{n} F_{i,z} = F_{1,z} + F_{2,z} + \ldots + F_{n,z} = 0 \end{aligned} \tag{4.10}$$

Now we introduce the concept of the free-body diagram to ease our task of determining net forces on objects.

Free-Body Diagram

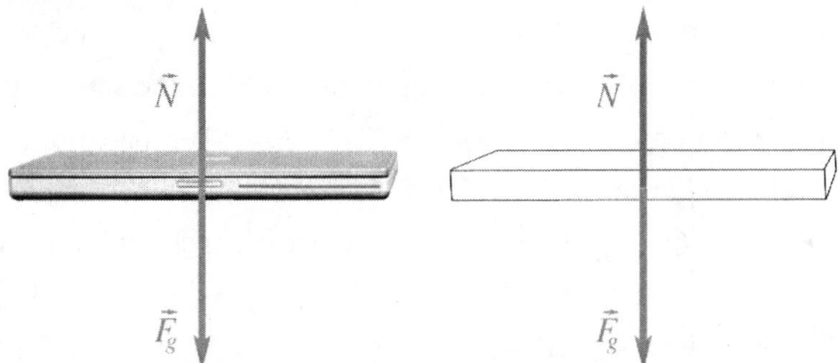

Figure 4.3: Left: forces on real object, a laptop computer;
right: abstraction of the object as a free body being acted upon by two forces.

We have represented the entire effect that the hand has in holding up the laptop computer by the force vector $\vec{N}$. We do not need to consider the influence of the hand, the arm, the person to which the arm belongs, or the entire rest of the world when we want to consider the forces acting on the laptop computer. We can just eliminate them from our consideration – see Figure 4.3, where we have removed everything but the laptop computer and the force vectors from the picture. For that matter, a realistic representation of the laptop computer is not necessary as well, and we can just draw some sort of box to represent it. This type of drawing of an object, where all connections to the rest of the world are ignored, and where only the force vectors that act on it are drawn, is called a free-body diagram.

Self-Test Opportunity:
Draw the free body diagram for a golf ball resting on a tee.

Two Objects' Forces on Each Other

Once we have understood the concept of the net force, we can also answer the question of what the force of object 2 is on object 1, provided we know what the force of object 1 is on object 2.

To start this deduction, let us again come back to our example of the hand holding the laptop computer. Because the laptop computer is at rest, the condition of zero net force had enabled us to calculate that the force that the hand exerts on the computer is directed upwards and has the same magnitude as the laptop's weight, mg. But we also know what the force of the laptop on the hand is: it is its weight, and it is directed downward. We know this force from our everyday experience.

A logical deduction can help us establish a much more general truth. We find that it is universally true that the forces two objects exert on each other are always equal in magnitude and opposite in direction.

To arrive at this conclusion, let us consider two arbitrary objects that are at rest and in contact with each other. We consider them in isolation, with no net external forces acting on them, $\vec{F}_{ext} = 0$. We can now add the two internal forces $\vec{F}_{1\to 2}$ (force of object 1 acting on object 2) and $\vec{F}_{2\to 1}$ (force of object 2 acting on object 1) to the sum of the external forces to obtain the total net force: $\vec{F}_{net} = \vec{F}_{ext} + \vec{F}_{1\to 2} + \vec{F}_{2\to 1}$. But because the external force is zero, $\vec{F}_{ext} = 0$, and because the objects are at rest, implying that $\vec{F}_{net} = 0$, we then arrive at: $\vec{F}_{1\to 2} + \vec{F}_{2\to 1} = 0 \Leftrightarrow \vec{F}_{1\to 2} = -\vec{F}_{2\to 1}$. This result is exactly what we predicted that we would find:

If an object 1 exerts a force $\vec{F}_{1\to 2}$ on object 2, then the force $\vec{F}_{2\to 1}$ that object two exerts on object 1 is exactly equal in magnitude and opposite in direction:

$$\vec{F}_{1\to 2} + \vec{F}_{2\to 1} = 0 \Leftrightarrow \vec{F}_{1\to 2} = -\vec{F}_{2\to 1} \tag{4.11}$$

This rule is also often called Newton's Third Law and will be elaborated on in greater detail further into this chapter. As simple as this rule seems to be, it allows us to treat complicated situations.

Example 4.1: Two Books on a Table

After we have considered the simple situation of one object supported from below and held at rest, let us now look at two objects at rest.

Figure 4.4: Two books on top of each other on a table

Question:

What is the magnitude of the force that the table exerts on the lower book?

Answer:

Start by drawing a free-body diagram of the book on top, book 1. This situation is not different from the example of the laptop computer held steady by the hand. The gravitational force due to the mass of the top book is indicated by $\vec{F}_1$. It has the magnitude $m_1 g$, where m_1 is the mass of the top book, and points straight down. The magnitude of the normal force $\vec{N}_1$ that the lower book exerts on the top book from below is then $N_1 = F_1 = m_1 g$ from the condition of zero net force on the top book. $\vec{N}_1$ points straight up, as shown in the free-body drawing; $\vec{N}_1 = -\vec{F}_1$.

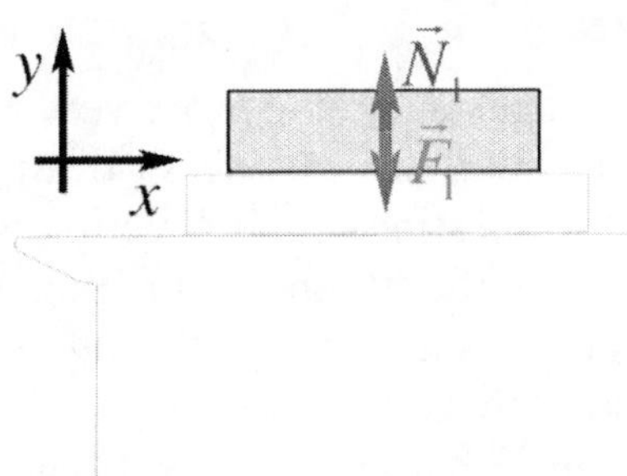

Figure 4.5: Free-body diagram for book 1.

The general principle that we introduced as Newton's Third Law now allows us to calculate the force that the upper book exerts on the lower book. It is equal in magnitude and directed opposite to the force that the lower book exerts on the upper one:

$$\vec{F}_{1,2} = -\vec{N}_1 = -(-\vec{F}_1) = \vec{F}_1 \tag{4.12}$$

This relationship says that the force that the top book exerts on the lower one is exactly equal to the gravitational force due to the mass of the top book, its weight. You may find

Example

this result trivial at this point, but the application of this general principle allows us to calculate even very complicated situations. Now consider the free-body diagram of the lower book, book 2.

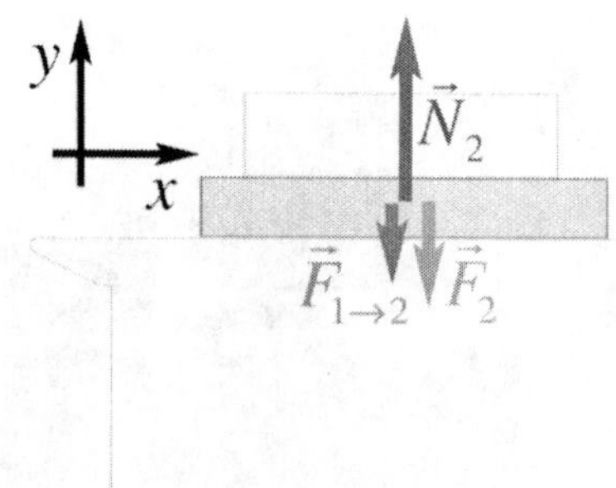

Figure 4.6: Free-body diagram for book 2.

This free-body diagram allows us to calculate the normal force that the table exerts on book 2. We simply sum up all forces acting on book 2:

$$\vec{F}_{1,2} + \vec{N}_2 + \vec{F}_2 = 0 \Rightarrow \vec{N}_2 = -(\vec{F}_{1\to2} + \vec{F}_2) = -(\vec{F}_1 + \vec{F}_2) \tag{4.13}$$

In the last step of this equation we used the result we had obtained from the free-body diagram of book 1. This result means that the force that the table exerts on book 2 is exactly equal in magnitude and opposite in direction to the sum of the forces of the weights of the books.

4.4. Ropes and Pulleys

Types of problems that involve ropes and pulleys are very common in many physical situations. In this chapter we consider only massless (idealized) ropes and pulleys. Whenever a rope is involved, the question of the direction of the force acting due to pulling on the rope involves a force exactly in the direction of the rope. The force with which we pull on the massless rope is transmitted through the entire rope unchanged. The magnitude of this force is referred to as the rope tension. Every rope can only withstand a certain maximum force, of course, but for now we will assume that all forces applied are below this limit. Ropes cannot support a compressional force.

If a rope is guided over a pulley, then we can redirect the direction of the force, but the magnitude of the force is still the same everywhere inside the rope. In the picture shown here, we have tied the right end of the green rope down and pull with a certain force, in this case 11.5 N on the rope. We have spliced the rope before and after it is guided across the pulley, and we have inserted force measurement devices. As one can clearly see, the magnitude of the force before and after the rope is guided across the pulley is the same. (The weight of the force measurement devices is a small real-world complication, but we have used enough force in pulling that it is reasonably safe to neglect this effect.)

Figure 4.7: A rope passing over a pulley with force measurement devices installed.

Example

Example 4.2: Modified Rope Tow

In the rope tow competition, two teams are trying to pull each other across a line. If we have two teams, and they are not able to move each other, they exert equal and opposite forces on each other. This is an immediate consequence of what we just learned about the net force and the forces that two objects exert on each other. So if the team shown here pulls with a force of magnitude F, the other team necessarily also has to pull with a force of the same magnitude, but in the opposite direction.

Now let us consider the situation where three ropes are tied together at one point, with a team pulling on each rope.

Figure 4.8: Rope tow on the beach.

Question:

Suppose team 1 is pulling due West with a force of 2,750 N, and team 2 is pulling due North with a force of 3,630 N. Can a third team pull in such a way that the whole rope tow still ends in a stand-still, i.e. that no team is able to move the rope? If yes, what is the magnitude and direction of the force needed to accomplish this?

Answer:

The answer to the first question is yes, no matter what force and direction teams 1 and 2 pull. This result is true because the two forces always add up to a combined force, and all that team 3 has to do is pull with a force equal and opposite to the direction of that combined force. Then all three forces will add up to 0, and we have achieved static equilibrium. Nothing moves.

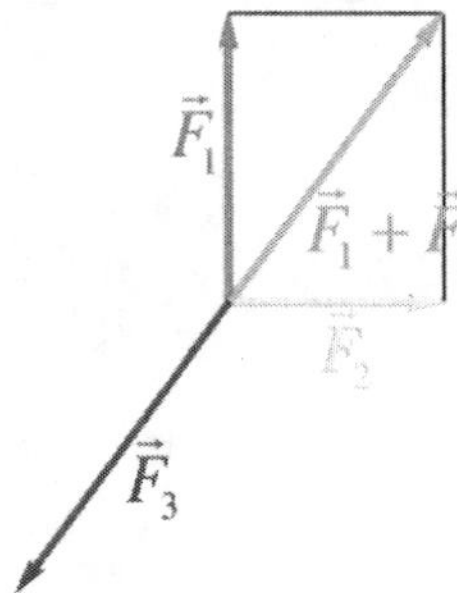

Figure 4.9: Addition of force vectors in the modified rope tow.

Example

Figure 4.9 represents this physical situation. The vector addition of the forces 1 and 2 is particularly simple, because the two forces are perpendicular to each other. We choose a convenient coordinate system such that its origin is at the point where all the ropes meet, and we designate the x-axis to be along the horizontal, along force vector $\vec{F}_1$. We can then see that $\vec{F}_2$ points along the y-axis (conventionally chosen in vertical direction) in this case:

$$\vec{F}_1 = (2750 \text{ N})\hat{x}$$
$$\vec{F}_2 = (3630 \text{ N})\hat{y}$$
$$\vec{F}_1 + \vec{F}_2 = (2750 \text{ N})\hat{x} + (3630 \text{ N})\hat{y}$$

The addition was made easier by the fact that the two forces pointed along the coordinate axes chosen. The general case would be the same. We have already stated that the sum of all three forces has to be 0, and so we obtain the force that the third team has to exert:

$$0 = \vec{F}_1 + \vec{F}_2 + \vec{F}_3$$
$$\Leftrightarrow \vec{F}_3 = -(\vec{F}_1 + \vec{F}_2)$$
$$= -(2750 \text{ N})\hat{x} - (3630 \text{ N})\hat{y}$$

This force vector is also indicated in Figure 4.9. Having the Cartesian components of the force vector we were looking for, we can get the magnitude and direction by using trigonometry:

$$F_3 = \sqrt{F_{3,x}^2 + F_{3,y}^2} = \sqrt{(-2750 \text{ N})^2 + (-3630 \text{ N})^2} = 4554 \text{ N}$$
$$\theta_3 = \arctan(F_{3,y} / F_{3,x}) = \arctan(3630 \text{ N}/2750 \text{ N}) + 180^\circ = 232.85^\circ$$

This result is our complete answer. The 180° had to be added to the angle because the inverse trigonometric functions are not defined over the entire range between 0 and 360°. When the arguments of the arctangent function are both negative, we have to add 180 degrees to the result to obtain the answer for the correct angle.

Because this type of problem is common, let's calculate another example.

Example

Example 4.3: Still Rings in Men's Gymnastics

Question 1:

A gymnast of mass 55 kg hangs vertically from a pair of parallel rings. If the ropes supporting the rings are attached to the ceiling vertically above, what is the tension in the ropes?

Figure 4.10: Still rings in men's gymnastics.

Answer 1:

In this example we again define the x–direction to be the horizontal and y–direction to be the vertical. The free-body diagram of the gymnast is shown Figure 4.11. For now, there are no forces in the x-direction.

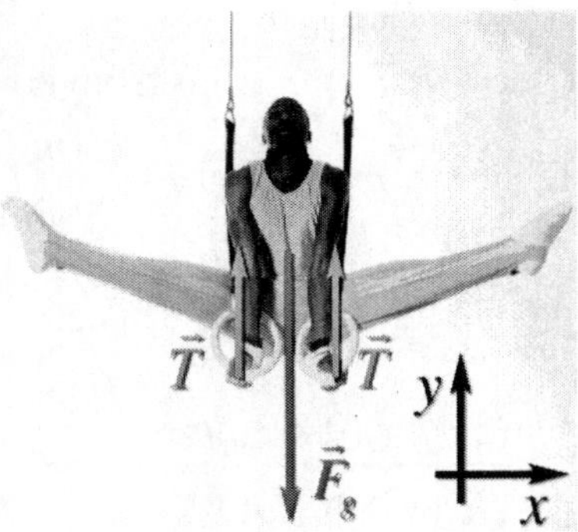

Figure 4.11: Forces acting in the still rings.

In the y-direction we have

$$\sum_i F_{y,i} = T_1 + T_2 - mg = 0 \tag{4.14}$$

Because both ropes support the gymnast equally, the tension has to be the same in both ropes, $T_1 = T_2 \equiv T$, and we get:

$$\begin{aligned} &T + T - mg = 0 \\ &\Rightarrow T = \tfrac{1}{2}mg = \tfrac{1}{2}(55 \text{ kg}) \cdot (9.81 \text{ m/s}^2) = 270 \text{ N} \end{aligned} \tag{4.15}$$

Question 2:

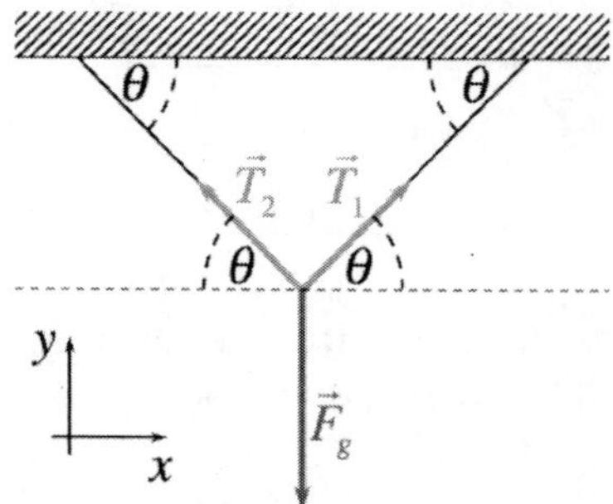

Figure 4.12: Free-body diagram for part 2 of the still ring problem.

If the ropes are supported so that they make an angle of 45° with the ceiling, what is the tension on the ropes?

Answer 2:
In this part, there are forces in the x- and y-directions. We will work this part for a general angle, and then plug in $\theta = 45°$ in the end:

In x-direction, we have for our equilibrium condition:

$$\sum_i F_{x,i} = T_1 \cos\theta - T_2 \cos\theta = 0 \tag{4.16}$$

and in y-direction our equilibrium condition is:

$$\sum_i F_{y,i} = T_1 \sin\theta + T_2 \sin\theta - mg = 0 \tag{4.17}$$

From equation (4.16) we again get $T_1 = T_2 \equiv T$, and from equation (4.17) we then obtain:

$$2T \sin\theta - mg = 0 \Rightarrow T = \frac{mg}{2\sin\theta} \tag{4.18}$$

Putting in the numbers, we obtain the tension in the ropes:

$$T = \frac{(55 \text{ kg})(9.81 \text{ m/s}^2)}{2\sin 45°} = 382 \text{ N}$$

Question 3:
How does the tension on the ropes change as the angle θ between the ceiling and the ropes becomes smaller and smaller?

Answer 3:
As the angle between the ceiling and the ropes becomes smaller, the angle θ between the vertical and the ropes approaches 90°. One can see from the previous formula that as θ approaches 90°, T becomes infinitely big. In reality, of course, the athlete has only a finite strength and cannot hold his position for arbitrary angles.

Example

In-class exercise:

Choose the set of three coplanar vectors, $\vec{F}_1 + \vec{F}_2 + \vec{F}_3$, that sums to a net force of zero:

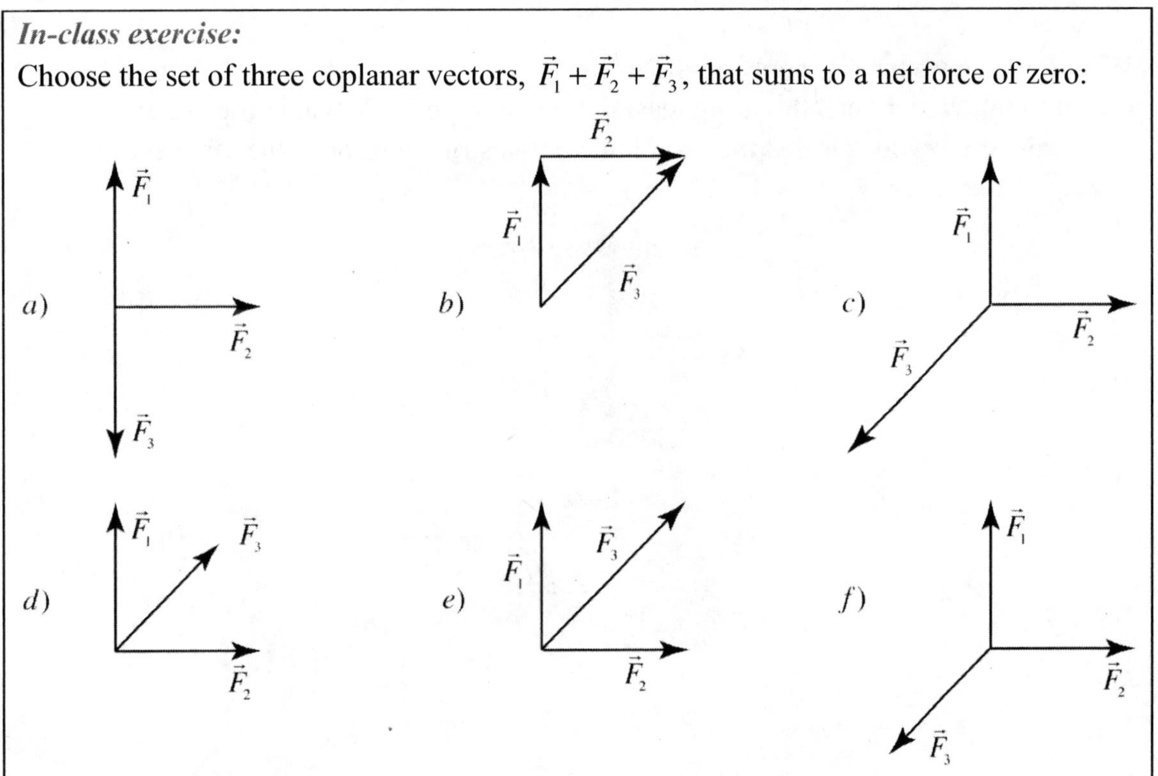

Force Multiplier

Ropes and pulleys can be combined to lift objects that would be too heavy to lift otherwise. In order to see how this can be done, consider Figure 4.13. The system shown here consists of a rope, 1, that is tied to the ceiling (upper right), and then guided over pulleys B and A. Pulley A is also tied to the ceiling with another rope, 2. Pulley B is attached to another rope, 3. The object of mass m, which we want to lift, is hanging from the other end of rope 3. We will assume that the two pulleys have negligible mass and that rope 1 can glide across the pulleys without friction.

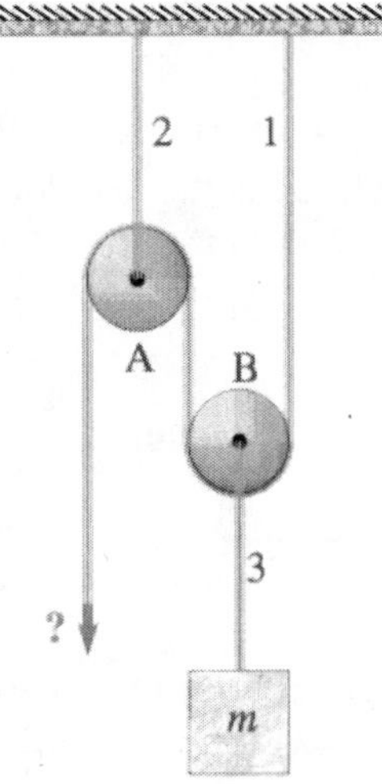

Figure 4.13: Rope guided over two pulleys.

What force do we need to apply on the free end of rope 1 to keep the system in static equilibrium? We will call the string tension force in rope 1, $\vec{T}_1$, that in rope 2, $\vec{T}_2$, and so on. Again, the key idea is that the magnitude of the string tension is the same everywhere in a given rope.

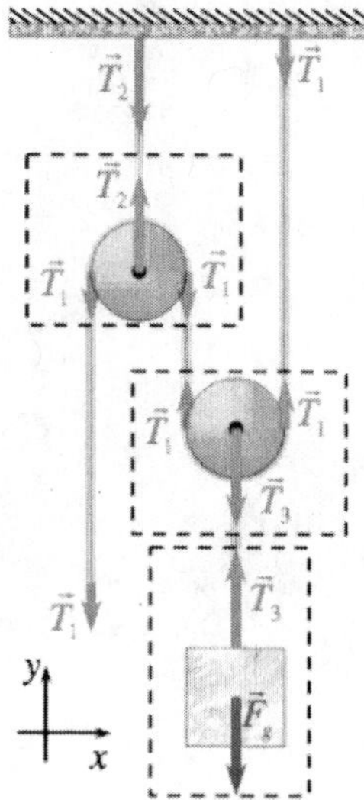

Figure 4.14: Free-body diagrams for the two pulleys and the mass to be lifted.

In Figure 4.14 we have repeated the same setup as in Figure 4.13, but now, by use of dashed lines and shaded areas, indicated the free-body diagrams of the two pulleys and the object of mass m. We start with the mass m. For the condition of zero net force and this zero acceleration to be fulfilled, we need

$$\vec{T}_3 + \vec{F}_g = 0 \tag{4.19}$$

or

$$F_g = mg = T_3 . \tag{4.20}$$

And from the free-body diagram of pulley B, we see that the string tension applied from rope 1 acts on both sides of pulley B. This has to balance the string tension from rope 3, giving us the condition:

$$2T_1 = T_3 . \tag{4.21}$$

Combining equations (4.20) and (4.21), we see that:

$$T_1 = \tfrac{1}{2} mg . \tag{4.22}$$

This result means that the force we need to apply to suspend the object of mass m in this way is only half as big as the one we would have had to use by simply holding it up with a rope, but without pulleys. This is what we mean by using the term “force multiplier”.

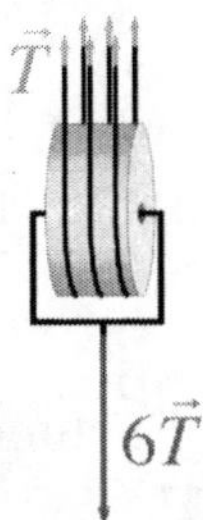

Figure 4.15: Pulley with 3 loops.

One can gain even larger force multipliers by guiding the rope 1 a total of n times over the same two pulleys. In this case, the force needed to suspend the object of mass m is then

$$T = \frac{1}{2n} mg \tag{4.23}$$

In Figure 4.15 the situation for $n = 3$ is shown. This results in $2n = 6$ force arrows of magnitude T each pointing up, thus being able to balance a downward force of $6T$, as expressed by (4.23).

In-class exercise:
We have a pulley with two loops and we can lift a weight of 440 N. We add two loops to the pulley and with the same force we can now lift
a) half the weight
b) twice the weight
c) one fourth the weight
d) four times the weight
e) the same amount of weight.

4.5. Newton's Laws

So far in this chapter we have only examined static cases, that is to say cases in which all forces and torques added up to zero, and in which the objects under consideration remained at rest. In the previous chapter, however, we looked at objects in motion, either with constant velocity, or with some kind of acceleration. And what remains to be answered is how this acceleration arises. The answer to this question is contained in Newton's Laws and will be the topic of the remainder of the present chapter.

Sir Isaac Newton (1642-1727) was perhaps the most influential scientist who ever lived. He is generally credited with being the founder of modern mechanics, as well as calculus (in competition with Leibnitz). Newtonian mechanics is what the first few chapters of this book are about. Although he formulated his famous three laws that govern forces in the 17th century, these laws are still the foundation of our understanding of forces. To begin this section, we will simply list the three laws. Newton's three laws, published in 1687, can be stated as:

Newton's First Law:

In the absence of a net force on an object, this object will remain at rest, if it was at rest. If it was moving, it will remain in motion with the same velocity.

Newton's Second Law:

If there is a net external force, $\vec{F}_{net}$, acting on an object with mass m, then the force will cause an acceleration, $\vec{a}$:

$$\vec{F}_{net} = m\vec{a}$$

Newton's Third Law:

The forces that two interacting objects exert on each other are always exactly equal in magnitude and opposite in direction to each other.

$$\vec{F}_{1\to 2} = -\vec{F}_{2\to 1}$$

Newton's First Law

In the absence of a net force on an object, this object will remain at rest, if it was at rest. If it was moving, it will remain in motion with the same velocity.

In previous sections of this chapter we have already encountered a restricted version of Newton's First Law for an object at rest, where we found that the condition of zero net external force is necessary for static equilibrium. But note that Newton's First Law also addresses the case when an object is already in motion with respect to some particular reference frame. For this case, it specifies that the acceleration is zero, provided the net external force is zero.

Newton's abstraction is not trivial, because it claims something that is at first sight in conflict with our everyday experience. Today we have the benefit that we have seen television pictures of objects floating in a spaceship, moving with unchanged velocities until the astronaut pushes them and thus exerts a force on them. This visual experience is in complete accordance with what Newton's First Law claims. But at Newton's time this experience was not the norm.

Consider the case of a car that is out of gas and needs to be pushed to the nearest gas station on a horizontal street. As long as we push the car, we can make it move. But as soon as we stop pushing, the car will slow down and come to a stop. It seems that as long as we push the car it can still go at constant velocity, but as soon as we stop exerting a force on it, it stops moving. This idea that a constant force is required to move with a constant speed was indeed the prevailing scientific view before Newton. It was the Aristotelian view, which originated from the ancient Greek philosopher Aristotle (384 BC – 322 BC) and his school of students.

What about the car that slows down once we stop pushing? This situation is not a case of zero net force. Instead, there is a force that is acting on the car to slow it down. This force is called the force of friction. Because the frictional force is acting as a non-vanishing net force, our example of the car slowing down turns out to not be an example for Newton's First Law, but one for Newton's Second Law instead. We will work more on friction later in this chapter.

Newton's Second Law

This law relates the concept of acceleration, for which we use the symbol $\vec{a}$, to the force. We have already introduced acceleration as the second derivative of the position with respect to time. And Newton's Second Law tells us what causes acceleration.

Newton's Second Law:

If there is a net external force, $\vec{F}_{net}$, acting on an object with mass m, then it will cause an acceleration, $\vec{a}$:

$$\vec{F}_{net} = m\vec{a} \tag{4.24}$$

This formula, "$F = ma$", is arguable the second-most famous in all of physics. (We will encounter the most famous formula, "$E = mc^2$", later in the book.) Equation (4.24) tells us that the magnitude of the acceleration of the object is proportional to the magnitude of the net external force acting on it. And it tells us that for a given external force the magnitude of the acceleration is inversely proportional to the mass of the object. All things being equal, more massive objects are harder to accelerate than less massive ones.

But the above formulation of Newton's Second Law tells us even more, because it is a vector equation. It says that the acceleration vector experienced by the object with mass m is in the same direction as the net external force vector that is acting on it to cause this acceleration. Because it is a vector equation, we can immediately write down the equations for the three spatial components:

$$F_x = ma_x \tag{4.25}$$

$$F_y = ma_y \tag{4.26}$$

$$F_z = ma_z \tag{4.27}$$

This result means that our familiar $F = ma$ holds independently for each Cartesian component of the force and acceleration vectors.

The use of Newton's Second Law enables us to perform a wide range of calculations. The following problem is a classic example that appears often in various forms in the introductory physics curriculum: Consider an object of mass m located on a plane that is inclined by an angle θ relative to the horizontal. For now we will assume that there is no frictional force between the plane and the object. (This "frictionless approximation" means that for the present problem we can safely ignore friction.)

Solved Problem 4.1: Snowboarding

Figure 4.16: Snowboarding as an example for motion on an inclined plane.

Question:

A snowboarder (mass 72.9 kg, height 1.79 m) glides down a slope with angle of 22° with respect to the horizontal. If we can neglect friction, what is the acceleration that he experiences?

Answer:

THINK:

The motion will be restricted to moving along the plane. The snowboarder cannot sink into the snow, and he cannot lift off from the plane. It is always advisable to start with a free-body diagram. Here we have drawn in the force vectors of gravity, $\vec{F}_g$, and the normal force, $\vec{N}$. Note that the normal force vector again is directed perpendicular to the contact surface, as required by the definition of the normal force. Also, please observe that now the normal force and the force of gravity do not point exactly in opposite direction to each other and thus do not cancel each other out completely.

Figure 4.17: Snowboarder with inclined plane and force vectors overlaid.

SKETCH:

Now we pick a convenient coordinate system. Choosing the coordinate system is important. Often the difference between very simple equations and very difficult ones is the clever choice of the coordinate system. Choosing the most advantageous coordinate system is an acquired skill gained through the experience of doing many problems of this type.

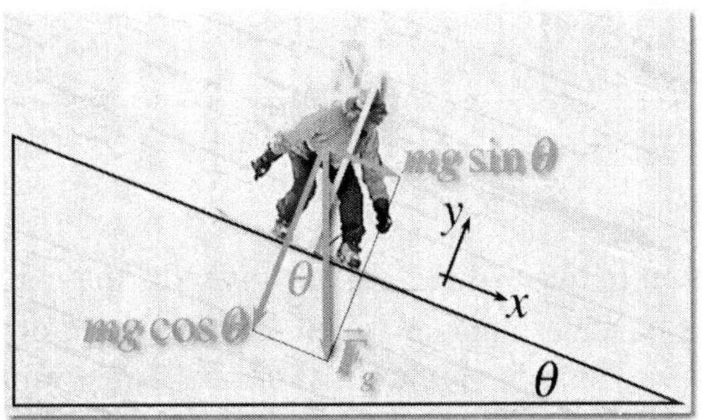

Figure 4.18: Same as previous figure, but now with a coordinate system.

Our choice of a coordinate system is such that the x-axis is along the direction of the inclined plane. This choice will ensure that the acceleration is only in x-direction. It is generally true that problems involving Newton's Second Law are simplified if one points an axis in the direction of the acceleration. Another advantage is that the normal force is pointing exactly along the y-direction. The price we pay for this convenience is that the gravitational force vector does not point along one of the major axes but now has an x- and a y-component in our coordinate system. The red arrows in the drawing indicate the two components of the gravitational force vector. Note that the angle of inclination of the plane, θ, also appears in the rectangle constructed from the two components of the gravity force vector, which is the diagonal of the rectangle. You can see this relationship by considering the similar triangles *abc* and *ABC*, as shown in Figure 4.19. Because *a* is perpendicular to *C* and *c* is perpendicular to *A*, it follows that the angle between *a* and *c* is the same as the angle between *A* and *C*.

Figure 4.19: Similar triangles in inclined-plane problems.

RESEARCH:

The x- and y-components of the gravitational force vector are given from trigonometry as:

$$F_{g,x} = F_g \sin\theta = mg\sin\theta \tag{4.28}$$

$$F_{g,y} = -F_g \cos\theta = -mg\cos\theta \tag{4.29}$$

SIMPLIFY:

Now we do the math in a straightforward way, separated by components. First, the y-direction: There is no motion in the y-direction, which means according to Newton's First Law that all external force-components in the y-direction have to add up to 0:

Solved Problem

Solved Problem

$$F_{g,y} + N = 0 \Rightarrow$$
$$-mg\cos\theta + N = 0 \Rightarrow$$
$$N = mg\cos\theta \qquad (4.30)$$

Our analysis of the motion in the y-direction has given us the magnitude of the normal force. The normal force balances the component of the weight of the snowboarder perpendicular to the slope. This is a very typical result. The normal force is almost always adjusted to balance the net force component perpendicular to the contact surface from all other forces. In this way objects do not sink into or lift off from surfaces.

The real physics information we are interested in comes from looking at the x-direction. In this direction, there is only one force component, the x-component of the gravitational force. And so according to Newton's Second Law we obtain:

$$F_{x,g} = mg\sin\theta = ma_x \Rightarrow$$
$$a_x = g\sin\theta \qquad (4.31)$$

So we now have our answer for the acceleration vector in the coordinate system specified:

$$\vec{a} = (g\sin\theta)\hat{x} \qquad (4.32)$$

Please note that the mass, m, dropped out of our answer. The answer for the acceleration does not depend on the mass of the snowboarder; it only depends on the angle of inclination of the plane. Thus the information on the mass of the snowboarder given in the question turns out to be just as irrelevant as the stated height of the person.

CALCULATE:

Putting in the given value for the angle leads to

$$a_x = (9.81 \text{ m/s}^2)\sin 22° = 3.67489 \text{ m/s}^2$$

ROUND:

Since the angle of the slope given is only specified to two digit accuracy, it makes no sense to give our result to a greater precision. Final answer:

$$a_x = 3.7 \text{ m/s}^2$$

DOUBLE-CHECK:

As a final step in the solution of this problem, let us check for consistency of our answer in a limiting case. In the case that $\theta \to 0°$, the sine also converges to 0, and the acceleration vanishes. This result is consistent because we expect no acceleration of the snowboarder if he rests on a horizontal surface. As $\theta \to 90°$, the sine approaches 1 and we obtain the results that the acceleration is the acceleration of gravity, as we expect as well. In this limiting case the snowboarded would be in free-fall.

Inclined-plane problems, like the one we have just solved, are very common, because they enable us to practice concepts of component-decomposition of forces. Another common set of problems involves redirection of forces via pulleys and strings. The next example shows how to proceed in a simple case.

Example 4.4: Two Blocks connected by a String

Here we present a second classic introductory physics problem. In this problem we use a hanging mass to generate a variable acceleration for a second mass on a horizontal surface. One mass, m_1, lies on a horizontal frictionless surface and is connected via a massless rope (for simplicity in the horizontal direction) running over a massless pulley to another mass, m_2, hanging from the rope.

Question:

What is the acceleration of mass m_1, and what is the acceleration of mass m_2?

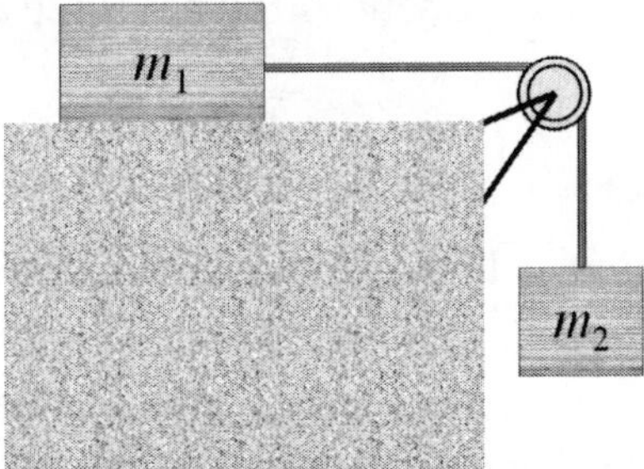

Figure 4.20: Object hanging from a rope connected over a pulley to a second object on a frictionless surface.

Answer:

Again we start with a free-body diagram for each object.

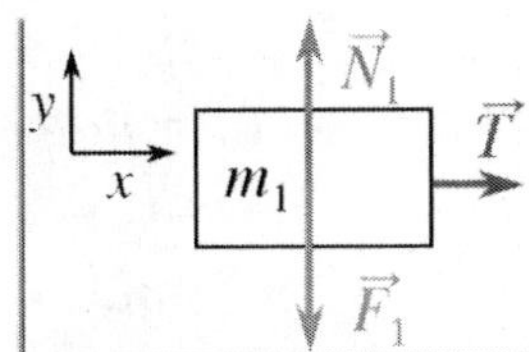

Figure 4.21: Free-body diagram for m_1.

For mass m_1, the free-body diagram is shown in Figure 4.21. The gravitational force vector points straight down and has the magnitude $F_1 = m_1 g$. The force due to the rope, $\vec{T}$, acts along the string and thus in the horizontal direction, which we have chosen as the x-coordinate. The normal force, $\vec{N}$, from the surface acting on m_1 acts perpendicular to the contact surface. Because the surface is horizontal, $\vec{N}$ acts in the vertical direction. From the requirement of zero net force in the y-direction, we get $N = F_1 = m_1 g$ for the magnitude of the normal force. The magnitude of the string force, T, remains yet to be

Example

Example

determined. Newton's Second Law gives us for the component of the acceleration in x-direction:

$$m_1 a = T \tag{4.33}$$

Now we turn to the free-body diagram for mass m_2. The same rope force, $\vec{T}$, that acts on m_1 also acts on m_2, but due to the redirection from the pulley, the force now acts in a different direction. However, we are interested in the magnitude of the tension, T, and this value is the same.

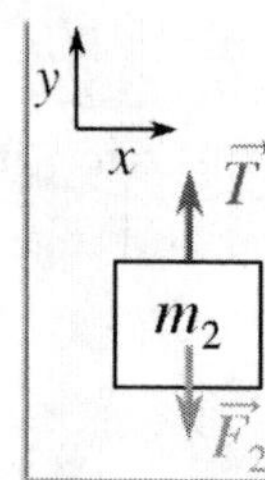

Figure 4.22: Free body diagram for m_2.

Newton's Second Law for the y-component of the net force acting on m_2 gives us:

$$T - m_2 g = -m_2 a \tag{4.34}$$

The magnitude of the acceleration a for m_2 that appears in this equation is the same as in the equation of motion for m_1, because the two masses are tied to each other by a rope and experience the same acceleration magnitude. This is a key insight: if two objects are tied to each other in this way, they must experience the same magnitude of acceleration, provided the rope is kept under tension! The negative sign on the right side of (4.34) indicates that m_2 will accelerate in the negative y-direction.

We can now combine equations (4.33) and (4.34) to eliminate the magnitude of the string force, T. We then obtain the answer for the common acceleration of the two masses:

$$m_1 a = T = m_2 g - m_2 a \Rightarrow$$

$$a = g \frac{m_2}{m_1 + m_2} \tag{4.35}$$

This result makes sense, because in the limit that m_1 is very large compared to m_2, there will be almost no acceleration, and if m_1 is very small compared to m_2, then m_2 will accelerate with almost the full acceleration due to gravity, as if m_1 were not there.

Finally we can calculate the magnitude of the string force by reinserting our result for the acceleration into one of the two equations we had obtained from Newton's Second Law:

$$T = m_1 a = g \frac{m_1 m_2}{m_1 + m_2} \tag{4.36}$$

Example 4.5: Atwood Machine

The Atwood machine consists of two masses (m_1 and m_2) connected via a rope running over a pulley. For now we will consider a friction-free case, where the pulley does not move, and the rope glides over it. (In chapter 10 on rotation we will return to this problem and solve it with friction, which causes the pulley to rotate). Let us also assume that $m_1 > m_2$. In this case the acceleration is as shown in Figure 4.23. (The formula derived below is correct for any case. If $m_1 < m_2$, then the acceleration, a, will come out with a negative sign, which we interpret to mean that the acceleration direction is opposite to what we assumed in working the problem.) In more complicated cases, it may not be clear at the beginning in which direction objects begin to accelerate. You just have to define a direction as positive and use this assumption consistently throughout your calculation. If the acceleration value that you obtain in the end turns out to be negative, this result means that the objects accelerate in the direction opposite to the one originally assumed. The calculation itself still will remain correct.

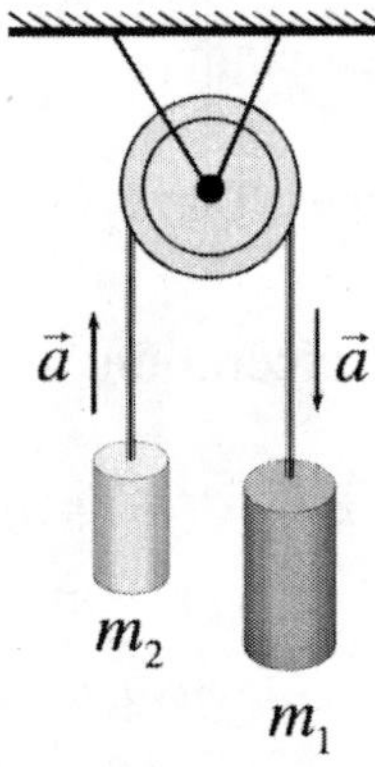

Figure 4.23: Atwood machine with the defined positive acceleration direction indicated.

We start by drawing free body diagrams for m_1 and m_2 as shown in Figure 4.24 and Figure 4.25. In both free-body diagrams we elect to point the positive y-axis up, and in both diagrams we indicate our choice for the direction of the acceleration. The rope exerts a tension T, of magnitude still to be determined, upward on both m_1 and m_2. With our choices of the coordinate system and the direction of the acceleration, the downward acceleration of m_1 is acceleration in a negative direction. This leads to an equation that be solved for T:

$$T - m_1 g = -m_1 a \quad \Rightarrow \quad T = m_1 g - m_1 a = m_1 (g - a) \tag{4.37}$$

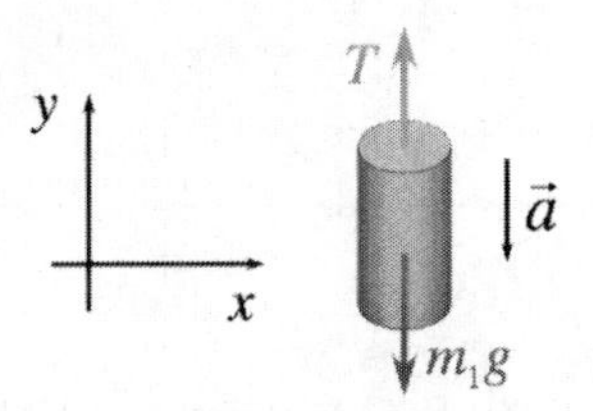

Figure 4.24: Free-body diagram for the mass on the right side.

Example

From the free body diagram for m_2 and the assumption that the upward acceleration of m_2 corresponds to acceleration in a positive direction, we get

$$T - m_2 g = m_2 a \;\Rightarrow\; T = m_2 g + m_2 a = m_2 (g + a) \qquad (4.38)$$

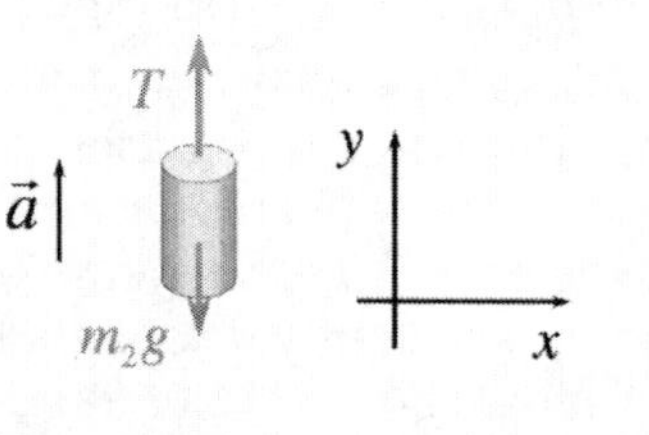

Figure 4.25: Free-body diagram for the mass on the left side.

Equating the two expressions for T we obtain

$$m_1 (g - a) = m_2 (g + a), \qquad (4.39)$$

which leads to an expression for the acceleration:

$$(m_1 - m_2) g = (m_1 + m_2) a \Rightarrow$$
$$a = g \frac{m_1 - m_2}{m_1 + m_2} \qquad (4.40)$$

From this equation you can see that the magnitude of the acceleration, a, in this case is always smaller than g. If both masses are equal, we obtain the expected result of no acceleration. By selecting the proper combination of masses, we can generate any value of the acceleration between 0 and g that we desire.

Self-Test Opportunity:
For the Atwood machine, can you calculate the string tension?

In-class exercise:
If you double the value of both masses in the Atwood machine, then the resulting acceleration will be
a) twice as large
b) half as large
c) the same
d) one quarter as large
e) four times as large

Newton's Third Law

If you have ever ridden a skateboard, you must have made the following observation: If you are standing at rest on your skateboard, and you step off your skateboard over the front or back, then skateboard shoots off into the opposite direction. In the process of stepping off, the skateboard exerts a force on your foot, and your foot exerts a force onto the skateboard. This experience seems to suggest that these forces point in opposite directions. This is one example for a general truth, one that is quantified in Newton's Third Law.

Newton's Third Law:

The forces that two interacting objects exert on each other are always exactly equal in magnitude and opposite in direction to each other.

$$\vec{F}_{1\to 2} = -\vec{F}_{2\to 1} \tag{4.41}$$

Note that these two forces do not act on the same body.

The Third Law is a consequence of the demand that internal forces, i.e. forces that act between different components of the same system under consideration, must add to 0; otherwise their sum would contribute to a net external force and cause an acceleration, according to Newton's Second Law. No object or group of objects can accelerate themselves without interacting with external objects. The fictional story of Baron Münchhausen, who claimed to have pulled himself out of a swamp by simply pulling very hard on his own hair, is then unmasked as untrue – courtesy of Newton's Third Law.

Example 4.6: Collision of two vehicles

Suppose an SUV with mass $M = 3{,}260$ kg has a head-on collision with a sub-compact car of mass $m = 1{,}194$ kg, and that during this process the SUV exerts a force of magnitude $2.9 \cdot 10^5$ N on the sub-compact.

Question:

What is the magnitude of the force that the sub-compact exerts on the SUV in this collision?

Answer:

As paradoxical as it may seem at first, the little sub-compact exerts just as much force on the SUV as the SUV on the sub-compact. This is a straightforward consequence of Newton's Third Law, equation (4.41). So our answer is $2.9 \cdot 10^5$ N.

The answer may be straightforward, but it is by no means intuitive at first. Obviously, the sub-compact will usually sustain much more damage, and its passengers have a much bigger chance of getting hurt in this collision. But this is simply due to Newton's Second Law, which teaches us that the same force applied to a less massive object yields higher acceleration than when it is applied to a more massive one. We will revisit this issue in the chapter 7 on momentum and collisions.

In-class exercise:
Follow-up on Example 4.7: we call the absolute value of the acceleration experienced by the SUV due to the collision a_{SUV} and that of the sub-compact car a_{car}, then we find approximately

a) $a_{SUV} \approx \frac{1}{9} a_{car}$

b) $a_{SUV} \approx \frac{1}{3} a_{car}$

c) $a_{SUV} \approx a_{car}$

d) $a_{SUV} \approx 3a_{car}$

e) $a_{SUV} \approx 9a_{car}$

4.8. Friction Force

So far, we have neglected the force of friction and only talked about frictionless approximations. However, in general this approach is not sufficient. Instead, we have to include friction into many of our calculations when we want to describe physically realistic situations.

There is a series of very simple experiments that one can conduct to learn about the basic characteristics of friction. Here are the findings of these experiments:

- If an object is at rest, then it takes a certain threshold magnitude of an external force acting along the contact surface between this object and the surface to overcome the frictional force.
- If an object is at rest, then the friction force that one needs to overcome to make the object move is bigger than the friction force that acts on a moving object.
- The friction force on a moving object is proportional to the normal force on the contact surface.
- The friction force is independent of the size of the contact area.
- The friction force is dependent on the "roughness" of the surface, i.e. a smoother surface interface generally provides less friction force than a rougher one.

From these findings, it seems clear that we need to distinguish between the case where an object is at rest relative to its supporting surface (static friction) and the case where an object is moving across the surface (kinetic friction).

Kinetic Friction

The case in which an object is moving across a surface is the easier one, and we treat it first.

The above observations related to moving objects can be summarized in the following approximate formula for the magnitude of kinetic friction force, f_k:

$$f_k = \mu_k N \tag{4.42}$$

Here N is the magnitude of the normal force, and μ_k is the coefficient of kinetic friction. This coefficient is always equal to or greater than 0. (The case of $\mu_k = 0$ corresponds to our frictionless approximation. In practice, however, it can never be reached perfectly.) In almost all cases, μ_k is also less than 1. (There are some special tire surfaces used for car racing where the coefficient of friction between street and tires can exceed the value of 1 quite significantly, though.)

The direction of the kinetic friction force is always opposite to the direction of motion of an object relative to the surface it moves on.

If you push with an external force along the contact surface, and the force has a magnitude exactly equal to that of the force of kinetic friction on an object, then the total net external force is zero, because the external force and the friction force cancel each other. In that case, according to Newton's First Law, the object will continue to slide across the surface with constant velocity.

Static Friction

If an object is at rest, it takes a certain threshold amount of external force to set it in motion. For example, if you push lightly with one finger against your refrigerator, it will not move. As you push harder and harder, you reach a point where the refrigerator finally slides across your kitchen floor.

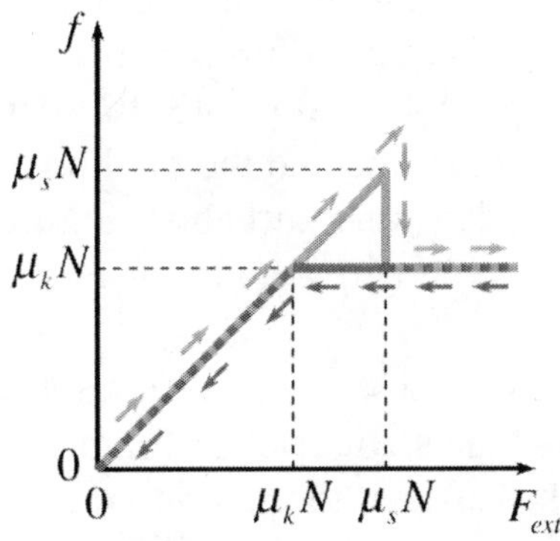

Figure 4.26: Force of friction as a function of the external force.

For any external force acting on an object that remains at rest, the friction force is exactly equal in magnitude and opposite in direction to the component of that external force that acts along the contact surface between the object and its supporting surface. However, there is a maximum of the magnitude of the static friction force, $f_s \le f_{s,\max}$. This maximum magnitude is again proportional to the normal force, but with a different proportionality constant than the force of kinetic friction, $f_{s,\max} = \mu_s N$. We can write for the magnitude of the force of static friction:

$$f_s \le \mu_s N = f_{s,\max} \tag{4.43}$$

In general, for any object on any supporting surface, the maximum force of static friction is greater than the force of kinetic friction. You may have experienced this by trying to slide a heavy object across a surface: as soon as the object starts moving, a lot less force is required to keep the object in constant sliding motion. We can write down this finding as a mathematical inequality between the two different friction coefficients:

$$\mu_s > \mu_k \tag{4.44}$$

We can now draw a diagram of how the friction force depends on an external force, F_{ext} applied to an object. If the object is initially at rest, a small external force results in a small force of friction, rising linearly with the external force until it reaches a value of $\mu_s N$. Then it drops rather quickly to a value of $\mu_k N$, when the object is set in motion. At this point the external force has a value of $F_{\text{ext}} = \mu_s N$, resulting in a sudden acceleration of the object. This dependence of the friction force on the external force is shown in Figure 4.26, red line.

On the other hand, if we start with a large external force, and the object is already in motion, then we can reduce the external force below a value of $\mu_s N$, but still above $\mu_k N$, and the object will still keep moving and accelerating, thus the friction coefficient retains a value of μ_k until the external force is reduced to a value of $\mu_k N$. At this point, the object will move with a constant velocity, because the external force and the friction force are equal in magnitude. If we reduce the external force further, the object decelerates and eventually comes to rest and the external force is not sufficient to move it any more. Thus the friction force is reduced proportionally to the external force until both reach 0. The blue line in Figure 4.26 illustrates this dependence of the friction force on the external force. Where the blue line and the red line overlap, we have alternated blue and red squares. The most interesting part about Figure 4.26 is that the blue and red lines do not follow each other between $\mu_k N$ and $\mu_s N$.

Suppose you want to move a refrigerator across your kitchen floor. Initially, the refrigerator sits on the floor, and the static friction force resists your effort to move it. Once you push hard enough, the refrigerator jars into motion. In this process, the friction coefficient between the refrigerator and the floor follows the red path in our diagram. Once the fridge moves, you can push less hard, and still keep the refrigerator moving. If you push with less force so that the fridge moves with constant velocity, you are following along the blue path in the diagram until your external force applied to the fridge is reduced to $F_{\text{ext}} = \mu_k N$. Then the friction force and the force you apply to the fridge just add up to 0, and there is no net force acting on the refrigerator, allowing it to move with constant velocity.

Example 4.7: Real Snowboarding

Downhill skiing and snowboarding are examples of moving down an inclined plane. So let us continue with the snowboarding discussion from Solved Problem 4.2, but now include friction. In this example a snowboarder moves down a slope of $\theta = 22°$. Suppose the coefficient of kinetic friction between his board and the snow is 0.21, and his velocity, which is along the direction of the slope, is measured as 8.3 m/s at this instant.

Question 1:
Assuming a constant slope, what will the speed of the snowboarder along the direction of the slope be, 100 m further down the slope?

Answer 1:
Figure 4.27 shows all forces at work. The gravitational force points downward and has the magnitude mg, where m is the mass of the snowboarder, including equipment. We introduce convenient x- and y-axes parallel and perpendicular to the slope, as indicated in Figure 4.27. The angle θ that the slope makes with the horizontal (22° in this case) also appears in the decomposition of the components of the gravitational force parallel and perpendicular to the slope. This analysis is a general feature of any inclined-plane problem. The force component along the plane is then $mg\sin\theta$, as shown in Figure 4.27. The normal force is given by $N = mg\cos\theta$, and the force of kinetic friction is $f_k = -\mu_k mg\cos\theta$, with the minus sign indicating that the force is acting in the negative x-direction, as given by our coordinate system. We thus get for the total force component in x-direction:

$$\begin{aligned} mg\sin\theta - \mu_k mg\cos\theta &= ma_x \Rightarrow \\ a_x &= g(\sin\theta - \mu_k\cos\theta) \end{aligned} \qquad (4.45)$$

Figure 4.27: Forces on a snowboarder, including the friction force.

Here we have used Newton's second law, $F_x = ma_x$, in the first line. The mass of the snowboarder drops out of the problem and the acceleration, a_x, along the slope is a constant. Inserting the numbers given in the problem, we obtain

$$a \equiv a_x = (9.81\ \text{m/s}^2)(\sin 22° - 0.21\cos 22°) = 1.76\ \text{m/s}^2$$

Thus we see that this situation is a problem of motion on a straight line in one direction with constant acceleration. We can thus apply the relationship between the squares of the initial and final velocities, the acceleration and the acceleration that we have derived for one-dimensional motion with constant acceleration,

$$v^2 = v_0^2 + 2a(x - x_0).$$

With $v_0 = 8.3 \text{ m/s}$ and $x - x_0 = 100 \text{ m}$, we then get for the final speed:

$$\begin{aligned} v &= \sqrt{v_0^2 + 2a(x - x_0)} \\ &= \sqrt{(8.3 \text{ m/s})^2 + 2 \cdot (1.76 \text{ m/s}^2)(100 \text{ m})} \\ &= 20.5 \text{ m/s} \end{aligned} \tag{4.46}$$

Question 2:
How long does it take to get to this speed?

Answer 3:
Since we now know the acceleration and the final speed, and we were given the initial speed, we use:

$$v = v_0 + at \Rightarrow t = \frac{v - v_0}{a} = \frac{(20.5 - 8.3) \text{ m/s}}{1.76 \text{ m/s}^2} = 6.95 \text{ s}$$

Example

Question 3:
Given the same coefficient of friction, what would have to be the angle of the slope for which the snowboarder would glide with constant velocity?

Answer 3:
Motion with constant velocity implies zero acceleration. We have already derived an equation for the acceleration as a function of the slope angle. Now we set this expression equal to zero and solve the resulting equation for the angle θ:

$$\begin{aligned} a_x = g(\sin\theta - \mu_k \cos\theta) = 0 &\Rightarrow \\ \sin\theta = \mu_k \cos\theta &\Rightarrow \\ \tan\theta = \mu_k &\Rightarrow \\ \theta = \arctan \mu_k & \end{aligned} \tag{4.47}$$

Because $\mu_k = 0.21$ was given, we get for the angle $\theta = \arctan 0.21 = 11.8°$. For a steeper slope, the snowboarder will accelerate, and for a shallower slope the snowboarder will slow down until he comes to a stop.

Air Resistance

So far we have ignored the friction of moving through the air. Unlike the force of kinetic friction that you encounter when dragging one object across the surface of another, air resistance increases as speed increases. We then need to express the friction force as a function of the velocity of the object relative to the medium it moves through. The direction of the force of air resistance is opposite to the direction of the velocity vector. In general the magnitude of the friction force due to air resistance can be expressed as $F_{frict} = K_0 + K_1 v + K_2 v^2 + ...$, with the constants $K_0, K_1, K_2, ...$ to be determined. For the force of friction of air resistance on macroscopic objects moving at relatively high speeds one can neglect the linear term in the velocity. The magnitude of this drag force is then approximated as

$$F_{drag} = Kv^2 \tag{4.48}$$

This equation means that the force due to air resistance is proportional to the square of the speed. When an object falls through air, the force from air resistance will increase as the object accelerates until it reaches a so-called "terminal velocity". At this point, the force of air resistance and gravity equal each other. Thus the net force is zero, and there is no more acceleration. Because there is no more acceleration, the falling object has constant terminal velocity:

$$F_g = F_{drag} \Rightarrow mg = Kv^2 \tag{4.49}$$

Solving this for the terminal velocity we obtain:

$$v = \sqrt{\frac{mg}{K}} \tag{4.50}$$

Note that this expression for the terminal velocity depends on the mass of the object, whereas when we neglected air resistance, the mass of the object did not enter into the acceleration of the object. In the absence of air resistance all objects fall at the same rate, and the presence of air resistance explains why heavy objects fall faster than light ones that have the same K.

To compute the terminal velocity for a falling object, we need to know the value of the constant K. This constant depends on many variables, including the size of the area exposed to the air stream. In general terms, the bigger the area, A, the bigger is the constant K. K also depends linearly on the air density, ρ. All other dependences on the shape of the object, on its inclination relative to the direction of motion, on air viscosity, and compressibility are usually collected in a drag coefficient, c_d:

$$K = \tfrac{1}{2} c_d A \rho \tag{4.51}$$

Equation (4.51) has the factor 1/2 to make calculations involving the energy of objects undergoing free-fall with air resistance simpler – we will return to this subject when we discuss energy in the next chapter.

In-class exercise:
(Unused) coffee filters reach their terminal velocity very quickly, if you let them fall. Suppose you have a single coffee filter and release it from a height of 1 m, from which height do you have to release a stack of 2 coffee filters at the same instant so that they hit the ground at the same time as the single coffee filter. (You can safely neglect the time needed to reach terminal speed.)
a) 0.5 m
b) 0.7 m
c) 1 m
d) 1.4 m
e) 2 m

Creating a low drag coefficient is an important consideration in automotive design, because it has a strong influence on the maximum speed of the car and its fuel consumption. Numerical computations are useful, but the drag coefficient is usually optimized experimentally by putting car prototypes into wind tunnels and testing the wind resistance at different speeds. The same wind tunnel tests are also used to optimize sporting equipment and athlete's performance in events such as downhill ski racing.

In very viscous environments and at low velocities, one cannot neglect the linear velocity term of the friction force. In this case the friction force can be approximated by the form $F_{frict} = K_1 v$. This form is the case for most biological processes, with large bio-molecules or even microorganisms like bacteria moving through liquids. This approximate form of the friction force is also useful when discussing the sinking of an object in a fluid, for example a small stone in water.

Example

Example 4.8: Sky Diving
An 80 kg skydiver falls through air with a density of 1.15 kg/m^3. Assume that his drag coefficient is $c_d = 0.57$. When he falls in the spread-eagle position, as shown Figure 4.28, his body presents an area of $A_1 = 0.94 \text{ m}^2$ to the wind, whereas when he dives head first, with arms close to the body and legs together, his area is reduced to $A_2 = 0.21 \text{ m}^2$.

Figure 4.28: Skydivers in the high-resistance position.

Question:
What are the terminal velocities in both cases?

Answer:
We use equation (4.50) for the terminal velocity and (4.51) for the air resistance constant, rearrange the formulas, and insert our numbers:

$$v = \sqrt{\frac{mg}{K}} = \sqrt{\frac{mg}{\frac{1}{2}c_d A\rho}} \tag{4.52}$$

$$v_1 = \sqrt{\frac{(80 \text{ kg})(9.8 \text{ m/s}^2)}{\frac{1}{2}0.57(0.94 \text{ m}^2)(1.15 \text{ kg/m}^3)}} = 50.4 \text{ m/s}$$

$$v_2 = \sqrt{\frac{(80 \text{ kg})(9.8 \text{ m/s}^2)}{\frac{1}{2}0.57(0.21 \text{ m}^2)(1.15 \text{ kg/m}^3)}} = 107 \text{ m/s}$$

This example shows that, by diving head first, the skydiver can reach higher velocities during free-fall than when he uses the spread-eagle position. Therefore it is possible to catch up to a person that has fallen out of an airplane, assuming that person is not diving head first, too. However, in general this technique cannot be used to save someone who jumped without a parachute because it is nearly impossible to hold onto that person during the sudden deceleration shock caused by opening the rescuer's parachute.

Tribology

What causes friction? The answer to this question is not at all easy or obvious. When surfaces rub against each other, different atoms (more on atoms in chapter 13) from the two surfaces make contact with each other in different ways. Atoms get dislocated in the process of dragging surfaces across each other. Electrostatic interaction (more on this in chapter 21) between the atoms on the surfaces causes additional friction in the static case. A true microscopic understanding of friction is beyond the scope of the present text and is still very much a topic of great research activity.

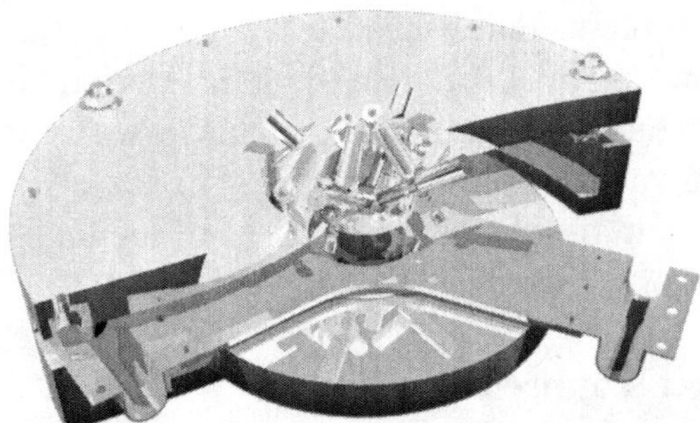

Figure 4.29: Cut-away drawing of a microscope used to study friction forces by dragging a sharp point across the surface to be studied.

The science of friction actually has a name, tribology. The laws of friction we have discussed above were already known 300 years ago. Their discovery is generally credited to Amontons and Coulomb, but even Da Vinci may have known them. And still, there are amazing new things to find out about friction, lubrication, and wear.

Perhaps the most interesting advance in tribology that occurred in the last two decades is the development of atomic and friction force microscopes. The basic principle that these microscopes employ is the dragging of a very sharp tip across a surface, employing cutting edge computer and sensor technology. With these friction force microscopes one can measure friction forces as small as 10 pN = 10^{-11} N. Shown in Figure 4.29 is a cut-away drawing of a schematic setup of one of these instruments, constructed by physicists at the University of Leiden, Netherlands. Present state-of-the-art microscopic theoretical simulations of friction are still not able to completely understand friction, and so this field is a current research area of great interest in the field of nanotechnology.

Friction is responsible for small particles breaking off the surfaces that rub against each other, causing wear. This phenomenon is of particular importance to high performance engines in cars, which require specially formulated engine lubricants. Understanding the influence of small surface impurities on the friction force is of great interest in this context.

Research into lubricants continues to try to find ways to reduce the coefficient of kinetic friction, μ_k, to a value as close to 0 as possible. For example, modern lubricants include buckyballs, molecules consisting of 60 carbon atoms in the shape of soccer balls, which were discovered only in the last decade. These can act like microscopic ball bearings.

Solving problems involving friction is also a big part of car racing. In the Formula 1 circuit, using the right tires that provide optimally high friction is essential for winning a race. While friction coefficients normally are in the range between 0 and 1, it is not unusual in top fuel racing, to have tires that have friction coefficients with the track surface of 3 or even larger.

4.9. Applications of the Frictional Force

There is a huge class of problems that we can solve now that we have Newton's three laws in our arsenal. Knowing about static and kinetic friction allows us to approximate real-world situations and come to meaningful conclusions. Because it is good to see these ideas of Newton's Law in various applications, we will solve several practice problems. These examples are designed to demonstrate a range of techniques that are useful in the solution of many kinds of problems.

Example

Example 4.9: Two Objects connected by a String – Version 2, with Friction

We have already solved this problem in Example 4.5 specifying that m_1 slides without friction across its horizontal support surface, and that the rope slides without friction across the pulley. Now we will allow for friction between m_1 and the surface it slides across. We will, for now, still keep the rope sliding without friction across the pulley. (In chapter 10 we will develop the techniques that let us also deal with the case that the pulley is set into rotational motion due to the rope moving across it.)

Example

Question 1:
Let the coefficient of static friction between mass $m_1 (= 2.3\text{ kg})$ and its support surface have a value of 0.73 and the kinetic friction coefficient have a value of 0.60. Will m_1 move, provided that the mass $m_2 = 1.9\text{ kg}$?

Answer 1:
All of our force considerations from the first version of the problem remain identical, except that the free-body diagram for mass m_1 shown in Figure 4.30 now also has a force arrow corresponding to the friction force, f. Please keep in mind that in order to draw the direction of the friction force arrow, you need to know in which direction the movement would be in the friction-free case. Because we have already solved the frictionless case, we know that in this case m_1 would move to the right. Because the friction force is directed opposite, the arrow will thus point to the left.

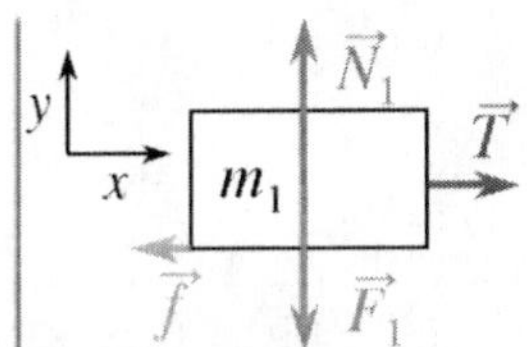

Figure 4.30: Free body diagram for m_1 including the force of friction.

The force equation that we had derived by using Newton's Second Law for m_1 then is changed from $m_1 a = T$ (equation (4.33)) to:

$$m_1 a = T - f \tag{4.53}$$

Combining this with the equation we obtained for m_2 via application of Newton's Second Law, $T - m_2 g = -m_2 a$, and eliminating again T gives us now:

$$m_1 a + f = T = m_2 g - m_2 a \Rightarrow$$
$$a = \frac{m_2 g - f}{m_1 + m_2} \tag{4.54}$$

We have so far avoided specifying any further details about the friction force. We now start by first calculating the maximum magnitude of the static friction force, $f_{s,\max} = \mu_s N$. For the magnitude of the normal force we had already found $N = m_1 g$, giving us the formula for the maximum static friction force

$$f_{s,\max} = \mu_s N = \mu_s m_1 g = 0.73 \cdot (2.3\text{ kg}) \cdot (9.81\text{ m/s}^2) = 16.5\text{ N} \tag{4.55}$$

We need to compare this value to $m_2 g$ in the numerator for the equation for the acceleration. If $f_{s,\max} \geq m_2 g$, then the static friction force will assume a value exactly equal to $m_2 g$, thus causing the acceleration to be 0, i.e. there will be no motion, because the pull due to mass m_2 hanging from the string is not sufficient to overcome the force of

Example

static friction between mass m_1 and its supporting surface. If $f_{s,\max} < m_2 g$, then there will be positive acceleration, and the two masses will start moving. In the present case, because $m_2 g = (1.9 \text{ kg}) \cdot (9.81 \text{ m/s}^2) = 18.6 \text{ N}$, the masses will start moving.

Question 2:
What is the acceleration?

Answer 2:
As soon as the static friction is overcome, kinetic friction takes over. We can then use equation (4.54) for the acceleration, insert $f = \mu_k N = \mu_k m_1 g$, and obtain

$$a = \frac{m_2 g - \mu_k m_1 g}{m_1 + m_2} = g \frac{m_2 - \mu_k m_1}{m_1 + m_2} \tag{4.56}$$

Inserting the numbers, we find:

$$a = (9.81 \text{ m/s}^2) \frac{(1.9 \text{ kg}) - 0.6 \cdot (2.3 \text{ kg})}{(2.3 \text{ kg}) + (1.9 \text{ kg})} = 1.21 \text{ m/s}^2$$

Example

Example 4.10: Pulling a sled
Suppose you are pulling a sled across a level snow-covered surface by pulling on a rope with constant force, at an angle of θ relative to the ground.

Question 1:
If the sled, including its load, has a mass of 95.3 kg, the coefficients of friction between the sled and the snow are $\mu_s = 0.076$, $\mu_k = 0.070$, and if you pull with a force of 145.3 N on a rope attached to the sled at an angle of 24.5° relative to the horizontal ground, what is the sled's acceleration?

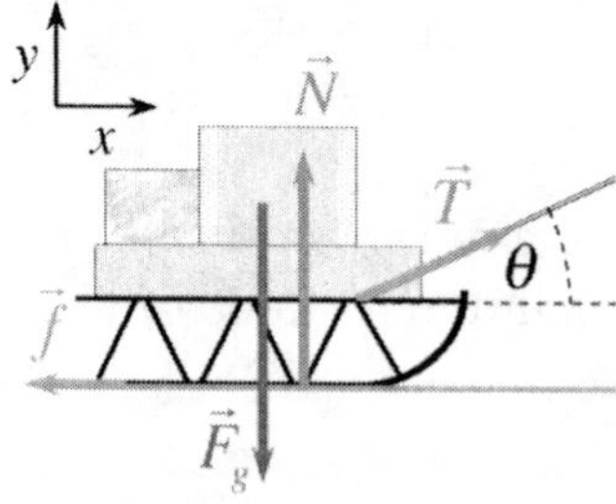

Figure 4.31: Drawing of a sled and its load showing the coordinate system and force vectors.

Answer 1:
Figure 4.31 shows the sled along with all forces acting on it. The force vectors' directions are correct, but the lengths not necessarily drawn to scale. The acceleration of the sled will, if at all, happen along the horizontal, the x-direction. In components, Newton's Second Law reads:

$$x: \quad ma = T\cos\theta - f \tag{4.57}$$

$$y: \qquad 0 = T\sin\theta - mg + N \tag{4.58}$$

For the friction force, we will simply use the form $f = \mu N$ for now, without specifying whether it is the kinetic or static friction, but in the end we will have to return to this point and answer it. The normal force can be calculated from the above equation for the y-components and inserted into the equation for the x-components:

$$\begin{aligned} N &= mg - T\sin\theta \\ ma &= T\cos\theta - \mu(mg - T\sin\theta) \Rightarrow \\ a &= \frac{T}{m}(\cos\theta + \mu\sin\theta) - \mu g \end{aligned} \tag{4.59}$$

Now we see that the normal force is actually smaller than the weight of the sled, because the force pulling on the rope has an upward component. So the vertical component of the force pulling on the rope also contributes to the acceleration of the sled as it affects the normal force and hence the horizontal frictional force.

When putting in the numbers, we first have to use the value of the coefficient of static friction to see if there is enough force applied by pulling on the rope to generate a positive acceleration. If the number for a turns out to be negative, this means that there is not enough force to overcome the force of static friction. With this choice, we obtain:

$$a' = \frac{145.3\text{ N}}{95.3\text{ kg}}(\cos 24.5° + 0.076\sin 24.5°) - 0.076(9.81\text{ m/s}^2) = 0.69\text{ m/s}^2$$

Because this attempt resulted in a positive value for a', we know that the force is strong enough to overcome the friction force. We now use the coefficient of kinetic friction to calculate our answer for the actual acceleration of the sled:

$$a = \frac{145.3\text{ N}}{95.3\text{ kg}}(\cos 24.5° + 0.070\sin 24.5°) - 0.070(9.81\text{ m/s}^2) = 0.74\text{ m/s}^2$$

Question 2:
If we have the choice of direction in which we pull the sled, which angle will lead to the maximum acceleration of the sled for this given value of the magnitude of the pulling force, T, and what is that maximum value of a?

Answer 2:
In calculus we learn that in order to find the extremum of a function we have to take the first derivative and find the value of the independent variable for which that derivative is 0.

$$\frac{d}{d\theta}a = \frac{d}{d\theta}\left(\frac{T}{m}(\cos\theta + \mu\sin\theta) - \mu g\right) = \frac{T}{m}(-\sin\theta + \mu\cos\theta) \tag{4.60}$$

Example

Example

Searching for the root of this equation results in

$$\left.\frac{da}{d\theta}\right|_{\theta=\theta_{\max}} = \frac{T}{m}(-\sin\theta_{\max} + \mu\cos\theta_{\max}) = 0$$

$$\Rightarrow \sin\theta_{\max} = \mu\cos\theta_{\max} \Rightarrow$$

$$\theta_{\max} = \arctan\mu \tag{4.61}$$

Inserting the value for the coefficient of kinetic friction, 0.070, into this equation results in a value of $\theta_{\max} = 4.0°$. This means that in this case we should pull in almost horizontal direction. The resulting value of the acceleration can again be obtained by inserting the numbers into the above equation for a:

$$a_{\max} \equiv a(\theta_{\max}) = 0.84 \text{ m/s}^2$$

Please note: a vanishing first derivative is only a necessary condition for a maximum, not a sufficient one. You can convince yourself in two ways that we have indeed found the maximum. First, we realize that we only obtained one root of the first derivative, meaning that the function $a(\theta)$ has only one extremum, and because we calculated the value of the acceleration at this point and found that it was bigger than the value we had previously obtained for 24.5°, we are assured that our single extremum is indeed a maximum. Alternatively, we could have also taken the second derivative and found that it is negative at the point $\theta_{\max} = 4.0°$; and then we could have compared the value of the acceleration obtained at that point with those at the boundaries of 0 and 90° angles.

What we have learned/Exam Study Guide:

- The net force on an object is the vector sum of the forces acting on the object, $\vec{F}_{net} = \sum_{i=1}^{n} \vec{F}_i$
- Mass is an intrinsic quality of an object that quantifies both an object's ability to resist acceleration and the gravitational force on the object.
- A free body diagram for an object is an abstraction showing all forces acting on that object.
- Newton's three laws are given by:
    - In the absence of a net external force on an object, this object will remain at rest, if it was at rest. If it was moving, it will remain in motion with the same velocity.
    - If there is a net external force, $\vec{F}_{net}$, acting on an object with mass m, then the force will cause an acceleration, $\vec{a}$, determined by the equation $\vec{F}_{net} = m\vec{a}$.
    - The forces that two interacting objects exert on each other are always

exactly equal in magnitude and opposite in direction to each other, $\vec{F}_{1\to2} = -\vec{F}_{2\to1}$.

- There are two types of friction, static and kinetic friction. Both types of friction are proportional to the normal force, N.
    - Static friction describes the force of friction between an object at rest on a surface in terms of the coefficient of static friction, μ_s. The static friction force, f_s opposes a force trying to move an object. f_s has a maximum value, $f_{s,\max}$ and $f_s \le \mu_s N = f_{s,\max}$.
    - Kinetic friction describes the force of friction between a moving object and a surface in terms of the coefficient of kinetic friction, μ_k. Kinetic friction is given by $f_k = \mu_k N$.
    - In general, $\mu_s > \mu_k$.

Additional Solved Problems

Solved Problem

Solved Problem 4.2: Wedge on Inclined Plane

Question:

A wedge of mass $m = 37.7$ kg is held in place on a fixed plane that is inclined by an angle $\theta = 20.5°$ with respect to the horizontal. A force $F = 309.3$ N in horizontal direction pushes on the wedge as shown in Figure 4.32.

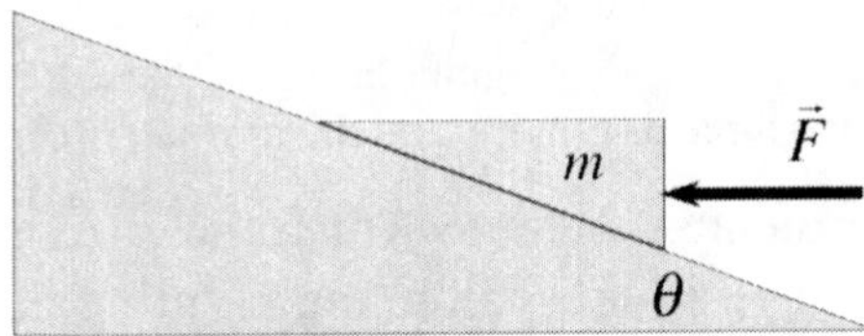

Figure 4.32: A wedge-shaped mass being pushed on an inclined plane.

The coefficient of kinetic friction between the wedge and the plane is $\mu_k = 0.171$. Assume that the coefficient of static friction is such that the net force will move the mass. What is the acceleration of m along the plane when the mass m is released?

Answer:

THINK: We want to know the acceleration a of the mass m along the plane, which requires us to determine the net force acting on the mass m parallel to the surface of the inclined plane. In addition, we need the net force acting on the mass m perpendicular to the plane to allow us to determine the force of kinetic friction.

The forces acting on the mass m are gravity, the normal force, the force of kinetic friction f_k, and the external force F. The coefficient of kinetic friction μ_k is given so we can calculate the friction force once we determine the normal force. Before we can continue with our analysis of the forces, we must determine which direction the mass m

will move after it is released when acted upon by the force F. Once we know which direction the mass will go, we can determine the direction of the friction force and we can complete our analysis.

To determine the net force before the mass begins to move, we need a free body diagram with the forces F, N, and mg. Once we determine the direction of motion, we can determine the direction of the friction force using a second free body diagram with the friction force added to our previous diagram.

SKETCH: A free body diagram of the forces acting on mass m before the mass is released is shown in Figure 4.33.

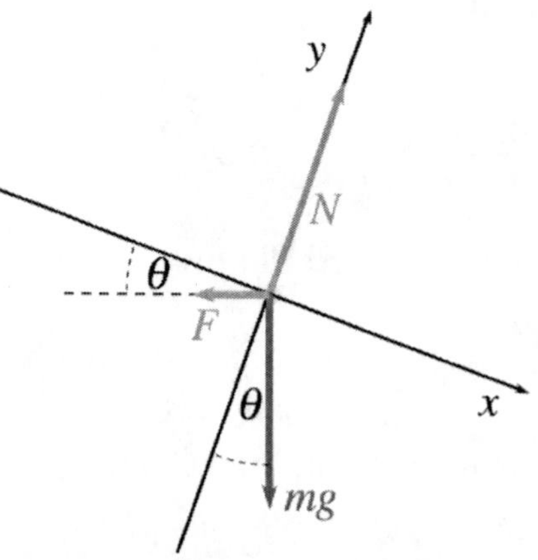

Figure 4.33: Free-body diagram including the external force, the force of gravity, and the normal force.

Here we have defined a coordinate system in which the x-axis is parallel to the surface of the inclined plane, with the positive x-direction pointing down the plane. The sum of the forces in the x-direction is

$$mg\sin\theta - F\cos\theta = ma \tag{4.62}$$

We need to determine if the mass will move to the right (positive x-direction or down the plane) or to the left (negative x-direction or up the plane). We can see from (4.62) that the quantity $mg\sin\theta - F\cos\theta$ will determine the direction of the motion. For the numerical values in this problem we have

$$\begin{aligned} mg\sin\theta - F\cos\theta &= (37.7 \text{ kg})(9.81 \text{ m/s}^2)\sin(20.5°) - (309.3 \text{ N})\cos(20.5°) \\ mg\sin\theta - F\cos\theta &= -160.193 \text{ N} \end{aligned} . \tag{4.63}$$

Thus the mass will move up the plane (to the left or in the negative x-direction) and we can redraw our free-body diagram as follows

Solved Problem

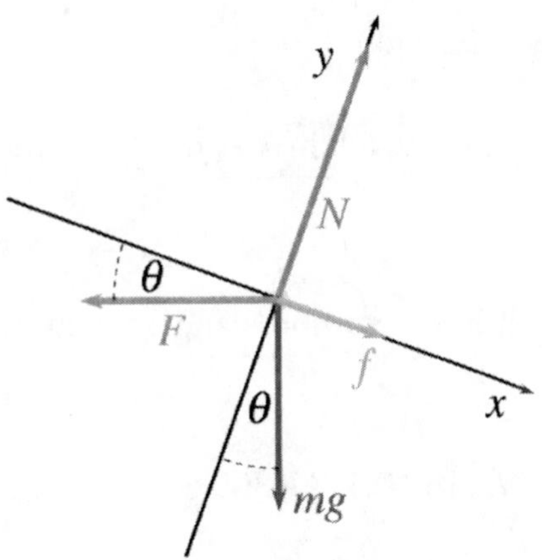

Figure 4.34: Free-body diagram including the external force, the force of gravity, the normal force, and the friction force.

We have now shown in Figure 4.34 the force of kinetic friction, f_k, pointing down the plane (in the $+x$-direction) because the friction force always opposes the direction of motion.

Solved Problem

RESEARCH: Now we can write down the components of the forces in the x- and y-directions based on our free-body diagram. For the x-direction we have

$$mg\sin\theta - F\cos\theta + f_k = ma. \qquad (4.64)$$

which is similar to (4.62) with the addition of the friction force down the plane. For the y-direction we have

$$N - mg\cos\theta - F\sin\theta = 0. \qquad (4.65)$$

From (4.65) we can get the normal force N that we need to calculate the friction force

$$f_k = \mu_k N = \mu_k\left(mg\cos\theta + F\sin\theta\right). \qquad (4.66)$$

SIMPLIFY: Having related all the known and unknown quantities to each other, we can get an expression for the acceleration of the mass using (4.64) and (4.66) given by

$$mg\sin\theta - F\cos\theta + \mu_k\left(mg\cos\theta + F\sin\theta\right) = ma. \qquad (4.67)$$

We can simplify this expression to get

$$\begin{aligned} mg\sin\theta - F\cos\theta + \mu_k\left(mg\cos\theta + F\sin\theta\right) &= ma \\ mg\sin\theta - F\cos\theta + \mu_k mg\cos\theta + \mu_k F\sin\theta &= ma \\ \left(mg + \mu_k F\right)\sin\theta + \left(\mu_k mg - F\right)\cos\theta &= ma \end{aligned} \qquad (4.68)$$

which we can solve for the acceleration

$$a = \frac{(mg + \mu_k F)\sin\theta + (\mu_k mg - F)\cos\theta}{m}. \tag{4.69}$$

CALCULATE: Now we put in the numbers and get a numerical result. The first term in the numerator of (4.69) is

$$((37.7 \text{ kg})(9.81 \text{ m/s}^2) + (0.171)(309.3 \text{ N}))\sin(20.5°) = 148.042 \text{ N} \tag{4.70}$$

Note that we have not rounded this result yet. The second term in the numerator of (4.69) is

$$((0.117)(37.7 \text{ kg})(9.81 \text{ m/s}^2) - (309.3 \text{ N}))\cos(20.5°) = \text{-}249.182 \text{ N} \tag{4.71}$$

Again we have not rounded the result yet. Now we calculate the acceleration using (4.69)

$$a = \frac{(148.042 \text{ N}) + (-249.182 \text{ N})}{37.7 \text{ kg}} = -2.68275 \text{ m/s}^2 \tag{4.72}$$

and we still have not rounded the result.

ROUND: Now we report our final result as

$$a = -2.68 \text{ m/s}^2 \tag{4.73}$$

because all of our known numerical values were quoted to three significant figures.

DOUBLE-CHECK: Looking at out answer, we see that the acceleration is negative, which means the acceleration is in the negative x-direction. We had determined that the mass would move to the left (up the plane or the negative x-direction), which agrees with our result for the sign of the acceleration. The magnitude of the acceleration is a fraction of the acceleration of gravity (9.81 m/s^2), which makes physical sense also.

Solved Problem 4.3: Accelerated Blocks

Question:

Two rectangular blocks are stacked on a table as shown in Figure 4.35. The upper block has a mass of 3.40 kg and the lower block has a mass of 38.6 kg. The coefficient of kinetic friction between the lower block and the table is 0.260. The coefficient of static friction between the upper and the lower blocks is 0.551. A string is attached to the lower block, and an external force $\vec{F}$ is applied in horizontal direction to pull on the string, as shown. What is the maximum force that one can apply without having the upper block slide off?

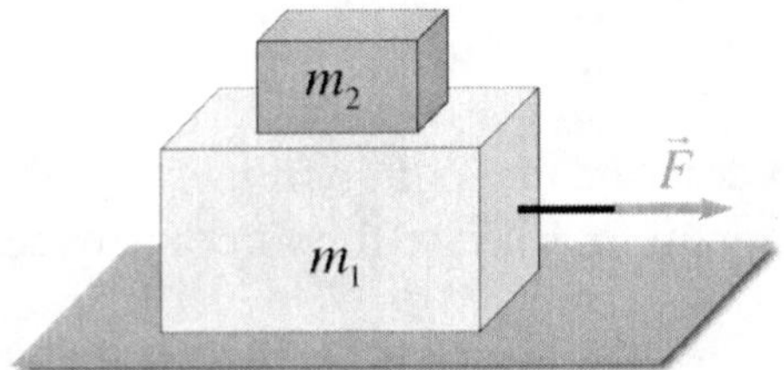

Figure 4.35: Two stacked blocks being pulled to the right.

Answer:

THINK: To begin this problem we note that as long as the force of static friction between the two blocks is not overcome, the two blocks will travel together. Thus if we pull gently on the bottom block, the top block will stay in its place on top of the bottom block and the two blocks will slide as one. If we pull hard on the bottom block, the force of static friction between the top block and the bottom block will not be sufficient to keep the top block in its place and it will begin to slide off the top block.

The forces acting in this problem are the external force F pulling the string, the force of kinetic friction f_k between the bottom block and the surface on which the blocks are sliding, the weight m_1g of the bottom block, the weight m_2g of the top block, and the force of static friction f_s between the bottom block and the top block.

SKETCH: We start with a free body diagram of the two blocks moving together as shown in Figure 4.36. We define the x-direction to be parallel to the surface on which the masses are sliding and parallel to the external force pulling the masses with the positive direction to the right, in the direction of the external force.

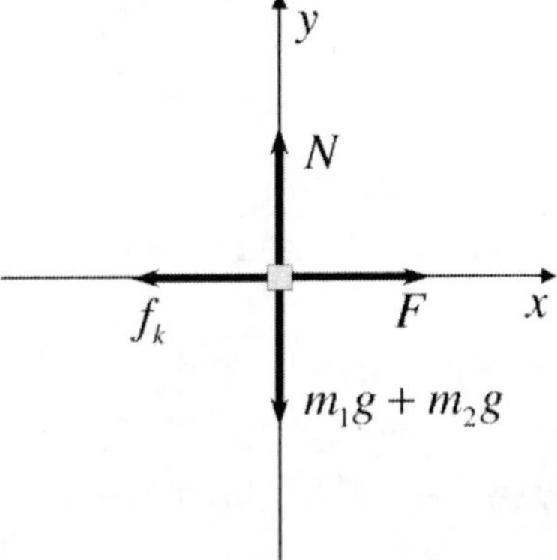

Figure 4.36: Free-body diagram for the two masses moving together.

The sum of the forces in the x-direction gives us

$$F - f_k = (m_1 + m_2)a . \tag{4.74}$$

The sum of the force in the y-direction gives us

Solved Problem

$$N - (m_1 g + m_2 g) = 0. \qquad (4.75)$$

Equations (4.74) and (4.75) describe the motion of the two blocks together. Now we need a second free-body diagram to describe the forces between the bottom block and the top block.

The forces in the free-body diagram for m_2 shown in Figure 4.37 are the normal force N_2 exerted by the bottom block, the weight $m_2 g$, and the force of static friction f_s.

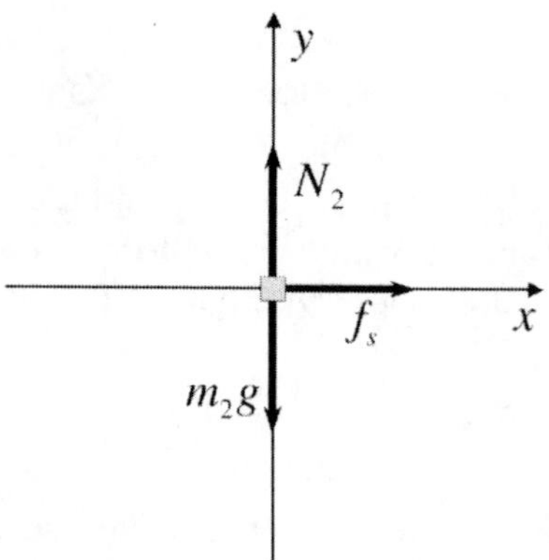

Figure 4.37: Free body diagram for m_2.

The sum of the forces in the x-direction gives us

$$f_s = m_2 a. \qquad (4.76)$$

The sum of the forces in the y-direction gives us

$$N_2 - m_2 g = 0, \qquad (4.77)$$

RESEARCH: The maximum value the force of static friction between the top block and the bottom is given by

$$f_s = \mu_s N_2 = \mu_s (m_2 g) \qquad (4.78)$$

where we have used (4.76) and (4.77). Thus the maximum acceleration that the top block can take without sliding is

$$a_{\max} = \frac{f_s}{m_2} = \frac{\mu_s m_2 g}{m_2} = \mu_s g. \qquad (4.79)$$

This maximum acceleration for the top block is also the maximum acceleration for both blocks together. From (4.75) we get the normal force between the bottom block and the sliding surface to be

$$N = m_1 g + m_2 g. \qquad (4.80)$$

The force of kinetic friction between the bottom block and the sliding surface is then

$$f_k = \mu_k(m_1 g + m_2 g). \tag{4.81}$$

SIMPLIFY: We can now relate the maximum acceleration to the maximum force F_{max} that can be exerted without the top mass sliding off using (4.74), (4.79), and (4.81)

$$F_{max} - \mu_k(m_1 g + m_2 g) = (m_1 + m_2)\mu_s g. \tag{4.82}$$

We can solve and simplify (4.82) to obtain

$$F_{max} = \mu_k(m_1 g + m_2 g) + (m_1 + m_2)\mu_s g = g(m_1 + m_2)(\mu_k + \mu_s). \tag{4.83}$$

CALCULATE: Putting in the numerical values for this problem we get

$$F_{max} = (9.81 \text{ m/s}^2)(38.6 \text{ kg} + 3.40 \text{ kg})(0.260 + 0.551) = 334.148 \text{ N}. \tag{4.84}$$

ROUND: All of the numerical values in this problem are specified to three significant figures, so we report our answer as

$$F_{max} = 334 \text{ N}. \tag{4.85}$$

DOUBLE-CHECK: This answer gives a positive value, implying a force to the right, which agrees with our free-body diagram in Figure 4.36.

The maximum acceleration is

$$a_{max} = \mu_s g = 0.551 \cdot 9.81 \text{ m/s}^2 = 5.41 \text{ m/s}^2. \tag{4.86}$$

which is a fraction of the acceleration of gravity, which seems reasonable. If there were no friction between the the bottom block and the sliding surface, the force required to accelerate both masses would be

$$F = (m_1 + m_2)a_{max} = (38.6 \text{ kg} + 3.40 \text{ kg})(5.41 \text{ m/s}^2) = 227 \text{ N}. \tag{4.87}$$

Thus our answer of 334 N for the maximum force in this problem seems reasonable because it is higher than the no-friction case.

Solved Problem

Chapter 5. Kinetic Energy, Work, and Power

What we will learn:

- Kinetic energy is the energy associated with the motion of an object.
- Work is defined as energy transferred to an object or transferred from a object due to the action of a force external to the object. Positive work is defined as a transfer of energy to the object, and negative work is a transfer of energy from the object. Positive work is work done *on* the object, while negative work is work done *by* the object.
- Work is the scalar product of the force vector and the displacement vector.
- The change in kinetic energy due to applied forces is equal to the work done by the forces.
- Power is the rate at which work is done.

5.1. Energy in our Daily Lives

No other physical quantity in our daily lives has a greater importance than energy. Energy consumption, energy efficiency, and energy "production" are all of the utmost economic importance and all lead to heated discussions over national policies and international agreements. (We will later see that the term "production" is a misnomer since energy is not produced but rather is converted from a less usable form to a more usable form.) Energy has also an important role in each individual person's daily routine: energy intake through food calories, and energy consumption through activities, work and exercise. Weight loss and weight gain are, at their most fundamental, results of positive or negative energy balances.

Figure 5.1: Wind farms harvest renewable energy.

Energy has many facets that will require several different approaches to cover completely. Thus energy is a recurring theme throughout this book. We start by investigating mechanical energy forms, kinetic energy and potential energy. Thermal energy is another form of energy, and will turn out to be one of the central pillars of thermodynamics. Chemical energy is stored in chemical compounds, and reactions between different reactants can either consume energy (endo-energetic reactions) or yield usable energy (exo-energetic reactions). Our petroleum economy makes use of heat, as do hydrogen fuel cells and our bodies (for their metabolic requirements).

Figure 5.2: The Glen Canyon Dam in Arizona provides renewable electrical energy

When we talk about light and electromagnetic waves, we will see that electromagnetic radiation contains energy. This energy is the basis for one "renewable" energy source, solar energy. Almost all other renewable energy sources on Earth can be traced back to solar energy as well. Solar energy is responsible for the wind that we can use in large wind turbines, currently in strong demand in Europe (see Figure 5.1). The Sun's radiation is also responsible for evaporating the water from the Earth's surface and moving it into the clouds, from where it will fall down as rain and eventually join rivers that we can dam (see Figure 5.2) to extract energy. Biomass, another form of renewable energy, utilizes the ability of plants and animals to store solar energy during their metabolic and growth processes.

In fact, the energy radiated onto the surface of Earth by the Sun exceeds the energy needs of the entire human population by a factor of more than 10,000. It is possible to convert solar radiation directly into electricity by using photovoltaic cells. There is great current research interest in increasing the efficiency and reliability while reducing the cost of these photocells. Early versions of solar cells are already in the stores to fill some needs, for example in patio and garden lights. Experimental solar farms like the one in Figure 5.3 are in operation as well. In our chapter on quantum physics, chapter 36, we will discuss in detail how photocells work.

Figure 5.3: Left: Solar farm with an adjustable array of mirrors; right: solar panel.

When we study nuclear physics, we will find out that splitting heavy nuclei like uranium or plutonium liberates energy. Conventional nuclear power plants work on this physical principle of nuclear fission. One can also obtain useful energy by merging very light atomic nuclei into heavier nuclei, a process called nuclear fusion. Our solar system's Sun and every other star in the universe uses nuclear fusion to generate energy that makes the stars shine.

The energy from nuclear fusion is thought by many to be the most likely answer to the long-term energy needs of a modern industrialized society. Our currently best hope to achieve progress towards controlled fusion reactions is the proposed international nuclear fusion reactor facility ITER ("The way" in Latin).

Related to energy are quantities such as work and power. They already have appeared in the paragraphs above, but before the end of this chapter we will explain how they relate to energy in physical terms.

You have seen from this introduction that energy occupies an essential place in our lives. One of our central goals is to give you a solid grounding in the fundamentals of the subject of energy by the time that you have reached the end of this introductory course in physics. Then you will be able to partake in some of the most important policy discussions of our time in an informed manner.

5.2. Kinetic Energy

The first kind of energy that we introduce is the energy contained in the motion of a moving object, kinetic energy. At this point we will first introduce the definition of the kinetic energy, and then work through a few examples so see why this definition makes sense and how it connects to the other physical quantities, such as force, displacement, and acceleration, which we have introduced so far. We define kinetic energy as one half of the product of the mass and the square of the speed:

$$K = \tfrac{1}{2}mv^2 \tag{5.1}$$

Note that by definition the kinetic energy is always greater or equal 0, and it is only 0 for an object at rest. The units of the kinetic energy are:

$$[K] = [m] \cdot [v]^2 = \text{kg m}^2/\text{s}^2 \tag{5.2}$$

Because energy is an important quantity, it has received its own unit, the Joule (J):

$$\text{Energy unit: } 1\text{ J} = 1\text{ kg m}^2/\text{s}^2 \tag{5.3}$$

Previously we had defined the force unit, N, as $1\text{ N}=1\text{ kg m/s}^2$. Comparing this definition with our definition for the J, we see that we can make a useful conversion:

$$1\text{ J} = 1\text{ N m} \tag{5.4}$$

Let us look at a few example numbers, to get a feeling for the size of the unit Joule. A car of mass 1,310 kg being driven at the speed limit of 55 mph (=24.6 m/s) has a kinetic energy of

$$K_{\text{car}} = \tfrac{1}{2}mv^2 = \tfrac{1}{2}(1310\text{ kg})(24.6\text{ m/s})^2 = 4.0 \cdot 10^5\text{ J}$$

The mass of the Earth is $6.0 \cdot 10^{24}$ kg, and it orbits the Sun with a speed of $3.0 \cdot 10^4$ m/s. The kinetic energy associated with this motion is

$$K_{\text{Earth}} = \tfrac{1}{2}mv^2 = \tfrac{1}{2}(6.0 \cdot 10^{24}\text{ kg})(3.0 \cdot 10^4\text{ m/s})^2 = 2.7 \cdot 10^{33}\text{ J}$$

In the same way, a person of mass 64.8 kg jogging at 3.5 m/s has a kinetic energy of 400 J, and a baseball (mass "5 ounces avoirdupois" = 0.142 kg) thrown at 80 mph (=35.8 m/s) has a kinetic energy of 91 J. These numbers give you an idea of the magnitudes of kinetic energies in the motion of different objects.

You can see from these examples that the range of energies in physical processes can be very large, even though we have not yet covered processes on atomic or astronomical scales. These vastly different energy scales provide motivation to introduce some other, frequently used, energy units: the electron-Volt (eV), the food-calorie (Cal), and the Mega-ton TNT (Mt).

$$1 \text{ eV} = 1.602 \cdot 10^{-19} \text{ J} \tag{5.5}$$

$$1 \text{ Cal} = 4186 \text{ J} \tag{5.6}$$

$$1 \text{ Mt} = 4.00 \cdot 10^{15} \text{ J} \tag{5.7}$$

1 eV is the kinetic energy that an electron gains when accelerated by an electric potential of 1 Volt. The energy content of the food we eat is usually (and mistakenly) listed in terms of calories but should be called food calories. As we'll see when we study Thermodynamics, 1 food calorie is equal to 1 kilocalorie. 1 Mt is the energy released by exploding one millions metric tons of the explosive TNT, an energy release only achieved by nuclear weapons. (All of these concepts will be discussed further in subsequent chapters).

Please note that for motion in more than one dimension we can write the total kinetic energy as the sum of the kinetic energies associated with the components of the velocity in each spatial dimension. To show this, we start with our definition of the kinetic energy (5.1) and then use $v^2 = v_x^2 + v_y^2 + v_z^2$:

$$\begin{aligned} K &= \tfrac{1}{2} m v^2 \\ &= \tfrac{1}{2} m \left(v_x^2 + v_y^2 + v_z^2 \right) \\ &= \tfrac{1}{2} m v_x^2 + \tfrac{1}{2} m v_y^2 + \tfrac{1}{2} m v_z^2 \\ K &= K(v_x) + K(v_y) + K(v_z) \end{aligned} \tag{5.8}$$

So we see that we can think of the kinetic energy as the sum of the kinetic energies contained in the motion in x-direction, y-direction, and z-direction. This is particularly useful for all ideal projectile problems, where the motion consists of free-fall in the vertical direction (the y-direction) and motion with constant velocity in horizontal direction (the x-direction). Since v_x is constant, we also find $K(v_x)$ remains constant in ideal projectile problems.

Example

Example 5.1: Falling Vase

Question:
A crystal vase (mass 2.40 kg) is dropped from a height of 1.30 m and falls to the floor. What is its kinetic energy just before impact?

Answer:
Once we know the velocity of the vase just before impact, we can put it into our equation for the kinetic energy. To obtain this velocity, we remind ourselves of the kinematics of free-falling objects. In this case, it is most straightforward to use the relationship

Example

$$v_y^2 = v_{y0}^2 - 2g(y - y_0)$$

between the initial and final velocities and heights that we had derived for free-fall motion in chapter 2. (Remember that the *y*-axis must be pointing up to use this relationship.) Since the vase is released from rest, the initial velocity components are: $v_{x0} = v_{y0} = 0$. Since there is no acceleration in x-direction, the x-component of the velocity remains zero during the fall of the vase, $v_x = 0$. Therefore we have in this case

$$v^2 = v_x^2 + v_y^2 = 0 + v_y^2 = v_y^2$$

We then obtain:

$$v^2 = v_y^2 = 2g(y_0 - y)$$

We use this result in our definition of the kinetic energy, resulting in

$$K = \tfrac{1}{2}mv^2 = \tfrac{1}{2}m\left(2g(y_0 - y)\right) = mg(y_0 - y)$$

With the numbers given in the problem, the numerical answer then works out to:

$$K = (2.40 \text{ kg})\cdot(9.81 \text{ m/s}^2)\cdot(1.30 \text{ m} - 0) = 30.6 \text{ J}$$

5.3. Work

In the previous example, the vase started out with a kinetic energy of 0, just before it was released. After falling a distance of 1.30 m, it had acquired a kinetic energy of 30.6 J. The greater the height is from which the vase is released, the greater the speed the vase will attain, and therefore the greater its kinetic energy becomes. In fact, we have just calculated that the kinetic energy of the vase depends linearly on the height it was allowed to fall, $K = mg(y_0 - y)$.

The gravitational force, $\vec{F}_g = -mg\hat{y}$, accelerates the vase and therefore gives the vase its kinetic energy. We have just deduced that the kinetic energy depends linearly on the distance that the object has fallen, so we can also see that the kinetic energy depends linearly on the magnitude of the gravitational force. If we were to double the mass of the object and thus double the gravitational force, we would also double the kinetic energy of that object.

Because the speed of an object can be increased or decreased by accelerating or decelerating it, respectively, we can also change its kinetic energy in this process. And we have just seen that the force of gravity was responsible for this change in our example. We account for this change in kinetic energy of an object caused by a force by introducing the concept of work, W. Formally we define work to be:

Work is defined as energy transferred to an object or transferred from an object due to the action of a force. Positive work is defined as a transfer of energy to the object, and negative work is a transfer of energy from the object. Positive work is work done *on* the object, while negative work is work done *by* the object.

Note that we have not restricted ourselves to "kinetic energy" in this definition. This definition holds also for kinetic energy. But as we have already discussed in the introductory remarks for this chapter, there are different kinds of energy. The relationship between work and energy, through which we have just defined the concept of work, still holds in the general case where different forms of energy besides kinetic energy are involved.

The definition of work that we have just introduced is not exactly the same as the meaning attached to the word "work" in common language use. The work we are referring to in this chapter is to be interpreted as mechanical work in connection with energy transfer. But the common use of work, physical as well as mental, does not necessarily involve the transfer of energy. So we need to be careful in the use of language.

5.4. Work Done by Constant Forces

Now we will let the vase slide along an inclined plane, with angle θ with respect to the horizontal. For now we will neglect the friction force, but we will come back to it later.

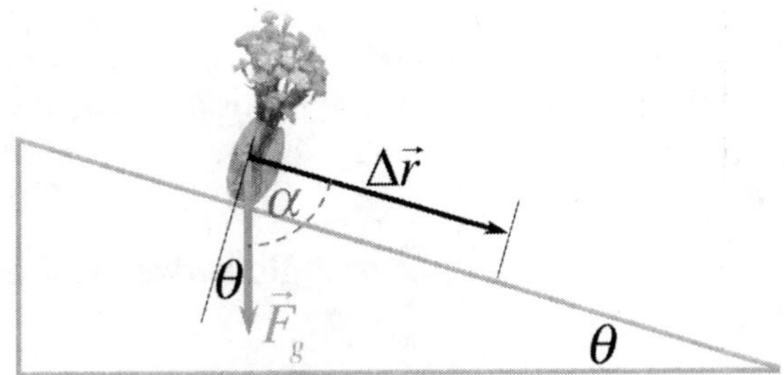

Figure 5.4: Object sliding without friction on an inclined plane.

As we showed in Chapter 4, in the absence of friction the acceleration along the plane is given by $a = g\sin\theta = g\cos\alpha$. (Here we have introduced the angle $\alpha = 90° - \theta$ as the angle between the gravitational force and the displacement vector, see Figure 5.4).

Self-Test Opportunity: Draw the free body diagram for the vase.

Now we can determine the kinetic energy that the vase has in this scenario as a function of the displacement $\Delta\vec{r}$. Most conveniently we can perform this calculation by using the relationship between the squares of initial and final velocities, the displacement, and the acceleration, which we had obtained for one-dimensional motion in chapter 2,

$$v^2 = v_0^2 + 2a\Delta r .$$

We set $v_0 = 0$, because we are again assuming that the vase is released from rest, i.e. with zero kinetic energy. Then we use the result for the acceleration, $a = g\cos\alpha$, that we just obtained. This results in

$$v^2 = 2g\cos\alpha\Delta r \Rightarrow K = \tfrac{1}{2}mv^2 = mg\Delta r\cos\alpha . \tag{5.9}$$

So we have found again in this case that the work done by the gravitational force on the vase, $W_g = mg\Delta r\cos\alpha$, is equal to the change in kinetic energy,

$$W_g = K = mg\Delta r\cos\alpha \tag{5.10}$$

There are two limiting cases of (5.10) that we can discuss right away:

- For $\alpha = 0$, where the gravitational force and the displacement are parallel, we recover the result already derived for the case of the falling vase. This is expected.
- For $\alpha = 90°$, when the gravitational force and the displacement are perpendicular to each other, we expect no acceleration, hence no change in the kinetic energy, and there is also no work done by the gravitational force on the vase.

Since $mg = \left|\vec{F}_g\right|$ and $\Delta r = \left|\Delta\vec{r}\right|$, we can also write the work as $W = \left|\vec{F}\right| \left|\Delta\vec{r}\right|\cos\alpha$ in this case. From the two limiting cases we have just discussed, we gain confidence that we can use the equation that we have just derived for the motion on the inclined plane as our definition for the work done by a constant force:

$$W = \left|\vec{F}\right| \left|\Delta\vec{r}\right|\cos\alpha, \text{ where } \alpha = \text{angle between } \vec{F} \text{ and } \Delta\vec{r} \tag{5.11}$$

This equation for the work done by constant force over a spatial displacement holds for all constant force vectors, arbitrary displacement vectors, and angles between the two vectors.

Mathematical Insert: Scalar Product of Vectors

The scalar product between two vectors $\vec{A}$ and $\vec{B}$ is defined as:

$$\vec{A} \bullet \vec{B} = \left|\vec{A}\right| \left|\vec{B}\right|\cos\alpha_{AB} \tag{5.12}$$

where α_{AB} is the angle between the vectors $\vec{A}$ and $\vec{B}$. Note that we introduce the symbol • as the multiplication sign for the scalar product between vectors, in contrast to the symbol ·, which we use for the multiplication of scalars. Because the symbol • resembles a dot, the scalar product is sometimes also referred to as the "dot-product".

If $\vec{A}$ and $\vec{B}$ are given in Cartesian coordinates as $\vec{A} = (A_x, A_y, A_z)$ and $\vec{B} = (B_x, B_y, B_z)$, then the scalar product has the value

$$\vec{A} \bullet \vec{B} = (A_x, A_y, A_z) \bullet (B_x, B_y, B_z) = A_x B_x + A_y B_y + A_z B_z \tag{5.13}$$

From this definition of the scalar product, we can also see that the scalar product has the commutative property:

$$\vec{A} \bullet \vec{B} = \vec{B} \bullet \vec{A} \tag{5.14}$$

This result is not surprising, because the commutative property also holds for the common multiplication of two scalars.

In particular, please note that we have for the scalar product of any vector with itself:

$$\vec{A} \bullet \vec{A} = A_x^2 + A_y^2 + A_z^2 \tag{5.15}$$

in the component notation, and from the definition (5.12):

$$\vec{A} \bullet \vec{A} = \left|\vec{A}\right| \left|\vec{A}\right| \cos\alpha_{AA} = \left|\vec{A}\right| \left|\vec{A}\right| = \left|\vec{A}\right|^2 \tag{5.16}$$

Combining these two results, we obtain in this special case the expression for the length of a vector that we introduced in chapter 1:

$$\left|\vec{A}\right| = \sqrt{A_x^2 + A_y^2 + A_z^2} \tag{5.17}$$

We can also use the definition of the scalar product to compute the angle between two arbitrary vectors in three-dimensional space:

$$\vec{A} \bullet \vec{B} = \left|\vec{A}\right| \left|\vec{B}\right| \cos\alpha_{AB} \Rightarrow \cos\alpha_{AB} = \frac{\vec{A} \bullet \vec{B}}{\left|\vec{A}\right| \left|\vec{B}\right|} \Rightarrow \alpha_{AB} = \arccos\left(\frac{\vec{A} \bullet \vec{B}}{\left|\vec{A}\right| \left|\vec{B}\right|}\right) \tag{5.18}$$

The following example puts the scalar product to use.

Example 5.2: Angle between two vectors

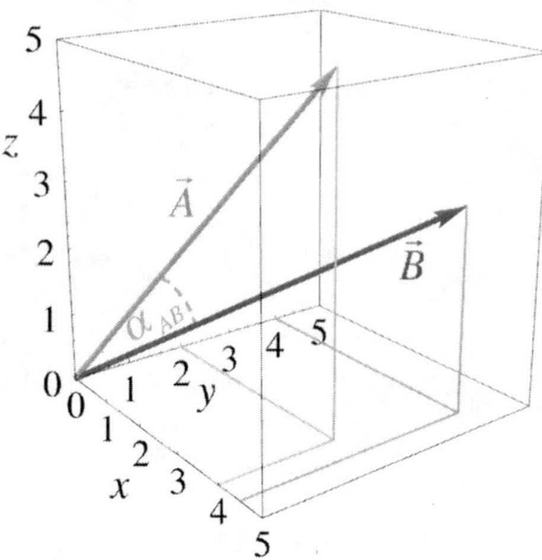

Figure 5.5: Illustration for calculation of the angle between two vectors.

Question:

What is the angle between two vectors $\vec{A} = (4.00, 2.00, 5.00)$ and $\vec{B} = (4.50, 4.00, 3.00)$?

Answer:

To solve the question posed, we have to put in the numbers for the components of the two vectors:

$$\left|\vec{A}\right| = \sqrt{4.00^2 + 2.00^2 + 5.00^2} = 6.71,\ \left|\vec{B}\right| = \sqrt{4.50^2 + 4.00^2 + 3.00^2} = 6.73$$

$$\vec{A} \bullet \vec{B} = A_x B_x + A_y B_y + A_z B_z = 4.00 \cdot 4.50 + 2.00 \cdot 4.00 + 5.00 \cdot 3.00 = 41.0$$

$$\Rightarrow \alpha_{AB} = \arccos\left(\frac{41.0}{6.71 \cdot 6.73}\right) = 24.7°$$

Geometrical Interpretation of the Scalar Product

In the definition equation $\vec{A} \bullet \vec{B} = \left|\vec{A}\right| \left|\vec{B}\right| \cos\alpha_{AB}$ (equation (5.12)) for the scalar product, we can interpret $\left|\vec{A}\right| \cos\alpha_{AB}$ as the projection of the vector $\vec{A}$ onto the vector $\vec{B}$, see Figure 5.6 (left side). In this drawing, we rotate $\left|\vec{A}\right| \cos\alpha_{AB}$ by 90 degrees to show the geometrical interpretation of the scalar product as the area of the rectangle with side lengths $\left|\vec{A}\right| \cos\alpha_{AB}$ and $\left|\vec{B}\right|$. In the same way we can also interpret $\left|\vec{B}\right| \cos\alpha_{AB}$ as the projection of the vector $\vec{B}$ on the vector $\vec{A}$ and construct a rectangle with side lengths $\left|\vec{B}\right| \cos\alpha_{AB}$ and $\left|\vec{A}\right|$, as done in the right side of Figure 5.6. The areas of the two yellow rectangles in the figure are identical and are equal to the scalar product between the two vectors $\vec{A}$ and $\vec{B}$.

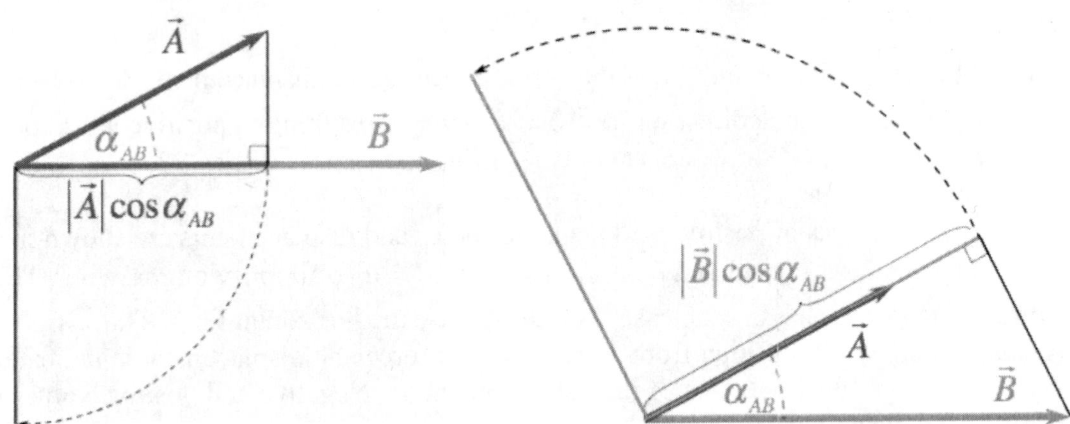

Figure 5.6: Geometrical interpretation of the scalar product as an area.

END OF INSERT

After this introduction of the scalar product, it is clear that we can write the work done by a constant force:

$$W = \vec{F} \bullet \Delta\vec{r} \tag{5.19}$$

This equation is the main result of the present section. It says that the work done by a constant force $\vec{F}$ in displacing an object by some $\Delta\vec{r}$ is the scalar product between the two vectors. In particular, if the displacement is perpendicular to the force, the scalar product is zero, and no work is done.

In-class exercise: Consider an object undergoing a displacement $\Delta\vec{r}$ and experiencing a force $\vec{F}$. In which of the three cases shown below is the work done by the force on the object zero?

$\vec{F}$ $\Delta\vec{r}$ *a)* $\vec{F}$ $\Delta\vec{r}$ *b)* $\Delta\vec{r}$ $\vec{F}$ *c)*

One-Dimensional Case

In all cases of motion in one dimension, the work is given by

$$W = F_x \cdot \Delta x = F_x \cdot (x - x_0) \tag{5.20}$$

The x-component of the force, F_x, and the x-component of the displacement, $\Delta x = x - x_0$, can either point in the same direction, $\alpha = 0 \Rightarrow \cos\alpha = 1$, resulting in positive work, or in opposite directions, $\alpha = 180° \Rightarrow \cos\alpha = -1$, resulting in negative work.

The four possible cases of positive and negative forces and displacements are shown in Figure 5.7. In all cases considered here, we have set $x_0 = 0$ to simplify our drawing. The force has a constant value in each case, as indicated by the horizontal lines. The magnitude of the work resulting from these values of force and displacement is indicated in each case as the (positive) area of the yellow rectangle. Negative and positive values of the work are indicated in each case.

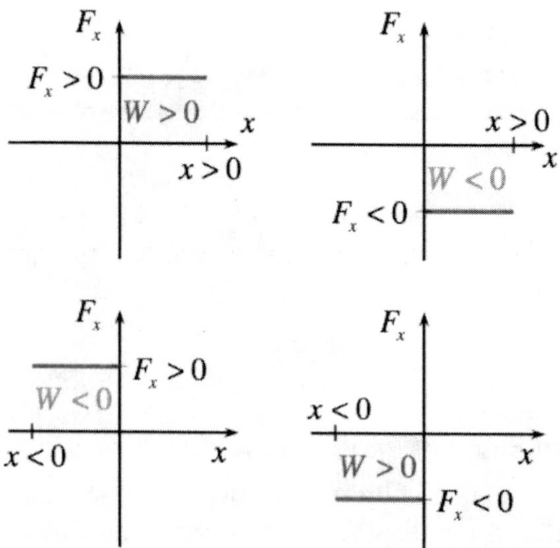

Figure 5.7: Positive and negative values of displacement and constant force and resulting signs of the work done by this force

Work-Kinetic Energy Theorem

Before we leave this section we formally write the relationship between kinetic energy of an object and the work done by the forces acting on it:

$$\Delta K \equiv K - K_0 = W \tag{5.21}$$

K is the kinetic energy that an object has after work W is done on it and K_0 is the kinetic energy before. Our definitions of W and K are such that Equation (5.21) is equivalent to Newton's Second Law. To see this, Let us first consider the case of one constant force in one dimension. Newton's Second Law is then $F_x = ma_x$, and the (also constant!) acceleration a_x of the object with mass m is related to the difference in the squares of the initial and final velocities via $v_x^2 - v_{x0}^2 = 2a_x(x - x_0)$, which is one of the five kinematic equations, which we derived in chapter 2. Multiplication of both sides with the factor $\frac{1}{2}m$ yields $\frac{1}{2}mv_x^2 - \frac{1}{2}mv_{x0}^2 = ma_x(x - x_0) = F_x\Delta x = W$. So we see that in this one-dimensional case the work-kinetic energy theorem is equivalent to Newton's Second Law.

Self-Test Opportunity: Show the equivalence between Newton's Second Law and the work-kinetic energy theorem for the case of a constant force in three dimensions.

Because of the equivalence that we have just established, we know that if there is more than one force acting we can just use the net force in calculating the work done. Alternatively, and more commonly in energy approaches, if there is more than one force acting we just calculate the work done by each force and then the W in Equation (5.21) represents their sum.

Equation (5.21) is often referred to as the "work-kinetic energy theorem". This equation is the main result of the present chapter. It specifies that the change in kinetic energy of the object is equal to the work done on the object by the forces acting on it. We can also rewrite this equation to solve it for K or K_0, resulting in

$$K = K_0 + W \tag{5.22}$$

or

$$K_0 = K - W. \tag{5.23}$$

Please note that by definition the kinetic energy cannot be less than 0. So in the case that an object has $K_0 = 0$, the work-kinetic energy theorem implies that $K = K_0 + W = W \geq 0$. So we see that then the object cannot do any work, which would imply $W < 0$. In this case we can only do work *on* the object, thus increasing its kinetic energy.

Work Done by the Gravitational Force

Because we now have the work-kinetic energy theorem at our disposal, we can take another look at the initial problem of an object falling under the influence of the gravitational force. On the way down, the work done by the gravitational force on the object is

$$W_g = +mgh, \tag{5.24}$$

where $h = |y - y_0| = |\Delta\vec{r}| > 0$. The displacement $\Delta\vec{r}$ and the force of gravity $\vec{F}_g$ point in the same direction, resulting in a positive scalar product and therefore a positive work. This situation is illustrated on the right side of Figure 5.8. Since the work is positive, this increases the kinetic energy of the object.

We can also reverse this problem and toss a projectile upwards, giving it an initial kinetic energy. This kinetic energy will decrease until the projectile reaches the top of its trajectory. Now the displacement vector $\Delta\vec{r}$ points up, in opposite direction to the force of gravity; compare the left side of Figure 5.8. Thus the work done by the gravitational force in this process of upward motion is:

$$W_g = -mgh, \tag{5.25}$$

So the work done by the gravitational force reduces the kinetic energy of the object during its upward motion. This result is consistent with our general formula for constant forces, $W = \vec{F} \bullet \Delta\vec{r}$, because in this case the displacement (pointing upward) and force (pointing downward) are in opposite directions.

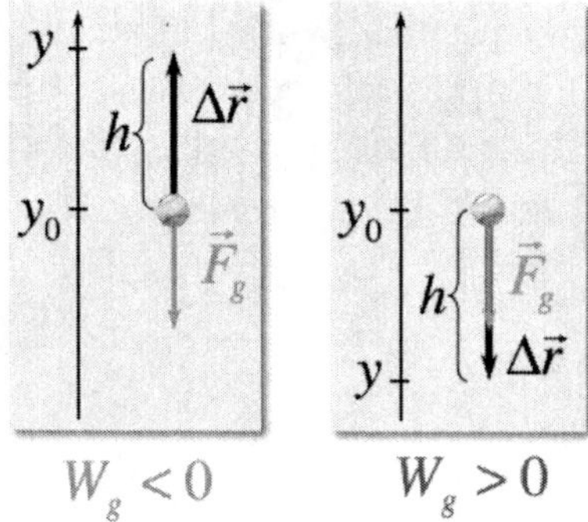

Figure 5.8: Work done by the gravitational force.

Work Done Lifting and Lowering an Object

Now we can consider the case of applying a vertical external force to an object, as for example is done by attaching the object to a rope and lifting it up or lowering it down. The work-kinetic energy theorem now has to include the work done by the gravitational force, W_g, and the work done by the external force, W_F:

$$K - K_0 = W_g + W_F \tag{5.26}$$

In the case where the object is initially at rest, $K_0 = 0$, and also finally at rest, $K = 0$, we then obtain from this equation:

$$W_F = -W_g \tag{5.27}$$

The work done by the lifting and lowering force is then:

$$W_F = -W_g = mgh \text{ (for lifting) and } W_F = -W_g = -mgh \text{ (for lowering)} \tag{5.28}$$

Example

Example 5.3: Weightlifting

Consider the Olympic sport of weightlifting, where the task is to pick up a weight as heavy as possible and lift it over your head and hold it there at rest for a moment. This is a perfect example of the concept of doing work by lifting and lowering a weight.

Question 1:
The German lifter Ronny Weller won the silver medal at the Olympic games in Sidney, Australia. In the process, he lifted 257.5 kg in the "jerk" competition. Assuming he lifted the weight to a height of 1.83 m and held it there, what was the mechanical work done by him in this process?

Answer 1:
This problem is an application of the formula just introduced to give us a feel for the magnitudes of mechanical work attainable by humans. The work is

$$W = mgh = (257.5 \text{ kg}) \cdot (9.81 \text{ m/s}^2) \cdot (1.83 \text{ m}) = 4.62 \text{ kJ}$$

Question 2:
Once Weller had successfully completed the lift and was holding the weight with outstretched arms above his head, what was the work done by him in lowering the weight slowly (with negligible kinetic energy) back down to the ground.

Answer 2:
Our calculation remains exactly the same as in the answer for question 1, but the only difference is that now the sign of the displacement changes. So our calculations give an answer of –4.62 kJ of work done by setting the weight back down. Exactly the opposite answer that we obtained for question 1!

Now is a good time to remind ourselves that we are dealing with strictly mechanical work. We make this remark at this point because every lifter knows that one can feel the muscles "burn" just as much when lowering the weight (in a controlled way) as lifting it. However, this physiological effect is *not* mechanical work, which is what we are presently interested in.

Lifting with Pulleys

When we studied pulleys and ropes in chapter 4 we learned that these systems act as force multipliers. For example, in the setup shown in Figure 5.9 the force needed to lift an object by pulling on the rope is only half of the gravitational force, $T = \frac{1}{2}mg$. The question then is in this context how the work in pulling an object up with ropes and pulleys compares to that of lifting it without mechanical aids.

In Figure 5.9 we show the initial and final positions of mass m and the ropes and pulleys used to lift it. By lifting it without mechanical aids, we would have had to use the force $\vec{T}_2$, as indicated, where the magnitude is given by $T_2 = mg$. The work done by force $\vec{T}_2$ in this example is $W_2 = \vec{T}_2 \bullet \vec{r}_2 = T_2 r_2 = mgr_2$, as indicated in the figure (please note that the displacement and force point in the same direction). Pulling on the rope with force $\vec{T}_1$ of magnitude $T_1 = \frac{1}{2}T_2 = \frac{1}{2}mg$ accomplishes the same. However, now the displacement is twice as long, $r_1 = 2r_2$, as you can see by examining the figure. So the work done in this case is $W_1 = \vec{T}_1 \bullet \vec{r}_1 = (\frac{1}{2}T_2)(2r_2) = mgr_2 = W_2$.

The result is the same work in both cases. We had to compensate for the reduced force by pulling the rope through a longer distance. This result is a general one for the use of pulleys or lever arms or any other mechanical force multiplier: the total work done is the same, and an advantage in the force is always going to be compensated by a proportional lengthening in the displacement.

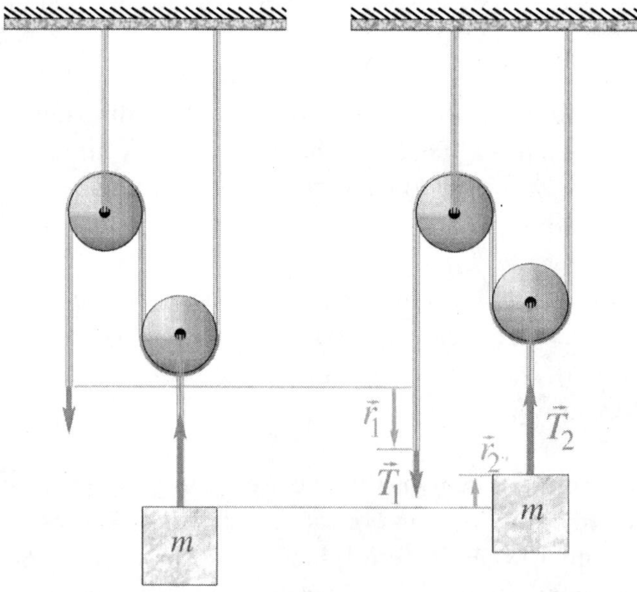

Figure 5.9: Forces and displacements for the process of lifting an object with the aid of a rope and pulley system.

5.5. Work Done by Variable Forces

Because we have already seen examples of forces that are not constant, we can ask what is the expression for work done by these forces. In a case of motion in one dimension with a variable x-component of force, $F_x(x)$, the work is:

$$W = \int_{x_0}^{x} F_x(x')dx' \tag{5.29}$$

The integrand uses x' as a variable to distinguish it from the integral limits. x' is called a dummy variable. Equation (5.29) shows that the work W is just the area under the curve of $F(x)$ versus x. For the general case of three-dimensional motion with a variable force $\vec{F}(\vec{x})$, the answer is

$$W = \int_{\vec{r}_0}^{\vec{r}} \vec{F}(\vec{r}') \bullet d\vec{r}' = \int_{x_0}^{x} F_x(\vec{r}')dx' + \int_{y_0}^{y} F_y(\vec{r}')dy' + \int_{z_0}^{z} F_z(\vec{r}')dz' \tag{5.30}$$

Note that the integral on the right hand side of this equation shows that the components of $\vec{F}$ depend on the path $\vec{r}'$ followed in three dimensions. This type of integral is called a path integral – an advanced calculus concept. The force could also depend on other variables such as the time.

Derivation 5.1:
If you have already taken a class on integral calculus, then you can skip this section. If this problem is your first exposure to integrals, then the following derivation is a useful introduction.

We derive the one-dimensional case and use our result for the constant force as a starting point.

In the case of a constant force, we had seen in the last section that the work is simply the area under the horizontal line that marks the value of the constant force in the interval between x_0 and x. For a variable force, the work is still the area under the curve $F_x(x)$, but is no longer a simple rectangle. In the case of a variable force the idea is to now divide the interval from x_0 to x into many small intervals, to approximate the area under the curve $F_x(x)$ by a series of rectangles, and to sum up their areas to approximate the work. As you can see from Figure 5.10, the area of the rectangle between x_i and x_{i+1} is given by $F_x(x_i)\cdot(x_{i+1}-x_i) = F_x(x_i)\cdot\Delta x$. We then obtain an approximation for the work by summing over all rectangles:

$$W \approx \sum_i W_i = \sum_i F_x(x_i)\cdot\Delta x \tag{5.31}$$

Derivation

Now we can space the points x_i closer and closer by using more and more of them. This method will make Δx smaller and smaller and will cause the series of rectangles to be a better and better approximation to the area under the curve $F_x(x)$. In the limit of $\Delta x \to 0$ we will approach the exact expression for the work,

$$W = \lim_{\Delta x \to 0}\left(\sum_i F_x(x_i)\cdot \Delta x\right) \quad (5.32)$$

This limit of the sum of the areas is exactly how the integral is defined:

$$W = \int_{x_0}^{x} F_x(x')dx' \quad (5.33)$$

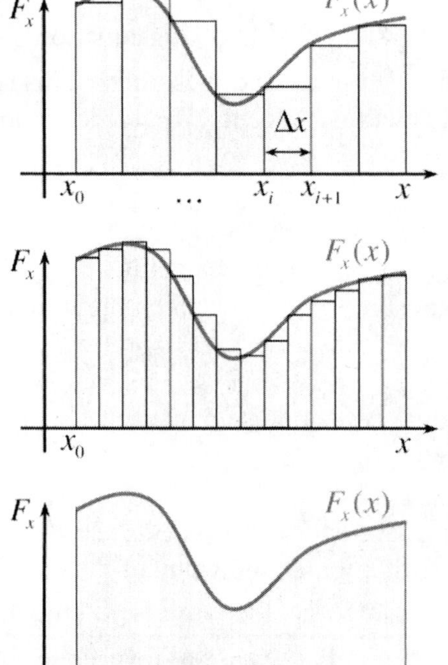

Figure 5.10: Upper part: Approximating the area under the curve of the force as a function of the displacement by a series of rectangles; middle part: better approximation by using rectangles of smaller width; lower part: exact area under the curve.

We have stated this result for the case of one-dimensional motion. The derivation of the three-dimensional case proceeds along similar lines, but is more involved in terms of algebra.

In-class exercise: A force x-component has the dependence $F_x(x) = -c \cdot x^3$ on the displacement x, with the constant $c = 19.1\ \text{N/m}^3$. How much work does it take to change the displacement from 0.810 m to 1.39 m?
a) 12.3 J
b) 0.452 J
c) -15.8 J
d) -3.76 J
e) 0.00 J

It is important to note that the Work-Kinetic Energy Equation, (5.21), is valid even when the force is variable. This is because the incremental changes in kinetic energy during each increment Δx of displacement add up to the total change $K - K_o$.

5.6. Spring Force

Let us examine the force that is needed to stretch or compress a spring. If you pull a little bit on a spring, then it offers only little resistance. The more you pull, the harder it gets to pull the spring. It turns out that, to a good approximation, the force needed to stretch or compress a spring is proportional to the change in length of the spring. So if the length that the spring would have if left alone is called x_0 (the equilibrium position), and the x-component of the displacement of the endpoint of the spring is called x as usual, then the force law for the spring is

$$F_s = k(x_0 - x). \tag{5.34}$$

(In this section we use F_s to represent the x-component of the spring force vector.) The constant k is positive because the spring force always points in the opposite direction to the displacement from equilibrium. Because we can choose the origin of our coordinate system at the point that is most convenient for us, we choose it to be x_0. This choice means that we set $x_0 = 0$. Our force law for the spring then becomes:

$$F_s = -kx \tag{5.35}$$

This simple force law is called Hooke's Law (Named after the British physicists Robert Hooke (1635-1703), a contemporary of Isaac Newton and Curator of Experiments for the Royal Society). Note that for a displacement $x > 0$, the force points in the negative direction, $F_s < 0$. The converse is also true; if $x < 0$, then $F_s > 0$. So in all cases the force F_s points towards the equilibrium position, $x = 0$. At exactly the equilibrium position, there is no force, $F_s(x = 0) = 0$. As a reminder from the previous chapter, zero force is one of the definition conditions for equilibrium.

The proportionality constant, k, that appears in the above force law, is called the "spring constant". It has units of $\text{N/m} = \text{kg/s}^2$.

The significance of Hooke's Law can be gleaned from a consideration of general forces for small displacements from equilibrium. To see this, we can examine a force that has an arbitrary functional dependence on the displacement from equilibrium. If the displacement is small, then we can expand the dependence of the force on the displacement in a Taylor series, $F(x) = F_0 + F_1x + F_2x^2 \ldots$. The lowest terms in this series are a constant term and a term that depends linearly on displacement. Since we wanted to examine a force where 0 displacement results in equilibrium, the constant term F_0 in the Taylor series is 0, and the dominant (leading) term is one that is linear in the displacement. (For small displacements from equilibrium, x is small and thus $|F_2x^2| \ll |F_1x|$.) Hooke's Law, where we set $F_1 = -k$, can serve as a good approximation for a wide class of force laws. This signals the importance that Hooke's Law has in physics. And this is why it is appropriate to study this force law and the resulting equations of motion in detail. In the present chapter we use this force to study the work done by it. In chapter 14 on oscillations we will analyze the motion of an object under the influence of the spring force.

Example

Example 5.4: Spring Constant

Question 1:

A spring has a length of 15.4 cm and is hanging vertically from a support point above as shown in Figure 5.11. A weight of 0.200 kg is then attached to the spring, causing it to extend to a length of 28.6 cm. What is the value of the spring constant?

Answer 1:

We choose the origin of our coordinate system at the top of the spring, with positive direction pointing up, as is customary. Then $x_0 = -15.4 \text{ cm}$ and $x = -28.6 \text{ cm}$. According to our force law, we have for the spring force:

$$F_s = -k(x - x_0) \tag{5.36}$$

On the other hand, we know the force extending the spring was provided by the weight of the 0.2 kg mass, $F = -mg = -(0.200 \text{ kg})(9.81 \text{ m/s}^2) = -1.962 \text{ N}$. Again, the minus sign indicates the direction.

Now we can solve our equation for the spring constant:

$$k = -\frac{F_s}{x - x_0} = -\frac{-1.962 \text{ N}}{-0.286 \text{ m} - (-0.154 \text{ m})} = 14.86 \text{ N/m} \tag{5.37}$$

Note that we would have obtained exactly the same result if we had put the origin of the coordinate system at another point, or if we had elected to designate the downward direction as positive.

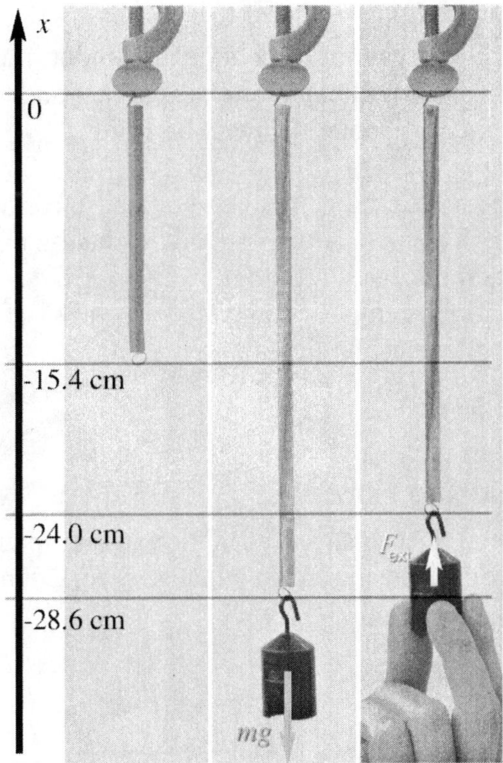

Figure 5.11: Mass on a spring
with corresponding coordinate system and forces drawn.

Question 2:
How much force is then needed to hold this weight at a position 4.6 cm above the $x = -28.6\,cm$ position?

Answer 2:
At first sight, this problem might look like a complicated calculation. But remember that the mass has stretched the spring to a new equilibrium position. To move the mass from that position takes an external force. If the external force moves the mass up 4.6 cm, then it has to be exactly equal in magnitude and opposite in direction to the spring force resulting from a displacement of 4.6 cm. So all we have to do is to use Hooke's Law for the spring force to obtain our result:

$$F_{\text{ext}} + F_s = 0 \Rightarrow F_{\text{ext}} = -F_s = kx = (0.046 \text{ m})(14.86 \text{ N/m}) = 0.68 \text{ N} \qquad (5.38)$$

At this point it is worthwhile to reflect on the observations made in this example and generalize it: Adding a constant force, for example by suspending a mass from the spring, only shifts the equilibrium position. This is generally true for all force laws that depend linearly on displacement. Moving the mass, up or down, away from this new equilibrium position then results again in a force law that is linearly proportional to the displacement out of this new equilibrium position. Adding another mass will only cause an additional shift to a new equilibrium position.

Of course, we all know that this cannot be continued without limit. At some point the addition of more and more mass will overstretch the spring and take it out of the elastic limit that we have to assume for Hooke's Law to be valid.

Self-Test Opportunity: Imagine a mass hanging vertically from a spring at the equilibrium displacement. The mass is then pulled down a bit and released from rest. Draw the free body diagram for mass in the following cases!
a) The mass is at the equilibrium displacement.
b) The mass is at its highest vertical point.
c) The mass is at its lowest vertical point.

Work Done by the Spring Force

The displacement of a spring is also a case of motion in one spatial dimension, and so we can apply our one-dimensional integral to calculate the work done by the spring force by moving from x_0 to x. The result is:

$$W_s = \int_{x_0}^{x} F_s(x')dx' = \int_{x_0}^{x} (-kx')dx' = -k\int_{x_0}^{x} x'dx' \tag{5.39}$$

The rule for integrating a polynomial, a function of the form x^n, is

$$\int_{x_0}^{x} x'^n \, dx' = \tfrac{1}{n+1} x'^{n+1}\Big|_{x_0}^{x} = \tfrac{1}{n+1} x^{n+1} - \tfrac{1}{n+1} x_0^{n+1} \tag{5.40}$$

So using the case for $n = 1$ in this rule of polynomial integration, we obtain for the work done by the spring force:

$$W_s = -k\int_{x_0}^{x} x'dx' = -\tfrac{1}{2}kx^2 + \tfrac{1}{2}kx_0^2 \tag{5.41}$$

If we set $x_0 = 0$ and start at the equilibrium position, as we have done in arriving at Hooke's Law in (5.35), then the second term becomes zero as well in the previous equation, and we retain

$$W_s = -\tfrac{1}{2}kx^2 . \tag{5.42}$$

Please note that because the spring constant is always positive, the work done by the spring force is negative for displacements from equilibrium. Equation (5.41) shows that the work done by the spring force is positive if the starting spring displacement is farther from equilibrium than the ending displacement. It takes external work done on a spring of $\frac{1}{2}kx^2$ to stretch or compress it out of its equilibrium position.

Solved Problem

Solved Problem 5.1: Compressing a Spring

A (mass-less) spring located on a smooth horizontal surface is compressed by a force of 63.5 N, which results in a compression of the spring by 4.35 cm. As shown in Figure 5.12 a steel ball of mass 0.075 kg is then placed in front of the spring and the spring is released.

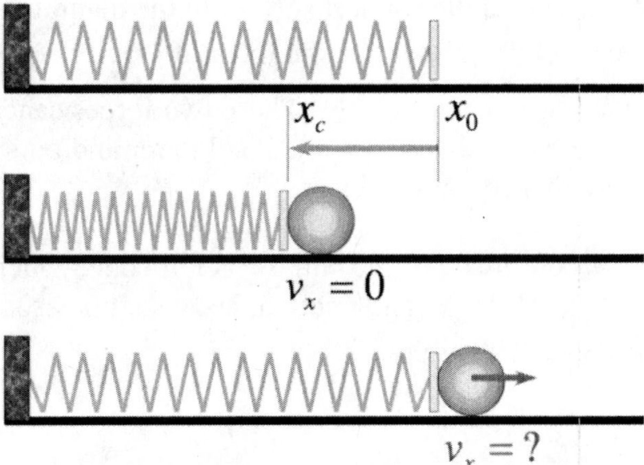

Figure 5.12: Top: spring in its equilibrium position; middle: compressing the spring; bottom: relaxing the compression and accelerating the steel ball.

Question:
What is the speed of the steel ball after it is shot off by the spring, i.e. right after the ball loses contact with the spring?

Answer:

THINK:

If we compress a spring with an external force, we do work against the spring force. Releasing the spring by withdrawing the external force enables the spring to do work on the steel ball. Thus the steel ball acquires kinetic energy in this process. Calculating the initial work done against the spring force enables us to figure out the kinetic energy that the steel ball will have and thus will lead us to the speed of the ball.

SKETCH:

We draw a free-body diagram at the instant before the external force is removed. At this instant the steel ball is at rest in equilibrium, because the external force and the spring force exactly cancel each other out.

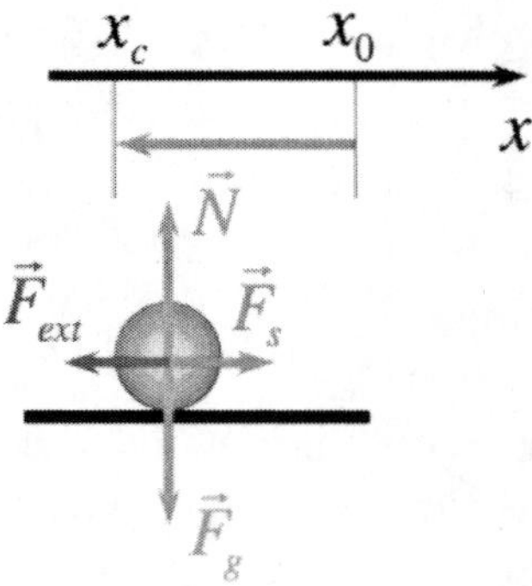

Figure 5.13: Free-body diagram of the ball before the external force is removed.

Please note that we also included the support surface in the diagram and indicated that there are two more forces acting on the ball, the force of gravity, $\vec{F}_g$, and the normal force from the support surface on the ball, $\vec{N}$. These two forces cancel each other out and thus will not enter into our calculations, but it is good to remind ourselves occasionally of the complete set of forces that act on an object.

Note that we mark the x-coordinate of the ball by its left edge, which is where it touches the spring. This is the physically relevant location, because it measures the elongation of the spring from its equilibrium position.

Solved Problem

RESEARCH:

The motion starts once the external force is removed. With the blue arrow absent in Figure 5.13, the spring force is the only unbalanced force in the problem, and will lead to the acceleration of the ball. That acceleration is not constant in time (as was the case for free-fall motion, for example), but changes. But it is the beauty of our energy considerations that we do not need to know the acceleration to calculate the final speed.

As mentioned before, we are free to chose our origin of the coordinate system, and we are going to put it at x_0, the equilibrium position of the spring. This implies that we set $x_0 = 0$. The relation of the x-component of the spring force at the moment of release and the maximum compression of the spring x_c is

$$F_s(x_c) = -kx_c \tag{5.43}$$

Since $F_s(x_c) = -F_{ext}$, we then find

$$kx_c = F_{ext} \tag{5.44}$$

The magnitude of this external force as well as the value of the compression are given, and so we can in principle calculate the value of the spring constant from this relation, as was done in example 5.4. Please note that with our choice of the coordinate system

$F_{ext} < 0$, because its vector arrow points in negative x-direction. In addition $x_c < 0$, because the deflection from equilibrium is in negative direction in this example.

We can now calculate the work W that it takes to compress this spring. Since the force that the ball exerts on the spring is always equal and opposite to the force that the spring exerts on the ball, then the definition of work allows us to set

$$W = -W_s = \tfrac{1}{2}kx_c^2 \tag{5.45}$$

According to the work-kinetic energy theorem, this work is related to the difference in kinetic energy of the steel ball via

$$K = K_0 + W = 0 + W = \tfrac{1}{2}kx_c^2 \tag{5.46}$$

And the kinetic energy is by definition

$$K = \tfrac{1}{2}mv_x^2 \tag{5.47}$$

Solved Problem

SIMPLIFY:

Now we solve (5.47) for the speed v_x and then use the above relations we have worked out:

$$v_x = \sqrt{\frac{2K}{m}} = \sqrt{\frac{2(\frac{1}{2}kx_c^2)}{m}} = \sqrt{\frac{kx_c^2}{m}} = \sqrt{\frac{F_{ext}x_c}{m}} \tag{5.48}$$

(In the second step we have used (5.47), in the third step we canceled out the factors 2 and 1/2, and in the fourth step we used (5.44).)

CALCULATE:

Now we are ready to insert the numbers!
With $x_c = -0.0435$ m, $m = 0.075$ kg , and $F_{ext} = -63.5$ N, our result is

$$v_x = \sqrt{\frac{(-63.5\text{ N})(-0.0435\text{ m})}{0.075\text{ kg}}} = 6.06877\text{ m/s}$$

Please note that we used the positive root for the x-component of the ball's velocity. By examining Figure 5.12 you can see that this is the appropriate choice, because the ball will move in positive x-direction after coming off the spring.

ROUND:

Rounding to the two-digit accuracy to which the mass was specified, we can state our result as

$$v_x = 6.1\text{ m/s}$$

DOUBLE-CHECK:

For now there are not a lot of checks we can perform to verify that our answer makes sense. This will only be possible once we study motion under the influence of the spring force in more detail in chapter 14. However, at least our solution passes the minimum requirements in that it has the proper units and that the order of magnitude of the number we have found seems in line with what, for example, realistic velocities for spring-loaded toy guns are.

In-class exercise:

How much work does it take to compress the same spring of the previous problem from 4.35 cm to 8.15 cm?

a) 4.85 J
b) 1.38 J
c) -3.47 J
d) -1.38 J
e) 3.47 J

5.7. Power

With what we have learned so far, we can calculate the work that it takes to accelerate a 3,410 lb (= 1,550 kg) car from a standing start to a speed of 60 mph (=26.8 m/s). The work is simply the difference in the final and initial kinetic energy. The initial kinetic energy is zero, and the final kinetic energy is $K = \frac{1}{2}mv^2 = \frac{1}{2}(1550\text{ kg})\cdot(26.8\text{ m/s})^2$ $= 557\text{ kJ}$, which is then also the amount of work that it takes. But if you are driving this car, you are really not so much interested in this fact. Probably, you would rather like to know how quickly your car is able to reach 60 mph. So the question that you need answered is the rate at which your car can do this work.

To this end, we define the power as the rate at which work is done. Mathematically, this concept means that the power, P, is the time derivative of the work

$$P = \frac{dW}{dt} \tag{5.49}$$

It is also useful to define the average power, $\overline{P}$, as

$$\overline{P} = \frac{W}{\Delta t} \tag{5.50}$$

The SI unit of power is the Watt (W). Please note that there is a possible confusion between the symbol for work, W (*italicized*), and the symbol the unit of power, W (non-italicized).

$$1 \text{ W} = 1 \text{ J/s} \tag{5.51}$$

Conversely, one Joule is then also one Watt times one second. This relationship is used in a very common energy unit, the kilowatt-hour (kWh):

$$1 \text{ kWh} = (1000 \text{ W})(3600 \text{ s}) = 3.6 \cdot 10^6 \text{ J} = 3.6 \text{ MJ} \tag{5.52}$$

This unit of kWh appears on our utility bills and quantifies the amount of electrical energy consumed. We can also use kWh to measure any kind of energy. So the kinetic energy of the 1550 kg car moving with a speed of 26.8 m/s, which we had calculated as 557 kJ, is expressed with equal validity as $(557{,}000 \text{ J})(1 \text{ kWh}/3.6 \cdot 10^6 \text{ J}) = 0.155 \text{ kWh}$.

The two most common non-SI power units are the horsepower (hp) and foot-pound per second (ft lb/s). Their conversions into SI-units are

$$1 \text{ hp} = 550 \text{ ft lb/s} = 746 \text{ W} \tag{5.53}$$

> ***In-class exercise:*** Select true or false for each statement.
>
> a) Work cannot be done in the absence of motion.
> b) More power is required to lift a box slowly than to lift a box quickly.
> c) A source of energy is required to do work.

Power for a Constant Force

For a constant force, we had found that the work was given by $W = \vec{F} \bullet \Delta\vec{r}$ and the differential work as $dW = \vec{F} \bullet d\vec{r}$. So in this case the time derivative is

$$P = \frac{dW}{dt} = \frac{\vec{F} \bullet d\vec{r}}{dt} = \vec{F} \bullet \vec{v} = Fv\cos\alpha_{Fv} \tag{5.54}$$

So in the case of a constant force the power is the scalar product of this force vector and the velocity vector.

Example 5.5: Accelerating Car

Question:
Returning to the accelerating car at the beginning of this section, let us assume that the car of mass 1,550 kg can reach the 60 mph (=26.8 m/s) mark in 7.1 seconds. What is the average power needed to accomplish this?

Example

Answer:
We had already stated that the car's kinetic energy at 60 mph is:

$$K = \tfrac{1}{2}mv^2 = \tfrac{1}{2}(1550\text{ kg})\cdot(26.8\text{ m/s})^2 = 557\text{ kJ}$$

The work to get this car to the 60 mph mark is then

$$W = \Delta K = K - K_0 = 557\text{ kJ}$$

The average power needed to get to the 60 mph mark in 7.1 seconds is therefore:

$$\bar{P} = \frac{W}{\Delta t} = \frac{5.57\cdot 10^5\text{ J}}{7.1\text{ s}} = 78.4\text{ kW} = 105\text{ hp}$$

If you own a car with a mass of at least 1,550 kg that has an engine with 105 horsepower, you know that your car cannot possibly reach 60 mph in 7.1 seconds. Instead, you probably need an engine with at least 180 hp to accelerate a car of mass 1,550 kg (including the driver, of course) to 60 mph in the desired time.

There are several reasons why our calculation is not quite correct. First, not all of the power output of the engine is available to do useful work such as accelerating the car. We will return to this question at the end of the next chapter, when we discuss questions of efficiency. Second, we also have to accelerate the car against friction and air resistance forces. We will address doing work against outside forces in the next chapter. Finally, a car's rated horsepower is a peak horsepower specification, listed at the most beneficial rpm-domain of the engine. As you accelerate the car from rest, this peak rating of the engine is not maintainable as you shift through the gears. Despite all of these qualifiers, you can still see that the concept of power that we introduced here has useful connections to everyday engineering experiences.

What we have learned/Exam Study Guide:

- Kinetic energy is the energy associated with the motion of an object, $K = \tfrac{1}{2}mv^2$.
- Energy unit: $1\text{ J} = 1\text{ kg m}^2/\text{s}^2$.
- Work is defined as energy transferred to an object or transferred from an object due to the action of a force. Positive work is defined as a transfer of energy to the object, and negative work is a transfer of energy from the object. Positive work is work done *on* the object, while negative work is work done *by* the object.
- Work done by a constant force: $W = |\vec{F}|\,|\Delta\vec{r}|\cos\alpha$, with α = angle between $\vec{F}$ and $\Delta\vec{r}$.

- Work done by a variable force in one dimension is $W = \int_{x_0}^{x} F_x(x')dx'$
- Work done by a variable force in three dimensions is
  $W = \int_{\vec{r}_0}^{\vec{r}} \vec{F}(\vec{r}\,')\bullet d\vec{r}\,' = \int_{\vec{r}_0}^{\vec{r}} F_x(\vec{r}\,')dx' + \int_{\vec{r}_0}^{\vec{r}} F_y(\vec{r}\,')dy' + \int_{\vec{r}_0}^{\vec{r}} F_z(\vec{r}\,')dz'$
- Work done by the gravitational force in the process of lifting an object is $W_g = -mgh < 0$ where $h = |y - y_0|$, and lowering an object: $W_g = +mgh > 0$.
- The spring force is given by Hooke's Law: $F_s = -kx$
- Work done by the spring force is $W = -k\int_{x_0}^{x} x'dx' = -\tfrac{1}{2}kx^2 + \tfrac{1}{2}kx_0^2$
- Work - kinetic energy theorem is $\Delta K \equiv K - K_0 = W$
- Power, P, is the time derivative of the work: $P = \dfrac{dW}{dt}$
- The average power, $\overline{P}$, is $\overline{P} = \dfrac{W}{\Delta t}$.
- The SI unit of power is the Watt (W): 1 W = 1 J/s.
- Power for a constant force is $P = \dfrac{dW}{dt} = \dfrac{\vec{F}\bullet d\vec{r}}{dt} = \vec{F}\bullet\vec{v} = Fv\cos\alpha_{Fv}$

Additional Solved Problems

Solved Problem

Solved Problem 5.2: Lifting Bricks

Question:

We have a load of bricks with a mass of 85.0 kg. We raise this load of bricks from the ground to a height of 50.0 m. The time required to raise the load is 60.0 s. What is the average power required for a crane to lift a load of bricks at a small, constant speed?

Answer:

THINK: Raising the bricks at a small, constant speed means that the kinetic energy is negligible and the work in this problem is done against gravity only. There is no acceleration and friction is negligible. The average power then is just the work done against gravity divided by the time it takes to raise the load of bricks the required height.

SKETCH: A sketch of the problem is shown in Figure 5.14.

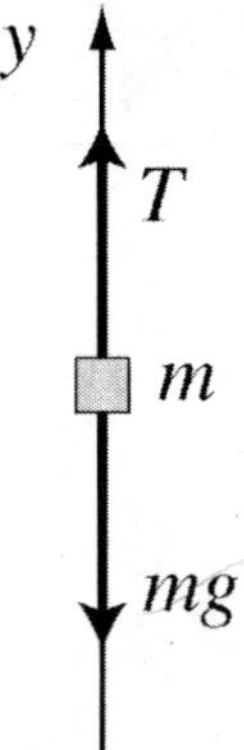

Figure 5.14: Sketch showing a mass m being lifted by a crane.

Here we have defined a coordinate system in which the y-axis is vertical. The tension T exerted by the cable of the crane is a force in upward direction and the weight mg of the mass is a force downward. Because the mass is moving at a constant speed, the sum of the tension and the weight is zero. The mass is moved vertically a distance h as shown in Figure 5.15.

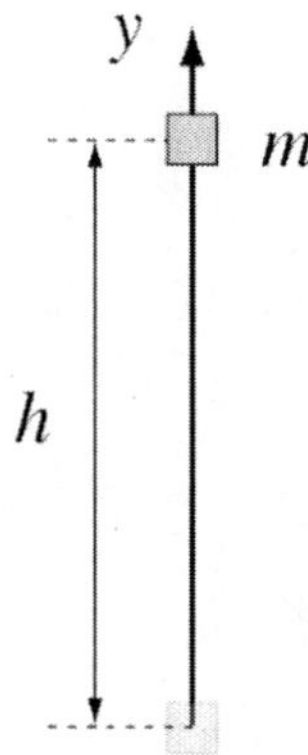

Figure 5.15. A mass m is lifted a distance h.

RESEARCH: The work W done by the crane against gravity is given by

$$W = mgh. \tag{5.55}$$

The average power $\bar{P}$ required to lift the mass in the given time Δt is

$$\bar{P} = \frac{W}{\Delta t}. \tag{5.56}$$

SIMPLIFY: Putting together (5.55) and (5.56) we get

$$\bar{P} = \frac{mgh}{\Delta t}. \tag{5.57}$$

Solved Problem

CALCULATE: Now we put in the numbers and get a numerical result.

$$\bar{P} = \frac{(85.0 \text{ kg})(9.81 \text{ m/s}^2)(50.0 \text{ m})}{60.0 \text{ s}} = 694.875 \text{ W}$$

ROUND: We report our final result as

$$\bar{P} = 695. \text{ W}$$

because all of our known numerical values were quoted to three significant figures.

DOUBLE-CHECK: To double-check our result for the required average power, we convert the average power in watts to average power in horsepower

$$\bar{P} = (695 \text{ W})\frac{1 \text{ hp}}{760 \text{ W}} = 0.914 \text{ hp}.$$

Thus a one horsepower motor is sufficient to lift the 85.0 kg load 50 m in 60 s, which seems reasonable, although surprisingly small. Because motors are not 100% efficient, the crane in reality would require a motor with somewhat higher rated power to actually lift the load.

Solved Problem

Solved Problem 5.3: Shot Put

Question:

Shot put competitions in track and field use metal balls with a mass of 7.26 kg. If you throw the shot at an angle of 43.3°, you release it from a height of 1.82 m above where it lands, and it lands a horizontal distance of 17.7 m from where you threw it, what was the kinetic energy of the shot as it left your hand?

Answer:

THINK:

We are given the horizontal distance $\ell = 17.7$ m, height of release $y_0 = 1.82$ m, and angle of the initial velocity $\theta_0 = 43.3°$, but not the initial speed v_0. If we can figure out the initial speed from the data given, then it will be easy to calculate the initial kinetic energy, because we also know the mass $m = 7.26$ kg of the shot.

Since the shot is very heavy, air resistance can be safely neglected. This is an excellent realization of ideal projectile motion. After the shot leaves the thrower's hand, the only force on the shot is the force of gravity and the shot will follow a parabolic trajectory until it lands on the ground. So our answer will likely result from the application of the lessons we learned from ideal projectile motion.

SKETCH:

The trajectory of the shot is shown in Figure 5.16.

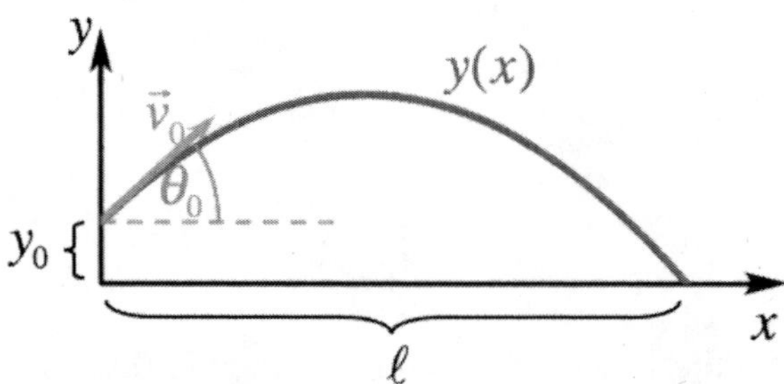

Figure 5.16: Parabolic trajectory of a shot.

RESEARCH:

The initial kinetic energy K of the shot with mass m is given by

$$K = \frac{1}{2} m v_0^2 . \quad (5.58)$$

So we need to answer the question how we obtain v_0. We are given the distance ℓ at which the shot hits the ground, but this is *not* equal to the range R, for which we had obtained an expression in chapter 3, because the range formula assumes that the heights of the start and end of the trajectory are equal. Here the initial height is y_0 and the final height is 0. Therefore we have to return to the full expression for the trajectory of an ideal projectile. In chapter 3 we had found:

$$y = y_0 + x \tan\theta_0 - \frac{x^2 g}{2 v_0^2 \cos^2\theta_0}$$

This expression describes the y-component of the trajectory as a function of the x-component.

In this particular problem, we are given the information that $y(x = \ell) = 0$, i.e. that the shot touches the ground at $x = \ell$. Inserting this information into the equation for the trajectory results in

$$0 = y_0 + \ell \tan\theta_0 - \ell^2 \frac{g}{2 v_0^2 \cos^2\theta_0} \quad (5.59)$$

SIMPLIFY:

Solved Problem

Solved Problem

We solve (5.59) for v_0^2 and find:

$$y_0 + \ell \tan\theta_0 = \frac{\ell^2 g}{2v_0^2 \cos^2\theta_0} \Rightarrow$$

$$2v_0^2 \cos^2\theta_0 = \frac{\ell^2 g}{y_0 + \ell \tan\theta_0} \Rightarrow$$

$$v_0^2 = \frac{\ell^2 g}{2\cos^2\theta_0 (y_0 + \ell \tan\theta_0)} \quad (5.60)$$

Inserting this result into our expression for the initial kinetic energy gives us the formula for our answer:

$$K = \tfrac{1}{2} m v_0^2 = \frac{m\ell^2 g}{4\cos^2\theta_0 (y_0 + \ell \tan\theta_0)}$$

CALCULATE:

Putting in the numerical values for this problem we get

$$K = \frac{(7.26\text{kg})(17.7\text{m})^2 (9.81\text{m/s}^2)}{4\cos^2(43.3°)\left[1.82\text{ m} + (17.7\text{m})\tan(43.3°)\right]} = 569.295\text{ J}.$$

ROUND:

All of the numerical values in this problem are specified to three significant figures, so we report our answer as

$$K = 569.\text{ J}.$$

DOUBLE-CHECK:

We can find the horizontal and vertical components of the initial velocity vector by calculating v_0 from (5.60) and then using

$$v_{x0} = v_0 \cos\theta_0 = 9.11\text{ m/s}$$

$$v_{y0} = v_0 \sin\theta_0 = 8.59\text{ m/s}$$

As we discussed in section 5.2 when we defined the concept of kinetic energy, we can split the total kinetic energy in ideal projectile motion up into contributions from the motion in horizontal and vertical directions (see (5.8)), and the kinetic energy contained in the motion in x-direction remains constant.

The kinetic energy contained in the motion in y-direction is initially

$$K(v_{y0}) = \tfrac{1}{2} m v_{y0}^2 \sin^2\theta_0 = 268.\text{ J}$$

At the top of the trajectory of the shot, just like for all projectile motion, the vertical velocity component is 0. This also means that the kinetic energy associated with the vertical motion is 0 at this point. All 268 Joules of the initial kinetic energy contained in the y-component of the motion have been used up to do work against the force of gravity, see section 5.3. This work is then (compare (5.25)) $W_g = mgh$, where $h = y_{max} - y_0$ is the maximum height of the trajectory. We thus find for h numerically:

$$h = \frac{268 \text{ J}}{mg} = \frac{268 \text{ J}}{(7.26\text{kg})(9.81\text{m/s}^2)} = 3.76 \text{ m}$$

Let's check what the maximum height would be for the initial velocity we have determined. In section 3.3 the maximum height H of a mass in projectile motion was shown to be

$$H = y_0 + \frac{v_{y0}^2}{2g}$$

Putting in the numbers, we find $v_{y0}^2 / 2g = 3.76 \text{ m}$. So the maximum height h of the trajectory above the initial release point that we find with our energy considerations is exactly the same as that found from our trajectory considerations, $h = H - y_0$.

Chapter 6. Potential Energy and Energy Conservation

What we will learn:

- Potential energy, U , is the energy stored in the configuration of a system of objects that exert forces on each other.
- A conservative force is a force for which the work it does on an object that travels on a path such that the object returns to where it started (a closed path) is zero. A force that does not fulfill this requirement is called a non-conservative force.
- A potential energy can be associated with any conservative force. The change in such a potential energy due to some spatial rearrangement of a system is equal to the negative of the work done by the conservative force during this spatial rearrangement.
- We define the mechanical energy, E, as the sum of kinetic energy and potential energy.
- The total mechanical energy is conserved (it remains constant in time) for any mechanical process inside an isolated system that involves only conservative forces.
- The total energy, the sum of all forms of energy – mechanical or otherwise, is always conserved in an isolated system. This holds for conservative as well as non-conservative forces.
- Small perturbations about stable equilibrium points result in small oscillations around the equilibrium, while for unstable equilibrium points small perturbations result in an accelerated movement away from that equilibrium point.

6.1. Potential Energy

We have examined in detail the relationship between kinetic energy and work. Now we are going to introduce another kind of energy besides the kinetic energy. This new energy form is called potential energy.

Potential energy, U, is the energy stored in the configuration of a system of objects that exert forces on each other.

For example, we have seen that it takes work to lift a load with an external force against the force of gravity, and this external work is given by $W = mgh$, where m is the mass of the load, and $h = y - y_0$ the difference in altitude to which the load is lifted. (In this chapter we will take the y axis to point up unless specified differently.) This lift can be accomplished without changing the kinetic energy, as for example in the case of the weightlifter, who has to lift the weight from rest and hold it still for a moment above his/her head. This means that there is energy stored in holding the weight above the head. If the weightlifter lets go of the weight, then this energy can be converted back into kinetic energy as the weight accelerates and falls to the ground. We see from this example that the gravitational potential energy can be expressed as

$$U_g = mgy, \tag{6.1}$$

and the change in gravitational potential energy as

$$\Delta U_g \equiv U_g(y) - U_g(y_0) = mg(y - y_0) = mgh. \tag{6.2}$$

(Equation (6.1) is only valid near the surface of the earth, where $F_g = mg$ is valid. We will encounter a more general expression for U_g later.) In the previous chapter, we had also calculated the work done by the gravitational force on an object that is lifted by a height h to be $W_g = -mgh$. From this, we see that the work done by the gravitational force and the gravitational potential energy for an object lifted from rest to a height h are related via

$$\Delta U_g = -W_g. \tag{6.3}$$

Equation (6.3) is even true for complicated paths involving horizontal as well as vertical motion, since the gravitational force does no work during horizontal segments of the motion. In horizontal motion the displacement is perpendicular to the force of gravity (which always points vertically down), and thus the scalar product between the force and the displacement vanishes; hence no work is done.

By doing work against the force of gravity, we can generate gravitational potential energy in lifting objects to a higher elevation. If we wish we can store this energy for later use. This principle is employed, for example, at many hydropower dams. The excess electricity generated by the water turbines is used to pump water up to a reservoir at higher altitude. There it constitutes a reserve that can be tapped into in times of high demand and/or low water supply. Stated in general terms, if ΔU_g is positive we have the potential (hence the name potential energy) to allow ΔU_g to be negative in the future, thereby extracting positive work since $W_g = -\Delta U_g$.

6.2. Conservative and Non-Conservative Forces

Before we can proceed to the calculation of the potential energy from a given force, we have to consider what kind of forces we can use to store potential energy for later retrieval. To do this, we need to ask what happens to the work done by this force when we reverse the direction of the path we take. In the case of the gravitational force we already have answered this question. As shown in Figure 6.1, the work done by F_g when an object of mass m is lifted from altitude y_A to y_B is the same in magnitude, but opposite in sign, to the work done by F_g when lowering the same object from altitude y_B to y_A. This means that the total work done by F_g in lifting the object from some altitude to a different one and then returning it to the same altitude is zero.

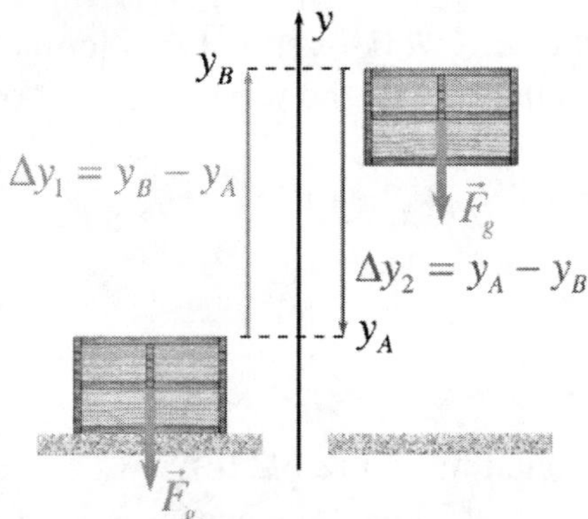

Figure 6.1: Gravitational force vectors and displacement vectors for lifting and lowering a box.

We now use this characteristic as the basis of definition of the term conservative force (compare Figure 6.2 (a)):

> A conservative force is a force for which the work done over any closed path is zero. A force that does not fulfill this requirement is called a non-conservative force.

For conservative forces, we can then immediately state two consequences of this definition (See Figure 6.2 (b).):

(1) If we know the work, $W_{A\to B}$, done by a conservative force on an object as it moves along a path from point A to point B, then we also know that the work, $W_{B\to A}$, that the same force does on the path in reverse direction from point B to point A. It is

$$W_{B\to A} = -W_{A\to B} \quad \text{(for conservative forces)} \tag{6.4}$$

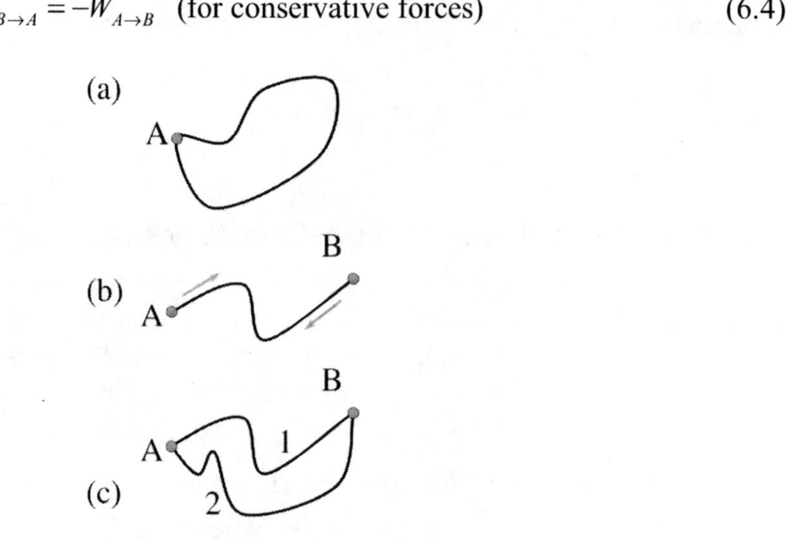

Figure 6.2: (a) Closed loop over which the total work is zero for a conservative force. (b) and (c) path-independence of the work done by a conservative force.

The proof is obtained from the zero work over a closed loop condition, because A to B to A forms a closed loop, and so the sum of the work contributions from the loop has to equal 0, in other words

$$W_{A\to B} + W_{B\to A} = 0,$$

from which equation (6.4) follows immediately.

Derivation

A second consequence is depicted in Figure 6.2 (c):
(2) If we know the work, $W_{A\to B,\text{path }1}$, done by a conservative force on path 1 going from point A to point B, then we also know the work, $W_{A\to B,\text{path }2}$, done by the same force using any other path 2 to go from point A to point B. It is the same; the work done by a conservative force is path-independent.

$$W_{A\to B,\text{path }2} = W_{A\to B,\text{path }1} \tag{6.5}$$

(for arbitrary paths 1 and 2, for conservative forces)

This statement is also easy to prove when we accept the definition of a conservative force as a force for which the work done over any closed path is zero, because the loop from point A to point B on path 1 and then back on path 2 is a closed one, therefore $W_{A\to B,\text{path }2} + W_{B\to A,\text{path }1} = 0$. Now we use the previous result of a sign change by reversing the path direction, $W_{B\to A,\text{path }1} = -W_{A\to B,\text{path }1}$. Combining these two results gives us $W_{A\to B,\text{path }2} - W_{A\to B,\text{path }1} = 0$, from which equation (6.5) follows.

Derivation

The gravitational force, as we have seen, is an example of a conservative force. Another example for a conservative force is the spring force. Not all forces conservative, however. Now the question arises: which forces are non-conservative?

Work Done by Friction Forces

Let us calculate the work done by sliding an object across a horizontal surface, from point A to point B and then back to point A, if the friction coefficient between the object and the surface is μ_k. (See Figure 6.3.) As we have learned, the friction force is given by $f = \mu_k N = \mu_k mg$ and always points in opposite direction to the direction of motion.

For the motion from A to B we can calculate the work from our general scalar product formula for work done by a constant force:

$$W_{f1} = \vec{f} \bullet \Delta\vec{r}_1 = -f \cdot (x_B - x_A) = -\mu_k mg \cdot (x_B - x_A) = \mu_k mgx_A - \mu_k mgx_B . \qquad (6.6)$$

Here we have assumed that the positive x-axis is pointing to the right, as conventional, and so the friction force points in negative x-direction.

For the motion from B back to A, on the other hand, the friction force now points in positive x-direction. So the work for this part of the path is

$$W_{f2} = \vec{f} \bullet \Delta\vec{r}_2 = f \cdot (x_A - x_B) = \mu_k mg \cdot (x_A - x_B) = \mu_k mgx_A - \mu_k mgx_B . \qquad (6.7)$$

This leads us to conclude that the total work done by the friction force on the closed path sliding the object across the surface from point A to point B and back to point A is not 0, but instead:

$$W_f = W_{f1} + W_{f2} = 2\mu_k mgx_A - 2\mu_k mgx_B < 0 . \qquad (6.8)$$

With our definition of a conservative force we find that the friction force is an example of a non-conservative force. Because the friction force is always in a direction opposite to the displacement, the work that it does will always be negative whether or not the path is closed.

The decisive fact is that the friction force switches direction as a function of the direction of motion. Thus the force for which we want to compute the work is dependent on the velocity vector. Any such force cannot be conservative! Another example of a non-conservative force is the force of air resistance. It is also velocity dependent and always points in opposite direction to the velocity vector, just like the force of kinetic friction. Yet another example for a non-conservative force is the damping force, which we will encounter in studying oscillations. It, too, is velocity dependent and has the form $-b\vec{v}$

where b is a constant. We will return to the damping force in chapter 14 on oscillations.

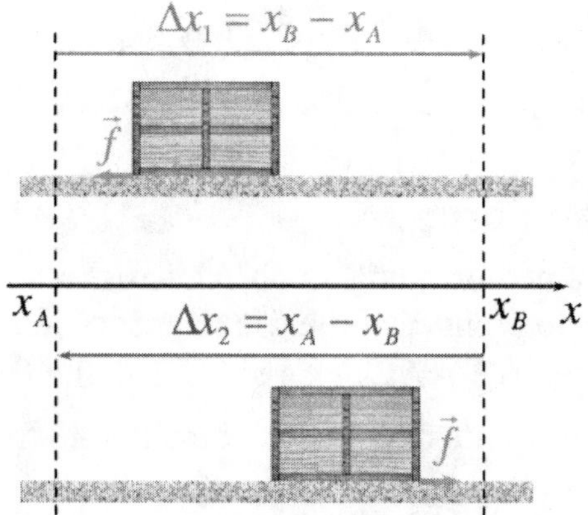

Figure 6.3: Friction force vector and displacement vector for the processes of sliding a box back and forth across a surface.

In-class exercise: A person pushes a box with mass 10.0 kg a distance of 5.00 m across a floor. The coefficient of kinetic friction between the box and the floor is 0.250. The person then picks up the box to a height of 1.00 m, carries the box back to the original starting point, and puts it back down on the floor. How much work has the person done on the box?
a) 74.3 J
b) 12.5 J
c) 98.1 J
d) 123 J
e) 25.0 J
f) 246 J

6.3. Work and Potential Energy

In our consideration of the work done by the gravitational force and its relationship to the gravitational potential energy, we have found at the beginning of this chapter that the change in potential energy is equal to the negative of the work done by the force, $\Delta U_g = -W_g$. This relationship is fulfilled for all conservative forces. In fact, we can define the concept of potential energy through this relationship.

For any conservative force, the change in potential energy due to some spatial rearrangement of a system is equal to the negative of the work done by the conservative force during this spatial rearrangement:

$$\Delta U = -W . \tag{6.9}$$

Since we have already found out that the expression for work is given as

$$W = \int_{\vec{r}_0}^{\vec{r}} \vec{F}(\vec{r}\,')\bullet d\vec{r}\,', \tag{6.10}$$

we then obtain from combining equations (6.9) and (6.10) the relationship between the conservative force and the potential energy:

$$\Delta U = U(\vec{r}) - U(\vec{r}_0) = -\int_{\vec{r}_0}^{\vec{r}} \vec{F}(\vec{r}\,')\bullet d\vec{r}\,'. \tag{6.11}$$

For motion in one dimension, this relationship reduces to:

$$\Delta U = U(x) - U(x_0) = -\int_{x_0}^{x} F_x(x')dx'. \tag{6.12}$$

This enables us to calculate the potential energy change for any given conservative force. Why does one bother with the potential energy concept when one can deal directly with the conservative force itself? It is because the change in potential energy depends only on the beginning and final state of the system and is independent of the path taken to get to the final state. Often we have a simple expression for a potential energy (and thus its change) prior to even working the problem! Whereas performing the integral on the right hand side of equation (6.12) could be quite complicated.

In the previous chapter, we have already evaluated this integral for the force of gravity and the spring force. The result for the gravitational force is:

$$\Delta U_g = U_g(y) - U_g(y_0) = -\int_{y_0}^{y} (-mg)dy' = mg\int_{y_0}^{y} dy' = mgy - mgy_0. \tag{6.13}$$

This is in accordance with our result we had found in the first section of this chapter. Consequently the gravitational potential energy is:

$$U_g(y) = mgy + \text{constant}. \tag{6.14}$$

Please note that we only were able to write down the potential energy at coordinate y to within an additive constant. The only physical observable, the work done, is related to the difference in the potential energy. If we add an arbitrary constant to the value of the potential energy everywhere, the difference in the potential energies remains unchanged.

For the spring force, we find in the same way:

$$\begin{aligned}\Delta U_s &= U_s(x) - U_s(x_0) \\ &= -\int_{x_0}^{x} F_s(x')dx' \\ &= -\int_{x_0}^{x} (-kx')dx' \\ &= k\int_{x_0}^{x} x'dx' \\ &= \tfrac{1}{2}kx^2 - \tfrac{1}{2}kx_0^2\end{aligned}$$

So the potential energy associated with elongating a spring from its equilibrium position at $x = 0$ is:

$$U_s(x) = \tfrac{1}{2}kx^2 + \text{constant} \tag{6.15}$$

Again, the potential energy is only determined up to an additive constant. However, please keep in mind that in physical situations we are often forced into a choice of the additive constant. The following examples will illustrate this in more detail.

Potential Energy and Force

How can we calculate the conservative force provided we have information on the corresponding potential energy?

In calculus, we are taught that taking the derivative is the inverse operation of integrating. And this is what is also used here. Therefore, we use equation (6.12) to obtain the force from the potential as:

$$F_x(x) = -\frac{dU(x)}{dx} \tag{6.16}$$

This is the answer for the case of motion in one dimension. As you can see from this expression, any constant that you add to the potential energy will not have any influence on the result you obtain for the force, because taking the derivative of a constant results in zero for that term. This is again evidence that the potential energy is only determined up to an additive constant.

We will not use more complicated three-dimensional scenarios in the present book. However, for completeness we can state the equivalent of the previous result for the case of three-dimensional motion. It is:

$$\vec{F}(\vec{r}) = -\left(\frac{\partial U(\vec{r})}{\partial x}\hat{x} + \frac{\partial U(\vec{r})}{\partial y}\hat{y} + \frac{\partial U(\vec{r})}{\partial z}\hat{z}\right) \equiv -\vec{\nabla}U(\vec{r}) \tag{6.17}$$

So in this general case the force components are given as the "partial derivatives" with respect to the corresponding coordinates. If you plan to have a deeper involvement with engineering or science, you will encounter partial derivatives in many situations. But for the purposes of this present introductory course we will refrain from using them. The mathematical operation performed on U in parentheses is so common that it has a special name, gradient, and symbol, $\vec{\nabla}$, which we define in the second part of equation (6.17), and which is a vector quantity.

In-class exercise: The potential energy $U(x)$ is shown in red as a function of position x in the figure. In which region is the magnitude of the force the highest?

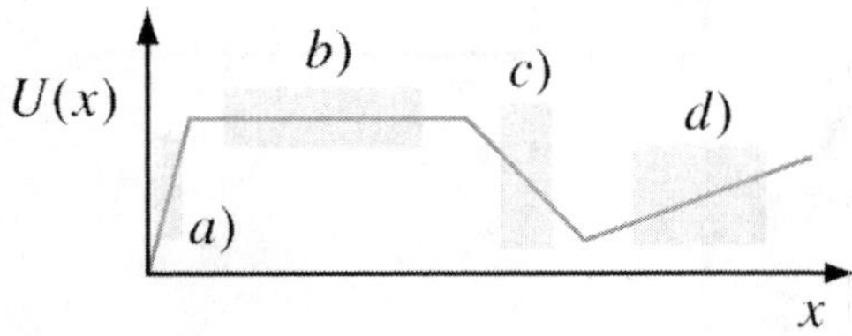

Example

Example 6.1: Force and Potential Energy

Question:
If the potential energy is given by the formula

$$U(x) = \frac{a}{x} + bx^2 + c \text{ with } a,b,c = \text{constant,} \tag{6.18}$$

what is the corresponding force?

Answer:
We simply have to take the negative of the derivative of the potential energy with respect to x:

$$\begin{aligned} F(x) &= -\frac{dU(x)}{dx} \\ &= -\frac{d}{dx}\left(\frac{a}{x} + bx^2 + c\right) \\ &= -a\frac{d}{dx}\left(\frac{1}{x}\right) - b\frac{d}{dx}(x^2) \\ &= \frac{a}{x^2} - 2bx \end{aligned} \tag{6.19}$$

As you can see, the additive constant c did not enter into the expression for the force.

Example

As an example, Figure 6.4 shows how $U(x)$ (blue line) and $F(x)$ (red line) depend on the coordinate x for a choice of the constants $a=-2, b=-1, c=-5$. As you can see, the force is zero where the potential energy has an extremum (a maximum in this case). This is clear from our knowledge of calculus: a function has an extremum at all points where its derivative is 0.

While we treat this potential energy function as an exercise, it is actually similar in its functional form (but with a different choice of constants!) to a common one used in particle physics to describe the potential energy of so-called "quarks" inside a nucleon (proton or neutron) – more of this in our chapter 39 on particle physics.

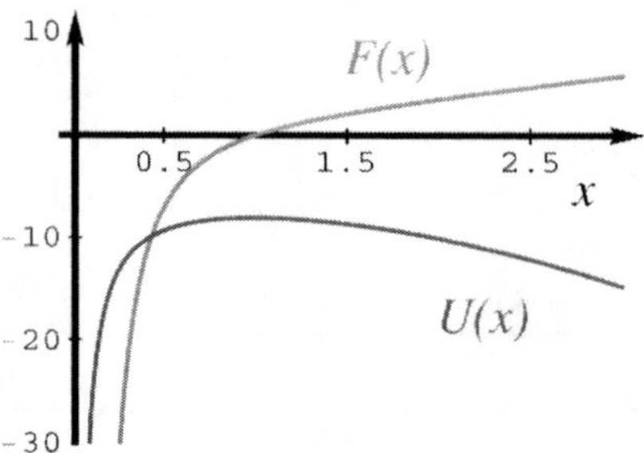

Figure 6.4: Dependence of the potential energy (blue line) and force (red line) on the coordinate for the potential energy function of equation (6.18), with $a=-2, b=-1, c=-5$.

Self-Test Opportunity: There are forces in nature that depend on the inverse of the distance between the objects squared. How does the potential energy associated with such a force depend on the distance between the objects?

6.4. Conservation of Mechanical Energy

We define the mechanical energy, E, as the sum of kinetic energy and potential energy:

$$E = K + U \tag{6.20}$$

Later, when we move beyond mechanics, we will add other kinds of energy to this sum and call it the total energy. For now, the energy sum is only one of mechanical energy.

We now look at the special case of an ***isolated system***, which by definition is a system of objects exerting forces on each other, but for which no force external to the system causes energy changes within the system. This means that no energy is transferred into or out of the system.

For any mechanical process inside this isolated system that involves only conservative forces, we show below that the total mechanical energy is conserved; it remains constant in time:

$$\Delta E = \Delta K + \Delta U = 0 \qquad (6.21)$$

An alternative way of writing the same result is:

$$K + U = K_0 + U_0 \qquad (6.22)$$

This relationship, which we call the Conservation of Mechanical Energy, does not imply that the kinetic energy of the system cannot change, or that the potential energy alone remains constant. Rather it states that their changes are exactly compensating and thus offset each other.

Derivation 6.1:
We have already found out in this chapter, equation (6.9), that if a conservative force does work, then the work causes a change in potential energy,

$$\Delta U = -W$$

(If the force under consideration is not conservative, this relationship does not hold in general, and conservation of mechanical energy is not valid.)

In the previous chapter, we had learned that the relationship between the change in kinetic energy and the work done by the force is (equation 5.21):

$$\Delta K = W$$

Combining these two results, we obtain:

$$\Delta U = -\Delta K \Rightarrow \Delta U + \Delta K = 0$$

Using $\Delta U = U - U_0, \Delta K = K - K_0$, we then find:

$$0 = \Delta U + \Delta K = U - U_0 + K - K_0 = U + K - (U_0 + K_0) \Rightarrow$$
$$U + K = U_0 + K_0$$

Note that this derivation did not make any use of the particular path on which the force did the work that caused the rearrangement. In fact we do not need to know any detail about the work or the force, other than that the force is conservative. Nor do we need to know how many conservative forces are acting. If there is more than one, you just need to interpret ΔU as the sum of all the potential energy changes and W as the total work done by all of the conservative forces and our derivation is still valid.

Energy conservation enables us to solve a huge number of problems involving just conservative forces in a streamlined fashion, problems which would have been very hard to solve without this conservation law. We do not yet have the more general Work-Energy Theorem for mechanics problems, as we need to include non-conservative forces. We will do this later in the chapter.

Equation (6.22) introduces a first conservation law, the Conservation of Mechanical Energy. In the chapters on heat (chapter 18) and thermodynamics (chapter 20), we will extend it slightly to also include thermal energy. In the next chapter a conservation law for the total momentum will follow. When we discuss rotations, we will encounter a conservation law for total angular momentum. In studying electricity and magnetism, we will find a conservation law for net charge (chapter 21), and in looking at elementary particle physics (chapter 39) we will find conservation laws for net lepton and baryon numbers, total strangeness, and other quantities. This list is not intended to confuse you, but to give you a flavor of a central theme of physics – the discovery of conservation laws and their use in determining the dynamics of systems under consideration.

Before we leave these general considerations and actually solve a few sample problems, one more remark on the concept of an isolated system is in order. In situations that involve the motion of objects under the influence of the gravitational force of Earth, the isolated system that we need for our energy conservation law really consists of the moving object plus the entire Earth. But in the approximation of the gravitational force as a constant that we are employing we assume that the Earth is infinitely heavy (and that we are close to the surface of earth). Therefore, no change in the kinetic energy of the Earth will result from the rearrangement of the system. So all changes in kinetic energy and potential energy are just calculated for the "junior partner", the object moving under the influence of the gravitational force. This force is conservative and internal to the system Earth-plus-moving-object, and so all of our conditions for the utilization of the law of energy conservation are fulfilled.

Specific examples for which these considerations apply are all projectile and pendulum motions occurring near the earth's surface.

Solved Problem

Solved Problem 6.1: Catapult

Your task is to defend castle Neuschwanstein from attackers. (See Figure 6.5.) You have a catapult at your disposal with which you can lob rocks with a launch speed of 14.2 m/s from the courtyard over the castle walls onto the attackers camped out in front of the castle, at an elevation of 7.20 m below that of the courtyard.

Question:

What is the speed with which your rocks will hit the ground at that elevation of 7.20 m below your position?

Figure 6.5: Illustration for a possible projectile path (red parabola) from the courtyard to the area below and in front of the castle gate. The blue line marks the horizontal.

Answer:

THINK: We can solve this problem with energy conservation techniques. Once the catapult launches the rocks, we are dealing with the conservative force of gravity. Thus the total mechanical energy is conserved, which means the sum of the kinetic energy and potential energy of the rocks always sum to the total mechanical energy.

SKETCH: The trajectory of the rocks is illustrated in Figure 6.6.

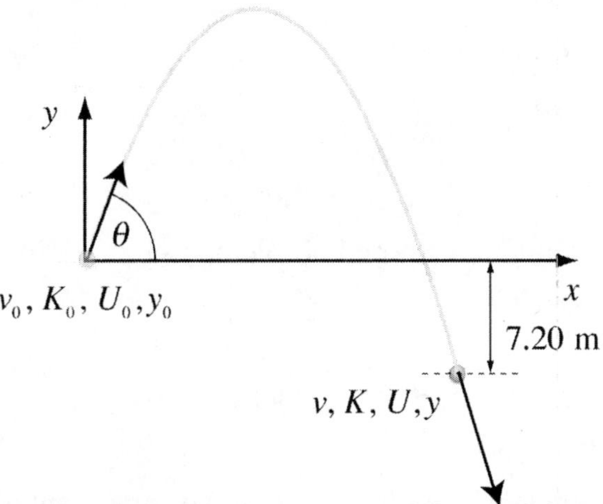

Figure 6.6: Trajectory of the rocks launched by the catapult.

We define the initial velocity of the rocks to be $\vec{v}_0$, the initial kinetic energy to be K_0, the initial potential energy to be U_0, and the initial height to be y_0. We also define the final speed to be $\vec{v}$, the final kinetic energy to be K, the final potential energy to be U, and the final height to be y.

Solved Problem

RESEARCH: We can use the conservation of mechanical energy to write

$$E = K + U = K_0 + U_0 \tag{6.23}$$

where E is the total mechanical energy. The kinetic energy of the projectile can be expressed as

$$K = \tfrac{1}{2}mv^2 \tag{6.24}$$

where m is the mass of the projectile and v is the speed of the projectile. The potential energy of the projectile can be expressed as

$$U = mgy \tag{6.25}$$

where y is the vertical component of the position vector of the projectile.

SIMPLIFY: We combine the previous three equations to get

$$E = \tfrac{1}{2}mv^2 + mgy = \tfrac{1}{2}mv_0^2 + mgy_0 \ . \tag{6.26}$$

We see that the mass of the rocks, m, cancels out, and we are left with:

$$\tfrac{1}{2}v^2 + gy = \tfrac{1}{2}v_0^2 + gy_0 \tag{6.27}$$

We solve this for the speed and obtain:

$$v = \sqrt{v_0^2 + 2g(y_0 - y)} \tag{6.28}$$

CALCULATE: According to the posed problem, $y_0 - y = 7.20$ m; $v_0 = 14.2$ m/s, and so we find for the final speed:

$$v = \sqrt{(14.2 \text{ m/s})^2 + 2(9.81 \text{ m/s}^2)(7.20 \text{ m})} = 18.51766724 \text{ m/s}$$

ROUND: The relative height was specified to three significant digits so we report our final answer to three significant digits

$$v = 18.5 \text{ m/s}.$$

DOUBLE-CHECK: Our answer for the speed of the rocks when they hit the ground in front of the courtyard is 18.5 m/s compared with the initial launch speed of 14.2 m/s, which seems reasonable.

Solved Problem

Since we were only interested in the impact speed, we did not even need to know the initial launch angle to solve our problem in which we were interested. All launch angles will give us the same result, which is a somewhat surprising finding. (But of course if you were in this situation, obviously you would still want to aim high enough to clear the castle wall and to aim accurately enough to strike the invaders.)

We can also get the answer for this problem using the techniques of projectile motion, which is also useful to double-check our answer and to show the power of applying the concepts of energy conservation. We start by writing the components of the initial velocity vector

$$v_{x0} = v_0 \cos\theta$$

and

$$v_{y0} = v_0 \sin\theta \,.$$

The final x-component of the velocity v_x is equal to the initial x-component of the initial velocity

$$v_x = v_{x0} = v_0 \cos\theta \,.$$

The final component of the velocity in the y-direction can be obtained from the analysis of projectile motion in Chapter 3

$$v_y^2 = v_{y0}^2 - 2g\left(y - y_0\right).$$

Therefore the final speed of rocks hitting the ground is

$$\begin{aligned} v &= \sqrt{v_x^2 + v_y^2} \\ &= \sqrt{\left(v_0 \cos\theta\right)^2 + \left(v_{y0}^2 - 2g\left(y - y_0\right)\right)} \\ &= \sqrt{v_0^2 \cos^2\theta + v_0^2 \sin^2\theta - 2g\left(y - y_0\right)} \end{aligned}$$

Remembering that $\sin^2\theta + \cos^2\theta = 1$ we can further simplify and get

$$v = \sqrt{v_0^2(\cos^2\theta + \sin^2\theta) - 2g\left(y - y_0\right)} = \sqrt{v_0^2 - 2g\left(y - y_0\right)} = \sqrt{v_0^2 + 2g\left(y_0 - y\right)}$$

which is the same result (equation (6.28)) we obtained using energy conservation techniques. Like the result using energy conservation concepts, the answer does not depend on the launch angle θ.

As you can see from this problem, the law of mechanical energy conservation provides us with a powerful technique to solve problems that seem rather complicated at first sight.

In general, we can determine speeds as a function of the altitude in situations where the gravitational force is at work. Consider the image sequence in Figure 6.7. Two balls are released at the same time from the same height at the top of two ramps of different shape. At the bottom end of the two ramps, they both reach the same lower altitude. So in both cases the height difference between initial and final point is the same, and in both cases the initial velocity was zero. These two balls also experience normal forces in addition to the gravitational force. But the normal forces do no work, because the forces are by definition perpendicular to the contact surface, and the motion is parallel to the surface; therefore the scalar product of the normal force and the displacement is zero. Thus our energy conservation considerations (see equation (6.28) in Solved Problem 6.1) then tell us that the speed of both balls on the bottom end of the ramps has to be the same,

$$v = \sqrt{2g(y_0 - y)} \tag{6.29}$$

This is a special case of the result of equation (6.28) with $v_0 = 0$. Note that, depending on the shape of the bottom surface, this result could be rather difficult to obtain using Newton's Second Law.

Figure 6.7: Race of two balls down inclines of different shape

However, even though the velocities at the top and at the bottom of the ramps are the same for both balls, one cannot conclude from this result that both balls arrive at the bottom at the same time. The image sequence clearly shows that this is not the case.

Self-Test Opportunity: Why does the lighter ball arrive at the bottom before the darker ball?

6.5. Work and Energy for the Spring Force

We have already calculated the potential energy stored in a spring; it is

$$U_s = \tfrac{1}{2}kx^2, \tag{6.30}$$

where k is the spring constant and x is the displacement from the equilibrium position. Using the principle of energy conservation, we can calculate the velocity as a function of the position. First, we can write in general for the total mechanical energy:

$$E = K + U_s = \tfrac{1}{2}mv^2 + \tfrac{1}{2}kx^2 \tag{6.31}$$

Once we know the total mechanical energy, we can solve this equation for the velocity. What is the total mechanical energy? We call the point of maximum elongation from equilibrium the amplitude, or A. When the displacement reaches the amplitude the velocity is zero. So we find for the total mechanical energy contained in an object oscillating on a spring

$$E = \tfrac{1}{2}kA^2 \tag{6.32}$$

Conservation of total mechanical energy then means that this is the value of the energy for any point in the oscillation. Inserting the value for the total energy into the previous equation then yields

$$\tfrac{1}{2}kA^2 = \tfrac{1}{2}mv^2 + \tfrac{1}{2}kx^2 \tag{6.33}$$

Then we can get an expression for the speed as a function of the position:

$$v = \sqrt{(A^2 - x^2)\frac{k}{m}} \ . \tag{6.34}$$

Please note that we did not rely on kinematics to get the solution as this approach is rather challenging – another piece of evidence that the techniques of using conservation laws (in this case energy conservation) can yield powerful results. We will return to solving the equation of motion for the problem of a mass on a spring in detail in chapter 14 on oscillations.

Solved Problem

Solved Problem 6.2: Human Cannonball

A favorite circus act is the "human cannonball", in which a person is shot from a long barrel, usually with a lot of smoke and a loud bang added for theatrical effect. Before the Italian Zacchini brothers invented the compressed air cannon to shoot human cannonballs in the 1920s, the Englishman George Farini used a spring-loaded cannon to do the same in the 1870s.

Suppose we want to recreate the spring-loaded human cannonball act with a spring inside of a barrel. Suppose the barrel is 4.00 m long, with a spring that extends the entire length of the barrel. Further, let's point the barrel vertically towards the ceiling of our auditorium. The human cannonball has been lowered into the barrel and is compressing the spring to some degree. An external force is added to compress the spring even further to a length of only 0.70 m. At a height of 7.50 m above the top of the barrel is a bar that our human cannonball of height 1.75 m and mass 68.4 kg is supposed to grab onto at the top of his trajectory. Removing the external force releases the spring and fires the human cannonball upwards.

Question 1:

What is the value of the spring constant needed to accomplish this stunt?

Answer 1:

THINK:

Energy conservation techniques can be applied to this problem. We can store potential energy in the spring and convert that potential energy to gravitational potential energy. As a reference point for all of our calculations we select the top of the barrel and place the origin of our coordinate system there. To accomplish our task we need to provide enough energy through compressing the spring that the top of the head of our human cannonball gets elevated to a height of 7.50 m above the zero-point we have chosen. Since the person has a height of 1.75 m, his feet only need to be elevated by $h = 7.50 \text{ m} - 1.75 \text{ m} = 5.75 \text{ m}$. This way we can specify all position values for the human cannonball on the y-coordinate as the position of the bottom of the feet.

SKETCH: To make this problem more transparent, let's consider energy conservation at different instances. On the left side of Figure 6.8 we show the initial equilibrium position of the spring (a). Then the external force $\vec{F}$ and the weight of the human cannonball compress the spring by 3.30 m (b) to a length of 0.70 m. When the spring is released, the cannonball gets accelerated and has a velocity $\vec{v}_c$ as he passes the spring's equilibrium position (c). From this position up he has to rise by 5.75 m and arrive at the top (e) with zero velocity.

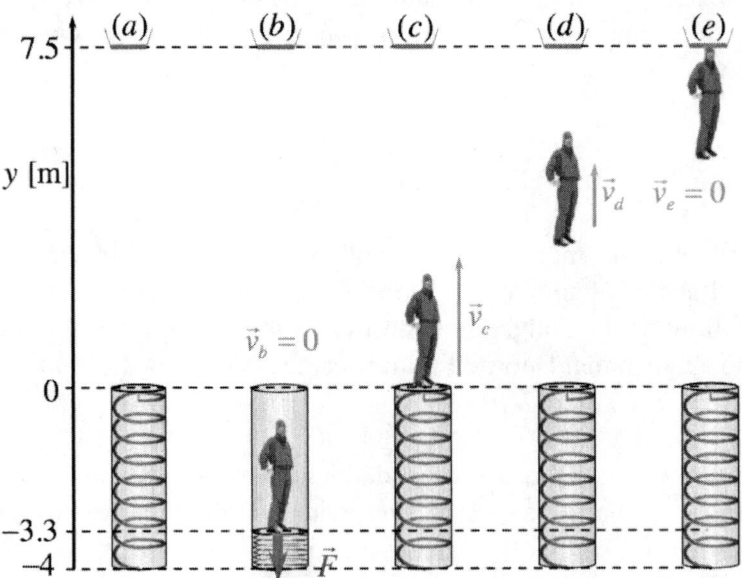

Figure 6.8: Illustration for the human cannonball stunt at five different instances.

RESEARCH: We are free to choose the zero point for the gravitational potential energy arbitrarily. So we elect to set the gravitational potential to zero at the equilibrium position of the spring without a load, as shown in the left panel (a) of Figure 6.8.

Solved Problem

At point (b) we have zero kinetic energy, and potential energies from spring and gravity. Therefore the total energy at this point is

$$E = \tfrac{1}{2}ky_b^2 + mgy_b\,. \tag{6.35}$$

At point (c) we only have kinetic energy and zero potential energy

$$E = \tfrac{1}{2}mv_c^2\,. \tag{6.36}$$

Right after crossing point (c) the human cannonball leaves the spring, then flies through the air as shown in panel (d), and finally reaches the top as shown in (e). At the top he will have only gravitational potential energy and no kinetic energy (since the spring is to be designed to allow the man to reach the top with no residual speed):

$$E = mgy_e\,. \tag{6.37}$$

SIMPLIFY: Energy conservation requires that the total energy remains the same. Setting the first and third expression equal, we obtain

$$\tfrac{1}{2}ky_b^2 + mgy_b = mgy_e \tag{6.38}$$

which we can rearrange to obtain the spring constant

$$k = 2mg\frac{y_e - y_b}{y_b^2}\,. \tag{6.39}$$

CALCULATE: According to the problem posed and the origin of our coordinate system selected, $y_b = -3.30$ m, $y_e = 5.75$ m. So we find for the spring constant needed:

$$k = 2(68.4 \text{ kg})(9.81 \text{ m/s}^2)\frac{5.75 \text{ m} - (-3.30 \text{ m})}{(3.30 \text{ m})^2} = 1115.26 \text{ N/m}\,.$$

ROUND: All of the numerical values are specified to three significant digits so our final answer is

$$k = 1.12 \cdot 10^3 \text{ N/m}\,.$$

DOUBLE-CHECK: When the spring is compressed initially, the potential energy stored in the spring is

$$U = \frac{1}{2}ky_b^2 = \frac{1}{2}\left(1.12 \cdot 10^3 \text{ N/m}\right)\left(3.30 \text{ m}\right)^2 = 6.07 \text{ kJ}\,.$$

Solved Problem

Solved Problem

The gravitational potential energy gained by the human cannonball is

$$U = mg\Delta y = (68.4 \text{ kg})(9.81 \text{ m/s}^2)(9.05 \text{ m}) = 6.07 \text{ kJ}$$

which is the same as the energy stored in the spring initially, so our calculated spring constant makes sense.

Note that the mass of the human cannonball enters this answer. Therefore the same cannon will shoot different people to different heights.

Question 2:
What is the speed that the human cannonball reaches as he passes the equilibrium position of the spring?

Answer 2:
We have already determined that our choice of origin implies that at this point the human cannon ball has only kinetic energy. Setting this kinetic energy equal to the potential energy reached a the top, we find

$$\tfrac{1}{2}mv_c^2 = mgy_e \Rightarrow$$
$$v_c = \sqrt{2gy_e} = \sqrt{2(9.81 \text{ m/s}^2)(5.75 \text{ m})} = 10.6 \text{ m/s}$$

This speed corresponds to a respectable 23.7 miles/hour.

In-class exercise:
What is the maximum acceleration that the human cannonball experiences?
a) 1.00g *b)* 2.14g *c)* 3.25g *c)* 4.48g *d)* 7.30g

In-class exercise: A ball with mass m is thrown vertically into the air with an initial speed v. Which of the following equations correctly describes the maximum height h of the ball?

a) $h = \sqrt{\dfrac{v}{2g}}$

b) $h = \dfrac{g}{\frac{1}{2}v^2}$

c) $h = 2mv/g$

d) $h = \dfrac{mv^2}{g}$

e) $h = \dfrac{v^2}{2g}$

Self-Test Opportunity:
Can you produce a drawing of the potential and kinetic energies as a function of the y-coordinate? For what value of the displacement is the speed of the human cannonball at maximum? (Hint: this occurs not exactly at $y=0$, but at a value of $y<0$.)

6.5.1 Potential Energy of a Mass hanging from a Spring

We have just seen that the potential energy of the human cannonball has contributions form the spring force and from the gravitational force. In Example 5.4 in the previous chapter we had worked out that hanging a mass m from a spring with spring constant k shifts the equilibrium position from 0 to y_0, which is given by the equilibrium condition (see Figure 6.9):

$$ky_0 = -mg \Rightarrow y_0 = -\frac{mg}{k} \tag{6.40}$$

with $g = 9.81\ \text{m/s}^2$, as usual.

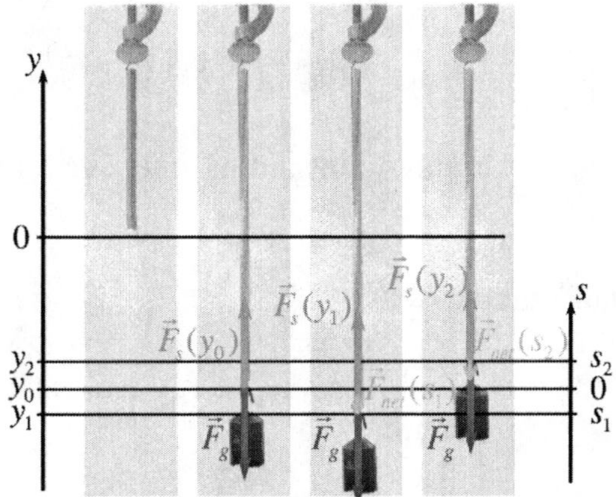

Figure 6.9: Forces acting on a mass hanging from a spring. The left coordinate axis (y-axis) has its origin at the equilibrium position of the spring without the mass hanging from it. The right coordinate axis has its origin at the equilibrium position of the spring with the mass hanging from it.

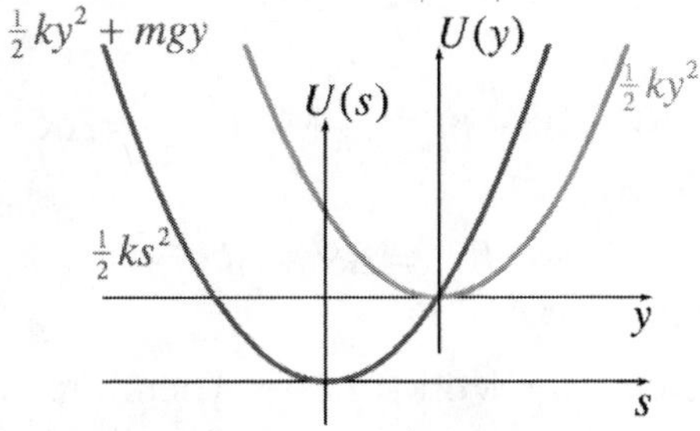

Figure 6.10: Potential energy functions for the two choices of vertical coordinate axes used in Figure 6.9

In Figure 6.9 we show the forces that act on the mass suspended from the spring in different positions. In this figure we use two different choices for the origin of the vertical coordinate axis. On the left side we show the vertical coordinate with choice of zero at the equilibrium position of the spring without the mass hanging from it. For this axis we use the letter y, and the new equilibrium point y_0 with the mass suspended from the spring is calculated according to (6.40). On the right side we chose this new equilibrium point as the origin of the axis and call the vertical coordinate s. In Figure 6.10 we show the potential energy functions for the choice of these two coordinate axes. The potential energy curves are parabolas in both case, which are only offset from each other by a simple constant.

6.6. Non-Conservative Forces and the Work-Energy Theorem

Is energy conservation violated in the presence of non-conservative forces? The name seems to imply that it is. And indeed, the total *mechanical* energy is not conserved. Where does the energy go then? The answer is that some or all of the work done by a non-conservative force is transformed into heat. Heat, as we will learn in chapter 18, is yet another form of energy, thermal energy. If we add this type of energy to our total mechanical energy, then we obtain the total energy,

$$E_{\text{total}} = E_{\text{mechanical}} + E_{\text{thermal}} = K + U + E_{\text{thermal}} \tag{6.41}$$

This total energy is conserved, i.e. stays constant in time, even for non-conservative forces.

This is an important point to stress:

> The total energy, the sum of all forms of energy – mechanical or other, is always conserved in an isolated system.

Since we do not know yet what thermal energy is and how to calculate it, it may seem that we cannot use any energy considerations when at least one of the forces acting is a non-conservative one. However, this is not the case. Consider the equation (5.21), $W = \Delta K$, where W represents the work done by all forces, W_c due to conservative forces and W_{nc} due to non-conservative external forces. Since we can represent the work done by conservative forces as $W_c = -\Delta U$, we have

$$W = W_c + W_{nc} = -\Delta U + W_{nc} = \Delta K$$

or

$$W_{nc} = \Delta K + \Delta U \tag{6.42}$$

This relationship, which we call the Work-Energy Theorem, is the most important result of this chapter. In the absence of non-conservative forces $W_{nc} = 0$, and equation (6.42) becomes the Conservation of Mechanical Energy, equation(6.22). In applying either of these two equations it is important to realize that one must select two times, a beginning and an end, in applying them. Usually this choice is obvious, but sometimes care must be taken as demonstrated when we use the Work-Energy Theorem in the following Solved Problem.

Solved Problem 6.3: Block Pushed off a Table

Consider a block on a table as in Figure 6.11. This block is pushed by the spring attached to the wall, slides across the table, and then falls to the ground. The block has a mass of $m = 1.35$ kg. The spring constant is $k = 560$ N/m, and the spring has been compressed by 0.11 m. The block slides a distance of $d = 0.65$ m across the table of height $h = 0.75$ m. The coefficient of friction between the block and the table is $\mu_k = 0.16$.

Question:
With what speed will the block land on the floor?

Answer:

THINK: At first look, this problem does not yield to our techniques of mechanical energy conservation, because the non-conservative force of friction is in play. However, here we can utilize the Work-Energy Theorem. To be certain that the block would actually leave the table, we first calculate the total energy imparted to the mass by the spring and make sure that the potential energy stored in the compressed spring is sufficient to overcome friction.

SKETCH: In Figure 6.11 a block with mass m is pushed by a spring. The mass slides on a table with friction a distance d and then falls to the floor, which is a distance h below the table.

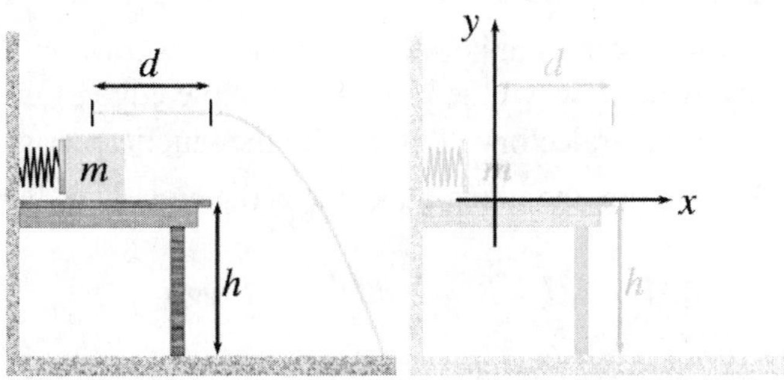

Figure 6.11: Block of mass m pushed off a table by a spring.
(On the right side the same sketch is shown with the coordinate system overlaid.)

Please note that we fix the origin of our coordinate system so that our block starts at $x = y = 0$. The origin of the coordinate system can be chosen at any point, but it is important to fix an origin, because all potential energies have to be expressed relative to some reference point.

Solved Problem

Solved Problem

RESEARCH:
Step 1: Same problem, but without friction force.
In this case, the block initially has potential energies from the spring and no kinetic energy, since it is at rest. Finally, when it hits the floor, it has kinetic energy and negative potential energy from gravity. Conservation of mechanical energy results in:

$$\begin{gathered} K_0 + U_0 = K + U \Rightarrow \\ 0 + \tfrac{1}{2}kx_0^{\ 2} + = \tfrac{1}{2}mv^2 - mgh + 0 \end{gathered} \qquad (6.43)$$

Usually, we would just solve this for the speed and put in the numbers later. However, since we will need this again, let us calculate the two contributions to the potential energy separately:

$$\tfrac{1}{2}kx_0^{\ 2} = 0.5 \cdot (560 \text{ N/m}) \cdot (0.11 \text{ m})^2 = 3.39 \text{ J}$$
$$mgh = (1.35 \text{ kg}) \cdot (9.81 \text{ m/s}^2) \cdot (0.75 \text{ m}) = 9.93 \text{ J}$$

Solving this for the speed results in

$$\begin{aligned} v &= \sqrt{\frac{2}{m}(\tfrac{1}{2}kx_0^{\ 2} + mgh)} \\ &= \sqrt{\frac{2}{1.35 \text{ kg}}(3.39 \text{ J} + 9.93 \text{ J})} \\ &= 4.44 \text{ m/s} \end{aligned}$$

Step 2: The same problem, but with friction
Our considerations remain almost unchanged, except that we now have to include the work done by the non-conservative force of friction, $W_f = -\mu_k mgd$. In applying the Work-Energy Theorem we choose the initial time to be that shown in Figure 6.11, while the final time will correspond to when the block reaches the edge of the table and is ready for the free-fall portion of the trajectory. Let K_{top} be the kinetic energy at the final time, a time we chose to make sure that the block makes it to the end of the table. Using equation (6.42) we find:

$$W_{nc} = \Delta K + \Delta U = K_{top} - \tfrac{1}{2}kx_0^{\ 2} = -\mu_k mgd$$
$$\begin{aligned} K_{top} &= \tfrac{1}{2}kx_0^{\ 2} - \mu_k mgd \\ &= 3.39 \text{ J} - 0.16 \cdot (1.35 \text{ kg}) \cdot (9.81 \text{ m/s}^2)(0.65 \text{ m}) \\ &= 3.39 \text{ J} - 1.38 \text{ J} = 2.01 \text{ J} \end{aligned}$$

Since the kinetic energy $K_{top} > 0$, the block can overcome friction and slide off the table. So now we can calculate our final answer.

SIMPLIFY: Now we will start the problem at the table's edge to exploit the

Solved Problem

calculations that we have already done. The end is when the block hits the floor. (If we had chosen the beginning to be that shown in in Figure 6.11 our result would be the same.)

$$W_{nc} = \Delta K + \Delta U = 0$$

$$\frac{1}{2}mv^2 - K_{top} + 0 - mgh = 0, or \qquad (6.44)$$

$$v = \sqrt{\frac{2}{m}(K_{top} + mgh)}$$

Calculate:

Putting in our numerical values gives us

$$v = \sqrt{\frac{2}{1.35 \text{ kg}}(2.01 \text{ J} + 9.93 \text{ J})} = 4.20757694 \text{ m/s}$$

Round:

All of the numerical values were specified to three significant digits so we have

$$v = 4.21 \text{ m/s}.$$

Double-Check:

As you can see, the main contribution to the speed of the block at impact originates from the free-fall portion in this case. Why did we go through the intermediate step of figuring out the value of K_{top} first, instead of simply using the formula $v = \sqrt{2(\frac{1}{2}kx_0^{\,2} - \mu_k mgd + mgh)/m}$ that we would get from equation (6.42)? The final number is certainly the same. However, we needed to calculate K_{top} first, to ensure that it is positive, meaning that the energy imparted on the block by the spring is sufficient to exceed the work needed to be done against the friction force. If K_{top} would have turned out negative, then the block would have simply stopped on the table. For example, if we had the exact same problem but with $\mu_k = 0.50$, then inserting all of our numbers into this formula would have resulted in an answer of 3.65 m/s, whereas the real answer in this case would have been that the block comes to rest on the table.

As this example shows, energy considerations are still a powerful tool to perform otherwise very difficult calculations and obtain answers in quite simple ways, even in the presence of non-conservative forces. However, the principle of conservation of mechanical energy cannot be applied quite as straightforwardly any more, and one has to account for the work done by these non-conservative forces.

In-class exercise: A curling stone with mass 19.96 kg is given an initial velocity of 2.46 m/s. The stone slides on the ice with a coefficient of kinetic friction of 0.0109. How far does the stone slide before it stops?
a) 18.7 m
b) 28.3 m
c) 34.1 m
d) 39.2 m
e) 44.5 m

6.7. General Considerations

We return to the question of the relationship between force and potential energy. Perhaps it may help you gain physical insight if you visualize the potential energy curve as the track of a roller coaster. This analogy is not a perfect one, because the roller coaster moves in a two-dimensional plane, not in one dimension. In addition, there is some small amount of friction between the cars and the track. But still, the motion of the roller coaster car can be described by the potential energy curves of the kind shown here.

Figure 6.12: Total, potential and kinetic energy for a roller coaster.

Shown in Figure 6.12 are the potential energy (yellow line following the outline of the track), the total energy (horizontal orange line), and the kinetic energy (difference between these two, the red line) for a segment of a roller coaster ride. You can see that at the top of the hump the kinetic energy has a minimum and therefore the speed of the cars is smallest, whereas the speed increase as the cars roll down the incline. All of these effects are a consequence of the conservation of total mechanical energy.

In Figure 6.13 we show an example for a potential energy function, upper panel, and the corresponding force, lower panel. Since the potential energy is only determined up to an additive constant, we have elected to define the zero-value of the potential energy at the lowest value. But for all physical considerations, this is irrelevant. On the other hand, the zero value for the force cannot be chosen arbitrarily.

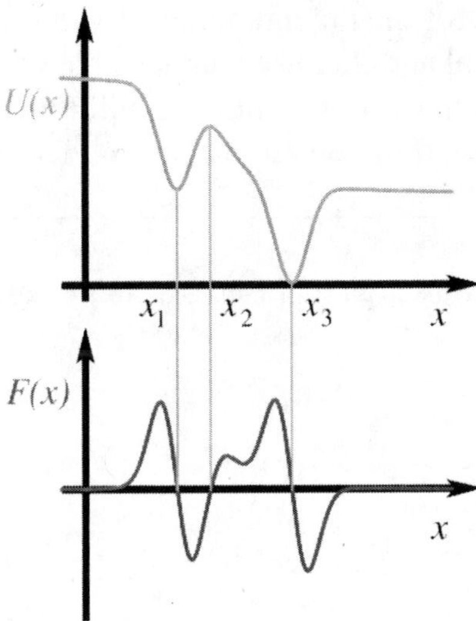

Figure 6.13: Upper drawing: potential energy as a function of the coordinate. Lower drawing: Force, as a function of position, corresponding to this potential energy function.

Equilibrium Points

We have marked three special points on the coordinate axis of Figure 6.13 by thin vertical gray lines. These are the points on the x-axis where the force has a value of 0. Since the force is the derivative of the potential energy with respect to the coordinate, it means that the potential energy has an extremum, maximum or minimum at this point. You can clearly see that the points x_1 and x_3 represent mimima, and x_2 is a maximum. At all three points an object would not experience an acceleration, because of the fact that it is located at an extremum. Since there is no acceleration, these points are then equilibrium points.

There are two different kinds of equilibrium points. x_1 and x_3 represent stable equilibrium points, and x_2 is an unstable equilibrium point. What distinguishes stable and unstable equilibrium points is the response to small perturbations.

> For **stable equilibrium points**, small perturbations result in small oscillations around the equilibrium, while for **unstable equilibrium points**, small perturbations result in an accelerating movement away from that equilibrium point.

The roller coaster analogy may help: If you would find yourself sitting in a roller coaster car at point x_1 or x_3 and someone gives you a push, you will just rock back and forth on the track, because you are sitting at the bottom of the well. However, if you get the same small push while you are sitting at x_2, then it will result in your car rolling down the hill.

What makes an equilibrium point stable or unstable from a mathematical standpoint is the value of the second derivative of the potential, the curvature. Negative curvature means a local maximum in the potential and therefore an unstable equilibrium point; and positive curvature indicates a stable equilibrium point. We will return to the discussion of equilibrium conditions in much more detail in chapter 11.

In-class exercise:
Which of the following four drawings represents a stable equilibrium for this ball on its supporting surface?

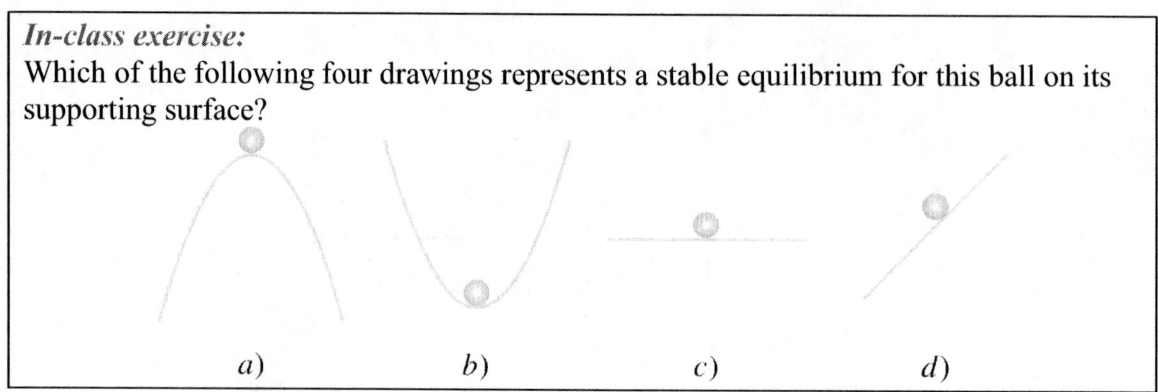

Turning Points

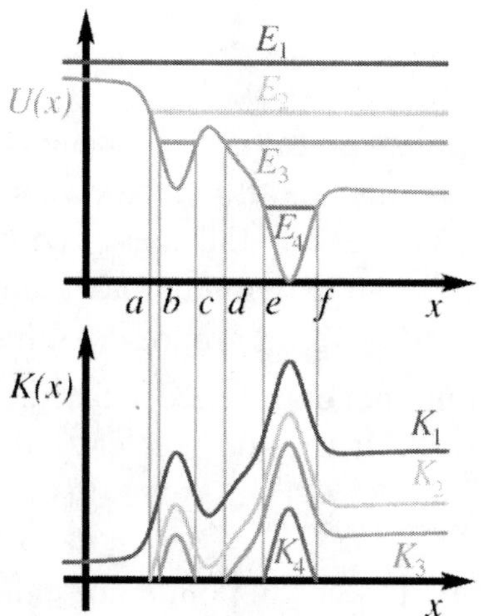

Figure 6.14: Upper drawing: same potential energy function as in the previous figure. Shown are four different values of the total energy. In the lower drawing, the corresponding kinetic energy functions for these four energies and the potential energy function in the upper drawing are shown. The gray vertical lines mark the turning points.

Figure 6.14 shows the same potential energy curve as Figure 6.13. But now we have included horizontal lines for four different values of the total mechanical energy (E_1 through E_4) in the drawing. For each value of the total energy, and for each point on the potential energy curve, we can then calculate the value of the kinetic energy by simple subtraction. Let us first consider the largest value of the total mechanical energy shown, E_1 (blue horizontal line):

$$K_1(x) = E_1 - U(x). \tag{6.45}$$

The resulting dependence of the kinetic energy $K_1(x)$ is shown in the lower part of the drawing by the line of the corresponding color. It is clearly just an upside-down version of the potential energy curve in the upper drawing. However, its absolute height is not arbitrary, it is a result of the above subtraction. We are, as already mentioned, always able to add an arbitrary additive constant to the potential energy, but then we are forced to add the same additive constant to the total mechanical energy so that their difference, the kinetic energy, remains unchanged.

For the other values of the total mechanical energy that we selected, there is an additional complication: we always have the condition that the kinetic energy has to be larger or equal to 0. This means that the kinetic energy is not defined in a region where the above subtraction turns out to be negative. For total mechanical energy E_2, the kinetic energy is only greater than 0 for $x \geq a$. This is indicated in the lower panel of Figure 6.14 by the green line. Thus an object moving with total energy E_2 from right to left in our diagram will reach the point $x = a$ and have zero velocity there. Comparing to the previous figure, you see that the force is positive, pushing the object to the right, i.e. making it turn around. This is why such a point is called a "turning point". On its move to the right, this object will pick up kinetic energy and follow the exact same kinetic energy curve from left to right, making its trajectory reversible. This is a consequence of the conservation of total mechanical energy.

Turning points are the points where the kinetic energy is zero, and where there is a net force moving the particle away from that point.

The object with total energy E_4 has two turning points in its trajectory, $x = e$, $x = f$. It can only move between these two points. This object is trapped in this interval and cannot escape. Perhaps the roller coaster analogy is again helpful: A car released from point $x = e$ will move through the valley to the right until it reaches the point $x = f$, where it will turn around and move back to $x = e$, never having enough total mechanical energy to escape the valley.

Perhaps the most interesting situation is found for energy E_3. If an object moves in from the right with energy E_3, then it will get reflected at the turning point marked with the letter d, in complete analogy to the situation we discussed for the object with energy E_2. However, there is another allowed region further to the left, in the interval $b \leq x \leq c$. If the object starts out in this interval, it remains just as trapped as the particle with energy E_4 in its valley. Between the allowed regions $b \leq x \leq c$ and $x \geq d$, there is a "forbidden region" that a particle with total mechanical energy E_3 cannot cross.

Preview: Atomic Physics

In atomic physics we will again encounter potential energy curves. We will learn that particles with energies like E_4 in Figure 6.14 that are trapped between two turning points are said to be in "bound states". One of the most interesting phenomena in atomic and nuclear physics, however, occurs in situations like the one shown for total mechanical energy E_3. From our considerations of classical mechanics, we would expect that a particle sitting in a bound state between $b \le x \le c$ could not escape. However, in atomic and nuclear physics applications the particle in this bound state has actually a small probability to leak out of this potential trap and escape through the classically forbidden region into the region $x \ge d$. This process is called **tunneling**. Depending on the height and width of the barrier, the tunneling probability can be quite large, leading to a fast escape, or quite small, leading to a very slow escape. For example, the isotope ^{235}U of the element Uranium, relevant for nuclear fission power plants and naturally occurring on Earth, has a mean lifetime of over 700 million years before an alpha particle (a tightly bound cluster of two neutrons and two protons in the nucleus) tunnels through its potential barrier, and thus causes the uranium nucleus to decay.

The previous paragraph was put in basically just to whet your appetite for things to come. In order to understand the processes of atomic and nuclear physics, we will have to introduce a few more concepts. However, the basic considerations of energy introduced here will remain virtually unchanged.

What we have learned/Exam Study Guide:

- Potential energy, U, is the energy stored in the configuration of a system of objects that exert forces on each other.
- Gravitational potential energy can then be defined in as $U_g = mgy$.
- The potential energy associated with elongating a spring from its equilibrium position at $x = 0$ is: $U_s(x) = \tfrac{1}{2}kx^2$
- A conservative force is a force for which the work done over any closed path is zero. A force that does not fulfill this requirement is called a non-conservative force.
- For any conservative force, the change in potential energy due to some spatial rearrangement of a system is equal to the negative of the work done by the conservative force during this spatial rearrangement.
- The relationship between a potential energy and the corresponding conservative force is $\Delta U = U(\vec{r}) - U(\vec{r}_0) = -\int_{\vec{r}_0}^{\vec{r}} \vec{F}(\vec{r}\,')\bullet d\vec{r}\,'$.
- We obtain the force component from the potential in one-dimensional problems as $F_x(x) = -\dfrac{dU(x)}{dx}$.
- We define the mechanical energy, E, as the sum of kinetic energy and potential energy: $E = K + U$
- The total mechanical energy is conserved for any mechanical process inside an

isolated system that involves only conservative forces, or $\Delta E = \Delta K + \Delta U = 0$

- An alternative way of writing mechanical energy conservation is: $K + U = K_0 + U_0$
- The total energy, the sum of all forms of energy – mechanical or other – is always conserved in an isolated system. This holds for conservative as well as non-conservative forces: $E_{\text{total}} = E_{\text{mechanical}} + E_{\text{thermal}} = K + U + E_{\text{thermal}}$=constant.
- Energy problems involving non-conservative forces can be solved using the Work-Energy Theorem $W_{nc} = \Delta K + \Delta U$.
- For stable equilibrium points, small perturbations result in small oscillations around the equilibrium, while for unstable equilibrium points, small perturbations result in an accelerating movement away from that equilibrium point.
- Turning points are points where the kinetic energy is zero, and where a net force acts to move the particle away from that point.

Additional Solved Problems

Solved Problem

Solved Problem 6.4: Trapeze

Question:

A trapeze artist in the circus starts her motion on the trapeze at rest with angle of 45.0 degrees relative to the vertical. Her swing has a length of 5.00 m. What is her speed at the lowest point in her trajectory?

Answer:

THINK: Initially we have only gravitational potential energy. Since we have arranged for $y = 0$ to be at her low point, the potential energy is zero at the lowest point of the arc. When the trapeze artist is at the lowest point, her kinetic energy will be a maximum. We can then equate the initial gravitational potential energy to the final kinetic energy of the trapeze artist.

SKETCH: We represent the trapeze artist in Figure 6.15 as a mass suspended by a rope of length ℓ.

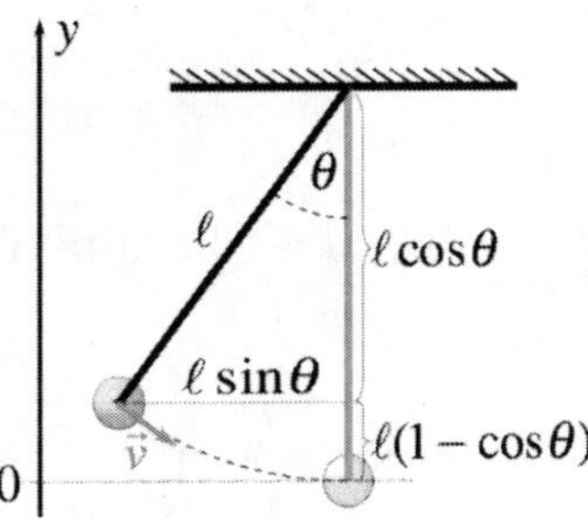

Figure 6.15: Trapeze.

The mass is pulled back to an angle θ relative to the vertical.

RESEARCH: According to the drawing in Figure 6.15, the potential energy at maximum deflection θ_0 is:

$$E = K + U = 0 + U = mg\ell(1-\cos\theta_0). \tag{6.46}$$

This result is also the value for the total mechanical energy, because we have zero kinetic energy at the point of maximum deflection. For any other deflection, the energy is the sum of kinetic and potential energy:

$$E = mg\ell(1-\cos\theta) + \tfrac{1}{2}mv^2. \tag{6.47}$$

SIMPLIFY: Solving this expression for the speed, we obtain:

$$\begin{aligned} mg\ell(1-\cos\theta_0) &= mg\ell(1-\cos\theta) + \tfrac{1}{2}mv^2 \Rightarrow \\ mg\ell(\cos\theta - \cos\theta_0) &= \tfrac{1}{2}mv^2 \Rightarrow \\ |v| &= \sqrt{2g\ell(\cos\theta - \cos\theta_0)}. \end{aligned} \tag{6.48}$$

CALCULATE: Per our initial condition, $\theta_0 = 45°$. We are interested in $v(\theta = 0)$. Inserting the numbers, we find:

$$v(0°) = \sqrt{2\cdot(9.81 \text{ m/s}^2)\cdot(5.00 \text{ m})\cdot(\cos 0° - \cos 45°)} = 5.360300809 \text{ m/s}$$

ROUND: All of the numerical values were specified to three significant digits so we report our answer as

$$v(0°) = 5.36 \text{ m/s}.$$

DOUBLE-CHECK: The speed of the trapeze artist at the lowest point is 5.36 m/s or 12.0 miles per hour, which seems reasonably in line with what we see in the circus.

Solved Problem 6.5: Potential Energy of a Cannonball

Question:
A cannonball of mass 4.00 kg is shot from a cannon an angle of 35.0° with respect to the horizontal. The initial speed of the cannonball is 55.0 m/s. When the cannonball reaches the highest point of its trajectory, what is the gain in potential energy of the

cannonball at this point relative to the point from which it was shot?

Answer:

THINK: Once the cannonball leaves the cannon, the only force acting on the cannonball is gravity, and the cannonball undergoes projectile motion. We define the potential energy of the cannonball to be zero at ground level. When the cannonball reaches the highest point of its trajectory, the gain in gravitational potential energy will be equal to the loss of kinetic energy because the total mechanical energy of the cannonball is conserved. The loss of kinetic energy can be easily related to the component of the velocity of the cannonball in the y-direction.

SKETCH: The trajectory of the cannonball is shown in Figure 6.16.

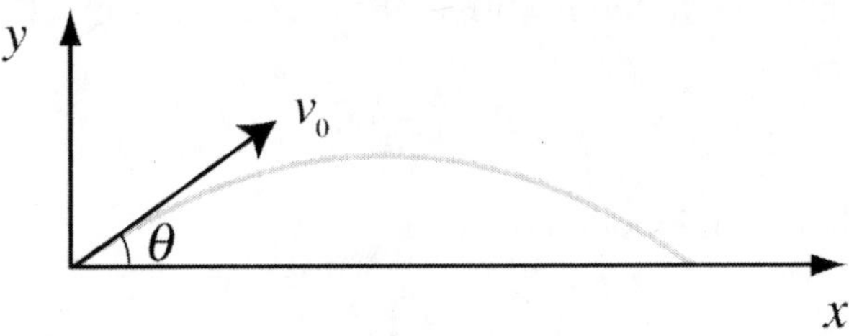

Figure 6.16: Parabolic trajectory of the cannonball.

The initial speed of the cannonball is v_0. The angle with respect to the horizontal is θ. We can resolve the x-component and y-component of the initial velocity as shown in Figure 6.17.

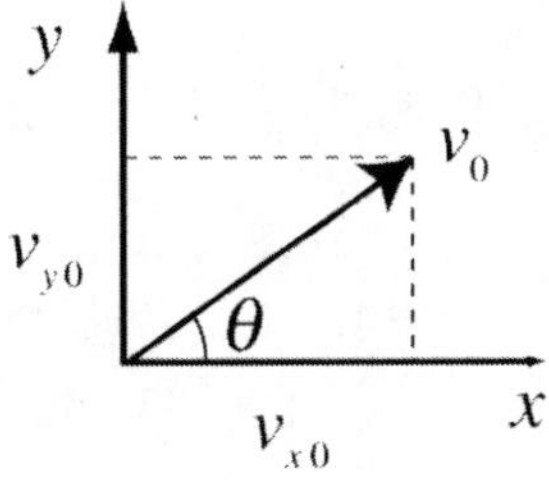

Figure 6.17: Components of the initial velocity vector.

The components of the initial velocity vector are

$$\begin{aligned} v_{x0} &= v_0 \cos\theta \\ v_{y0} &= v_0 \sin\theta \end{aligned} . \tag{6.49}$$

The velocity vector at the maximum height with be in the x-direction and will have the magnitude v_{x0} as shown in Figure 6.18.

Solved Problem

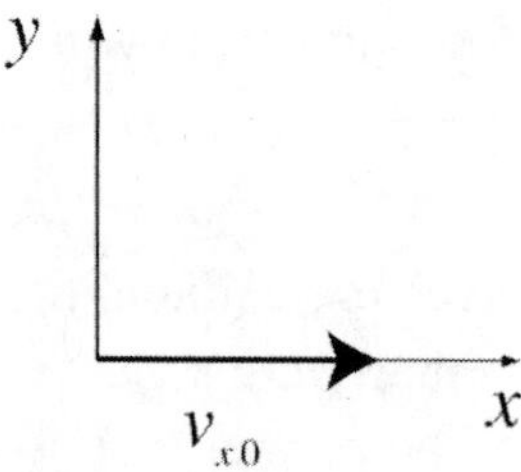

Figure 6.18: Velocity vector of the cannonball at maximum height.

At the maximum height, the speed of the cannonball is given by $v = v_{x0} = v_0 \cos\theta$.

RESEARCH: The conservation of mechanical energy tells us that the change in potential energy ΔU is equal to the negative of the change in kinetic energy ΔK

$$\Delta U = -\Delta K . \qquad (6.50)$$

We can express the change in kinetic energy as

$$\Delta K = K_f - K_i = \frac{1}{2}mv_{x0}^2 - \frac{1}{2}mv_0^2 \qquad (6.51)$$

where K_i is the initial kinetic energy and K_f is the final kinetic energy. Here we refer to the shooting of the cannonball as the initial state and the point in the trajectory where the cannonball is at its highest as the final state.

SIMPLIFY: We can combine (6.50) and (6.51) to get

$$\Delta U = -\Delta K = -\left(\frac{1}{2}mv_{x0}^2 - \frac{1}{2}mv_0^2\right) = \frac{1}{2}mv_0^2 - \frac{1}{2}mv_{x0}^2 = \frac{1}{2}m\left(v_0^2 - v_{x0}^2\right). \qquad (6.52)$$

The magnitude of the initial velocity vector can be written as

$$v_0 = \sqrt{v_{x0}^2 + v_{y0}^2} \Rightarrow v_0^2 = v_{x0}^2 + v_{y0}^2 . \qquad (6.53)$$

Substituting (6.53) into (6.52) gives us

$$\Delta U = \frac{1}{2}m\left(v_0^2 - v_{x0}^2\right) = \frac{1}{2}m\left((v_{x0}^2 + v_{y0}^2) - v_{x0}^2\right) = \frac{1}{2}mv_{y0}^2 . \qquad (6.54)$$

Remembering that $v_{y0} = v_0 \sin\theta$ we can write

Solved Problem

$$\Delta U = \frac{1}{2}mv_{y0}^2 = \frac{1}{2}m\left(v_0 \sin\theta\right)^2 = \frac{1}{2}mv_0^2 \sin^2\theta \quad (6.55)$$

CALCULATE: Putting in the numerical values for this problem we get

$$\Delta U = \frac{1}{2}(4.00 \text{ kg})(55.0 \text{ m/s})^2 (\sin 35.0°)^2 = 1990.389066 \text{ J}.$$

ROUND: All of the numerical values in this problem are specified to three significant figures, so we report our answer as

$$\Delta U = 1.99 \text{ kJ}.$$

DOUBLE-CHECK: We can double-check our answer by referring back to Chapter 3. For projectile motion, the maximum height H reached by a body in projectile motion can be expressed as

$$H = \frac{v_0^2}{2g}\sin^2\theta \quad (6.56)$$

where v_0 is the initial speed and θ is the initial angle with respect to the horizontal. The change in potential energy of a body raised a distance H is given by $\Delta U = mgH$. Using (6.56) we can write

$$\Delta U = mgH = mg\left(\frac{v_0^2}{2g}\sin^2\theta\right) = \frac{1}{2}mv_0^2\sin^2\theta \quad (6.57)$$

which is the expression (6.55). Our answer is thus reasonable because we got the same answer using a previously derived kinematical technique compared to the result we derived using energy conservation concepts.

Solved Problem

Solved Problem 6.6: Mass on a Spring

Question:
A mass of 0.450 kg connected to spring with spring constant 205 N/m oscillates horizontally with amplitude 55.0 cm. The mass slides on a frictionless surface. What is the speed of the mass at a distance of 25.0 cm from the equilibrium position?

Answer:

THINK: For a mass connected to a spring, mechanical energy is conserved, which means that the sum of the kinetic energy and potential energy of the mass/spring system

Solved Problem

must remain constant. In addition, we know that the total energy of the mass/spring system can be expressed in terms of the amplitude of the oscillation of the mass. The amplitude of the oscillation is specified so we can get an expression for the total energy. We know the potential energy can be related to the distance of the mass from the equilibrium point. Knowing the total energy and the potential energy at a given position, we can extract the kinetic energy of mass at that point and from the kinetic energy we can calculate the speed of the mass.

SKETCH: The mass connected to a spring is shown in Figure 6.19 sliding on a frictionless surface.

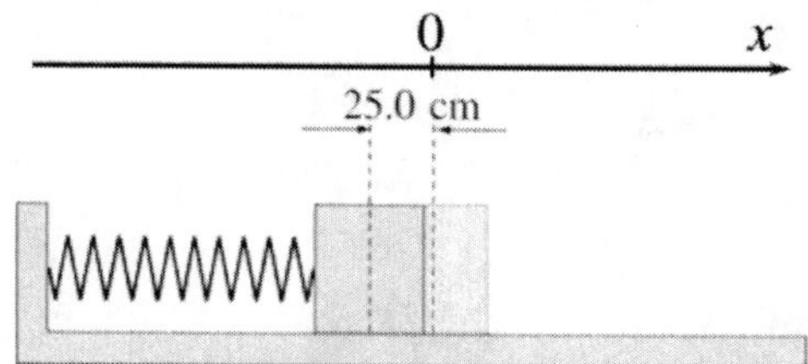

Figure 6.19: Sketch of a mass connected to a spring. The mass is sliding on a frictionless surface.

The mass is 25.0 cm from the equilibrium position at the present time.

RESEARCH: The conservation of mechanical energy tells us that the total mechanical energy E is constant and that the total mechanical energy is the sum of the kinetic energy of the moving mass K_{mass} and the potential energy U_{spring} stored in the spring

$$E = K_{\text{mass}} + U_{\text{spring}} . \tag{6.58}$$

The total energy of a mass oscillating on a spring with spring constant k can be related to the amplitude A of the oscillation using (6.32)

$$E = \frac{1}{2}kA^2 . \tag{6.59}$$

The kinetic energy of the mass is given by

$$K_{\text{mass}} = \frac{1}{2}mv^2 \tag{6.60}$$

where v is the speed of the that we are working to obtain. The potential energy stored in the spring is given by

$$U_{\text{spring}} = \frac{1}{2}kx^2 \tag{6.61}$$

Solved Problem

where x is the distance from the equilibrium position.

SIMPLIFY: We can combine the previous four equations to obtain

$$E = K_{\text{mass}} + U_{\text{spring}} = \frac{1}{2}kA^2 = \frac{1}{2}mv^2 + \frac{1}{2}kx^2 . \tag{6.62}$$

We can rewrite this equation as

$$kA^2 = mv^2 + kx^2 . \tag{6.63}$$

Solving for the speed v at position x we get

$$v = \sqrt{\frac{kA^2 - kx^2}{m}} = \sqrt{\frac{k\left(A^2 - x^2\right)}{m}} . \tag{6.64}$$

CALCULATE: Putting in the numerical values for this problem we get

$$v = \sqrt{\frac{k\left(A^2 - x^2\right)}{m}} = \sqrt{\frac{(205 \text{ N/m})\left((0.550 \text{ m})^2 - (0.250 \text{ m})^2\right)}{0.450 \text{ kg}}} = 10.45625 \text{ m/s} .$$

ROUND: All of the numerical values in this problem are specified to three significant figures, so we report our answer as

$$v = 10.5 \text{ m/s} .$$

DOUBLE-CHECK: We can double-check our answer by comparing our result for the speed of the mass at the position of $x = 25.0$ cm from the equilibrium point to the speed of the mass at the equilibrium point, v_{max}. At the equilibrium point, the potential energy stored in the spring is zero and the total mechanical energy of the mass/spring system will equal the kinetic energy of the mass so we can write

$$E = K_{\text{mass}} = \frac{1}{2}mv_{\text{max}}^2 . \tag{6.65}$$

Solving for the maximum speed we get

$$v_{\text{max}} = \sqrt{\frac{2E}{m}} = \sqrt{\frac{2\left(\frac{1}{2}kA^2\right)}{m}} = \sqrt{\frac{kA^2}{m}} = A\sqrt{\frac{k}{m}} . \tag{6.66}$$

Solved Problem

Putting in our numerical values we obtain

$$v_{\text{max}} = (0.550 \text{ m})\sqrt{\frac{205 \text{ N/m}}{0.450 \text{ kg}}} = 11.7 \text{ m/s}.$$

Thus our answer for speed at $x = 25.0$ cm of $v = 10.5$ m/s makes sense because it is less than the maximum speed $v_{\text{max}} = 11.7$ m/s.

Chapter 7. Momentum and Collisions

Figure 7.1: Collision test of a fighter plane.

What we will learn:

- The momentum of an object is the product of its velocity and mass. It is a vector quantity and points in the same direction as the velocity vector.
- Newton's Second Law can be phrased more generally as: the net force equals the time derivative of the momentum.
- The change of momentum, impulse, is the time integral of the net force that causes the momentum change.
- In all collisions, the total momentum is conserved. The law of the conservation of momentum is the second conservation law that we encounter, after the law of energy conservation.
- Besides momentum conservation, elastic collisions also have the property that the total kinetic energy is conserved.
- In totally inelastic collisions, the maximum amount of kinetic energy is removed, and the colliding objects stick to each other. Total kinetic energy is not conserved, but total momentum is.
- Collisions that are neither elastic nor totally inelastic are partially inelastic, and the change in kinetic energy is proportional to the square of the coefficient of restitution.
- Through the physics of collisions we can make a connection to the current physics frontier of chaos science.

7.1. Linear Momentum

When we introduced the words "force", "position", "velocity", and "acceleration", we found out that their precise physical definitions were actually quite close to their use in our everyday language. With the term "momentum" the situation is more analogous to "energy", another term where one can make a vague connection between conversational use and precise physical meaning.

In politics, one sometimes hears that the campaign of a particular candidate gains momentum, or that legislation gains momentum in Congress. And, of course, sports teams or individual players can gain or lose momentum. What one implies with these statements is that the objects said to gain momentum are now harder to stop. However, Figure 7.1 shows that even objects with a large momentum can be stopped!

Definition

The physics definition of momentum is simply the product of an object's mass and its velocity,

$$\vec{p} = m\vec{v} . \tag{7.1}$$

As you can see, we are using the lowercase letter p as the notation for momentum. The velocity, $\vec{v}$, is a vector; and we multiply this vector by a scalar quantity, the mass m. The product is then a vector as well. The momentum vector, $\vec{p}$, and the velocity vector, $\vec{v}$, are parallel to each other, i.e. they point in the same direction. As a simple consequence of (7.1), the magnitude of the linear momentum is then given by

$$p = mv\,. \tag{7.2}$$

The momentum is also referred to as "linear momentum", to distinguish it from the angular momentum, a concept we will study in chapter 10 on rotation.

Momentum and Force

Let us take the time derivative of the above definition equation (7.1). We obtain

$$\frac{d}{dt}\vec{p} = \frac{d}{dt}(m\vec{v}) = m\frac{d\vec{v}}{dt} + \frac{dm}{dt}\vec{v}\,, \tag{7.3}$$

where we have used the product rule of differentiation. For now, we will assume that the mass of the object does not change, and therefore the second term is zero. Because the time derivative of the velocity is the acceleration, we then get

$$\frac{d}{dt}\vec{p} = m\frac{d\vec{v}}{dt} = m\vec{a} = \vec{F}\,,$$

according to Newton's Second Law. The relationship

$$\vec{F} = \frac{d}{dt}\vec{p} \tag{7.4}$$

is then an equivalent formulation of Newton's Second Law. This form actually is more general than the $\vec{F} = m\vec{a}$ form, because it also holds in the cases where the mass is not constant in time. This distinction will become important when we examine rocket motion in the next chapter. Because this equation is a vector equation, we can also write it in Cartesian components:

$$F_x = \frac{dp_x}{dt}; F_y = \frac{dp_y}{dt}; F_z = \frac{dp_z}{dt}\,. \tag{7.5}$$

Momentum and Kinetic Energy

We have already established a relationship, $K = \frac{1}{2}mv^2$ (equation (5.1)), between kinetic energy K, the speed v, and the mass m. We use $p = mv$ and get

$$K = \frac{mv^2}{2} = \frac{m^2v^2}{2m} = \frac{p^2}{2m}$$

So we have the important relationship between kinetic energy, mass, and momentum:

$$K = \frac{p^2}{2m} \tag{7.6}$$

At this point you may ask yourself why it is useful to re-formulate much of what we have learned about velocity in terms of momentum. This reformulation is far more than an idle game with mathematics. We will see that momentum is conserved in collisions; and this principle will provide an extremely helpful way to find solutions to complicated problems. But first, we need to explore the physics of changing momentum in a little more detail.

> ***In-class exercise:***
> A typical scene from a Saturday afternoon college football game: A linebacker of mass 95 kg runs with a speed of 7.8 m/s, and a wide receiver of mass 74 kg runs with a speed of 9.6 m/s. Let us denote the momentum (magnitude) and kinetic energy of the linebacker by p_l, K_l, respectively, and the momentum (magnitude) and kinetic energy of the wide receiver by p_w, K_w. We then have:
> a) $p_l > p_w$; $K_l > K_w$
> b) $p_l < p_w$; $K_l > K_w$
> c) $p_l > p_w$; $K_l < K_w$
> d) $p_l < p_w$; $K_l < K_w$

7.2. Impulse

The change in momentum is defined as the difference between the final (index f) and initial (index i) momentum:

$$\Delta\vec{p} \equiv \vec{p}_f - \vec{p}_i \,. \tag{7.7}$$

To see why this definition is useful, we have to engage in a few lines of math. Let us start by exploring the relationship between force and momentum just a little further. We can integrate each component of the equation $\vec{F} = d\vec{p}/dt$ over time. For the integral over F_x, for example (compare the upper part of Figure 7.2), we then obtain:

$$\int_{t_i}^{t_f} F_x dt = \int_{t_i}^{t_f} \frac{dp_x}{dt} dt = \int_{p_{x,i}}^{p_{x,f}} dp_x = p_{x,f} - p_{x,i} \equiv \Delta p_x \,. \tag{7.8}$$

This equation requires some explanation. In the second step, we have performed a substitution of variables to transform a time integration into a momentum integration. The upper part of Figure 7.2 illustrates this relationship: the area under the $F_x(t)$ curve is the change in momentum Δp_x. Of course, we obtain similar equations for the y- and z-components. Combining them into one vector equation then yields the following result:

$$\int_{t_i}^{t_f} \vec{F}dt = \int_{t_i}^{t_f} \frac{d\vec{p}}{dt}dt = \int_{\vec{p}_i}^{\vec{p}_f} d\vec{p} = \vec{p}_f - \vec{p}_i \equiv \Delta\vec{p}. \tag{7.9}$$

The time integral of the force has a name. It is called impulse:

$$\vec{J} \equiv \int_{t_i}^{t_f} \vec{F}dt. \tag{7.10}$$

With this definition we now of course immediately have a relationship between the impulse and the momentum change,

$$\vec{J} = \Delta\vec{p}. \tag{7.11}$$

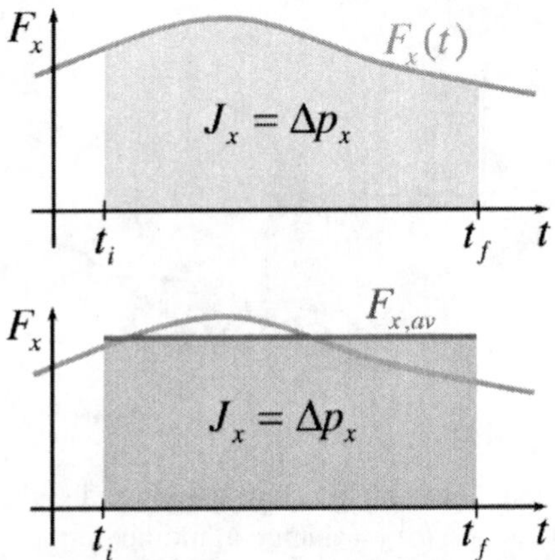

Figure 7.2: Upper part: Impulse = time-integral of the force = yellow area; lower part: same impulse resulting from an average force.

From this equation we can calculate the momentum change over some time interval, if we know the time dependence of the force. If the force is constant or has some form that we can integrate, then we can simply evaluate the integral of equation (7.10). But formally we can define an average force

$$\vec{F}_{av} = \frac{\int_i^f \vec{F}dt}{\int_i^f dt} = \frac{1}{t_f - t_i}\int_i^f \vec{F}dt = \frac{1}{\Delta t}\int_i^f \vec{F}dt \tag{7.12}$$

and then get:

$$\vec{J} = \vec{F}_{av}\Delta t \tag{7.13}$$

You may think that this transformation trivially tells the same information as (7.11). After all, the integration is still there, only hidden in the definition of the average force. This is true, but sometimes one is only interested in the average force. Measuring the time interval Δt over which the force acts as well as the resulting impulse an object receives will then tell us the average force that this object experiences during that time interval. The lower part of Figure 7.2 illustrates the relationship between the time-averaged force, the momentum change, and the impulse.

Example

Example 7.1: Baseball Home Run

(Compare also example 3.2) A major league pitcher throws a fastball that crosses the plate with a speed of 90.0 mph (= 40.23 m/s) and an angle of 5.0 degrees below the horizontal. A batter slugs it for a home run, launching it with a speed of 110.0 mph (= 49.17 m/s) at an angle of 35.0 degrees above the horizontal. The legal mass of a baseball is between 5 and 5.25 ounces. So let's say that the mass of the baseball hit here was 5.10 ounces (= 0.145 kg).

Question 1:
What is the magnitude of the impulse the baseball receives from the bat?

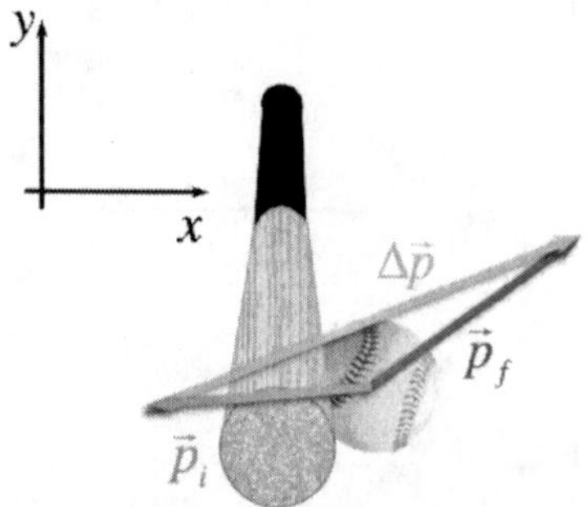

Figure 7.3: Baseball being hit by a bat, with initial and final momentum vectors, as well as impulse vector (= change in momentum vector) arrows indicated.

Answer 1:
The impulse is equal to the momentum change that the baseball receives. Unfortunately, there is no shortcut, but to calculate $\Delta\vec{v} \equiv \vec{v}_f - \vec{v}_i$ for the x and y components separately, and then add them in as vectors, and finally multiply with the mass of the baseball:

$$\Delta v_x = (49.17 \text{ m/s})\cos 35° - (40.23 \text{ m/s})\cos(185°) = 80.35 \text{ m/s}$$
$$\Delta v_y = (49.17 \text{ m/s})\sin 35° - (40.23 \text{ m/s})\sin(185°) = 31.71 \text{ m/s}$$
$$\Delta v = \sqrt{\Delta v_x^2 + \Delta v_y^2} = \sqrt{80.35^2 + 31.71^2} \text{ m/s} = 86.38 \text{ m/s}$$
$$\Delta p = m\Delta v = (0.145 \text{ kg})(86.38 \text{ m/s}) = 12.52 \text{ kg m/s}$$

Avoiding a Common Mistake:
It is tempting to just add the magnitude of the initial momentum and final momentum, because they point approximately in opposite directions. This method would lead to $\Delta p_{\text{wrong}} = m(v_1 + v_2) = 12.96$ kg m/s. As you can see, numerically this answer is pretty close to the correct one, only about 3% off. It would serve as a first estimate, if you realize that the vectors almost point in opposite directions, and that in that case vector subtraction implies an addition of the two magnitudes. But if you want the right answer,

Example

you have to go through the work above.

Question 2:
Precise measurements show that the ball-bat contact lasts only about 1 millisecond. Suppose that for our home run the contact lasted 1.2 milliseconds. What was the magnitude of the average force exerted on the ball by the bat during that time?

Answer 2:
The force can be simply calculated by using the formula for the impulse,

$$\Delta\vec{p} = \vec{J} = \vec{F}_{av}\Delta t$$

$$\Rightarrow F_{av} = \frac{\Delta p}{\Delta t} = \frac{12.53 \text{ kg m/s}}{0.0012 \text{ s}} = 10.4 \text{ kN}$$

This force is approximately the same as the weight of an entire baseball team! The collision of the bat and the ball results in significant compression of the baseball.

In-class exercise:
In the previous example, if the same incoming baseball would have been hit so that it would have received the same speed of 110 mph after it left the bat, but would have been hit so that it left the bat with an angle of 38 degrees instead of 35 degrees, would the impulse the baseball received have been:
a) bigger
b) smaller
c) the same

Before we leave the concept of impulse, it is useful to consider it in technical applications. Some of the most important safety devices make use of the relationship (7.13) between impulse, average force, and time.. Airbags and seatbelts are installed in cars, and they use the principles implied in equation (7.13). If the car you are driving has a collision with another vehicle or a stationary object, then the impulse, the momentum change of your car, is rather large, and it can happen over a very short time interval. Equation (7.13) then results in a very large average force,

$$\vec{F}_{av} = \frac{\vec{J}}{\Delta t} \tag{7.14}$$

If there were no safety devices such as seat belts and air bags installed in your car, then your car suddenly stopping would result in your head hitting the windshield and experiencing the impulse during a very short time of only a few milliseconds, resulting in a big average force on your head that usually causes injury or even death. Air bags and seat belts are designed to make the time over which the momentum change occurs as long as possible. Maximizing this contact time and letting the driver's body decelerate in contact with the airbag surface minimizes the force acting on the driver, greatly reducing injuries.

In-class exercise:
Several luxury cars are designed with active crumple zones that get severely damaged during head-on collisions. This is done to
a) reduce the impulse experienced by the driver during the collision.
b) increase the impulse experienced by the driver during the collision.
c) reduce the collision time and thus reduce the force acting on the driver.
d) increase the collision time and thus reduce the force acting on the driver.
e) make the repair as expensive as possible.

7.3. Conservation of Linear Momentum

Suppose we have two objects that collide with each other. The collision can be, for example, that of two billiard balls on a billiard table. This collision is called an elastic collision (at least approximately, as we will see later!). Another example is the collision of a subcompact car with an 18-wheeler on a highway, where the two vehicles stick to each other. This collision is called a totally inelastic collision. In a moment we will obtain exact definitions of what is meant by the use of the terms "elastic" and "inelastic". But first, let us look at what is happening to the momenta, $\vec{p}_1$ and $\vec{p}_2$, of the two colliding partners during the collision.

We find that the sum of the two momenta after the collision in the same as the sum of the two momenta before the collision (index *i*1 implies *i*nitial value for particle 1, just before the collision, and index *f*1 the *f*inal value for the same particle):

$$\vec{p}_{f1} + \vec{p}_{f2} = \vec{p}_{i1} + \vec{p}_{i2} \qquad (7.15)$$

This equation is the basic expression of the law of the conservation of total momentum, the most important result of this present chapter. Let us first have a look at how to derive it and then think about its consequences.

Derivation 7.1:

During the collision, object 1 exerts a force on object 2. Let's call this force $\vec{F}_{1\to2}$. Using our definition of the impulse and its relationship to the momentum change, we then get for the momentum change of object 2 during the collision:

$$\int_{t_i}^{t_f} \vec{F}_{1\to2}dt = \Delta\vec{p}_2 = \vec{p}_{f2} - \vec{p}_{i2}. \qquad (7.16)$$

Here we neglect external forces; if they exist, they are usually negligible compared to $\vec{F}_{1\to2}$ during the collision. The initial and final times are selected to contain the time of the collision process. Of course, there is also a force $\vec{F}_{2\to1}$ which object 2 exerts on object 1. The same argument as before now leads to:

Derivation

$$\int_{t_i}^{t_f} \vec{F}_{2\to1}dt = \Delta\vec{p}_1 = \vec{p}_{f1} - \vec{p}_{i1}. \tag{7.17}$$

Newton's Third Law (see chapter 4) tells us that the forces are equal and opposite to each other, $\vec{F}_{12} = -\vec{F}_{21}$, or

$$\vec{F}_{1\to2} + \vec{F}_{2\to1} = 0. \tag{7.18}$$

Integration of this equation immediately results in:

$$0 = \int_{t_i}^{t_f} (\vec{F}_{2\to1} + \vec{F}_{1\to2})dt = \int_{t_i}^{t_f} \vec{F}_{2\to1}dt + \int_{t_i}^{t_f} \vec{F}_{1\to2}dt = \vec{p}_{f1} - \vec{p}_{i1} + \vec{p}_{f2} - \vec{p}_{i2}. \tag{7.19}$$

Collecting the initial momentum vectors on one side, and the final momentum vectors on the other, we then obtain the equation:

$$\vec{p}_{f1} + \vec{p}_{f2} = \vec{p}_{i1} + \vec{p}_{i2}$$

Derivation

Equation (7.15) expresses the principle of conservation of linear momentum. The sum of the final momentum vectors is exactly equal to the sum of the initial momentum vectors. Note that this equation does not refer to any particular conditions that the collision must follow. It is valid for all two-body collisions, elastic or inelastic. All we have used in the derivation is Newton's Third Law.

You may object now that there also may be other, external, forces present. In the collision of billiard balls, for example, there is also the friction force due to each ball rolling or sliding across the table. Or in the collision of two cars, there is also friction between the tires and the road. But what characterizes a collision is the occurrence of very large impulses due to very large contact forces during relatively short collision times. If you integrate the external forces during these collision times, you obtain only very small or moderate impulses. Thus these external forces can usually be safely neglected in the calculation of the collision dynamics, and we can treat the two-body collisions as if there were only internal forces at work.

In addition, the same argument can be made if there are more than two partners taking part in the collision, or if there is no collision at all. As long as the net external force is zero, the total momentum will be conserved,

$$\text{if} \quad \vec{F}_{net} = 0 \quad \text{then} \quad \sum_{i=1}^{n} \vec{p}_i = \text{constant} \tag{7.20}$$

This equation is the general formulation of the law of the conservation of momentum, the most important result of the present chapter. We will return to this general formulation again in the next chapter when we talk about systems of particles. For the remainder of the present chapter we will only consider cases in which the net external force vanishes, and thus the total momentum is always conserved in all processes we consider.

7.4. Elastic Collisions in 1 Dimension

Figure 7.4 shows the collision of two carts on an almost frictionless track. The collision was videotaped, and we show seven frames of this video, each frame six hundredths of a second apart. The cart marked with the green circle is initially at rest. The one marked with the orange square has a larger mass than the other cart and is approaching from the left. The collision happens in the frame marked with the time stamp $t = 0.12$ s. We can see that after the collision both carts move to the right, but the lighter cart moves with a significantly larger speed. (The speed is proportional to the horizontal distance between the markings in neighboring video frames.) We will now derive equations that can be used to determine the velocities of the carts after the collision.

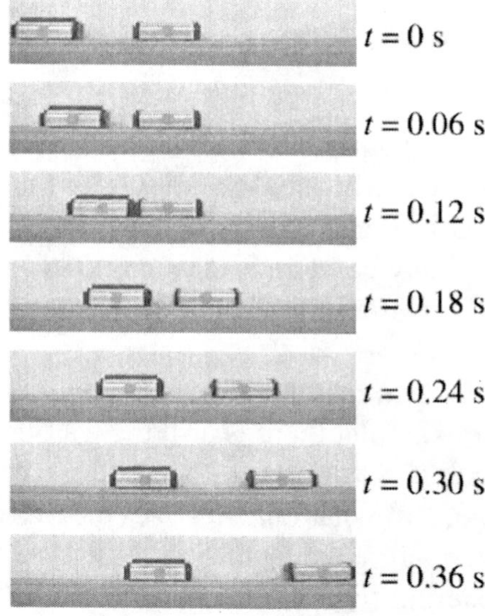

Figure 7.4: Video sequence of a collision between two carts of non-equal mass on the air track. The cart with the orange dot carries a black metal bar to increase its mass.

What exactly is an elastic collision? The answer, as in so many cases, is an idealization. In practically all collisions, at least some kinetic energy is converted into other forms of energy. This energy can be heat or the energy to deform an object, for example. But we will talk of elastic collisions in the limit that the total kinetic energy of the colliding objects is conserved.

This definition does not mean that each object involved in the collision retains its kinetic energy. Kinetic energy can be transferred from one object to the other, but for an elastic collision the sum of the kinetic energies has to remain constant. Let us use the notation of $p_{i1,x}$ for the one-dimensional initial momentum vector of particle 1, and $p_{f1,x}$ for the final momentum. (We use the subscript x to remind ourselves that this could equally be considered the x-component of the 2- or 3-dimensional momentum vector.) In the same way we denote the initial and final momentum vector of particle 2 by $p_{i2,x}$ and $p_{f2,x}$. Because we want to restrict ourselves to collision in one dimension for now, the equation for kinetic energy conservation can then be written as:

$$\frac{p_{f1,x}^2}{2m_1} + \frac{p_{f2,x}^2}{2m_2} = \frac{p_{i1,x}^2}{2m_1} + \frac{p_{i2,x}^2}{2m_2} \tag{7.21}$$

because for motion in one dimension the square of the x-component of the vector is also the square of the absolute value of the vector. The equation for momentum conservation in the x-direction can be written as:

$$p_{f1,x} + p_{f2,x} = p_{i1,x} + p_{i2,x} \tag{7.22}$$

(Remember: momentum is conserved in any collision in which the external forces are negligible.)

Let's look at the two equations for momentum and energy conservation. What is known, and what is unknown? Typically, we would know the two masses and initial momentum vectors, and we would want to calculate the final momentum vectors after the collision. This calculation can be done because we have two equations for two unknowns, $p_{f1,x}$ and $p_{f2,x}$. This result is by far the most common use of these equations, but it is also possible, for example, to calculate the two masses, if the initial and final momentum vectors are known. So let us go ahead and calculate the final momentum vectors. Here is what we will get:

$$\begin{aligned} p_{f1,x} &= \frac{m_1 - m_2}{m_1 + m_2} p_{i1,x} + \frac{2m_1}{m_1 + m_2} p_{i2,x} \\ p_{f2,x} &= \frac{2m_2}{m_1 + m_2} p_{i1,x} + \frac{m_2 - m_1}{m_1 + m_2} p_{i2,x} \end{aligned} \tag{7.23}$$

Now let's figure out how to get to this result. The derivation is very instructive, because it will help you solve similar problems. So here it is:

Derivation 7.2:
We start with the equations for energy and momentum conservation and collect all quantities connected with object 1 on the left side, and all those connected with object 2 on the right. The equation for the (conserved) kinetic energy then becomes:

$$\frac{p_{f1,x}^2}{2m_1} - \frac{p_{i1,x}^2}{2m_1} = \frac{p_{i2,x}^2}{2m_2} - \frac{p_{f2,x}^2}{2m_2}$$

or

$$m_2(p_{f1,x}^2 - p_{i1,x}^2) = m_1(p_{i2,x}^2 - p_{f2,x}^2), \tag{7.24}$$

where we have used the fact that in this case the momentum vectors only have x components. For the equation of momentum conservation we obtain by rearranging

$$p_{f1,x} - p_{i1,x} = p_{i2,x} - p_{f2,x}. \tag{7.25}$$

Now we divide equation (7.24) by equation (7.25) by dividing the left-hand sides of the equations by each other and the right hand sides by each other. To do this division, we use the algebraic identity $a^2 - b^2 = (a+b)(a-b)$. This process results in

$$m_2(p_{i1,x} + p_{f1,x}) = m_1(p_{i2,x} + p_{f2,x}). \tag{7.26}$$

Now we can solve (7.25) for $p_{f1,x} = p_{i1,x} + p_{i2,x} - p_{f2,x}$ and insert this equation into (7.26):

$$\begin{aligned}
m_2(p_{i1,x} + [p_{i1,x} + p_{i2,x} - p_{f2,x}]) &= m_1(p_{i2,x} + p_{f2,x}) \\
2m_2 p_{i1,x} + m_2 p_{i2,x} - m_2 p_{f2,x} &= m_1 p_{i2,x} + m_1 p_{f2,x} \\
p_{f2,x}(m_1 + m_2) &= 2m_2 p_{i1,x} + (m_2 - m_1)p_{i2,x} \\
p_{f2,x} &= \frac{2m_2 p_{i1,x} + (m_2 - m_1)p_{i2,x}}{m_1 + m_2}
\end{aligned}$$

This result gives us one of the two desired equations above. The other equation can be obtained easily by solving (7.25) for $p_{f2,x} = p_{i1,x} + p_{i2,x} - p_{f1,x}$ and inserting this equation into (7.26).

Perhaps it is even easier to obtain the result for $p_{f1,x}$ from the result for $p_{f2,x}$ that we just derived by exchanging the indices 1 and 2 of the two objects. It is, after all, arbitrary which object we gave the labels 1 and 2, and so the resulting equations should be symmetric under the exchange of the two labels. Use of this type of symmetry principle is very powerful and very convenient. (But it does take some getting used to at first!)

Derivation

With the result for the final momentum vectors in hand, we can also easily obtain expressions for the final velocities, just by using $p_x = mv_x$. This rearrangement results in

$$
\begin{aligned}
v_{f1,x} &= \frac{m_1 - m_2}{m_1 + m_2} v_{i1,x} + \frac{2m_2}{m_1 + m_2} v_{i2,x} \\
v_{f2,x} &= \frac{2m_1}{m_1 + m_2} v_{i1,x} + \frac{m_2 - m_1}{m_1 + m_2} v_{i2,x}
\end{aligned} \tag{7.27}
$$

The two equations for the final velocities look, at first sight, very similar to those for the final momentum vectors (7.23). But there is one important difference: In the second term of the right hand side of the upper equation the numerator is now $2m_2$ instead of $2m_1$; and conversely it is now $2m_1$ instead of $2m_2$ in the first term of the lower equation.

As a last point in this general section, let us calculate the relative velocity, $v_{f1,x} - v_{f2,x}$, after the collision,

$$
\begin{aligned}
v_{f1,x} - v_{f2,x} &= \frac{m_1 - m_2 - 2m_1}{m_1 + m_2} v_{i1,x} + \frac{2m_2 - (m_2 - m_1)}{m_1 + m_2} v_{i2,x} \\
&= -v_{i1,x} + v_{i2,x} = -(v_{i1,x} - v_{i2,x})
\end{aligned} \tag{7.28}
$$

So we see that the relative velocity just changes sign in elastic collisions, $\Delta v_f = -\Delta v_i$. We will return to this result later in this chapter.

Special Case 1: Equal Masses

If $m_1 = m_2$, the general equations (7.23) simplify considerably, because the terms proportional to $m_1 - m_2$ vanish, and the ratios $2m_1/(m_1 + m_2)$ and $2m_2/(m_1 + m_2)$ become unity. We then obtain the extremely simple result

$$
\begin{aligned}
p_{f1,x} &= p_{i2,x} \\
p_{f2,x} &= p_{i1,x}
\end{aligned} \quad \text{(for special case } m_1 = m_2) \tag{7.29}
$$

This result means that in any elastic collision of two objects of equal mass in one dimension the two objects simply *exchange* their momenta. The initial momentum of object 1 becomes the final momentum of object 2. The same is true for the velocities:

$$
\begin{aligned}
v_{f1,x} &= v_{i2,x} \\
v_{f2,x} &= v_{i1,x}
\end{aligned} \quad \text{(for special case } m_1 = m_2) \tag{7.30}
$$

Special Case 2: One Object Initially at Rest

Now we want to look into the case where the two masses are not necessarily the same, but where one of the two objects is initially at rest, i.e. has zero momentum. Without loss of generality we can say that object 1 is the one at rest. (Remember: the equations are invariant under exchange of the two indices 1 and 2.) By using the general equations (7.23) for the momentum vectors and setting $p_{i,1,x} = 0$, we then get:

$$\begin{aligned} p_{f1,x} &= \frac{2m_1}{m_1 + m_2} p_{i2,x} \\ p_{f2,x} &= \frac{m_2 - m_1}{m_1 + m_2} p_{i2,x} \end{aligned} \quad \text{(for special case } p_{i,1,x} = 0\text{)} \tag{7.31}$$

In the same way we obtain for the final velocities:

$$\begin{aligned} v_{f1,x} &= \frac{2m_2}{m_1 + m_2} v_{i2,x} \\ v_{f2,x} &= \frac{m_2 - m_1}{m_1 + m_2} v_{i2,x} \end{aligned} \quad \text{(for special case } p_{i,1,x} = 0\text{)} \tag{7.32}$$

Suppose $v_{i2,x} > 0$, i.e. the object would move from left to right, with the conventional assignment of the positive x-axis pointing to the right. This situation is the case in Figure 7.4. Depending on which mass is larger, we can then have four cases:

1. $m_2 > m_1 \Rightarrow (m_2 - m_1)/(m_2 + m_1) > 0$: The final velocity of object 2 still points in the same direction, but is now reduced in magnitude.
2. $m_2 = m_1 \Rightarrow (m_2 - m_1)/(m_2 + m_1) = 0$: After the collision object 2 is now at rest, and object 1 moves with the initial velocity of object 2.
3. $m_2 < m_1 \Rightarrow (m_2 - m_1)/(m_2 + m_1) < 0$: Now object 2 bounces back; it changes direction of its velocity vector.
4. $m_2 << m_1 \Rightarrow (m_2 - m_1)/(m_2 + m_1) \approx -1$ and $2m_2/(m_1 + m_2) \approx 0$: Object 1 would still remain at rest, and object 2 approximately reverses its velocity in the collision process. This situation occurs, for example, in the collision of a ball with the ground. In this collision object 1 is the entire Earth, and object 2 is the ball. If the collision is sufficiently elastic, the ball bounces back with the same speed it had right before the collision, but in the opposite direction - up instead of down.

In-class exercise:
Suppose we have an elastic collision in one dimension like the one shown in Figure 7.4, where the cart marked with the green dot was initially at rest, and the cart with the red dot initially had $v_{red} < 0$, i.e. was moving from right to left. What can we say about the masses of the two carts?

a) $m_{red} < m_{green}$

b) $m_{red} > m_{green}$

c) $m_{red} = m_{green}$

In-class exercise:
Instead of the scenario shown in Figure 7.4, if the mass of the red cart would have been very much larger than that of the green cart, what outcome would you expect then?
a) about the same as the one shown in the figure.
b) the red cart moves with an almost unchanged velocity after the collisions, and the green cart moves with a velocity almost twice as large as the initial velocity of the red cart.
c) both carts move with almost the same speed as the red cart had before the collision
d) the red cart stops, and the green cart moves with the same speed to the left that the red cart had originally.

In-class exercise:
Instead of the scenario shown in Figure 7.4, if the mass of the green cart (the one originally at rest) would have been very much larger than that of the red cart, what outcome would you expect then?
a) about the same as the one shown in the figure.
b) the red cart moves with an almost unchanged velocity after the collisions, and the green cart moves with a velocity almost twice as large as the initial velocity of the red cart.
c) both carts move with almost the same speed as the red cart had before the collision
d) the green cart remains almost at rest and only receives a very small velocity to the left, and the red cart bounces back to the right with almost the same speed it had originally.

Self-Test Opportunity:
In this figure we show a high-speed video sequence of the collision of a driver with a golf ball. The ball experiences significant deformation, but this deformation is sufficiently restored before the ball leaves the clubface. Thus it is justified to approximate this collision as a 1-dimensional elastic collision. Discuss what the speed of the ball after the collision is relative to that of the driver, and how this finding fits with the cases that we have discussed.

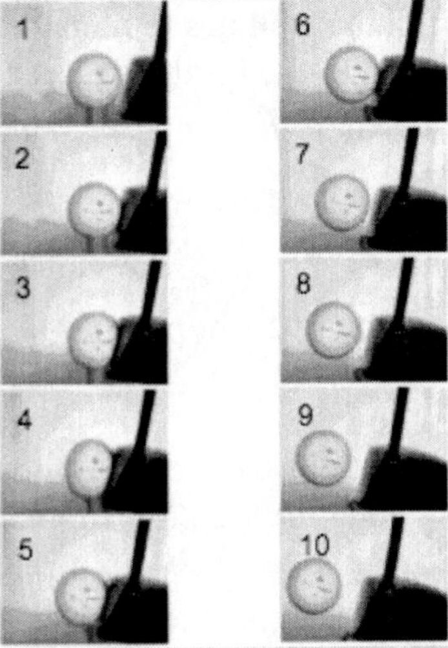

(High-speed video images courtesy of Photron)

7.5. Elastic Collisions in 2 or 3 Dimensions

Collisions with Walls

To begin our discussion of two- and three-dimensional collisions, we consider the elastic collision of an object with a solid wall. In our chapter on forces, we had seen that solid surfaces exert forces on objects that attempt to penetrate the wall. These forces are normal forces, i.e. are directed perpendicular to the surface. If this normal force acts on an object colliding with the wall, it can only give it an impulse that is perpendicular to the wall; the normal force has no component that is parallel to the wall.

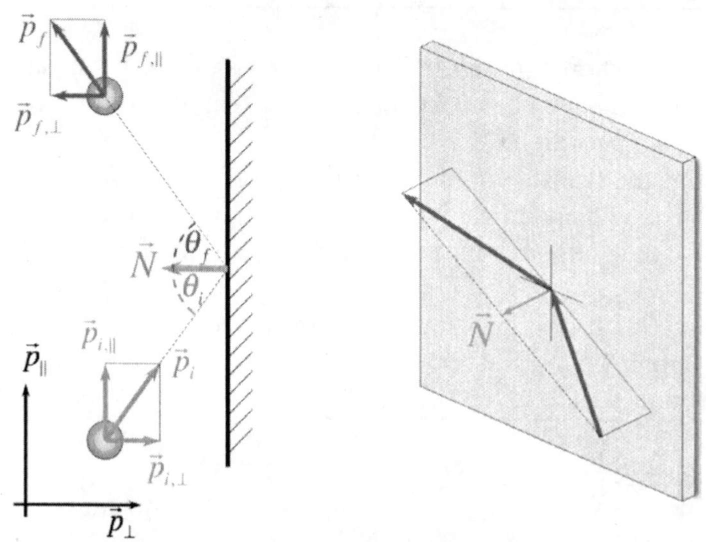

Figure 7.5: Elastic collision of an object with a wall.

So we find that the momentum component of the object along the wall does not change, $p_{f,\parallel} = p_{i,\parallel}$. In addition, for an elastic collision, we have the condition that the kinetic energy of the object colliding with the wall has to remain the same. After all, the wall stays at rest (because it is connected to the Earth and has a *much* bigger mass than the ball). The kinetic energy of the object is $K = p^2/2m$, and so we see that $p_f^2 = p_i^2$. Because $p_f^2 = p_{f,\parallel}^2 + p_{f,\perp}^2$ and $p_i^2 = p_{i,\parallel}^2 + p_{i,\perp}^2$, we find that $p_{f,\perp}^2 = p_{i,\perp}^2$. The only two solutions are then $p_{f,\perp} = p_{i,\perp}$ and $p_{f,\perp} = -p_{i,\perp}$. Obviously, only for the second solution does the perpendicular momentum component point away from the wall after the collision. Thus it is the only physical solution.

To summarize, we find that the length of the momentum vector remains unchanged, as does the momentum component along the wall; the momentum component perpendicular to the wall changes sign, but retains the same absolute value. The angle of incidence, θ_i on the wall (compare Figure 7.5) is then also the same as the angle of reflection, θ_f,

$$\theta_i = \cos^{-1}\frac{p_{i,\perp}}{p_i} = \cos^{-1}\frac{p_{f,\perp}}{p_f} = \theta_f \tag{7.33}$$

We will see the same relationship again when we study light and its reflection off a mirror.

In-class exercise:
Choose the correct statement:
a) In an elastic collision of an object with a wall, energy may or may not be conserved.
b) In an elastic collision of an object with a wall, momentum may or may not be conserved.
c) In an elastic collision of an object with a wall, the incident angle is equal to the final angle.
d) In an elastic collision of an object with a wall, the original momentum vector does not change as a result of the collision.
e) In an elastic collision of an object with a wall, the wall cannot change the momentum of the object because momentum is conserved.

Collisions of Two Objects in Two Dimensions

We have just seen that elastic collisions in 1 dimension are always solvable if we have the initial velocity or momentum conditions for the two colliding objects, as well as their masses. Again, this result is due to the fact that we have two equations for the two unknown quantities, $p_{f1,x}$ and $p_{f2,x}$.

For collisions in 2 dimensions, each of the final momentum vectors now has two components. So this situation leaves four unknown quantities to be determined. How many equations do we have at our disposal? Conservation of kinetic energy again provides one of them. Conservation of linear momentum provides independent equations for the x- and y-directions. Thus we only have a total of 3 equations for the 4 unknown quantities. Thus without specifying an additional condition for the collision, we cannot solve for the final momenta.

For collisions in 3 dimensions the situation is even worse. Now we have two vectors with three components each, for a total of 6 unknown quantities. And we only have four equations that we can use, one from energy conservation, and three from the conservation equations for the x-, y-, and z-components of the momentum.

Incidentally, this fact is what makes billiards an interesting game. The final momenta after the collision are determined by where on their surface the two balls in the collision hit each other.

Speaking of billiards: we can make an interesting statement that applies here. Suppose object 2 is initially at rest, and both objects have the same mass. Then momentum conservation results in:

$$\vec{p}_{f1} + \vec{p}_{f2} = \vec{p}_{i1}$$
$$(\vec{p}_{f1} + \vec{p}_{f2})^2 = (\vec{p}_{i1})^2 \qquad (7.34)$$
$$p_{f1}^2 + p_{f2}^2 + 2\vec{p}_{f1} \bullet \vec{p}_{f2} = p_{i1}^2$$

Here we squared the equation for momentum conservation and then used the properties of the scalar product. On the other hand, conservation of kinetic energy leads to:

$$\frac{p_{f1}^2}{2m} + \frac{p_{f2}^2}{2m} = \frac{p_{i1}^2}{2m} \qquad (7.35)$$
$$p_{f1}^2 + p_{f2}^2 = p_{i1}^2$$

for $m_1 = m_2 \equiv m$. If we subtract this equation from the previous one, we obtain

$$2\vec{p}_{f1} \bullet \vec{p}_{f2} = 0 \qquad (7.36)$$

But the scalar product of two vectors can only be 0 if the two vectors are perpendicular to each other, or if one of them has length 0. The latter case is in effect in a head-on collision of the two billiard balls, after which the cue ball remains at rest ($\vec{p}_{f1} = 0$) and the other ball moves on with the momentum that the cue ball had initially. In all non-central collisions both balls move after the collision; and they move in directions that are perpendicular to each other.

In-class exercise:
Choose the correct statement:

a) When a moving object strikes a stationary object, the angle between the velocity vectors of the two objects after the collision is always $90°$.
b) For a real-life collision between a moving object and a stationary object, the angle between the velocity vectors of the two objects after the collision is never less than $90°$.
c) When a moving object has a head-on collision with a stationary object, the angle between the two velocity vectors after the collision is $90°$.
d) When a moving object collides elastically head-on with a stationary object of the same mass, the ball that was moving stops and the second ball moves with original velocity of the moving ball.
e) When a moving object collides elastically with a stationary object of the same mass, the angle between the two velocity vectors after the collision cannot be $90°$.

There is an experiment that you can do quite easily to see if this result of a 90-degree angle works out quantitatively. (We acknowledge Harvard's Eric Mazur, who suggested this demonstration experiment to us). You can put two coins on a piece of paper, as shown in Figure 7.6. Mark one of them on the paper by drawing a circle around it. Then flick the other coin with your fingers into the one that you marked, which we call the target (a). The coins will bounce off each other and slide briefly, before friction forces slow them down to rest (b). Then you can draw a line from the final position of the target coin back to the circle that you have drawn, as shown in (c), and therby deduce the trajectory of the other coin. In (c) we also superimpose the two frames from (a) and (b) to show the motion of the coins before and after the collision, as indicated by the red arrows.

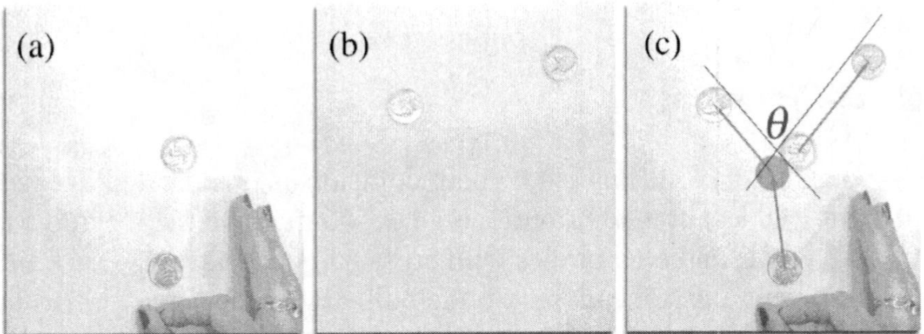

Figure 7.6: Collision of two nickels.

Measuring the angle between the two blue lines in Figure 7.6 results in the answer $\theta = 80°$. So our theoretically derived result of $\theta = 90°$ is not quite true for this experiment. Why?

What we have neglected is the rotation in the coins after the collision and the transfer of energy to that motion, as well as the fact that this collision is not quite elastic. However, this does not change the fact that the 90-degree rule just derived by us is a good first approximation to the problem of two colliding coins. You can perform another simple experiment of this kind on any billiard table. Again, you will find that the scattering angle is not quite 90 degrees, but that this approximation will give you a good idea on where your cue ball will move to after you hit the ball that you want to sink.

Self-Test Opportunity:
The above discussion only specifies the angle between the two coins after the collision, but not what the individual deflection angles are. In order to obtain these individual angles, one also has to know how far off center the collision takes place, the so-called impact parameter. Quantitatively, the impact parameter is the distance that the original trajectory would need to be moved parallel to itself to have a head-on collision (see the drawing). Can you produce a sketch of the dependence of the deflection angles as a function of impact parameter? (You can do this experimentally in the way shown above, or you can think about limiting cases first and then try to interpolate between them).

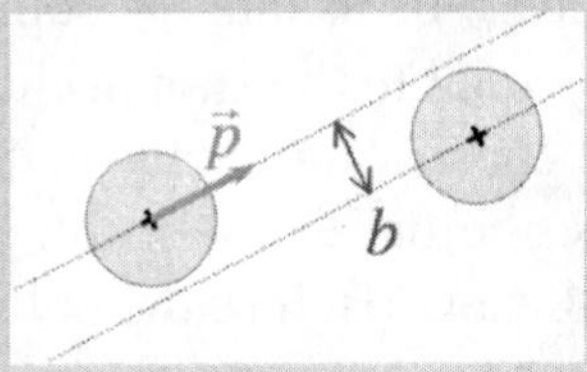

Self-Test Opportunity:
Suppose we had done exactly the same experiment as shown in Figure 7.6, but replaced one of the coins with a less heavy dime or a heavier quarter. What changes? (Again, you can explore the answer by doing the experiment).

Solved Problem

Solved Problem 7.1: Curling

The great Canadian sport of curling is all about collisions. As indicated in Figure 7.7 one slides a 42.0 lb (= 19.0 kg) granite "stone" about 35-40 m down the ice into a target area (= concentric red, white, and blue circles with cross hairs on the ice). The teams take turns sliding stones, and the stone closest to the bull's eye in the end wins. When a stone of the other team is the closest, the other team attempts to knock that stone out of the way, as shown in Figure 7.7.

Question:
Suppose that the red stone shown here had an initial velocity of 1.60 m/s in the x direction and got deflected to an angle of 32.0° relative to the $x-$axis, what are the two final momentum vectors right after this elastic collision, and what is the sum of their kinetic energies?

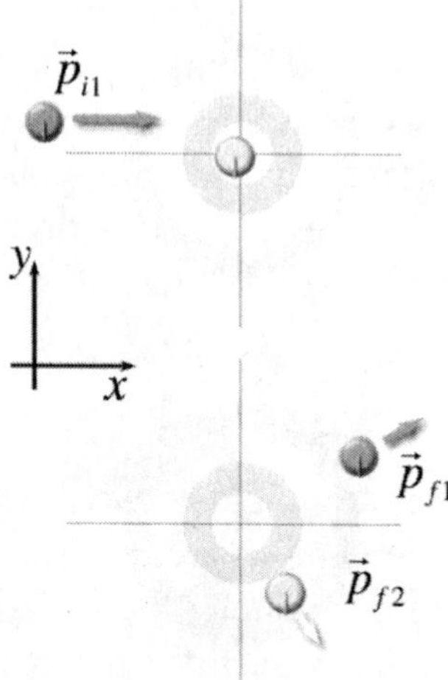

Figure 7.7: Collision of two curling stones.

Answer:

THINK: Momentum conservation tells us that the sum of the momentum vectors of both stones before the collision is equal to the sum of the momentum vectors of both stones after the collision. Energy conservation tells us that in an elastic collision the sum of the kinetic energy of both stones before the collision is equal to the sum of the kinetic energy of both stones after the collision. Before the collision, the red stone has momentum and kinetic energy because it is moving and the yellow stone is a rest and thus has no momentum or kinetic energy. After the collision, both stones have momentum and kinetic energy. We must calculate the momentum in terms of x-components and y-components.

SKETCH: A sketch of the two stones before and after the collision is shown in Figure 7.8.

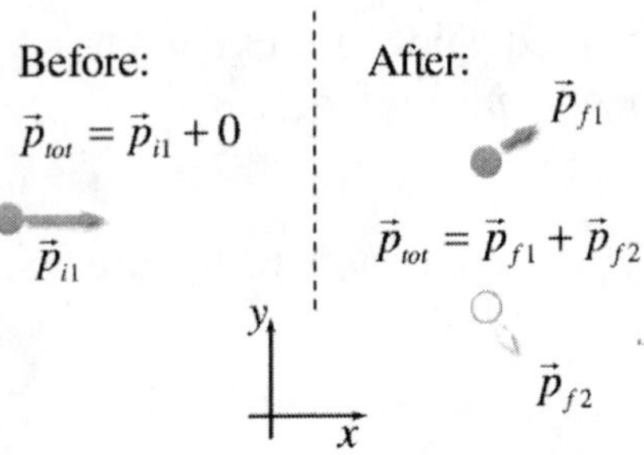

Figure 7.8: Sketch before the two stones collide and after the two stones collide.

The x-components and y-components of the momentum vectors after the collision of the two stones are shown in Figure 7.9.

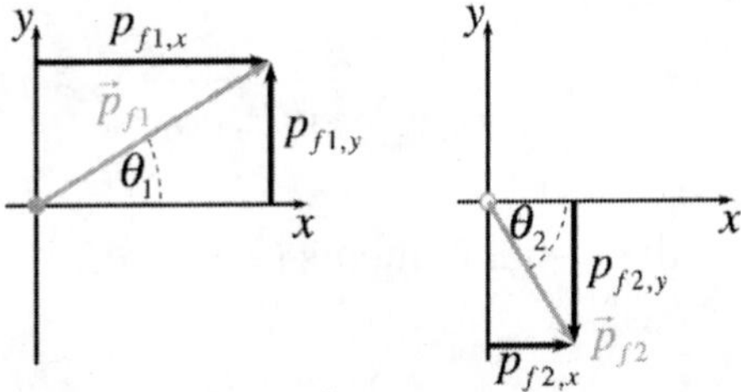

Figure 7.9: x- and y-components of the momentum vectors of the two stones after the collision.

RESEARCH: Momentum conservation dictates that the sum of the momenta of the two stones before the collision must equal the sum of the momenta of the two stones after the collision. The momenta of both stones before the collision are specified in the problem and our task is to calculate the momenta of the two stones after the collision based on the additional information supplied about the momenta of the two stones after the collision. For the x-components we can write

$$p_{i1,x} + 0 = p_{f1,x} + p_{f2,x}. \tag{7.37}$$

For the y-components we can write

$$0 + 0 = p_{f1,y} + p_{f2,y}. \tag{7.38}$$

The problem specifies that stone 1 gets deflected to $\theta_1 = 32.0°$. According to the 90°-rule that we derived for perfectly elastic collisions between equal masses, stone 2 has to be deflected to $\theta_2 = -58.0°$. So we obtain in the x-direction:

Solved Problem

$$p_{i1,x} = p_{f1,x} + p_{f2,x} = p_{f1}\cos\theta_1 + p_{f2}\cos\theta_2 \qquad (7.39)$$

and in the y-direction:

$$0 = p_{f1,y} + p_{f2,y} = p_{f1}\sin\theta_1 + p_{f2}\sin\theta_2. \qquad (7.40)$$

This problem is a system of two equations for two unknown quantities, which are the magnitudes of the final momenta, p_{f1} and p_{f2}.

SIMPLIFY: We solve this system of equations by direct substitution. We can solve (7.40) for p_{f1}

$$p_{f1} = -p_{f2}\sin\theta_2 / \sin\theta_1 \qquad (7.41)$$

and insert it into (7.39) to get

$$p_{i1,x} = (-p_{f2}\sin\theta_2 / \sin\theta_1)\cos\theta_1 + p_{f2}\cos\theta_2$$

which we can rearrange to get

$$p_{f2} = \frac{p_{i1,x}}{\cos\theta_2 - \sin\theta_2\cot\theta_1}.$$

Inserting this result back into the y-components (7.41) results in

$$p_{f1} = -p_{f2}\frac{\sin\theta_2}{\sin\theta_1}.$$

CALCULATE: First, we calculate the magnitude of the initial momentum of stone 1

$$p_{i1,x} = mv_{i1,x} = 19.0 \text{ kg} \cdot 1.60 \text{ m/s} = 30.4 \text{ kg m/s}. \qquad (7.42)$$

We can then calculate the magnitude of the final momentum of stone 2 as

$$p_{f2} = \frac{30.4 \text{ kg m/s}}{\cos(-58.0°) - \sin(-58.0°)\cot(32.0°)} = 16.10954563 \text{ kg m/s}.$$

The magnitude of the final momentum of stone 1 is

$$p_{f1} = -p_{f2}\frac{\sin(-58.0°)}{\sin(32.0°)} = 25.78066212 \text{ kg m/s}.$$

We can finish the second part of the question concerning the sum of the kinetic energies of the two stones after the collision. Because this collision is elastic, we can simply

Solved Problem

calculate the initial kinetic energy of the red stone, because the yellow one was at rest. So our answer is:

$$K = \frac{p_{i1}^2}{2m} = \frac{(30.4 \text{ kg m/s})^2}{2 \cdot 19.0 \text{ kg}} = 24.32 \text{ J}$$

ROUND: Because all the numerical values were specified to three significant figures, we report the magnitude of the final momentum of the first stone as

$$p_{f1} = 25.8 \text{ kg m/s}.$$

The direction of the first stone is $+32.0°$ with respect to the horizontal. We report the magnitude of the final momentum of the second as

$$p_{f2} = 16.1 \text{ kg m/s}.$$

The direction of the second stone is $-58.0°$ with respect to the horizontal. The total kinetic energy of the two stones after the collision is

$$K = 24.3 \text{ J}.$$

Self-Test Opportunity: Double-check the reported results for the final momenta of the two stones by calculating the kinetic energies of the two stones individually after the collision to verify if their sum is indeed equal to the initial kinetic energy.

7.6. Totally Inelastic Collisions

In all collisions that are not completely elastic we can no longer make use of the conservation of kinetic energy. These collisions are called inelastic, because some of the initial kinetic energy gets converted into internal excitation, deformation, or eventually into heat. At first sight this loss of energy may make our task of calculating the final momentum or velocity vectors of the colliding objects appear to be more complicated. However, that is not the case. In particular, the algebra actually becomes considerably easier when we deal with the limiting case of completely inelastic collisions.

We speak of a completely inelastic collision if the colliding objects stick to each other after the collision. This result implies that both objects have the same velocity vector after the collisions: $\vec{v}_{f1} = \vec{v}_{f2} \equiv \vec{v}_f$. (Thus the relative velocity between the two colliding objects is zero after the collision.)

Using $\vec{p} = m\vec{v}$ and momentum conservation, we then get for the final velocity vector:

$$\vec{v}_f = \frac{m_1\vec{v}_{i1} + m_2\vec{v}_{i2}}{m_1 + m_2} \tag{7.43}$$

While this formula enables you to solve practically all problems involving totally inelastic collisions, it does not tell you how it was obtained. We show this in the following (very short) derivation.

Derivation 7.3:
We start with the conservation law for total momentum (7.15):

$$\vec{p}_{f1} + \vec{p}_{f2} = \vec{p}_{i1} + \vec{p}_{i2}$$

Now we use $\vec{p} = m\vec{v}$ and get:

$$m_1\vec{v}_{f1} + m_2\vec{v}_{f2} = m_1\vec{v}_{i1} + m_2\vec{v}_{i2} \tag{7.44}$$

Having already stated that the collision is completely inelastic implies that the final velocities of the two objects are the same. This assumption results in:

$$\begin{aligned} m_1\vec{v}_f + m_2\vec{v}_f &= m_1\vec{v}_{i1} + m_2\vec{v}_{i2} \\ (m_1 + m_2)\vec{v}_f &= m_1\vec{v}_{i1} + m_2\vec{v}_{i2} \\ \vec{v}_f &= \frac{m_1\vec{v}_{i1} + m_2\vec{v}_{i2}}{m_1 + m_2} \end{aligned}$$

Note that the condition of totally inelastic collision only implies that the final velocities are the same for both objects, but that in general their momentum vectors can have quite different magnitudes.

In-class exercise:
In a totally inelastic collision between a moving object and a stationary object, the two objects will
a) stick together.
b) bounce off of each other, losing energy.
c) bounce off of each other, without losing energy.

We know from Newton's Third Law (see chapter 4) that the forces that two objects exert on each other during a collision are equal in magnitude. But it should also be made clear that the changes in velocity, i.e. the accelerations that the two objects experience in a totally inelastic collision can be drastically different. The following example illustrates this effect.

Example 7.2: Head-On Collision
Consider a head-on collision of a full-size SUV, with mass M=3,023 kg, and a compact car, with mass m=1,184 kg. Let us assume that each had an initial speed of v=50 mph (=22.35 m/s), moving in opposite directions, of course. For the sake of clarity, let's then state that the SUV initially moves with a velocity of $-v_x$ and the compact car with $+v_x$.

If the two cars crash into each other and become entangled, we have our idealized case of a totally inelastic collision.

Figure 7. 10: Head-on collision of two vehicles with identical speeds.

Question:
What are the velocity changes of the two cars' velocities in the collisions? (You may safely neglect friction between the tires and the road in this problem!)

Answer:
We can first calculate the final velocity that the pair has immediately after the collision. To do this calculation, we simply use the above formula and get:

$$v_{f,x} = \frac{mv_x - Mv_x}{m+M} = \frac{m-M}{m+M}v_x$$
$$= \frac{1184\text{ kg} - 3023\text{ kg}}{1184\text{ kg}+3023\text{ kg}}(22.35\text{ m/s}) = -9.77\text{ m/s}$$

So the velocity change for the SUV turns out to be:

$$\Delta v_{\text{SUV,x}} = -9.77\text{ m/s} - (-22.35\text{ m/s}) = 12.58\text{ m/s}$$

But the velocity change for the compact car is:

$$\Delta v_{\text{compact,x}} = -9.77\text{ m/s} - (22.35\text{ m/s}) = -32.12\text{ m/s}$$

One obtains the corresponding average accelerations by dividing by the time interval, Δt, during which the collision takes place. This time interval is obviously the same for both cars. But this equal time interval means that the magnitude of the acceleration experienced by the body of the driver of the compact car is a factor of $32.12/12.58 = 2.55$ bigger than that experienced by the body of the driver of the SUV.

Just from this consideration alone it is clear that it is much safer to be in the SUV in this head-on collision than in the compact car. Keep in mind that this result is true even though Newton's Third Law teaches us that the forces exerted by the two vehicles on each other are the same (compare Example 4.7).

Example

Self-Test Opportunity: We can start with Newton's Third Law and make use of the fact that the forces that the two cars exert on each other are equal. Use the values of the masses given in the example. What is the ratio of the accelerations of the two vehicles that you obtain then?

Ballistic Pendulum

A ballistic pendulum is a device that can be used to measure muzzle speeds of projectiles shot from firearms. The ballistic pendulum consists of a block of material into which the bullet is fired. This block of material is suspended so that it forms a pendulum. From the deflection angle of the pendulum and the known masses of bullet, m, and block, M, the speed of the bullet right before it hit the block can be calculated, as we will show in the following.

Figure 7.11: Ballistic pendulum as used in an introductory physics laboratory.

In order to calculate the deflection angle, we have to calculate the speed of the bullet plus block combination right after the bullet gets stuck in the block. This collision is a prototypical totally inelastic collision, and thus we can apply equation (7.43). Because the pendulum is at rest before the bullet hits it, the speed of block plus bullet is

$$v = \frac{m}{m+M} v_b \tag{7.45}$$

where v_b is the speed of the bullet before it hits the block, and v is the speed of the block and bullet system right after impact. The kinetic energy of the bullet was $K_b = \frac{1}{2} m v_b^2$, whereas right after the collision the block plus bullet system has the kinetic energy

$$K = \tfrac{1}{2}(m+M)v^2 = \tfrac{1}{2}(m+M)\left(\frac{m}{m+M} v_b\right)^2 = \tfrac{1}{2} m v_b^2 \frac{m}{m+M} = \frac{m}{m+M} K_b \tag{7.46}$$

Obviously kinetic energy is not conserved in this process of the bullet getting stuck in the block. (In the case of a real ballistic pendulum this kinetic energy is transferred into deformation of bullet and block, and in this lecture demonstration version it is transferred into frictional work between the bullet and the block.) We have just shown in (7.46) that the total kinetic energy (and with it the total mechanical energy) is reduced by a factor of $m/(m+M)$. However, after the collision the block plus bullet system retains its remaining total energy in the ensuing pendulum motion, converting all of the initial kinetic energy of equation (7.46) into potential energy at the highest point,

$$U_{max} = (m+M)gh = K = \tfrac{1}{2}\frac{m^2}{m+M}v_b^2 \tag{7.47}$$

As you can see from Figure 7.11, the height h and angle θ are related via $h = \ell(1-\cos\theta)$, where ℓ is the length of the pendulum. (We have previously found this result in Solved Problem 6.4). Inserting this result into equation (7.47) yields

$$(m+M)g\ell(1-\cos\theta) = \tfrac{1}{2}\frac{m^2}{m+M}v_b^2 \Rightarrow$$

$$v_b = \frac{m+M}{m}\sqrt{2g\ell(1-\cos\theta)} \tag{7.48}$$

It is clear from this expression that one can measure practically any bullet speed in this way, provided one selects the mass of the block, M, appropriately.

For example, if you shoot a 357 Magnum caliber round (mass $m = 0.125$ kg) into a block of mass $M = 40.0$ kg suspended by a 1.00 m long rope and you get a deflection of 25.4 degrees, then equation (7.48) lets you deduce that the muzzle speed of this bullet fired from this particular gun that you used was 442 m/s (which is a typical value for this type of ammunition).

Self-Test Opportunity: If instead you use a bullet of half the mass of a 357 Magnum caliber round, what is then your deflection angle?

In-class exercise:
A ballistic pendulum is used to measure the speed of a bullet shot from a gun. The mass of the bullet is 50.0 g and the mass of the block is 20.0 kg. When the bullet strikes the block, the bullet/block system rises a vertical distance of 5.00 cm. What was the speed of the bullet as it struck the block?

a) 397 m/s.
b) 426 m/s.
c) 457 m/s.
d) 479 m/s.
e) 503 m/s.

Kinetic Energy Loss in Totally Inelastic Collisions

Because the total kinetic energy is not conserved in totally inelastic collisions, as we have just seen, we can ask exactly how much kinetic energy is lost in the general case. This loss can be calculated by taking the difference between the total initial kinetic energy, $K_i = p_{i1}^2/2m_1 + p_{i2}^2/2m_2$, and the total final kinetic energy. We calculate the total kinetic energy for the case that the two objects stick together and move as one with the total mass of $m_1 + m_2$ and velocity $\vec{v}_f$. It is:

$$K_f = \frac{1}{2}(m_1 + m_2)v_f^2 = \frac{1}{2}(m_1 + m_2)\left(\frac{m_1\vec{v}_{i1} + m_2\vec{v}_{i2}}{m_1 + m_2}\right)^2 = \frac{(m_1\vec{v}_{i1} + m_2\vec{v}_{i2})^2}{2(m_1 + m_2)} \qquad (7.49)$$

Now we can take the difference of the final and initial kinetic energy and obtain for the kinetic energy loss:

$$\Delta K = K_i - K_f = \frac{1}{2}\frac{m_1 m_2}{m_1 + m_2}(\vec{v}_{i1} - \vec{v}_{i2})^2 \qquad (7.50)$$

The derivation of this result involves a bit of algebra and is omitted here. What matters, though, is that the difference in the initial velocities, i.e. the initial relative velocity, enters in the energy loss. We will return to the significance of this fact in the following section, and then again in the next chapter, when we talk about center-of-mass motion.

In-class exercise:

Suppose mass 1 is initially at rest, and mass 2 moves initially with a speed $v_{i,2}$. The loss of kinetic energy is largest for

a) $m_1 \ll m_2$

b) $m_1 \gg m_2$

c) $m_1 = m_2$

Solved Problem

Solved Problem 7.2: Forensic Science

In Figure 7.12, a traffic accident is sketched. The white full size pickup truck (car 1) with mass m_1=2,209 kg is traveling north and hits the westbound red car (car 2) with mass m_2=1,474 kg. As the two vehicles smash into each other, they become entangled, i.e. stick to each other. Skid marks on the road reveal the exact location of the accident, and the direction in which the two vehicles were sliding immediately after the accident. This direction is measured to be 38° relative to the initial direction of the white pickup truck (car 1). The white pickup truck had the right of way, because the red car (car 2) had a stop sign. The driver of the red car (car 2), however, claimed that the driver of the white pickup truck (car 1) was moving with a speed of at least 50 mph (=22.35 m/s), whereas the speed limit was 25 mph (=11.18 m/s) for these roads. Furthermore, the driver of the red car (car 2) claimed that he had stopped at the stop sign and then driven through the intersection with a speed of less that 25 mph when the white pickup truck (car 1) hit him. Since the driver of the white pickup truck (car 1) was speeding, he would legally forfeit the right of way and have to be declared responsible for the accident.

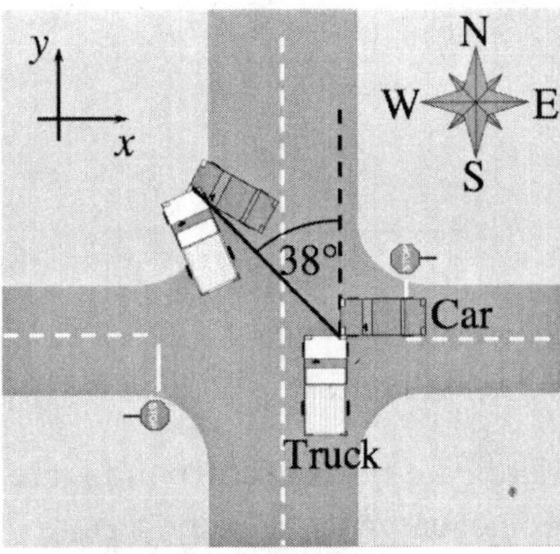

Figure 7.12: Sketch of the accident scene.

Question:
Can this version of the accident be correct?

Answer:

THINK: This collision is clearly a totally inelastic collision, and so we know that the velocity of the pair of colliding cars after the collision is given by (7.43). We are given the angles of the initial velocity of both cars and the angle of final velocity vector of the two cars joined together. However, we are not given the magnitudes of these three velocities. Thus we have one equation and three unknowns. However, for this problem it suffices to determine the ratio of the magnitude of the initial velocity of car 1 to the magnitude of the initial velocity of car 2. Here the initial velocity means the velocity of the vehicles just before the collision occurred.

SKETCH: A sketch of the velocity vectors of the two vehicles before and after the collision is shown in Figure 7.13.

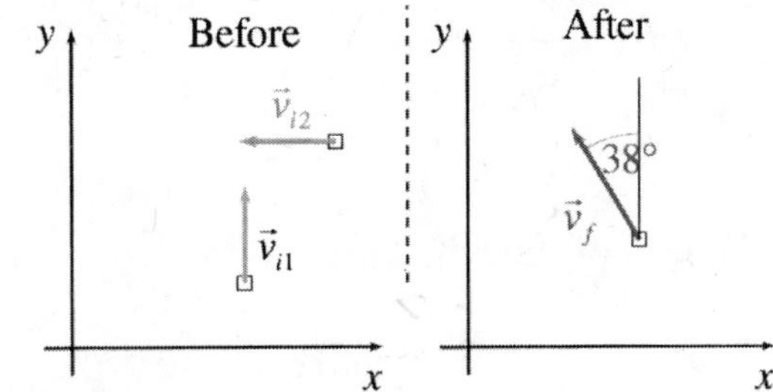

Figure 7.13: Velocity vectors of the two cars before and after the collision.

A sketch of the velocity vector of the two cars joined together after the collisions is shown in Figure 7.14.

Solved Problem

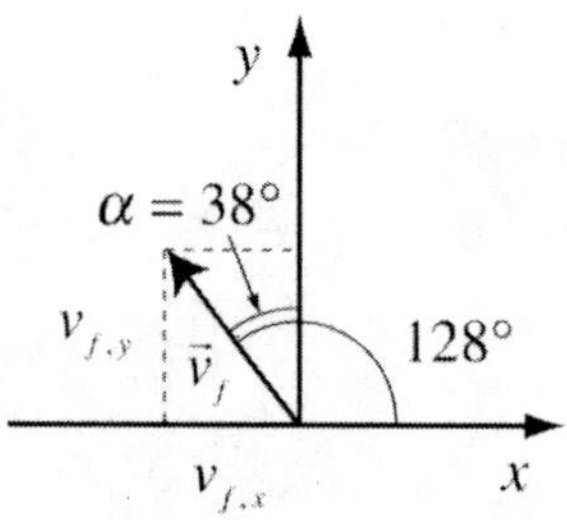

Figure 7.14: Velocity vector of the two cars after the collision.

Solved Problem

RESEARCH: Using the coordinate system shown in Figure 7.13, the white pickup truck (car 1) has only a y-component in its velocity vector, $\vec{v}_{i1} = v_{i1}\hat{y}$, where v_{i1} is the initial speed of the white pickup truck (car 1). The red car (car 2) has only a velocity component in the negative x direction, $\vec{v}_{i2} = -v_{i2}\hat{x}$. The final velocity $\vec{v}_f$ of the two cars after the collision expressed in terms of the initial velocities is given by

$$\vec{v}_f = \frac{m_1\vec{v}_{i1} + m_2\vec{v}_{i2}}{m_1 + m_2}$$

SIMPLIFY: Inserting the specified initial velocities into this equation for the final velocity leads to

$$\vec{v}_f = v_{fx}\hat{x} + v_{fy}\hat{y} = \frac{-m_2 v_{i2}}{m_1 + m_2}\hat{x} + \frac{m_1 v_{i1}}{m_1 + m_2}\hat{y}.$$

From trigonometry, we obtain an expression for the tangent of the angle of the final velocity as the ratio of its y and x components

$$\tan\alpha = \frac{v_{fy}}{v_{fx}} = \frac{\dfrac{m_1 v_{i1}}{m_1 + m_2}}{\dfrac{-m_2 v_{i2}}{m_1 + m_2}} = -\frac{m_1 v_{i1}}{m_2 v_{i2}}.$$

Thus we find for the initial speed of the white pickup truck (car 1)

$$v_{i,1} = -\frac{m_2 \tan\alpha}{m_1} v_{i,2}$$

in terms of the initial speed of the red car (car 2). We have to be careful with the value of the angle α. It is *not* $38°$, as one might conclude from a casual examination of Figure 7.14. Instead, it is $38° + 90° = 128°$, because angles must be measured relative to the positive x-axis when using the tangent formula $\tan\alpha = \dfrac{v_{fy}}{v_{fx}}$.

Solved Problem

CALCULATE: With this result, and the known values of the masses of the two cars, we find:

$$v_{i1} = -\frac{1474 \text{ kg} \cdot \tan 128°}{2209 \text{ kg}} v_{i2} = 0.854066983 v_{i2}$$

ROUND: The angle that the two cars moved after the collision was specified to two significant digits, so we report our answer to two significant digits

$$v_{i1} = 0.85 v_{i2}$$

So it follows that the white pickup truck (car 1) drove at a slower speed than the red car (car 2). The story of the driver of the red car (car 2) is not consistent with the facts. Apparently the driver of the white pickup truck (car 1) was not speeding at the time of the collision and the driver of the red car (car 2) running the stop sign caused the accident.

Self-Test Opportunity: To double-check these results for the traffic accident, give an estimate of what the angle would have been had the white pickup truck been traveling with a speed of 50 mph and the red car had been traveling with a speed of 25 mph just before the collision.

Explosions

In totally inelastic collisions two or more objects merge into one and move in unison with the same momentum after the collision. The reverse is also possible. If one object moves with initial momentum $\vec{p}_i$ and then explodes into fragments, the process of the explosion only generates internal forces between the fragments. Because an explosion takes place over a very short time, the impulse due to external forces usually can be neglected. In this case, according to Newton's third law, the total momentum is conserved. This result implies that the sum of the fragment momentum vectors has to add up to the initial momentum vector,

$$\vec{p}_i = \sum_{i=1}^{n} \vec{p}_f \tag{7.51}$$

This equation relating the momentum of the exploding object just before the explosion to the sum of the fragment momentum vectors after the explosion is exactly the same as the one for a totally inelastic collision, except that the indices for the initial and final states are exchanged.

In particular, if an object breaks up into two fragments, equation (7.51) is exactly equivalent to equation (7.43), with the indices i and f exchanged,

$$\vec{v}_i = \frac{m_1\vec{v}_{f1} + m_2\vec{v}_{f2}}{m_1 + m_2} \tag{7.52}$$

This relationship allows us, for example, to reconstruct the initial velocity, if the fragment velocities and masses are known. Further, the energy release in such a two-body breakup can be calculated from equation (7.50), again with the indices i and f exchanged,

$$\Delta K = K_f - K_i = \frac{1}{2}\frac{m_1 m_2}{m_1 + m_2}(\vec{v}_{f1} - \vec{v}_{f2})^2 \tag{7.53}$$

Example 7.3: Particle Physics

Use of the conservation laws of momentum and energy is essential in the work of particle physicists when they analyze the products of collisions of particles at high energies, such as the ones produced at Fermilab's Tevatron, near Chicago, Illinois, currently the World's highest energy proton-antiproton accelerator. (There is an accelerator called LHC that is planned to turn on in 2007 at the CERN Laboratory in Geneva Switzerland that will be more powerful than the Tevatron. However the LHC is a proton-proton accelerator.)

At the Tevatron accelerator particle physicists collide protons and antiprotons at total energies of 1.96 TeV (Hence the name!) Remember that 1 eV = $1.602\cdot 10^{-19}$ J; so 1.96 TeV = $1.96\cdot 10^{12}$ eV = $3.2\cdot 10^{-7}$ J. The Tevatron is set up so that the protons and antiprotons circulate in the collider ring in opposite directions with for practical purposes exactly opposite momentum vectors. The main detectors, DØ and CDF, are located at the interaction regions, where protons and antiprotons collide.

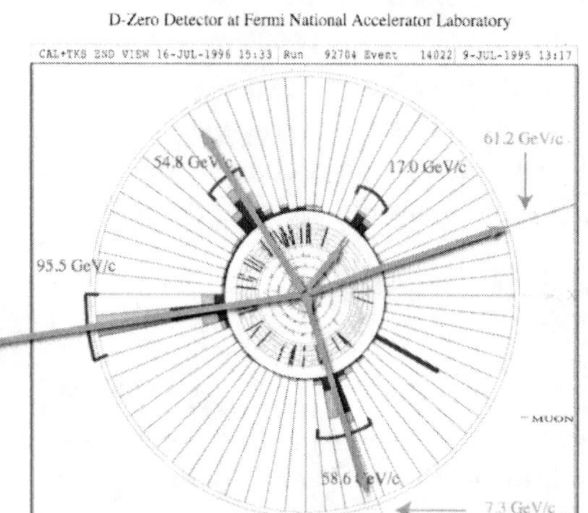

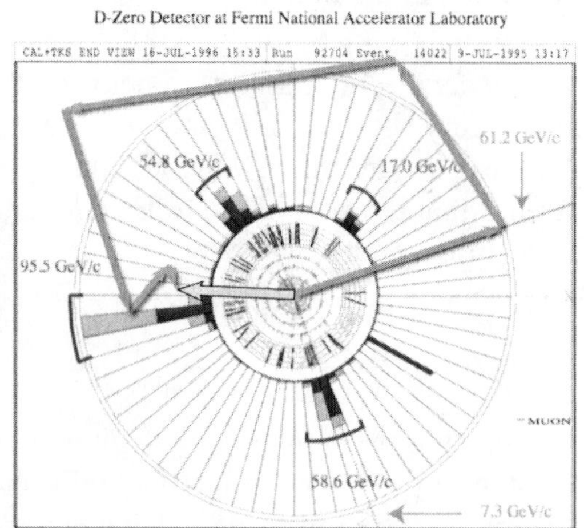

Figure 7.15: Event display generated by the DØ collaboration and the education office at Fermilab, showing a top-quark event. Left: momentum vectors of the detected produced particles; right: graphical addition of the momentum vectors, showing that they add up to a non-zero sum, indicated by the thicker green arrow.

In Figure 7.15 we show an example of such a collision. In this computer-generated event display of the DØ detector and of one particular collision event, the proton's initial

Example

momentum vector points exactly into the page and that of the antiproton exactly out of the page. Thus the total initial momentum of the proton-antiproton system is zero. The explosion produced by this collision produces several fragments, almost all of which are registered by the detector. These measurements are indicated in gray line segments inside of the inner circle in the event display shown in Figure 7.15. We superimposed on this event display the momentum vectors of the corresponding parent particles of these fragments, with their length and direction given by the information produced by the computer analysis of the detector response. (The momentum unit of GeV/*c*, commonly used in high-energy physics and shown in the figure, is simply the energy unit GeV divided by the speed of light.) On the right side of this figure, we add up the momentum vectors graphically, finding a non-zero vector sum, as indicated by the thicker green arrow.

However, momentum conservation absolutely requires that the sum of the momentum vectors of all particles produced in this collision must be zero. The conservation of momentum allows us to assign the missing momentum that would balance the momentum conservation to a particle that escaped undetected, a neutrino. With the aid of this missing-momentum analysis, physicists in the DØ collaboration were able to show that the event displayed here was one in which an elusive top-quark was produced.

Self-Test Opportunity: The length of the vector arrows is proportional to the magnitude of the momentum vector of the individual particles. Can you find out how big the momentum of the non-detected particle (green arrow) is in this example?

7.7. Partially Inelastic Collisions

You can now ask what happens if a collision is neither elastic nor totally inelastic. Most real collisions are somewhere in between these two extremes, as we have seen in Figure 7.6 and the associated coin collision experiment. And so it is important to take a look at partially inelastic collisions in more detail. We have already seen that the relative velocity of the two collision partners in one-dimensional elastic collisions simply changes sign. This is also true in two- and three- dimensional elastic collisions, although we do not prove this here. The relative velocity becomes zero in totally inelastic collisions. So it seems logical to have a definition of the elasticity of a collision that involves the ratio of initial and final relative velocities.

Thus we define the coefficient of restitution as the ratio of the magnitudes of the final to the initial relative velocities in the collision,

$$\varepsilon = \frac{|\vec{v}_{f1} - \vec{v}_{f2}|}{|\vec{v}_{i1} - \vec{v}_{i2}|} \tag{7.54}$$

With this definition, we obtain a coefficient of restitution of $\varepsilon = 1$ for elastic collisions, and $\varepsilon = 0$ for totally inelastic collisions.

First, let us examine what happens in the limit that one of the two colliding partners is the ground (for all intents and purposes, infinitely massive) and the other one a ball. If you release the ball from some height, h_i, we know that it reaches a speed of $v_i = \sqrt{2gh_i}$ immediately before it collides with the ground. If the collision is elastic, its speed just after the collision is the same, $v_f = v_i = \sqrt{2gh_i}$, and it bounces back to the exact same height from which it was released. If the collision is totally inelastic, as is the case for a ball of putty that falls to the ground and then just stays there, then the final speed is 0. For all cases in between, one can measure the coefficient of restitution from the height h_f that the ball returns to:

$$h_f = \frac{v_f^2}{2g} = \frac{\varepsilon^2 v_i^2}{2g} = \varepsilon^2 h_i \Rightarrow$$
$$\varepsilon = \sqrt{h_f / h_i} \tag{7.55}$$

Using this method to measure the coefficient of restitution, one finds for baseballs that $\varepsilon = 0.58$ for typical relative velocities that would be involved in ball-bat collisions in major-league games.

In general, we state (without proof) that we can calculate the kinetic energy loss in partially inelastic collisions as:

$$\Delta K = K_i - K_f = \frac{1}{2}\frac{m_1 m_2}{m_1 + m_2}(1-\varepsilon^2)(\vec{v}_{i1} - \vec{v}_{i2})^2 \tag{7.56}$$

In the limit of $\varepsilon \to 1$ we obtain $\Delta K = 0$, i.e. no loss in kinetic energy, as required for elastic collisions. And in the limit $\varepsilon \to 0$ of (7.56) we find the limit for totally inelastic collisions already shown in (7.53).

Self-Test Opportunity: The maximum kinetic energy loss is obtained in the limit of a totally inelastic collision. What fraction of this maximum possible energy loss is obtained in the case of $\varepsilon = \frac{1}{2}$?

Partially Inelastic Collision with a Wall

If you play racquetball or especially squash, you know that the ball loses energy when you hit it against the wall. While we have seen above that the angle with which a ball bounces off the wall in an elastic collision is the same as the angle with which it hit the wall, the answer of the final angle is not so clear for the present partially elastic case (depicted in Figure 7.16).

The key to obtaining a first approximation to this situation is to consider only the normal force, which acts in a perpendicular direction to the wall. Then the momentum component along the wall still remains unchanged, just like in the elastic case. But now the momentum component perpendicular to the wall does not simply get inverted, but also reduced in magnitude by the coefficient of restitution, $\vec{p}_{f,\perp} = -\varepsilon \vec{p}_{i,\perp}$. In this approximation we obtain a larger angle of reflection relative to the normal than the initial angle,

$$\theta_f = \operatorname{arc\,cot}\frac{p_{f,\perp}}{p_{f,\parallel}} = \operatorname{arc\,cot}\frac{\varepsilon p_{i,\perp}}{p_{i,\parallel}} > \theta_i \tag{7.57}$$

The magnitude of the final momentum vector is also changed and reduced to

$$p_f = \sqrt{p_{f,\parallel}^2 + p_{f,\perp}^2} = \sqrt{p_{i,\parallel}^2 + \varepsilon^2 p_{i,\perp}^2} < p_i \tag{7.58}$$

If we want a more quantitative description, we also need to include the effect of a friction force between ball and wall, acting for the duration of the collision. (This is why squash-balls and racquetballs leave blue marks on the walls.) Further, the collision with the wall also changes the rotation of the ball, and thus additionally alters the direction and kinetic energy of the ball bouncing off. But equation (7.57) and (7.58) still provide a very reasonable first approximation to partially inelastic collisions with walls.

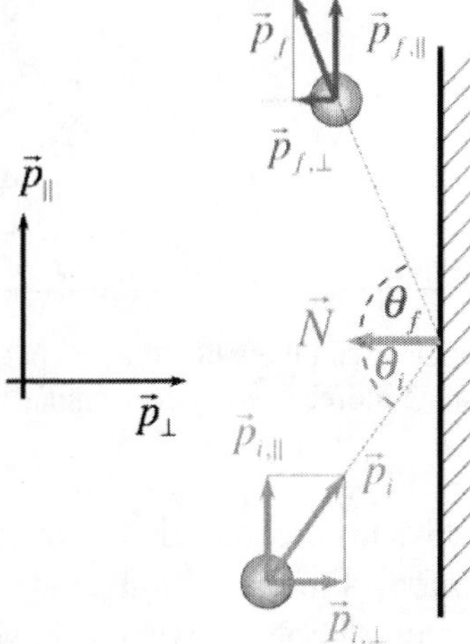

Figure 7.16: Partially inelastic collision of a ball with a wall.

7.8. Billiards and Chaos

Let us look at billiard systems in an abstract way. Our "billiard" is going to be a rectangular (or even square) area, in which particles can bounce around and have elastic collisions with the wall. Between collisions, these particles move on straight trajectories without energy loss. When we start two particles close to each other, as in the left part of the drawing in Figure 7.17, they stay close to each other. In the left panel, we show the trajectories (red and green lines) of two particles, which started close to each other and with the same initial momentum (indicated by the red arrow). And you can clearly see that the two particles stay close the entire time.

The situation becomes qualitatively different when you add a circular wall in the middle of the billiard. Now each collision with the circle drives the two trajectories farther apart. In the right panel, you can see that one collision with the circle was enough to separate the red and green line for good. This type of billiard is called a Sinai-billiard, named after the Russian Academician Yakov Sinai (1935-) who studied it first in 1970. While the conventional billiard system shows regular motion, the Sinai-billiard exhibits chaotic motion. And surprisingly these billiard systems are still not fully explored. Cutting edge modern physics research gains new knowledge of these systems all the time, and thus explores the physics of chaos.

Here is one example from the authors' own research. Only in the last decade have we begun to understand the decay properties of these systems. If you cut a small hole into the wall of a conventional billiard table and measure the time it takes a particle to hit this hole and escape, you obtain a power-law decay time distribution. If you do the same for the Sinai-billiard, you obtain an exponential time dependence of the escape.

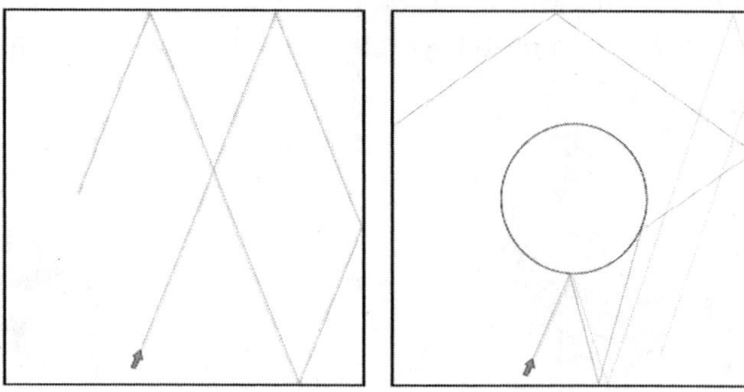

Figure 7.17: Collision of particles with the walls for two particles starting out very close to each other and with the same momentum. Left: regular billiard, right: Sinai-billiard

These types of investigations are by no means idle theoretical speculations. If you want, you can do the following experiment. Place a billiard ball on the surface of a table and hold on to the ball. Then hold a second one as exactly as you can over the first one and release it from a height of a few inches (or centimeters). You will see that the upper one cannot be made to bounce on the lower one more than three or four times, before falling off in some uncontrollable direction. Even if you could fix the location of the two balls to atomic precision, the upper ball would fall off after only ten to fifteen bounces. This result means that after only a few collisions your ability to predict the outcome of this experiment has completely vanished. This limitation of predictability goes to the heart of chaos science. It is one of the main reasons, for example, that exact long-time weather forecasting is impossible. Air molecules, after all, bounce off each other too, and we have just examined how unpredictable these scatterings become after only short time spans.

Laplace's Demon

Marquis Pierre-Simon Laplace (1749-1827) was an eminent French physicist and mathematician of the 18th century. He lived during the time of the French Revolution and other great societal upheavals, characterized by the struggle for self-determination and freedom. No painting symbolizes this better than "*Liberty Leading the People*" (1830) by Eugène Delacroix, shown here in Figure 7.18.

Figure 7.18: "Liberty Leading the People", Eugène Delacroix (Louvre, Paris, France).

Laplace had an interesting idea, now known as Laplace's Demon. He reasoned that everything is made out of atoms, and all atoms obey differential equations governed by the forces acting on them. If one were to feed all initial positions and velocities of all atoms, together with all force laws, into a huge computer (he called this an "intellect"), then "for such an intellect nothing could be uncertain and the future just like the past would be present before its eyes". This situation implies that everything is predetermined, and we are all only cogs in a huge clockwork. If you think this line of reasoning through to its ultimate consequence, it means that nobody has free will. And Laplace came up with this idea in a period when quite a few people believed that they could achieve free will, if they only killed enough people presently in power.

The rescue from Laplace's Demon comes from the combination of two areas of physics. One is chaos science that tells us that long-term predictability is sensitively dependent on the knowledge of the initial conditions, as seen in the example of bouncing billiard balls above. And of course the same principle applies to molecules bouncing off each other, as for example air molecules do. The other ingredient is the impossibility to specify both the position and the momentum of any object exactly at the same time. We will return to this point when we discuss the Uncertainty Relation in quantum physics (chapter 36). But what we can already take from this discussion is the certainty that the concept of free will is still alive and well – the concept of long-term predictability of large systems like the weather or the human brain is impossible. The combination of chaos theory and quantum theory ensure that Laplace's Demon or any computer cannot possibly calculate and predict what your individual decisions will turn out to be.

What we have learned/Exam Study Guide:

- Momentum is defined to be the product of mass times velocity: $\vec{p} = m\vec{v}$.
- Newton's Second Law can be written as $\vec{F} = d\vec{p}/dt$.
- The impulse is the momentum change and is equal to the time integral over the

applied external force: $\vec{J} = \Delta\vec{p} = \int_{t_i}^{t_f} \vec{F}dt$.

- In collisions of two objects, momentum can be exchanged, but the sum of the momenta of the colliding objects remains constant, $\vec{p}_{f1} + \vec{p}_{f2} = \vec{p}_{i1} + \vec{p}_{i2}$.
- We distinguish between elastic, totally inelastic, and partially elastic collisions.
- In elastic collisions, the total kinetic energy also remains constant, $\frac{p_{f1}^2}{2m_1} + \frac{p_{f2}^2}{2m_2} = \frac{p_{i1}^2}{2m_1} + \frac{p_{i2}^2}{2m_2}$.
- One-dimensional elastic collisions can be solved in general, and the final velocities of the two colliding objects can be expressed as a function of the initial velocities:
$$v_{f1,x} = \frac{m_1 - m_2}{m_1 + m_2} v_{i1,x} + \frac{2m_2}{m_1 + m_2} v_{i2,x}$$
$$v_{f2,x} = \frac{2m_1}{m_1 + m_2} v_{i1,x} + \frac{m_2 - m_1}{m_1 + m_2} v_{i2,x}$$
- In totally inelastic collisions, the colliding partners stick together after the collision and have the same velocity, $\vec{v}_f = (m_1\vec{v}_{i1} + m_2\vec{v}_{i2})/(m_1 + m_2)$.
- All partially inelastic collisions between the two extremes are characterized by a coefficient of restitution, defined as the ratio of the magnitudes of the final and the initial relative velocity, $\varepsilon = |\vec{v}_{f1} - \vec{v}_{f2}|/|\vec{v}_{i1} - \vec{v}_{i2}|$. The kinetic energy loss in partially inelastic collisions is then given by
$$\Delta K = K_i - K_f = \frac{1}{2}\frac{m_1 m_2}{m_1 + m_2}(1 - \varepsilon^2)(\vec{v}_{i1} - \vec{v}_{i2})^2$$

Additional Solved Problems

Solved Problem

Solved Problem 7.3: Egg Drop

Question:

An egg in a special container is dropped from a height of 3.70 m. The container and egg have a mass of 144.0 g. A force of 4.42 N will break the egg. What is the minimum time over which the egg in its container can come to a stop without breaking the egg?

Answer:

THINK: When the egg and its container are released, they will accelerate with the acceleration of gravity. When the egg/container strikes the ground, the velocity of the egg/container will go from the final velocity resulting from the gravitational acceleration to zero. As the egg/container is coming to a stop, the force stopping the egg/container times the time interval will equal the mass of the egg/container times the change in speed. The time interval over which the velocity change takes place will determine whether the

Solved Problem

force exerted on the egg by the collision with the floor will break the egg or not.

SKETCH: The egg/container is dropped from rest from a height of $h = 3.70$ m as shown in Figure 7.19.

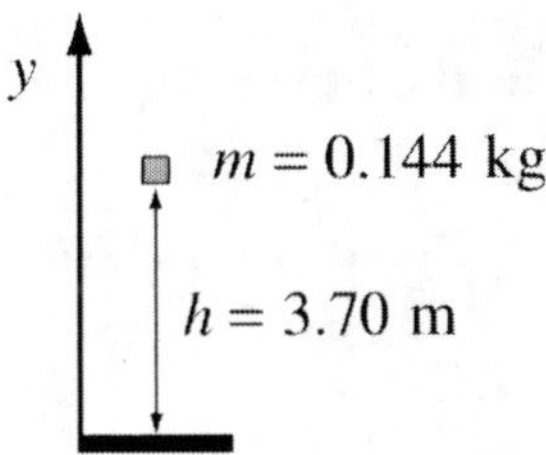

Figure 7.19: An egg in special container is dropped from a height of 3.70 m.

RESEARCH: The kinematics of free-fall tell us that the final velocity v_y of the egg/container resulting from free-fall from a height of y_0 to a final height of y starting with an initial velocity v_{y0} is given by

$$v_f^2 = v_{f0}^2 - 2g(y - y_0). \tag{7.59}$$

We know that $v_{f0} = 0$ because the egg/container was release from rest. We define the final height to be $y = 0$ and the initial height to be $y_0 = h$ as shown in Figure 7.19. Thus our expression for the final speed in the y-direction (7.59) reduces to

$$v_y = \sqrt{2gh}. \tag{7.60}$$

When the egg/container strikes the ground, the impulse $\vec{J}$ exerted on the egg-container is given by

$$\vec{J} = \Delta\vec{p} = \int_{t_1}^{t_2} \vec{F}dt \tag{7.61}$$

where $\Delta\vec{p}$ is the change in momentum of the egg/container and $\vec{F}$ is the force exerted to stop the egg/container. In this problem, the force is assumed to be constant so we can re-write the integral as

$$\int_{t_1}^{t_2} \vec{F}dt = \vec{F}(t_2 - t_1) = \vec{F}\Delta t. \tag{7.62}$$

The momentum of the egg/container will change from $p = mv_y$ to $p = 0$ when the egg/container strikes the ground so we can write

$$\Delta p_y = 0 - (-mv_y) = mv_y = F_y\Delta t \tag{7.63}$$

Solved Problem

where the term $-mv_y$ is negative because the velocity of the egg/container just before impact is in the negative y-direction.

SIMPLIFY: We can now solve for the time interval using (7.60) and (7.63)

$$\Delta t = \frac{mv_y}{F} = \frac{m\sqrt{2gh}}{F} \tag{7.64}$$

CALCULATE: Putting our numerical values into (7.64) we get

$$\Delta t = \frac{(0.144 \text{ kg})\sqrt{2(9.81 \text{ m/s}^2)(3.70 \text{ m})}}{4.42 \text{ m}} = 0.277581543 \text{ s}.$$

ROUND: All of the numerical values in this problem are specified to three significant digits so we report our answer as

$$\Delta t = 0.278 \text{ s}.$$

DOUBLE-CHECK: Slowing the egg/container from its final velocity to zero over a time interval of 0.278 s seems reasonable. Looking at (7.64) we see that the force exerted on the egg as it hits the ground is given by

$$F = \frac{mv_y}{\Delta t}.$$

For a given height, we could reduce the force exerted on the egg in several ways. We could make Δt larger by making some kind of crumple zone in the container. Second, we could make the egg/container as light as possible. Third, we could construct the container such that it had a large area and thus had significant air resistance, which would reduce v_y from its frictionless free-fall value.

Solved Problem

Solved Problem 7.4: Collision with Parked Car

Question:
A moving truck strikes a parked car. During the collision, the cars stick together and then slide to a stop together. The moving truck has a total mass of 1982 kg (including the driver), and the parked car has a total mass of 966.0 kg. If the cars slide 10.5 m before coming to rest, how fast was the truck going? The coefficient of sliding friction between the tires and the road is 0.350.

Answer:

THINK: This problem involves the totally inelastic collision of a moving truck with a parked car. After the collision, the two vehicles slide to a stop. The kinetic energy of the combined truck/car system just after the collision is reduced by the work done by friction while the cars are sliding. The kinetic energy of the truck/car system can be related to the initial speed of the truck before the collision.

SKETCH: In Figure 7.20 we show a sketch of the moving truck m_1 and parked car m_2. Before the collision, the truck is moving with an initial speed of $v_{i,1}$. After the truck collides with the car, the two vehicles slide together with an initial speed of v_f.

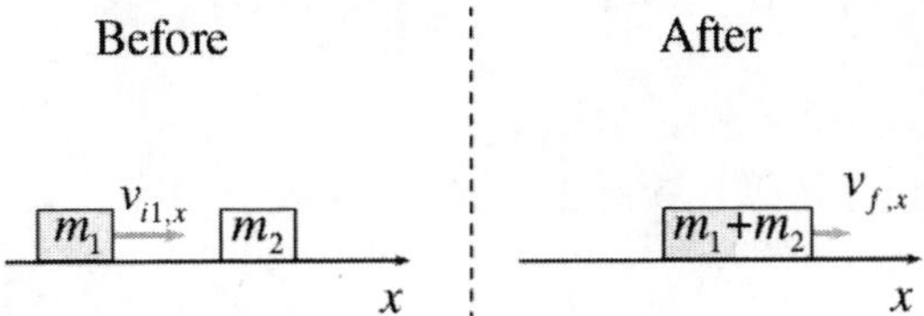

Figure 7.20: Sketch of collision of a moving truck with a parked car.

RESEARCH: Momentum conservation tells us that the $x-$ component of velocity of the two cars just after the totally inelastic collision is given by

$$v_{f,x} = \frac{m_1 v_{i1,x}}{m_1 + m_2}. \tag{7.65}$$

The kinetic energy of the combined truck/car system just after the collision is

$$K = \frac{1}{2}(m_1 + m_2)v_f^2 \tag{7.66}$$

where, as usual, v_f is the final speed.

We can solve this remainder of this problem using the Work-Energy Theorem from Chapter 6, $W_{nc} = \Delta K + \Delta U$. The work done by friction, W_f, on the truck/car system is equal to the change in kinetic energy ΔK of the truck/car system since $\Delta U = 0$ in this case. The change in kinetic energy is equal to zero (since the truck and car finally stop) minus the kinetic energy of the truck/car system just after the collision. We can then write

$$W_f = \Delta K. \tag{7.67}$$

The truck/car system slides a distance d. The $x-$ component of the frictional force

Solved Problem

Solved Problem

slowing down the truck/car system is given by $f_x = -\mu_k N$ where μ_k is the coefficient of kinetic friction and N is magnitude of the normal force. In this case, the normal force has a magnitude equal to the weight of the truck/car system, or $N = (m_1 + m_2)g$. The work is equal to the $x-$component of the force of friction times the distance that the truck/car system slides along the x axis, so we can write

$$W_f = f_x d = -\mu_k (m_1 + m_2) gd. \tag{7.68}$$

SIMPLIFY: We can combine (7.65) and (7.66) and get

$$K = \frac{1}{2}(m_1 + m_2)v_f^2 = \frac{1}{2}(m_1 + m_2)\left(\frac{m_1 v_{i1}}{m_1 + m_2}\right)^2 = \frac{(m_1 v_{i1})^2}{2(m_1 + m_2)}. \tag{7.69}$$

Combining this equation with (7.67) and (7.68) we get

$$\Delta K = W_f = 0 - \frac{(m_1 v_{i1})^2}{2(m_1 + m_2)} = -\mu_k (m_1 + m_2) gd. \tag{7.70}$$

Solving for v_{i1} finally leads us to

$$v_{i1} = \frac{(m_1 + m_2)}{m_1}\sqrt{2\mu_k gd}. \tag{7.71}$$

CALCULATE: Putting in our numerical values into (7.71) we get

$$v_{i1} = \frac{1982 \text{ kg} + 966 \text{ kg}}{966 \text{ kg}}\sqrt{2 \cdot 0.350 \cdot 9.81 \text{ m/s}^2 \cdot 10.5 \text{ m}} = 25.91364626 \text{ m/s}$$

ROUND: All of the numerical values in this problem were specified to three significant digits so we report our result as

$$v_{i1} = 25.9 \text{ m/s}.$$

DOUBLE-CHECK: The initial speed of the truck was 25.9 m/s, which corresponds to 57.9 miles per hour, which is at least within the range of normal speeds for vehicles on highways.

Chapter 8. Systems of Particles and Extended Objects

What we will learn:

- The center of mass, interchangeably also called center of gravity, is the point at which we can represent an extended object by a point-like object.
- We can calculate the position of the combined center of mass of two or more objects by taking the sum of their position vectors, weighted by their individual masses.
- It is possible to calculate the location of the center of mass of an extended object by an integration of its mass density over its entire volume, weighted by the coordinate vector, and then divided by the total mass.
- The integration procedure can be greatly simplified if there is a mirror-symmetry in the object under consideration. The center of mass then lies in the symmetry plane. If there is more than one symmetry plane, the center of mass lies on the line or point of intersection of the planes.
- The translational motion of the center of mass of extended objects can be described by Newtonian mechanics.
- The center of mass linear momentum is the sum of the linear momenta of the parts of the system. Its time derivative is equal to the total net external force acting on the system, an extended formulation of Newton's Second Law.
- For systems of two particles, we can work in terms of center of mass momentum and relative momentum instead of the individual momenta, giving us deeper insight into the physics of collisions and recoil phenomena.
- For rocket motion we have to consider systems with varying mass. This variation

leads to a logarithmic dependence of the velocity of the rocket on the initial versus final mass ratio.

8.1. Center of Mass / Center of Gravity

In our discussion so far, we have always represented the location of objects by coordinates of a single point. For example, when we use the phrase "a car is located at $x = 3.2$ m", we surely do not want to imply that the entire car is located at that point. So what does it mean to give the coordinate of one particular point to represent an extended object? Of course there are many answers to this question, and they depend on the particular application that one has in mind. In auto racing, for example, the cars' locations are represented by the coordinate of the front-most part of the car. When this point crosses the finish line, the race is decided. On the other hand, in soccer a goal is only counted when the entire ball has crossed the goal line, and in this case it makes sense to represent the soccer ball's location by the coordinates of the back-most part of the ball. These are exceptions however, and for almost all situations there is a natural choice of a point that represents the location of an extended object. This point is called the *center of mass*.

> The center of mass is defined as the point in which we can imagine all of the mass of the object to be concentrated.

As a consequence of this definition, the center of mass is also the point in which we can imagine the force of gravity acting on the entire object to be concentrated. Of course, if we can imagine all of the mass to be concentrated in that point, when calculating the force due to gravity, it is also legitimate to call this point the *center of gravity*, another commonly used expression that can be used interchangeably with "center of mass". (To be precise, however, we should note that these two terms are only equivalent in situations where gravity is constant everywhere throughout the object. In chapter 12 we will see that this is not the case for very large objects.)

As a motivation for what is to follow, we just mention that the center of mass / center of gravity is located in the geometrical center of an object, if its mass density is constant. So for most objects in our everyday experience it is a reasonable first guess that the center of gravity is the "middle" of the object. The derivations in this chapter will bear out this conjecture.

Combined Center of Mass for Several Objects

If we have two identical objects of equal mass and want to calculate the center of mass / center of gravity of the combination of the two objects, then it is reasonable from symmetry considerations that the combined center of mass of this system is exactly in the middle between the individual centers of gravity of the two objects. If one of the two objects is heavier, then it is equally reasonable to assume that the combined center of mass is closer to that of the heavier one. We postulate that the general method of calculating the location of the center of mass, $\vec{R}$, for two masses m_1 and m_2 located at positions $\vec{r}_1$ and $\vec{r}_2$ relative to an arbitrary coordinate system is (see Figure 8.1):

$$\vec{R} = \frac{\vec{r}_1 m_1 + \vec{r}_2 m_2}{m_1 + m_2} \tag{8.1}$$

This definition implies that the center of mass coordinate is a sum of the coordinates of the individual objects, weighted by their mass. It is consistent with the empirical evidence that we have just cited. For now we will work with this as a working definition and gradually work out its consequences. However, further in this chapter and in the following chapters we will also see that there are additional reasons why this definition makes sense.

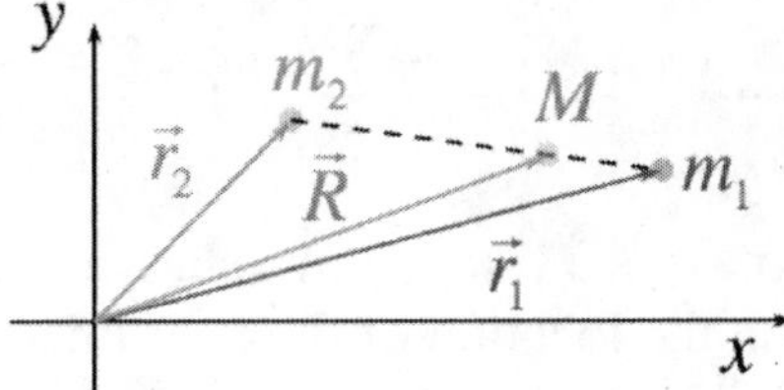

Figure 8.1: Location of center of mass for a system of two masses.

In-class exercise:
In the case sketched in Figure 8.1, what can we say about the relative magnitude of the two masses m_1 and m_2?

a) $m_1 < m_2$

b) $m_1 > m_2$

c) $m_1 = m_2$

d) Based solely on the information given in this figure, it is not possible to decide which of the two masses is larger.

Self-Test Opportunity:
In Figure 8.1 we have drawn the location of the center of mass exactly onto the straight line (dashed black line) that connects the two masses. Is this a general result, i.e. does the center of mass always lie on this line? If yes, why? If no, what is the special condition that is needed for this to be the case?

We can immediately generalize this definition of the center of mass to the case where a total of n objects with different masses m_i are located at different positions $\vec{r}_i$, and get in this general case

$$\vec{R} = \frac{\vec{r}_1 m_1 + \vec{r}_2 m_2 + \ldots + \vec{r}_n m_n}{m_1 + m_2 \ldots + m_n} = \frac{\sum_{i=1}^{n} \vec{r}_i m_i}{\sum_{i=1}^{n} m_i} = \frac{1}{M}\sum_{i=1}^{n} \vec{r}_i m_i \tag{8.2}$$

Here we use the symbol M for the combined mass of all objects,

$$M = \sum_{i=1}^{n} m_i \tag{8.3}$$

Writing (8.2) in Cartesian components we obtain

$$X = \frac{1}{M}\sum_{i=1}^{n} x_i m_i; \quad Y = \frac{1}{M}\sum_{i=1}^{n} y_i m_i; \quad Z = \frac{1}{M}\sum_{i=1}^{n} z_i m_i \tag{8.4}$$

The location of the center of mass is a fixed point relative to the object or system of objects and does not depend on the location of the coordinate system used to describe the center of mass. We can see this by taking the system described in (8.2) and moving the whole system by $\vec{r}_0$, resulting in a new center of mass position $\vec{R} + \vec{R}_0$. Using the above formulation we find

$$\vec{R} + \vec{R}_0 = \frac{\sum_{i=1}^{n} (\vec{r}_0 + \vec{r}_i) m_i}{\sum_{i=1}^{n} m_i} = \vec{r}_0 + \frac{1}{M}\sum_{i=1}^{n} \vec{r}_i m_i$$

So $\vec{R}_0 = \vec{r}_0$ and thus the center of mass location does not change relative to the object.

In-class exercise:
The Earth has a mass of $5.97 \cdot 10^{24}$ kg and the Moon has a mass of $7.36 \cdot 10^{22}$ kg. The distance between the Earth and the Moon is 384,000 km. How far from the center of the Earth is the center of mass of the Earth-Moon system?
a) 504 km b) 1,240 km c) 3,200 km d) 4,680 km e) 192,000 km

In-class exercise:
How does the location of the center of mass of the Earth-Moon system compare with radius of the Earth ($R_E = 6{,}380$ km)?
a) inside the radius of the Earth
b) outside the radius of the Earth
c) same as the radius of the Earth

8.2. Three-Dimensional Non-Cartesian Coordinate Systems

In chapter 1 we introduced a three-dimensional orthogonal coordinate system, the Cartesian coordinate system with coordinates x, y, z. But for some applications it is useful to represent the position vector in different coordinate systems. Here we give a very brief introduction to the two most commonly used three-dimensional orthogonal coordinate systems. In each of these cases we need to specify a vector in three-dimensional space by three values of the individual coordinates. We define the three coordinates used for each coordinate system and give the mapping between these coordinates and the Cartesian coordinates.

Spherical Coordinates

In spherical coordinates we represent the position vector $\vec{r}$ by giving its length, r, its polar angle relative to the positive z-axis, ϑ, and the azimuthal angle of the vector's projection into the xy-plane relative to the positive x-axis, φ. (See Figure 8.2)

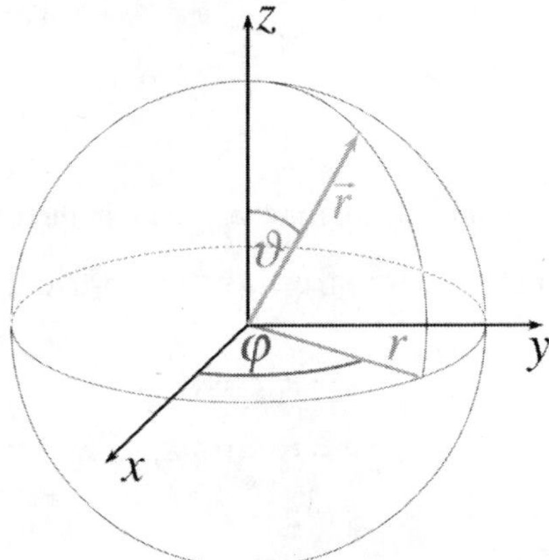

Figure 8.2: Spherical coordinate system in three dimensions.

We can obtain the Cartesian coordinates of the same vector from the spherical coordinates via the transformation

$$\begin{aligned} x &= r\cos\varphi\sin\vartheta \\ y &= r\sin\varphi\sin\vartheta \, . \\ z &= r\cos\vartheta \end{aligned} \tag{8.5}$$

The inverse transformation from Cartesian to spherical coordinates is

$$\begin{aligned} r &= \sqrt{x^2+y^2+z^2} \\ \vartheta &= \cos^{-1}\left(\frac{z}{\sqrt{x^2+y^2+z^2}}\right) . \\ \varphi &= \tan^{-1}\left(\frac{y}{x}\right) \end{aligned} \tag{8.6}$$

Cylindrical Coordinates

Cylindrical coordinates can be thought of as some sort of compromise between Cartesian and spherical coordinate systems, in the sense that we are retaining the Cartesian z-coordinate, but replace the Cartesian coordinates x and y by the coordinates $r_\perp$ and φ. $r_\perp$ specifies the length of the projection of the vector $\vec{r}$ onto the xy plane. So it is the perpendicular distance to the z-axis. And just like for spherical coordinates, φ is the angle of the vector's projection into the xy-plane relative to the positive x-axis.

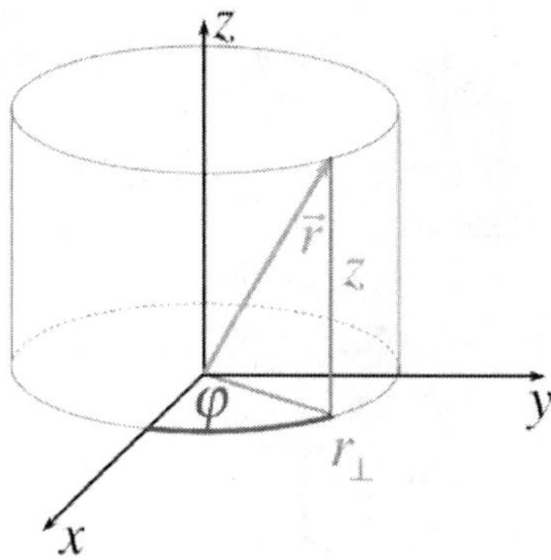

Figure 8.3: Cylindrical coordinate system in three dimensions

We can obtain the Cartesian coordinates from the cylindrical coordinates via

$$\begin{aligned} x &= r_\perp \cos\varphi \\ y &= r_\perp \sin\varphi \\ z &= z \end{aligned} \tag{8.7}$$

In this case the inverse transformation from Cartesian to cylindrical coordinates is

$$\begin{aligned} r_\perp &= \sqrt{x^2+y^2} \\ \varphi &= \tan^{-1}\left(\frac{y}{x}\right) \\ z &= z \end{aligned} \tag{8.8}$$

As a rule of thumb, you should use a Cartesian coordinate system as your first attempt in any physical situations that you want to describe. However, often cylindrical and spherical coordinate systems are preferable for "round" objects. As we proceed further in this chapter we will make use of a cylindrical coordinate system to perform a three-dimensional volume integral. In the next chapter, we will give a more extensive discussion of polar coordinates, which can be thought of as the two-dimensional equivalent of either cylindrical or spherical coordinates. And in chapter 10 we will return to the use of spherical and cylindrical coordinates to solve somewhat more complicated integration problems.

8.3. Calculating the Center of Mass

So far we have avoided asking the central question: How does one calculate the location of the center of mass for an arbitrarily shaped object? To answer this question, we examine Figure 8.4. Shown is a hammer, for which we want to calculate the location of the center of mass. To do this, we can represent the hammer by little identical-sized cubes, as shown in the lower part of the figure. The centers of the cubes are their individual centers of gravity and are marked with red dots. The red arrows are the coordinate vectors of the cubes. If we accept the collection of cubes as a good approximation for the hammer, we can use (8.2) to find the center of mass of the collection of cubes and with it that of the hammer.

Figure 8.4: Calculating the center of mass for a hammer.

Obviously, not all cubes have the same mass, though, because the densities of the wooden handle and the iron head are vastly different. The relationship between mass density ρ, mass, and volume is given by:

$$\rho = \frac{dm}{dV}. \tag{8.9}$$

If the mass density is uniformly constant throughout an object, then we simply have

$$\rho = \frac{M}{V} \quad (\text{for constant } \rho). \tag{8.10}$$

We can then use the mass density and re-write (8.2) as:

$$\vec{R} = \frac{1}{M}\sum_{i=1}^{n} \vec{r}_i m_i = \frac{1}{M}\sum_{i=1}^{n} \vec{r}_i \rho(\vec{r}_i) V_i. \tag{8.11}$$

Here we have assumed that the mass density inside each of our little cubes is constant (but still possibly different from one cube to another), and that each cube has the same (small) volume V.

We can obtain a better and better approximation by shrinking the volume of each cube and using a larger and larger number of cubes. This procedure should look very familiar to you, because it is exactly what is done in calculus to arrive at the limit of the integral. In this limit, we obtain for the location of the center of mass for an arbitrarily shaped object:

$$\vec{R} = \frac{1}{M}\int_V \vec{r}\rho(\vec{r})dV \, . \tag{8.12}$$

Here the three-dimensional volume integral extends over the entire volume of the object under consideration.

Mathematical Insert: Volume Integrals

Even though calculus is a prerequisite for physics, many universities allow the introductory physics sequence and the calculus sequence of courses to proceed simultaneously. In general this approach works well, but when one introduces multi-dimensional integrals in physics, it usually means that this is the first time that students have encountered this notation. Therefore at this point we introduce the basic procedure that one follows to perform these integrations, without trying to give an exhaustive treatment of the subject.

If we want to integrate any function over a volume in three dimensions, we need to find an expression for the volume element dV in an appropriately selected set of coordinates. Unless there is an extremely important reason not to, you should always select orthogonal coordinate systems. The three sets of orthogonal coordinates in three dimensions that we have introduced so far, Cartesian, cylindrical, and spherical, are also the only ones in practical use.

It is by far easiest to express the volume element dV in Cartesian coordinates. Then it is simply the product of the three individual coordinate elements, and the three-dimensional volume integral written in Cartesian coordinates becomes

$$\int_V f(\vec{r})dV = \int_{z_{\min}}^{z_{\max}} \left(\int_{y_{\min}}^{y_{\max}} \left(\int_{x_{\min}}^{x_{\max}} f(\vec{r})dx \right) dy \right) dz \tag{8.13}$$

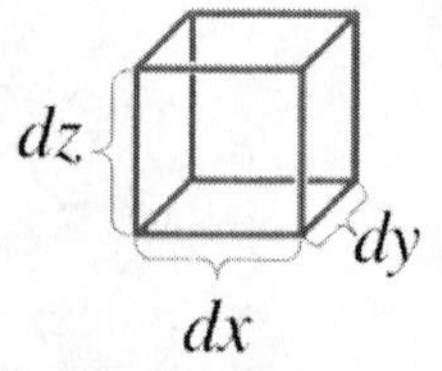

dz
dy
dx

Figure 8.5: Volume element in Cartesian coordinates

In this equation $f(\vec{r})$ can be an arbitrary function of the position. The lower and upper boundaries for the individual coordinates are denoted by $x_{\min}, x_{\max}, \ldots$ The convention is to solve the inner-most integral first, and then work our way outside. For (8.13) this would mean that we first execute the x-integration, then the y-integration, and finally the z-integration. But any other order is also possible. An equally valid way of writing the integral in (8.13) would be

$$\int_V f(\vec{r})dV = \int_{x_{\min}}^{x_{\max}} \left(\int_{y_{\min}}^{y_{\max}} \left(\int_{z_{\min}}^{z_{\max}} f(\vec{r})dz \right) dy \right) dx, \tag{8.14}$$

which implies that the order of integrations is now z, y, x. Why would this make a difference? The only time that the order of the integration matters is when the integration boundaries in a coordinate depend on one or both of the other coordinates. We will show this explicitly below in an example, but first we introduce the volume elements in cylindrical and spherical coordinates.

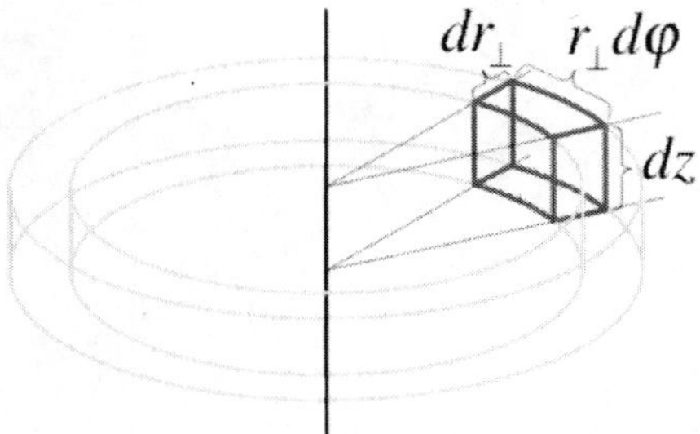

Figure 8.6: Volume element in cylindrical coordinates.

Because we are using the angle φ as one of the coordinates in cylindrical coordinates, our volume element is not cube-shaped any more. For a given differential angle $d\varphi$ the size of the volume element depends on how far away from the z-axis the volume element is located. It grows linearly with the distance $r_\perp$ from the z-axis (see Figure 8.6) and is given by

$$dV = r_\perp dr_\perp d\varphi dz. \tag{8.15}$$

The volume integral is then

$$\int_V f(\vec{r})dV = \int_{z_{\min}}^{z_{\max}} \left(\int_{\varphi_{\min}}^{\varphi_{\max}} \left(\int_{r_{\perp\min}}^{r_{\perp\max}} f(\vec{r})r_\perp dr_\perp \right) d\varphi \right) dz. \tag{8.16}$$

Again the order of integrations is arbitrary and can be chosen to make the task as simple as possible.

Finally, in spherical coordinates we use two angular variables. This case is shown in Figure 8.7. Here the size of the volume element for a given value of the differential coordinates depends on the distance r to the origin as well as the angle relative to the $\vartheta = 0$ axis (equivalent to the z-axis in Cartesian or cylindrical coordinates. The differential volume element in spherical coordinates is

$$dV = r^2 dr \sin\vartheta d\vartheta d\varphi \tag{8.17}$$

Then the volume integral in spherical coordinates is given by

$$\int_V f(\vec{r})dV = \int_{r_{\min}}^{r_{\max}} \left(\int_{\varphi_{\min}}^{\varphi_{\max}} \left(\int_{\vartheta_{\min}}^{\vartheta_{\max}} f(\vec{r}) \sin\vartheta d\vartheta \right) d\varphi \right) r^2 dr \tag{8.18}$$

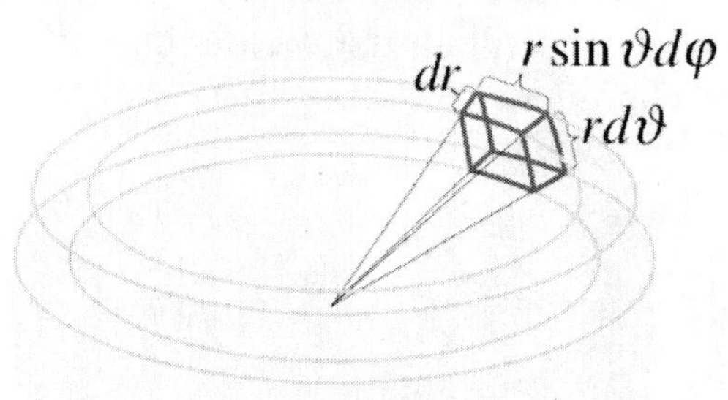

Figure 8.7: Volume element in spherical coordinates.

As an illustration showing why it may be useful to use non-Cartesian coordinates in the right circumstances, let us calculate the volume of a cylinder with radius R and height H. We have to integrate a function $f(\vec{r}) = 1$ over the entire cylinder to obtain the volume. (Of course we know that the answer should be $V = \pi R^2 H$, but in the following we will show how to get there by using the volume integrals.)

In Cartesian coordinates we select the origin of our coordinate system as the center of the circular part of the cylinder-bottom plate, so that the shape in the xy plane that we have to integrate over is a circle with radius R, see Figure 8.8. Our volume integral in Cartesian coordinates is then from (8.13):

$$\int_V dV = \int_0^H \left(\int_{y_{\min}}^{y_{\max}} \left(\int_{x_{\min}(y)}^{x_{\max}(y)} dx \right) dy \right) dz \tag{8.19}$$

The innermost integral has to be done first and is straightforward,

$$\int_{x_{\min}(y)}^{x_{\max}(y)} dx = x_{\max}(y) - x_{\min}(y) \tag{8.20}$$

But the integration boundaries depend on y as $x_{\max} = \sqrt{R^2 - y^2}$, $x_{\min} = -\sqrt{R^2 - y^2}$, and so the solution of (8.20) becomes $x_{\max}(y) - x_{\min}(y) = 2\sqrt{R^2 - y^2}$. We insert this into (8.19) and obtain

$$\int_V dV = \int_0^H \left(\int_{-R}^{R} 2\sqrt{R^2 - y^2}\, dy \right) dz \tag{8.21}$$

The inner of these two remaining integrals evaluates to

$$\int_{-R}^{R} 2\sqrt{R^2 - y^2}\, dy = \left(y\sqrt{R^2 - y^2} + R^2 \tan^{-1}\left(\frac{y}{\sqrt{R^2 - y^2}} \right) \right)\Bigg|_{-R}^{R} = \pi R^2 \tag{8.22}$$

Inserting this result back into (8.21) finally yields our answer

$$\int_V dV = \int_0^H \pi R^2 dz = \pi R^2 \int_0^H dz = \pi R^2 H \tag{8.23}$$

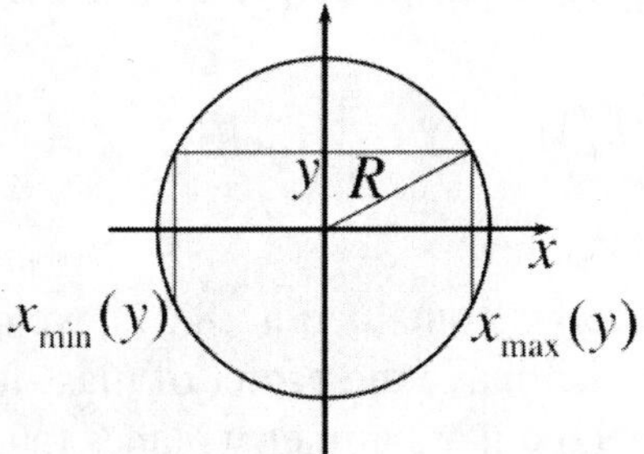

Figure 8.8: Bottom surface of a right cylinder of radius R.

As you can see, obtaining the volume of a cylinder was rather cumbersome in Cartesian coordinates. What about using cylindrical coordinates? According to (8.16) our integral to solve is then

$$\begin{aligned} \int_V f(\vec{r}) dV &= \int_0^H \left(\int_0^{2\pi} \left(\int_0^R r_\perp dr_\perp \right) d\varphi \right) dz = \int_0^H \left(\int_0^{2\pi} \left(\tfrac{1}{2} R^2 \right) d\varphi \right) dz \\ &= \tfrac{1}{2} R^2 \int_0^H \left(\int_0^{2\pi} d\varphi \right) dz = \tfrac{1}{2} R^2 \int_0^H 2\pi dz = \pi R^2 H \end{aligned} \quad . \tag{8.24}$$

As you can see, in this case the use of cylindrical coordinates was vastly easier, a consequence of the geometry of the object we had to integrate over.

Self-Test Opportunity: Using spherical coordinates, show that the volume V of a sphere with radius R is $V = \frac{4}{3}\pi R^3$!

End of Mathematical Insert

After this discussion of volume integrals we can return to our problem of calculating the center of mass location, equation (8.12). For the Cartesian components of the position vector we find from equation (8.12):

$$X = \frac{1}{M}\int_V x\rho(\vec{r})dV; \quad Y = \frac{1}{M}\int_V y\rho(\vec{r})dV; \quad Z = \frac{1}{M}\int_V z\rho(\vec{r})dV \tag{8.25}$$

If the mass density for the entire object is constant, $\rho(\vec{r}) \equiv \rho$, then we can remove this constant factor from the integral and obtain as a special case of equation (8.12) for constant mass density:

$$\vec{R} = \frac{\rho}{M}\int_V \vec{r}dV = \frac{1}{V}\int_V \vec{r}dV \quad \text{(for constant } \rho\text{)}, \tag{8.26}$$

where we have used (8.10) in the last step. Expressed in Cartesian components, we obtain for this case:

$$X = \frac{1}{V}\int_V xdV; \quad Y = \frac{1}{V}\int_V ydV; \quad Z = \frac{1}{V}\int_V zdV \tag{8.27}$$

From (8.26) and the three equations contained in (8.27), we can now see that any object that that has a symmetry plane will have the center of mass located in that plane. An object having 3 mutually perpendicular symmetry planes (such as a cylinder, a rectangular solid, or a sphere) has its center of mass where these three planes intersect, which is the geometric center. The following example is intended to develop this idea further.

Example 8.1: Center of mass for a half-sphere

Question:

Consider the solid half-sphere of constant mass density with Radius R_0 shown in Figure 8.9, left side. Where is its center of mass?

Answer:

As shown in the center part of Figure 8.9, we can draw symmetry planes through this object, so that exactly half of the object is located on one side of the plane, and the other half is a mirror image. Drawn are two perpendicular planes in red and yellow, but any plane through the vertical symmetry axis (indicated by the thin black line) is possible.

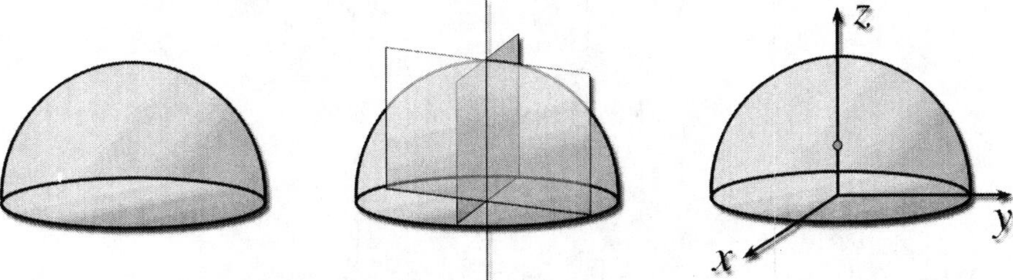

Figure 8.9: Determination of the center of mass; Left: half-sphere; center symmetry planes and symmetry axis; right: coordinate system, with possible location of center of mass marked by red dot.

Example

We now position our coordinate system so that one axis (the z -axis in this case) coincides with this symmetry axis. We are then assured that the center of mass is located exactly on this axis. Because the mass distribution is symmetric, and the integrands of (8.26) or (8.27) are odd powers of $\vec{r}$, the integral for X or Y has to have a value 0. Specifically,

$$\int_{-a}^{a} x dx = 0 \text{ for all values of the constant } a. \tag{8.28}$$

Positioning our coordinate system such that the z -axis is the symmetry axis thus ensures that $X = Y = 0$. This is done in the right part of Figure 8.9, where we have elected to assign the origin of the coordinate system to the center of the circle at the bottom of the half-sphere.

Now we have to find out the value of the integral 3 in (8.27):

$$Z = \frac{1}{V} \int_V z dV$$

The volume of the half-sphere is half the volume of a sphere,

$$V = \frac{2\pi}{3} R_0^3 \tag{8.29}$$

To solve the integral, we use cylindrical coordinates, in which the differential volume element is given as $dV = r_\perp dr_\perp d\varphi dz$. The integral is then calculated as:

Example

$$\begin{aligned}
\int_V z dV &= \int_0^{R_0}\left(\int_0^{\sqrt{R_0^2-z^2}}\left(\int_0^{2\pi} z r_\perp d\varphi\right)dr_\perp\right)dz \\
&= \int_0^{R_0} z\left(\int_0^{\sqrt{R_0^2-z^2}} r_\perp\left(\int_0^{2\pi} d\varphi\right)dr_\perp\right)dz \\
&= 2\pi\int_0^{R_0} z\left(\int_0^{\sqrt{R_0^2-z^2}} r_\perp dr_\perp\right)dz \\
&= \pi\int_0^{R_0} z(R_0^2-z^2)dz \\
&= \frac{\pi}{4}R_0^4
\end{aligned} \tag{8.30}$$

Combining the results (8.29) and (8.30), we obtain for the z -coordinate of the center of mass:

$$Z = \frac{1}{V}\int_V z dV = \frac{3}{2\pi R_0^3}\frac{\pi R_0^4}{4} = \frac{3}{8}R_0 \tag{8.31}$$

Self-Test Opportunity: A plate with height h is cut from a thin metal sheet with uniform mass density as shown.

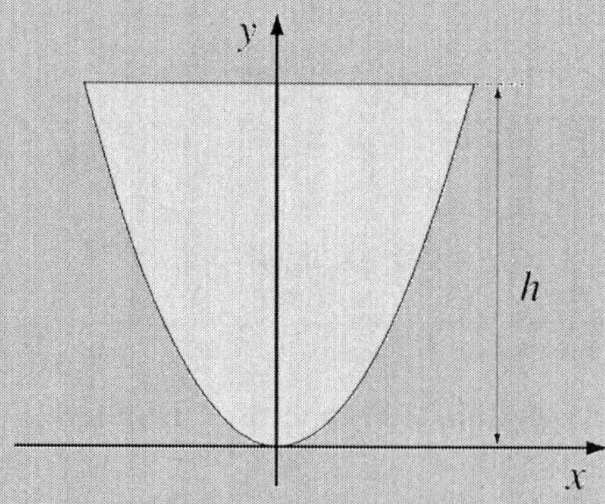

The lower boundary of the plate is defined by $y = 2x^2$. Show that the center of mass of this plate is located at $x = 0$ and $y = \frac{3}{5}h$.

General Considerations

Before we leave the discussion of the center of mass or center of gravity, we would like to point out that the center of mass of an object does not always have to be located inside of it. The most obvious example is shown in Figure 8.10. From our symmetry considerations, it follows that the center of mass of the donut is exactly in the center of its hole, at a point where there is no dough.

Figure 8.10: Donut - an object with center of mass outside of its mass distribution.

A perhaps even more relevant case of the center of mass' location outside of an object was discovered and then experimentally realized by US track and field star Dick Fosbury. During the 1968 Olympic Games in Mexico City he introduced a new high jump technique, now called the Fosbury Flop and with it won the gold medal. Properly executed, it allows the athlete to cross over the bar, while her/his center of mass remains below it, thus adding effective height to the jump.

Extended solid objects can have motions that appear, at first sight, rather complicated. Figure 8.11 shows such a case of a wrench twirling through the air, shown here in a multiple exposure shot with equidistant time intervals between sequential frames.

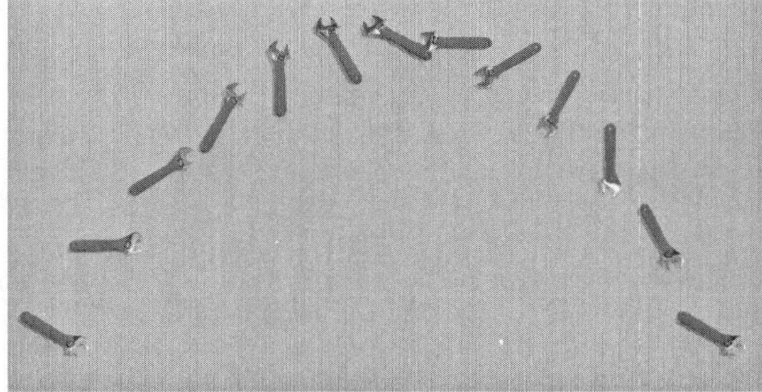

Figure 8.11: Digitally processed multiple exposure series of a wrench being tossed through the air.

While this motion looks complicated, we can actually use what we know about the center of mass to perform a fairly straightforward analysis of this motion. If we assume that all mass of the wrench is concentrated in a point, then this point would move on a parabola through the air under the influence of gravity. We had found this in chapter 3. It is no surprise that the center of mass of the wrench is also moving on the same parabolic trajectory. Superimposed on this motion is a rotation of the wrench about its center of mass. We can see this very clearly in Figure 8.12, where we have overlaid a parabola (green line) that passes through the location of the center of mass of the wrench in each exposure. In addition we have drawn black lines that rotate with a constant rate about the center of mass of the wrench. You can clearly see that the handle of the wrench is always aligned with the black lines, indicating that the wrench indeed rotates with constant rate about its center of mass, a motion that we can easily analyze with the tools provided later in chapter 10.

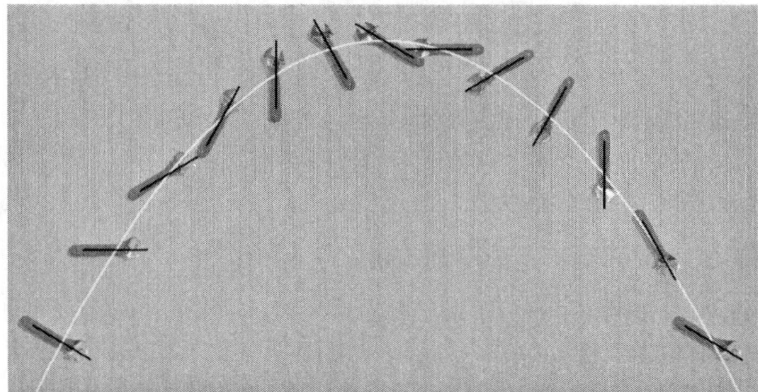

Figure 8.12: Same as previous figure, but now with a parabola for the center of mass motion overlaid.

Thus the techniques introduced here allow us to attack many kinds of complicated problems of moving solid objects and identify them as a superposition of the motion of the center of mass and a rotation of the object about the center of mass.

8.4. Center of Mass Momentum

Now that we have introduced the position vector of the center of mass, we can take the time derivative of this quantity to get $\vec{V}$, the velocity vector of the center of mass. However, in taking the derivative, several interesting effects can be observed. Using (8.2) and taking the time derivative:

$$\vec{V} \equiv \frac{d}{dt}\vec{R} = \frac{d}{dt}\left(\frac{1}{M}\sum_{i=1}^{n}\vec{r}_i m_i\right) = \frac{1}{M}\sum_{i=1}^{n} m_i \frac{d}{dt}\vec{r}_i = \frac{1}{M}\sum_{i=1}^{n} m_i \vec{v}_i = \frac{1}{M}\sum_{i=1}^{n} \vec{p}_i \,. \qquad (8.32)$$

For now, we have assumed that the total mass M and the masses m_i of the individual objects remain constant. (Later in this chapter we will give up this assumption and study the consequences for rocket motion). Equation (8.32) gives us an expression for the velocity vector of the center of mass, $\vec{V}$. Multiplication of both sides of (8.32) with M yields then:

$$\vec{P} = M\vec{V} = \sum_{i=1}^{n} \vec{p}_i \,. \tag{8.33}$$

We thus find that the center of mass momentum $\vec{P}$ is the product of the total mass M and the center of mass velocity $\vec{V}$ and is simply the sum over all individual momenta.

Taking another time derivative, this time of both sides of (8.33), yields Newton's Second Law for the center of mass:

$$\frac{d}{dt}\vec{P} = \frac{d}{dt}(M\vec{V}) = \frac{d}{dt}\left(\sum_{i=1}^{n}\vec{p}_i\right) = \sum_{i=1}^{n}\frac{d}{dt}\vec{p}_i = \sum_{i=1}^{n}\vec{F}_i \,. \tag{8.34}$$

In the last step we have used the result of the previous chapter that the time derivative of the momentum of particle i is given by the net force, $\vec{F}_i$ acting on it. Please note that if these particles in the sum over i exert forces on each other, then these do not make a net contribution to the sum. Why? According to Newton's Third Law, the forces that two objects exert on each other are equal in magnitude an opposite in direction. So adding them yields 0. Thus we obtain for Newton's Second Law for the center of mass:

$$\frac{d}{dt}\vec{P} = \vec{F}_{net} \,, \tag{8.35}$$

where $\vec{F}_{net}$ is the sum over all *external* forces acting on the system of particles. Thus the center of mass has the same relationships between position, velocity, momentum, force, and mass that we established earlier for point particles. It is thus possible to consider the center of mass of extended objects or groups of objects as point particles. After the fact, this result justifies the point particle approximation for extended objects that we had utilized in all chapters of mechanics up to this point.

Two-body Collisions

Consider a system consisting of only two objects. In this case the total momentum, the sum over individual momenta in (8.33), is then just

$$\vec{P} = \vec{p}_1 + \vec{p}_2 \,. \tag{8.36}$$

In the previous chapter, we had seen that the relative velocity between the two colliding partners plays a big role in two-body collisions. So it is natural to now also introduce the relative momentum as one half of the momentum difference:

$$\vec{p} = \tfrac{1}{2}(\vec{p}_1 - \vec{p}_2) \,. \tag{8.37}$$

Why do we use the factor of ½ in this definition? The answer is that then the momentum of object 1 is $\vec{p}$ and that of object 2 is $-\vec{p}$ in the center-of-momentum frame, i.e. a frame in which the center of mass has zero momentum.

In Figure 8.13(a), we illustrate the relationship between center of mass momentum, $\vec{P}$ (red arrow), relative momentum, $\vec{p}$ (blue arrow), and the momenta of the two objects 1 and 2 (black arrows). Of course, one can also express the individual momenta in terms of the center of mass momentum and relative momentum. This relationship is given by:

$$\begin{aligned}\vec{p}_1 &= \tfrac{1}{2}\vec{P} + \vec{p} \\ \vec{p}_2 &= \tfrac{1}{2}\vec{P} - \vec{p}\end{aligned} \tag{8.38}$$

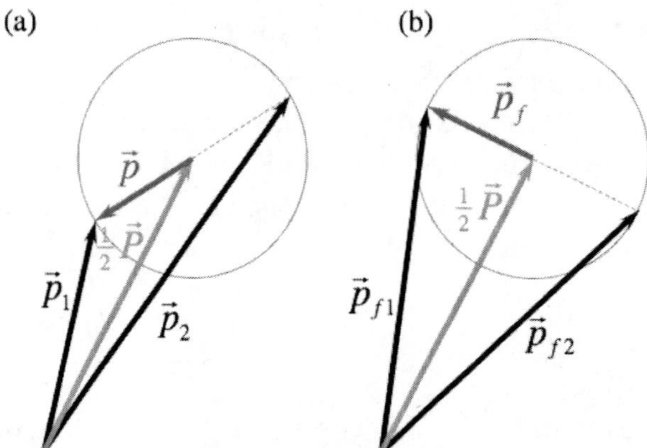

Figure 8.13: Relationship between momentum vectors 1 and 2, center of mass momentum, and relative momentum. (a): Before an elastic collision; (b): After the elastic collision.

The biggest advantage of thinking in terms of center of mass and relative momentum becomes obvious when we consider a collision between the two objects. During this collision, the dominant forces that act on the objects are the forces that the objects exert on each other. They are thus internal forces that do not enter into the sum of equation (8.34), and so we obtain in this case for the collision of two objects

$$\frac{d}{dt}\vec{P} = 0. \tag{8.39}$$

In other words, the center of mass momentum does not change; it remains the same during a two-body collision. This is true for elastic or totally inelastic or partially inelastic collisions.

In inelastic collisions, where the two objects stick together after the collision, we had already derived in chapter 7 that the velocity with which the combined object moves is

$$\vec{v}_f = \frac{m_1\vec{v}_{i1} + m_2\vec{v}_{i2}}{m_1 + m_2}.$$

If we compare this equation with our result of (8.32), we see that this velocity is just the center of mass velocity. In this case of a totally inelastic collision the relative momentum after the collision is 0.

For elastic collisions, the total kinetic energy has to be conserved. If we compute the total kinetic energy in terms of the total momentum $\vec{P}$ and the relative momentum $\vec{p}$, then the contribution from the total momentum has to remain constant, because $\vec{P}$ is constant. This finding implies that the kinetic energy contained in the relative motion also has to remain constant. Because this kinetic energy in turn is proportional to the square of the relative momentum vector, the length of the relative momentum vector has to remain unchanged during an elastic collision. Only the direction of the relative momentum vector can change. This relationship is shown in Figure 8.13(b), where the new relative momentum vector after the elastic collision now lies on the perimeter of a circle with radius of the initial relative momentum vector and with center at the endpoint of the total momentum vector. The situation depicted in Figure 8.13 implies that the motion is restricted to 2 spatial dimensions. For two-body collisions in three dimensions, the final state relative momentum vector is located on the surface of a sphere instead of the perimeter of a circle.

Recoil

When firing a bullet from a gun, the gun recoils, i.e. it moves in opposite direction to the one the bullet is fired in. Another example for the same physical principle occurs when you are sitting in a boat that is at rest and you throw an object off the boat: the boat moves in the opposite direction. You will experience the identical effect when you stand on a skateboard and toss a (reasonably heavy) ball. This is the well-known recoil effect and can be understood from the framework we have just developed for two-body collisions. It is of course also a consequence of Newton's Third Law.

Solved Problem

Solved Problem 8.1: Cannon Recoil

Suppose you need to fire a cannonball of mass 13.7 kg to a target that is 2.30 km away from your cannon of mass 249.0 kg. The distance of 2.30 km is also the maximum range of the cannon. The target and cannon are at the same altitude, and the cannon is resting on a horizontal surface.

Question:
What is the velocity with which your cannon will recoil?

Answer:

THINK: First we realize that the cannon can only recoil in the horizontal direction, because the normal force from the ground will prevent it from acquiring a vertical velocity component. We use the fact that the $x-$component of the center of mass momentum of the system cannon + cannonball remains unchanged in the process of firing the cannon, because the explosion of the gunpowder inside the cannon, which sets the cannonball in motion, constitutes a force internal to the system. There is no net external force component in horizontal direction because the two external forces (normal plus gravity) are both vertical. The $y-$component of the center of mass velocity changes because there is a net external force component in the $y-$direction when the normal force increases to prevent the cannon from penetrating the ground. Because the ball and cannon are initially both at rest, the center of mass momentum of this system is initially zero and its $x-$component remains this way after the firing of the cannon.

SKETCH: We show a sketch of the cannon just after the cannonball is shot out of the cannon in Figure 8.14.

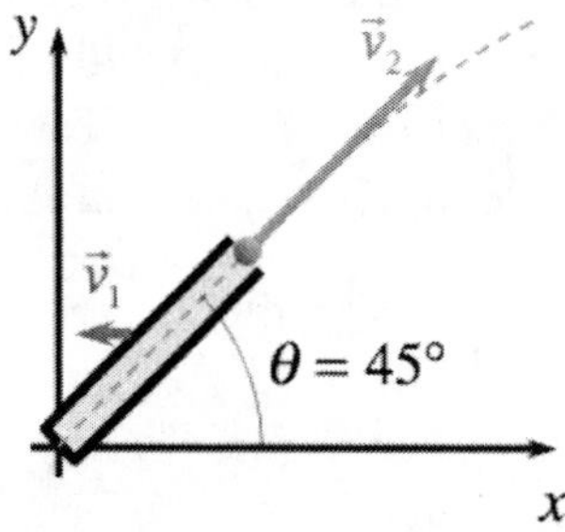

Figure 8.14: Sketch of cannonball fired from a cannon.

In Figure 8.15 we show a sketch of the velocity vector of the cannonball $\vec{v}_2$ including the x- and y-components.

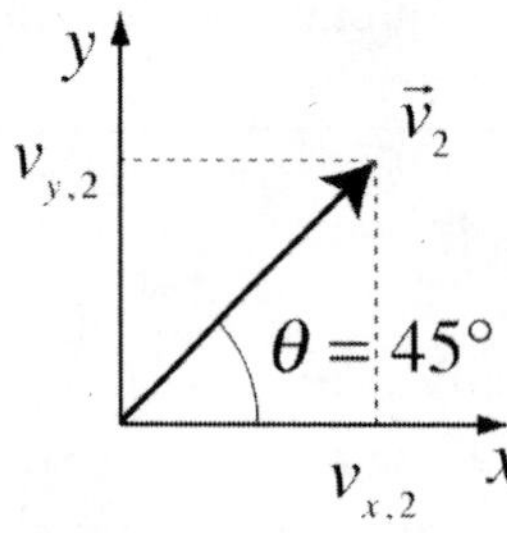

Figure 8.15: The initial velocity vector of the cannonball.

RESEARCH: Using (8.36) we then obtain (we use index 1 for the cannon and 2 for the cannonball):

$$\vec{P} = \vec{p}_1 + \vec{p}_2 = m_1\vec{v}_1 + m_2\vec{v}_2 = 0 \Rightarrow \vec{v}_1 = -\frac{m_2}{m_1}\vec{v}_2. \tag{8.40}$$

For the horizontal component of the velocity we then obtain:

$$v_{1,x} = -\frac{m_2}{m_1} v_{2,x} . \tag{8.41}$$

We can obtain the horizontal component of the cannonball's velocity at firing from knowing that the range of the cannon is 2.30 km. In Chapter 3 we had seen that the range of the cannon is related to the initial velocity via: $R = (v_0^2 / g)\sin 2\theta_0$. The maximum range is reached for $\theta_0 = 45^\circ$ and is $R = v_0^2 / g \Rightarrow v_0 = \sqrt{gR}$.

For $\theta_0 = 45^\circ$, the initial speed and horizontal velocity component are related via $v_{2,x} = v_0 \cos 45^\circ = v_0 / \sqrt{2}$. Combining these two results, we can relate the maximum range to the initial horizontal component of the velocity of the cannonball via:

$$v_{2,x} = v_0 / \sqrt{2} = \sqrt{gR / 2} . \tag{8.42}$$

SIMPLIFY: Inserting result (8.42) into our recoil equation (8.41) gives us the result we are looking for:

$$v_{1,x} = -\frac{m_2}{m_1} v_{2,x} = -\frac{m_2}{m_1}\sqrt{\frac{gR}{2}} . \tag{8.43}$$

CALCULATE: Inserting the numbers given in the problem, we obtain

$$v_{1,x} = -\frac{m_2}{m_1}\sqrt{\frac{gR}{2}} = -\frac{13.7 \text{ kg}}{249 \text{ kg}}\sqrt{\frac{(9.81 \text{ m/s}^2)(2.30 \cdot 10^3 \text{ m})}{2}} = -5.84392 \text{ m/s} .$$

ROUND: Expressing our answer to three significant digits gives us

$$v_{1,x} = -5.84 \text{ m/s} .$$

DOUBLE-CHECK: The minus sign means that the cannon moves in the opposite direction to the one that the cannonball takes, which is reasonable. The cannonball should have a much larger initial velocity than the cannon because the cannon is much more massive. The initial speed of the cannonball was

$$v_0 = \sqrt{gR} = \sqrt{\left(9.81 \text{ m/s}^2\right)\left(2.3 \cdot 10^3 \text{ m}\right)} = 475 \text{ m/s} .$$

Solved Problem

The fact that our answer for the speed of the cannon is much less than the initial speed of the cannonball also seems reasonable.

Of course, there are also cases where mass gets ejected continuously and there is a continuous recoil process. As an example, let us consider the spraying of water from a fire hose.

Example

Example 8.2: Fire hose

Question:
What is the magnitude of the force that acts on a firefighter holding a fire hose that ejects 360 liters of water per minute with a muzzle velocity of 39.0 m/s?

Answer:
Let us first find the total mass of the water that gets ejected per minute. The mass density of water is $\rho = 1000 \text{ kg/m}^3 = 1.0 \text{ kg/liter}$. Because $\Delta V = 360$ liters of water get ejected, we get for the total mass ejected in a minute:

$$\Delta m = \Delta V \rho = (360 \text{ liter})(1.0 \text{ kg/liter}) = 360 \text{ kg}.$$

The momentum of the water is then $\Delta p = v\Delta m$, and the momentum per unit time is:

$$F = \frac{v\Delta m}{\Delta t} = \frac{(39.0 \text{ m/s})(360 \text{ kg})}{60 \text{ s}} = 234 \text{ N}$$

Here we have used the definition of the average force as $F = \Delta p / \Delta t$. This force is sizeable and explains why it is so dangerous for firemen to let go of fire hoses, which would allow them to whip around, potentially causing injury.

In-class exercise:
A garden hose is used to fill a 20 liter bucket in one minute. The velocity of the water leaving the hose is 1.05 m/s. What force is required to hold the hose in place?
a) 0.35 N
b) 2.1 N
c) 9.8 N
d) 12 N
e) 21 N

8.5. Rocket Motion

Up to now we have only considered cases of motion where the mass of the moving object does not change. However, this is not the case for rocket motion, in which part of the mass of the rocket is ejected through a nozzle in the back of the rocket as shown in Figure 8.16. This scenario is an important case of the recoil that we have just considered. A rocket does not have to "push against" anything. Instead, its forward thrust is simply gained from ejecting its propellant out its rear nozzle and the law of conservation of total momentum.

Figure 8.16: Space Shuttle riding its rocket engines.

In order to obtain an expression for the acceleration of a rocket, we first consider shooting discrete amounts of mass out of the rocket as indicated in Figure 8.17. Then we can approach the continuum limit.

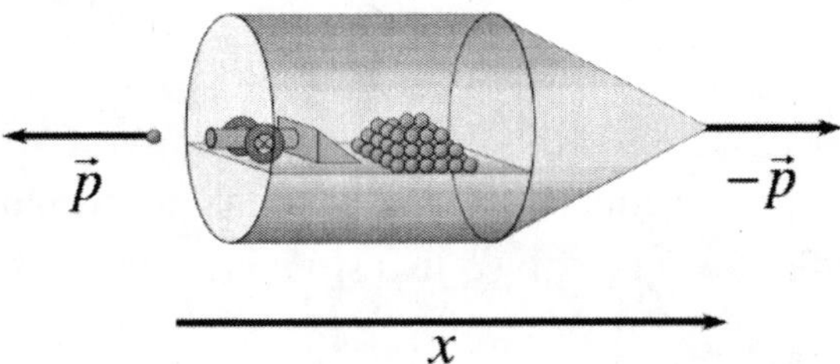

Figure 8.17: Toy model for rocket propulsion: firing cannonballs.

Let's start our rocket motion discussion by using a toy model of a rocket in interstellar space that propels itself forward by shooting cannon balls out its nozzle. (That the rocket is in interstellar space implies that we can treat it and its components as an isolated system, for which we can neglect outside forces.) Initially, the rocket is at rest. All motion is in x-direction; so we can use our notation for one-dimensional motion, with the sign of the velocity $x-$components (which, for simplicity, we will refer to as velocities) indicating their direction. Each cannonball has a mass of Δm and the initial mass of the space ship including all cannonballs is m_0. Each cannonball is fired off with a velocity of v_c relative to the rocket, resulting in a cannonball momentum of $v_c\Delta m$. After firing off the first cannonball, the mass of the space ship is then reduced to $m_0 - \Delta m$. Firing off the cannonball does not change the center of mass momentum of the system rocket plus cannonball. (Remember, this is an isolated system, on which no net external forces act!) So the rocket receives a recoil momentum opposite to that of the cannonball, $p_r = -v_c \Delta m$. We then obtain the velocity change, Δv_1, of the spaceship after firing of one cannonball:

$$\Delta v_1 = -\frac{v_c \Delta m}{m_0 - \Delta m}. \tag{8.44}$$

The total velocity, v_1, of the rocket is then also $v_1 = \Delta v_1 + 0 = \Delta v_1$.

In the moving system of the rocket, we can then fire off the second cannonball. This reduces the mass of the rocket from $m_0 - \Delta m$ to $m_0 - 2\Delta m$. This results in an additional recoil velocity of

$$\Delta v_2 = -\frac{v_c \Delta m}{m_0 - 2\Delta m}, \tag{8.45}$$

increasing the total velocity of the spacecraft to $v_2 = v_1 + \Delta v_2$. When firing the nth cannonball, the velocity change is then:

$$\Delta v_n = -\frac{v_c \Delta m}{m_0 - n\Delta m} \tag{8.46}$$

Thus the velocity of the rocket after firing the nth cannonball is:

$$v_n = v_{n-1} + \Delta v_n \tag{8.47}$$

This set of equations, where the equation for n depends on the equation for $(n-1)$, is called a recursion relation. It can be solved in a straightforward manner by using a computer.

However, there is a very useful approximation for the case that the mass emitted per time interval is constant and small as compared to m, the overall (time-dependent) mass of the rocket. In this limit we obtain from (8.46):

$$\Delta v = -\frac{v_c \Delta m}{m} \Rightarrow \frac{\Delta v}{\Delta m} = -\frac{v_c}{m} \tag{8.48}$$

v_c is the velocity with which the propellant is ejected. In the limit of $\Delta m \to 0$ we then obtain the derivative:

$$\frac{dv}{dm} = -\frac{v_c}{m} \tag{8.49}$$

The solution of this differential equation is:

$$v(m) = -v_c \int_{m_0}^{m} \frac{1}{m'} dm' = -v_c \ln m \Big|_{m_0}^{m} = v_c \ln\left(\frac{m_0}{m}\right) \tag{8.50}$$

(You can verify that this is indeed the solution of (8.49) by taking the derivative of (8.50) with respect to m, which should result in (8.49).)

By going from a total mass m_i down to a final mass m_f, the velocity difference between the final and initial velocity of the rocket is then:

$$v_f - v_i = v_c \ln\left(\frac{m_0}{m_f}\right) - v_c \ln\left(\frac{m_0}{m_i}\right) = v_c \ln\left(\frac{m_i}{m_f}\right) \tag{8.51}$$

Example

Example 8.3: Rocket launch to Mars

One proposal to send astronauts to Mars involves assembling a spaceship in orbit around Earth, thus avoiding the need for this spaceship to overcome most of Earth's gravity at the start. Suppose such a spaceship has a payload of 50,000 kg, carries 2,000,000 kg of fuel, and is able to eject the propellant with a velocity of 23.5 km/s. (Current chemical propellant rockets allow propellant velocities of up to approximately 5 km/s, but electromagnetic propulsion schemes are predicted to yield up to perhaps 40 km/s propellant velocities.)

Question:
What is the final velocity that this rocket can reach relative to the velocity it already had in its orbit around earth before ignition?

Answer:
Using our rocket equation (8.51), we find for the numbers given in this problem

$$v_f - v_i = v_c \ln\left(\frac{m_i}{m_f}\right) = (23.5 \text{ km/s}) \ln\left(\frac{2{,}050{,}000 \text{ kg}}{50{,}000 \text{ kg}}\right) (23.5 \text{ km/s}) \ln 41 = 87.3 \text{ km/s}$$

For comparison, the Saturn V multi-stage rocket that carried the astronauts to the moon in the late 1960s and early 1970s was able to reach a speed of only approximately 12 km/s.

But even with the advanced technology that this problem implies, it would still take several months to send astronauts to Mars, even under the most favorable conditions. The Mars Rover took 207 days to travel from Earth to Mars.

There is another and perhaps easier way to think of rocket motion. For this approach, we do not start from discrete quantities of mass that we eject, but go back to the definition of the momentum as the product of mass and velocity, then take the time derivative to obtain the force. However, this time we consider explicitly that the mass of the object can change as well:

$$\vec{F}_{net} = \frac{d}{dt}\vec{p} = \frac{d}{dt}(m\vec{v}) = m\frac{d\vec{v}}{dt} + \vec{v}\frac{dm}{dt} \tag{8.52}$$

where the last step in this equation results from the application of the product rule of differentiation in calculus. If there is no external force acting on an object, then this means that we obtain from (8.52) the equation:

$$m\frac{d\vec{v}}{dt} = -\vec{v}\frac{dm}{dt} \tag{8.53}$$

In the case of rocket motion, the outflow of propellant, dm/dt, is constant and creates the change in mass of the rocket, and the propellant flows out with a constant velocity $\vec{v}_c$ relative to the rocket. So we obtain

$$m\frac{d\vec{v}}{dt} = m\vec{a} = -\vec{v}_c\frac{dm}{dt} \tag{8.54}$$

The combination $v_c dm/dt$ is called the thrust of the rocket and is measured in Newtons (or in pounds in the British system). The thrust generated by the space shuttle engines and solid rocket boosters is approximately 31.3 MN (31.3 mega-Newton, or approximately 7 million pounds in the British system, NASA fact sheet FS-1995-07-013-MSFC). The initial total mass of the space shuttle, including payload, fuel tanks and rocket fuel, is slightly greater than 2.0 million kg, thus allowing the space shuttle's rocket engines and boosters to produce an initial acceleration of

$$a = \frac{3.13\cdot 10^7 \text{ N}}{2.0\cdot 10^6 \text{ kg}} = 16 \text{ m/s}^2 .$$

This acceleration is sufficient to lift the shuttle off the launch pad against the acceleration of gravity (-9.81 m/s^2). As the shuttle rises and its mass decreases, it can generate larger accelerations. As the shuttle expends its fuel, the main engines are throttled back to make sure that accelerations do not exceed $3g$ (three times gravitational acceleration) in order to avoid damaging the cargo or insuring the astronauts.

What we have learned/Exam Study Guide:

- The center of mass, also called center of gravity, is defined as the point in which we can imagine all of the mass of the object to be concentrated.
- We can calculate the location of the center of mass for an arbitrarily shaped object as $\vec{R} = \frac{1}{M}\int_V \vec{r}\rho(\vec{r})dV$, where the mass density is defined as $\rho = \frac{dm}{dV}$, the integration extends over the entire volume V of the object, and M is its mass.

- In the special case that the mass density is a uniformly constant throughout the object, $\rho = \frac{M}{V}$, the center of mass is $\vec{R} = \frac{1}{V}\int_V \vec{r}dV$.
- If an object exhibits a mirror-symmetry, the location of the center of mass must be in the symmetry plane.
- The location of the combined center of mass of several objects can be found by the mass-weighted average of the location of the centers of mass of the individual objects, $\vec{R} = \frac{\vec{r}_1 m_1 + \vec{r}_2 m_2 + ... + \vec{r}_n m_n}{m_1 + m_2 ... + m_n} = \frac{1}{M}\sum_{i=1}^{n}\vec{r}_i m_i$.
- The motion of extended rigid objects can be described by the motion of the center of mass, superimposed with a possible rigid-body rotation of the object around this center of mass.
- The velocity of the center of mass is given by the derivative of the position vector of the center mass, $\vec{V} \equiv \frac{d}{dt}\vec{R}$.
- The center of mass momentum for a combination of several objects is defined as $\vec{P} = M\vec{V} = \sum_{i=1}^{n}\vec{p}_i$, and it obeys Newton's Second Law, $\frac{d}{dt}\vec{P} = \frac{d}{dt}(M\vec{V}) = \sum_{i=1}^{n}\vec{F}_i = \vec{F}_{net}$. Internal forces between objects in the sum do not contribute to the net external force and thus do not change the center of mass momentum, because they always come in action-reaction force pairs adding up to 0.
- For a system of two objects, we can introduce the total momentum $\vec{P} = \vec{p}_1 + \vec{p}_2$ and relative momentum $\vec{p} = \frac{1}{2}(\vec{p}_1 - \vec{p}_2)$. In collisions between these two objects, the total momentum remains unchanged.
- Rocket motion is an example of motion during which the mass of the moving object is not constant. The equation of motion for the rocket is given by $m\frac{d\vec{v}}{dt} = m\vec{a} = -\vec{v}_c\frac{dm}{dt}$, where $\vec{v}_c$ is the velocity of the propellant relative to the rocket, $\frac{dm}{dt}$ is the rate of mass outflow, and the product $\vec{v}_c\frac{dm}{dt}$ is called the thrust.
- The velocity of the rocket as a function of its mass is given by $v_f - v_i = v_c \ln\left(\frac{m_i}{m_f}\right)$, where the indices i, f indicate "initial" and "final" masses and velocities.

Additional Solved Problems

Solved Problem 8.2: Long Thin Rod

Question:

A long, thin rod lies along the x-axis. One end of the rod is located at $x = 1.00$ m and the other end of the rod is located at $x = 3.00$ m. The linear mass density of the rod is given by $\lambda = ax^2 + b$ where $a = 0.300$ kg/m^3 and $b = 0.600$ kg/m. What are the mass of the rod and the x-coordinate of the center of mass of the rod?

Answer:

THINK: The linear mass density of the rod is not uniform. The linear mass density depends on the x-coordinate. Therefore, to get the mass we must integrate the linear mass density over the length of the rod. To get the center of mass, we need to integrate the linear mass density weighted by the distance in the x-direction and then divide by the mass of the rod.

SKETCH: The long thin rod oriented along the x-axis is shown in Figure 8.18.

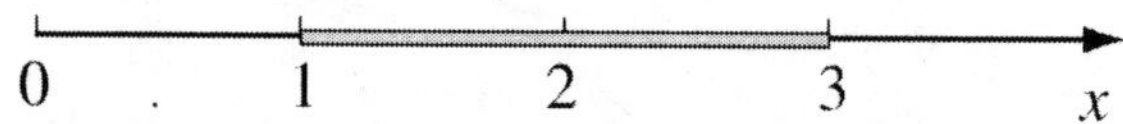

Figure 8.18: A long, thin rod oriented along the x-axis.

RESEARCH: The mass of the rod can be obtained by integrating the linear mass density λ over the rod from $x_1 = 1.00$ m to $x_2 = 3.00$ m

$$m = \int_{x_1}^{x_2} \lambda(x)dx = \int_{x_1}^{x_2} \left(ax^2 + b\right)dx = \left[a\frac{x^3}{3} + bx\right]_{x_1}^{x_2}. \tag{8.55}$$

The x-coordinate of the center of mass of the rod X can be obtained by calculating the integral of the differential mass times the x position and then dividing by the mass calculated in (8.55)

$$X = \frac{1}{m}\int_{x_1}^{x_2} \lambda(x)xdx = \frac{1}{m}\int_{x_1}^{x_2} \left(ax^2 + b\right)xdx = \frac{1}{m}\int_{x_1}^{x_2} \left(ax^3 + bx\right)dx = \frac{1}{m}\left[a\frac{x^4}{4} + b\frac{x^2}{2}\right]_{x_1}^{x_2}. \tag{8.56}$$

SIMPLIFY: Carrying out the definite integral in (8.55) for the mass of the rod we get

$$m = \left(a\frac{x_2^3}{3} + bx_2\right) - \left(a\frac{x_1^3}{3} + bx_1\right) = \frac{a}{3}\left(x_2^3 - x_1^3\right) + b\left(x_2 - x_1\right).$$

Solved Problem

Carrying out the definite in (8.56) for the x-coordinate of the center of mass of the rod we obtain

$$X = \frac{1}{m}\left[a\frac{x^4}{4} + b\frac{x^2}{2}\right]_{x_1}^{x_2} = \frac{1}{m}\left\{\left(a\frac{x_2^4}{4} + b\frac{x_2^2}{2}\right) - \left(a\frac{x_1^4}{4} + b\frac{x_1^2}{2}\right)\right\}$$

which we can further simplify to

$$X = \frac{1}{m}\left\{\frac{a}{4}\left(x_2^4 - x_1^4\right) + \frac{b}{2}\left(x_2^2 - x_1^2\right)\right\}.$$

CALCULATE: Putting our numerical values and calculating the mass of the rod we get

$$m = \frac{0.300 \text{ kg/m}^3}{3}\left((3.00 \text{ m})^3 - (1.00 \text{ m})^3\right) + (0.600 \text{ kg/m})(3.00 \text{ m} - 1.00 \text{ m}) = 3.8 \text{ kg}.$$

Putting in our numerical values for the x-coordinate of the rod we obtain

$$X = \frac{1}{3.8 \text{ kg}}\left\{\frac{0.300 \text{ kg/m}^3}{4}\left((3.00 \text{ m})^4 - (1.00 \text{ m})^4\right) + \frac{0.600 \text{ kg/m}}{2}\left((3.00 \text{ m})^2 - (1.00 \text{ m})^2\right)\right\}$$

which gives us

$$X = 2.210526316 \text{ m}.$$

ROUND: All of the numerical values in this problem were specified to three significant digits so we report our results as

$$m = 3.80 \text{ kg}$$

and

$$X = 2.21 \text{ m}.$$

DOUBLE-CHECK: To get a double-check of our answer for the mass of the rod, let's assume that the rod had a constant linear mass density equal to the linear mass density from our formula with $x = 2$ m (the middle of the rod) given by

$$\lambda = (0.3 \cdot 4 + 0.6) \text{ kg/m} = 1.8 \text{ kg/m}.$$

The mass of the rod would then by $m \approx 2 \text{ m} \cdot 1.8 \text{ kg/m} = 3.6 \text{ kg}$, which is reasonable because it is close to our exact calculation of $m = 3.80$ kg.

To get a double-check of the x-coordinate of the center of mass of the rod, we again assume that the linear mass density is constant. Then the center of mass would be located

Solved Problem

at the middle of the rod or $X \approx 2$ m. Our answer was $X = 2.21$ m, which is slightly right of the middle of the rod. Looking at the function for the linear mass density, we see that the linear mass of the rod increases as we move to the right, which means that the center of mass of the rod must be to the right of the center of the rod. Our result is to the right of the center of the rod, which seems reasonable.

Solved Problem

Solved Problem 8.3: Thruster Firing

Question:

Suppose a spacecraft has an initial mass of 1,850,000 kg. Without its fuel, the spacecraft has a mass of 50,000 kg. The rocket that powers the spacecraft is designed to eject its propellant with a speed of 25 km/s at a constant rate of 15,000 kg/s. The spacecraft is initially at rest in space and travels in a straight line. How far will the spacecraft travel before its rocket shuts down from fuel exhaustion?

Answer:

THINK: The rocket ejects its propellant at a fixed rate. The total mass of propellant is the total mass of the spacecraft minus the mass of the spacecraft after all the propellant is ejected. Thus, we can calculate amount of time during which the rocket operates. As the propellant is used up, the speed of the spacecraft increases and the mass of the spacecraft decreases. If the spacecraft starts from rest, the speed $v(t)$ at any time while the rocket is operating can be obtained from (8.51) replacing the final mass of the spacecraft with the mass of the spacecraft at a given time. The distance traveled before all the propellant is exhausted is given by an integral over the speed as a function of time.

SKETCH: A sketch of the flight of the spacecraft as the propellant is being ejected is shown in Figure 8.19.

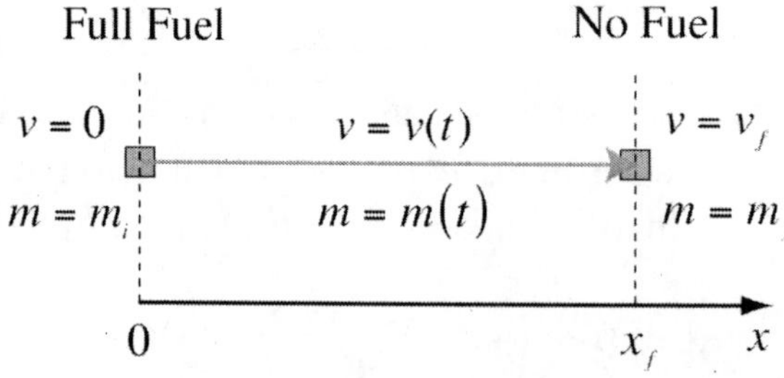

Figure 8.19: A sketch showing the various parameters of the spacecraft as the rocket operates.

RESEARCH: We define the rate at which the propellant is ejected as r_p. The time t_{max} that rocket will operate then is given by

$$t_{\max} = \frac{(m_i - m_f)}{r_p},$$

where m_i is the initial mass of the spacecraft and m_f is the mass of the spacecraft after all the propellant is ejected. The total distance that the rocket travels in this time interval is the integral of the speed over time,

$$x_f = \int_0^{t_{\max}} v(t)dt$$

In order to obtain the speed as a function of time, we need to go back to our rocket equations. While the rocket is operating, the mass of the spacecraft at a time t is given by

$$m(t) = m_i - r_p t$$

The speed of the spacecraft at any given time after the rocket starts to operate and the time all the propellant is exhausted is given by (compare (8.51))

$$v(t) = v_c \ln\left(\frac{m_i}{m(t)}\right) = v_c \ln\left(\frac{m_i}{m_i - r_p t}\right) = v_c \ln\left(\frac{1}{1 - r_p t / m_i}\right)$$

where v_c is the speed of the ejected propellant.

Solved Problem

SIMPLIFY:

Now we insert the time dependence of the speed of the spacecraft into the integral for the displacement and obtain:

$$x_f = \int_0^{t_{\max}} v(t)dt = \int_0^{t_{\max}} v_c \ln\left(\frac{1}{1 - r_p t / m_i}\right)dt = -v_c \int_0^{t_{\max}} \ln\left(1 - r_p t / m_i\right)dt$$

Since $\int \ln(1-ax)dx = -x + x\ln(1-ax) - a^{-1}\ln(ax-1)$ (You can look this result up in an integral table!), the integral evaluates to

$$\begin{aligned}\int_0^{t_{\max}} \ln(1 - r_p t / m_i)dt &= \left[-t + t\ln(1 - r_p t / m_i) - (m_i / r_p)\ln(r_p t / m_i - 1)\right]_0^{t_{\max}} \\ &= \left[-t_{\max} + t_{\max}\ln(1 - r_p t_{\max} / m_i) - (m_i / r_p)\ln(r_p t_{\max} / m_i - 1)\right] \\ &\quad - \left[-(m_i / r_p)\ln(-1)\right] \\ &= -t_{\max} + t_{\max}\ln(1 - r_p t_{\max} / m_i) - (m_i / r_p)\ln(1 - r_p t_{\max} / m_i) \\ &= -t_{\max} + (t_{\max} - (m_i / r_p))\ln(1 - r_p t_{\max} / m_i)\end{aligned}$$

Our distance traveled is then

$$x_f = -v_c\left[-t_{\max} + (t_{\max} - (m_i / r_p))\ln(1 - r_p t_{\max} / m_i)\right].$$

CALCULATE: The time that the rocket is operating is

$$t_{\max} = \frac{(m_i - m_f)}{r_p} = \frac{1{,}850{,}000 \text{ kg} - 50{,}000 \text{ kg}}{15{,}000 \text{ kg/s}} = 120 \text{ s}.$$

Putting in our numerical values for the factor $1 - r_p t_{\max} / m_i$ give us

$$1 - r_p t_{\max} / m_i = 1 - \frac{15{,}000 \text{ kg/s} \cdot 120 \text{ s}}{1{,}850{,}000 \text{ kg}} = 0.027027$$

So we find for the distance traveled

$$x_f = -(25 \cdot 10^3 \text{ m/s})\left[-(120 \text{ s}) + \{(120 \text{ s}) - (1.85 \cdot 10^6 \text{ kg})/(15 \cdot 10^3 \text{ kg/s})\}\ln(0.027027)\right]$$
$$= 2.69909 \cdot 10^6 \text{ m}$$

ROUND: Since the expellant speed was only given to two significant digits, we need to round to that accuracy. Expressing our result in two significant digits gives us

$$x_f = 2.7 \cdot 10^6 \text{ m}$$

DOUBLE-CHECK: To double-check our answer for the distance traveled, we use (8.51) to calculate the final velocity of the spacecraft

$$v_f = v_c \ln\left(\frac{m_i}{m_f}\right) = (25 \text{ km/s})\ln\left(\frac{1.85 \cdot 10^6 \text{ kg}}{5 \cdot 10^4 \text{ kg}}\right) = 90.3 \text{ km/s}.$$

If the spacecraft accelerated at a constant rate, the speed would increase linearly in time and the average speed during the fuel burn would be $\bar{v} = v_f / 2$. Taking this average speed and multiplying by the time the fuel was burning gives us

$$x_{a-const} \approx \bar{v} t_{\max} = (v_f / 2) t_{\max} = (90.2 \text{ km/s} \cdot 120 \text{ s})/2 = 5.4 \cdot 10^6 \text{ m}.$$

This approximate distance must be bigger than the exact result, because in the exact calculation the velocity increases logarithmically in time until it reaches the value of 90.3

km/s. As we can see the approximation is about twice the distance we calculated, giving us confidence that our exact answer is at least of the right order of magnitude.

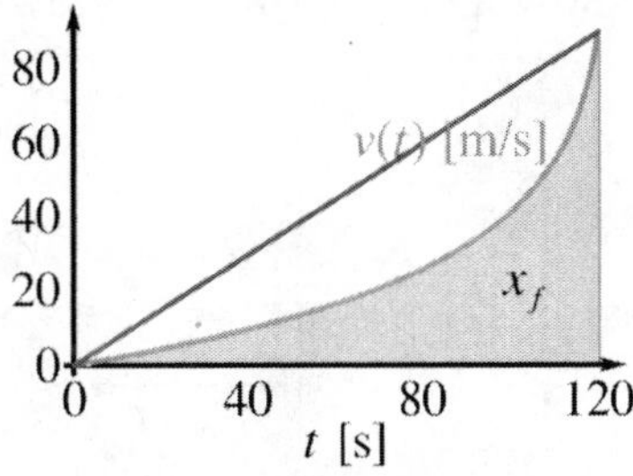

Figure 8.20: Comparison of the exact solution (red) to one for constant acceleration (blue).

In Figure 8.20 we show the exact solution for $v(t)$ (red curve). The final distance traveled, x_f, is the area under the red curve. The blue line shows the comparison case of constant acceleration that would lead to the same final velocity. As one can see, the area under the blue line is approximately twice that under the red line. Since we just calculated the area under the blue line, $x_{a-const}$, and found that it is twice as big as our exact solution, we gain confidence that our integrals were solved correctly.

Solved Problem 8.4: Center of mass of a disk with a hole in it

Question:
Where is the center of mass of the disk with a rectangular hole in it, as depicted in Figure 8.21? The height of the disk is $h = 11.0$ cm, and its radius is $R = 11.5$ cm. There is a rectangular hole cut in it as shown, with a width of $w = 7.0$ cm and depth of $d = 8.0$ cm. The right side of the hole is located such that its middle coincides with the central axis of the disk.

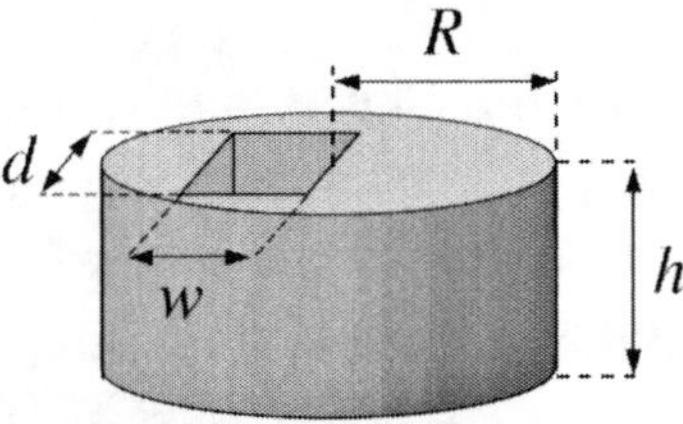

Figure 8.21: A disk with a rectangular hole in it.

Answer:

THINK: One way to approach this problem is to define explicitly the geometry of the volume of the disk with a hole in it, and then to integrate over that volume to obtain the coordinates of the center of mass. We would then be faced with several difficult integrals. A simpler way to approach this problem is to think of the disk with a hole in it as a solid disk minus a rectangular hole. Using the symmetry of the solid disk and the hole in the disk, we can specify the coordinates of the center of mass of the solid disk and the hole. We can then calculate the coordinates of the center of mass of the original disk with a hole in it.

SKETCH: In Figure 8.22 we show a sketch of a top view of the disk, defining the x-axis and the y-axis.

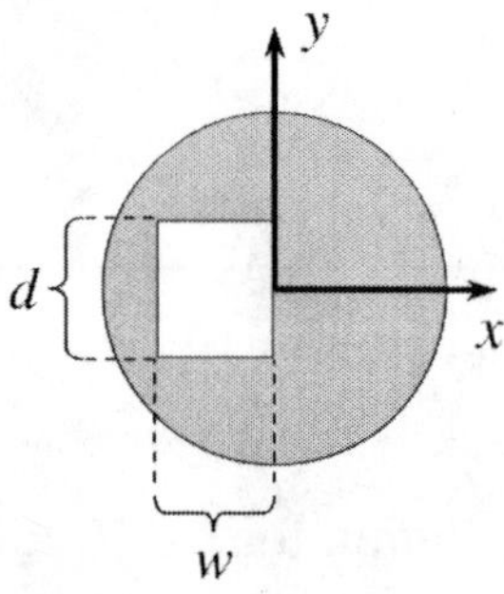

Figure 8.22: Top view of the disk with assumed coordinate system.

In Figure 8.23 we show a sketch of the two symmetry planes of the disk with a rectangular hole in it.

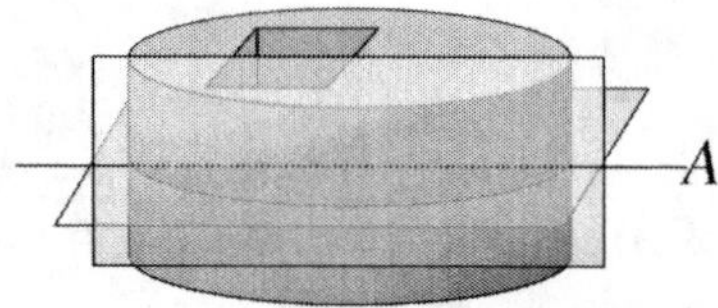

Figure 8.23: Symmetry planes of the disk with a rectangular hole in it.

One plane corresponds to the $x-y$ plane and the second plane corresponds to a plane along the x-axis perpendicular to the $x-y$ plane. The line where the two planes intersect is marked with the letter A.

RESEARCH: The center of mass must lie along the intersection of the two planes of symmetry. Therefore, we know that the center of mass can only be located along the x-axis. The center of mass for the disk without the hole is located at the origin of our coordinate system at $x_d = 0$, and the volume of the solid disk is $V_d = \pi R^2 h$. If the hole were a solid object with the same dimensions as the hole (height $h = 11.0$ cm, width $w = 7.0$ cm, and depth $d = 8.0$ cm), the hole would have a volume of $V_h = hwd$. If this imagined solid object were located where our hole is located, then its center of mass would be in the middle of the hole at $x_h = -3.5$ cm. We can now multiply each of the volumes with the mass density ρ of the material of the disk to get the corresponding masses and then use (8.1) to get the x-coordinate of the center of mass

$$X = \frac{x_d V_d \rho - x_h V_h \rho}{V_d \rho - V_h \rho}. \tag{8.57}$$

Solved Problem

This method of treating the absence of matter as a hole, and then using this hole in calculations just like a regular object, but with negative mass (or charge) is very common in atomic and subatomic physics. We will encounter it again in the chapters on atomic physics (chapter 37) and nuclear and particle physics (chapters 39 and 40).

SIMPLIFY: We can simplify (8.57) by realizing that $x_d = 0$ and that ρ is a common factor

$$X = \frac{-x_h V_h}{V_d - V_h}.$$

Substituting the expressions describing the volumes of the solid disk and hole we get

$$X = \frac{-x_h V_h}{V_d - V_h} = \frac{-x_h(hwd)}{\pi R^2 h - hwd} = \frac{-x_h wd}{\pi R^2 - wd}.$$

Defining the area in the $x-y$ plane of the disk to be $A_d = \pi R^2$ and the area in the $x-y$ plane of the hole to be $A_h = wd$ we can write

$$X = \frac{-x_h wd}{\pi R^2 - wd} = \frac{-x_h A_h}{A_d - A_h}.$$

CALCULATE: Inserting the numbers, we find that the area of the disk is

$$A_d = \pi R^2 = \pi (11.5 \text{ cm})^2 = 415.475 \text{ cm}^2.$$

and the area of the hole is

$$A_h = wd = (7.0 \text{ cm})(8.0 \text{ cm}) = 56 \text{ cm}^2.$$

Therefore the location of the center of mass of the disk with hole (remember, $x_h = -3.5$ cm !):

$$X = \frac{-x_h A_h}{A_d - A_h} = \frac{-(-3.5 \text{ cm})(56 \text{ cm}^2)}{(415.475 \text{ cm}^2) - (56 \text{ cm}^2)} = 0.545239 \text{ cm}$$

ROUND: Expressing our answer with two significant figures, we report the x-coordinate of the center of mass of the disk with a hole as

$$X = 0.55 \text{ cm}.$$

Solved Problem

DOUBLE-CHECK: This result is slightly to the right of the center of the solid disk. This distance is a small fraction of the radius of the disk. This result seems reasonable because taking material out of the disk to the left of $x = 0$ should shift the center of gravity to the right, just as we calculated.

Chapter 9. Circular Motion

What we will learn:

- To describe the motion of objects traveling in a circle rather than in a straight line.
- To use coordinates involving radius and angle rather than Cartesian coordinates to describe circular motion.
- To understand the relationship between linear motion and circular motion.
- To describe the angular coordinate, the angular frequency, and the period of circular motion.
- To express the angular velocity and angular acceleration of an object undergoing circular motion.

Figure 9.1: Circular motion in the horizontal and in the vertical plane.

9.1. Polar Coordinates

In chapter 2 we discussed motion in one dimension. Here we examine the case of special motion in a two-dimensional plane, motion along the perimeter of a circle. This circular motion is surprisingly common. Riding on a carrousel or on many other amusement park rides, such as the ones depicted in Figure 9.1, qualifies as circular motion. So does Indy racing, where the cars usually alternate between going down straight sections and half-circle segments of the track. A record turntable is a good example for circular motion as well, but turntables are hard to find. CD- and DVD-players still operate with circular motion, but this motion is usually hidden from the eye.

We need an appropriate coordinate system to study circular motion. During the motion, both x- and y-coordinates change in continuous fashion, but the distance to the center stays the same. We take advantage of this fact by introducing polar coordinates. Shown in Figure 9.2 is the vector $\vec{r}$. It can change as a function of time, but its tip has to move on the perimeter of the circle. We can specify $\vec{r}$ by giving its x- and y-components but we can also specify the same vector by two other numbers, angle of $\vec{r}$ relative to the x-axis, θ, and the length of $\vec{r}$, $r = |\vec{r}|$ as shown in Figure 9.2.

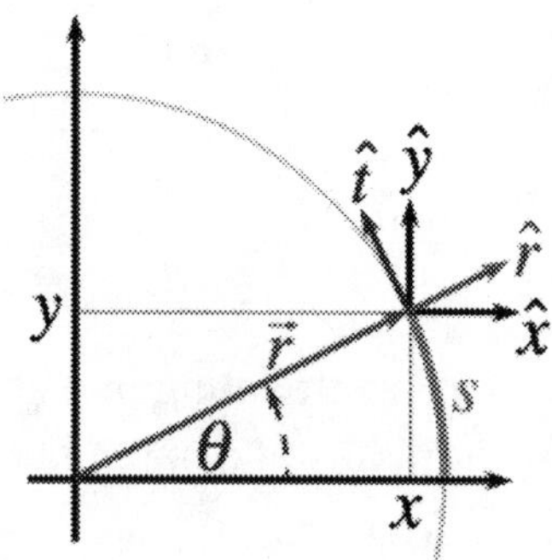

Figure 9.2: Polar coordinate system for circular motion.

Trigonometry then reveals the relationship between the Cartesian coordinates x and y, and the polar coordinates angle θ and radius r:

$$r = \sqrt{x^2 + y^2} \tag{9.1}$$

$$\theta = \arctan(y/x) \tag{9.2}$$

The inverse transformation is given by:

$$x = r\cos\theta \tag{9.3}$$

$$y = r\sin\theta \tag{9.4}$$

The major advantage of using polar coordinates for circular motion is that r never changes. It remains the same as long as the tip of the vector $\vec{r}$ moves along the perimeter of the circle. In this way we can reduce the two-dimensional motion on the perimeter of a circle to a one-dimensional problem for the angle θ.

Figure 9.2 also shows the unit vectors in radial and tangential direction, $\hat{r}$ and $\hat{t}$, respectively. The angle between $\hat{r}$ and $\hat{x}$ is the same angle θ that we just introduced. So the Cartesian components of the radial unit vector can be written as (compare Figure 9.3)

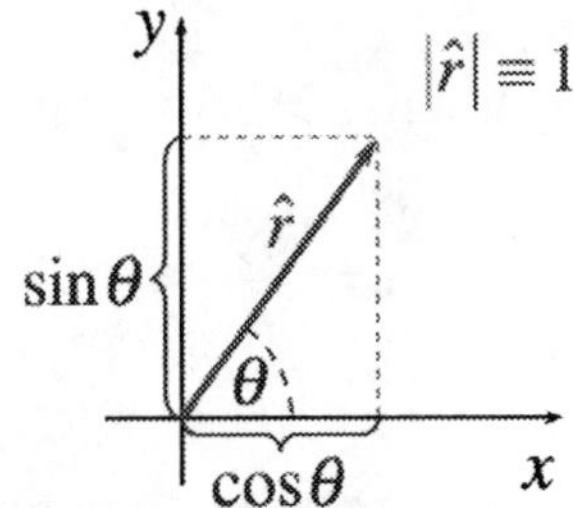

Figure 9.3: Relationship between the radial unit vector and the sine and cosine of the angle.

$$\hat{r} = \frac{x}{r}\hat{x} + \frac{y}{r}\hat{y} = \cos\theta\hat{x} + \sin\theta\hat{y} \equiv (\cos\theta, \sin\theta) \tag{9.5}$$

And in the same way we obtain the Cartesian components of the tangential unit vector as

$$\hat{t} = \frac{-y}{r}\hat{x} + \frac{x}{r}\hat{y} = -\sin\theta\hat{x} + \cos\theta\hat{y} \equiv (-\sin\theta, \cos\theta) \tag{9.6}$$

(Note that the unit tangent vector $\hat{t}$ always is denoted with a caret and can thus be distinguished from the time t). It is easy to verify that the radial and tangential unit vectors are perpendicular to each other by taking the scalar product of the two unit vectors:

$$\hat{r} \bullet \hat{t} = (\cos\theta, \sin\theta) \bullet (-\sin\theta, \cos\theta) = -\cos\theta\sin\theta + \sin\theta\cos\theta = 0 \tag{9.7}$$

Similarly, we find that the lengths of the two unit vectors have the value 1, as required:

$$\begin{aligned} \hat{r} \bullet \hat{r} &= (\cos\theta, \sin\theta) \bullet (\cos\theta, \sin\theta) = \cos^2\theta + \sin^2\theta = 1 \\ \hat{t} \bullet \hat{t} &= (-\sin\theta, \cos\theta) \bullet (-\sin\theta, \cos\theta) = \sin^2\theta + \cos^2\theta = 1 \end{aligned} \tag{9.8}$$

9.2. Angular Coordinate and Angular Displacement

The angle θ is measured relative to the positive x-axis. The two most commonly used measures for angles are degrees and radians. 360 degrees correspond to 2π radians, which represent the angle subtended by one complete circle. The conventional notation for angular specification in degrees is the symbol "°", whereas we will use "rad" to denote angular measures in radians. Neither degrees nor radians have a physical dimension, but we use these symbols to specify that the numbers specifying angles have a certain meaning and are measured in certain units.

Because 360 degrees correspond to 2π radians, the unit conversion between the two angular measures is:

$$\theta\text{ (degrees)}\frac{\pi}{180} = \theta\text{ (radians)} \Leftrightarrow \theta\text{ (radians)}\frac{180}{\pi} = \theta\text{ (degrees)}$$
$$1\text{ radian} = \frac{180°}{\pi} \approx 57.3° \tag{9.9}$$

We will discuss angular coordinates in a manner analogous to our discussion of linear coordinates. Like the linear position, x, the angle, θ, can have positive and negative values. But there are subtle differences. Most obvious among the differences is the fact that θ is periodic; any time you add a complete turn around the circle (2π, or $360°$), you end up at the same point in space.

As we defined the linear displacement, Δx, as the difference between two positions x_2 and x_1, we define the angular displacement, $\Delta\theta$, as the difference between two angles

$$\Delta\theta = \theta_2 - \theta_1 \tag{9.10}$$

Here the notation $\theta_1 \equiv \theta(t_1)$; $\theta_2 \equiv \theta(t_2)$ is used.

Arc Length

In Figure 9.2 we have also marked the path on the perimeter of the circle that the tip of the radius vector arrow has traveled by going from an angle of 0 to θ. We call this the arc length, s. It is related to the radius and angle via

$$s = r\theta \tag{9.11}$$

For this relationship to work out numerically, the angle has to be measured in radians. The fact that the circumference of a circle is $2\pi r$ is a special case of (9.11) with $\theta = 2\pi$ corresponding to one full turn around the circle. The arc length has the same unit as the radius, meters.

For small angles, say a degree or less, the sine of an angle is approximately equal to the angle measured in radians. Because of this and because of (9.11), the preferred unit for angular coordinates is the radian. But the use of degrees is common, and we will use both in this book.

Self-Test Opportunity: Use polar coordinates and calculus to show that the circumference of a circle with radius R is $2\pi R$.

Self-Test Opportunity: Use polar coordinates and calculus to show that the area of a circle with radius R is πR^2.

Example

Example 9.1: CD Track

Let us look at the track on a CD. The track is of spiral shape, originates from an inner radius of $r_1 = 25$ mm and terminates at a maximal outer radius of $r_2 = 58$ mm. The spacing between sequential loops of the track is a constant $\Delta r = 1.6\ \mu\text{m}$; therefore the track density, i.e. the number of times we cross the track per unit length as we move outward, is $\lambda = 1/\Delta r = 625{,}000\ \text{m}^{-1}$.

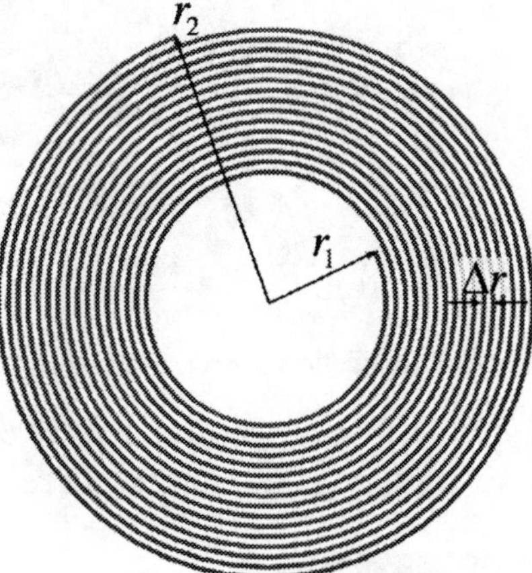

Figure 9.4: Sketch of a compact disk.

Question:
What is the total length of this track?

Answer:
At a given radius r between r_1 and r_2 the track is almost perfectly circular, and this segment of the spiral track has a length of $2\pi r$, growing steadily longer as we move from the inside to the outside. So we obtain the overall length of the track by integrating the length of each turn from r_1 to r_2, multiplied by the number of turns we encounter per unit length:

$$L = \lambda \int_{r_1}^{r_2} 2\pi r dr = \lambda \pi r^2 \Big|_{r_1}^{r_2} = \lambda \pi \left(r_2^2 - r_1^2 \right)$$

Inserting the numbers for the inner and outer radii, as well as for the track density, we then obtain

$$L = (625{,}000\ \text{m}^{-1})\pi\left((0.058\ \text{m})^2 - (0.025\ \text{m})^2\right) = 5{,}378\ \text{m}$$

So we find that the length of a track on a CD is more than 3.3 miles! (For a DVD, by the way, the track density is higher by a factor of 2.2, resulting in a track that is 7.2 miles long.)

In Figure 9.5 we show a small portion of the track of CDs, displayed at a magnification of a factor of 500. The picture on the left is of a factory-pressed CD, with the individual aluminum bumps visible. Displayed on the right is a read-write CD, for which a laser induces a phase change in the continuous track in the process of "burning". The lower right portion of this picture shows a portion of the track that has not been written on.

Figure 9.5: Microscope pictures (magnification 500x) of a CD (left) and re-writeable CD (right).

We can even look at a CD in greater magnification. This is done in Figure 9.6, where we show an image of a CD obtained by using an Atomic Force Microscope.

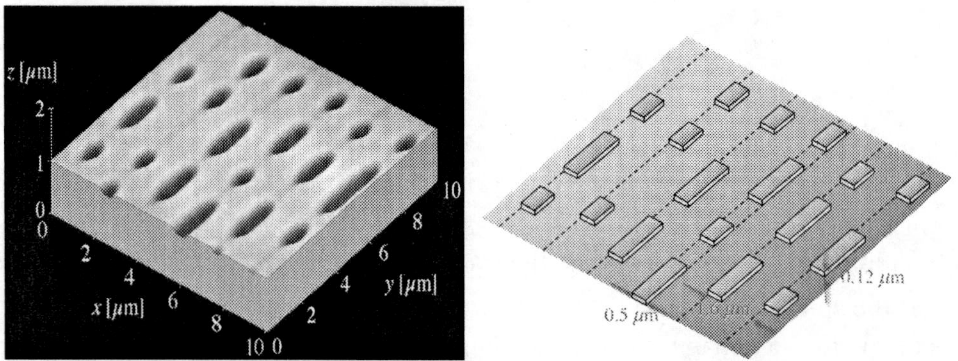

Figure 9.6: Right side: Atomic Force Microscope image of the surface of a CD (image courtesy of B. Bi, MSU; Left: idealized drawing.

9.3. Angular Velocity, Angular Frequency, and Period

In the same way that the change of the linear coordinate in time is the velocity, the change of the angular coordinate in time is the angular velocity. The average angular velocity is defined as

$$\bar{\omega} = \frac{\theta_2 - \theta_1}{t_2 - t_1} = \frac{\Delta\theta}{\Delta t} \tag{9.12}$$

Again, we have used the notation of a horizontal bar above the symbol indicating a time average. By taking the limit of the time interval as approaching zero, we find the instantaneous value of the angular velocity

$$\omega = \lim_{\Delta t \to 0} \bar{\omega} = \lim_{\Delta t \to 0} \frac{\Delta\theta}{\Delta t} \equiv \frac{d\theta}{dt} \tag{9.13}$$

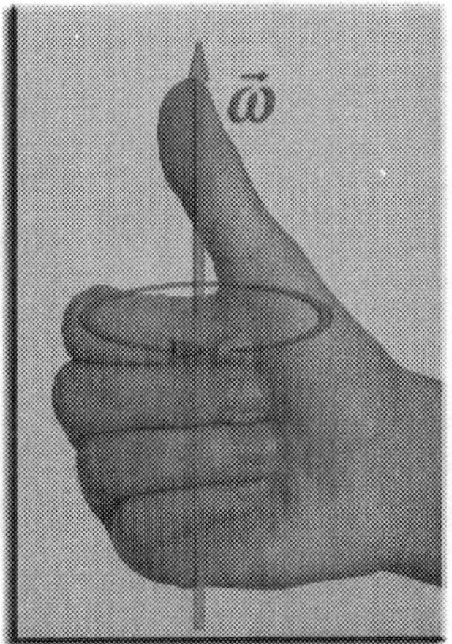

Figure 9.7: The right hand rule for determining the direction of the angular velocity.

Note that the unit of the angular velocity is radians per second. The unit "degrees per second" is not used in practice.

$$[\omega] = \text{rad/s}. \tag{9.14}$$

The angular velocity is also a vector. Its direction is that of the rotation axis, through the center of the circle, and perpendicular to the plane of the circle. This definition leaves two different possibilities where the vector $\vec{\omega}$ could point: either up or down. The right-hand rule helps us decide which is the correct way. For this right hand rule, the fingers point in the direction of rotation along the circle's perimeter. Then the thumb points in the direction of $\vec{\omega}$ as shown in Figure 9.7.

The angular velocity measures how fast the angle changes in time. There is another quantity that measures how fast the angle changes in time, the angular frequency, or simply the frequency, f. For example, the rpm number on the tachometer in your car indicates how many times per minute the engine cycles and thus specifies the frequency of engine revolution. Figure 9.8 shows a tachometer, where the units are specified as

"$1/\text{min} \times 1{,}000$"; the engine hits the red zone at 6,000 revolutions per minute. The quantity that measures cycles per unit time, the frequency, f, (instead of radians per unit time as the angular velocity does) is then related to the angular velocity (also often called the "angular frequency"), ω, by

$$f = \frac{\omega}{2\pi} \Leftrightarrow \omega = 2\pi f \tag{9.15}$$

This relationship makes sense because one complete turn around the circle requires 2π radians in angle. However, care must be taken because both frequency and angular velocity have the same units of inverse seconds (the "rad" is not a dimensional quantity) and can be easily confused.

Figure 9.8: Tachometer of a car. This instrument measures the revolutions per minute of the engine.

Finally, because the unit of inverse second is so common, it was given a new name, the Hertz (Hz). The unit is named for the German physicist Heinrich Rudolf Hertz (1857-1894):

$$1 \text{ Hz} = 1 \text{ s}^{-1} \tag{9.16}$$

The period of rotation, T, is defined as the inverse of the frequency:

$$T = \frac{1}{f} \tag{9.17}$$

The period measures the time interval between two sequential instances where the angle assumes the same value, i.e. the time it takes to pass once around the circle. The unit of the period is that of time, seconds. Given the relationship between period and frequency, and between frequency and angular velocity, we also obtain:

$$\omega = 2\pi f = \frac{2\pi}{T}. \tag{9.18}$$

Angular Velocity and Linear Velocity

If we take the time derivative of the coordinate vector, then we obtain the linear velocity vector. It is most convenient for our purpose to write the vectors in Cartesian coordinates and perform the derivatives component by component:

$$\begin{aligned} \vec{r} &= x\hat{x} + y\hat{y} = (x,y) = (r\cos\theta, r\sin\theta) = r(\cos\theta, \sin\theta) = r\hat{r} \Rightarrow \\ \vec{v} &= \frac{d\vec{r}}{dt} = \frac{d}{dt}(r\cos\theta, r\sin\theta) = \left(\frac{d}{dt}(r\cos\theta), \frac{d}{dt}(r\sin\theta) \right). \end{aligned} \tag{9.19}$$

Now we can use the fact that for motion on a circle the distance r to the origin does not change in time, $r = \text{constant}$. This results in

$$\begin{aligned} \vec{v} &= \left(\frac{d}{dt}(r\cos\theta), \frac{d}{dt}(r\sin\theta) \right) = \left(r\frac{d}{dt}(\cos\theta), r\frac{d}{dt}(\sin\theta) \right) \\ &= \left(-r\sin\theta\frac{d\theta}{dt}, r\cos\theta\frac{d\theta}{dt} \right) \\ &= r\frac{d\theta}{dt}(-\sin\theta, \cos\theta) \end{aligned} \tag{9.20}$$

Here we used the chain rule of differentiation in line 2 and then factored out the common factor $rd\theta / dt$. We already know that the time derivative of the angle is the angular velocity (see the definition equation (9.13)). In addition, we recognize the vector $(-\sin\theta, \cos\theta)$ as the tangential unit vector (compare equation (9.6)). So we finally find for the relationship between angular and linear velocities

$$\vec{v} = r\omega\hat{t} \, . \tag{9.21}$$

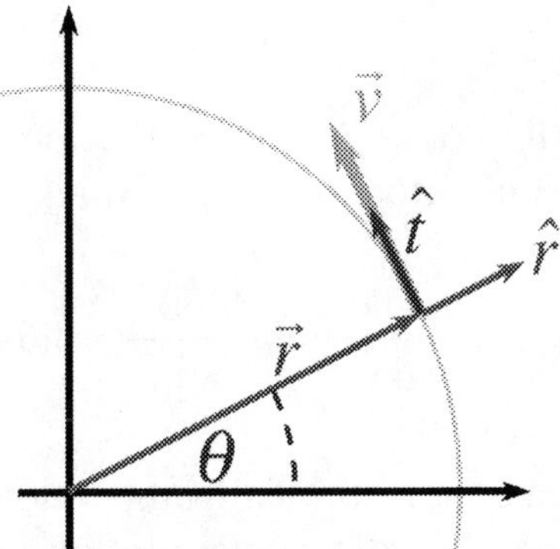

Figure 9.9: Linear velocity and coordinate vectors.

Because the velocity vector is in the direction of the tangent to the trajectory at any given time, it is tangential to the circle's perimeter, in the direction of the arc length. Note that the velocity vector points in the tangential direction and is perpendicular to the position vector, which points in radial direction! If two vectors are perpendicular to each other, their scalar product vanishes. Thus, for circular motion we always find

$$\vec{r}\bullet\vec{v} = (r\cos\theta, r\sin\theta)\bullet(-r\omega\sin\theta, r\omega\cos\theta) = 0 \tag{9.22}$$

If we take the absolute values of the left- and right-hand sides of equation (9.21), we obtain the important relationship between the magnitude of the linear and angular speeds:

$$v = r\omega\,. \tag{9.23}$$

Remember that this result is a relationship between the magnitudes of the linear and angular velocities! Their vector arrows point in different directions and for uniform circular motion are perpendicular to each other, $\vec{\omega}$ pointing in the direction of the rotation axis, and $\vec{v}$ tangential to the perimeter of the circle.

In-class exercise: A bicycle has wheels with a radius of 33.0 cm. The bicycle is traveling with a speed of 6.5 m/s. What is the angular speed of the front tire?
a) 0.197 Hz
b) 1.24 Hz
c) 5.08 Hz
d) 19.7 Hz
e) 215 Hz

Example

Example 9.2: Earth

Question:
The Earth orbits around the Sun and revolves around its own pole-to-pole axis. What are the corresponding angular velocities, frequencies, and linear speeds?

Answer:
Any point on the surface of Earth moves in circular motion around the rotation axis (pole-to-pole) axis, with a rotation period of 1 day. Expressed in seconds, this period is:

$$T_{earth} = 1\text{ day}\cdot\frac{24\text{ hour}}{\text{day}}\cdot\frac{3600\text{ s}}{\text{hour}} = 8.64\cdot10^4\text{ s} \tag{9.24}$$

The Earth moves around the Sun on an elliptical path, which is very close to circular. We will treat the Earth's orbit as a problem of circular motion for the present example. The orbital period for the motion of the Earth around the Sun is 1 year. If we express this period in seconds, we obtain:

$$T_{sun} = 1\text{ year}\cdot\frac{365\text{ day}}{\text{year}}\cdot\frac{24\text{ hour}}{\text{day}}\cdot\frac{3600\text{ s}}{\text{hour}} = 3.15\cdot10^7\text{ s} \tag{9.25}$$

Example

Both circular motions have constant angular velocity. Thus, we can use $T = 1/f$ and $\omega = 2\pi f$ to obtain our answers:

$$f_{earth} = 1/T_{earth} = 1.16 \cdot 10^{-5} \text{ Hz}; \ \omega_{earth} = 2\pi f_{earth} = 7.27 \cdot 10^{-5} \text{ Hz} \quad (9.26)$$

$$f_{sun} = 1/T_{sun} = 3.17 \cdot 10^{-8} \text{ Hz}; \ \omega_{sun} = 2\pi f_{sun} = 1.99 \cdot 10^{-7} \text{ Hz} \quad (9.27)$$

Note that the 24-hour period that was used as the length of a day is the period that it takes for the Sun to have the same position in the sky. Because the Earth also moves around the Sun during these 24 hours, the time that it takes the Earth to actually complete one complete rotation so that the stars have the same position again in the night sky is only 23 hours, 56 minutes and a little more than 4 seconds, or 86,164.09074 seconds ($\approx (1 - 1/365.2425) \cdot 86{,}400$ seconds). This time reference is called *sidereal* time. (We have also used that it takes a fraction of a day more than 365 to complete an orbit around the Sun – this is where leap years come in.)

Figure 9.10: Earth with its rotational axis indicated by the vertical line. Points on different latitudes on the Earth's surface move at different orbital speeds.

Now consider the velocity of the Earth orbiting the Sun. Because we assume circular motion, the relationship between the orbital speeds and angular velocities are given by $v = r\omega$. To get our answer, we need to know the radius of the orbit. The radius of this orbit is the distance Earth-Sun, $r_{sun-earth} = 1.49 \cdot 10^{11}$ m. So the linear orbital speed, the speed with which the Earth moves around the Sun is

Example

$$v = r\omega = (1.49\cdot 10^{11}\ \text{m})\cdot(1.99\cdot 10^{-7}\ \text{s}^{-1}) = 2.97\cdot 10^{4}\ \text{m/s}$$

This speed is large, over 66,000 miles per hour!

Now we want to find the orbital speed of a point on the surface of the Earth, relative to the center of the earth, due to the rotation of the Earth around itself. We note that points at different latitudes have different distances to the axis of rotation as shown in Figure 9.10. At the equator, the radius of the orbit is $r = R_{earth} = 6{,}380\ \text{km}$. As we move away from the equator, the orbital radius as a function of the latitude angle is: $r = R_{earth}\cos\theta$. We obtain, in general, for the orbital speed the following formula:

$$\begin{aligned} v &= \omega r = \omega R_{earth}\cos\theta \\ &= (7.27\cdot 10^{-5}\ \text{s}^{-1})(6.38\cdot 10^{6}\ \text{m})\cos\theta \\ &= (464\ \text{m/s})\cos\theta \end{aligned} \tag{9.28}$$

At the poles, with $\theta = 90°$, we have zero orbital speed, and at the equator, with $\theta = 0°$, the full 464 m/s. Seattle, with $\theta = 47.5°$, moves with $v = 313\ \text{m/s}$, and Miami, with $\theta = 25.7°$, has a speed of $v = 418\ \text{m/s}$.

9.4. Angular and Centripetal Acceleration

Now we address angular acceleration, the rate of change of the angular velocity. The definition of angular acceleration is analogous to the definition of the linear acceleration. We will use the letter α for the angular acceleration, and its time average is defined as:

$$\bar{\alpha} = \frac{\Delta\omega}{\Delta t}. \tag{9.29}$$

The instantaneous angular acceleration is then obtained in the limit of the averaging time interval approaching zero,

$$\alpha = \lim_{\Delta t\to 0}\bar{\alpha} = \lim_{\Delta t\to 0}\frac{\Delta\omega}{\Delta t} \equiv \frac{d\omega}{dt} = \frac{d^2\theta}{dt^2}. \tag{9.30}$$

Just as we related the velocity vector to the angular velocity, we can also relate the tangential acceleration to the angular acceleration. We start with our definition of the linear acceleration vector as the time derivative of the linear velocity vector and insert the expression we obtained for the linear velocity in circular motion in equation (9.20),

$$\vec{a}(t) = \frac{d}{dt}\vec{v}(t) = \frac{d}{dt}(v\hat{t}) = \left(\frac{dv}{dt}\right)\hat{t} + v\left(\frac{d\hat{t}}{dt}\right). \tag{9.31}$$

In the last step of this equation, we executed the derivative using the product rule of differentiation. Thus, we see that there are two physical contributions to the acceleration in circular motion. The first arises from the change in the magnitude of the velocity, and the second from the fact that the velocity vector always points in tangential direction and thus has to change its direction continuously as the radius vector moves around the circle.

Let us look at these two terms individually. First we can calculate the time derivative of the linear speed, v, by using the relationship between linear speed and angular speed that we found in equation (9.23) and by again invoking the product rule:

$$\frac{dv}{dt} = \frac{d}{dt}(r\omega) = \left(\frac{dr}{dt}\right)\omega + r\frac{d\omega}{dt}. \tag{9.32}$$

Since for circular motion $r =$ constant, we find $dr/dt = 0$; so the first term in the sum is 0. In equation (9.30) we have introduced that $d\omega/dt = \alpha$, and so the second term in our sum is equal to $r\alpha$. So we see that the change in speed is related to the angular acceleration via

$$\frac{dv}{dt} = r\alpha\,. \tag{9.33}$$

However, let us not forget that the acceleration vector in equation (9.31) also contains another term that is proportional to the time derivative of the tangential unit vector. If we calculate this quantity, we find

$$\begin{aligned}\frac{d}{dt}\hat{t} &= \frac{d}{dt}(-\sin\theta,\cos\theta) = \left(\frac{d}{dt}(-\sin\theta),\frac{d}{dt}(\cos\theta)\right)\\ &= \left(-\cos\theta\frac{d\theta}{dt},-\sin\theta\frac{d\theta}{dt}\right) = -\frac{d\theta}{dt}(\cos\theta,\sin\theta)\,.\\ &= -\omega\hat{r}\end{aligned} \tag{9.34}$$

Therefore, we find that the time derivative of the tangential unit vector points in opposite direction of the radial unit vector. With this result, we can finally write for the linear acceleration vector of equation (9.31)

$$\vec{a}(t) = r\alpha\hat{t} - v\omega\hat{r} \tag{9.35}$$

Again, for circular motion the acceleration vector has two physical components: the first results from a change in speed and points in tangential direction, and the second component comes from the continuous change of the direction of the velocity vector and points in negative radial direction, towards the center of the circle. This latter acceleration component is present even if the circular motion proceeds at constant speed. If the angular velocity is constant, and therefore the angular acceleration is 0, the velocity vector still changes direction continuously as the object moves in its circular trajectory. The acceleration that changes the direction of the velocity vector without changing its magnitude is called centripetal (or "center-seeking"), and is in the radial inward direction.

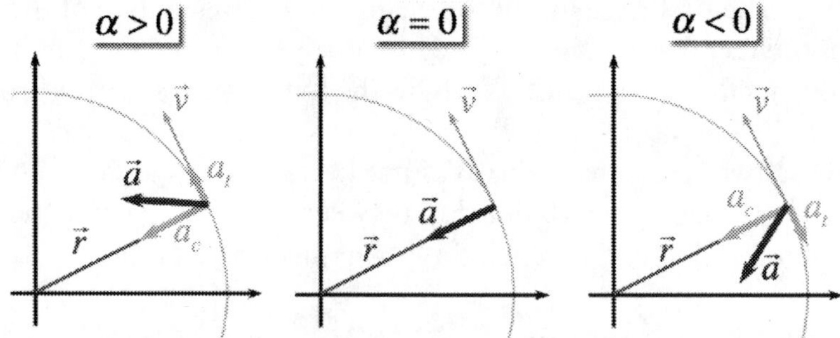

Figure 9.11: Relationship between linear acceleration, centripetal acceleration, and angular acceleration for increasing speed (left), constant speed (center), and decreasing speed (right).

The magnitude of the centripetal acceleration is:

$$a_c = v\omega = \frac{v^2}{r} = \omega^2 r . \tag{9.36}$$

The first expression for the centripetal acceleration in (9.36) can be simply read off from equation (9.35) as the coefficient of the unit vector pointing in negative radial direction. And for the second and third way of writing the centripetal acceleration we have used th relationship between linear and angular speeds, and the radius (9.23).

Example

Example 9.3: Centripetal acceleration due to Earth's rotation

Because the Earth rotates, and points on its surface move with an orbital velocity, it is interesting to compute the corresponding centripetal acceleration and discuss the correction to the commonly stated value of the acceleration due to gravity on the surface of Earth that this motion implies. Since we have just given the formula for the magnitude of the centripetal acceleration in equation 5.27, we can insert the data for the Earth and find:

$$\begin{aligned} a_c &= \omega^2 r = \omega^2 R_{earth} \cos\theta \\ &= (7.27 \cdot 10^{-5}\ \text{s}^{-1})^2 \cdot (6.37 \cdot 10^6\ \text{m}) \cdot \cos\theta . \\ &= (0.034\ \text{m/s}^2) \cdot \cos\theta \end{aligned} \tag{9.37}$$

This result shows that the typical corrections of the centripetal acceleration due to the rotation of Earth to the effective gravitational acceleration observed on the surface of Earth are between 0.33 percent (at the equator) and 0 (at the poles). Using Seattle and Miami again as our example cities, we obtain a centripetal acceleration of $0.02\ \text{m/s}^2$ for Seattle and $0.03\ \text{m/s}^2$ for Miami. These results are relatively small as compared with the quoted value for the acceleration of gravity, $9.81\ \text{m/s}^2$, but not always negligible.

Self-Test Opportunity: We just found that the centripetal acceleration due to the Earth's rotation has approximately the maximum value of $g / 300$? Can you determine what the corresponding value of the centripetal acceleration from the Earth's orbit around the Sun is?

In-class exercise:
The period of rotation of the Earth on its axis is 24 hours. At this angular velocity, the centripetal acceleration at the surface of the Earth is small compared with the acceleration of gravity. What would the period of rotation of the Earth be if the magnitude of the centripetal acceleration at the surface of the Earth at the equator due to the rotation of the Earth were equal to the magnitude of the acceleration of gravity? (With this rotation you could levitate just above the earth's surface!)

a) 0.043 hours
b) 0.340 hours
c) 0.841 hours
d) 1.41 hours
e) 3.89 hours
f) 12.0 hours

Self-Test Opportunity: We are standing on the surface of the Earth at the equator. If the Earth stopped rotating on its axis, would we feel lighter or heavier, or the same?

If we want a large centripetal acceleration for a given orbital speed, then we need a small radius. The following example illustrates this point.

Solved Problem

Solved Problem 9.1: Roller Coaster

Perhaps the biggest thrill in an amusement park can be had when riding a roller coaster with a vertical loop in it, as in Figure 9.12, where one can feel almost weightless at the top of the loop.

Question:
Suppose the loop has a radius of 5.00 m, what does the linear speed of the roller coaster car have to be at the top of the loop for the passengers to feel weightless?

Answer:

THINK:
Note that we feel weightless when there is no supporting force, such as from a seat or a restraint. Our mass is not zero, however. The supporting force from the seat is a kind of normal force. For us to feel weightless at the top of the loop, we then have to make sure

Solved Problem

that at this point there is no normal force acting. How can we accomplish this?

Figure 9.12: Modern roller coaster with a loop.

SKETCH:

The free-body diagram shown in the left-hand side of Figure 9.13 may help to conceptualize the situation. Here we show the force of gravity and the normal force acting on the person in the roller coaster at the top of the loop. The sum of these two forces is the net force, which has to equal the centripetal force in circular motion. If the net force (= centripetal force here) is equal to the gravitational force, then the normal force is zero, and we feel weightlessness. This situation is illustrated on the right-hand side of Figure 9.13.

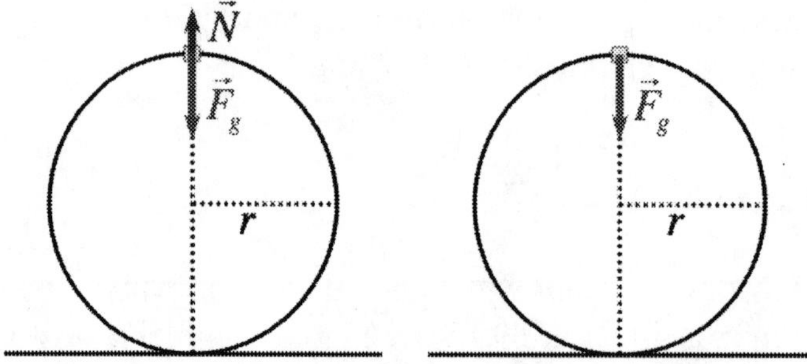

Figure 9.13: Left: general free-body diagram for the top of the roller coaster;
Right: special case of feeling of weightlessness.

RESEARCH:

We have just stated that the net force is equal to the centripetal force, and that the net force is the sum of the normal force and the force of gravity:

$$\vec{F}_c = \vec{F}_{net} = \vec{F}_g + \vec{N}$$

Solved Problem

For the feeling of weightlessness at the top of the loop, we need $\vec{N} = 0$, and thus

$$\vec{F}_c = \vec{F}_g \Rightarrow F_c = F_g$$

As always we have $F_g = mg$. And for the magnitude of the centripetal force we have just found (9.39):

$$F_c = ma_c = m\frac{v^2}{r}$$

SIMPLIFY:

Inserting the expressions for the centripetal and the gravitation forces we can solve for the linear speed:

$$F_c = F_g \Rightarrow m\frac{v_{top}^2}{r} = mg \Rightarrow v_{top} = \sqrt{rg}\,. \tag{9.38}$$

CALCULATE:

Using the standard number of $g = 9.81\ \text{m/s}^2$ and the value of 5.00 m given for the radius we obtain: $v_{top} = \sqrt{(5.00\ \text{m})(9.81\ \text{m/s}^2)} = 7.00357\ \text{m/s}$.

ROUND:

Rounding our result to the 3-digit precision, we can state for the speed at the top

$$v_{top} = 7.00\ \text{m/s}$$

DOUBLE-CHECK:

Is our finding of 7.00 m/s for the speed at the top reasonable? Converting this result to mph, we find 15.7 mph, which seems very much in line from what we know about the speeds with which roller coasters move.

Let us go one step further and calculate the velocity vectors at the 3-o'clock and 9 o'clock positions in the loop, supposing that our roller coast moves counter-clockwise through the loop. The directions of the velocity vectors in circular motion are always perpendicular to the perimeter of the circle. This leads to velocity vector directions as shown in Figure 9.14.

How do we obtain the magnitude of the velocities v_3 (at 3 o'clock) and v_9 (at 9 o'clock)? To find out, we have to remind ourselves of the results of chapter 6, where we had found that the total energy is the sum of kinetic and potential energy, $E = K + U$, and where we had found that the kinetic energy is $K = \frac{1}{2}mv^2$ and that the gravitational potential energy is proportional to the height above ground, $U = mgy$. In Figure 9.14 we display a coordinate system, where the 0 of the y-axis is chosen as the bottom of the loop. We then can write the equation for the conserved mechanical energy and find:

Solved Problem

$$E = K_3 + U_3 = K_{top} + U_{top} = K_9 + U_9 \Rightarrow$$
$$\tfrac{1}{2}mv_3^2 + mgy_3 = \tfrac{1}{2}mv_{top}^2 + mgy_{top} = \tfrac{1}{2}mv_9^2 + mgy_9$$

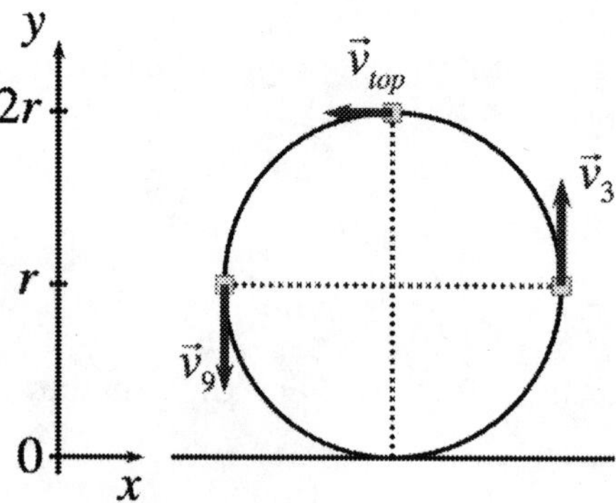

Figure 9.14: Directions of the velocity vectors in the roller coaster loop.

We can see right away that the y-coordinates and therefore the potential energies at the 3 o'clock and 9 o'clock positions are the same; therefore the kinetic energies at both points have to be the same; consequently the absolute values of the speeds at both points are the same, $v_3 = v_9$. Solving the above equation for v_3 we obtain

$$\tfrac{1}{2}mv_3^2 + mgy_3 = \tfrac{1}{2}mv_{top}^2 + mgy_{top} \Rightarrow$$
$$\tfrac{1}{2}v_3^2 + gy_3 = \tfrac{1}{2}v_{top}^2 + gy_{top} \Rightarrow$$
$$v_3 = \sqrt{v_{top}^2 + 2g(y_{top} - y_3)}$$

We see that the mass again cancels out in this calculation. Further, only the difference in the y-coordinates enters into our answer; therefore the choice of the origin of the coordinate system is irrelevant. The difference in the y-coordinates between the two points is $y_{top} - y_3 = r$. Inserting the numbers, we use the given value of $r = 5.00$ m and the result of $v_{top} = 7.00$ m/s that we have found above. Then we see that the speed at the 3 o'clock and that at the 9 o'clock position in the loop is:

$$v_3 = \sqrt{(7.00 \text{ m/s})^2 + 2(9.81 \text{ m/s}^2)(5.00 \text{ m})} = 12.1 \text{ m/s}$$

In-class exercise: In the above roller coaster problem, what is the speed with which the roller coaster car has to enter at the bottom of the loop of 5.00 m radius in order to achieve the feeling of weightlessness at the top?

a) 7.00 m/s
b) 12.1 m/s
c) 13.5 m/s
d) 15.6 m/s
e) 21.4 m/s

Self-Test Opportunity: What is the required speed of the roller coaster at the top of the loop to accomplish the same feeling of weightlessness if we double the radius of the loop?

In-class exercise: In Figure 9.13 we show on the left the general free-body diagram for the forces acting on the rider of the roller coaster at the top, where there is a normal force present that acts on the rider and is exerted on him/her by the car. In this drawing that normal force arrow points up and is smaller than that for the gravitational force. Providing that the speed of the roller coaster car is also 7.00 m/s, what would the radius of the loop have to be for this free-body diagram to be correct?
a) less than 5 m
b) 5 m
c) more than 5 m

"Centrifugal" Acceleration/Force

For circular motion, one often talks about centrifugal (or "center-fleeing", in the radial outward direction) acceleration or centrifugal force (= mass times acceleration). You can experience the sensation of seemingly being pulled outward on many rotating amusement park rides. This sensation is due to your body's inertia, which "resists" the centripetal acceleration towards the center, and is thus felt as a seemingly outward pointing force, the centrifugal force. Keep in mind that this perception is due to your body moving in an accelerated reference frame and that there is no centrifugal force. The real force that acts on your body and forces it to move on a circular path is called the centripetal force and points inward. The centripetal force F_c is not an additional fundamental force of nature but is simply the name given to the net inward force, which is the product of the mass of the object times the centripetal acceleration required to force it onto a circular path

$$F_c = ma_c = m\frac{v^2}{r}. \tag{9.39}$$

You have also experienced a similar effect in straight-line motion. When you are sitting in your car at rest and then step on the gas pedal, you feel like you are pressed back into your seat. This sensation of a force that presses you in backward direction into your seat also comes from the inertia of your body that gets accelerated forward by your car. Both of these sensations of forces acting on your body, the "centrifugal force" and the "pushing into the seat force", are the result of your body experiencing an acceleration in the opposite direction and putting up resistance, inertia, against this acceleration.

9.5. Circular and Linear Motion

Let us start with a short summary of the relationship between linear and angular quantities that we have found so far. This comparison is done in form of a table.

Table 9.1: Comparison of kinematical variables for linear and circular motion.

Quantity	Linear	Circular	Relationship
Displacement	s	θ	$s = r\theta$
Velocity	v	ω	$v = r\omega$
Acceleration	a	α	$\vec{a} = r\alpha\,\hat{t} - r\omega^2\hat{r}$
			$a_t = r\alpha$
			$a_c = \omega^2 r$

The relationships shown in the table relate the angular quantities (θ, ω, α) to the linear quantities (s, v, a). r, the radius of the orbit, is constant and provides the connection between the two sets of quantities. In the next chapter we will add several more lines to this table as we look at moment of inertia, rotational kinetic energy, angular momentum, and torque, all of which have counterparts in linear motion.

As we have just shown, we can make a formal connection between moving on a straight line with constant velocity and moving in circular motion with constant angular velocity. However, there is a one big difference! As we have seen in our section on relative motion in chapter 3, one cannot tell if one is moving with constant velocity, or if one is at rest. This is because we are free to define our origin of our coordinate system at any point. This point can even move with constant velocity, and the physics of translational motion does not change under this Galilean transformation, as we have seen in chapter 3. In contrast, in circular motion one is always moving on a circular path with a well-defined center. Experiencing the "centrifugal" force that we have talked about in the previous section is then a sure sign that one is in circular motion, and the strength of that force experience is a measure for the magnitude angular velocity. You may argue that while reading this you are in circular motion around the center of the Earth, around the center of the solar system, and around the center of the Milky Way, but that you do not feel the effects of those circular motions. True, but this is because of the very small magnitudes of the angular velocities involved in these motions, which cause the effects of these circular motion to be negligible for most applications in our daily lives.

9.5.1 Constant Angular Acceleration

If you look back at our chapter 2 on straight-line motion in one spatial dimension, you see that we spent much of our effort on the discussion of the special case of a constant acceleration. Under this assumption we managed to derive five kinematical equations that proved useful in solving all kinds of problems. For ease of reference, let us repeat these five equations of linear motion with constant acceleration here:

$$
\begin{array}{ll}
(i) & x = x_0 + v_{x0}t + \tfrac{1}{2}a_x t^2 \\
(ii) & x = x_0 + \bar{v}_x t \\
(iii) & v_x = v_{x0} + a_x t \\
(iv) & \bar{v}_x = \tfrac{1}{2}(v_x + v_{x0}) \\
(v) & v_x^2 = v_{x0}^2 + 2a_x(x - x_0)
\end{array}
\tag{9.40}
$$

Now let us take the same steps as in chapter 2 to derive the equivalent equations for constant angular acceleration. We start with (9.30) and integrate

$$\alpha(t) = \frac{d\omega}{dt} \Rightarrow$$

$$\int_{t_0}^{t} \alpha(t')dt' = \int_{t_0}^{t} \frac{d\omega(t')}{dt'}dt' = \omega(t) - \omega(t_0) \Rightarrow$$

$$\omega(t) = \omega_0 + \int_{t_0}^{t} \alpha(t')dt', \tag{9.41}$$

where we have used the usual notation convention of $\omega_0 \equiv \omega(t_0)$. This relationship is the inverse relationship to (9.30) and holds in general. If we now demand that the angular acceleration α is constant in time, then we can execute the integral and obtain

$$\omega(t) = \omega_0 + \alpha\int_0^t dt' = \omega_0 + \alpha t \tag{9.42}$$

For convenience, we have set $t_0 = 0$, just as we had done in chapter 2 at this juncture. In the next step we use (9.13), expressing that the angular velocity is the derivative of the angle with respect to time,

$$
\begin{aligned}
\frac{d\theta(t)}{dt} &= \omega(t) = \omega_0 + \alpha t \Rightarrow \\
\theta(t) &= \theta_0 + \int_0^t \omega(t')dt' = \theta_0 + \int_0^t (\omega_0 + \alpha t')dt' \Rightarrow \\
&= \theta_0 + \omega_0\int_0^t dt' + \alpha\int_0^t t'dt' \Rightarrow \\
\theta(t) &= \theta_0 + \omega_0 t + \tfrac{1}{2}\alpha t^2,
\end{aligned}
\tag{9.43}
$$

where we have used the notation of $\theta_0 = \theta(t=0)$. Comparing (9.42) and (9.43) to the first and second equations of (9.40), we find that these two equations are the circular motion equivalent of the first two kinematical equations for straight-line linear motion in one dimension. With the straightforward substitutions $x \to \theta$, $v_x \to \omega$, and $a_x \to \alpha$ we can write down our five kinematical equations for circular motion under constant angular acceleration

$$
\begin{array}{ll}
(i) & \theta = \theta_0 + \omega_0 t + \tfrac{1}{2}\alpha t^2 \\
(ii) & \theta = \theta_0 + \bar{\omega} t \\
(iii) & \omega = \omega_0 + \alpha t \\
(iv) & \bar{\omega} = \tfrac{1}{2}(\omega + \omega_0) \\
(v) & \omega^2 = \omega_0^2 + 2\alpha(\theta - \theta_0)
\end{array}
\qquad (9.44)
$$

Self-Test Opportunity: We have shown the derivation of the first two of these five kinematical equations for circular motion. Can you provide the derivation for the remaining ones? (Hint: the chain of reasoning proceeds exactly along the same lines as Derivation 2.1 in chapter 2.)

Example

Example 9.4: Hammer Throw

One of the most interesting events in track and field competitions is the hammer throw. The task is to throw the "hammer", a 12 cm diameter ball attached to a grip by a steel cable, a maximum distance. The hammer's total length is 121.5 cm, and its total weight is 7.26 kg. The athlete has to accomplish the throw while not leaving a circle of radius 7 feet (= 2.135 m), and the best way to throw the hammer is for the athlete to spin, allowing the hammer to move in a circle around him before releasing it. At the 1988 Seoul Olympic Games, the Russian thrower Sergey Litvinov won the gold medal with an Olympic record of 84.80 m. He took seven turns before releasing the hammer, and we timed the periods to complete each turn by examining the video recording frame by frame. They were 1.52 s, 1.08 s, 0.72 s, 0.56 s, 0.44 s, 0.40 s, and 0.36 s, respectively.

Question 1:
What was the angular acceleration during this process, assuming that it is constant?

Answer 1:
In order to find the average angular acceleration, we have to add all time intervals for the seven turns, to obtain the total time,

$$t_{all} = 1.52 \text{ s} + 1.08 \text{ s} + 0.72 \text{ s} + 0.56 \text{ s} + 0.44 \text{ s} + 0.40 \text{ s} + 0.36 \text{ s} = 5.08 \text{ s}$$

During this time, the hammer thrower completed seven full turns, resulting in a total angle of

$$\theta_{all} = 7 \cdot 2\pi \text{ rad} = 14\pi \text{ rad} \approx 44.0 \text{ rad} .$$

Because we can assume constant acceleration according to the question posed, we can solve for the angular acceleration by using

$$\theta = \tfrac{1}{2}\alpha\, t^2 \Rightarrow \alpha = \frac{2\theta}{t^2} = \frac{2 \cdot 44.0 \text{ rad}}{(5.08 \text{ s})^2} = 3.41 \text{ rad/s}^2 . \quad (9.45)$$

This is our answer. However, since we have information on how long it took to complete each turn, we can generate a plot of the angle of the hammer in the horizontal plane as a function of time.

This is done in Figure 9.15 by the red dots that represent the data points. The blue line is a fit to these data that assumes a constant angular acceleration of $\alpha = 3.41 \text{ s}^{-2}$. As you can see the assumption of constant angular acceleration is not quite fulfilled, but it is still close enough that the process of spinning with the hammer in the hammer throw competition can serve as a useful example for us.

Example

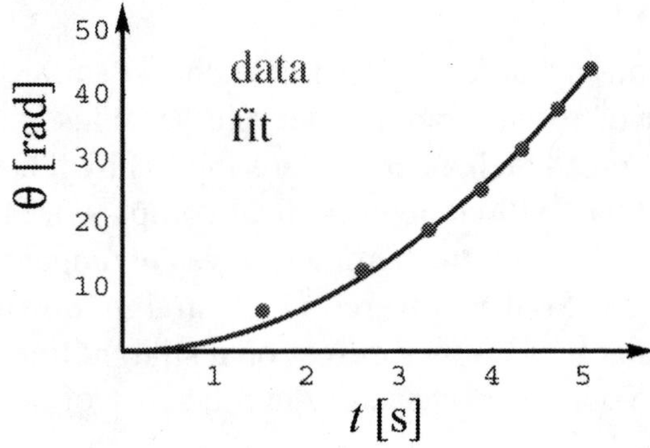

Figure 9.15: Angle as a function of time for Sergey Litvinov's 1988 gold medal hammer throw.

Question 2:
Assuming that the radius of the circle on which the hammer moves is 1.67 m (= length of hammer + arms of the athlete), what is the linear speed with which the hammer gets released?

Answer 2:
Under constant angular acceleration from rest for a period of 5.08 s, the final angular velocity reached is

$$\omega = \alpha\, t = (3.41 \text{ s}^{-2}) \cdot (5.08 \text{ s}) = 17.3 \text{ s}^{-1} . \quad (9.46)$$

Using the relationship between linear and angular velocity, we obtain for the linear speed at release:

$$v = r\omega = (1.67 \text{ m}) \cdot (17.3 \text{ s}^{-1}) = 28.9 \text{ m/s} \quad (9.47)$$

Question 3:
What is the centripetal force that the hammer thrower has to exert on the hammer right before the hammer gets released?

Answer 3:
The centripetal acceleration right before release is given by:

$$a_c = v\omega = (28.9 \text{ m/s}) \cdot (17.3 \text{ s}^{-1}) = 500. \text{ m/s}^2 \quad (9.48)$$

With a mass of 7.26 kg for the hammer, the centripetal force required is then:

$$F_c = ma_c = (7.26 \text{ kg}) \cdot (500 \text{ m/s}^2) = 3630 \text{ N}$$

This is an astonishingly large force, equivalent to the gravitational force on an object of mass of 370 kg! This is why world-class hammer throwers need to be very strong.

Question 4:
After release, what is the direction in which the hammer moves?

Answer 4:
It is a common misconception that the hammer somehow "spirals" in some sort of circular motion with ever-increasing radius after release. This is wrong; if there is no horizontal component of force (such as had been supplied by the athlete), Newton's Second Law tells us that there will be no horizontal component of acceleration and hence no centripetal acceleration. Instead, the hammer moves in tangential direction to the circle at the point of release. So if you were to look straight down on the stadium from an airplane, you would see that the hammer moves on a straight line as in Figure 9.16. Viewed from the side, of course, the shape of the trajectory of the hammer is a parabola, as shown in chapter 3.

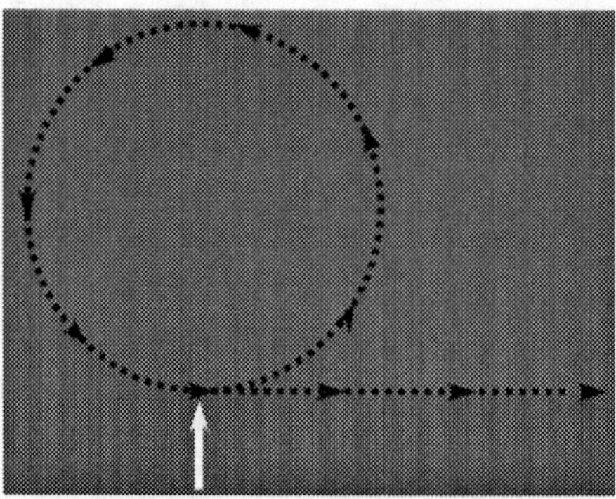

Figure 9.16: Schematic top-view diagram of the trajectory of the hammerhead (black dots, with the arrows indicating the direction of the velocity vector) during the time that the athlete holds on to it (circular path) and after release (straight line). The white arrow marks the point of release.

Example

9.6. Applications of Circular Motion

Let us look at a few examples and solved problems to see how useful the concepts developed in our study of circular motion are.

Example 9.5: Formula 1 Racing

If you watch a Formula 1 race, you can see that racers approach curves from the outside, cut through to the inside and then drift again to the outside, as shown by the red trajectory in Figure 9.17. The blue trajectory is shorter. Why don't the drivers follow the shortest path?

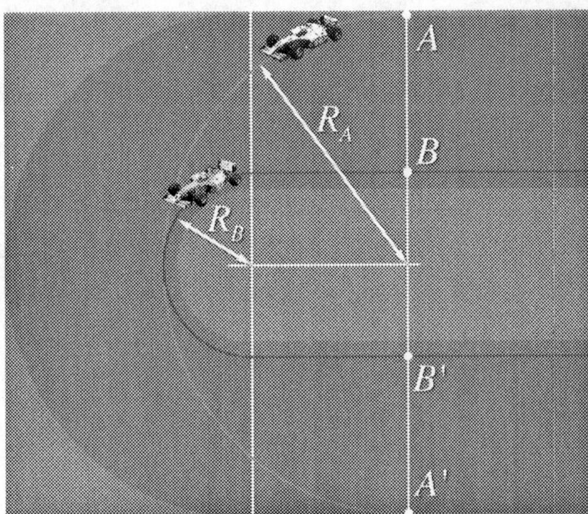

Figure 9.17: Motion of racecars negotiating a turn on an oval track in two different ways.

Example

Question:
Suppose cars move through the U-turn shown here at constant speed, and suppose that the coefficient of friction between the tires and the road is $\mu_s = 1.2$. (Note: we again point out what we already said in chapter 4: modern race car tires can have coefficients of friction that exceed 1, if they are heated to race temperature and thus very sticky.) If the inner radius of the curve shown is $R_B = 10.3$ m and the outer radius is $R_A = 32.2$ m, how much time will it take to move from point A to A', and how much from point B to B', if the drivers use their maximal possible speeds?

Answer:
We start with drawing a free-body diagram, as is done on the right side of Figure 9.18. We show all forces that act on the car and attach their force arrows to the center of mass of the car (black dot). The force of gravity, acting downwards with magnitude $F_g = mg$, is shown in red. This force is exactly balanced by the normal force with which the road acts on the car, shown in green. As the car makes the turn a net force is required to change the car's velocity vector and act as the centripetal force that pushes the car onto a circular motion path. This net force is generated by the friction force (shown in blue) between the car's tires and the road. This force arrow points horizontally inwards, towards the center of the curve. As usual, the magnitude of the friction force is the product of the normal force and the coefficient of friction. Therefore $f_{\max} = \mu_s mg$. (Note: in this case we use the $=$ sign, because the race car drivers push their cars and tires to the limit and thus use the maximum possible static friction force.) The arrow for the friction force is a factor of 1.2 longer than that for the normal force, because $\mu_s = 1.2$.

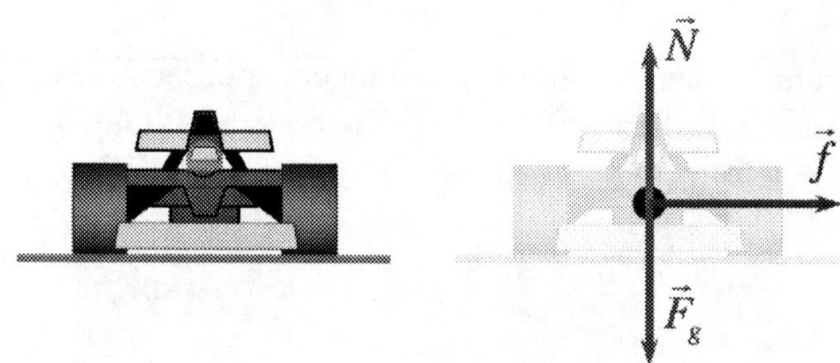

Figure 9.18: Left: frontal view of the racecar; right: Free-body diagram for the racecar in a curve.

Example

First, we need to calculate the maximum velocity that we can use on each trajectory. For each radius of curvature R, the resulting centripetal force, $F_c = mv^2 / R$, must be provided by the friction force, $f_{\max} = \mu_s mg$:

$$m\mu_s g = m\frac{v^2}{R} \Rightarrow v = \sqrt{\mu_s gR} \qquad (9.49)$$

So we get for the red and blue curves:

$$v_{red} = \sqrt{\mu_s gR_A} = \sqrt{1.2 \cdot (9.81 \text{ m/s}^2) \cdot (32.2 \text{ m})} = 19.5 \text{ m/s}$$
$$v_{blue} = \sqrt{\mu_s gR_B} = \sqrt{1.2 \cdot (9.81 \text{ m/s}^2) \cdot (10.3 \text{ m})} = 11.0 \text{ m/s}$$

Note that these speeds are only about 43.6 mph and 24.6 mph, respectively! On the other hand, this curve is a very tight one typically encountered on a city course like Monaco.

Even though you can drive much faster on the red curve, the blue trajectory is shorter than the red one. For the path length of the red curve, we simply have the length of the semicircle $\ell_{red} = \pi R_A = 101.$ m, and for the blue trajectory path length we have to add the two straight sections plus the semicircle curve with the smaller radius:

$$\ell_{blue} = \pi R_B + 2(R_A - R_B) = 76.2 \text{ m}$$

We then get for the time to go from A to A' on the red trajectory:

$$t_{red} = \frac{\ell_{red}}{v_{red}} = \frac{101. \text{ m}}{19.5 \text{ m/s}} = 5.18 \text{ s}$$

To travel through the curve on the blue trajectory from B to B', it takes:

$$t_{blue} = \frac{\ell_{blue}}{v_{blue}} = \frac{76.2 \text{ m}}{11.0 \text{ m/s}} = 6.92 \text{ s}.$$

So we see that in the limit that the cars have to use constant speeds, it is clearly a huge advantage to cut through the curve, as shown by the red trajectory.

Discussion:
In a race situation, it is unreasonable to expect the blue car to drive the straight-line segments with constant velocity. Instead, the driver will come in to point B with the maximum speed that allows him to slow down to 11.0 m/s when entering the circular segment. The friction between the tires and the road provides the deceleration on the straight segment from point A to point B. The maximum deceleration is achieved by braking with the maximum possible force of friction between tires and road, $f_{\max} = \mu_s mg$. We can calculate the speed v_B at point B by utilizing the work-energy theorem that we developed in chapter 6. The work done by the maximum friction force is simply the product of this (constant!) force, the net displacement, and the cosine of the angle between these two. Since the friction force acts in opposite direction to the displacement, the angle between these two vectors is 180 degrees, and so the cosine of the angle is -1, resulting in the work done by the friction force

$$W_f = f_{\max}\Delta r\cos\alpha = (\mu_s mg)(R_B - R_A)(-1) = -\mu_s mg(R_B - R_A)$$

Now we can use the work-energy theorem, which says that the kinetic energy at point B is equal to the kinetic energy at point A plus the work done by the friction force,

$$K_B = K_A + W_f \Rightarrow$$
$$\tfrac{1}{2}mv_B^2 = \tfrac{1}{2}mv_A^2 - \mu_s mg(R_B - R_A)$$

The speed at B can thus be calculated as:

$$v_B = \sqrt{v_A^2 - 2\mu_s g(R_B - R_A)}\,. \tag{9.50}$$

Inserting the numbers, this works out to:

$$v_B = \sqrt{(11.0\text{ m/s})^2 - 2\cdot 1.2\cdot(9.81\text{ m/s}^2)\cdot(10.3\text{ m} - 32.2\text{ m})} = 25.2\text{ m/s}\,.$$

Then the time that it would take on the blue line to travel from B to B' is:

$$t_{blue} = \frac{\pi R_B}{v_{blue}} + \frac{2(R_A - R_B)}{\tfrac{1}{2}(v_B + v_{blue})} = 5.36\text{ s}\,. \tag{9.51}$$

The blue path is still slower, but not by much. In addition, the car following the blue line can reach point B with a slightly higher speed than the red car can reach point A. So there is a careful tradeoff that one has to consider before declaring a winner in this problem.

Example

In real racing situations, cars slow down as they approach the curve and then accelerate as they come out of the curve. The most advantageous trajectory for cutting through a curve is not the red semicircle, but a trajectory that looks closer to elliptical, starting out on the outside, cutting to the extreme inside in the middle of the turn, and then drifting to the outside again while accelerating out of the turn.

Formula 1 racing generally involves flat tracks and tight turns. Indy and NASCAR racing takes place on tracks with bigger turning radii as well as banked curves. To study the forces involved with this type of racing we must combine concepts of static equilibrium on the inclined plane with the concepts of circular motion.

Solved Problem

Solved Problem 9.2: NASCAR Racer

As a NASCAR racer moves through a banked curve, the banking helps him achieve higher speeds. In Figure 9.19 we show a drawing of a racer on a banked curve.

Figure 9.19: Racecar on a banked curve.

Question:
If the coefficient of friction between the racetrack surface and the tires of the racecar is $\mu_s = 0.620$ and the radius of the turn is $R = 110.\text{ m}$, what is the maximum speed with which the driver can take this curve banked at $\theta = 21.1°$?

Answer:

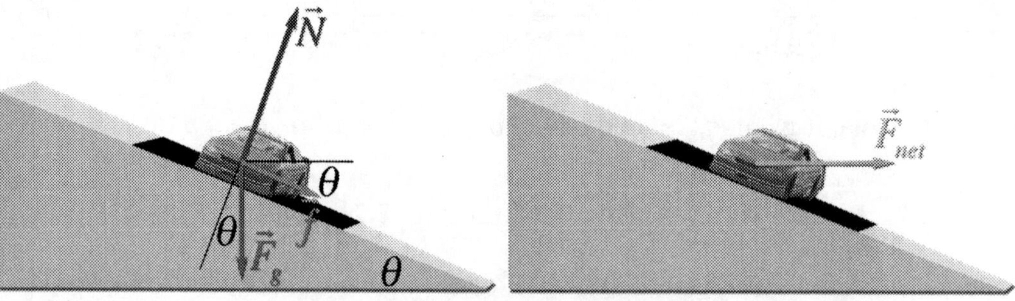

Figure 9.20: Left: Forces on a racecar going around a banked curve on a racetrack; right: net force, the sum of the three forces in the left diagram.

THINK: In Figure 9.20 we have drawn vectors for the force of gravity $\vec{F}_g$, the normal force $\vec{N}$, and the force of friction $\vec{f}$. The curve is banked at an angle of θ, and the same angle appears between the normal to the road surface and the gravity force vector, as shown. To draw the vector for the force of friction, we have assumed that the racer has entered the curve at high speed so that the direction of the force of friction is down the road. In contrast to the situation for static equilibrium considerations, these three forces do not add up to zero, but instead add up to the net force $\vec{F}_{net}$. This net force $\vec{F}_{net}$ has to provide the centripetal force, $\vec{F}_c$, which forces the car to move on the perimeter of a circle. Thus the net force has to act in horizontal direction.

SKETCH: A sketch showing a free body diagram for the racer in the banked curve is shown in Figure 9.21. In order to produce our free-body diagram we have to pick an orientation for our coordinate system. We select a horizontal x-axis and vertical y-axis.

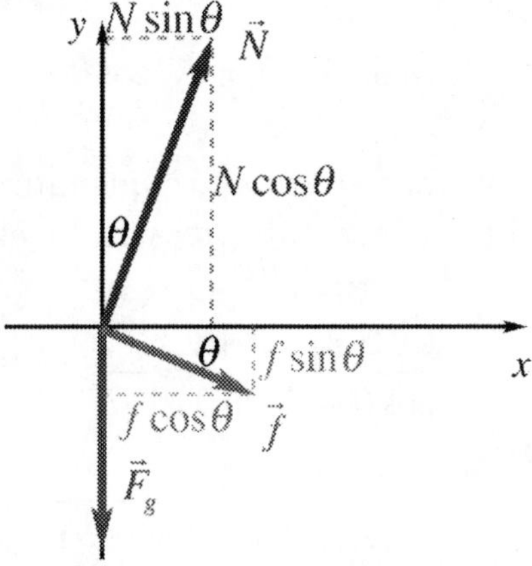

Figure 9.21: Free body diagram for a racer on a banked curve.

RESEARCH: Just like for the problems in linear motion, we can also solve the problems of circular motion by starting from our familiar Newton's Second Law, $\sum \vec{F} = m\vec{a}$. And just like in the linear case, we can in general work the problems in Cartesian components. In the free body diagram of Figure 9.21 we can see that the x-components of the forces acting on the racer are

$$N \sin\theta + f \cos\theta = F_{net} . \qquad (9.52)$$

In a similar manner, we can see that the forces acting in the y-direction are

$$N \cos\theta - F_g - f \sin\theta = 0 \qquad (9.53)$$

As usual, the friction force is given by the product of the friction coefficient and the normal force, $f = \mu_s N$, and the gravitational force is the product of mass and gravitational acceleration, $F_g = mg$.

However, the key to the solution of the problem is the realization that the net force has to be the force that causes the racecar to move through the curve, i.e. provide the centripetal force. Therefore

$$F_{net} = F_c = m\frac{v^2}{R}, \tag{9.54}$$

where we have used the expression for the centripetal force derived in (9.39), and where R is the radius of the curve given in the problem.

SIMPLIFY: We can insert the expressions for the maximal friction force, the gravitational force and the net force into (9.52) and (9.53), resulting in

$$N\sin\theta + \mu_s N\cos\theta = m\frac{v^2}{R} \Rightarrow N(\sin\theta + \mu_s\cos\theta) = m\frac{v^2}{R} \tag{9.55}$$

$$N\cos\theta - mg - \mu_s N\sin\theta = 0 \Rightarrow N(\cos\theta - \mu_s\sin\theta) = mg \tag{9.56}$$

This is a system of two equations for two unknown quantities, the magnitude of the normal force N and the speed of the car v. It is easiest to get rid of N, if we divide the two equations by each other:

$$\frac{\sin\theta + \mu_s\cos\theta}{\cos\theta - \mu_s\sin\theta} = \frac{v^2}{gR}$$

We solve for v and obtain:

$$v = \sqrt{\frac{Rg(\sin\theta + \mu_s\cos\theta)}{\cos\theta - \mu_s\sin\theta}} \tag{9.57}$$

Note that the mass of the car, m, cancels out of this calculation.

CALCULATE: Putting in the numbers, we obtain:

$$v = \sqrt{\frac{(110.\text{ m})\cdot(9.81\text{ m/s}^2)\cdot(\sin 21.1° + 0.620\cdot\cos 21.1°)}{\cos 21.1° - 0.62\cdot\sin 21.1°}} = 37.7726\text{ m/s}$$

ROUND: Expressing our result to three significant digits gives us

$$v = 38.8\text{ m/s}.$$

DOUBLE-CHECK: To double-check our results, we compare our result for a banked curve to the maximum speed a racer can achieve for the same radius curve without banking. Without banking, the only force keeping the racer on the circular path is the force of friction. Therefore we can use (9.49) and our numerical values to obtain the maximum speed around a flat curve of the same radius and coefficient of friction

Solved Problem

Solved Problem

$$v = \sqrt{\mu_s g R} = \sqrt{0.620 \cdot 9.81 \text{ m/s}^2 \cdot 110. \text{ m}} = 25.9 \text{ m/s}.$$

Our result for the maximum speed around a banked curve of 37.8 m/s (84.6 mph) is considerably larger than the result for a flat curve of 25.9 m/s (57.9 mph), so our result seems reasonable.

Note that we have drawn the force of friction pointing along the surface of the ramp and downward toward the inside of the curve, following what was done for the non-banked curve. However, as the banking angle increases, you can see that there is a value for which the denominator of our velocity formula, equation (9.57), approaches zero. This situation is the case when $\cot\theta = \mu_s$. For the given value of $\mu_s = 0.620$, this angle is 58.2 degrees. For larger angles, the friction force arrow will point along the surface of the ramp and toward the outside of the curve; for these angles it takes a minimum speed to drive through the curve and prevent the car from sliding off to the bottom of the incline.

What we have learned/Exam Study Guide:

- The conversion between Cartesian coordinates, x and y, and polar coordinates, r and θ, is given by
$$r = \sqrt{x^2 + y^2}$$
$$\theta = \arctan(y/x).$$
- The conversion between polar coordinates and Cartesian coordinates is given by
$$x = r\cos\theta$$
$$y = r\sin\theta.$$
- The linear displacement s is related to the angular displacement θ by $s = r\theta$ where r is the radius of the circular motion and θ is measured in radians.
- The instantaneous angular velocity ω is given by $\omega = \dfrac{d\theta}{dt}$.
- The magnitude of the angular velocity is related to the magnitude of the linear velocity v by $v = r\omega$.
- The instantaneous angular acceleration α is given by $\alpha = \dfrac{d\omega}{dt} = \dfrac{d^2\theta}{dt^2}$.
- The magnitude of the angular acceleration is related to the magnitude of the tangential acceleration a_t by $a_t = r\alpha$.
- The centripetal acceleration a_c required to keep an object moving in a circle with constant angular velocity is given by $a_c = \omega^2 r = \dfrac{v^2}{r}$
- The total acceleration of an object in circular motion is $a = \sqrt{a_t^2 + a_c^2}$

Additional Solved Problems

Solved Problem 9.3: Carnival Ride

Question:

One of the amusements at many carnivals is a rotating cylinder. The customers step inside and stand with their backs to the wall. The cylinder spins very rapidly, and at some angular velocity the floor is pulled away. The thrill-seekers now hang like flies on the wall. If the radius of the cylinder is $r = 2.10$ m, and the coefficient of static friction between the people and the wall is $\mu_s = 0.390$, what is the minimum angular velocity, ω, at which the floor can be withdrawn?

Answer:

THINK: When the floor drops away, the magnitude of the force of static friction between the customer and the wall of the rotating cylinder must equal the magnitude of the force of gravity on the customer. The static friction between the customer and the wall of the rotating cylinder depends on the normal force being exerted on the customer and the coefficient of static friction. As the cylinder spins up, the normal force (which acts as the centripetal force) being exerted on the customers increases. At a certain angular velocity, the magnitude of the maximum force of static friction will equal magnitude of the force of gravity. That angular velocity is the minimum angular velocity at which the floor can be withdrawn.

SKETCH: A sketch showing a top view of the rotating cylinder is shown in Figure 9.22.

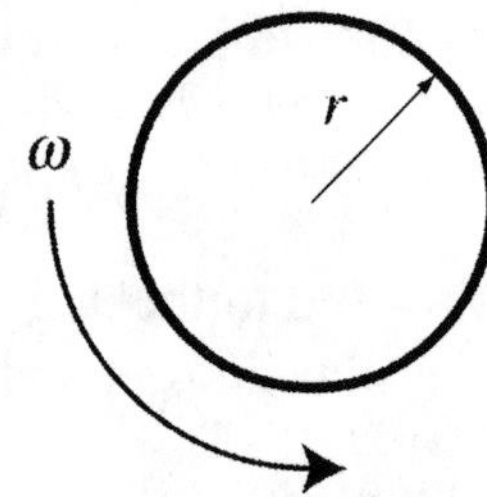

Figure 9.22: Top view of rotating cylinder.

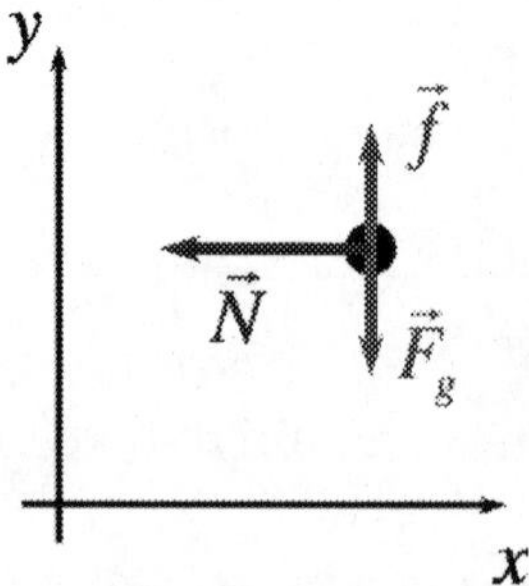

Figure 9.23: Free body diagram for one of the customers in the carnival ride.

The free-body diagram for one of the customers in the carnival ride is shown in Figure

Solved Problem

9.23, where the rotation axis was assumed to be the y-axis. In this sketch, $\vec{f}$ is the force of static friction, $\vec{N}$ is the normal force exerted on the customer with mass m by the wall of the cylinder, and $\vec{F}_g$ is the force of gravity on the customer.

RESEARCH: At the minimum angular velocity required to keep the customer from falling, the magnitude of the force of static friction between the customer and the wall is equal to the magnitude of the force of gravity on the customer. To analyze these forces we start with the free body diagram shown in Figure 9.23. In the free body diagram, we define the x-direction to be along the radius of the cylinder and the y-direction to be vertical. In the x-direction, the normal force exerted by wall on the customer provides the centripetal force that force the customer to move in a circle,

$$F_c = N. \tag{9.58}$$

In the y-direction, we know that the thrill-seeking carnival ride user only sticks to the wall, if the force of gravity is balanced by the force of static friction between the customer and the wall. The force of gravity on the customer is the weight of the customer; so we can write

$$f = F_g = mg. \tag{9.59}$$

We know that the centripetal force is given by

$$F_c = mr\omega^2 \tag{9.60}$$

and the force of static friction is given by

$$f \le f_{\max} = \mu_s N. \tag{9.61}$$

SIMPLIFY: We can combine (9.59) and (9.61) to obtain

$$mg \le \mu_s N. \tag{9.62}$$

Inserting (9.58) into (9.60) we find

$$N = mr\omega^2. \tag{9.63}$$

Combining (9.62) and (9.63) we have

$$mg \le \mu_s mr\omega^2,$$

which we can solve for ω and find

$$\omega \ge \sqrt{\frac{g}{\mu_s r}}.$$

Thus the minimum value of the angular velocity is given by:

$$\omega_{\min} = \sqrt{\frac{g}{\mu_s r}}. \tag{9.64}$$

Solved Problem

Note that the mass of the customer cancelled out! This is very important if people of different mass want to ride this attraction at the same time!

CALCULATE: Putting our numerical values into (9.64) gives us

$$\omega_{\min} = \sqrt{\frac{g}{\mu_s r}} = \sqrt{\frac{9.81 \text{ m/s}^2}{(0.390)(2.10 \text{ m})}} = 3.46093 \text{ rad/s}.$$

ROUND: Expressing our result to three significant digits we find

$$\omega_{\min} = 3.46 \text{ rad/s}.$$

DOUBLE-CHECK: To double-check our answer, let's express our result for the angular velocity in revolutions per minute (rpm)

$$3.46 \frac{\text{rad}}{\text{s}} = \left(3.46 \frac{\text{rad}}{\text{s}}\right)\left(\frac{60 \text{ s}}{1 \text{ min}}\right)\left(\frac{1 \text{ rev}}{2\pi \text{ rad}}\right) = 33 \text{ rpm}.$$

An angular velocity of 33 rpm for the rotating cylinder seems reasonable. If you have ever been on one of these rides or at least watched one, you know that the answer is in the right ballpark.

Note that of course the coefficient of friction μ_s between the clothes of the riders and the wall of the ride is not identical in all cases. So the people who design this ride need to make sure that they take the smallest coefficient of friction into account that can be expected to occur. Obviously, the want to have a somewhat sticky contact surface on their ride, just to make sure!

Solved Problem

Solved Problem 9.4: Flywheel

Question:

The flywheel of a steam engine starts to rotate from rest with a constant angular acceleration of $\alpha = 1.43 \text{ rad/s}^2$. The flywheel undergoes this constant angular acceleration for $t = 25.9$ s and then continues to rotate at a constant angular velocity ω. After the wheel has been rotating for 59.5 s, what is the total angle through which the flywheel has rotated since it began rotating?

Answer:

THINK: Here we are trying to determine the total angular displacement θ. Since we are only interested in the angular displacement since the start of the ride, we can set

$\theta_0 = 0$ and gain a little efficiency in out notation. We can determine the angular displacement using an analogy with one-dimensional linear kinematics. We can relate the linear displacement x with the angular displacement θ, the linear velocity v with the angular velocity ω, and the linear acceleration a with the angular acceleration α. While the flywheel is undergoing angular acceleration, we can use the angular analog of $x = (1/2)at^2$, which is $\theta = (1/2)\alpha t^2$. While the flywheel is rotating at a constant angular velocity, we can use the angular analog of $x = vt$, which is $\theta = \omega t$. The angular velocity reached by the flywheel after undergoing angular acceleration is can be obtained using the angular analog of $v = at$, which is $\omega = \alpha t$. To get the total angular displacement, we add these two angular displacements.

SKETCH: A top view of the rotating flywheel is shown in Figure 9.24.

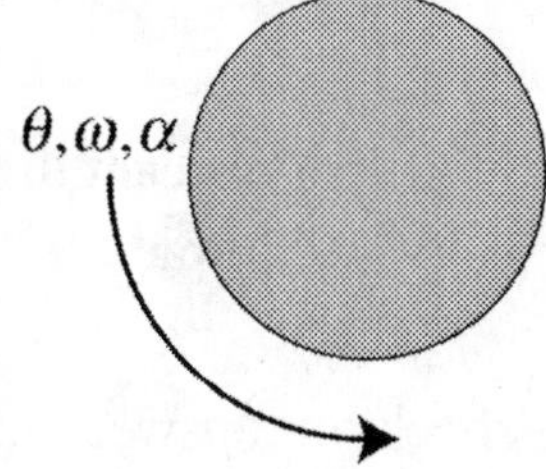

Figure 9.24: Top view of rotating flywheel.

RESEARCH: We call the time that the flywheel is undergoing angular acceleration t_1. We call the total time that the flywheel is rotating t_2. Thus the flywheel will rotate at a constant angular velocity for time $t_2 - t_1$. The angular displacement θ_1 that occurs while the flywheel is undergoing angular acceleration is given by

$$\theta_1 = \frac{1}{2}\alpha t_1^2. \tag{9.65}$$

The angular displacement θ_2 that occurs while the flywheel is rotating at a constant angular velocity ω is given by

$$\theta_2 = \omega(t_2 - t_1). \tag{9.66}$$

The angular velocity ω reached by the flywheel after undergoing angular acceleration α for a time t_1 is given by

$$\omega = \alpha t_1. \tag{9.67}$$

The total angular displacement is given by

$$\theta = \theta_1 + \theta_2. \tag{9.68}$$

SIMPLIFY: We can combine (9.66) and (9.67) to obtain the angular displacement while the flywheel is rotating at a constant angular velocity

Solved Problem

$$\theta_2 = (\alpha t_1)(t_2 - t_1) = \alpha t_1 t_2 - \alpha t_1^2 . \qquad (9.69)$$

We can combine (9.69), (9.68) and (9.65) to get the total angular displacement of the flywheel

$$\theta = \theta_1 + \theta_2 = \frac{1}{2}\alpha t_1^2 + \left(\alpha t_1 t_2 - \alpha t_1^2\right) = \alpha t_1 t_2 - \frac{1}{2}\alpha t_1^2 . \qquad (9.70)$$

CALCULATE: Putting our numerical values into (9.70) gives us

$$\theta = \alpha t_1 t_2 - \frac{1}{2}\alpha t_1^2 = \left(1.43 \text{ rad/s}^2\right)\left(25.9 \text{ s}\right)\left(59.5 \text{ s}\right) - \frac{1}{2}\left(1.43 \text{ rad/s}^2\right)\left(25.9 \text{ s}\right)^2 = 1724.07 \text{ rad} .$$

ROUND: Expressing our result to three significant digits gives us

$$\omega = 1720 \text{ rad} .$$

DOUBLE-CHECK: To double-check our answer, let's calculate the angular displacement in two steps. The first step is to calculate the angular displacement while the flywheel is accelerating

$$\theta_1 = \frac{1}{2}\alpha t_1^2 = \frac{1}{2}\left(1.43 \text{ rad/s}^2\right)\left(25.9 \text{ s}\right)^2 = 480 \text{ rad} .$$

The angular velocity of the flywheel after the angular acceleration is complete is

$$\omega = \alpha t_1 = \left(1.43 \text{ rad/s}^2\right)\left(25.9 \text{ s}\right) = 37.0 \text{ rad/s} .$$

Now we calculate the angular displacement while the flywheel is coasting

$$\theta_2 = \omega\left(t_2 - t_1\right) = \left(37.0 \text{ rad/s}\right)\left(59.5 \text{ s} - 25.9 \text{ s}\right) = 1240 \text{ rad} .$$

The total angular displacement then is

$$\theta = \theta_1 + \theta_2 = 480 \text{ rad} + 1240 \text{ rad} = 1720 \text{ rad}$$

which agrees with our answer.

Chapter 10. Rotation

Figure 10.1: Left: Rotating air masses form a hurricane; right: rotation on the largest scale – spiral galaxy M74.

What we will learn:

- We will determine that the kinetic energy contained in rotational motion of an object is proportional to the square of the angular speed, times the rotational inertia of the object.
- We will find that for the case of rotation about an axis through the center of mass of an object, the rotational inertia of this object is proportional to product of its mass and the square of the largest perpendicular distance from any part of the object to the axis of rotation. The proportionality constant has a value between 0 and 1 and depends on the shape of the object.
- We will show that for the case of a rotation about an axis parallel to an axis through the center of mass, the rotational inertia is equal to the center of mass rotational inertia plus the product of the mass of the object and the square of the distance between the two axes.
- We will learn how to evaluate the integrals to obtain the rotational inertia for different shapes.
- We will find that for rolling objects, the kinetic energy of rotation and translation are related, and we will use this relationship to investigate the dynamics of rolling objects.
- We will investigate torque and introduce the concept of a vector product. The torque is the vector product of the position vector and the force vector.
- We will derive a version of Newton's Law for rotational motion.
- We will introduce the concept of the angular momentum, defined as the vector product of the position vector and momentum vector.
- We will find relationships between angular momentum, torque, rotational inertia, angular velocity, and angular acceleration.
- Finally, we will discover another fundamental conservation law, the law of conservation of angular momentum.

10.1. Kinetic Energy of Rotation

In chapter 8 we have seen that one can describe the motion of an extended object by the trajectory that its center of mass follows, combined with a rotation of the objects around the center of mass. However, even though we have already covered circular motion for point-like particles in the previous chapter, we have not yet specified how to calculate the rotation of an extended object such as shown in Figure 10.1, which will be the purpose of the present chapter.

Point Particle in Circular Motion

In the previous chapter we introduced the kinematic quantities of circular motion. Angular velocity, ω, and angular acceleration, α, were defined in terms of the time derivatives of the angular displacement, θ, as

$$\omega = \frac{d\theta}{dt}$$
$$\alpha = \frac{d\omega}{dt} = \frac{d^2\theta}{dt^2} \tag{10.1}$$

We found that the angular quantities are related to the linear quantities as:

$$s = r\theta$$
$$v = r\omega$$
$$a_t = r\alpha \tag{10.2}$$
$$a_c = \omega^2 r$$
$$a = \sqrt{a_c^2 + a_t^2}$$

where s is the arc length, v the linear velocity of the center of mass, and a the linear acceleration. The most straightforward way to introduce the physical observables for the description of rotation is through the kinetic energy of rotation of an extended object. The kinetic energy is a concept we have introduced in the chapter on work and energy, where we have defined the kinetic energy of an object as

$$K = \tfrac{1}{2}mv^2 . \tag{10.3}$$

If the motion of this object is circular, then we can use the relationship between linear and angular velocity to obtain

$$K = \tfrac{1}{2}mv^2 = \tfrac{1}{2}m(r\omega)^2 = \tfrac{1}{2}mr^2\omega^2 , \tag{10.4}$$

which is the kinetic energy of rotation for a point particle's motion on the perimeter of a circle with radius r about a fixed axis.

Several Point Particles

Just as we proceeded in the chapter on systems of particles in our calculation of the location of the center of mass, we start with a sum of individual objects, before we approach the continuous limit.

The kinetic energy of a collection of objects is given as

$$K = \sum_{i=1}^{n} K_i = \tfrac{1}{2}\sum_{i=1}^{n} m_i v_i^2 = \tfrac{1}{2}\sum_{i=1}^{n} m_i r_i^2 \omega_i^2 . \tag{10.5}$$

This result is simply a consequence of using (10.4) for several point particles and writing the total kinetic energy as the sum of the individual kinetic energies. ω_i is the angular velocity of particle i, and r_i is its perpendicular distance to the axis of rotation.

Next, we assume that all of these point particles in our sum of equation (10.5) keep their distances fixed with respect to each other and with respect to the axis of rotation. In this way, we force all point particles in this sum to undergo circular motion around the common axis of rotation with a common angular velocity. Inserting this constraint into the previous equation, we obtain:

$$K = \tfrac{1}{2}\sum_{i=1}^{n} m_i r_i^2 \omega^2 = \tfrac{1}{2}\left(\sum_{i=1}^{n} m_i r_i^2\right)\omega^2 = \tfrac{1}{2} I \omega^2 . \tag{10.6}$$

The quantity I that we have introduced in this way is called the "rotational inertia." It only depends on the masses of the individual particles and their distances to the axis of rotation,

$$I = \sum_{i=1}^{n} m_i r_i^2 . \tag{10.7}$$

In the previous chapter, we saw that all quantities associated with circular motion have equivalents in linear motion. The angular velocity ω and the linear velocity v form such a pair. By comparing the expressions for the kinetic energy of rotation (10.6) and kinetic energy of linear motion (10.3), we find that the rotational inertia I plays the same role for circular motion as the mass m does for linear motion.

In-class exercise: Consider two masses each of mass m. They are connected by a thin, massless rod. In the three drawings below, the two masses spin in a horizontal plane around a vertical axis represented by dashed line. Which of the systems has the highest rotational inertia?

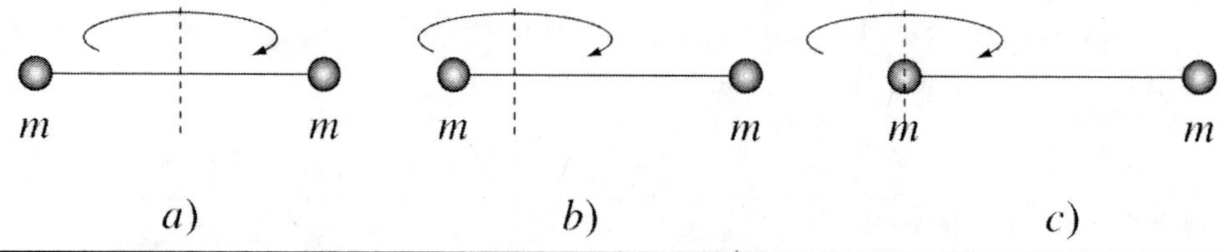

10.2. Calculation of Rotational Inertia

Now we use our discrete sum for the rotational inertia of several point particles, (10.7), as a starting point to calculate the rotational inertia for extended objects. This calculation proceeds in the same way in which we introduced the continuous limit for the center of mass location in the chapter 8. We again represent an extended object by a collection of small identical-sized cubes of volume V of possibly different mass density ρ. Then (10.7) becomes:

$$I = \sum_{i=1}^{n} \rho(\vec{r}_i) r_i^2 V . \tag{10.8}$$

Again, just like we proceeded in chapter 8, we follow the conventional calculus approach, in which the volume of the cubes approaches zero, $V \to 0$. In this limit the sum in Equation (10.8) approaches the integral. We then obtain our final expression for the rotational inertia of an extended object,

$$I = \int_V r_\perp^2 \rho(\vec{r}) dV . \tag{10.9}$$

The symbol $r_\perp$ indicates the perpendicular distance of the infinitesimal volume element to the axis of rotation as indicated in Figure 10.2.

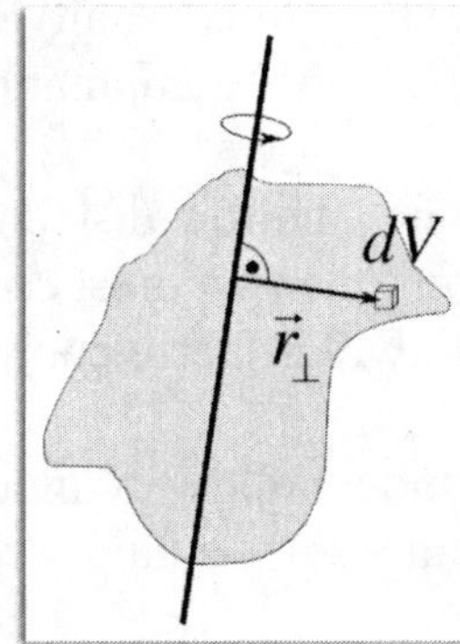

Figure 10.2: Definition of the symbol $r_\perp$ as the perpendicular distance from the axis of rotation.

We also know that the total mass can be obtained by the integration of the density over the total volume,

$$M = \int_V \rho(\vec{r}) dV . \tag{10.10}$$

Equations (10.9) and (10.10) are the most general expressions for the rotational inertia and mass of an object. However, just like in our calculations of the center of mass, some of the physically most interesting cases are those where the mass density is constant throughout the volume. In this case, equations (10.9) and (10.10) reduce to:

$$I = \rho \int_V r_\perp^2 dV \text{ (for constant density } \rho \text{)}, \tag{10.11}$$

$$M = \rho \int_V dV = \rho V \text{ (for constant density } \rho \text{)}, \tag{10.12}$$

and we obtain for the rotational inertia in this special case:

$$I = \frac{M}{V} \int_V r_\perp^2 dV \text{ (for constant density } \rho \text{)}. \tag{10.13}$$

We can now calculate moments of inertia for some special cases. First we assume that the axis of rotation passes through the center of mass of the object. Then we will construct a general theorem that connects this special case in a simple way to the general case, for which the axis of rotation does not pass through the center of mass.

Rotation about an Axis through the Center of Mass

For any object with constant density, we can use (10.13) to calculate the rotational inertia with respect to a rotation about a fixed axis that passes through the center of mass of the object. For convenience, the location of the center of mass is usually chosen as the origin of the coordinate system. Because the integral in (10.13) is a three-dimensional volume integral, the choice of the coordinate system is usually extremely important, if we want to obtain a solution of the integral with as little computational work as possible.

In this section we solve two cases, one a hollow disk and the other a sphere. We select these two cases because they represent the two most common classes of object that can roll, and they illustrate the choice of two different coordinate systems for the integral.

Figure 10.3 shows a solid cylinder and a hollow cylinder rotating about their symmetry axis (left panel and central panel) and a solid cylinder rotating about an axis perpendicular to its symmetry axis.

$$I = \tfrac{1}{2} M \left(R_1^2 + R_2^2 \right) \text{ (hollow cylinder)} \qquad (10.14)$$

The expression in (10.14) is the general result for the rotational inertia of a hollow cylinder rotating about its symmetry axis.

Two special cases of equation (10.14) deserve explicit mention:

- We can obtain the rotational inertia for a solid cylinder by setting $R_1 = R; R_2 = 0$. This results in:

$$I = \tfrac{1}{2} MR^2 \text{ (solid cylinder)} \qquad (10.15)$$

- We can also obtain the limiting case of a thin cylindrical shell or hoop, where all of the mass is concentrated on the perimeter by setting $R_1 = R_2 = R$. In this case we find:

$$I = MR^2 \text{ (hoop or cylinder thin shell)} \qquad (10.16)$$

Finally, the rotational inertia for the solid cylinder rotating about an axis through its center of mass, but perpendicular to its symmetry axis is given by

$$I = \tfrac{1}{4} MR^2 + \tfrac{1}{12} Mh^2 \text{ (solid cylinder, perpendicular)} \qquad (10.17)$$

In the case that the radius R is very small as compared to the height h, as is the case for a thin long rod, then the rotational inertia in that limit is given by dropping the first term of equation (10.17):

$$I = \tfrac{1}{12}Mh^2 \text{ (thin rod of length } h\text{, perpendicular)} \quad (10.18)$$

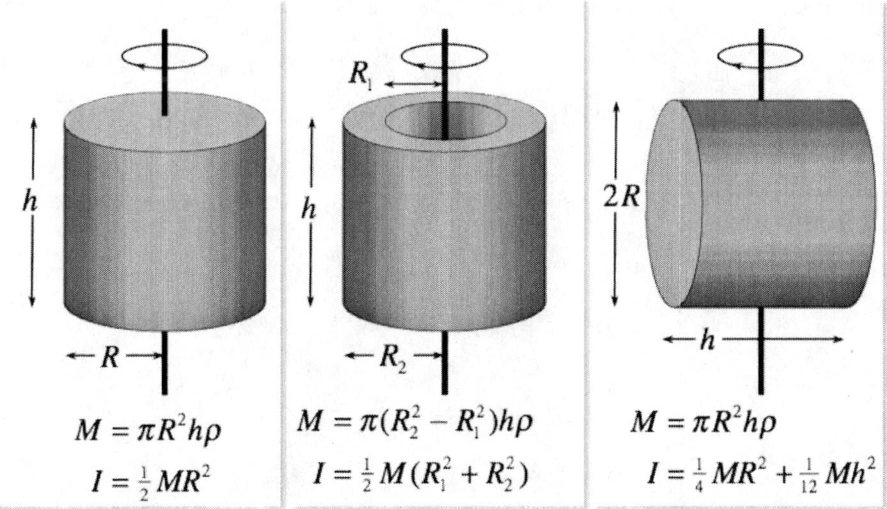

Figure 10.3: Rotational inertia for a cylinder (left) and hollow cylinder (center) rotating about its symmetry axis. Right: Rotational inertia for a cylinder rotating about an axis through its center of mass, but perpendicular to the symmetry axis.

We will derive the case of the hollow cylinder and leave the other cases as exercises for the reader.

Derivation 10.1: Rotational Inertia for a Wheel

In order to derive the rotational inertia of a hollow disk of constant density ρ, height h, inner radius R_1, and outer radius R_2 with its symmetry axis as the axis of rotation (see center panel of Figure 10.3) we use cylindrical coordinates.

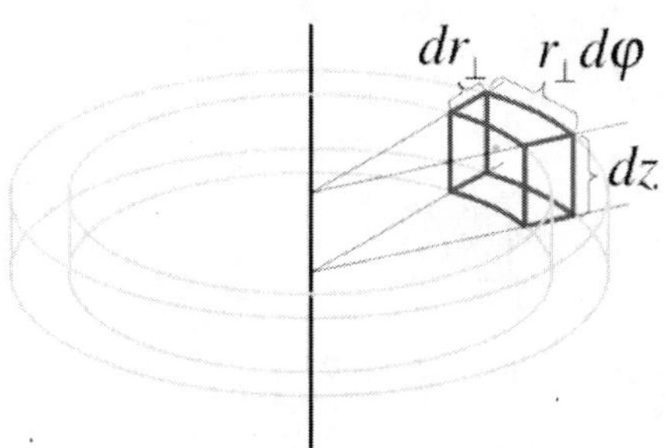

Figure 10.4: Volume element in cylindrical coordinates.

For most problems involving disks, our first try for a coordinate system should be cylindrical coordinates. In cylindrical coordinate systems (compare Mathematical Insert in Chapter 8), the volume element is given by (see Figure 10.4):

Derivation

$$dV = r_\perp dr_\perp d\varphi dz$$

For cylindrical coordinate (and only for cylindrical coordinates!) the perpendicular distance $r_\perp$ is the same as the radial coordinate r. With this in mind, we can perform the integrals for the hollow cylinder. For the mass, we obtain:

$$\begin{aligned}
M = \rho\int_V dV &= \rho\int_{R_1}^{R_2}\left(\int_0^{2\pi}\left(\int_{-h/2}^{h/2} dz\right)d\varphi\right)r_\perp dr_\perp \\
&= \rho h\int_{R_1}^{R_2}\left(\int_0^{2\pi} d\varphi\right)r_\perp dr_\perp \\
&= \rho h 2\pi\int_{R_1}^{R_2} r_\perp dr_\perp \\
&= \rho h 2\pi\left(\tfrac{1}{2}R_2^2 - \tfrac{1}{2}R_1^2\right) \\
&= \pi\left(R_2^2 - R_1^2\right)h\rho
\end{aligned}$$

Alternatively, we can also express the density as a function of the mass:

$$M = \pi\left(R_2^2 - R_1^2\right)h\rho \Leftrightarrow \rho = \frac{M}{\pi\left(R_2^2 - R_1^2\right)h}$$

Why we perform this last step may not be entirely obvious right now, but should become so after we evaluate the integral for the rotational inertia. That integral yields:

$$\begin{aligned}
I = \rho\int_V r_\perp{}^2 dV &= \rho\int_{R_1}^{R_2}\left(\int_0^{2\pi}\left(\int_{-h/2}^{h/2} dz\right)d\varphi\right)r_\perp^3 dr_\perp \\
&= \rho h\int_{R_1}^{R_2}\left(\int_0^{2\pi} d\varphi\right)r_\perp^3 dr_\perp \\
&= \rho h 2\pi\int_{R_1}^{R_2} r_\perp^3 dr_\perp \\
&= \rho h 2\pi\left(\tfrac{1}{4}R_2^4 - \tfrac{1}{4}R_1^4\right)
\end{aligned}$$

Now we can insert the result for the density that we just obtained and find:

$$I = \tfrac{1}{2}\rho h\pi\left(R_2^4 - R_1^4\right) = \frac{M}{\pi\left(R_2^2 - R_1^2\right)h}\tfrac{1}{2}h\pi\left(R_2^4 - R_1^4\right)$$

Derivation

Finally we make use of the identity $a^4 - b^4 = (a^2 - b^2)(a^2 + b^2)$ and obtain our solution:

$$I = \tfrac{1}{2}M\left(R_1^2 + R_2^2\right)$$

For other objects, the choice of cylindrical coordinates may not be advantageous. The most important non-disk-like objects are spheres and rectangular blocks.

The rotational inertia for a sphere rotating about any axis through its center of mass is given by:

$$I = \tfrac{2}{5}MR^2 \text{ (solid sphere)} \tag{10.19}$$

The rotational inertia for a thin spherical shell rotating about any axis through its center of mass is found to be:

$$I = \tfrac{2}{3}MR^2 \text{ (thin spherical shell)} \tag{10.20}$$

And the rotational inertia for a rectangular block with side length a, b, c rotating about an axis through the center of mass and parallel to side c is:

$$I = \tfrac{1}{12}M(a^2 + b^2) \text{ (rectangular block)} \tag{10.21}$$

Again we only derive the case of the solid sphere in order to illustrate working in a different coordinate system and we leave the other cases such as the rectangular solid in the left panel of Figure 10.5 as exercises.

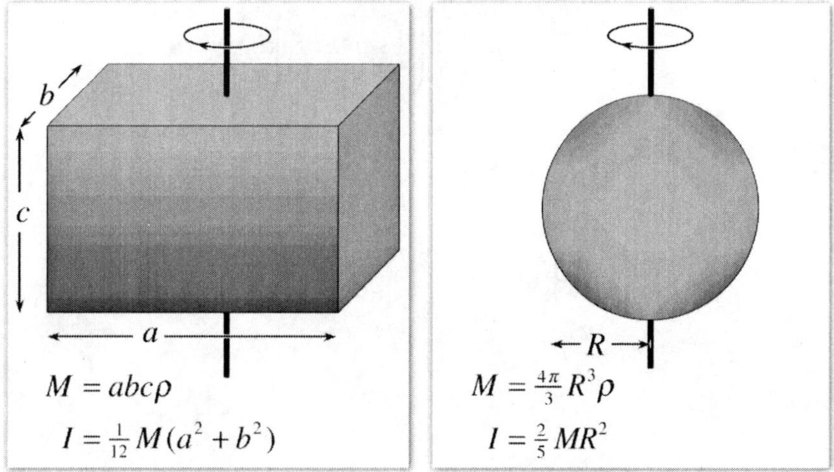

Figure 10.5: Moments of inertia of a block and a sphere.

Derivation 10.2: Rotational Inertia for a Sphere

To calculate the rotational inertia for a sphere (see the right panel of Figure 10.5) of constant density ρ and radius R for a rotation about an axis through its center, it is not appropriate to use cylindrical coordinates, but one should utilize spherical coordinates instead. In spherical coordinates the volume element is (see Figure 10.6):

$$dV = r^2 \sin\vartheta dr d\vartheta d\varphi .$$

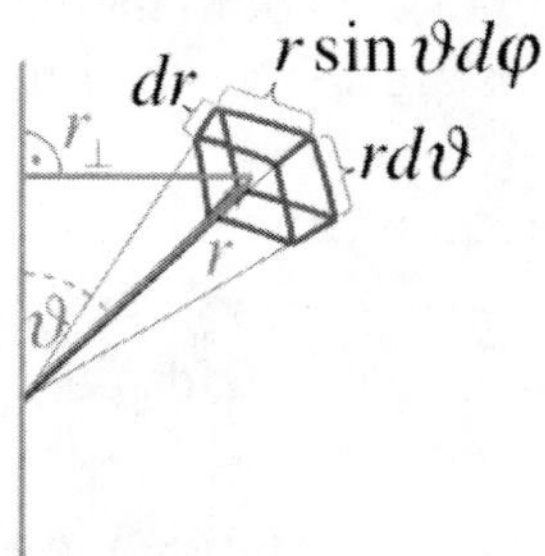

Figure 10.6: Volume element in spherical coordinates.

Please note that for spherical coordinates the radial coordinate r and the perpendicular distance $r_\perp$ are not identical. Instead they are related via (see Figure 10.6):

$$r_\perp = r\sin\vartheta .$$

(It is a very common source or errors in calculations to omit the sine of the angle, and you need to keep this point in mind if you are using spherical coordinates!)

Again, we first solve the integral for the mass,

$$\begin{aligned}
M = \rho\int_V dV = \rho\int_0^R\left(\int_0^{2\pi}\left(\int_0^{\pi}\sin\upsilon d\vartheta\right)d\varphi\right)r^2 dr \\
= 2\rho\int_0^R\left(\int_0^{2\pi}d\varphi\right)r^2 dr \\
= 4\pi\rho\int_0^R r^2 dr \\
= \frac{4\pi}{3}R^3\rho \\
\rho = \frac{3M}{4\pi R^3}
\end{aligned}$$

Now we can solve the integral for the rotational inertia in a similar way

Derivation

$$\begin{aligned}
I &= \rho \int_V r_\perp^2 dV = \rho \int_V r^2 \sin^2 \vartheta dV \\
&= \rho \int_0^R \left(\int_0^{2\pi} \left(\int_0^{\pi} \sin^3 \vartheta d\vartheta \right) d\varphi \right) r^4 dr \\
&= \rho \frac{4}{3} \int_0^R \left(\int_0^{2\pi} d\varphi \right) r^4 dr \\
&= \rho \frac{8\pi}{3} \int_0^R r^4 dr \\
&= \rho \frac{8\pi}{15} R^5
\end{aligned}$$

Derivation

Inserting the relation between the density and the mass that we had found in the previous integral, we then obtain:

$$I = \rho \frac{8\pi}{15} R^5 = \frac{3M}{4\pi R^3} \frac{8\pi}{15} R^5 = \tfrac{2}{5} MR^2$$

Finally, let us make an important general observation: If R is the largest perpendicular distance of any part of the rotating object from the axis of rotation, then the rotational inertia is always related to the mass of an object by the relationship

$$I = cMR^2 \text{, with } 0 < c \leq 1. \tag{10.22}$$

The constant c can be calculated from the geometrical configuration of the rotating object and always has a value between 0 and 1. This equation is a consequence of the mean value theorem of integral calculus. For the cylinder rotating around its symmetry axis, $c_{cyl} = \frac{1}{2}$, and for the sphere, $c_{sph} = \frac{2}{5}$, as we have seen in the above examples. The more the bulk of the mass is pushed towards the axis of rotation, the smaller the value of the constant c turns out to be. And if all mass is located on the perimeter, as for example for the hoop, c approaches the value 1.

Example

Example 10.1: Rotational Kinetic Energy of Earth

Assume that the entire Earth is a solid sphere of constant density, mass $5.98 \cdot 10^{24}$ kg, and radius 6370 km.

Question:

What is the rotational inertia of Earth with respect to the rotation about its axis, and what is the kinetic energy of this rotation?

Answer:

Example

Since Earth can be approximated by a sphere of constant density, its rotational inertia is:

$$I = \tfrac{2}{5}MR^2$$

Inserting the numbers for the mass and radius of Earth given in the question, we obtain:

$$I = \tfrac{2}{5}MR^2 = \tfrac{2}{5}(6.0\cdot 10^{24}\ \text{kg})(6.37\cdot 10^{6}\ \text{m})^2 = 9.7\cdot 10^{37}\ \text{kg m}^2$$

The angular frequency of the rotation of Earth is:

$$\omega = \frac{2\pi}{1\ \text{day}} = \frac{2\pi}{86164\ \text{s}} = 7.29\cdot 10^{-5}\ \text{Hz}$$

Please note that the sidereal day was used here; see the previous chapter.

Combining the two results for the rotational inertia and the angular frequency gives us the answer for the kinetic energy of rotation that is contained in the Earth's rotation:

$$K = \tfrac{1}{2}I\omega^2 = 0.5\cdot(9.7\cdot 10^{37}\ \text{kg}\cdot\text{m}^2)\cdot(7.29\cdot 10^{-5}\ \text{s}^{-1})^2 = 2.6\cdot 10^{29}\ \text{J}$$

It is perhaps instructive to compare this to the kinetic energy of the motion of the Earth on its path around the Sun. In the previous chapter, we had calculated the orbital speed of Earth to be $v = 2.97\cdot 10^4\ \text{m/s}$. So the kinetic energy contained in Earth's motion around the Sun is:

$$K = \tfrac{1}{2}mv^2 = 0.5\cdot(6.0\cdot 10^{24}\ \text{kg})\cdot(2.97\cdot 10^{4}\ \text{m/s})^2 = 2.6\cdot 10^{33}\ \text{J},$$

a factor of 10,000 times bigger.

Parallel Axes Theorem

Once we have solved the problem for a rotation axis through the center of mass of an object, the question immediately arises as to what the rotational inertia is for a rotation about an axis that does not pass through the center of mass. The parallel axes theorem answers this question. It states that the rotational inertia $I_{\parallel}$ for rotation about an axis located a distance d away from the center of mass and parallel to an axis through the center of mass, for which the rotational inertia is I_{cm}, is given by

$$I_{\parallel} = I_{cm} + Md^2 \tag{10.23}$$

Again M is the total mass of this object.

Derivation 10.3: Parallel Axes Theorem

For this derivation, please consider Figure 10.7. Suppose we have already calculated the rotational inertia of an object for rotation about the blue axis, and that this axis contains the point at which the center of mass of this object is located. We then move the origin of our *xyz* coordinate system to the center of mass, and align the z-axis with the rotation axis.

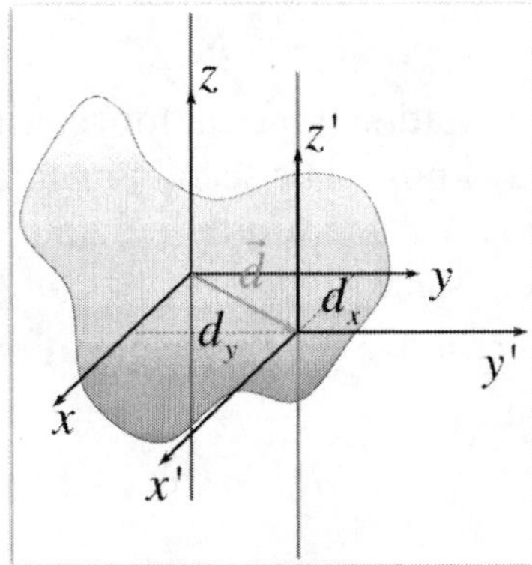

Figure 10.7: Illustration of the parallel axes theorem.

Any axis parallel to the rotation axis can then be described by a simple shift in the xy plane with the vector $\vec{d}$, with components d_x and d_y, as indicated in the figure.

If we now shift our coordinate system in the xy plane such that the new vertical axis, the z' axis, coincides with the new rotation axis, then the coordinate transformation from the old xyz to the new $x'y'z'$ coordinates is given by

$$x' = x - d_x;\ \ y' = y - d_y;\ \ z' = z$$

If we want to calculate the rotational inertia of this object in the new coordinate system, for the rotation about the new axis, then we can simply use (10.9), the most general form that includes the case where the mass density is not constant,

$$I_{\parallel} = \int_V r'^2_{\perp} \rho dV$$

But according to our coordinate transformation:

$$\begin{aligned} r'^2_{\perp} &= x'^2 + y'^2 = (x - d_x)^2 + (y - d_y)^2 = \\ &= x^2 - 2xd_x + d_x^2 + y^2 - 2yd_y + d_y^2 \\ &= (x^2 + y^2) + (d_x^2 + d_y^2) - 2xd_x - 2yd_y \\ &= r_{\perp}^2 + d^2 - 2xd_x - 2yd_y \end{aligned}$$

Derivation

(Keep in mind that $\vec{r}_\perp$ lies in the xy-plane by construction of our coordinate system.) Now we insert this back into our integral and obtain:

$$I_{\parallel} = \int_V r'^2_\perp \rho dV$$
$$= \int_V r_\perp^2 \rho dV + d^2 \int_V \rho dV - 2d_x \int_V x\rho dV - 2d_y \int_V y\rho dV$$

The first of these integrals is the rotational inertia for rotation about the center of mass, which we assume that we already know. The second integral is simply equal to the mass (compare equation (10.10)). The third and fourth integrals were introduced in chapter 8 and calculate the location of the x- and y-coordinates of the center of mass. By construction they are thus 0, because we put the origin of the xyz coordinate system at the center of mass. So we obtain

$$I_{\parallel} = I_{cm} + d^2 M$$

Derivation

Note that, according to equations (10.22) and (10.23), the rotational inertia with respect to rotation about an arbitrary axis parallel to an axis through the center of mass can then be written as:

$$I = (cR^2 + d^2)M \text{, with } 0 < c \leq 1 \qquad (10.24)$$

R is the maximum perpendicular distance of any part of the object from its axis of rotation through the center of mass, and d is the distance of the rotation axis from a parallel axis through the center of mass.

Self-Test Opportunity: Show that the rotational inertia of a thin rod of mass m and length L rotating around one end of the rod is $I = \frac{1}{3}mL^2$.

10.3. Rolling

There is a special case of rotational motion for round objects of radius R that move across a surface without slipping. This is rolling motion. For rolling motion, we can connect the linear and angular quantities by realizing that the linear distance moved by the center of mass is the same as a corresponding perimeter arc. Thus we find the relationship between linear displacement of the center of mass, r, and rotation angle:

$$r = R\theta \text{.} \qquad (10.25)$$

Taking the time derivative and keeping in mind that the radius remains a constant, we then obtain for the relationship between linear and angular velocities and accelerations:

$$v = R\omega \qquad (10.26)$$

and

$$a = R\alpha . \quad (10.27)$$

The total kinetic energy of an object in rolling motion is the sum of its translational and rotational kinetic energies,

$$K = K_{trans} + K_{rot} = \tfrac{1}{2}mv^2 + \tfrac{1}{2}I\omega^2 . \quad (10.28)$$

We can now insert the result of (10.26) relating angular and linear velocities, as well as equation (10.22) relating mass and rotational inertia and obtain:

$$\begin{aligned} K &= \tfrac{1}{2}mv^2 + \tfrac{1}{2}I\omega^2 \\ &= \tfrac{1}{2}mv^2 + \tfrac{1}{2}(cR^2m)(v/R)^2 \\ &= \tfrac{1}{2}mv^2 + \tfrac{1}{2}mv^2c \Rightarrow \\ K &= (1+c)\tfrac{1}{2}mv^2 \end{aligned} \quad (10.29)$$

where $0 < c \le 1$ is the constant that we had introduced in (10.22). This implies that the kinetic energy of a rolling object is always greater than that of an object that is sliding, provided they have the same mass and linear velocity.

With the kinetic energy suitably modified to include the contribution of the rotation, we can now again apply the same considerations of total mechanical energy as the sum of kinetic and potential energy that we applied in chapter 6.

In-class exercise: A bicycle is moving with a speed of 4.02 m/s. If the radius of the front wheel is 0.450 m, how long does it take for the front wheel to make a complete revolution?

a) 0.703 s
b) 1.23 s
c) 2.34 s
d) 4.04 s
e) 6.78 s

Solved Problem

Solved Problem 10.1: Sphere Rolling Down an Inclined Plane

Question:
A solid sphere with mass 5.15 kg and radius 0.340 m starts from rest at a height 2.10 m above the base of an inclined plane and rolls down under the influence of gravity. What is the linear speed of the center of mass of the sphere just as it leaves the incline and rolls onto a horizontal surface?

Solved Problem

Answer:

THINK: At the top of the incline, the sphere is at rest. At that point, the sphere has gravitational potential energy and no kinetic energy. As the sphere starts to roll, it will give up potential energy and gain kinetic energy of linear motion and kinetic energy of rotation. At the bottom of the inclined plane, all of the original potential energy will now be in the form of kinetic energy of linear motion plus the kinetic energy of rotation. The kinetic energy of linear motion is linked to the kinetic energy of rotation through the radius of the sphere.

SKETCH: A sketch of the problem is shown in Figure 10.8, where we have put the origin of the y-coordinate at the bottom of the incline.

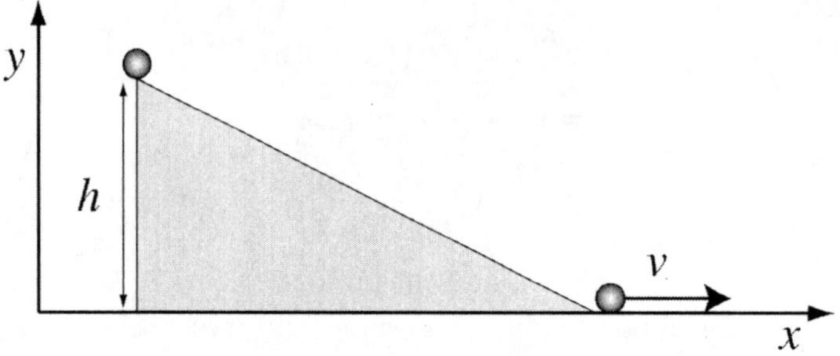

Figure 10.8: Sphere rolling down an inclined plane.

RESEARCH: At the top of the incline the sphere is at rest and therefore has zero kinetic energy. At the top its energy is therefore its potential energy mgh,

$$E_{top} = K_{top} + U_{top} = 0 + mgh = mgh \qquad (10.30)$$

where m is the mass of the sphere, h is the height of the sphere above the horizontal surface, and g is the acceleration of gravity. At the bottom of the incline, just as the sphere starts rolling on the horizontal surface, the potential energy is zero. According to (10.29) the sphere has a total kinetic energy (= sum of translational and rotational kinetic energy) of $(1+c)\frac{1}{2}mv^2$, and so the total energy at the bottom of the incline is

$$E_{bottom} = K_{bottom} + U_{bottom} = (1+c)\tfrac{1}{2}mv^2 + 0 = (1+c)\tfrac{1}{2}mv^2 \qquad (10.31)$$

Since the moment of inertia of a sphere is $I = \frac{2}{5}mR^2$ (compare (10.19)), the constant c in (10.31) has the value of $c = \frac{2}{5}$.

SIMPLIFY: We can combine (10.30), (10.31) to find due to the conservation law of energy

$$mgh = (1+c)\tfrac{1}{2}mv^2 . \qquad (10.32)$$

Solving for the linear velocity gives us

Solved Problem

$$v = \sqrt{\frac{2gh}{1+c}}. \tag{10.33}$$

For the sphere we have, as stated $c = \frac{2}{5}$, and so (10.33) is in this case

$$v = \sqrt{\frac{2gh}{1+\frac{2}{5}}} = \sqrt{\tfrac{10}{7}gh} \tag{10.34}$$

CALCULATE: Putting our numerical values into (10.33) gives us

$$v = \sqrt{\frac{10}{7} \cdot 9.81 \text{ m/s}^2 \cdot 2.10 \text{ m}} = 5.42494 \text{ m/s}.$$

ROUND: Expressing our result with three significant digits leads to

$$v = 5.42 \text{ m/s}.$$

DOUBLE-CHECK: If the sphere did not roll but rather slid down the inclined plane without friction, the final speed would be

$$v = \sqrt{2gh} = \sqrt{2 \cdot 9.81 \text{ m/s}^2 \cdot 2.10 \text{ m}} = 6.42 \text{ m/s}$$

which is faster than our result for the rolling sphere. It seems reasonable that our result for the final linear velocity for the rolling sphere would be somewhat less than the final linear velocity of the sliding sphere, because we have to spend some of our initial potential energy on rotational kinetic energy, and this energy is then not available for kinetic energy of the linear motion of the center of mass of the sphere.

Galileo Galilei famously showed that the acceleration of an object in free fall is independent of its mass. This result is still valid for an object rolling down an incline, as we have just seen in this solved problem for the sphere. However, while the total mass of the object does not matter, the distribution of the mass within the rolling object does matter. The following example shows this very impressively.

Example

Example 10.2: Race down an incline

Question:
A solid sphere, a solid cylinder, and a hollow cylinder, all of the same mass m and the same outer radius R, are released from rest and start rolling down an incline. In which order do they arrive at the bottom of the incline?

Example

Answer:

We can answer this question again entirely by using energy considerations. Since the total mechanical energy is conserved for each of the three objects during its rolling motion, we can write for each of them

$$E = K + U = K_0 + U_0$$

We have just written down the expression for the total kinetic energy in (10.29). According to the question, the objects were released from rest, implying that $K_0 = 0$. For the potential energy, we again use $U = mgh$, and for the kinetic energy we use the result that we just obtained in equation (10.29). Therefore, we obtain:

$$K_{bottom} = U_{top} \Rightarrow (1+c)\tfrac{1}{2}mv^2 = mgh \Rightarrow$$
$$v = \sqrt{\frac{2gh}{1+c}}$$

which is again the result we obtained in (10.33).

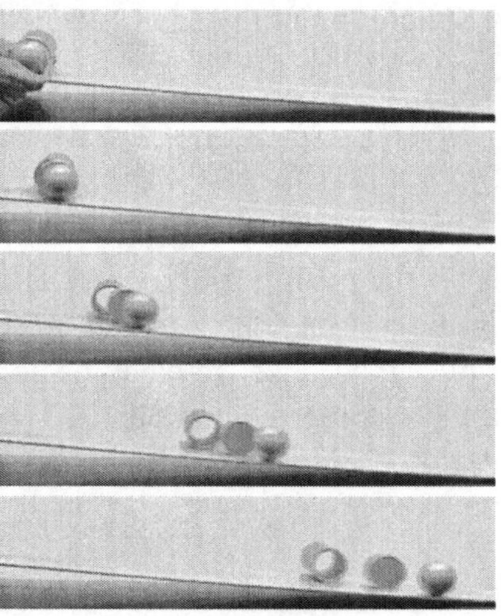

Figure 10.9: Race of a sphere, a solid cylinder, and a hollow cylinder of the same mass and radius down an inclined plane. The time between each two frames shown is 1/2 s.

We have already stated in the previous solved example that the mass of the object has again cancelled out of our final answer. But there are two additional important observations we need to make: (1) the radius of the rotating object does not appear in our final answer above, (2) and the constant c that is determined by the distribution of the mass appears in the denominator. For our three racing objects, we have already found the value of this constant: $c_{sphere} = 2/5$, $c_{cylinder} = 1/2$, and $c_{tube} \approx 1$. Since the denominator for the sphere is the smallest, its velocity for any given height h is the largest, implying that the sphere will win the race. Physically we see that since all balls have the same mass and thus have the same change in potential energy, all final kinetic energies are equal and thus the object with the higher c will have relatively more of its kinetic energy in rotation and thus a lower translational kinetic energy and thus a lower speed. The solid cylinder will come in second, followed by the tube, the hollow cylinder. Figure 10.9 shows frames from a videotaped experiment and verifies experimentally that our conclusion reached is indeed correct.

In-class exercise:
If we repeat the same race as above, but now let an unopened soft drink can participate, in which place will this can finish?

1st
2nd
3rd
4th

***Self-Test Opportunity*:**
Can you explain why the soft drink can finishes in this position?

Solved Problem

Solved Problem 10.2: Ball Rolling Through a Loop

A solid sphere is released from rest and rolls down an incline, from which it rolls into a circular loop of radius R as shown in Figure 10.10.

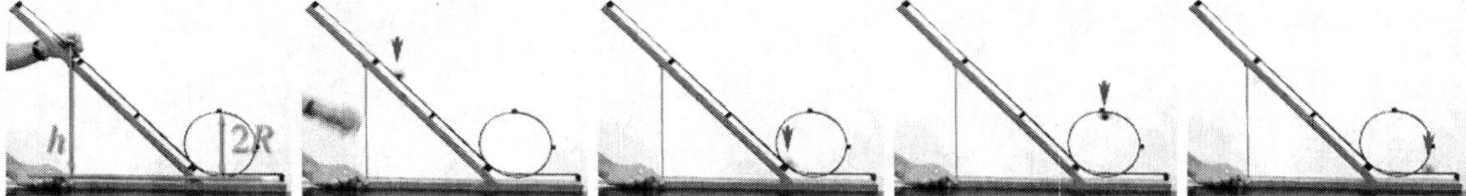

Figure 10.10: Ball rolling through a loop. The time between each two frames shown is 1/4 s.

Question:
What is the minimum height h from which the sphere has to be released so that it does not fall off the track?

Answer:

THINK: When we release the sphere at the top of the loop from rest, the sphere has gravitational potential energy but no kinetic energy. As the sphere rolls down the track and around the loop, gravitational potential energy is converted to kinetic energy. At the top of the loop, the sphere has dropped a distance of $h-2R$. The key to solving this problem is to realize that at the top of the loop the centripetal acceleration has to be equal to or larger than the gravitational acceleration. (When these accelerations are equal you have the "weightless" case worked out in Solved Problem 9.1. When the centripetal acceleration is greater there must be a downward supporting force, which the track can supply. When the centripetal acceleration is less, there must be an upward supporting force, which the track cannot supply.) What is unknown is the speed v at the top of the loop. We can again employ our energy conservation considerations to allow us to calculate the minimum velocity required and then the minimum height required for the sphere to remain on the track.

SKETCH: A sketch of the sphere rolling on the roller coaster track is shown in Figure 10.11.

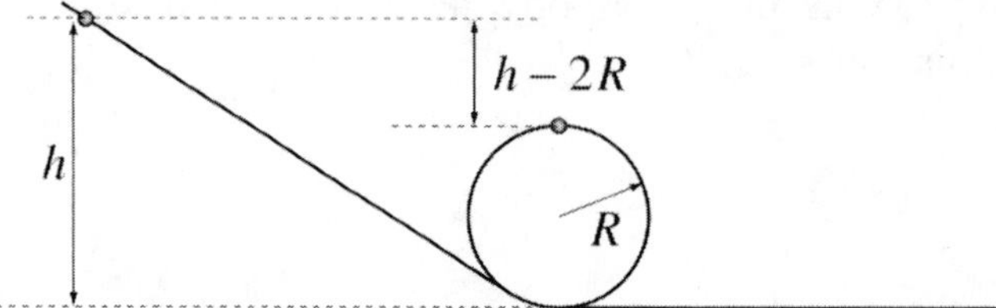

Figure 10.11: sphere rolling on a roller coaster track.

RESEARCH:

When the sphere is released, it has potential energy $U_0 = mgh$ and zero kinetic energy. At the top of the loop, the potential energy is $U = mg2R$, and the total kinetic energy is, according to equation (10.29), $K = (1+c)\frac{1}{2}mv^2$, where $c_{sphere} = \frac{2}{5}$. So conservation of total mechanical energy tells us

$$E = K + U = (1+c)\tfrac{1}{2}mv^2 + mg2R = K_0 + U_0 = mgh. \quad (10.35)$$

At the top of the loop the centripetal acceleration a_c has to be equal to or larger than the gravitational acceleration g

$$g \le a_c = \frac{v^2}{R}. \quad (10.36)$$

SIMPLIFY: We can solve (10.35) for v^2 to obtain

$$v^2 = \frac{2g(h-2R)}{1+c}.$$

If we then insert this result into (10.36), we find

$$g \le \frac{2g(h-2R)}{R(1+c)}.$$

Multiplying both sides of this equation with the denominator of the fraction on the right leads to

$$R(1+c) \le 2h - 4R.$$

And thus

Solved Problem

Solved Problem

$$h \geq \frac{5+c}{2} R.$$

CALCULATE: This result is valid for any rolling object, with the constant c determined from its geometry. For this problem we have a sphere, therefore $c = \frac{2}{5}$. Thus the result is

$$h \geq \frac{5+\frac{2}{5}}{2} R = \frac{27}{10} R.$$

ROUND: This problem dealt with variables rather than numerical values, so we can quote our result exactly as

$$h \geq 2.7R.$$

DOUBLE-CHECK: If the sphere were not rolling, but sliding without friction, we could equate the kinetic energy of the sphere at the top of the loop with the change in gravitational potential energy

$$\tfrac{1}{2}mv^2 = mg(h-2R).$$

We could then express the inequality (10.36) as

$$g \leq a_c = \frac{v^2}{R} = \frac{2g(h-2R)}{R}.$$

Solving this equation for h gives us

$$h \geq \frac{5}{2} R = 2.5R.$$

This result for a sliding sphere is slightly lower than our result for a rolling sphere. We would expect that less energy would be required in the form of gravitation potential energy to keep the sphere on the track it if were not rolling since its kinetic energy is entirely translational. Thus, our result for a rolling sphere on the roller coaster loop seems reasonable.

10.4. Torque

There is one general question that we have not addressed so far in our discussion of forces. Where do we attach the force vectors acting on an object in our free-body drawing of an object?

When an object is connected to a string, held by a string or pulled by a string, then the force that the string exerts acts in the direction of the string and its force vector is attached to the object in the same place that the string is. What about forces that do not act on a single point? In chapter 8 on systems of particles and extended objects we defined the center of mass (or center of gravity) as the point in space for an extended object where we can imagined all of its mass to be concentrated, or equivalently, where the force vector of the force of gravity is attached.

Moment Arm

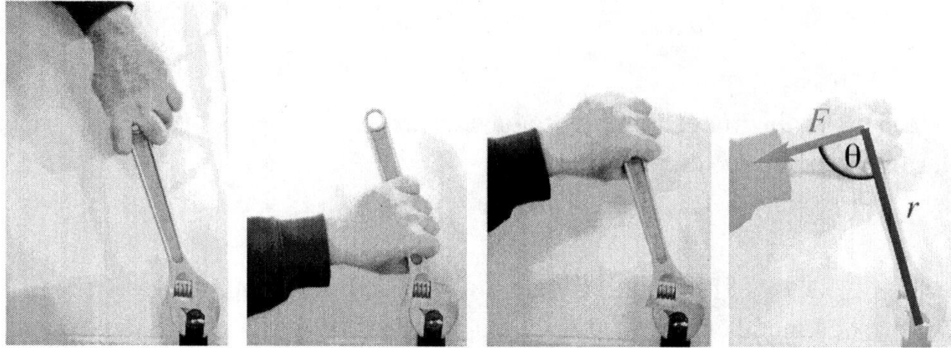

Figure 10.12: Photographs showing three ways to use a wrench to loosen a bolt. In the right panel, the force F and moment arm r are shown along with the angle θ between the two.

Look at the hand pulling on the wrench to loosen the screw in Figure 10.12. It is clear that it will be easiest to turn the screw in the case on the right, quite a bit harder in the case in the middle, and downright impossible in the case on the left.

This example shows us that knowing the magnitude of the force is not the only relevant quantity, but that the distance of the force to the axis of rotation, the moment arm, is also important. In addition, the angle at which we apply the force relative to the moment arm matters as well. In the right and middle cases, this angle is 90°. (The same would hold for 270°, but then the force would act in the opposite direction.) An angle of 180° or 0° provides no means to turn the bolt.

We can quantify these considerations by introducing the concept of torque, τ. Torque is the vector product of the force $\vec{F}$ and the position vector $\vec{r}$

$$\vec{\tau} = \vec{r} \times \vec{F} . \tag{10.37}$$

where the symbol "×" denotes the vector product. In section 5.4 we had seen that one can multiply two vectors to yield a scalar quantity. This scalar product was denoted with the symbol "•". Now we also find that one can multiply two vectors in such way that the result is another vector.

The magnitude of the torque is the product of the magnitude of the force and the distance (= magnitude of the position vector, also often called "moment arm") times the sine of the angle between the force vector and the position vector at which the force attaches (see the far right drawing of Figure 10.12):

$$\tau = rF\sin\theta \,. \tag{10.38}$$

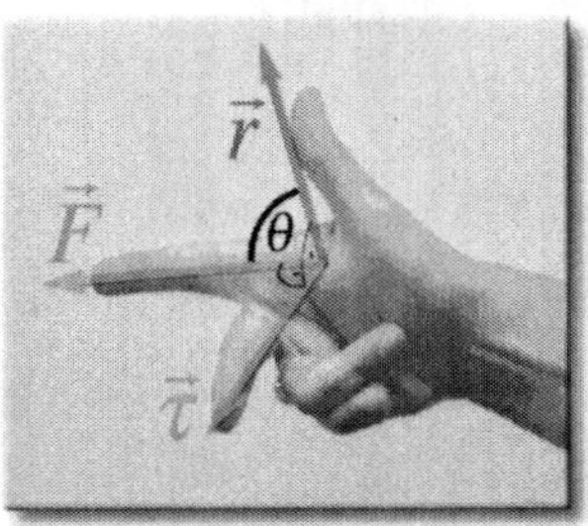

Figure 10.13: Right hand rule for the direction of the torque for a given force and position vector.

In chapter 9 we remarked that angular quantities are also vectors, so-called axial vectors. (Reminder: The term "axial vector" simply refers to a vector that points along the rotation axis.) The torque is an example of an axial vector, and its magnitude is given by equation (10.38). The direction of the torque is given by the right-hand-rule (see Figure 10.13). The torque is pointing perpendicular to the plane spanned by the force and position vectors. So if the position vector points along the thumb, and the force along the index finger, then the direction of the torque axial vector is given by the direction of the middle finger, as shown in Figure 10.13. Note that the torque vector is perpendicular to the force vector and also perpendicular to the position vector!

Mathematical Insert: Vector Product

The vector product (sometimes also called "cross-product") between two vectors $\vec{A} = (A_x, A_y, A_z)$ and $\vec{B} = (B_x, B_y, B_z)$ is defined as

$$\begin{aligned} \vec{C} &= \vec{A} \times \vec{B} \\ C_x &= A_y B_z - A_z B_y \\ C_y &= A_z B_x - A_x B_z \\ C_z &= A_x B_y - A_y B_x \end{aligned} \tag{10.39}$$

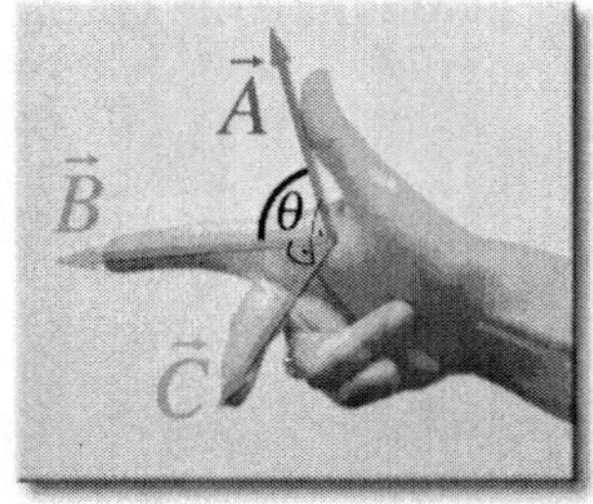

Figure 10.14: Vector product.

The absolute magnitude of the vector $\vec{C}$ is given by:

$$\left|\vec{C}\right| = \left|\vec{A}\right|\left|\vec{B}\right|\sin\theta . \qquad (10.40)$$

Here θ is the angle between $\vec{A}$ and $\vec{B}$ as in Figure 10.14. This result also implies that the magnitude of the vector product of the two vectors is at its maximum when $\vec{A} \perp \vec{B}$, and zero for the case $\vec{A} \parallel \vec{B}$. We can also interpret the right-hand-side of equation (10.40) either as the product of the magnitude of vector $\vec{A}$ times the component of $\vec{B}$ perpendicular to $\vec{A}$, or as the product of the magnitude of $\vec{B}$ times the component of $\vec{A}$ perpendicular to $\vec{B}$, $\left|\vec{C}\right| = \left|\vec{A}\right| B_{\perp A} = \left|\vec{B}\right| A_{\perp B}$.

The direction of the vector $\vec{C}$ can be found via the right-hand-rule: If vector $\vec{A}$ points along the direction of the thumb, and vector $\vec{B}$ along the direction of the index finger, then the vector product of the two is perpendicular to *both* vectors and points along the direction of the middle finger, as shown.

It is important to realize that for the vector product, the order of the factors matters:

$$\vec{B} \times \vec{A} = -\vec{A} \times \vec{B} \qquad (10.41)$$

END OF INSERT

With the mathematical definition of the torque, its magnitude, and its relation to the force vector, position vector, and their relative angle, we can now revisit Figure 10.12 and understand that the picture on the right yield maximum torque for a given magnitude of the force, whereas the situation in the left picture yields zero torque. We see that the magnitude of the torque is the decisive factor for how easy or hard it is to loosen (or tighten) a bolt.

There are clockwise torques and counter-clockwise torques. As indicated by the force arrow in Figure 10.12, the torque generated by the hand pulling on the wrench would be counter-clockwise.

We thus define the net torque as the difference between the sum of all clockwise torques and the sum of all counter-clockwise torques:

$$\tau_{\text{net}} = \sum_i \tau_{\text{counter-clockwise},i} - \sum_j \tau_{\text{clockwise},j} \qquad (10.42)$$

In-class exercise:
Choose the combination of the position vector, $\vec{r}$, and the force vector, $\vec{F}$, that produces the highest magnitude of torque around the point shown by the black circle.

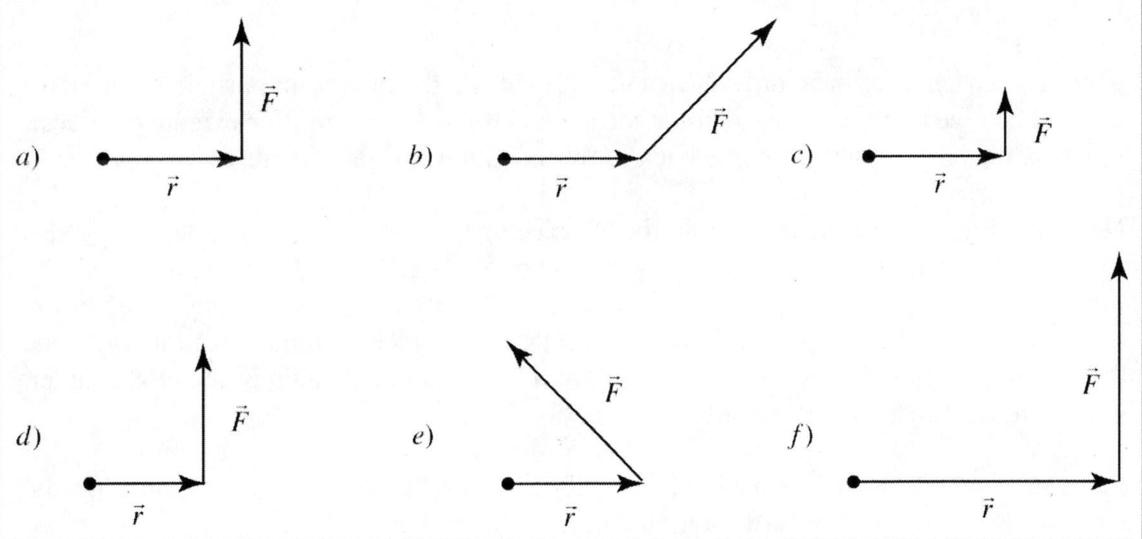

10.5. Newton's Second Law for Rotation

We finished section 10.1 by noting that the rotational inertia I is the rotational equivalent to the mass. From chapter 4 we know that the product of the mass and the linear acceleration is the force, as expressed by Newton's Second Law, $F = ma$. So the obvious question now is: what is the equivalent to Newton's Second law for rotational motion?

Let us start with some considerations for a point particle of mass M moving around an axis at a distance R. If we multiply the rotational inertia for rotation about an axis parallel to the center of mass with the angular acceleration, we obtain

$$I\alpha = (R^2 M)\alpha = RM(R\alpha) = RMa = RF$$

To obtain this result, we used equation (10.22) in the first step, then used the relationship between angular and linear acceleration for motion on a circle, and then used Newton's Second Law. We thus see that the product of the rotational inertia and the angular acceleration is proportional to the product of a force quantity and a distance quantity. In the previous section we had seen that this product is a torque, τ. This consideration motivates the following form of Newton's Second Law for rotational motion:

$$\tau = I\alpha \qquad (10.43)$$

The final result of the equations of this section is the combination of equations (10.37) and (10.43):

$$\vec{\tau} = \vec{r} \times \vec{F} = I\vec{\alpha} \tag{10.44}$$

This result for rotational motion is analogous to Newton's Second Law, $\vec{F} = m\vec{a}$, for linear motion.

Note that, strictly, we have only shown that (10.44) holds for a point particle in circular orbit. Then we motivated that it holds for general rotational inertia for extended objects. Later in this chapter we will come back to this equation and provide its general proof.

Newton's First Law stipulates that in the absence of forces there is no acceleration and thus no change in velocity. The equivalent case of Newton's First Law for rotational motion is that there is no angular acceleration and thus no change in angular velocity for vanishing net torque. In particular this means that for objects to remain stationary the net torque on them has to be zero. We will return to this statement again in the next chapter, where we investigate static equilibrium situations.

For now, however, we can already use Newton's Second Law of rotation (10.44) to solve several interesting problems of rotational motion, such as the following one.

Example 10.3: Toilet Paper

This may have happened to you: You are trying to put a new role of toilet paper into its holder in the bathroom. But you drop the role, managing just to hold on to the first sheet. On its way to the ground, the toilet paper roll then unwinds as in Figure 10.15.

Question:

How long does it take the role of toilet paper to hit the ground, if it was released from a height of 0.73 m? The role has an inner radius $R_1 = 2.7$ cm and outer radius $R_2 = 6.1$ cm, and a mass of 274 g.

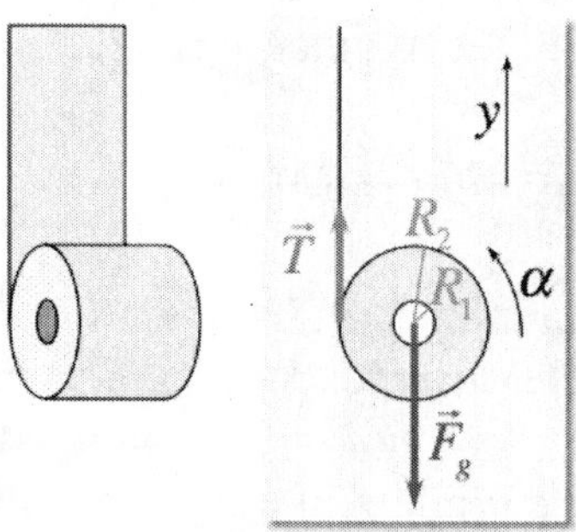

Figure 10.15: Unrolling toilet paper.

Answer:

Let us first review the case of free-fall. In this case the acceleration would have been $a_y = -g$, and in chapter 2 we have found that for free-fall from rest the position as a function of time is given in general as $y = y_0 + v_0 t - \frac{1}{2} g t^2$. In this case the initial velocity is 0; therefore $y = y_0 - \frac{1}{2}gt^2$. If we put the origin at ground level, then we have to find the time at which $y = 0$. This implies $y_0 = \frac{1}{2}gt^2$ for the time it takes to hit the ground. Therefore the time it would take in free-fall for the toilet paper roll to hit the ground is in this case

$$t_{\text{free}} = \sqrt{\frac{2y_0}{g}} = \sqrt{\frac{2\cdot(0.73\text{ m})}{9.81\text{ m/s}^2}} = 0.386\text{ s}$$

But since we are holding on to the first sheet and the toilet paper unwinds on its way down, this causes the toilet paper to roll without slipping (in the sense in which we defined "rolling without slipping"). And so we expect the acceleration to change to a different value from the free-fall case. Once we know the value of this acceleration, we can use the same formula relating the initial height and fall-time that we just used.

How do we calculate the acceleration that the toilet paper experiences? The answer lies again in a free-body diagram. On the right-hand side of Figure 10.15 we show the toilet paper role in side view and indicate the forces of gravity, $\vec{F}_g = mg(-\hat{y})$ and the "string" tension from the paper that is held by the hand, $\vec{T} = T\hat{y}$. Newton's Second Law then allows us to connect the net force acting on the toilet paper to the acceleration of the roll,

$$T - mg = ma_y \tag{10.45}$$

The string tension and acceleration are both unknown; so we need to find a second equation relating these quantities. This second equation can be obtained from the rotational motion of the roll, for which the net torque is the product of the rotational inertia and the angular acceleration, $\tau = I\alpha$. The rotational inertia of the toilet paper roll is that of a hollow cylinder, $I = \frac{1}{2}m(R_1^2 + R_2^2)$, see equation (10.14).

We can again relate the linear and the angular accelerations to each other via $a_y = R_2\alpha$, where R_2 is the outer radius of the toilet paper roll. In order to do this, we need to specify which way we count as the positive angular acceleration, other wise we could get the sign wrong and thus obtain a false result. In order to be consistent with the choice of up as the positive y-direction, we need to select a counter-clockwise rotation as the positive angular direction, as indicated in the free-body diagram of Figure 10.15.

For the torque about the central symmetry axis of the toilet paper roll, we then have $\tau = -R_2T$ with our sign convention for positive angular acceleration that we just established. The force of gravity does not contribute to the torque about the symmetry axis, because its moment arm has a length of 0. Newton's Second Law for rotational motion then results in:

Example

$$\tau = I\alpha$$

$$-R_2 T = (\tfrac{1}{2}m(R_1^2 + R_2^2))\frac{a_y}{R_2}$$

$$-T = \tfrac{1}{2}m\left(1+\frac{R_1^2}{R_2^2}\right)a_y \qquad (10.46)$$

Equations (10.45) and (10.46) form our set of two equations for our two unknown quantities T and a. Adding them results in

$$-mg = \tfrac{1}{2}m\left(1+\frac{R_1^2}{R_2^2}\right)a_y + ma_y$$

As we can easily see, the mass of the toilet paper roll cancels out, and we find for the acceleration

$$a_y = -\frac{g}{\frac{3}{2}+\frac{R_1^2}{2R_2^2}} \qquad (10.47)$$

Example

Using our values of the inner radius $R_1 = 2.7$ cm and outer radius $R_2 = 6.1$ cm, then find numerically for the acceleration

$$a = -\frac{9.81 \text{ m/s}^2}{\frac{3}{2}+\frac{(2.7 \text{ cm})^2}{2(6.1 \text{ cm})^2}} = -6.14 \text{ m/s}^2$$

Inserting this value of the acceleration for our fall-time, we finally find our answer

$$t = \sqrt{\frac{2y_0}{(-a_y)}} = \sqrt{\frac{2\cdot(0.73 \text{ m})}{6.14 \text{ m/s}^2}} = 0.488 \text{ s},$$

approximately $1/10^{\text{th}}$ of a second longer than for the free-falling role of toilet paper released from the same height.

Discussion:
Please note that we used the assumption that the outer radius of the roll of toilet paper does not change as the paper unwinds. For the short distance of less than 1 m this is justified. However, if you want to calculate how long it takes for the toilet paper to unwind over a distance of, say, 10 m, then you need to take this effect into account. Of course, then you also would need to take into account the effects of air resistance!

As an extension of the previous example, we can consider a yoyo. A yoyo consists of two solid disks of radius R_2, with a thin smaller disk of radius R_1 mounted between them, around which a rope is strung (see Figure 10.16).

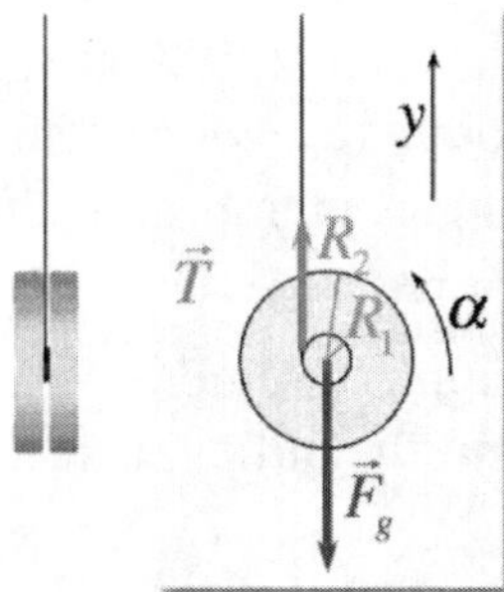

Figure 10.16: Left: yoyo; right: free-body diagram.

For the purpose of the following calculation, we can consider the rotational inertia of the yoyo to be that of a solid disk with radius R_2, $I = \frac{1}{2}mR_2^2$. Comparing the free-body diagrams of Figure 10.15 and Figure 10.16, you can see that they are almost identical. Except for one detail: for the yoyo the string tension acts on the surface of the inner radius R_1, as opposed to the outer radius R_2, as was the case for the role of toilet paper. This also implies that angular and linear acceleration are proportional to each other with proportionality constant R_1 instead of R_2 for the toilet paper roll. Thus the torque equation for the yoyo rolling without slipping along the string is now

$$-TR_1 = (\tfrac{1}{2}mR_2^2)\frac{a_y}{R_1}$$

$$-T = \tfrac{1}{2}m\frac{R_2^2}{R_1^2}a_y \qquad (10.48)$$

It is instructive to compare this equation to (10.46), which we derived for the toilet paper. They look very similar, but the ratio of the radii is different. On the other had, the equation derived from Newton's Second Law is the same in both cases,

$$T - mg = ma_y \qquad (10.49)$$

Combining (10.48) and (10.49) the tells us the acceleration of the yoyo:

$$-mg = ma_y + \tfrac{1}{2}m\frac{R_2^2}{R_1^2}a_y \Rightarrow$$

$$a_y = -\frac{g}{1+\tfrac{1}{2}\dfrac{R_2^2}{R_1^2}} = -\frac{2R_1^2}{2R_1^2 + R_2^2}g \qquad (10.50)$$

For example, if $R_2 = 5R_1$ we find: $a_y = -g/(1+\tfrac{1}{2}25) = -g/13.5 = 0.727 \text{ m/s}^2$.

Atwood Machine

In chapter 4 we had a first look at the so-called Atwood machine. It consists of two masses m_1 and m_2 connected by a string, which is guided over a pulley. In chapter 4 we solved this problem under the condition that the rope glides without friction over the pulley so that the pulley does not rotate (or, equivalently, that the pulley is massless). In that case, we found that the common acceleration of the two masses is $a = g(m_1 - m_2)/(m_1 + m_2)$. Now that we have developed the concepts of rotational dynamics, we can take another look at the same problem and solve it for the case that there is friction between the rope and the pulley, causing the pulley to rotate.

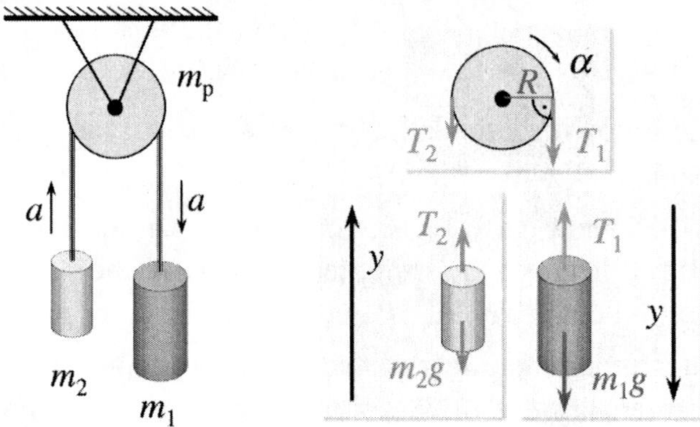

Figure 10.17: Atwood machine. Left side: physical setup; right side: free-body diagrams

Note that in chapter 4 we stated that the magnitude of the tension, T, is the same everywhere in a string. But since there are now friction forces involved that keep the string attached to the pulley, we cannot assume any more that the tension is constant. Instead, the string tension is only the same in each segment of the string from which the two masses hang. Thus, we have two different string tensions T_1 and T_2 in the free-body diagrams for the two masses (as shown in the right side of Figure 10.17). Just like in the previous case in chapter 4, Newton's Second Law applied individually to each free-body diagram leads to:

$$-T_1 + m_1 g = m_1 a \tag{10.51}$$

$$T_2 - m_2 g = m_2 a \tag{10.52}$$

Here we again used the (arbitrary) sign convention that we consider a positive acceleration ($a > 0$) to be one for which m_1 moves downward and m_2 upward. This convention is indicated in the free-body diagrams by the direction of the positive y-axis.

We also show a free-body diagram for the pulley. However, we only drew in the forces that can cause a torque, the two string tensions T_1 and T_2. We left out the forces of gravity and the force of the support structure on the pulley. The pulley does not have a translational motion, and so all forces acting on the pulley add up to 0. However, there is a net torque acting on the pulley. According to (10.38) the magnitude of the torque due to the string tensions is given by:

$$\tau = \tau_1 - \tau_2 = RT_1 \sin 90° - RT_2 \sin 90° = R(T_1 - T_2) \tag{10.53}$$

These two torques have opposite signs, because one is acting clockwise and the other counterclockwise. According to (10.43) the net torque is related to the rotational inertial of the pulley and its angular acceleration as $\tau = I\alpha$. The rotational inertia of the pulley is that of a disk, $I = \frac{1}{2}m_p R^2$. Since the rope moves across the pulley without slipping, and acceleration of the rope (and masses m_1 and m_2) is related to the angular acceleration α via $\alpha = a / R$, in the same way that we have established the correspondence between linear and angular acceleration for a point particle moving on the perimeter of a circle in the last chapter. Inserting this expression for the rotational inertia and the angular acceleration results in $\tau = I\alpha = (\frac{1}{2}m_p R^2)(a / R)$, and inserting this expression for the torque into (10.53) we find

$$\begin{aligned} R(T_1 - T_2) = \tau = (\tfrac{1}{2}m_p R^2)(a / R) \Rightarrow \\ T_1 - T_2 = \tfrac{1}{2}m_p a \end{aligned} \tag{10.54}$$

Equations (10.51), (10.52), and (10.54) form a set of three equations for three unknown quantities, the two values of the string tension, T_1 and T_2, as well as the acceleration a. The easiest way to solve this system for the acceleration is to add all equations. We then find:

$$\begin{aligned} m_1 g - m_2 g = (m_1 + m_2 + \tfrac{1}{2}m_p)a \Rightarrow \\ a = \frac{m_1 - m_2}{m_1 + m_2 + \frac{1}{2}m_p} g \end{aligned} \tag{10.55}$$

Note that this final expression is very much like the expression for the case of a massless pulley (or the case in which the rope slides over the pulley without friction), except for the additional term of $\frac{1}{2}m_p$ in the denominator, which represents the contribution of the pulley to the overall inertia of the system. The factor $\frac{1}{2}$ reflects the shape of the pulley, a disk, because we had found for disks that $c = \frac{1}{2}$ in the relationship between rotational inertia, mass, and radius (compare equation (10.22)).

10.6. Work Done by Torque

In chapter 5 we have found that the work W done by force $\vec{F}$ is given by the integral

$$W = \int_{\vec{r}_0}^{\vec{r}} \vec{F}(\vec{r}\,') \bullet d\vec{r}\,' = \int_{\vec{r}_0}^{\vec{r}} F_x(\vec{r}\,')dx' + \int_{\vec{r}_0}^{\vec{r}} F_y(\vec{r}\,')dy' + \int_{\vec{r}_0}^{\vec{r}} F_z(\vec{r}\,')dz'$$

We can now ask what the work done by a torque $\vec{\tau}$ is. The torque is the angular equivalent of the force. The angular equivalent of the displacement $d\vec{r}$ is the angular displacement $d\vec{\theta}$. Since both the torque and the angular displacement are axial vectors and point in the direction of the axis of rotation, we can write their scalar product as $\vec{\tau} \bullet d\vec{\theta} = \tau d\theta$. So the work done by a torque is

$$W = \int_{\theta_0}^{\theta} \tau(\theta')d\theta' \qquad (10.56)$$

In the special case that the torque is constant and thus does not depend on θ, then this integral simply evaluates to

$$W = \tau(\theta - \theta_0) \qquad (10.57)$$

Also in chapter 5 we have developed a first version of the work-kinetic energy theorem. This work-kinetic energy theorem is simply $\Delta K \equiv K - K_0 = W$. The rotational equivalent to this work-kinetic energy relationship can then simply be written with the aid of (10.6) as

$$\Delta K \equiv K - K_0 = \tfrac{1}{2}I\omega^2 - \tfrac{1}{2}I\omega_0^2 = W \qquad (10.58)$$

For the case of a constant torque we can use (10.57) and find for the work-kinetic energy theorem for constant torque

$$\tfrac{1}{2}I\omega^2 - \tfrac{1}{2}I\omega_0^2 = \tau(\theta - \theta_0) \qquad (10.59)$$

Example

Example 10.4: Tightening a Bolt

Question:
What is the total work required to screw the nut shown in Figure 10.18 onto the bolt? The total number of turns is 30.5, the diameter of the screw is 0.86 cm, and the friction force between the nut and the bolt is a constant 14.5 N.

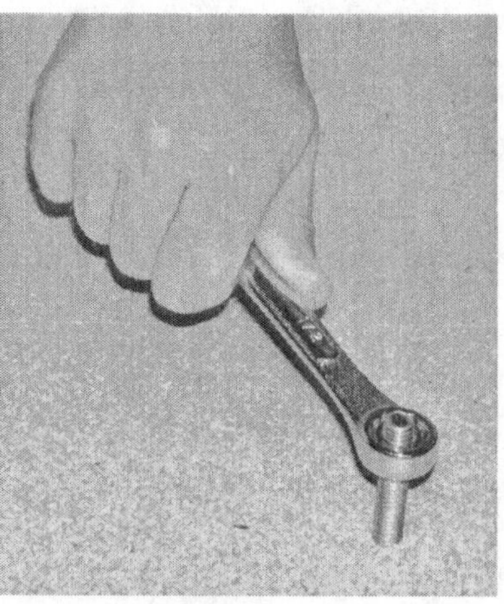

Figure 10.18: Tightening a bolt.

Answer:
Since the friction force is constant and since the diameter of the screw is constant, we can easily calculate the torque needed to turn the nut,

$$\tau = Fr = \tfrac{1}{2}Fd = \tfrac{1}{2}(14.5 \text{ N})(0.86 \text{ cm}) = 0.125 \text{ Nm}$$

In order to calculate the total work required to screw the nut onto the bolt, we need to figure out the total angle. Each turn corresponds to an angle of 2π rad; so the total angle is in this case $\Delta\theta = 30.5 \cdot 2\pi = 278.5$ rad .

The total work required is then simply obtained by making use of (10.57):

$$W = \tau\Delta\theta = (0.125 \text{ Nm})(278.5) = 35.8 \text{ J}$$

As you can see, there is not much difficulty in figuring out the work required for a constant torque. But in many physical situations the torque cannot be considered to be constant. The next example illustrates such a case.

Example 10.5: Screwing

The friction force between a drywall screw and a block of wood is proportional to the contact area between the screw and the wood. Since the drywall screw has a constant diameter, this means that the torque required for turning the screw increases linearly with the depth that the screw has already penetrated into the wood.

Question:
Suppose it takes 27.3 turns to screw the drywall screw shown in Figure 10.19 completely into the block of wood. The torque needed to turn the screw increases linearly from 0 at the beginning to a maximum of 12.4 Nm at the end. What is the total work required to screw in the screw?

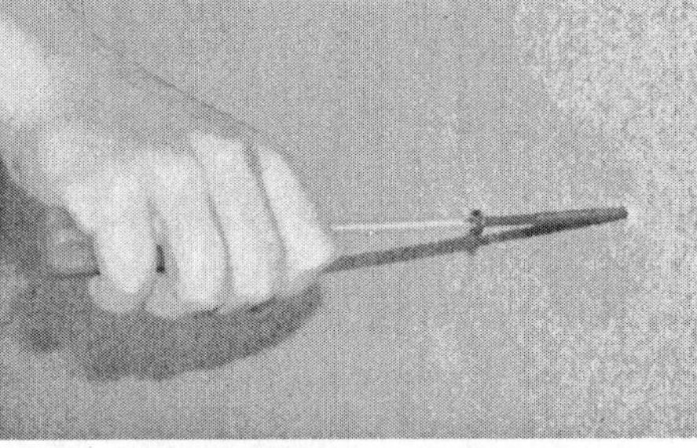

Figure 10.19: Screwing a drywall screw into a block of wood.

Answer:
Clearly τ is now a function of the angle and not constant any more. Thus we have to use the full integral (10.56) to find our answer. First, let us calculate the total angle θ_{total} that the screw is turned. 27.3 turns means that $\theta_{total} = 27.3 \cdot 2\pi = 171.5$ rad . Now we need to

Example

find an expression for $\tau(\theta)$. A linear increase with θ from zero to 12.4 Nm means

$$\tau(\theta) = \theta \frac{\tau_{\max}}{\theta_{total}} = \theta \frac{12.4 \text{ Nm}}{171.5} = \theta \cdot 0.0722 \text{ Nm}$$

Now we can execute the integral as follows:

$$W = \int_0^{\theta_{total}} \tau(\theta')d\theta' = \int_0^{\theta_{total}} \theta' \frac{\tau_{\max}}{\theta_{total}} d\theta' = \frac{\tau_{\max}}{\theta_{total}} \int_0^{\theta_{total}} \theta' d\theta' = \frac{\tau_{\max}}{\theta_{total}} \tfrac{1}{2}\theta'^2 \Big|_0^{\theta_{total}} = \tfrac{1}{2}\tau_{\max}\theta_{total}$$

Inserting the numbers we obtain:

$$W = \tfrac{1}{2}\tau_{\max}\theta_{total} = \tfrac{1}{2}(12.4 \text{ Nm})(171.5 \text{ rad}) = 1.06 \text{ kJ}$$

In-class exercise: If you want to reduce the torque required to screw in the screw, you can rub soap on the thread beforehand. Suppose this reduces the coefficient of friction between the screw and the wood by a factor of 2, but how much does it change the total work to screw the screw into the wood?

a) It leaves the work the same
b) It reduces the work by a factor of 2
c) It reduces the work by a factor of 4

In-class exercise: If you get tired before you get done screwing in the screw completely and you only manage to screw it in halfway, how does this change the total work you have done?

a) It leaves the work the same
b) It reduces the work by a factor of 2
c) It reduces the work by a factor of 4

Solved Problem

Solved Problem 10.3: Atwood Machine

Question:
Two masses $m_1 = 3.00$ kg and $m_2 = 1.40$ kg are connected by a very light rope that runs without sliding over a (solid disk) pulley of mass $m_p = 2.30$ kg, as shown in Figure 10.20. The two masses initially hang at the same height and are kept at rest. Obviously, once released the heavier mass m_1 will descend and lift up the lighter mass m_2. What is the speed that m_2 will have at a height $h = 0.16$ m?

Answer:

THINK:

We could try to calculate the acceleration of the two masses and then use kinematic equations to relate this acceleration to the vertical displacement. But we can also try our energy considerations. The latter will lead to a fairly easy solution, and so let us discuss the steps involved. Initially the two hanging masses and the pulley are at rest. So the total kinetic energy is 0. We also can use a coordinate system that implies that the initial potential energy is zero, and thus the total energy is zero. As one of the masses is lifted, it gains gravitational potential energy, and the other one loses potential energy. Both masses gain translational kinetic energy, and the pulley gains rotational kinetic energy. Since the kinetic energy is proportional to the square of the speed, we can use energy conservation to solve for the speed.

SKETCH:

On the left side of our sketch we show the initial state of the Atwood machine with both hanging masses at the same height. We decide to set that height as the origin of our vertical axis, thus ensuring that the initial potential energy and therefore the total energy is zero.

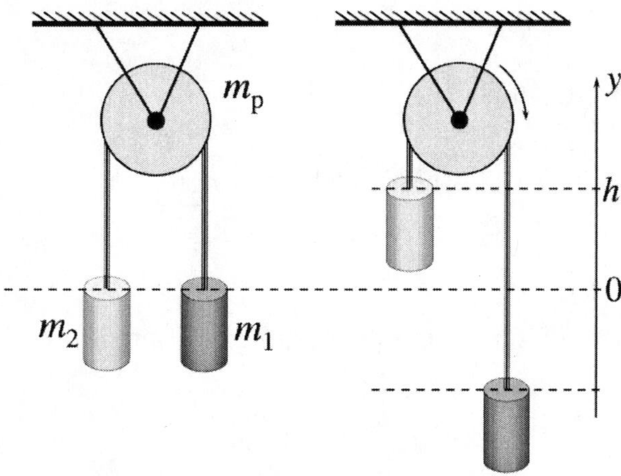

Figure 10.20: One more Atwood machine.

RESEARCH:

The gravitational potential energy gain for mass 2 is $U_2 = m_2gh$. At the same time mass is lowered the same distance and so its potential energy is $U_1 = -m_1gh$. The kinetic energy of mass 1 is $K_1 = \frac{1}{2}m_1v^2$, and the kinetic energy of mass 2 is $K_2 = \frac{1}{2}m_2v^2$. Note that the same speed v is used in both expressions for the two masses. This is assured, because they are connected by a rope. (We assume that the rope does not stretch!)

What about the rotational kinetic energy of the pulley? The pulley is a solid disk with rotational inertia $I = \frac{1}{2}m_pR^2$. Its rotational kinetic energy is $K_r = \frac{1}{2}I\omega^2$. Since the rope runs over the pulley without slipping, and since the rope also moves with the same speed v as the two masses, points on the surface of the pulley also have to move with that same linear speed. Just like for a rolling solid disk, we then find that the linear speed is connected to the angular speed via $\omega R = v$. This results in a rotational kinetic energy of

Solved Problem

the pulley of

$$K_r = \tfrac{1}{2} I\omega^2 = \tfrac{1}{2}(\tfrac{1}{2} m_p R^2)\omega^2 = \tfrac{1}{4} m_p R^2 \omega^2 = \tfrac{1}{4} m_p v^2$$

Now we are in the position to write down the entire energy. It is the sum of the potential and translational and rotational kinetic energies. This overall sum has to be 0, because this was its initial value, and because of energy conservation:

$$\begin{aligned} 0 &= U_1 + U_2 + K_1 + K_2 + K_r \\ &= -m_1 gh + m_2 gh + \tfrac{1}{2} m_1 v^2 + \tfrac{1}{2} m_2 v^2 + \tfrac{1}{4} m_p v^2 \end{aligned}$$

SIMPLIFY:

We can rearrange the previous equation to isolate the speed v and find:

$$(m_1 - m_2)gh = (\tfrac{1}{2} m_1 + \tfrac{1}{2} m_2 + \tfrac{1}{4} m_p)v^2 \Rightarrow$$

$$v = \sqrt{\frac{2(m_1 - m_2)gh}{m_1 + m_2 + \tfrac{1}{2} m_p}} \qquad (10.60)$$

CALCULATE:

Now it is time to insert the numbers:

$$v = \sqrt{\frac{2(3.00\text{ kg} - 1.40\text{ kg})(9.81\text{m/s}^2)(0.16\text{ m})}{3.00\text{ kg} + 1.40\text{ kg} + \tfrac{1}{2} 2.30\text{ kg}}} = 0.951312\text{ m/s}$$

ROUND:

The displacement h was given with the fewest digits of precision, 2. So we round our result to

$$v = 0.95\text{ m/s}$$

DOUBLE-CHECK:

We are in the fortunate situation that we have calculated the acceleration of the masses in the previous section on the Atwood machine. So we can use the final result of that calculation, which is (10.55)

$$a = \frac{m_1 - m_2}{m_1 + m_2 + \tfrac{1}{2} m_p} g$$

Already back in chapter 2 we developed kinematic equations for the case of one-dimensional linear motion. One of these, which relates the initial and final speeds and the displacement and the acceleration now comes in handy:

$$v^2 = v_0^2 + 2a(y - y_0)$$

In our case $v_0 = 0$ and $y - y_0 = h$. Inserting the value of a we then find

$$v^2 = 2ah = 2\frac{m_1 - m_2}{m_1 + m_2 + \frac{1}{2}m_p}hg \Rightarrow v = \sqrt{\frac{2(m_1 - m_2)gh}{m_1 + m_2 + \frac{1}{2}m_p}}$$

This results is identical to (10.60), which we obtained with our energy methods. However, if you go back and see how much effort it took to calculate the acceleration, it becomes clear that the energy method that we selected for the solution is the quicker way to proceed.

General Hint on Problem Solving:
Newton's Second Law and the work-kinetic energy theorem provide two powerful and complementary tools to solve a wide variety of problems in mechanics. As a general guideline on which one to try for which problem, we suggest the following: In rotational mechanics problems, just as in translational problems, one should try an approach based on Newton's Second Law and free-body diagrams when the task involves the calculation of accelerations, and an approach based on the work-energy theorem when there is a need to calculate speeds.

10.7. Angular Momentum

While we have discussed the rotational equivalents of mass, velocity, acceleration, and force, we have not yet introduced the rotational analog to the linear momentum. Since the linear momentum is the product of the velocity and the mass, we may speculate by analogy that the angular momentum should be the product of angular velocity and rotational inertia. Later in this section we will find that this relationship is true for extended objects with fixed rotational inertia. But before we get there we have to do a bit of work, starting from a definition for a point particle. While this definition may at first seem not to be connected to what you may expect, the following subsections will allow us to get from one to the other.

Definition for a Point Particle

As a starting point, one usually defines the angular momentum $\vec{L}$ of a point particle as the vector product of its position and momentum vectors.

$$\vec{L} = \vec{r} \times \vec{p} \tag{10.61}$$

Because the angular momentum is defined as a vector product, we can make very similar statements to the ones made in the previous section on torque, replacing "force" by "momentum":

The magnitude of the angular momentum is given by:

$$L = rp\sin\theta \qquad (10.62)$$

θ is now the angle between the position and momentum vectors. Just like the torque's direction, the direction of the angular momentum vector is given by a right-hand-rule. Let the thumb of the right hand point along the position vector and the index finger along the momentum vector; then the middle finger will indicate the direction of the angular momentum $\vec{L}$ of this point particle with position vector $\vec{r}$ and momentum vector $\vec{p}$. This procedure is depicted in Figure 10.21.

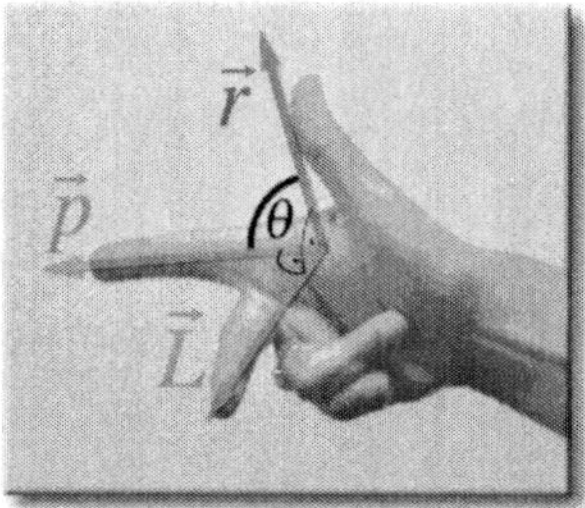

Figure 10.21: Right hand rule for the direction of the angular momentum: The thumb is aligned with the position vector and the index finger with the momentum vector; then the angular momentum vector points along the middle finger, as shown.

With the definition of the angular momentum as introduced in equation (10.61), we can now take the time derivative. This results in:

$$\frac{d}{dt}\vec{L} = \frac{d}{dt}(\vec{r}\times\vec{p}) = \left(\left(\frac{d}{dt}\vec{r}\right)\times\vec{p}\right) + \left(\vec{r}\times\frac{d}{dt}\vec{p}\right) = (\vec{v}\times\vec{p}) + \left(\vec{r}\times\vec{F}\right)$$

To take the derivative of the vector product, we have applied the product rule of calculus. The term $\vec{v}\times\vec{p}$ is always zero, because $\vec{v}\parallel\vec{p}$. And from equation (10.37) we already know that $\vec{r}\times\vec{F} = \vec{\tau}$. So we obtain for the time derivative of the angular momentum vector:

$$\frac{d}{dt}\vec{L} = \vec{\tau} \qquad (10.63)$$

The time derivative of the angular momentum vector for a point particle is the torque acting on that point particle. Again this result is analogous to the linear motion case, where the time derivative of the linear momentum is equal to the force.

System of Point Particles

It is straightforward to generalize the concept of angular momentum to a system of n point particles. The total angular momentum of this system of point particles is simply the sum of the individual angular momenta of the individual particles:

$$\vec{L} = \sum_{i=1}^{n} \vec{L}_i = \sum_{i=1}^{n} \vec{r}_i \times \vec{p}_i = \sum_{i=1}^{n} m_i \vec{r}_i \times \vec{v}_i \tag{10.64}$$

Again we take the time derivative of this expression in order to obtain the relationship between the total angular momentum of this system and the torque:

$$\begin{aligned} \frac{d}{dt}\vec{L} &= \frac{d}{dt}\left(\sum_{i=1}^{n} \vec{L}_i\right) = \frac{d}{dt}\left(\sum_{i=1}^{n} \vec{r}_i \times \vec{p}_i\right) = \sum_{i=1}^{n} \frac{d}{dt}(\vec{r}_i \times \vec{p}_i) \\ &= \sum_{i=1}^{n} \underbrace{\underbrace{\left(\frac{d}{dt}\vec{r}_i\right)}_{=\vec{v}_i} \times \vec{p}_i}_{=0,\text{ because } \vec{v}_i \| \vec{p}_i} + \vec{r}_i \times \underbrace{\left(\frac{d}{dt}\vec{p}_i\right)}_{\vec{F}_i} = \sum_{i=1}^{n} \vec{r}_i \times \vec{F}_i = \sum_{i=1}^{n} \vec{\tau}_i = \vec{\tau}_{net} \end{aligned} \tag{10.65}$$

As expected, we find that the time derivative of the total angular momentum for a system of particles is given by the total net external torque acting on this system. We stress that this is the net *external* torque due to *external* forces $\vec{F}_i$.

Self-test opportunity: Can you show that internal toques, i.e. torques due to internal forces between particles in a system, do not contribute to the total net torque?

Hint: you should use Newton's third Law, $\vec{F}_{i \to j} = -\vec{F}_{j \to i}$.

Rigid Objects

Rigid objects rotate about fixed axes with an angular velocity $\vec{\omega}$ that is the same for every part of the object. In this case the angular momentum is proportional to the angular velocity, and the proportionality constant is the rotational inertia:

$$\vec{L} = I\vec{\omega} \tag{10.66}$$

Derivation 10.4

Here we restrict ourselves to showing that the magnitude of the angular momentum is equal to the rotational inertia times the magnitude of the angular velocity. We omit the more complicated discussion of the direction and instead simply state the result.

We then obtain for the magnitude of $\vec{L}$ from equation (10.64):

$$L = \left|\vec{L}\right| = \left|\sum_{i=1}^{n} m_i \vec{r}_i \times \vec{v}_i\right| = \sum_{i=1}^{n} m_i \left|\vec{r}_i \times \vec{v}_i\right|$$

We represent the rigid object by collection of point particles. In this way we can use the

Derivation

Derivation

results of the previous section as a starting point. In order for our point particles to represent the rigid object we demand that their relative distances to each other remain constant (= rigid). Then all of these point particles will rotate with a constant angular velocity $\vec{\omega}$ about the common rotation axis, and each individual point particle's velocity will be given by $v_i = \omega r_{i\perp}$, where $r_{i\perp}$ is the perpendicular distance to the axis of rotation.

The magnitude of the vector product is $\left|\vec{r}_i \times \vec{v}_i\right| = r_i v_i \sin\theta = r_{i\perp} v_i$.

Inserting the results of the previous two paragraphs into the above equation yields:

$$L = \sum_{i=1}^{n} m_i \left|\vec{r}_i \times \vec{v}_i\right| = \sum_{i=1}^{n} m_i r_{i\perp} v_i = \sum_{i=1}^{n} m_i r_{i\perp}(\omega r_{i\perp}) = \omega \sum_{i=1}^{n} m_i r_{i\perp}^2$$

Now we can recognize the sum as the definition of the rotational inertia for a collection of point particles, and so we indeed obtain:

$$L = I\omega$$

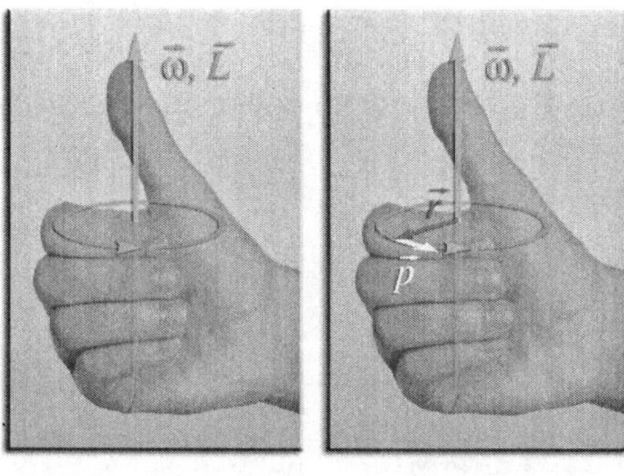

Figure 10.22: Right hand rule for the direction of the angular momentum (along the thumb) as a function of the direction of rotation (along the fingers). Shown on the right are the momentum and position vector of a point particle in circular motion.

The direction of the angular momentum vector is the same as that of the angular velocity vector, because the moment of inertia is a scalar. Figure 10.22 shows the right-hand rule use to determine the direction of the angular momentum vector (arrow along the direction of the thumb) as a function of the sense of rotation (direction of the fingers).

Example

Example 10.6: Angular Momentum of a Golf Ball

Question:

What is the magnitude of the angular momentum of a golf ball ($m = 4.59 \cdot 10^{-2}$ kg, $R = 2.13 \cdot 10^{-2}$ m) spinning at 4250 rpm (= revolutions per minute), which is a typical value after a good hit with a driver?

Example

Answer:
First we need to find out the angular frequency of the golf ball. This is a useful refresher of the concepts introduced in chapter 9.

$$\omega = 2\pi f = 2\pi(4250 \text{ min}^{-1}) = 2\pi(4250/60 \text{ s}^{-1}) = 445.0 \text{ s}^{-1}$$

The rotational inertia of the golf ball is

$$I = \tfrac{2}{5}mR^2 = 0.4 \cdot (4.59 \cdot 10^{-2} \text{ kg}) \cdot (2.13 \cdot 10^{-2} \text{ m})^2 = 8.33 \cdot 10^{-6} \text{ kg m}^2$$

The magnitude of the angular momentum of the golf ball is then simply the product of these two numbers:

$$L = (8.33 \cdot 10^{-6} \text{ kg m}^2) \cdot (445.0 \text{ s}^{-1}) = 3.71 \cdot 10^{-3} \text{ kg m}^2 \text{ s}^{-1}$$

Using our expression for the angular momentum of a rigid object, equation (10.66), we can easily show that the relationship between the rate of change of the angular momentum and the torque is still valid. Taking the time derivative of equation (10.66), and assuming a rigid body with rotational inertia that is constant in time, we obtain:

$$\frac{d}{dt}\vec{L} = \frac{d}{dt}(I\vec{\omega}) = I\frac{d}{dt}\vec{\omega} = I\vec{\alpha} = \vec{\tau} \quad (10.67)$$

When we motivated equation (10.44), we strictly only showed that this was true for a point particle. But after introducing the concept of angular momentum, (10.67) provides an easy proof that (10.44) indeed hold for all objects with fixed (= constant in time) rotational inertia.

The time derivative of the angular momentum is equal to the torque, like the time derivative of the linear momentum is equal to the force. Equation (10.63) is another formulation of Newton's Second Law for rotation and is more general than equation (10.44), because it also encompasses the case of a rotational inertia that is not constant in time.

Conservation of Angular Momentum

If the net external torque is zero, then according to equation (10.67) the time derivative of the angular momentum is also zero. And if the time derivative of a quantity is zero, then it is constant in time. So we can write down the conservation law for angular momentum:

$$\text{if } \vec{\tau}_{net} = 0 \Rightarrow \vec{L} = \text{constant} \Rightarrow \vec{L}(t) = \vec{L}(t_0) \equiv \vec{L}_0 . \quad (10.68)$$

This result is the third major conservation law that we have encountered, after those for total mechanical energy (chapter 6) and linear momentum (chapter 7). And like these conservation laws, we can now solve problems that would otherwise be very hard to attack.

If we use our relationship between angular momentum and rotational inertia, equation (10.66), then we arrive at a very useful formulation of the law of conservation of angular momentum:

$$I\vec{\omega} = I_0\vec{\omega}_0 \quad (\text{for } \vec{\tau}_{net} = 0) \qquad (10.69)$$

or, equivalently:

$$\frac{\omega}{\omega_0} = \frac{I_0}{I} \quad (\text{for } \vec{\tau}_{net} = 0) \qquad (10.70)$$

This conservation law is the basis for the functioning of gyroscopes. (See Figure 10.23, left panel.) Gyroscopes are objects (usually cylinders) that spin around their symmetry axis at high angular velocities. Their axis of rotation is able to spin on ball bearings, almost without friction. The suspension system of a gyroscope is able to rotate freely in all directions. This way one ensures that there is no net external torque that can act on the gyroscope. Without torque the angular momentum of the gyroscope remains constant and thus points in the same direction, no matter what the object carrying the gyroscope does. Airplanes rely on gyroscopes, as do satellites. The Hubble Space Telescope for example, is equipped with 6 separate gyroscopes, at least 3 of which must work for the space telescope to be able to orient itself in space.

Figure 10.23: Practical applications of angular momentum conservation: Left: Toy gyroscopes; right: Platform diver tucking in knees to reduce his rotational inertia.

Equation (10.69) is of importance in many sports, most notably gymnastics, platform diving, and figure skating. (See Figure 10.23, right panel.) In all three sports the athletes rearrange their bodies and thus adjust their moments of inertia to manipulate their rotation frequencies. While performing a pirouette in figure skating or in ballet, the athletes typically start a rotation with their arms stretched out away from their bodies. Pulling the arms close reduces the rotational inertia of their bodies by some factor,

$I' = I/k$, $k > 1$. Conservation of angular momentum then increases the angular velocity by the same factor k: $\omega' = k\omega$ Thus the performer can control the rate of rotation. The same is true in platform diving or gymnastics, where tucking in the knees can increase the rate of rotation by more than a factor of 2, as compared to the stretched-out position.

Example 10.7: Death of a Star

At the end of the life of a massive star (more than five times as massive as our sun), the core of the star consists almost entirely of nuclei of the metal iron. Once this stage is reached, the core becomes unstable and collapses (as indicated in Figure 10.24) in a process that lasts only about one second. This event is the initial phase of a supernova explosion, one of the most powerful energy release events in the universe. This explosion is thought to create most of the elements heavier than iron in the universe by throwing off the debris of the explosion into outer space. It leaves behind a neutron star, which is stellar material that is compressed to a density millions of times higher than the highest densities found on earth.

Question:
If the iron core initially spins with a rotation frequency of $f_0 = 3.2/\text{s}$, and if the core's radius decreases during the collapse by a factor of 22.7, what is the angular velocity of the iron core at the end of the collapse? Hint: We cannot really assume that the iron core has a constant density. Instead, computer simulations show that it falls off exponentially in the radial direction. However, the same simulations show that the rotational inertia of the iron core is still approximately proportional to the square of its radius during the collapse process.

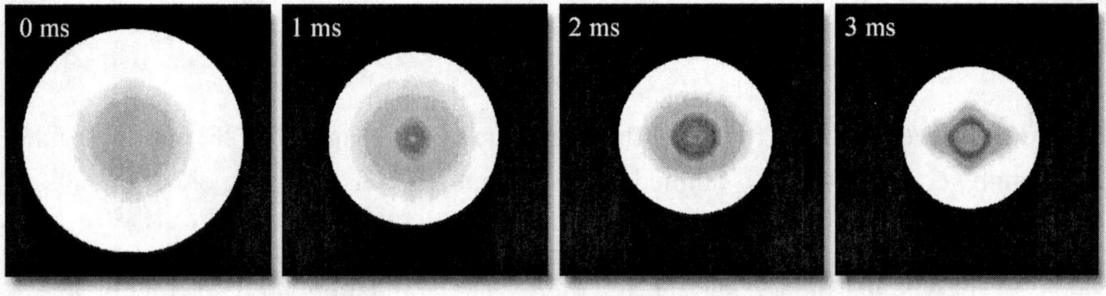

Figure 10.24: Computer simulation of the initial stages of a star's core collapse.

Answer:
Because the collapse of the iron core is under the influence of its own gravitational pull, no net external torque acts on the core. Thus, according to equation (10.63), angular momentum is conserved. From equation (10.69) we then obtain

$$\frac{\omega}{\omega_0} = \frac{I_0}{I} = \frac{R_0^2}{R^2} = 22.7^2 = 515.3$$

With $\omega_0 = 2\pi f_0 = 2\pi(3.2 \text{ s}^{-1}) = 20.1 \text{ s}^{-1}$, we can then see that the magnitude of the final angular velocity is:

$$\omega = 515\omega_0 = 515 \cdot 20.1 \text{ s}^{-1} = 10.4 \text{ kHz}$$

Thus the neutron star that results from this collapse rotates with a high angular frequency of more than 10,000 radians per second.

10.8. Precession

Spinning tops were popular toys when your parents were kids. When you put them in rapid rotational motion, they stand upright without falling down. What's more, you can actually tilt them at angle relative to the vertical, and they will still not fall down. Instead their rotation axis moves on the surface of a cone as a function of time. This motion is called "precession". What causes it?

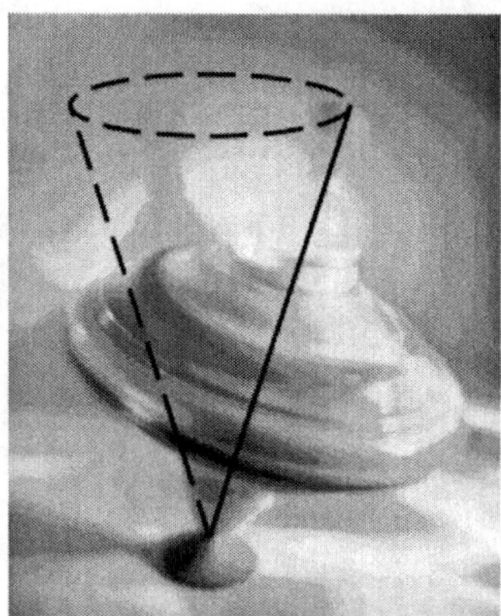

Figure 10.25: Spinning top.

To find an answer, we need to realize that the spinning top (Figure 10.25) has an angular momentum vector $\vec{L}$, which is aligned with its symmetry axis, pointing either up or down, depending on if it is spinning clockwise or counterclockwise (Figure 10.26). Since the top is tilted, its center of mass (marked with a black dot) is not located above the contact point with the support surface any more. The gravitational force acting on the center of mass then results in a torque $\vec{\tau}$ about the contact point, as indicated in the figure, pointing in this case straight out of the page. The position vector $\vec{r}$ of the center of mass relative to the rotation axis that enters into the torque is exactly aligned with the angular momentum vector. We call the angle of the symmetry axis of the top with respect to the vertical ϕ. The angle between the gravitational force vector and the position vector is then $\pi - \phi$, see Figure 10.26. Since $\sin(\pi - \phi) = \sin\phi$, we can then write for the magnitude of the torque as a function of the angle ϕ

$$\tau = rF\sin\phi = rmg\sin\phi \tag{10.71}$$

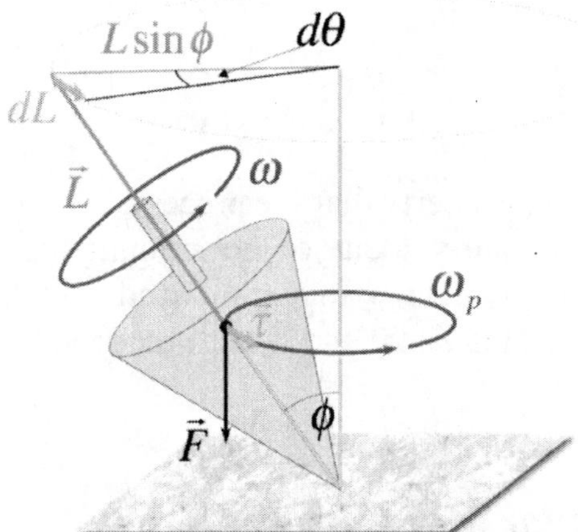

Figure 10.26: Precession of a spinning top.

Since $d\vec{L}/dt = \vec{\tau}$, the change in the angular momentum vector, $d\vec{L}$, points in the same direction as the torque and is thus perpendicular to the angular momentum vector. This forces the angular momentum vector to sweep along the surface of a cone of angle ϕ as a function of time, with the tip of the angular momentum vector following a circle in the horizontal plane, as indicated in gray color in Figure 10.26.

We can even calculate the magnitude of the angular velocity ω_p for this precession motion. In Figure 10.26 we see that the radius of the circle that the tip of the angular momentum vector sweeps out as a function of time is given by $L\sin\phi$. The differential change in angular momentum, dL, is the arc length of this circle, and it can be calculated as the product of the circle's radius and the differential angle swept out by the radius, $d\theta$: $dL = (L\sin\phi)d\theta$. Consequently we find for the time derivative of the angular momentum dL/dt:

$$\frac{dL}{dt} = (L\sin\phi)\frac{d\theta}{dt} \tag{10.72}$$

The time derivative of this deflection angle θ is the angular velocity of precession, ω_p. Since $dL/dt = \tau$ we finally find from (10.72) and using the expression for the torque of equation (10.71):

$$rmg\sin\phi = \tau = \frac{dL}{dt} = (L\sin\phi)\frac{d\theta}{dt} = (L\sin\phi)\omega_p \Rightarrow$$

$$\omega_p = \frac{rmg\sin\phi}{L\sin\phi} \tag{10.73}$$

Now we see that the term $\sin\phi$ cancels out of this expression. The precession angular frequency is the same for all tilt angles ϕ of the rotation axis! This result may seem a bit surprising, but experiments verify that this is indeed the case. For the final step, we use the fact that the angular momentum for a rigid object is the product of the rotational inertia, I, and its angular velocity, ω. Inserting this into (10.73) gives us our final result for the precession angular velocity

$$\omega_p = \frac{rmg}{I\omega} \tag{10.74}$$

This formula has the interesting property that the precession angular velocity is inversely proportional to the spinning angular velocity of the spinning top. As the top slows down due to friction, its angular velocity gets gradually reduced, and therefore the precession frequency increases gradually. This faster and faster precession eventually causes the top to wobble and to fall down.

10.9. Quantized Angular Momentum

Before we leave our discussion of angular momentum and rotation, we would like to touch on the question of the smallest quantity of angular momentum that an object can have. If we return to our definition of the angular momentum of a point particle (10.61), $\vec{L} = \vec{r} \times \vec{p}$, $L = rp\sin\theta$, then it would appear that there is no smallest amount of angular momentum, because we can always reduce either the distance to the rotation axis r or the momentum p by a factor between 0 and 1, and we would reduce the corresponding angular momentum by the same factor.

However, when it comes to atoms and subatomic particles, we are forced to give up the notion of a continuously variable angular momentum. Instead we have to introduce a quantum of angular momentum. This quantum of angular momentum is called Planck's constant,

$$h = 6.626 \cdot 10^{-34} \text{ J s} \tag{10.75}$$

Very often one needs Planck's constant divided by the factor 2π, and physicists have given this ratio the name $\hbar$. (Pronounced: "h bar", which incidentally is also the name of the coffee shop in the physics building of the University of Washington in Seattle!)

$$\hbar \equiv \frac{h}{2\pi} = 1.055 \cdot 10^{-34} \text{ J s} \tag{10.76}$$

In chapter 36, we will return to a much more expanded discussion of what experimental observations necessitated the introduction of this fundamental constant. However, here we only state the amazing result: all elementary particles have intrinsic angular momentum, also often called "spin", of either integer multiples ($0,\ 1\hbar,\ 2\hbar,\ ...$) of this Planck's quantum of the angular momentum or half integer multiples ($\frac{1}{2}\hbar,\ \frac{3}{2}\hbar,\ ...$). Astonishingly, the integer or half-integer spin values of particles makes all the difference in the way they interact with each other. The particles with integer-valued spin include the photons, which we will learn are the elementary particle of light. And the particles with half-integer values spin include electrons, protons, and neutrons, the elementary particles that constitute the building blocks of matter. We will return to the fundamental importance of angular momentum in atoms and subatomic particles in chapters 37 through 40. But at this point we would just like to mention these facts as way to motivate you to take a deeper look at angular momentum in the future.

What we have learned/Exam Study Guide:

- The kinetic energy of rotation is given by $K = \frac{1}{2}I\omega^2$. This relationship holds for point particles as well as solid objects.
- The rotational inertia for a rotation about an axis through the center of mass is defined as the integral $I = \int_V r_\perp^2 \rho(\vec{r})dV$, where $r_\perp$ is the perpendicular distance of the volume element dV to the axis of rotation and $\rho(\vec{r})$ is its mass density.
- In the case that the mass density is constant, we can express the rotational inertia as $I = \frac{M}{V}\int_V r_\perp^2 dV$, where M is the total mass of the rotating object, and V its volume.
- The rotational inertia of round objects can always be written as $I = cMR^2$ with $c \in [0,1]$.
- The parallel axes theorem: the rotational inertia $I_{\parallel}$ for rotation about an axes parallel to the one through the center of mass is given by $I_{\parallel} = I_{cm} + Md^2$, where d is the distance between the two axes, and I_{cm} is the rotational inertia for rotation about the axes through the center of mass.
- For a object that is rolling without slipping, the center of mass coordinate $\vec{r}$ and the rotation angle $\vec{\theta}$ are related via $r = R\theta$, where R is the radius of the object.
- The kinetic energy of a rolling object is the sum of its translational and rotational kinetic energies, $K = K_{trans} + K_{rot} = \frac{1}{2}mv_{cm}^2 + \frac{1}{2}I_{cm}\omega^2 = \frac{1}{2}(1+c)mv_{cm}^2$, again with $c \in [0,1]$ and with c depending on the shape of the object.
- The torque is defined as the vector product of position vector and force vector, $\vec{\tau} = \vec{r} \times \vec{F}$.
- The angular momentum of a point particle is defined as $\vec{L} = \vec{r} \times \vec{p}$.
- The rate of change of the angular momentum is equal to the torque, $\frac{d}{dt}\vec{L} = \vec{\tau}$. This is the rotational equivalent of Newton's Second Law.
- For rigid objects, the angular momentum is given as $\vec{L} = I\vec{\omega}$, and the torque is $\vec{\tau} = I\vec{\alpha}$.
- In the case of vanishing net external torque, angular momentum is conserved, $I\vec{\omega} = I_0\vec{\omega}_0$ (for $\vec{\tau}_{net} = 0$).
- Finally, we can compile a table of the equivalent quantities for linear and circular motion.

Quantity	Linear	Circular	Relationship
Displacement	$\vec{s}$	$\vec{\theta}$	$s = r\theta$
Velocity	$\vec{v}$	$\vec{\omega}$	$v = r\omega$
Acceleration	$\vec{a}$	$\vec{\alpha}$	$\vec{a} = r\alpha\,\hat{t} + r\omega^2\hat{r}$ $a_t = r\alpha$ $a_c = \omega^2 r$
Momentum	$\vec{p}$	$\vec{L}$	$\vec{L} = \vec{r} \times \vec{p}$
Mass/rotational inertia	m	I	
Kinetic energy	$\frac{1}{2}mv^2$	$\frac{1}{2}I\omega^2$	
Force/torque	$\vec{F}$	$\vec{\tau}$	$\vec{\tau} = \vec{r} \times \vec{F}$

Additional Solved Problems

Solved Problem

Solved Problem 10.4: Falling Horizontal Rod

We suspend a thin horizontal rod of length $L = 2.50$ m and mass $m = 3.50$ kg by a pair of vertical strings attached to each end, as shown in Figure 10.27. The string that is supporting end B is then cut.

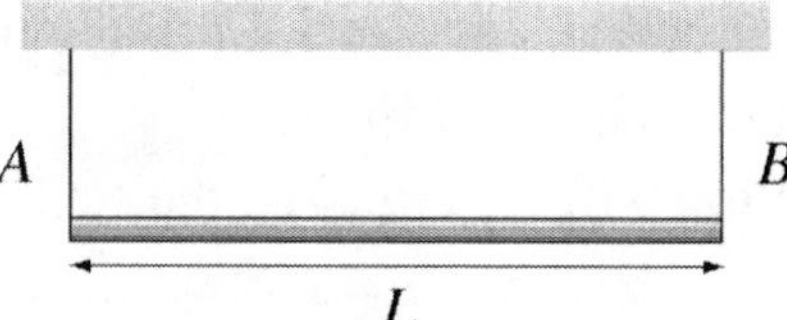

Figure 10.27: A horizontal thin rod supported by a vertical string from each end.

Question:

What is the linear acceleration of end B of the rod just after the string is cut?

Answer:

THINK: Before the string is cut, the rod is in equilibrium. When the string that is supporting end B is cut, there is a net torque acting on the rod. The pivot point is end A of the rod. The torque is a result of the force of gravity acting on the rod. We can consider the mass of the rod as a point mass at the center of mass of the rod, which is located at $L/2$. The initial torque will be equal to the weight of the rod times the moment arm, which is $L/2$. The resulting initial angular acceleration can be related to the linear acceleration of end B of the rod.

SKETCH: A sketch of the rod after the string that is supporting end B is cut is shown in Figure 10.28.

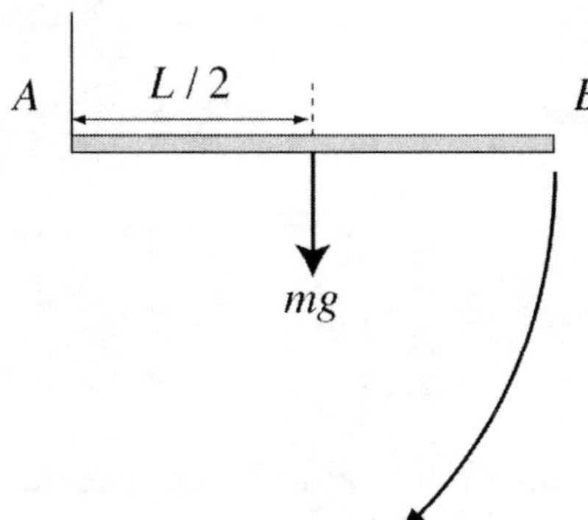

Figure 10.28: The horizontal thin rod just after the string that is supporting end B is cut.

Solved Problem

RESEARCH: When the string that is supporting end B is cut, the torque on the rod τ will be due to the force of gravity F_g acting on the rod times the moment arm $r_\perp = L/2$

$$\tau = r_\perp F_g = (L/2)(mg) = \frac{mgL}{2}. \tag{10.77}$$

The angular acceleration α is given by

$$\tau = I\alpha \tag{10.78}$$

where the rotational inertia I of the thin rod rotating around end A is given by

$$I = \frac{1}{3}mL^2. \tag{10.79}$$

The linear acceleration a of end B can be related to the angular acceleration through

$$a = L\alpha \tag{10.80}$$

because we can think of end B of the rod as undergoing circular motion as the rod pivots around end A.

SIMPLIFY: We can combine (10.77) and (10.78) to get

$$\tau = I\alpha = \frac{mgL}{2}. \tag{10.81}$$

Substituting (10.79) and (10.80) into (10.81) gives us

$$I\alpha = \left(\frac{1}{3}mL^2\right)\left(\frac{a}{L}\right) = \frac{mgL}{2}. \tag{10.82}$$

Solved Problem

Dividing out the common factors, we obtain

$$\frac{a}{3}=\frac{g}{2} \tag{10.83}$$

or

$$a=\tfrac{3}{2}g\,. \tag{10.84}$$

CALCULATE: Putting the numerical value for the acceleration of gravity into (10.84) gives us

$$a=1.5\cdot\left(9.81\text{ m/s}^2\right)=14.715\text{ m/s}^2.$$

ROUND: Expressing our result with three significant digits leads to

$$a=14.7\text{ m/s}^2.$$

DOUBLE-CHECK: Perhaps this answer is somewhat surprising, because you may have guessed that the acceleration cannot exceed the free-fall acceleration g. If both strings were cut at the same time, the acceleration of the entire rod would be $a=g$. Our result that the initial acceleration of the end B is $a=1.5g$ when the string-supporting end B is cut seems reasonable because the full force of gravity is acting on the rod and end A of the rod remains fixed. Therefore the end that is cut loose is not just accelerated by the free fall, but in addition it receives acceleration from the rotation of the rod.

Chapter 11. Static Equilibrium

Figure 11.1: This 440 kg installation created by Alexander Calder hangs from the ceiling at the National Gallery of Art (Washington, DC) in perfect static equilibrium.

What we will learn:

- Static equilibrium is defined as mechanical equilibrium for the special case that the object in equilibrium is at rest.
- An object (or a collection of objects) can only be in static equilibrium, if the net external force is zero and the net external torque is zero.
- A sufficient condition for static equilibrium is that the first derivative of the potential energy function is zero at the equilibrium point.

- An object, which is not rigidly attached to other objects, can only remain at rest if its center of mass is either supported from directly below or suspended from directly above.
- Stable equilibrium is achieved at points where the potential energy function has a minimum.
- Unstable equilibrium is given at points where the potential energy function has a maximum.
- Indifferent equilibrium exists at points where the first and second derivative of the potential energy function are both zero.

11.1. Equilibrium Conditions

In chapter 4 we explored the conditions for mechanical equilibrium. We found that the necessary condition for mechanical equilibrium is the absence of a net external force. In that case Newton's First Law stipulates that an object in mechanical equilibrium stays at rest or moves with constant velocity. But most often we want to explore the conditions that are needed for an object to stay at rest, in *static* equilibrium, and this is the topic of the current chapter.

An object (or collection of objects) is in static equilibrium, if it is at rest and not experiencing translational or rotational motion. A famous example for such a collection of objects in static equilibrium is shown in Figure 11.1. Part of what makes this installation by Alexander Calder so amazing is that the eye does not want to accept that the configuration it is in is a stable static equilibrium.

The requirement of no translational or rotational motion means that the linear and angular velocities of this object are zero at all times. And since the values of the linear and angular velocities do not change in time, this also implies that the linear and angular accelerations are zero at all times. In chapter 4 we learned that Newton's Second Law,

$$\vec{F}_{net} = m\vec{a}\,, \tag{11.1}$$

then implies that the external net force $\vec{F}_{net}$ is zero, if we demand zero linear acceleration $\vec{a}$. In the same way we saw in chapter 10 that Newton's Second Law for rotation,

$$\vec{\tau}_{net} = I\vec{\alpha}\,, \tag{11.2}$$

then implies that the external net torque $\vec{\tau}_{net}$ is zero, if we demand that the angular acceleration $\vec{\alpha}$ is zero. This leads us to our two conditions for static equilibrium:

Static Equilibrium Condition 1:

An object can only stay at rest if the net force acting on it is 0.

Static Equilibrium Condition 2:

An object can only stay at rest, if the net torque acting on it is 0.

Even if Newton's First Law is satisfied and there is no net force on an object and thus no translational motion, an object will still rotate if it experiences a net torque. It is also important to realize that the torque is always defined with respect to a pivot point. When one computes the net torque, the pivot point (the point where the axis of rotation intersects the plane define by $\vec{F}$ and $\vec{r}$) has to be the same for all forces in the problem. If we try to solve a problem of static equilibrium, with vanishing net torque, the net torque has to be zero for any pivot point selection. So we have the freedom to select a pivot point that best suits our purpose. A clever selection of a pivot point is often the key to a quick solution. For example, if there is an unknown force in the problem, you can select the pivot point as the point where the force acts. Then this force will not enter the equation for your torques because it has a moment arm of length zero.

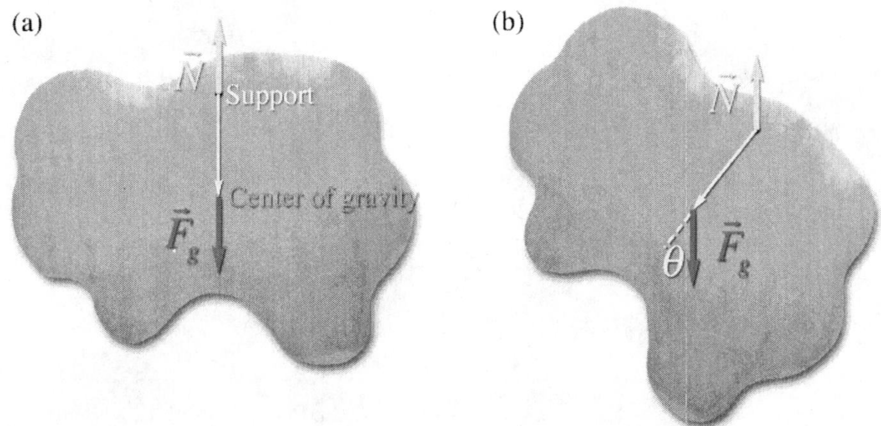

Figure 11.2: (a) Zero net torque, because the object is supported by a pin exactly above the center of gravity; (b) Net torque resulting from the center of gravity of the same object at a location not exactly below the support point.

If we support an object directly above the center of gravity by a pin, as done in Figure 11.2(a), then this object stays balanced, i.e. does not start to rotate. Why? Because in this case there are only two forces acting on the object, the force of gravity and the normal force from the pin, and they lie on the same line, see Figure 11.2(a). The two forces then cancel each other out and produce no net torque, resulting in static equilibrium and thus we have an object in balance. In Figure 11.2 we have marked the center of gravity of the object by a red dot. We represent the force of gravity with the blue arrow, whereas the normal force from the support pin is indicated in green. The line connecting the center of gravity and the support point is drawn in yellow.

On the other hand, if the object is supported from the same pin but the center of gravity is not below the support point, then we obtain a situation as shown in Figure 11.2(b). The normal and gravitational force vectors still point in opposite directions. However, now there is non-zero net torque acting, because the angle θ between the force vector $\vec{F}_g$ and the moment arm (yellow line) is not 0 any more. So the zero net torque condition for static equilibrium is violated. This leads to a practical recipe for finding the center of gravity for an object, even strangely shaped ones like the one in Figure 11.2.

Experimentally Locating the Center of Gravity

To locate the center of gravity experimentally, support the object by a pin in such a way that it can freely rotate around the pin and let it come to rest. In that position, the center of gravity will be located on the line directly below the pin. If you do this for two different points, the intersection of the two lines will mark the precise location of the center of gravity. This technique is shown in Figure 11.3. We have hung a plum bob from the same pin used to support our object in order to show the line directly below the support point in each case. Then we simply support the object in two different points and obtain two different lines. The point where these two lines intersect is the center of gravity.

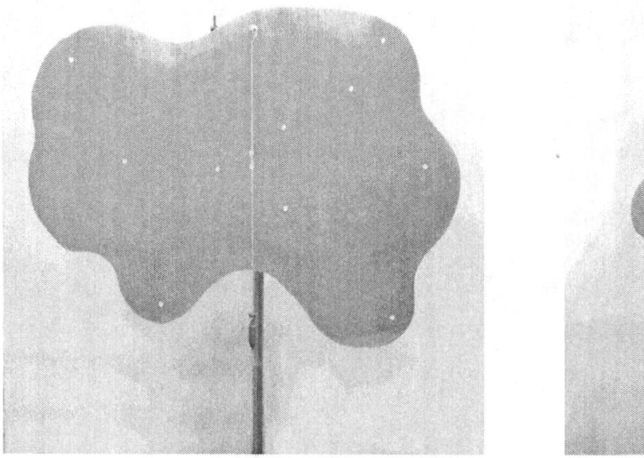

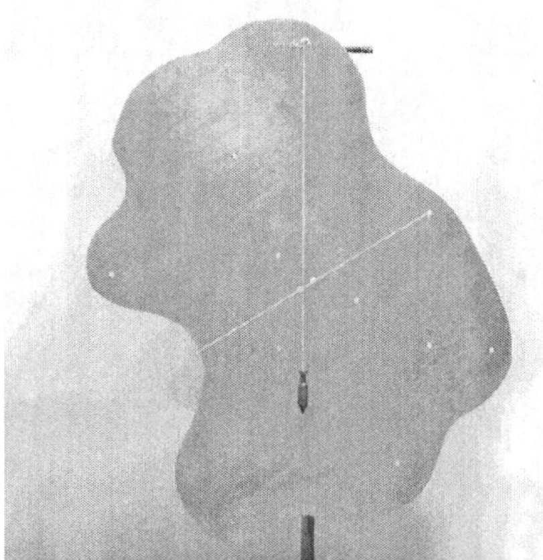

Figure 11.3: Finding the center of gravity for an arbitrarily shaped object.

There is a similar technique that you can use to determine the location of the center of gravity for many objects. It is a simple experiment that you can do at home and is shown in Figure 11.4. It simply involves suspending the object on two fingers and sliding the fingers closer to each other. Initially, the fingers need to be placed in such a way that the center of gravity is located somewhere between the fingers. (If this is not the case, you will know right away, because the object will fall.) Then you simply need to slowly slide the fingers closer to each other. At the point where they meet, they are directly below the center of gravity, and the object is balanced on top.

Why does this process work? The finger that is closer to the location of the center of gravity acts with a larger normal force. Thus, when moving, this finger exerts a larger friction force on the object than the one that is farther away. Consequently, if you slide the fingers towards each other, the finger that is closer to the center of gravity will take the suspended object along with it. This will happen until the other finger becomes closer to the center of gravity, upon which the effect is reversed. In this way, the two fingers always keep the center of gravity located between them. Sliding the fingers next to each other thus locates the center of gravity.

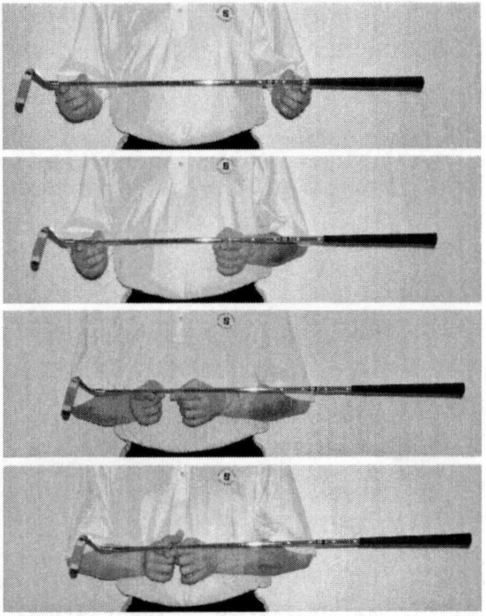

Figure 11.4: Determining the center of gravity of a golf club experimentally.

For the process of holding up our laptop computer in chapter 4 we drew the force vector $\vec{N}$ exerted by the hand on the laptop at the laptop center, just like the gravitational force vector but in the opposite direction. This placement was selected with a definite purpose. For our hand to be able to hold up the computer in this case, it needed to be placed directly below the center of mass. Otherwise, if the center of mass were not supported from directly below, the computer would tip over.

We can, in fact, elevate this idea to a general principle. Let us consider an object that is not rigidly attached to other objects:

An object can only remain at rest if its center of mass is either supported from directly below or suspended from directly above.

Equilibrium Equations

Now that we have a qualitative understanding of the concepts and conditions for static equilibrium, we can formulate the equilibrium conditions for a more quantitative analysis. Already in chapter 4 we remarked that the condition of zero net force translates into three independent equations in a three-dimensional space. They are

$$F_{net,x} = \sum_{i=1}^{n} F_{i,x} = F_{1,x} + F_{2,x} + ... + F_{n,x} = 0 \tag{11.3}$$

$$F_{net,y} = \sum_{i=1}^{n} F_{i,y} = F_{1,y} + F_{2,y} + ... + F_{n,y} = 0 \tag{11.4}$$

$$F_{net,z} = \sum_{i=1}^{n} F_{i,z} = F_{1,z} + F_{2,z} + \ldots + F_{n,z} = 0 \tag{11.5}$$

In chapter 10 we elaborated that the net torque is the difference of the sum of the counter-clockwise torques and the sum of the clockwise torques. The static equilibrium condition of zero net torque can then be written as

$$\tau_{\text{net}} = \sum_{i} \tau_{\text{counter-clockwise},i} - \sum_{j} \tau_{\text{clockwise},j} = 0 \tag{11.6}$$

The four equations (11.3)–(11.6) form the basis for the quantitative analysis of all static equilibrium problems. We will apply these equations to various examples and physical situations throughout this chapter.

11.2. Static Equilibrium Examples

The two conditions for static equilibrium (zero net force and zero net torque) are the complete set of conditions that we need to solve a very large class of problems on static equilibrium. To solve these problems, there is no need for calculus yet, and all that enters into these calculations is algebra and trigonometry.

Example

Example 11.1: Seesaw

Let us start with an example where the answer seems clear right away. But this will help us practice our concepts and methods and convince us that they will lead to the right answer. The seesaw is a playground toy, which consists of a pivot and a bar, of mass M, that is placed over it so that its ends can move up or down freely as shown in Figure 11.5.

If you place a an object of m_1 on one end at a distance r_1 from the center axle, as shown in Figure 11.5, then obviously that end goes down, simply because of the force and torque that the object exerts on it.

Question 1:

Where do you have to place an object of mass m_2 (for now assumed to be of equal mass to m_1) to get the see saw to be balanced, so that the bar is horizontal and neither end touches the ground?

Answer 1:

Let us first construct a free-body drawing of the bar and the masses located on it. It only needs to show the forces and have them located at the points where they act on the bar.

The force that m_1 exerts on the bar is simply $m_1 g$, acting downward as shown in Figure 11.5. The same is true for the force from m_2 acting on the bar. In addition, because the bar also has a mass M of its own, it will experience a gravitational force Mg. We draw the force arrow at its proper location, the center of gravity of the bar, right in the middle of the bar. The final force that is acting on the bar is the normal force N from the bar's support structure. It is acting exactly at the axle of the seesaw (marked with an orange dot).

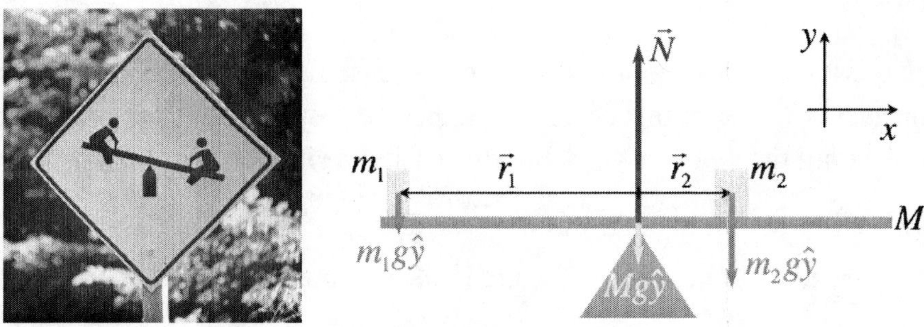

Figure 11.5: Forces and moment arms for a playground seesaw.

Our equilibrium force condition equation for the y-components of the forces is therefore:

$$\begin{aligned} F_{net,y} &= \sum_i F_{i,y} = -m_1 g - m_2 g - Mg + N = 0 \\ &\Rightarrow N = g(m_1 + m_2 + M) \end{aligned} \tag{11.7}$$

The signs in front of the individual force components indicate that they act upward (positive) or downward (negative). As in previous examples, this equation fixes the value of the normal force.

Because all forces only act in the y-direction, it is not necessary to construct equations for the net force components in x- or z-directions.

What remains then is the equation for the net torque. The selection of the proper pivot point is important, if we want to make our computations simple. For the see saw, the "natural" selection is the point where the bar is attached to its support structure, the axle, marked with a black dot in the center of the bar in our drawing. Because the normal force, N, and the weight force of the bar, Mg, act exactly through this point, their moment arms have length 0. Thus these two forces do not contribute to the torque equation for this particular selection of the pivot point. What remains are the forces $F_1 = m_1 g$ and $F_2 = m_2 g$. The force F_1 generates a counter-clockwise torque, and F_2 a clock-wise one. So our torque equation then reads:

$$\begin{aligned} \tau_{\text{net}} &= \sum_i \tau_{\text{clockwise},i} - \sum_j \tau_{\text{counter-clockwise},j} \\ &= m_2 g r_2 \sin 90° - m_1 g r_1 \sin 90° = 0 \\ &\Rightarrow m_2 r_2 = m_1 r_1 \\ &\Rightarrow r_2 = r_1 \frac{m_1}{m_2} \end{aligned} \tag{11.8}$$

Example

Example

In the first line of this set of equations we explicitly wrote down the factors of $\sin 90°$, to remind ourselves that the angle between force and moment arm enters for the calculation of the torques.

Because the question was where to put m_2 for the case that the two masses were the same, the answer is $r_2 = r_1$ in this case. This expected result shows that our systematic way of approaching the solution works in this easily verifiable case.

Question 2:
How big does m_2 need to be, if $r_1 = 3r_2$, i.e. if m_2 is 3 times closer to the pivot point than m_1?

Answer 2:
We can use the same free-body diagram as before. And we arrive at the same general equation relation between the masses and distances that we just derived. Solving it for m_2 we obtain:

$$\begin{aligned} m_2 r_2 &= m_1 r_1 \\ \Rightarrow m_2 &= m_1 \frac{r_1}{r_2} \end{aligned} \tag{11.9}$$

Using now $r_1 = 3r_2$, we obtain:

$$m_2 = m_1 \frac{r_1}{r_2} = m_1 \frac{3r_2}{r_2} = 3m_1 \tag{11.10}$$

So our solution for this case is that the mass m_2 has to be three times bigger than m_1 for the establishment of static equilibrium.

Self-test opportunity:
If you do not pick the pivot point at the center of the seesaw, but for example at the center of mass of the mass 2, can you derive the same result as (11.10)?

The following example expands on our statement that the center of mass has to be supported from directly below as a minimum condition for static equilibrium, shows an application of the formulas to compute the center of gravity that we introduced in chapter 8, and at the same time it has a very surprising outcome.

Example 11.2: Stacking blocks

Question:
Consider a collection of identical blocks on a table. How far can we push out the leading edge of the top block without the pile of blocks falling off the table?

Example

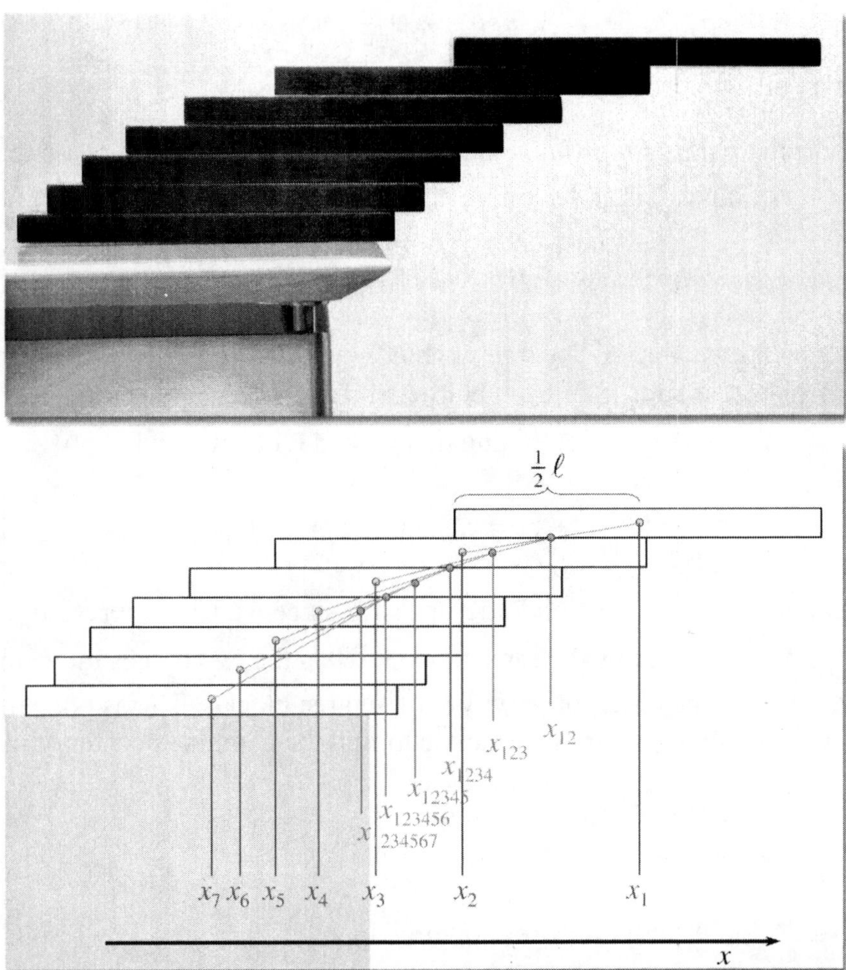

Figure 11.6: Stack of seven identical blocks piled on a table. Top: Photograph – please note that the left edge of the top block is to the right of the right edge of the support table. Bottom: Location of the positions of the centers of gravity of the individual blocks (x_1 through x_7) and location of the combined centers of gravity of the topmost blocks (x_{12} through $x_{1234567}$).

Answer:
Let us start with one block. If the block has a length ℓ and uniform mass density, then its center of gravity will be located at $\frac{1}{2}\ell$. Clearly, it can stay at rest as long as it is at least halfway on the table, with its center of gravity supported by the table from below. The leading edge of the block can then stick out just an infinitesimal amount less than $\frac{1}{2}\ell$ outside the support, and it will remain at rest.

Next, we consider two identical blocks. If we call the x-coordinate of the center of gravity of the upper block x_1 and that of the lower block x_2, we obtain for the x-coordinate of the center of gravity of the combined system, according to section 1 in chapter 8

$$x_{12} = \frac{x_1 m_1 + x_2 m_2}{m_1 + m_2} = \tfrac{1}{2}(x_1 + x_2), \tag{11.11}$$

because for identical blocks $m_1 = m_2$. Since $x_1 = x_2 + \frac{1}{2}\ell$ in the limiting case that the center of gravity of block 1 is still supported from below by block 2, we obtain then

$$x_{12} = \tfrac{1}{2}(x_1 + x_2) = \tfrac{1}{2}((\tfrac{1}{2}\ell + x_2) + x_2) = x_2 + \tfrac{1}{4}\ell. \tag{11.12}$$

Now we can go to three blocks. The top two blocks will not topple, if the combined center of gravity, x_{12}, is supported from below. Shifting x_{12} to the very edge of block three, we obtain $x_{12} = x_3 + \frac{1}{2}\ell$. Combining this with (11.12), we find

$$x_{12} = x_2 + \tfrac{1}{4}\ell = x_3 + \tfrac{1}{2}\ell \Rightarrow x_2 = x_3 + \tfrac{1}{4}\ell. \tag{11.13}$$

Note the equation (11.12) is still valid after the shift since we have expressed x_{12} in terms of x_2, and x_{12} and x_2 change by the same amount when the two blocks move together. We can then calculate the center of gravity for the three blocks. This is done in the same way as before, by applying the same principle to find the combined center of mass again.

$$x_{123} = \frac{x_{12}(2m) + x_3 m}{2m + m} = \tfrac{2}{3}x_{12} + \tfrac{1}{3}x_3 = \tfrac{2}{3}(x_3 + \tfrac{1}{2}\ell) + \tfrac{1}{3}x_3 = x_3 + \tfrac{1}{3}\ell. \tag{11.14}$$

Requiring that the top three blocks are supported by block 4 from below results in $x_{123} = x_4 + \frac{1}{2}\ell$. Combined with the previous equation, this establishes:

$$x_{123} = x_3 + \tfrac{1}{3}\ell = x_4 + \tfrac{1}{2}\ell \Rightarrow x_3 = x_4 + \tfrac{1}{6}\ell. \tag{11.15}$$

You can now see how this series continues. If you have $n-1$ blocks supported in this way by the nth block, then the coordinates of the $n-1^{\text{st}}$ and n^{th} block are related as:

$$x_{n-1} = x_n + \frac{\ell}{2n-2}. \tag{11.16}$$

We can now add up all terms and find out how far x_1 can be away from the edge:

$$x_1 = x_2 + \tfrac{1}{2}\ell = x_3 + \tfrac{1}{4}\ell + \tfrac{1}{2}\ell = x_4 + \tfrac{1}{6}\ell + \tfrac{1}{4}\ell + \tfrac{1}{2}\ell = \ldots = x_{n+1} + \tfrac{1}{2}\ell\left(\sum_{i=1}^{n}\frac{1}{i}\right). \tag{11.17}$$

You may remember from calculus that the sum $\sum_{i=1}^{n} i^{-1}$ does not converge, i.e. does not have an upper limit for $n \to \infty$. This gives us the astonishing result that you can move x_1 *infinitely* far away from the edge, provided you have enough blocks, and provided that

Example

the edge of the table can support their weight without significant deformation! The upper part of Figure 11.6 shows a case for only 7 blocks stacked on a table, and already then we can see that the left edge of the top block is to the right of the right edge of the support table.

Let us do one more example that involves the center of mass of a composite extended object. This solved problem also serves to review the concept for calculation of the center of mass of extended objects, which we developed in chapter 8.

Solved Problem

Solved Problem 11.1: Sculpture

An alumnus of your university has donated a sculpture to be displayed in the atrium of your new physics building. It consists of a rectangular block of marble of dimensions $a \times b \times c = (0.71 \text{ m}) \times (0.71 \text{ m}) \times (2.74 \text{ m})$ and a cylinder of wood with length $\ell = 2.84$ m and diameter $d = 0.71$ m, which is attached to the marble so that its upper edge is a distance $e = 1.47$ m from the top of the marble block (see Figure 11.7).

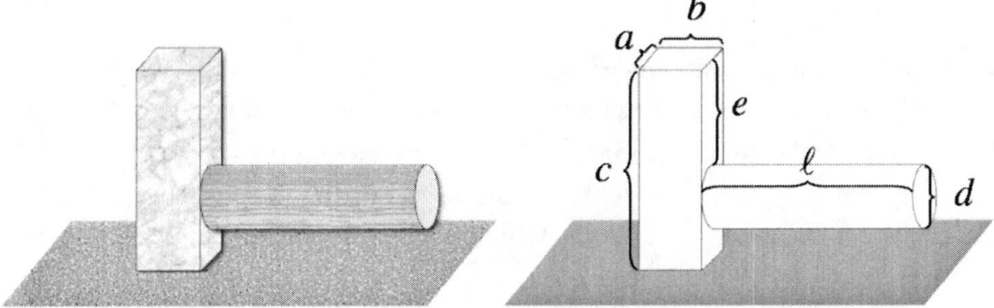

Figure 11.7: Sculpture.

Question:
Knowing that the mass density of the marble used is $2.85 \cdot 10^3$ kg/m^3 and that of the wood is $4.40 \cdot 10^2$ kg/m^3, can this sculpture stand upright on the floor of the building atrium, or does it need to be supported by additional bracing?

Answer:

THINK:

In chapter 4 we had learned that a stability condition for an object is that the center of mass of that object needs to be directly supported from below. In order to decide if this sculpture can stand upright as designed without additional support, we therefore need to determine the location of the center of mass of the sculpture and find out of it is located at a point inside the marble block. Since the block is supported from below by the floor, the sculpture will be able to stand upright if this is the case. If the center of mass of the sculpture is located outside the support base, then the sculpture will need additional bracing.

SKETCH:

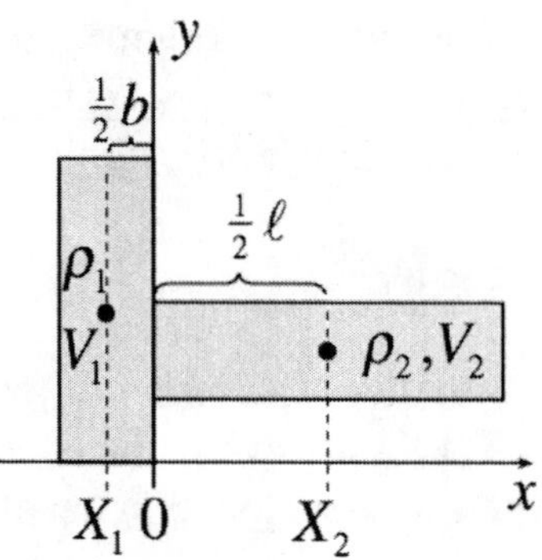

Figure 11.8: Sketch to calculate the center of mass of the sculpture.

We draw a side view of the sculpture (Figure 11.8), representing the marble block by rectangle 1 and the wood cylinder by rectangle 2. We also indicate a coordinate system with a horizontal x-axis and a vertical y-axis and choose the origin as the right edge of the marble column. (What about the z-coordinate? We can use symmetry arguments in the same way as was done in chapter 8 and find that the z-component of the center of mass is located in the center.)

Solved Problem

RESEARCH:

With this choice of the coordinate system, we also do not need to worry about calculating the y-coordinate of the center of mass of the sculpture. Our stability condition does not depend on how high the center of mass is off the ground. So the only task that is left is to calculate the x-component of the center of mass. According to our general principles to calculate the center of mass coordinates, which we developed in chapter 8, we can then write

$$X = \frac{1}{M}\int_V x\rho(\vec{r})dV$$

where the mass M is the mass of the sculpture and V is the entire volume of the sculpture. Note that in this case the density is not homogeneous, but depends in where in the sculpture the point $\vec{r}$ is located.

In order to perform the integration we can split the integration volume V into convenient parts: $V = V_1 + V_2$, where V_1 is the volume of the marble column and V_2 is the volume of the wood cylinder. Then the above integral becomes

$$\begin{aligned} X &= \frac{1}{M}\int_{V_1} x\rho(\vec{r})dV + \frac{1}{M}\int_{V_2} x\rho(\vec{r})dV \\ &= \frac{1}{M}\int_{V_1} x\rho_1 dV + \frac{1}{M}\int_{V_2} x\rho_2 dV \\ &= \frac{\rho_1}{M}\int_{V_1} xdV + \frac{\rho_2}{M}\int_{V_2} xdV \end{aligned}$$

SIMPLIFY:

If we want to calculate the location of the x-component of the center of mass of the marble block alone, we can also use the equations for constant density from chapter 8 and write

$$X_1 = \frac{1}{M_1}\int_{V_1} x\rho_1 dV = \frac{\rho_1}{M_1}\int_{V_1} xdV$$

(Since the density is constant over the entire volume, we were able to move it out of the integral.) In the same way we can write for the center of mass of the wood cylinder

$$X_2 = \frac{\rho_2}{M_2}\int_{V_2} xdV$$

Therefore the expression for the center of mass of the composite object, i.e. the entire sculpture becomes

$$\begin{aligned} X &= \frac{\rho_1}{M}\int_{V_1} xdV + \frac{\rho_2}{M}\int_{V_2} xdV \\ &= \frac{M_1}{M}\frac{\rho_1}{M_1}\int_{V_1} xdV + \frac{M_2}{M}\frac{\rho_2}{M_2}\int_{V_2} xdV \\ &= \frac{M_1}{M}X_1 + \frac{M_2}{M}X_2 \end{aligned}$$

This is a very important general result. It says that even for extended objects the combined center of mass of these objects can be calculated in the same way that we have introduced for point particles. Since the total mass of the sculpture is the combined mass of its two parts, $M = M_1 + M_2$, the above expression for the location of the combined center of mass becomes

$$X = \frac{M_1}{M_1 + M_2}X_1 + \frac{M_2}{M_1 + M_2}X_2 \qquad (11.18)$$

It is important to note that this relationship between the combined center of mass and the individual center of mass coordinates of composite objects is even true in the case of more than two objects. Further, it still holds in the case that the density inside a given object is not constant. Formally, (11.18) only relies on the fact that one can always split volume integrals into a set of integrals over disjoint sub-volumes that add up to the whole.

This step has simplified our complicated problem greatly, because the center of mass coordinates of the two individual objects can be calculated easily. Since the density inside each of them is constant, their center of mass locations are identical to their geometrical centers. One look at Figure 11.8 is enough to then convince us that $X_2 = \frac{1}{2}\ell$ and that

$X_1 = -\frac{1}{2}b$. (Remember, we have chosen the origin of our coordinate system as the right edge of the marble block!)

All that is left now is to calculate the masses of the two individual objects. Since we know their densities, we only need to figure out each object's volume, and then their masses are given by $M = \rho V$.

Since the marble block is rectangular, its volume is $V = a \cdot b \cdot c$, and so we get for M_1:

$$M_1 = \rho_1 \cdot a \cdot b \cdot c$$

The horizontal wood part is a cylinder; thus its mass is:

$$M_2 = \rho_2 \cdot \ell \cdot \pi d^2 / 4$$

Calculate:

Inserting the numbers given in the problem we obtain for the masses

$$M_1 = (2850 \text{ kg/m}^3) \cdot (0.71 \text{ m}) \cdot (0.71 \text{ m}) \cdot (2.74 \text{ m}) = 3942.26 \text{ kg}$$

$$M_2 = (731 \text{ kg/m}^3) \cdot (2.84 \text{ m}) \cdot \pi (0.71 \text{ m})^2 / 4 = 494.741 \text{ kg}$$

and thus for the combined mass

$$M = M_1 + M_2 = 3942.26 \text{ kg} + 494.741 \text{ kg} = 4437.001 \text{ kg}$$

Then the location of the x-component of the center of mass of the sculpture follows from (11.18):

$$X = \frac{3942.26 \text{ kg}}{4437.001 \text{ kg}}(-0.5 \cdot 0.71 \text{ m}) + \frac{494.741 \text{ kg}}{4437.001 \text{ kg}}(0.5 \cdot 2.84 \text{ m}) = -0.157082 \text{ m}$$

Round:

The densities were given to three significant digits, but the length dimensions were only given to two significant digits. Rounding to the least amount of significant digits then results in our final answer:

$$X = -0.16 \text{ m}$$

Since this number is negative, this means that the center of mass of the sculpture is located to the left of the right edge of the marble column. Thus it is located above the base of the marble column and supported from directly below. The sculpture is stable and can stand without additional bracing.

Double-Check:

If you look at Figure 11.7, it seems hardly possible that this sculpture would be able to stand up straight without tipping over. But our eyes can be deceiving, because they cannot properly determine the weight by multiplying the volume by the density. The ratio of the densities of the two materials used is $\rho_1 / \rho_2 = (2850 \text{ kg/m}^3)/(440 \text{ kg/m}^3) = 6.48$. So we would obtain the same location of the center of mass if we replaced the 2.84 m

Solved Problem

Solved Problem

long cylinder made of wood by a factor of $2.55 = \sqrt{6.48}$ thinner cylinder of the same length made of marble, with its central axis located at the same place at that of the wood column. The resulting object is shown in Figure 11.9. It has the same location of its center of mass as the sculpture in Figure 11.7. A visual examination of Figure 11.9 makes it much more convincing that the sculpture is able to stand in stable equilibrium without additional bracing.

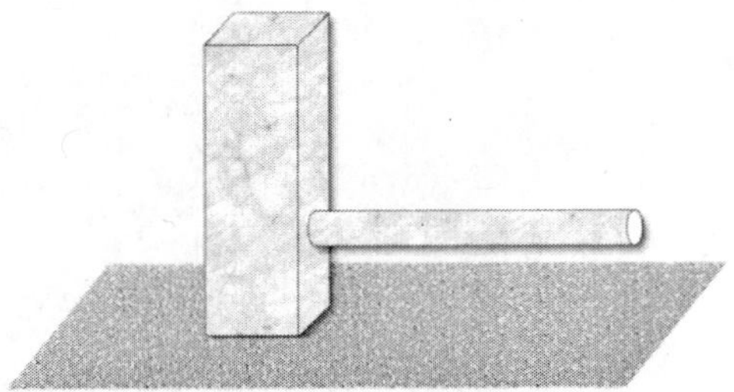

Figure 11.9: Equivalent sculpture made entirely of marble.

In-class exercise:
If you put a point mass at the very right end of the wood cylinder in our sculpture, how big can this mass be before the sculpture tips over?
a) 2.4 kg
b) 29.1 kg
c) 37.5 kg
d) 245 kg
e) 1210 kg

The following example makes use of the force of static friction. Static friction forces help to keep many arrangements of objects in equilibrium. Absent the force of static friction the following example would not result in equilibrium.

Example 11.3: Person standing on a Ladder
In a typical use of a ladder, it stands on a horizontal surface, the floor, and leans against a vertical surface, the wall. Let us consider the following scenario: A ladder of length $\ell = 3.04\text{ m}$, with mass $m_l = 13.3\text{ kg}$, rests against a smooth wall at an angle of $\theta = 24.8°$. A student, who has a mass of $m_m = 62.0\text{ kg}$, stands on the ladder as shown. The student is standing on a rung that is $r = 1.43\text{ m}$ along the ladder, as measured from where the ladder touches the ground.

Example

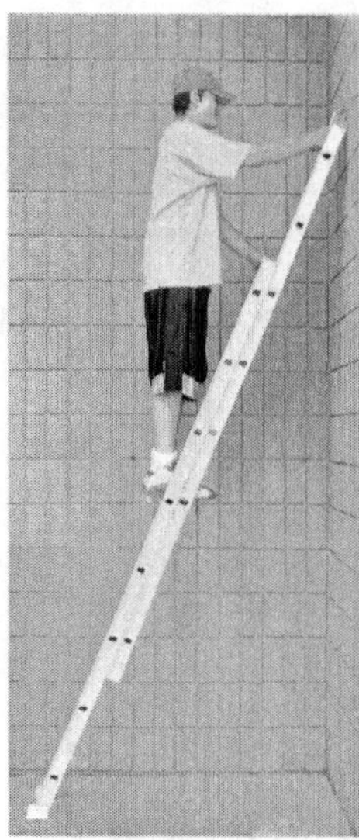

Figure 11.10: Person standing on a ladder.

Question 1:
What frictional force must act on the bottom of the ladder to keep it from slipping? You may neglect the (small) force of friction between the smooth wall and the ladder.

Answer 1:

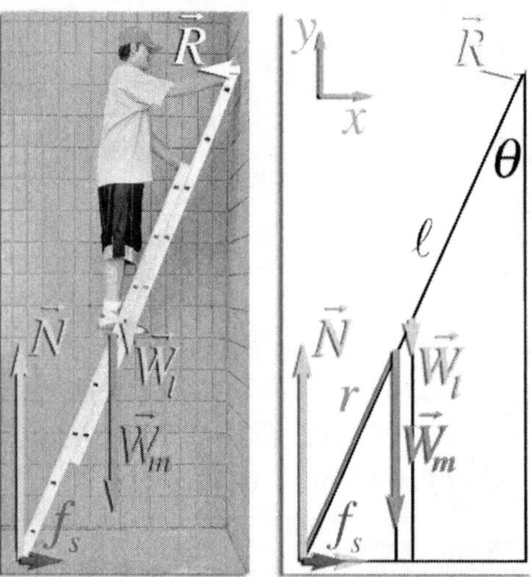

Figure 11.11: Left: picture with force vectors superimposed; right: free-body diagram of the ladder.

Let's start with the free body diagram shown in the right half of Figure 11.11. $\vec{R} = -R \cdot \hat{x}$ is the normal force exerted by the wall on the ladder. $\vec{N} = N \cdot \hat{y}$ is the normal force from the floor, and $\vec{W}_m = -m_m g \cdot \hat{y}$ and $\vec{W}_l = -m_l g \cdot \hat{y}$ are the weights of the student and the ladder. $m_m g = (62.0 \text{ kg})(9.81 \text{ m/s}^2) = 608. \text{ N}$ and $m_l g = (13.3 \text{ kg})(9.81 \text{ m/s}^2) = 130. \text{ N}$.

$\vec{f}_s = f_s \hat{x}$ is the force of static friction that the floor exerts of on the ladder, the answer to this problem. Note the direction of that force vector, in positive x-direction. This situation arises because if the ladder slips, its bottom will slide in negative x-direction, and the friction force must necessarily oppose that motion. As instructed, we are going to neglect the force of friction between wall and ladder.

In this example, the ladder and the student are in translational and rotational equilibrium; so we can write down the three equilibrium conditions introduced earlier in this chapter:

$$\sum_i F_{x,i} = 0; \ \sum_i F_{y,i} = 0; \ \sum_i \tau_i = 0 \tag{11.19}$$

Let us start with the equation for the force components in horizontal direction:

$$\sum_i F_{x,i} = f_s - R = 0 \Rightarrow R = f_s \tag{11.20}$$

From this we only learn that the force that the wall exerts on the ladder and the friction force between ladder and wall have exactly the same magnitude.

$$\sum_i F_{y,i} = N - m_m g - m_l g = 0 \Rightarrow N = g(m_m + m_l) \tag{11.21}$$

The normal force that the floor exerts on the ladder is exactly equal in magnitude to the sum of the weight of ladder and man, $N = 608 \text{ N} + 130 \text{ N} = 738 \text{ N}$. (Again, we were instructed to neglect the friction force between wall and ladder, which would otherwise have come in here.)

Now we perform the sum of the torques, assuming the pivot point is at the point where the ladder touches the ground. This assumption has the advantage that we do not need to know the forces acting at that point, because their moment arm will be zero.

$$\sum_i \tau_i = (m_l g)(\ell/2)\sin\theta + (m_m g) r \sin\theta - R\ell\cos\theta = 0 \tag{11.22}$$

Please note that the torque from the wall's normal force acts counter-clockwise, whereas the two torques from the weight of the student and the ladder act clockwise. Also, the angle between the normal force $\vec{R}$ and its moment arm $\vec{\ell}$ is $90° - \theta$, and $\sin(90° - \theta) = \cos\theta$. Now we solve this for R, using the information we already obtained:

$$R = \frac{\frac{1}{2}(m_l g)\ell\sin\theta + (m_m g) r \sin\theta}{\ell\cos\theta} = \left(\tfrac{1}{2} m_l g + m_m g \frac{r}{\ell}\right)\tan\theta \tag{11.23}$$

Numerically, this works out to:

$$R = \left(\tfrac{1}{2}(130 \text{ N}) + (608 \text{ N})\frac{1.43 \text{ m}}{3.04 \text{ m}}\right)\tan 24.8° = 162. \text{ N}$$

But remember that we had already found that $f_s = R$, and so we get as our answer to this

Example

Example

problem: $f_s = 162.\text{ N}$.

Question 2:
Suppose that the coefficient of static friction between ladder and floor is 0.31. Will the ladder slip?

Answer 2:
Remember that the normal force was calculated earlier $N = g(m_m + m_l) = 738.\text{ N}$, and it is related to the maximum static friction force via $f_{s,\max} = \mu_s N$. Then the maximum static fraction force is 229 N, well above the 162 N that we just found for static equilibrium. Thus the ladder will not slip. We have indicated the maximum force of static friction in the free body diagram in Figure 11.11 by the semitransparent gray arrow. Since it is longer than the arrow for the actual force of static friction, the ladder does not slip.

In general, the ladder will not slip as long as the reaction force is smaller than the maximum force of static friction, leading to the condition

$$R = \left(\tfrac{1}{2} m_l + m_m \frac{r}{\ell} \right) \tan\theta \le \mu_s (m_l + m_m) \qquad (11.24)$$

Question 3:
What happens as the student climbs higher?

Answer 3:
From equation (11.24) you see that the reaction force R grows bigger with increasing r. Eventually, this force will overcome the maximum force of static friction, and the ladder will slip. We now understand why it is not a good idea to climb too high on the ladder in this situation.

Question 4:
What can the student do, if he really still needs to get up a little bit higher?

Answer 4:
The student can reduce the angle θ between ladder and wall. Examining equation (11.24) again, we see that the tangent then decreases, thus reducing the normal force from the wall and with it the friction force needed to stay in equilibrium. (However, if he makes the angle too steep and happens to lean back, the ladder might fall over backwards with him.)

11.3. Stability

If you are building a skyscraper or a bridge, it is not enough to design it so that it is standing freely. Instead, we also need to worry about the ability of the structure to remain standing under the influence of external forces, for example due to winds blowing against the structure from different directions. Neglecting to properly take into account the force of wind led to the famous collapse of the Tacoma Narrows Bridge in the State of Washington on November 7, 1940. The strong wind did not directly blow the bridge over, but excited a resonance, which destroyed it. We will discuss this in more detail in chapter 14. But for now this bridge collapse and other architectural disasters simply serve to remind us that stability of structures is of paramount concern.

Figure 11.12: Collapse of the midsection of the Tacoma Narrows Bridge on November 7, 1940. (credit: University of Washington Libraries, Special Collections, UW 21422)

Let us try to quantify the concept of stability by looking at the example shown in Figure 11.13. Here a box is show resting on a horizontal surface in static equilibrium. Our experience tells us that the box remains in the same position, if we use our finger to push with a small force in the way shown in Figure 11.13. The small force we exert with our finger on the box is exactly balanced by the force of friction between the box and the supporting surface. The net force is zero, and there is no motion.

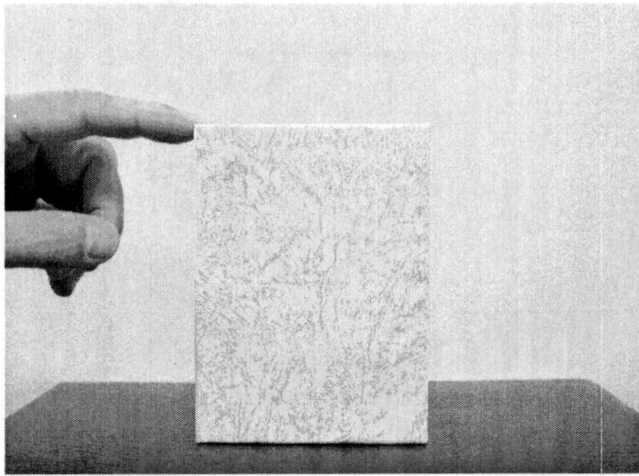

Figure 11.13: Pushing with a small force against the upper edge of a box.

If we now steadily increase the magnitude of the force, there are two possible outcomes. Either the friction force is not sufficient to counter-balance the force exerted by the finger, and the box begins to slide to the right, or the box starts to tilt in the way shown in

Figure 11.14. So the static equilibrium of the box is stable with respect to small perturbations by external forces, but a sufficiently large external force destroys the equilibrium. This simple example shows the characteristic of stability. Engineers need to be able to calculate the maximum external forces and torques that still allow for stability of structures.

Figure 11.14: Exerting a larger force on the box results in tilting it.

Quantitative Stability Condition

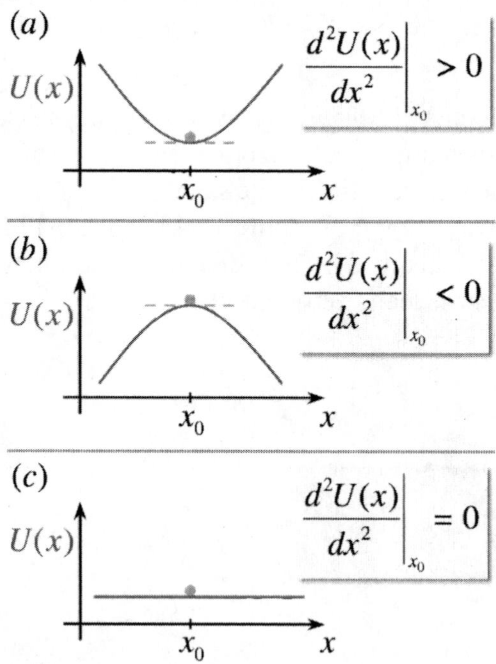

Figure 11.15: Local shape of the potential energy function at an equilibrium point. (*a*) stable equilibrium; (*b*) unstable equilibrium; (*c*) indifferent equilibrium.

In order to be able to quantify when an equilibrium situation is stable or not, we return to the connection between potential energy and force, for which we found in chapter 6

$$\vec{F}(\vec{r}) = -\vec{\nabla}U(\vec{r}) \tag{11.25}$$

or, in one dimension

$$F_x(x) = -\frac{dU(x)}{dx} \tag{11.26}$$

If we demand a vanishing net force as one of our equilibrium conditions, we can also state that same equilibrium condition as $\vec{\nabla}U(\vec{r}) = 0$ or in one dimension $dU(x)/dx = 0$ at a given point in space. So far the condition of vanishing first derivative adds no new insight. However, if we examine the second derivative of the potential energy, then we can distinguish three different cases, depending on the sign of the second derivative.

Case 1: Stable Equilibrium

$$\text{Stable equilibrium: } \left.\frac{d^2U(x)}{dx^2}\right|_{x=x_0} > 0 \tag{11.27}$$

If the second derivate of the potential energy with respect to the coordinate is positive, then the potential energy has a local minimum, and the sytem is in *stable* equilibrium. In this case a small deviation from the equilibrium position creates a restoring force that drives the system back to the equilibrium point. This situation is illustrated in part (*a*) of Figure 11.15. If you move the red dot away form its equilibrium position at x_0 in either positive or negative direction and release it, it will return to its equilibrium position.

Case 2: Unstable Equilibrium

$$\text{Unstable equilibrium: } \left.\frac{d^2U(x)}{dx^2}\right|_{x=x_0} < 0 \tag{11.28}$$

If the second derivative of the potential energy with respect to the coordinate is negative, then the potential energy has a local maximum, and the system is in *unstable* equilibrium. In this case a small deviation from the equilibrium position creates a force that drives the system away from the equilibrium point. This situation is illustrated in part (*b*) of Figure 11.15. If you move the red dot even only every so slightly away form its equilibrium position at x_0 in either positive or negative direction and release it, it will run away from its equilibrium position.

Case 3: Indifferent Equilibrium

$$\text{Indifferent equilibrium: } \left.\frac{d^2U(x)}{dx^2}\right|_{x=x_0} = 0 \tag{11.29}$$

There is, of course, also the case where the sign of the second derivative of the potential energy function with respect to the coordinate is neither positive nor negative. This case is called an *indifferent* equilibrium, also called *neutral* or *marginally stable*. This situation is illustrated in part (*c*) of Figure 11.15. If the system is displaced by a small amount, then it will neither return to nor run away form its old equilibrium position. Instead it will simply stay in the new position, which is also an equilibrium position.

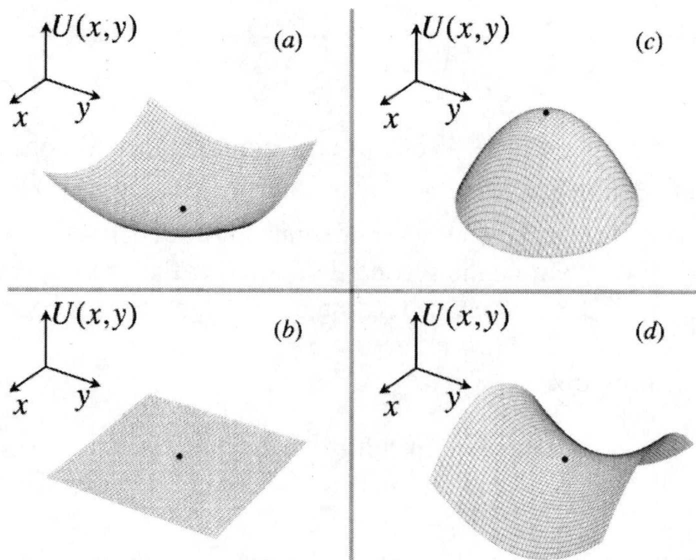

Figure 11.16: Different types of equilibrium in for two-dimensional potential surfaces.

Multidimensional Surfaces, Saddle Points

The three cases above constitute all possible cases in one-dimensional systems. They are easily generalized to two-and three-dimensional potential energy functions that depend on more than one coordinate. Instead of looking at only the derivative with respect to one coordinate, as done in (11.27), (11.28), and (11.29), we now have to examine all partial derivatives. For the two-dimensional potential energy surface $U(x,y)$ the equilibrium condition is

$$\left.\frac{\partial U(x,y)}{\partial x}\right|_{(x_0,y_0)} = \left.\frac{\partial U(x,y)}{\partial y}\right|_{(x_0,y_0)} = 0 \tag{11.30}$$

In addition stable equilibrium requires

$$\left.\frac{\partial^2 U(x,y)}{\partial x^2}\right|_{(x_0,y_0)} > 0 \text{ and } \left.\frac{\partial^2 U(x,y)}{\partial y^2}\right|_{(x_0,y_0)} > 0, \tag{11.31}$$

unstable equilibrium implies

$$\left.\frac{\partial^2 U(x,y)}{\partial x^2}\right|_{(x_0,y_0)} < 0 \text{ and } \left.\frac{\partial^2 U(x,y)}{\partial y^2}\right|_{(x_0,y_0)} < 0, \tag{11.32}$$

and indifferent equilibrium means

$$\left.\frac{\partial^2 U(x,y)}{\partial x^2}\right|_{(x_0,y_0)} = \left.\frac{\partial^2 U(x,y)}{\partial y^2}\right|_{(x_0,y_0)} = 0. \tag{11.33}$$

Figure 11.16 shows in part (*a*) – (*c*) the three cases that we have just discussed. However in more than one spatial dimension there is also the possibility that the partial derivative in one spatial direction is positive, whereas in another it is negative. These points are called *saddle* points, because the potential energy function is locally shaped like a saddle. In Figure 11.16 (*d*) we show such a saddle point, where one of the second partial derivatives is negatives and one is positive, in this case

$$\left.\frac{\partial^2 U(x,y)}{\partial x^2}\right|_{(x_0,y_0)} < 0 \text{ and } \left.\frac{\partial^2 U(x,y)}{\partial y^2}\right|_{(x_0,y_0)} < 0 . \tag{11.34}$$

So the equilibrium at this saddle point is stable with respect to small displacements in the y-direction, but unstable with respect to small displacements in the x-direction.

In-class exercise:
In Figure 11.16, which of the panels contains additional equilibrium points, in addition to the central one marked with the black dot?
a)
b)
c)
d)

Note: in the strict mathematical sense the conditions for the second derivative above are sufficient for the existence of maxima and minima, but not necessary. There are also cases for which the first derivative of the potential energy function is not continuous, but for which extrema can still exists, as the following example shows.

Example 11.4: Pushing a box
Question 1:
What is the force that is force that is required to hold the box that we showed in Figure 11.13 and Figure 11.14 in equilibrium at a given tilt angle?

Answer 1:
Before we push on it, the box is resting on a level surface. The only two forces acting on it are the force of gravity and a balancing normal force. There is no net force and no net torque; the box is in equilibrium. (see upper part of Figure 11.17).

Once the finger starts pushing in horizontal direction on the upper edge of the box and start tilting the box, the normal force vector acts on the contact point, as shown in the lower part of Figure 11.17. In addition, the force of static friction acts on the same point, but in horizontal direction. Since the box does not slip, the friction force vector has exactly the same magnitude, but acts in opposite direction to the external force vector due to the action of the finger.

Example

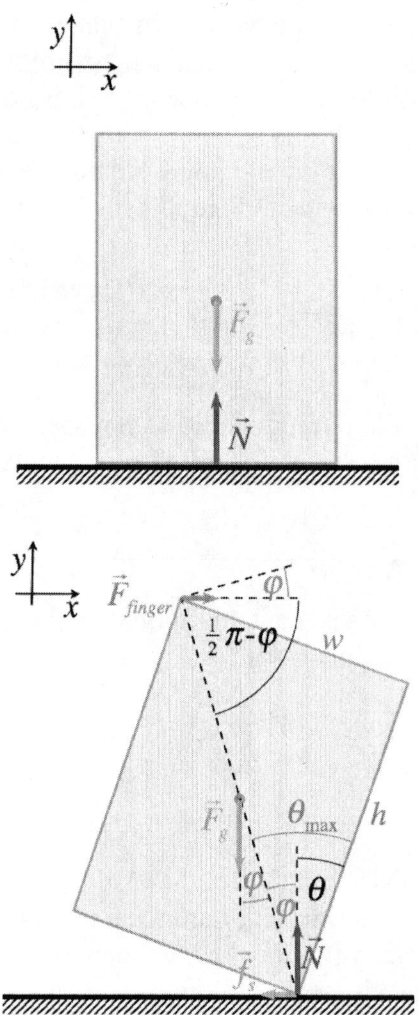

Figure 11.17: Free-body diagram for the box resting on the level surface (upper part) and being tilted by the finger pushing in horizontal direction (lower part).

We can now calculate the torques of these forces and find the conditions for equilibrium, i.e. how much force it takes for the finger to hold the box at an angle θ with respect to the vertical, as indicated in Figure 11.17. In the same figure we also indicate the angle θ_{max}, which is a geometric property of the box and can be calculated from the ratio of the width w and height h of the box as $\theta_{max} = \tan^{-1}(w/h)$. Of crucial importance in this problem is the angle φ, which is the difference between these two angles (see Figure 11.17), $\varphi = \theta_{max} - \theta$. This angle φ decreases with increasing angle θ until $\theta = \theta_{max} \Rightarrow \varphi = 0$, upon which the box falls over into the horizontal position.

Using (11.6) we can calculate the net torque. The natural pivot point in the present case is the contact point between box and support surface. The friction force and the normal force then have moment arms of zero length and thus do not contribute to the torque. The only clockwise torque is due to the force from the finger, and the only counter-clockwise torque results from the force of gravity. The length of the moment arm for the force from the finger is (see Figure 11.17) $\ell = \sqrt{h^2 + w^2}$, and the length of the moment arm for the force of gravity is half of this value, $\ell / 2$. This means that our torque equation becomes

$$(F_g)(\tfrac{1}{2}\ell)\sin\varphi - (F_{finger})(\ell)\sin(\tfrac{1}{2}\pi - \varphi) = 0 . \tag{11.35}$$

We can use $\sin(\tfrac{1}{2}\pi - \varphi) = \cos\varphi$, and $F_g = mg$, and then solve (11.35) for the force of the finger needed to keep the box at equilibrium at a given angle

$$F_{finger}(\theta) = \tfrac{1}{2} mg \tan(\tan^{-1}(w/h) - \theta) \tag{11.36}$$

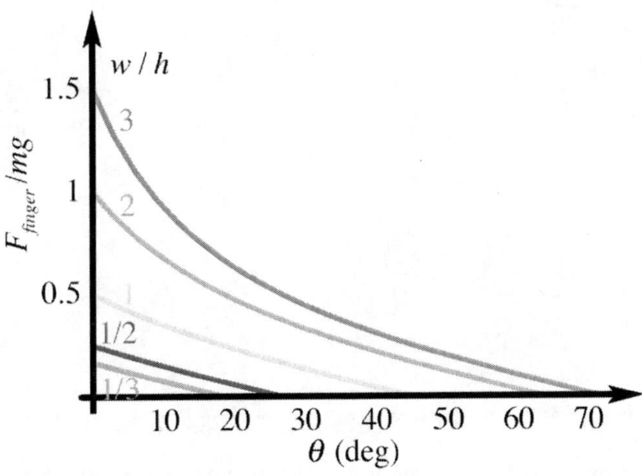

Figure 11.18: Ratio of the force of the finger divided by the weight of the box that is needed to hold the box in equilibrium as a function of the angle, shown for different representative values of the ratio of the width to the height of the box.

In Figure 11.18 we plot the force of the finger needed to hold the box at equilibrium at a given angle in this situation. For the plot we take the ratio of the force of the finger divided by the weight of the box, and we show the result of (11.36) for different ratios of width to height of the box. We only show the curves for values of the angle θ between 0 and $\theta_{\max}$, which is the point where the force form the finger required is 0, and where the box tips over.

Question 2:
Sketch the potential energy function for this box!

Answer 2:
The answer to this question is much more straightforward than the first part of this example. The potential energy is the gravitational potential energy, $U = mgy$, where y is the vertical coordinate of the center of mass of the box. In Figure 11.19 we show (red curve) the location of the center of mass of the box for different tipping angles. It traces out a segment of a circle with center at the lower right corner. The dashed red line shows the same, but now for angles $\theta > \theta_{\max}$, for which the box tips over into the horizontal position without the finger exerting a force on it. One can clearly see that this potential

Example

energy function has a maximum at the point where the box stands on edge and its center of mass is exactly above the contact point with the surface. We also draw the same curve for the location of the center of mass when tilting the box to the left. Now we can see that the potential energy function has a minimum at the point where the box rest flat on the table.

Note: at this equilibrium point the first derivative does not exist in the mathematical sense, but it is apparent from the drawing that the function still has a minimum, which is sufficient for stable equilibrium.

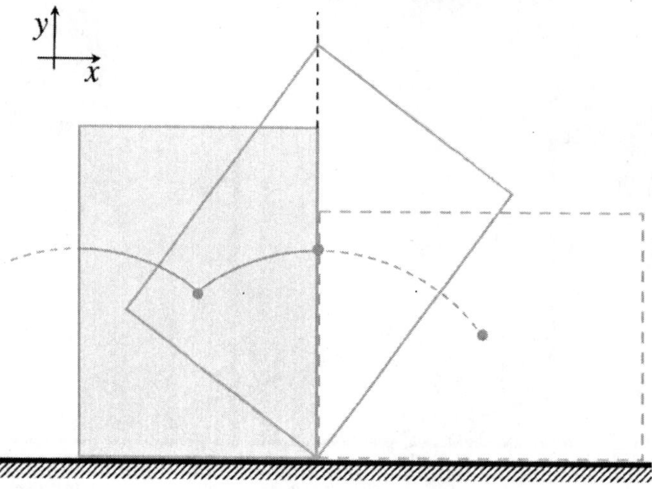

Figure 11.19: Location of the center of mass of the box as a function of tipping angle.

Self-test opportunity:
What is the minimum value of the coefficient of static friction that is needed to push over a box in the manner shown in the preceding example, if the ratio of the width to the height of the box is 0.4?

What we have learned:

- Static equilibrium is defined as mechanical equilibrium for the special case that the object in equilibrium is at rest.
- An object (or a collection of objects) can only be in static equilibrium, if the net external force is zero and the net external torque is zero:

$$F_{net,x} = \sum_{i=1}^{n} F_{i,x} = F_{1,x} + F_{2,x} + ... + F_{n,x} = 0$$

$$F_{net,y} = \sum_{i=1}^{n} F_{i,y} = F_{1,y} + F_{2,y} + ... + F_{n,y} = 0$$

$$F_{net,z} = \sum_{i=1}^{n} F_{i,z} = F_{1,z} + F_{2,z} + ... + F_{n,z} = 0$$

$$\tau_{\text{net}} = \sum_i \tau_{\text{counter-clockwise},i} - \sum_j \tau_{\text{clockwise},j} = 0$$

- The condition for force equilibrium can also be expressed as $\vec{\nabla} U(\vec{r})\big|_{\vec{r}_0} = 0$, that is to say that the first derivative of the potential energy function with respect to the coordinate is zero at the equilibrium point.
- The condition for stable equilibrium is that the potential energy function has a minimum at that point. A sufficient condition for stability is that the second derivative of the potential function with respect to the coordinate at the equilibrium point is positive.
- The condition for unstable equilibrium is that the potential energy function has a maximum at that point. A sufficient condition for instability is that the second derivative of the potential function with respect to the coordinate at the equilibrium point is negative.
- If the second derivative of the potential function with respect to the coordinate is zero at the equilibrium point, then we call this type of equilibrium indifferent or marginal.

Additional Solved Problems

Solved Problem

Solved Problem 11.2: Storefront Sign

It is not uncommon for businesses to hang signs over the sidewalk that are suspended from their front wall. To do this, one can use a post that is attached to the wall by a hinge and held horizontal by a cable that is also attached to the wall. The sign is then suspended from the post. Here the mass of the sign is $M = 33.1$ kg, and the mass of the post is $m = 19.7$ kg. The length of the post is $l = 2.40$ m, and the sign is attached to the post as shown at a distance of $r = 1.95$ m. The cable is attached to the wall a distance $d = 1.14$ m above the post.

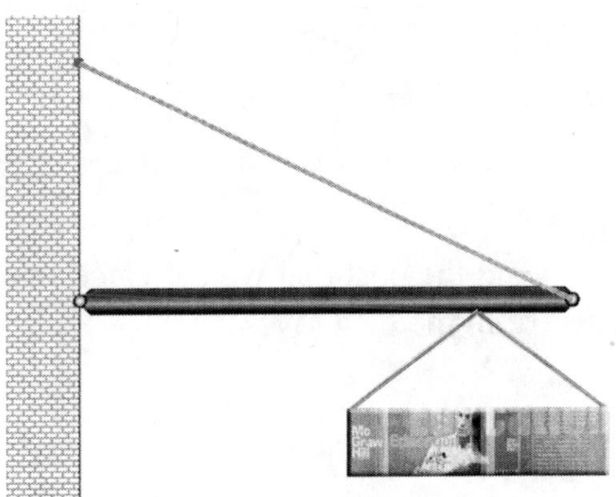

Figure 11.20: Hanging storefront sign.

Question:

What is the tension in the cable holding the post? What is the magnitude and direction of the force, $\vec{F}$, that the wall exerts on the post?

Answer:

THINK:

This question addresses the problem of equilibrium, moment arms and torques. Equilibrium means vanishing net external force and torque. In order to figure out the torques, we have to pick a pivot point. It seems natural to pick the point where the hinge attaches the post to the wall. Because we use a hinge, the post can rotate about this point. Picking this point also has the advantage that we do not need to pay attention to the force that the wall exerts on the post, because it will act at the contact point, the hinge, and thus have a vanishing moment arm and consequently no contribution to the torque.

SKETCH:

To start our calculation of the net torque, we first draw arrows representing all of the forces acting on the post. We already know that the weight force of the sign acts at the point where the sign is suspended from the post (red arrow). The gravitational force acting on the post can be represented by the blue force arrow, which attached to the center of gravity of the post. Finally, we know that the string tension, $\vec{T}$, is acting along the direction of the cable (yellow arrow).

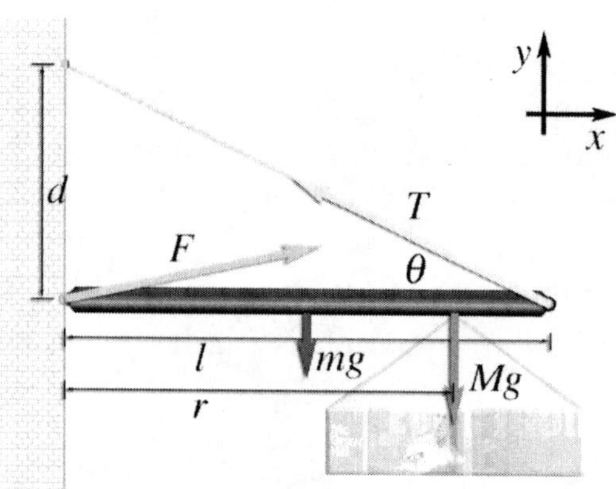

Figure 11.21: Free-body diagram for the post.

RESEARCH:

The angle θ between the cable and the post that we indicated in the free-body diagram Figure 11.21 can be calculated from the data given:

$$\theta = \arctan\left(\frac{d}{l}\right) \tag{11.37}$$

The equation for the torques about the point where the post touches the wall is then:

$$mg\frac{l}{2}\sin 90° + Mgr\sin 90° - Tl\sin\theta = 0 \tag{11.38}$$

Solved Problem

We have also drawn in Figure 11.21 an arrow for the force that the wall exerts on the post (green arrow), but the direction and magnitude of this force vector still is to be determined in the second part of our answer. Equation (11.38) cannot be used to find this force, because we have used the point where this force attaches as our pivot point, and thus the corresponding moment arm has length zero.

One the other hand, once we have found the tension in the cable, we have already determined all other forces in the problem, and we know from our static equilibrium conditions that the net force has to be 0 in this problem. Then we can write this condition down for the horizontal and vertical force components separately.

In the horizontal direction, we only have two force components, those of the string tension and of the force from the wall:

$$F_x - T\cos\theta = 0 \Rightarrow F_x = T\cos\theta \qquad (11.39)$$

In the vertical direction, we have the weight of the beam and sign in addition to the vertical components of the string tension and force from the wall:

$$F_y + T\sin\theta - mg - Mg = 0 \Rightarrow F_y = (m+M)g - T\sin\theta \qquad (11.40)$$

Simplify:

We solve equation (11.38) for the tension and get our answer:

$$T = \frac{(ml + 2Mr)g}{2l\sin\theta} \qquad (11.41)$$

For the magnitude of the force that the wall exerts on the post we find

$$F = \sqrt{F_x^2 + F_y^2}$$

and the direction of this force is given by

$$\theta_F = \arctan(F_y / F_x)$$

Calculate:

Inserting the numbers given in the problem, we find for the angle

$$\theta = \arctan(1.14 \text{ m}/2.40 \text{ m}) = 25.4°$$

and thus for the tension in the cable we then obtain from (11.41):

$$T = \frac{((19.7 \text{ kg})\cdot(2.40 \text{ m}) + 2\cdot(33.1 \text{ kg})\cdot(1.95 \text{ m}))\cdot(9.81 \text{ m/s}^2)}{2\cdot(2.40 \text{ m})\cdot\sin 25.4°} = 840.351 \text{ N}$$

Solved Problem

For the components of the force that the wall exerts on the post we find numerically

$$F_x = (840.351 \text{ N})\cos 25.4° = 759.119 \text{ N}$$

$$F_y = (19.7 \text{ kg}+33.1 \text{ kg})(9.81 \text{ m/s}^2) - (840.351 \text{ N})\sin 25.4° = 157.512 \text{ N}$$

and therefore its magnitude and direction are given by

$$F = \sqrt{(157.512 \text{ N})^2 + (759.119 \text{ N})^2} = 775.288 \text{ N}$$

$$\theta_F = \arctan(759.119 / 157.512) = 11.7°$$

ROUND:

All of our input quantities were specified to three significant digits, and so we round our final answers to three digits as well, obtaining $T = 840.$ N and $F = 775.$ N.

DOUBLE-CHECK:

The two forces that we calculated have rather large magnitudes, considering that the combined weight of the post and attached sign is only $F_g = (m + M)g = (19.7 \text{ kg} + 33.1 \text{ kg})(9.81 \text{ m/s}^2) = 518 \text{ N}$. So the sum of the magnitudes of the forces from the cable on the post, T, and from the wall on the post, F, is more than a factor of 3 larger than the combined weight of the post and the sign. Can we understand this? Yes, because the two force vectors $\vec{T}$ and $\vec{F}$ have rather large horizontal components that have to cancel each other. And when we calculate the magnitudes of these forces their horizontal components also enter. As the angle θ between the cable and the post approaches 0, the horizontal components of the two vectors $\vec{T}$ and $\vec{F}$ become larger and larger. Thus we see that selecting a distance d in Figure 11.21 that is too small compared to the length of the post results in huge tension in the cable and thus a very stressed suspension system.

Chapter 12. Gravitation

Figure 12.1: The Earth as observed from the surface of our moon. Earth and moon orbit around each other and are kept together by their gravitational interaction.

What we will learn:

- The gravitational attraction between two point masses is proportional to the product of their masses and inversely proportional to the square of their distance apart.
- The gravitational force on an object inside a homogeneous solid sphere, like a planet, rises linearly with the distance that the object is from the center of the solid sphere.

- Close to the surface of the Earth, it is a very good approximation to use a constant value of the gravitational acceleration ($= g$). We will see how we can recover our previous value of g for the free-fall case from the more general gravitational force law.
- We will also find a more general form of the gravitational potential energy, which is inversely proportional to the distance between two objects.
- From the gravitational potential energy we will derive the escape speed, which is the minimum speed with which we need to shoot off a projectile so that it will escape to infinity from the gravitational pull.
- We will investigate Kepler's three laws of planetary motion around the Sun, which state that planets move on elliptical orbits with the Sun at one focal point, that the radius vector connecting the Sun and a planet sweeps out equal areas in equal times, and that the square of the orbit's period for any planet is proportional to the cube of its semi-major axis.
- We will find that the kinetic, potential, and total mechanical energy of satellites in orbit have a fixed relationship with each other, and we will calculate the radius of geostationary orbits.
- Finally, we will examine the evidence for dark matter and dark energy in the universe.

12.1. Newton's Law of Gravity

Up to now we have introduced the gravitational force only in the form of a constant gravitational acceleration with the value $g = 9.81 \text{ m/s}^2$, multiplied by the mass of the object. However, because we have seen the videos of astronauts running and jumping on the moon, we all know that gravity is different on the moon. (See Figure 12.2.) So the approximation of a constant gravitational force that only depends on the mass of object that gravity acts on cannot be correct, if we move away from the surface of the Earth.

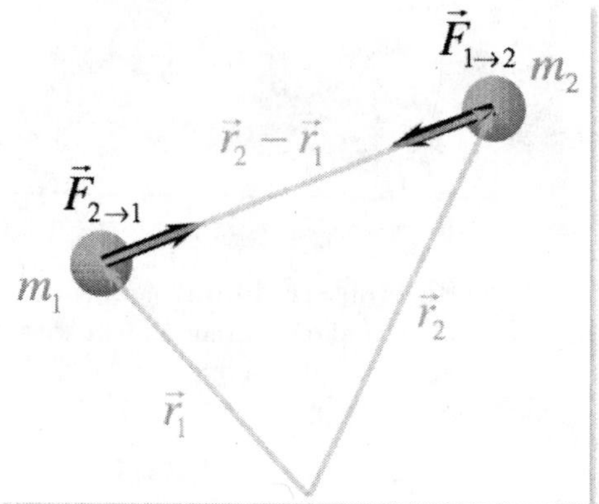

Figure 12.2: Nomenclature used for the gravitational interaction of two massive objects.

The general expression for the magnitude of the attraction interaction between two point masses m_1 and m_2 at a distance $r = |\vec{r}_2 - \vec{r}_1|$ away from each other, as in Figure 12.2, is:

$$F(r) = G\frac{m_1 m_2}{r^2}. \tag{12.1}$$

This relationship is an empirical law, deduced from experiments, and has been verified extensively. The proportionality constant G is called the universal gravitational constant and has the value:

$$G = 6.674 \cdot 10^{-11} \text{ m}^3\text{kg}^{-1}\text{s}^{-2}. \tag{12.2}$$

Equation (12.1) tells us that the strength of the gravitational interaction is proportional to each of the two masses involved in the interaction, and that it is inversely proportional to the square of the distance between them. For example, doubling one of the masses will double the strength of the interaction, doubling the distance will reduce the interaction strength by a factor of four.

Because the force is a vector, we need to address the question of the direction of the force. The gravitational force $\vec{F}_{2\to1}$ acting from object 2 on object 1 always points towards object 2. We can write this concept in the form of an equation,

$$\vec{F}_{2\to1} = -F(r)\frac{\vec{r}_1 - \vec{r}_2}{\left|\vec{r}_1 - \vec{r}_2\right|}.$$

Combining this result with equation (12.1) results in

$$\vec{F}_{2\to1} = -G\frac{m_1 m_2}{\left|\vec{r}_1 - \vec{r}_2\right|^3}\left(\vec{r}_1 - \vec{r}_2\right). \tag{12.3}$$

This equation represents the general form of the gravitational force acting on object 1 due to object 2. It is strictly valid for the case of point particles, as well as for the case of extended spherically symmetric objects, in which case the position vector is the position of the center of mass coordinate. We can also use it as a very good approximation for non-spherical extended objects, representing them by their center-of-mass coordinate. Note that the center of gravity is identical to the center of mass for spherically symmetric objects that are small compared to the relative distance between the objects.

In chapter 4 we introduced Newton's Third Law. It states that the force $\vec{F}_{1\to2}$ acting on object 2 from object 1 has to be of the same magnitude and reverse direction as the force $\vec{F}_{2\to1}$ exerted on object 1 by object 2.

$$\vec{F}_{1\to2} = -\vec{F}_{2\to1} \tag{12.4}$$

One can see that the force of equation (12.3) fulfills the requirement of Newton's Third Law. This check is performed by exchanging the indices "1" and "2" in equation (12.3) and observing that then the magnitude of the force remains the same, but the sign changes. Equation (12.3) is the basis for the motion of the planets in our solar system around the Sun just as it is the foundation for the description of objects in free-fall on the surface of the Earth.

Superposition of Gravitational Forces

If more than one other object has a gravitational interaction with object 1, then it is straightforward to generalize the gravitational force by using the superposition principle. This superposition principle states that the vector sum of all gravitational forces on a specific object simply add up to form the total force on that object. So we find the total gravitational force acting on object one by adding the contributions from all other objects:

$$\vec{F}_1 = \vec{F}_{2\to1} + \vec{F}_{3\to1} + \ldots = \sum_{i=2}^{n} \vec{F}_{i\to1} \qquad (12.5)$$

The individual forces $\vec{F}_{i1}$ can be found from equation (12.3):

$$\vec{F}_{i\to1} = -G\frac{m_i m_1}{\left|\vec{r}_1 - \vec{r}_i\right|^3}\left(\vec{r}_1 - \vec{r}_i\right)$$

Conversely, the total gravitational force on any one of the n objects in mutual gravitational interaction can be written as

$$\vec{F}_j = \sum_{i=1,i\neq j}^{n} \vec{F}_{i\to j} = G\sum_{i=1,i\neq j}^{n} \frac{m_i m_j}{\left|\vec{r}_i - \vec{r}_j\right|^3}\left(\vec{r}_i - \vec{r}_j\right) \qquad (12.6)$$

The notation $i \neq j$ in the summation is meant to indicate that the sum is taken over all n objects, except for the object's interaction with itself. While the superposition of forces is straightforward, the solution of the resulting equations of motion can become complicated. Even in a system of three approximately equal masses that interact with each other, some initial conditions can lead to regular trajectories, whereas others lead to chaotic motion. The numerical investigation of this system started to become possible with the advent of computers. But during the last twenty years, this field has developed into one of the most interesting in all of physics, and many more results are likely to emerge.

Derivation 12.1: Gravitational Force from a Sphere

Above we have stated that we can treat the gravitational interaction of an extended spherically symmetric object as that of a point particle with the same mass located at the center of the extended sphere. We can prove this statement with the aid of calculus and some elementary geometry.

To start our proof we treat a sphere as a collection of concentric very thin spherical shells. If we can prove that a thin spherical shell has the same gravitational interaction as a point particle located at its center, then we can use the above superposition principle to show that we can do the same for a solid sphere.

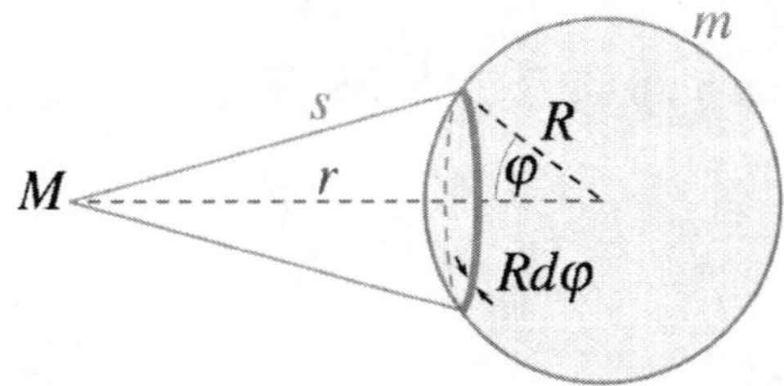

Figure 12.3: Gravitational force from a hollow sphere.

In Figure 12.3 we show a point particle of mass M located outside a spherical shell of mass m. We want to calculate the value of the x-component of the force on the mass M due to a ring of angular width $d\varphi$. This ring has a radius of $a = R\sin\varphi$ and thus circumference of $2\pi R\sin\varphi$. It has a width of $Rd\varphi$, as shown, and thus a total area of $2\pi R^2 \sin\varphi d\varphi$. Since the mass m is homogeneously distributed over the spherical shell of area $4\pi R^2$, the differential mass of the ring is

$$dm = m\frac{dA}{A} = m\frac{2\pi R^2 \sin\varphi d\varphi}{4\pi R^2} = \tfrac{1}{2} m \sin\varphi d\varphi$$

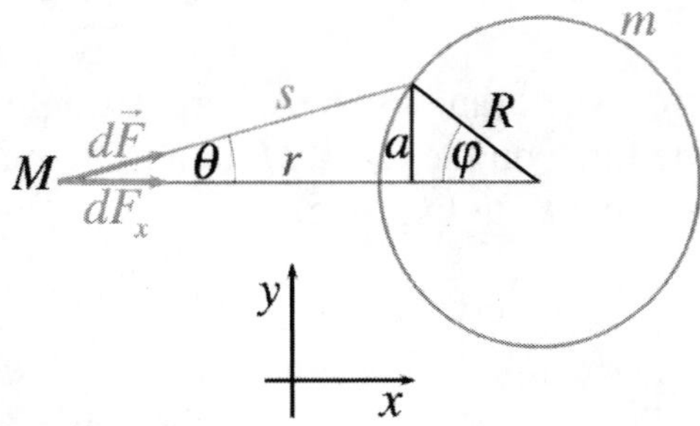

Figure 12.4: Cut through the center of the shell of the previous figure.

Since the ring is arranged symmetric around the horizontal axis, there is no net force in vertical direction from the ring acting on the mass M. The horizontal force component is (see Figure 12.4)

$$dF_x = \cos\theta \; G\frac{Mdm}{s^2} = \cos\theta \; G\frac{Mm\sin\varphi d\varphi}{2s^2}$$

Now we can relate $\cos\theta$ to s, r, and R via the law of cosines.

Derivation

Derivation

$$\cos\theta = \frac{s^2 + r^2 - R^2}{2sr},$$

and in the same way:

$$\cos\varphi = \frac{R^2 + r^2 - s^2}{2Rr}.$$

If we take the differential on both sides of this relation, we obtain

$$-\sin\varphi d\varphi = -\frac{s}{Rr}ds$$

Inserting the expression for $\sin\varphi d\varphi$ and $\cos\theta$ into our above expression of the differential force component we find

$$\begin{aligned} dF_x &= \frac{s^2 + r^2 - R^2}{2sr} G\frac{Mm}{2s^2}\frac{s}{Rr}ds \\ &= G\frac{Mm}{r^2}\frac{s^2 + r^2 - R^2}{4s^2R} \end{aligned}$$

Now we can integrate over ds from the minimum value of $s = r - R$ to the maximum value of $s = r + R$ and obtain:

$$F_x = \int_{r-R}^{r+R} G\frac{Mm}{r^2}\frac{(s^2 + r^2 - R^2)}{4s^2R}ds = G\frac{Mm}{r^2}\underbrace{\int_{r-R}^{r+R}\frac{s^2 + r^2 - R^2}{4s^2R}ds}_{=1} = G\frac{Mm}{r^2}$$

Thus we find that the spherical shell (and by the superposition principle therefore also a solid sphere) exerts the same force on the mass M as a point mass located at the center of the sphere, which is what we set out to prove.

Self-Test Opportunity: The derivation above assumes that $r > R$, which implies that the mass M is located outside the spherical shell. What changes if $r < R$?

The Solar System

We all know that the solar system consists of the Sun, which contains the overwhelming majority of all mass in the solar system, the four Earth-like inner planets (Mercury, Venus, Earth, and Mars), the Asteroid Belt between the orbits of Mars and Jupiter, the four gas giants (Jupiter, Saturn, Uranus, and Neptune), Pluto, and finally the Kuiper Belt. Figure 12.5 shows all of the planets at their respective orbits and with their relative sizes. The horizontal scale is in units of Astronomical Units [AU], 1 AU = 149.6 million km, the radius of Earth's orbit around the Sun. Table 12.1 shows the data for all planets.

Figure 12.5: Solar system. The tips of the blue arrows mark the radii of the planets' orbits on the horizontal scale. On this scale the sizes of the planets themselves are too small to be seen on this page. The small yellow dot at the origin of the axis marks the Sun, but is drawn a factor of 30 bigger than what the Sun would appear if it were drawn to scale. The pictures of the planets (all courtesy of NASA) and the Sun (lower part of the figure) are all magnified by a factor of 30,000 relative to the scale displayed.

Not listed as a planet is Pluto, and this deserves a bit of an explanation. The planet Neptune was discovered in 1846. This discovery was predicted because of observed small irregularities in the orbit of Uranus that hinted that another planet's gravitational interaction with Uranus was the cause. After careful observations of the Neptune orbit, more irregularities were found, which pointed towards the existence of yet another planet, and Pluto (mass $1.3 \cdot 10^{22}$ kg) was found in 1930. Since then all children were taught that our solar system has nine planets. However, in 2003 Sedna (mass $\sim 5 \cdot 10^{21}$ kg) and Eris (mass $\sim 3 \cdot 10^{22}$ kg) were discovered in the Kuiper Belt, which is the name for the asteroid-like objects that orbit the Sun between 30 and 48 AU. When the moon Dysnomia of Eris was discovered in 2006 and allowed astronomers to calculate that Eris is heavier than Pluto, then the discussion of what a planet is started again. The choice was to either give Sedna, Eris, the dwarf-planet Ceres in the Asteroid Belt (which was actually classified as a planet from 1801 to ~1850), and many other Pluto-like objects in the Kuiper Belt the status of a planet, or to reclassify Pluto as a dwarf-planet. In August 2006 the International Astronomical Union thus decided to remove the planet status from Pluto.

Table 12.1: Data for all planets in our solar system.

Planet	**Radius (km)**	**Mass (10^{24}kg)**	g **(m/s^2)**	**Escape v (km/s)**	***a*-orbit (10^6 km)**	**Eccent.**	***T*-orbit (years)**
Mercury	2,440	0.330	3.7	4.3	57.9	0.205	0.241
Venus	6,050	4.87	8.9	10.4	108.2	0.007	0.615
Earth	6,370	5.97	9.8	11.2	149.6	0.017	1
Mars	3,400	0.642	3.7	5.0	227.9	0.094	1.88
Jupiter	71,500	1,890	23.1	59.5	778.6	0.049	11.9
Saturn	60,300	568	9.0	35.5	1433	0.057	29.4
Uranus	25,600	86.8	8.7	21.3	2872	0.046	83.8
Neptune	24,800	102	11.0	23.5	4495	0.009	164
Sun	696,000	1,990,000	274	618	-	-	-

As the story of Pluto shows, the solar system still holds many mysteries and the potential for many discoveries. Take for example the Asteroid Belt. Almost 400,000 asteroids are currently known, and an average of 5,000 additional ones are discovered each month. The total mass of all asteroids in the Asteroid Belt is less than 5% of the mass of the Earth's moon. But more than 200 of these asteroids are of a diameter of more than 100 km! Finding and tracking them is very important, considering the damage that they could cause when they hit Earth. Another example of currently ongoing research is the investigation of the objects in the Kuiper Belt. Some models postulate that the combined mass of all Kuiper Belt objects is up to thirty times the mass of Earth, but the observed combined mass is perhaps a factor of 100 smaller than this value.

Example

Example 12.1: Influence of other Planets

Astronomy is the science of the stars, galaxies, and the universe as a whole. But the similarly named astrology has no scientific basis whatsoever. It may be fun to read the daily horoscope, but constellations of stars and/or alignments of planets have no influence on our lives. The only way that the other planets can interact with us is through the gravitational force. In this example we will calculate how big the gravitational force is.

Question:

If Mars (Figure 12.6) and Earth are at their minimum distance, they are $r_M = 5.6 \cdot 10^{10}$ m apart. The mass of Mars is $M_M = 6.4 \cdot 10^{23}$ kg. How far away from you does a truck of mass 16,000 kg have to be to have the same gravitation interaction with your body as Mars at closest approach?

Answer:

If the two gravitational forces are to be equal in magnitude, then we can write:

Example

$$G\frac{M_M m}{r_M^2} = G\frac{m_T m}{r_T^2},$$

where m is your mass, m_T is the mass of the truck, and r_T is the distance we want to solve for. Canceling out the mass and the universal gravitational constant, we then find:

$$r_T = r_M\sqrt{\frac{m_T}{M_M}}$$

Inserting the numerical values leads us to:

$$r_T = (5.6\cdot 10^{10}\text{ m})\sqrt{\frac{1.6\cdot 10^4\text{ kg}}{6.4\cdot 10^{23}\text{ kg}}} = 8.8\text{ m}$$

This result means that if you get closer to this truck than 8.8 m, it has a bigger gravitational pull on you than Mars at closest approach.

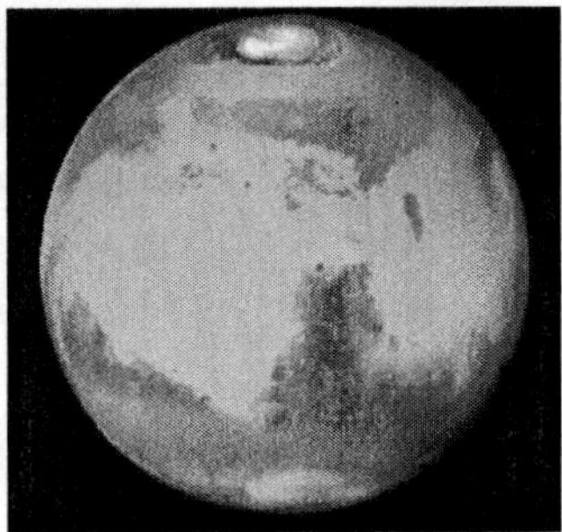

Figure 12.6: Hubble Space Telescope picture of Mars.

12.2. Gravitation Near the Surface of the Earth

Now that we have a general expression for the gravitational interaction between two objects, we can ask what gravitational force acts on an object near the surface of the Earth due to the Earth. To study this problem we can neglect the gravitational interaction of our object with any other objects, because the magnitude of the gravitational interaction with Earth is many orders of magnitudes larger, due to the very large mass of the Earth.

Because we can represent extended objects by point particles of the same mass located at the center of gravity, any object on the surface of the Earth is experiencing a gravitational force directed towards the center of the Earth. This direction is straight down anywhere on the surface of the Earth, completely in accordance with our empirical evidence.

More interesting is the determination of the magnitude of the gravitational force that our object experiences near the surface of the Earth. Inserting the mass of the Earth, M_E, for one object, and introducing the altitude h above the surface of the Earth as $h+R_E=r$, where R_E is the radius of the Earth, we find from equation (12.1) for this special case:

$$F=G\frac{M_E m}{(R_E+h)^2} \tag{12.7}$$

Because $R_E=6{,}370$ km, we can neglect the altitude, h, above ground for many applications. If we make this assumption, we find that $F=mg$, with

$$g=\frac{GM_E}{R_E^2}=\frac{\left(6.67\cdot10^{-11}\ \text{m}^3\text{kg}^{-1}\text{s}^{-2}\right)\left(5.97\cdot10^{24}\ \text{kg}\right)}{\left(6.37\cdot10^{6}\ \text{m}\right)^2}=9.81\ \text{m/s}^2 \tag{12.8}$$

As expected, near the surface of the Earth the gravitational acceleration can be approximated by the constant g that we had introduced in chapter 2 as the gravitational acceleration. So we see that equation (12.1) indeed contains as a special case the near-constant gravitational acceleration with magnitude $g=9.81\ \text{m/s}^2$ that we had previously introduced. Of course we can insert the mass and radius of other planets, moons, or stars into equation (12.8) and find the surface gravity of these objects as well (see Table 12.1). For example, one finds that the gravitational acceleration at the surface of the Sun is approximately 28 times higher than on the surface of the Earth.

If we need to find a result for altitudes where we cannot safely neglect h, we can expand equation (12.7) in powers of h/R_E and obtain to first order

$$g(h)=GM_E(R_E+h)^{-2}=\frac{GM_E}{R_E^2}\left(1+\frac{h}{R_E}\right)^{-2}=g\left(1+\frac{h}{R_E}\right)^{-2}=g\left(1-2\frac{h}{R_E}+\ldots\right) \tag{12.9}$$

This result implies that the gravitational acceleration falls off approximately linearly as a function of the altitude above ground. At the top of Mount Everest, the Earth's highest peak at an altitude of 8,850 meters, the gravitational acceleration is reduced by 0.27%, or less than 0.03 m/s^2. The international space station is at an altitude of 365 km, and there the gravitational acceleration is reduced by 11.4% down to a value of 8.7 m/s^2.

However, if we want to obtain a more precise determination of the gravitational acceleration, we also need to consider other effects. First, the Earth is not an exact sphere, but has a slightly larger radius at the equator than at the poles. (The value of 6,370 km that we use in Table 12.1 is the mean radius of Earth; it varies from 6,357 km polar radius to 6,378 km equatorial radius). Second, the density of the Earth is not uniform and for a precision determination of the gravitational acceleration, the density of the ground right below the measurement makes a difference. Perhaps most importantly, there is a systematic variation of the apparent gravitational acceleration as a function of polar angle ϑ due to the rotation of the Earth and the associated centripetal acceleration;

see Figure 12.7. From the chapter on circular motion, chapter 9, we know that the centripetal acceleration is given by $a_c = \omega^2 r$, where r is the radius of the circular motion. For the rotation of the Earth, this radius is the perpendicular distance to the rotation axis. At the poles this distance is 0, and we have no contribution from the centripetal acceleration. At the equator, $r = R_E$, and we obtain for a_c the maximum value of

$$a_{c,\max} = \omega^2 R_E = \left(7.29 \cdot 10^{-5}\ \text{Hz}\right)^2 (6{,}378\ \text{km}) = 0.034\ \text{m/s}^2$$

So we find that the reduction of the apparent gravitational acceleration at the equator due to the Earth's rotation is approximately equal to the reduction at the top of Mount Everest.

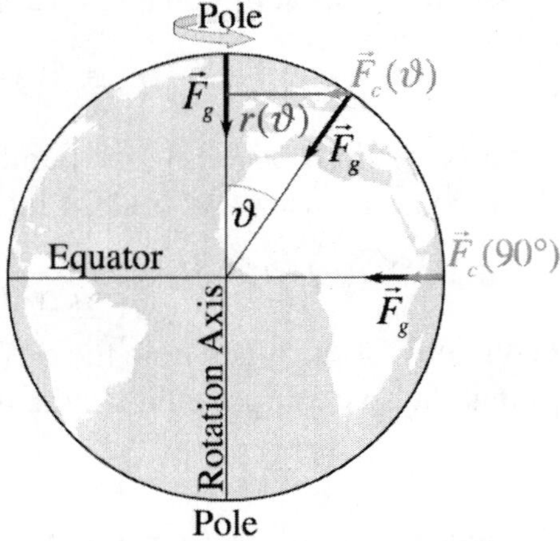

Figure 12.7: Illustration of the variation of the effective force of gravity due to the Earth's rotation. (The force arrows for the centripetal force are scaled up by a factor of 200 in length relative to the arrows representing the gravitational force.)

It is worth noting that the same considerations also hold for the gravitational acceleration near the surface of other planets, moons, and stars.

Self-Test Opportunity: What is the acceleration due to the Earth's gravity at a distance $d = 3R_E$ from the center of the Earth, where R_E is the radius of the Earth?

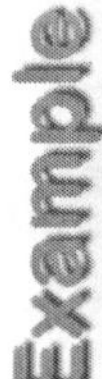

Example 12.2: Gravitational Tear from a Black Hole

A black hole is a very massive and extremely compact object, such that light emitted from its surface cannot escape. (Hence, from the outside, it appears black.) Suppose a black hole has a mass of $6.0 \cdot 10^{30}$ kg, three times the mass of our Sun.

Question:

If a spaceship of length 85 m approaches the black hole to a distance of 13,500 km, what is the difference in gravitational acceleration between the front and the back of the space ship?

0 R $R+h$

Figure 12.8: Coordinate system with the Black Hole at the origin.

Answer:

We can determine the gravitational acceleration at the front of the ship from the black hole via

$$g_{bh} = \frac{GM_{bh}}{R^2} = \frac{(6.67\cdot 10^{-11}\ \text{m}^3\text{kg}^{-1}\text{s}^{-2})(6.0\cdot 10^{30}\ \text{kg})}{(1.35\cdot 10^{7}\ \text{m})^2} = 2.2\cdot 10^{6}\ \text{m/s}^2 .$$

Now we can use the linear approximation of equation (12.9) and obtain

$$g_{bh}(h) - g_{bh}(0) = g_{bh}\left(1 - 2\frac{h}{R}\right) - g_{bh}(0) = -2g_{bh}\frac{h}{R}.$$

where h is the length of the space ship. Inserting the numbers, we find for the difference in the gravitational acceleration at the front and back of the ship:

$$g_{bh}(h) - g_{bh}(0) = -2\cdot(2.2\cdot 10^{6}\ \text{m/s}^2)\frac{85\ \text{m}}{1.35\cdot 10^{7}\ \text{m}} = -276\ \text{m/s}^2$$

So you can see that in the vicinity of the black hole the differential acceleration between front and back is so large that the spaceship would need a robust design to prevent being torn apart!

(Near a Black Hole Newtonian gravity needs to be modified. We will return to this point in chapter 35 on relativity. However, for this instructional example we have neglected this effect.)

Example

The difference in gravitational attraction between the side of the Earth closer to the Moon and the side further away from the Moon is the reason for the ocean tides. With the same techniques we have just used for Example 12.2 we can estimate the fractional difference between the attraction that the center of Earth experiences from the Moon and the water on the near/far side. It is $(1 \pm R_E / R)$, where $R = 3.84\cdot 10^{8}\,\text{m}$ is the distance between the centers of the Earth and Moon, and $R_E = 6.37\cdot 10^{6}\,\text{m}$ is the radius of Earth. (Since $R_E \ll R$ the approximation we derived above is applicable in this case as well.) So we find that the water in the "near side" experiences a 1.66% ($= R_E / R$) greater gravitational attraction from the Moon, and the far side a 1.66% smaller value. This causes water to pile up in the oceans in the direction to and in the direction away form the Moon, which is the physical reason for the tides. (see Figure 12.9)

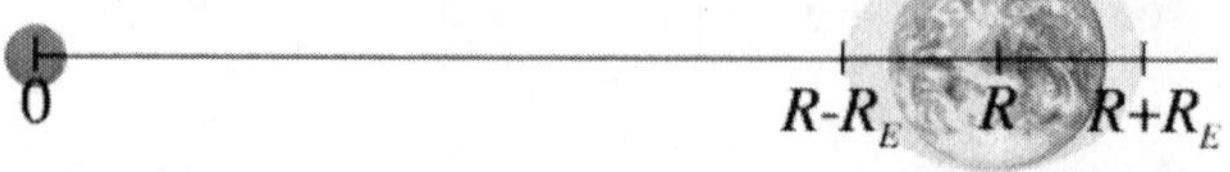

Figure 12.9: Physical reason for the ocean tides. (The tide amplitude is vastly exaggerated for this illustration).

12.3. Gravitation Inside Earth

We have already stated that one can represent the gravitational interaction of a mass m with a spherically symmetric mass distribution (where m is located outside the sphere) by replacing the sphere with a point particle with the same total mass, located at its center of mass (or center of gravity). In addition, one can show that on the inside of a spherical shell of uniform density the net gravitational force is zero.

Derivation 12.2: Force of Gravity inside a Hollow Sphere

We want to show that the gravitational force acting on a point mass inside a homogeneous hollow spherical shell is zero everywhere inside this shell. In order to do so, we can use calculus and construct a mathematical law that is commonly called Gauss's Law. We will return to Gauss's Law when we discuss electrostatic interaction and the Coulomb force, which is a another force that falls of as $1/r^2$. Here, however, we want to show a geometrical argument that was already presented by Newton in his book "Principia" (Proposition LXX, Theorem XXX).

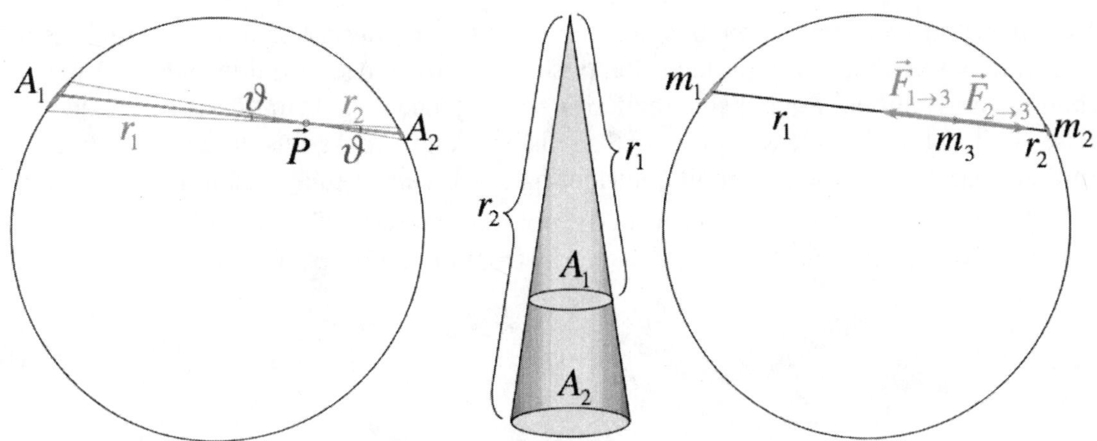

Figure 12.10: Gravitational interaction of a point with the surface of a hollow sphere.

Consider the (infinitesimally thin) spherical shell shown in Figure 12.10. We mark a point $\vec{P}$ at an arbitrary location inside the shell and then draw a straight line through this point. This straight line intersects with the shell in two points, and we call the distances between these two intersection points and $\vec{P}$ the radii r_1 and r_2. Now we draw circular cones with tips at $\vec{P}$ and with small opening angle ϑ around our line. The areas where the two cones intersect with the shell are called A_1 and A_2. These areas have the same "tilt" and are proportional to the angle ϑ, which is the same for both of them. Area A_1 is proportional to r_1^2, and area A_2 is proportional to r_2^2 (see middle part of Figure 12.10). Further, since the shell is homogeneous, the mass of any segment of the shell is proportional to its area. So we find that $m_1 = cr_1^2$ and $m_2 = cr_2^2$.

The gravitational force $\vec{F}_{1\to3}$ of the mass m_1 of area A_1 acting on the mass m_3 at point $\vec{P}$

then points along r_1 towards the center of A_1, and $\vec{F}_{2\to3}$ points exactly in the opposite direction. We can also calculate the magnitude of the two forces:

$$F_{1\to3} = Gm_1m_3 / r_1^2 = G(cr_1^2)m_3 / r_1^2 = Gcm_3$$
$$F_{2\to3} = Gm_2m_3 / r_2^2 = G(cr_2^2)m_3 / r_2^2 = Gcm_3$$

Since the dependence on the distance cancels out, we find the results that the magnitudes of the two forces are the same. Since the magnitudes are exactly the same, and since they point in opposite directions, the forces $\vec{F}_{1\to3}$ and $\vec{F}_{2\to3}$ cancel each other out exactly (see right part of Figure 12.10).

Since the line drawn was arbitrary, the same statement is true for any line and for any point inside the spherical shell. Hence the net force of gravity inside this spherical shell is indeed 0.

Derivation

We can use this concept to gain physical insight into the gravitational force acting inside the Earth by thinking of the Earth as composed of many concentric thin spherical shells. Then the gravitational force inside the Earth at a distance of r from the center is due to those shells with radius less than r. All shells with a greater radius do not contribute. Furthermore the mass $M(r)$ of all contributing shells can be imagined to be concentrated in the center, at a distance r away from the point of interest. The gravitational force acting on an object of mass m at a distance r from the center of the Earth is then

$$F(r) = G\frac{M(r)m}{r^2} \tag{12.10}$$

This equation is again equation (12.1) for Newtonian gravity, with a mass yet to be determined. In order to calculate the enclosed mass, we make the simplifying assumption of a constant density ρ_E inside Earth. Then we obtain:

$$M(r) = \rho_E V(r) = \rho_E \tfrac{4}{3}\pi r^3 \tag{12.11}$$

We can calculate the Earth's mass density from its total mass and radius:

$$\rho_E = \frac{M_E}{V_E} = \frac{M_E}{\frac{4}{3}\pi R_E^3} = \frac{\left(5.97\cdot 10^{24}\text{ kg}\right)}{\frac{4}{3}\pi\left(6.38\cdot 10^6\text{ m}\right)^3} = 5.5\cdot 10^3\text{ kg/m}^3 \tag{12.12}$$

Inserting the expression for the mass obtained from equation (12.11) back into equation(12.10), we then obtain the radial dependence of the gravitational force inside Earth as:

$$F(r) = G\frac{M(r)m}{r^2} = G\frac{\rho_E \frac{4}{3}\pi r^3 m}{r^2} = \tfrac{4}{3}\pi G\rho_E mr \tag{12.13}$$

This equation states that the magnitude of the gravitational force increases linearly with the distance from the center of the Earth. In particular, there is zero gravitational force acting on our test object, if this object is located exactly at the center of the Earth.

Now we can combine the radial dependence of the gravitational acceleration divided by g (acted on by just the force due to the Earth) inside and outside of the Earth. In Figure 12.11 we show the linear rise inside the Earth, as well as the inverse square law fall-off outside. At the surface of the Earth both curves intersect, and the gravitational acceleration has the value of g. Also shown is the linear approximation (12.9) to the dependence of the gravitational acceleration as a function of the height above the Earth's surface: $g(h) = g(1-2h/R_E+...) \Rightarrow g(r) = g(3-2r/R_E+...)$, because $r = h + R_E$. One can clearly see that this approximation is valid for altitude of a few hundred kilometers above the surface of the Earth.

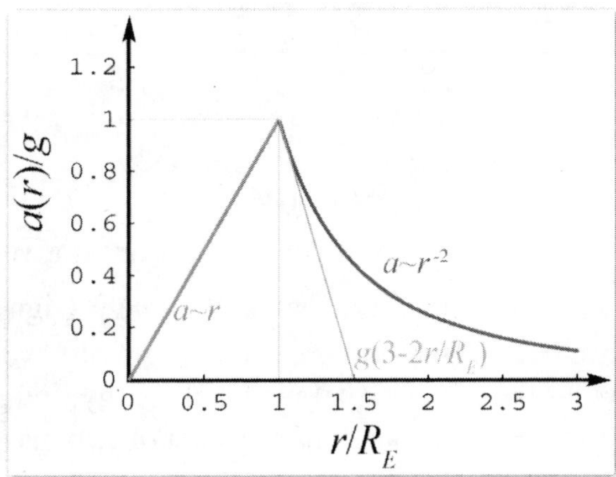

Figure 12.11: Dependence of the gravitational acceleration on the radial distance from the center of the Earth.

Note the functional form of the force in equation (12.13) is that of a spring force, with a linearly rising restoring force as a function of displacement from equilibrium at $r = 0$. In equation (12.13) we specify the magnitude of the force. Because the force always points towards the center of the Earth, we can also write the force as a one-dimensional vector equation as a function of x, the displacement from equilibrium. The result is:

$$F_x(x) = -\tfrac{4}{3}\pi G\rho_E mx = -\frac{mg}{R_E}x = -kx \tag{12.14}$$

This result is Hooke's Law for the spring, which we encountered in chapter 5. Therefore, we find that the "spring constant" of this force is

$$k = \tfrac{4}{3}\pi G \rho_E m = \frac{mg}{R_E} \tag{12.15}$$

Similar considerations also apply to the insides of other spherically symmetrical mass distributions such as planets or stars.

In-class exercise: The Moon can be considered a sphere with uniform density with mass M_M and radius R_M. At the center of the Moon, the gravitation force on a mass m due to the mass of the Moon is

a) mGM_M / R_M^2

b) $\frac{1}{2} mGM_M / R_M^2$

c) $\frac{3}{5} mGM_M / R_M^2$

d) 0

e) $2mGM_M / R_M^2$

12.4. Gravitational Potential Energy

In chapter 6 we found that the gravitational potential energy is given by $U = mgh$, provided we start with a gravitational force that is $\vec{F} = -mg\hat{y}$ (sign convention: + points straight up). Now that we have Newton's force law for gravity, we can determine the more general expression for the gravitational potential energy. Integrating (12.1), we obtain for the gravitational potential energy of a system of two masses m_1 and m_2 separated by a distance r:

$$\begin{aligned}\Delta U &= U(r) - U(\infty) \\ &= -\int_\infty^r \vec{F}(\vec{r}\,') \bullet d\vec{r}\,' = \int_\infty^r F(r')dr' = \int_\infty^r G\frac{m_1 m_2}{r'^2}dr' \\ &= Gm_1 m_2 \int_\infty^r \frac{1}{r'^2}dr' = -Gm_1 m_2 \left.\frac{1}{r'}\right|_\infty^r = -G\frac{m_1 m_2}{r}\end{aligned} \tag{12.16}$$

The first part of this equation is the general relation between a conservative force and potential energy. For the gravitational interaction the force is only dependent on the radial separation and points outward, $\vec{F}(\vec{r}) = \vec{F}(r)$. In our integration we are bringing the two masses together in the radial direction from an initial infinite separation to a final separation r. So our integration $d\vec{r}$ points opposite to the force $\vec{F}(\vec{r})$. Thus $\vec{F}(\vec{r}) \bullet d\vec{r} = -F(r)dr$.

Note that (12.16) only tells us the *difference* between the gravitational potential energy at separation r and at separation infinity. We choose $U(\infty)=0$, which implies that the gravitational potential energy vanishes between two objects that are separated by an infinite distance. This leaves us for the gravitational potential energy as a function of the separation of two masses the expression:

$$U(r) = -G\frac{m_1 m_2}{r} \tag{12.17}$$

The gravitational potential energy is then always less than 0. This result of a $1/r$-dependence of the gravitational potential energy is shown in red in Figure 12.12 for the case of the gravitational potential of an arbitrary mass near the surface of the Earth.

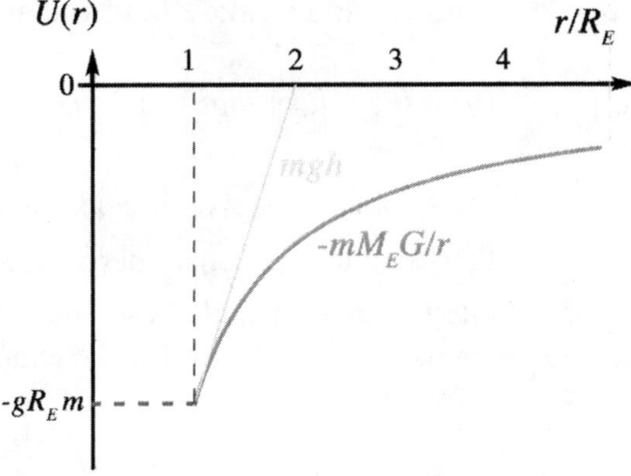

Figure 12.12: Dependence of the gravitational potential energy on the distance to the center of the Earth, for distances larger than the radius of the Earth. Red curve: exact expression; green line: previous linear approximation for values of r not much larger than the radius of the Earth, R_E.

In the case that we have more than two objects to consider, we can write down the pair-wise interaction between each two of them and integrate. The gravitational potential energies from these interactions simply add to give us the total gravitational potential energy. For three point particle we then find, for example:

$$U = U_{12} + U_{13} + U_{23} = -G\frac{m_1 m_2}{|\vec{r}_1 - \vec{r}_2|} - G\frac{m_1 m_3}{|\vec{r}_1 - \vec{r}_3|} - G\frac{m_2 m_3}{|\vec{r}_2 - \vec{r}_3|} \tag{12.18}$$

An important special case that we need to consider is when one of the two interacting partners is the Earth. For altitudes h that are small as compared to the radius of the Earth, we expect to recover our previous result. Because the Earth is many orders of magnitude more massive than any object on the surface of the Earth for which we want to calculate the gravitational potential energy, the combined center of mass of the Earth and this object is practically identical to the center of mass of the Earth, which we then select as the origin of our coordinate system. Using the result from (12.17), this results in:

$$U(h) = -G\frac{M_E m}{R_E + h} = -G\frac{M_E m}{R_E}\left(1+\frac{h}{R_E}\right)^{-1} \approx -\frac{GM_E m}{R_E} + \frac{GM_E m}{R_E^2}h = -gmR_E + mgh \Rightarrow$$

$$U(h) \approx -gmR_E + mgh \qquad (12.19)$$

In the second step of this equation, we have used the fact that $h \ll R_E$ and expanded. Our result (shown in green in Figure 12.12) almost looks like the expression $U = mgh$ that we are used to, except that the constant term $-gmR_E$ is added. This is a result of the choice of our integration constant in equation (12.17). However, as we already have stressed in chapter 6, one can always add any additive constant to the potential energy without a change in the physical results for the motion of objects. The only physically relevant quantity is the difference in potential energy between two different locations. Taking the difference between altitude h and altitude 0 results in:

$$\Delta U = U(h) - U(0) = (-gmR_E + mgh) - (-gmR_E) = mgh \qquad (12.20)$$

As advertised, the additive constant $-gmR_E$ cancels out, and we obtain the same result for low altitudes h, $\Delta U = mgh$, that we had previously derived. A final note: independent of the choice of the integration constant above, the important result is that ΔU increases if the separation increases. This is true for the exact result as well as the approximation close to the surface of earth.

Escape Speed

With our result for the gravitational potential energy, we can now write down the mechanical energy E for any object of mass m_1 and moving with speed v_1, having a gravitational interaction with another object of mass m_2 and speed v_2, if the two objects are separated by a distance $r = |\vec{r}_1 - \vec{r}_2|$. It is:

$$E = K + U = \tfrac{1}{2}m_1 v_1^2 + \tfrac{1}{2}m_1 v_2^2 - \frac{Gm_1 m_2}{|\vec{r}_1 - \vec{r}_2|} \qquad (12.21)$$

Of particular interest is the case where one of the objects is the Earth ($m_1 \equiv M_E$). If we move to the rest frame of the Earth ($v_1 = 0$), it has no kinetic energy in this frame. Again, we put the origin of our coordinate system at the center of the Earth. Then the expression for the total energy in this system is just the kinetic energy of object 2 (where we have now omitted the subscript 2 for its mass and speed), plus the gravitational potential energy

$$E = \tfrac{1}{2}mv^2 - \frac{GM_E m}{R_E + h}, \tag{12.22}$$

Here we have used the same notation as before, with h as the altitude of the object with mass m above sea level.

If we want to find out what speed it takes to fire a projectile so that it escapes to infinity, then we can use energy conservation. At infinite separation, the gravitational potential energy is 0, and the minimum kinetic energy is also 0; thus the total energy with which a projectile can barely escape to infinity from the Earth's gravitational pull is 0. Energy conservation then implies, starting from the surface:

$$E(h=0) = \tfrac{1}{2}mv_E^2 - \frac{GM_E m}{R_E} = 0$$

Solving this for v_E we obtain the minimum escape speed as:

$$v_E = \sqrt{\frac{2GM_E}{R_E}} \tag{12.23}$$

Inserting the numerical value of these constants, we finally obtain:

$$v_E = \sqrt{\frac{2\left(6.67\cdot10^{-11}\ \text{m}^3\text{kg}^{-1}\text{s}^{-2}\right)\left(5.97\cdot10^{24}\ \text{kg}\right)}{\left(6.37\cdot10^{6}\ \text{m}\right)}} = 11.2\ \text{km/s} \tag{12.24}$$

This escape speed is approximately equal to 25,000 mph. The same exercise can also be performed for other planets, moons, and stars by inserting the relevant constants (see Table 12.1).

In-class exercise: The escape speed from the surface of our Moon (mass $7.35\cdot10^{22}$ kg, diameter 3476 km) is

a) 2.38 km/s
b) 1.68 km/s
c) 11.2 km/s
d) 5.41 km/s

Note that the angle with which the projectile was shot off into space does not enter into the answer at all. Therefore, it does not matter if you shoot the projectile straight up or almost in horizontal direction. However, we have neglected air resistance, and so the launch angle would make a difference, if this effect were included. An even bigger effect results from the rotation of the Earth. Since the Earth rotates once around its own axis per day, a point on the surface of the Earth located at the equator has a speed of $v = 2\pi R_E / (1 \text{ day}) \approx 0.46$ km/s, decreasing to zero at the poles. The direction of the corresponding velocity vector points tangential to the Earth's surface, in the direction East. Therefore, the launch angle matters most at the equator, and for a projectile fired in the Eastern direction the escape speed then reduces to approximately 10.7 km/s.

Can a projectile that is launched from the surface of the Earth with a speed of 11.2 km/s escape the solar system? Does the gravitational potential energy of our projectile in its interaction with the Sun play a role? At first glance, it would appear not to be the case. After all, the force of the Sun on an object located near the surface of the Earth is negligible compared to the force the Earth exerts on that object. Proof: if we jump up in the air, we land at the same place, independent of what time of day it is, i.e. where the Sun is in the sky. So we can indeed neglect the Sun's force near the surface of the Earth.

However, it is a different story as far as the gravitational potential energy is concerned. In contrast to the force, which falls off as r^{-2}, the potential energy falls off much slower, proportional to r^{-1}. It is straightforward to generalize (12.23) for the escape from any planet or star with mass M, if one is initially separated a distance R from the center of that planet or star, resulting in

$$v = \sqrt{\frac{2GM}{R}}. \tag{12.25}$$

Inserting the mass of the Sun and the size of the orbit of the Earth we find

$$v_S = \sqrt{\frac{2\left(6.67\cdot10^{-11} \text{ m}^3\text{kg}^{-1}\text{s}^{-2}\right)\left(2.0\cdot10^{30} \text{ kg}\right)}{\left(1.49\cdot10^{11} \text{ m}\right)}} = 42 \text{ km/s} \tag{12.26}$$

where v_s is the speed needed for an object to escape from the sun if it is initially a distance from it equal to the radius of the Earth's orbit.

This is a quite astonishing result: the escape speed needed to take off from the orbit of the Earth and leave the solar system is almost 4 times larger than the escape speed to flee from the gravitational attraction of just the Earth.

If we want to launch our projectile from the surface of the Earth with enough speed to leave the solar system, we need to overcome the combined gravitational potential energy of the Earth and Sun. Since the two potential energies add, we find the combined escape speed as

$$v_{ES} = \sqrt{v_E^2 + v_S^2} = 43.5 \text{ km/s} \tag{12.27}$$

While we found above that the rotation of the Earth has a non negligible, but still fairly small, effect on the escape speed, we find a much bigger effect from the orbiting motion of the Earth around the Sun. The Earth orbits the Sun with an orbital speed of $v_O = 2\pi R_{ES} / (1 \text{ year}) = 30$ km/s, where R_{ES} is the distance between Earth and Sun, 149 million km. If we launch our projectile in the direction of this orbital velocity vector, we only need a launch velocity of $v_{ES,\min} = (43.5-30)$ km/s $= 13.5$ km/s, whereas if we launch it in the opposite direction we need $v_{ES,\max} = (43.5+30)$ km/s $= 73.5$ km/s. Other angles produce all values between these two extremes.

When NASA launches satellites to explore the outer planets or even to leave the solar system, like for example Voyager 2, then they use the gravity assist technique to lower the required launch velocities. This technique is illustrated in Figure 12.13. On the left, the Jupiter fly-by of a spacecraft is sketched as seen by an observer at rest relative to Jupiter. You can observe that the velocity vector changes direction, but has the same length at the same distance from Jupiter when the spacecraft approaches and when it leaves. This is a consequence of energy conservation.

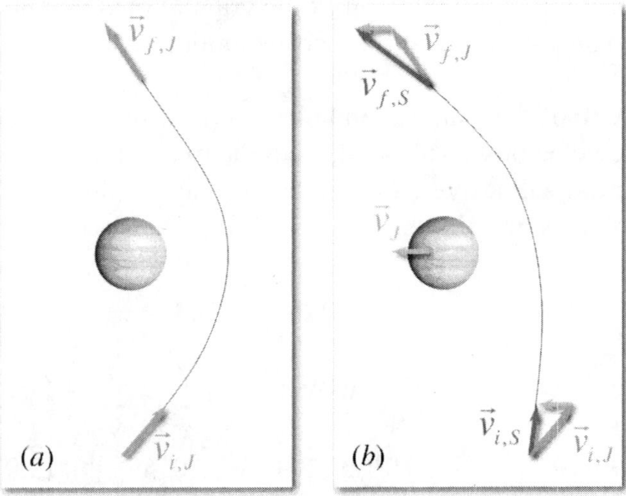

Figure 12.13: Gravity assist technique; left: trajectory of a spacecraft passing Jupiter, as seen in the frame of Jupiter; right: the same velocity vectors as seen in the frame of the Sun, in which Jupiter moves with a velocity of approximately 13 km/s.

The right frame of the figure contains a sketch of Jupiter's trajectory as seen by an observer at rest relative to the Sun. In this frame, Jupiter moves with an orbital velocity of approximately 13 km/s. To transform from Jupiter's rest frame, we have to add the velocity of Jupiter to the velocities observed in Jupiter's frame (red arrows), in order to obtain the velocities in the Sun's frame (blue arrows). As you can see from the result of this velocity addition, in the Sun's frame the length of the final velocity vector is significantly greater than that of the initial one. This means that the satellite has acquired significant additional kinetic energy (and that Jupiter has lost this kinetic energy) during the fly-by that allows it climb further out of the gravitational grip of the Sun.

Example 12.3: Asteroid Impact

One of the most likely scenarios for the extinction of dinosaurs is a large asteroid hitting the Earth. This example takes a look at the energy released during an asteroid impact.

Example

Question:
Consider a spherical asteroid of negligible speed in our solar system. It has a radius of 1.00 km and a mass density of 4750 kg/m^3. Suppose this asteroid collides with Earth in such a way that it hits Earth from a radial direction with respect to the sun. What kinetic energy will this asteroid have in the earth's reference frame just before impact on Earth?

Answer:
First we calculate the mass of the asteroid. It is:

$$m_a = V_a \rho_a = \tfrac{4}{3}\pi r_a^3 \rho_a = \tfrac{4}{3}\pi(1.00\cdot 10^3\text{ m})^3(4750\text{ kg/m}^3) = 1.99\cdot 10^{13}\text{ kg}$$

If the asteroid hits the earth in a radial direction with respect to the sun, the Earth's velocity vector will be perpendicular to that of the asteroid at impact, because the Earth moves tangentially around the Sun. So we get three contributions to the kinetic energy of the asteroid as measured from Earth: 1. Conversion of the gravitational potential energy between Earth and asteroid; 2. Conversion of the gravitational potential energy between Sun and asteroid; 3. Kinetic energy of the Earth's motion relative to the asteroid.

We could now insert all of the numbers and obtain our result. But since we have already calculated the escape velocities corresponding to the two potential energy terms, and since the falling asteroid will arrive with the kinetic energy sum that corresponds to these escape velocities, we can simply calculate;

$$K = \tfrac{1}{2}m_a(v_E^2 + v_S^2 + v_O^2)$$

where we use the numerical values from above:

$$K = 0.5\cdot(1.99\cdot 10^{13}\text{ kg})((1.1\cdot 10^4\text{ m/s})^2 + (4.2\cdot 10^4\text{ m/s})^2 + (3.0\cdot 10^4\text{ m/s})^2)$$
$$= 2.8\cdot 10^{22}\text{ J}$$

This is equivalent to the energy release of approximately 300 million nuclear weapons of the magnitude that were used to destroy Hiroshima and Nagasaki. Thus one can begin to understand the destructive power of an asteroid impact of this magnitude. An event like this could wipe out human life from Earth! A somewhat bigger asteroid of perhaps 6 to 10 km diameter hit Earth near the tip of the Yucatan peninsula in the Gulf of Mexico approximately 65 million years ago. It is believed to be responsible for the K-T (Cretaceous-Tertiary) extinction, which killed off the dinosaurs.

Figure 12.14: Barringer asteroid impact crater in Central Arizona.

Discussion:
Figure 12.14 shows a photo of the approximately 1.5 km diameter and almost 200 m deep Barringer asteroid impact crater, which was left behind by such an asteroid impact. This crater was formed approximately 50,000 years ago by a meteorite of approximately 50 m diameter (a factor of 20 smaller than what we assumed in this example!), with a mass of approximately 300,000 ton = ($3 \cdot 10^8$ kg), hitting Earth with a speed of approximately 12 km/s. So this is a much smaller object than envisioned in this example. But still, the impact had a distractive power of 150 atomic bombs of the Hiroshima/Nagasaki class.

Gravitational Potential

We have seen in equation (12.17) that the gravitational potential energy of any object is proportional to that object's mass. When we employed energy conservation to calculate the escape speed, we saw that the mass of the objects cancels out, because kinetic energy as well as gravitational potential energy are proportional to the object's mass. So we can make certain statements about the kinematics that are independent of the object's mass. Let us, for example, take the gravitational potential energy of a mass m interacting with Earth:

$$U_E(r) = -\frac{GM_E m}{r} \tag{12.28}$$

We define the Earth's gravitational potential $V_E(r)$ as the ratio of the gravitational potential energy and the mass of the object, $V_E(r) = U_E(r)/m$:

$$V_E(r) = -\frac{GM_E}{r} \tag{12.29}$$

This definition has the advantage that it gives us the information on the gravitational interaction with Earth, independent of the other mass that is involved. We will explore the concept of potentials in much more depth when we investigate static electricity.

12.5. Kepler's Laws and Planetary Motion

Johannes Kepler (1571-1630) used empirical observations, mainly from the data gathered by Tycho Brahe, and sophisticated calculations to arrive at his famous laws of planetary motion, published in 1609 and 1619. This observation occurred decades before Isaac Newton was born in 1643. What is particularly significant about these laws is that they changed the prevailing world-view at the time, with the Earth in the center of creation, and the Sun and all planets orbiting around it, just like the moon does. The main problem with that view was that it was hard to understand the epicycles of the planets, where the planets seemed to "loop back". Kepler and other pioneers, like Galileo Galilei, changed this geocentric worldview into a heliocentric worldview. Now we have direct observations from vantage points outside the Earth's atmosphere and can easily verify that Kepler and Galilei were correct. But the simplicity with which their heliocentric model was able to explain the observations won intelligent people over to their view long before external observations were possible.

Kepler's First Law: Orbits

All planets move in elliptical orbits with the sun at one focal point.

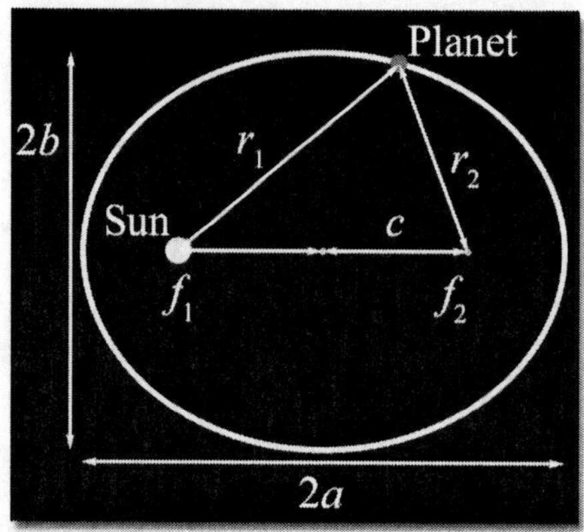

Figure 12.15: Illustration of parameters used in describing ellipses and elliptical orbits.

Mathematical Insert: Ellipses

An ellipse is a closed curve in a two-dimensional plane. It has two focal points (f_1, f_2) separated by a distance $2c$, as shown. The points on the ellipse are characterized by the condition that the sum of the distance to the two focal points is a constant,

$$r_1 + r_2 = 2a$$

The length a is the semi-major axis of the ellipse, as shown in Figure 12.15. (Note: unfortunately the standard notation for the semi-major axis of an ellipse uses the same letter, a, as the one conventionally used for the acceleration. Thus one needs to be careful to avoid confusion.) One can also define a semi-minor axis, b, and it is related to a and c via

$$b^2 \equiv a^2 - c^2$$

In terms of the Cartesian coordinates x, y, the points on the ellipse then satisfy the equation:

$$\frac{x^2}{a^2} + \frac{y^2}{b^2} = 1$$

Here the origin is assumed to reside in the center of the ellipse.

If $a = b$, then we obtain a circle as a special case of the ellipse. It is useful to introduce the eccentricity, e, of the ellipse. It is defined as

$$e = \frac{c}{a} = \sqrt{1 - \frac{b^2}{a^2}}$$

An eccentricity of 0, the smallest possible value, leads to a circle. The ellipse shown in Figure 12.15 has an eccentricity of 0.6.

End of Mathematical Insert

The eccentricity of the Earth's orbit around the Sun is only 0.017. If we were to plot an ellipse with this value of e, then it would not be distinguishable form a circle by visual inspection. The semi-minor axis' length of the Earth's orbit is approximately 99.98% of that of the semi-major axis. At its closest approach to the Sun, the perihelion, the Earth is 147.1 million km away from the Sun. The aphelion, the furthest point from the Sun, is 152.6 million km away from the Sun. The difference between these two distances is 5.5 million km , less than 3% of the average distance between Earth and Sun.

It is important to note that the change in seasons is *not* caused primarily by the eccentricity of the Earth's orbit. (The point of closest approach to the Sun is reached in early January each year, in the middle of the cold season in the Northern hemisphere.) Instead, the seasons are caused by the fact that the Earth's axis of rotation is tilted by an angle of 23.4 degrees relative to the plane of the orbital ellipse, exposing more of the Northern hemisphere to the Sun's rays in the summer months.

Of the orbits of the other planets in our solar system, Mercury's has the largest eccentricity with 0.205. (Pluto's orbit's eccentricity is even larger at 0.249, but since August 2006 we do not count Pluto as a planet any more.) Venus's orbit has the smallest eccentricity with 0.007, followed by Neptune with 0.009.

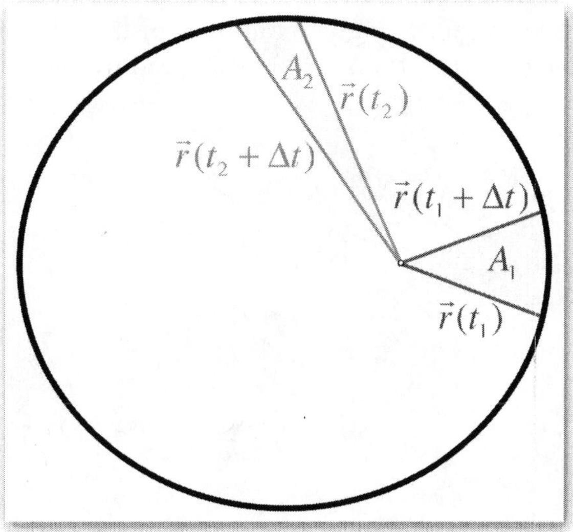

Figure 12.16: Illustration of Kepler's Second Law. Here $A_1 = A_2$.

Kepler's Second Law: Areas

A straight line connecting the center of the Sun and the center of any planet, such as in Figure 12.16) sweeps out an equal area in any given time interval:

$$\frac{dA}{dt} = const. \tag{12.30}$$

Kepler's Third Law: Periods

The square of the period of a planet is proportional to the cube of the semi-major axis of the orbit:

$$\frac{T^2}{a^3} = const. \tag{12.31}$$

Derivation 12.3: Kepler's Laws

The general proof of Kepler's Laws uses the Newtonian force law for the gravitational force, equation (12.1), and the conservation law of angular momentum. Using quite a bit of algebra and calculus, it is then possible to prove all three of Kepler's Laws. Here we will derive Kepler's 2nd and 3rd Laws for circular orbits with the Sun in the center, so that we can put the Sun into the origin of our coordinate system and neglect the motion of the Sun around the common center of mass of the Sun-planet system.

First we show that circular motion is indeed possible. From chapter 9 on circular motion we know that in order to obtain a closed circular orbit, the centripetal force needs to be equal to the gravitational force:

$$m\frac{v^2}{r} = G\frac{Mm}{r^2} \Rightarrow v = \sqrt{\frac{GM}{r}}$$

This result establishes two important facts: First, the mass of the orbiting object cancels out. All objects can have the exact same orbit, provided of course that their mass is small compared to the Sun. Second, for any given radius r of the orbit there is a unique orbital velocity that follows from it. Also, for a given orbital radius we obtain a constant value of the angular velocity:

$$\omega = \frac{v}{r} = \sqrt{\frac{GM}{r^3}}$$

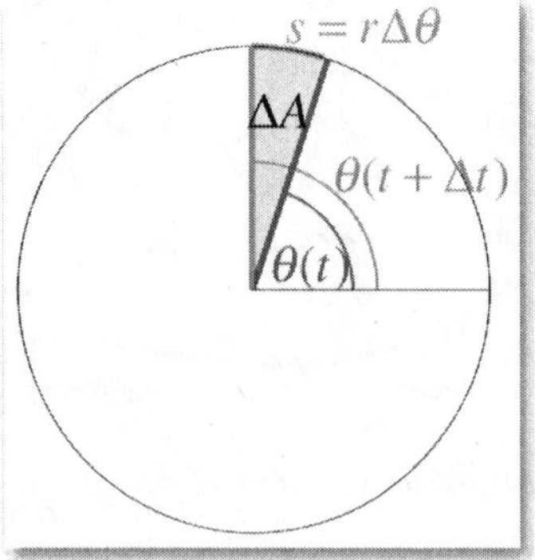

Figure 12.17: Angle, arc length, and area as a function of time.

Derivation

Now we examine the area swept out by the radius vector connecting the Sun and the planet. As indicated in Figure 12.17, the area swept out by it is $\Delta A = \frac{1}{2} rs = \frac{1}{2} r^2 \Delta\theta$. Taking the derivative results in:

$$\frac{dA}{dt} = \tfrac{1}{2} r^2 \frac{d\theta}{dt} = \tfrac{1}{2} r^2 \omega$$

Since, according to the above, ω and r are constant, we thus have shown Kepler's Second Law, which states that $dA/dt = const.$

Finally, for Kepler's Third Law, we use $T = 2\pi / \omega$ and the expression derived above for the angular velocity. This results in:

$$T = 2\pi \sqrt{\frac{r^3}{GM}}$$

We can rearrange this equation and find:

$$\frac{T^2}{r^3} = \frac{4\pi^2}{GM} \tag{12.32}$$

This proves Kepler's Third Law and even gives the value for the proportionality constant between the square of the orbital period and the cube of the orbital radius.

Derivation

Again, keep in mind that Kepler's Laws are valid for general elliptic orbits, not just for the circular orbits for which we have shown their proof. Instead of referring to the radius of the circle, r has to be taken as the semi-major axis of the ellipse in this more general case. A perhaps even more useful formulation of Kepler's Third Law is written as:

$$\frac{T_1^2}{a_1^3} = \frac{T_2^2}{a_2^3} \tag{12.33}$$

In this formulation, we can easily find relationship for orbital periods and radii for two different orbiting objects.

Solved Problem

Solved Problem 12.1: The Dwarf-Planet Sedna

Question:
On November 14, 2003, astronomers discovered a previously unknown dwarf-planet in our solar system. They have named this object Sedna, after the Inuit goddess of the sea. The average distance of Sedna from the Sun is $17 \cdot 10^9$ km. How long does it take Sedna to complete one orbit around the Sun?

Solved Problem

Answer:

THINK: We can use Kepler's Laws to relate the distance of Sedna from the Sun to the period of Sedna's orbit around the Sun.

SKETCH: A sketch of the distance of Sedna from the Sun compared with the distance of Pluto from the Sun is shown in Figure 12.18.

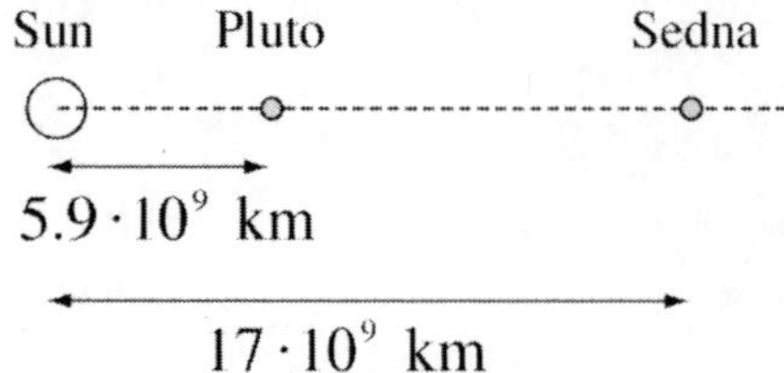

Figure 12.18: Sketch showing the distance of Sedna from the Sun compared with the distance of Pluto from the Sun.

RESEARCH: We can relate the orbit of Sedna to the known orbit of the Earth using Kepler's Laws

$$\frac{T_{\text{Earth}}^2}{a_{\text{Earth}}^3} = \frac{T_{\text{Sedna}}^2}{a_{\text{Sedna}}^3} \tag{12.34}$$

where T_{Earh} is the period of the Earth's orbit, r_{Earth} is the radius of the Earth's orbit, T_{Sedna} is the period of Sedna's orbit, and r_{Sedna} is the radius of Sedna's orbit.

SIMPLIFY: We can solve (12.34) for the period of Sedna's orbit

$$T_{\text{Sedna}} = T_{\text{Earth}} \left(\frac{a_{\text{Sedna}}}{a_{\text{Earth}}} \right)^{3/2} \tag{12.35}$$

CALCULATE: Putting in our numerical values we get

$$T_{\text{Sedna}} = (1 \text{ year}) \left(\frac{17 \cdot 10^9 \text{ km}}{0.150 \cdot 10^9 \text{ km}} \right)^{3/2} = 1206.53 \text{ years}$$

ROUND: We report our result to two significant figures

$$T_{\text{Sedna}} = 1.2 \cdot 10^3 \text{ years}.$$

DOUBLE-CHECK: We can compare our result to the tabulated values of the semi-major axes of the orbits of the planets and their orbital periods. As Figure 12.19 shows, our calculated result falls nicely onto the extrapolation of the data from the planets.

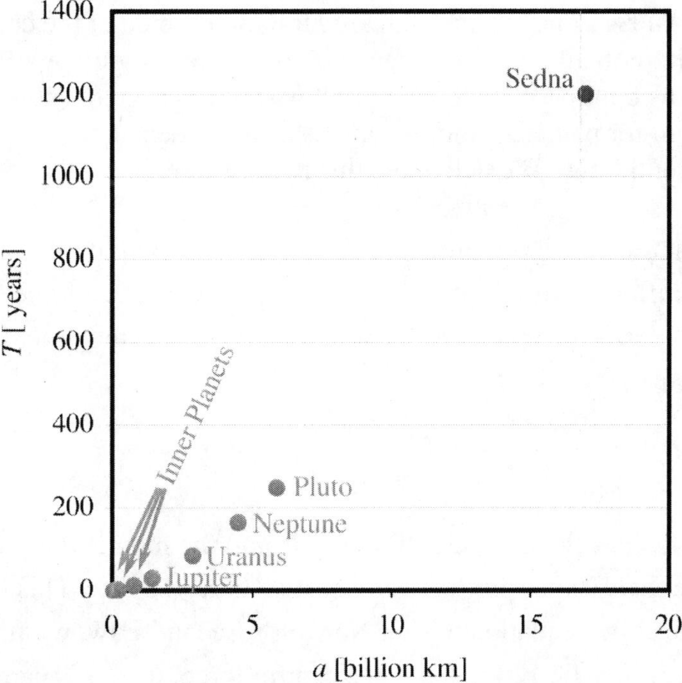

Figure 12.19: Orbital periods versus length of the semi-major axis of the orbits in the solar system.

One can also use Kepler's Third Law to determine the mass of the Sun. We obtain this result by using the Third law in the form of equation (12.32) and solve for the mass of the Sun:

$$M = \frac{4\pi^2 a^3}{GT^2} \tag{12.36}$$

Inserting the data for Earth's orbital period and radius results in:

$$M = \frac{4\pi^2 (1.496 \cdot 10^{11} \text{ m})^3}{(6.67 \cdot 10^{-11} \text{ m}^3\text{kg}^{-1}\text{s}^{-2})(3.15 \cdot 10^7 \text{ s})^2} = 1.99 \cdot 10^{30} \text{ kg}$$

Using the same formula it is also possible to determine the mass of the Earth from the period and radius of the moon's orbit around Earth.

Self-Test Opportunity: Use the fact that the gravitational interaction between Earth and Sun provides the centripetal force that keeps Earth on its orbit to proof (12.36). (You may assume a circular orbit.)

Kepler's Second Law and Angular Momentum Conservation

In the chapter 10 on rotation, we have stressed the importance of the concept of angular momentum, and in particular the importance of the conservation law of angular momentum. It turns out that it is quite straightforward to prove the conservation of angular momentum for planetary motion and as a consequence of this conservation law also Kepler's Second Law. We will show this in the following.

First we show that the angular momentum $\vec{L} = \vec{r} \times \vec{p}$ of a point particle is conserved, if it moves under the influence of a central force. A central force is a force that acts in the radial direction, $\vec{F}_c = F\hat{r}$. To prove this statement, let us take the time derivative of the angular momentum

$$\frac{d\vec{L}}{dt} = \frac{d}{dt}(\vec{r} \times \vec{p}) = \frac{d\vec{r}}{dt} \times \vec{p} + \vec{r} \times \frac{d\vec{p}}{dt} \tag{12.37}$$

For a point particle the velocity vector $\vec{v} = d\vec{r} / dt$ and the momentum vector $\vec{p}$ are parallel; therefore their vector product vanishes: $(d\vec{r} / dt) \times \vec{p} = 0$. This leaves only the second term in the above equation. Using Newton's Second Law, we find (see chapter 7 on momentum) $d\vec{p} / dt = \vec{F}$. If this force is a central force, then it is parallel (or anti-parallel) to the vector $\vec{r}$. Thus for a central force the vector product in the second term also vanishes:

$$\frac{d\vec{L}}{dt} = \vec{r} \times \frac{d\vec{p}}{dt} = \vec{r} \times \vec{F}_c = \vec{r} \times F\hat{r} = 0 \tag{12.38}$$

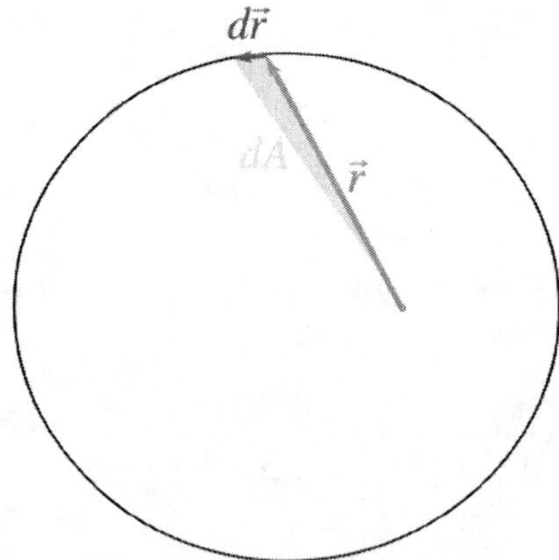

Figure 12.20: Area swept out by the radius vector.

Since $d\vec{L} / dt = 0$, we have shown that angular momentum is conserved for a central force. The Newtonian force of gravity is such a central force, and therefore angular momentum is conserved for any planet moving on its orbit.

How does this general result help in proving Kepler's Second Law? If we can show that the area dA swept out by the radius vector $\vec{r}$ during some infinitesimal time is proportional to the absolute value of the angular momentum, then we are done, because the angular momentum is conserved.

As you can see in Figure 12.20, the infinitesimal area dA swept out by the radius vector $\vec{r}$ is the triangle spanned by the radius vector and the differential change in the radius vector $d\vec{r}$.

$$dA = \tfrac{1}{2}\left|\vec{r}\times d\vec{r}\right| = \tfrac{1}{2}\left|\vec{r}\times\frac{d\vec{r}}{dt}dt\right| = \tfrac{1}{2}\left|\vec{r}\times\frac{1}{m}m\frac{d\vec{r}}{dt}dt\right| = \frac{dt}{2m}\left|\vec{r}\times\vec{p}\right| = \frac{dt}{2m}\left|\vec{L}\right| \tag{12.39}$$

So we find that the area swept out per time interval dt is

$$\frac{dA}{dt} = \frac{\left|\vec{L}\right|}{2m} = \text{constant}, \tag{12.40}$$

which is exactly what Kepler's Second Law states.

12.6. Satellite Orbits

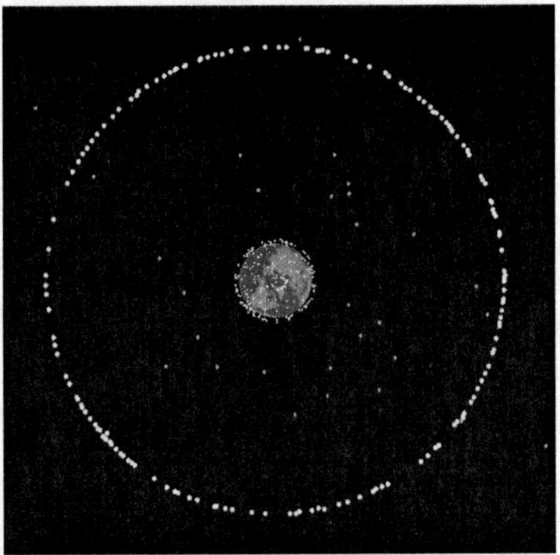

Figure 12.21: Positions of some of the satellites in orbit around Earth. This is a snapshot taken on June 23, 2004, looking down on Earth's North Pole. This illustration was produced with data that are available from NASA.

Figure 12.21 shows the positions of many of the several hundreds of satellites in orbit around Earth. Each dot represents the position of a satellite in the afternoon of June 23, 2004. In low orbits, only a few hundred kilometers above sea level are communication satellites for satellite phone systems, the International Space Station, the Hubble Space Telescope, and others. The perfect circle of satellites formed around Earth at a distance of approximately 5.6 Earth radii above ground is composed of the geostationary satellites. In between the geostationary and the low-orbit satellites are mainly the satellites used for the Global Positioning System, but also research instruments like the Chandra X-ray satellite.

Solved Problem

Solved Problem 12.2: Satellite in Orbit

Question:
A satellite is in a circular orbit around the Earth. The radius of this circular orbit is 3.75 times the radius of the Earth. What is the linear speed of the satellite?

Answer:

THINK: The force of gravity provides the centripetal force keeping the satellite in orbit around the Earth. We can obtain the velocity by equating the centripetal force expressed in terms of the linear speed with the force of gravity between the satellite and the Earth.

SKETCH: A sketch of the problem is shown in Figure 12.22.

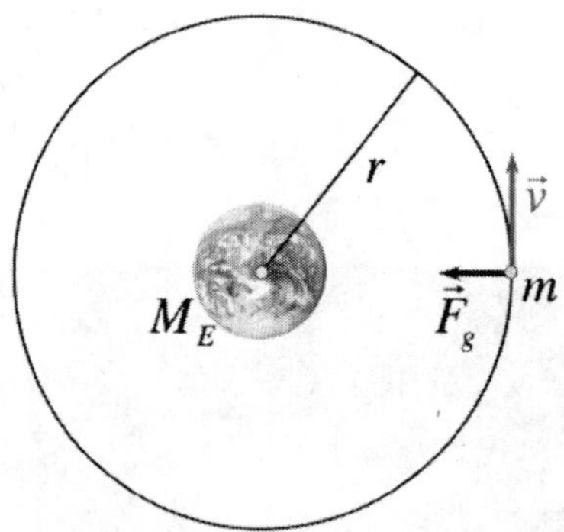

Figure 12.22: Satellite in circular orbit around the Earth.

RESEARCH: The centripetal force that keeps the satellite moving in a circle is the force of gravity. For the satellite with mass m moving with linear speed v the centripetal force required to keep the satellite moving in a circle with radius r is

$$F_c = \frac{mv^2}{r}. \tag{12.41}$$

The gravitational force F_g between the satellite and the Earth is

$$F_g = G\frac{M_E m}{r^2} \tag{12.42}$$

where G is the universal gravitational constant and M_E is the mass of the Earth. Equating (12.41) and (12.42) we get

Solved Problem

$$F_c = F_g \Rightarrow$$

$$\frac{mv^2}{r} = G\frac{M_E m}{r^2} \tag{12.43}$$

SIMPLIFY: The mass of the satellite cancels out; thus the orbital speed of a satellite does not depend on its mass. We obtain

$$v^2 = G\frac{M_E}{r} \Rightarrow$$

$$v = \sqrt{\frac{GM_E}{r}} \tag{12.44}$$

CALCULATE: Now we use the information specified in the problem that the radius of the orbit of the satellite is $r = 3.75R_E$ where R_E is the radius of the Earth. Putting in the known numerical values gives us

$$v = \sqrt{\frac{GM_E}{3.75R_E}} = \sqrt{\frac{(6.67\cdot 10^{-11}\ \text{m}^3\text{kg}^{-1}\text{s}^{-2})(5.97\cdot 10^{24}\ \text{kg})}{3.75\cdot 6.37\cdot 10^6\ \text{m}}} = 4082.86\ \text{m/s}.$$

ROUND: Expressing our result with three significant figures gives us

$$v = 4080\ \text{m/s} = 4.08\ \text{km/s}.$$

DOUBLE-CHECK: The time it takes for the satellite in this problem to complete one orbit is

$$T = \frac{2\pi r}{v} = \frac{2\pi\cdot 3.75R_E}{v} = \frac{2\pi\cdot 3.75\cdot 6.37\cdot 10^6\ \text{m}}{4080\ \text{m/s}} = 36800\ \text{s} = 10.2\ \text{hours},$$

which seems reasonable compared with communication satellites, which take 24 hours, but are at higher altitudes, and the Hubble Space Telescope, which take 1.6 hours at a significantly lower altitude.

If we compare this result for the orbital speed as a function of the orbital radius r in (12.44) to the escape speed $v_{esc}(r)$, i.e. the speed you need to escape from a point that is at an altitude r above the center of that planet, which we had calculated earlier (12.25), then we find that the orbital velocity of a satellite is always

$$v(r) = \frac{1}{\sqrt{2}}v_{esc}(r) \tag{12.45}$$

The Earth is, of course, a satellite of the Sun, and we have determined (12.26) that the escape speed from the Sun is 42 km/s, if one starts from the orbital radius of the Earth. Using (12.45), we then can predict that the orbital speed of the Earth moving around the Sun is $42/\sqrt{2}$ km/s, approximately 30 km/s, which is the value of the orbital speed that we had found earlier.

In-class exercise: The elliptical orbit of a small satellite orbiting a spherical planet is shown:

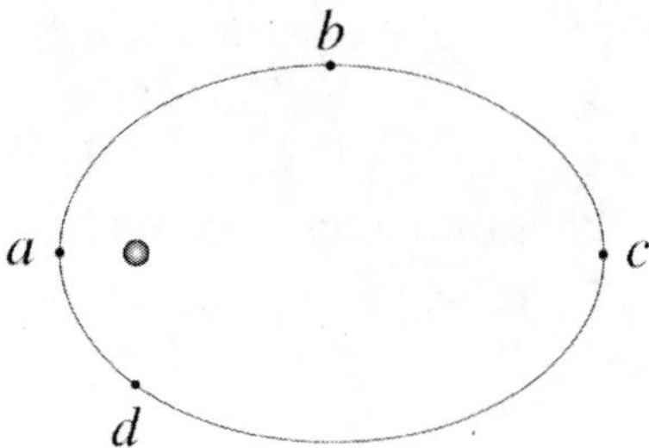

At which point along the orbit (*a, b, c,* or *d*) is the linear speed of the satellite maximum?

Energy of a Satellite

Having solved the above problem, it is straightforward to obtain an expression for the kinetic energy of the satellite in orbit. Multiplication of both sides of equation (12.43) with $r/2$ yields

$$\tfrac{1}{2}mv^2 = \tfrac{1}{2}G\frac{M_E m}{r} \tag{12.46}$$

The left-hand side of this equation is the kinetic energy of the satellite. Comparing the right hand side with our expression for the gravitational potential energy, $U = -GM_E m/r$, we see that this term is just $-\tfrac{1}{2}U$. So we obtain for the kinetic energy of a satellite in circular orbit:

$$K = -\tfrac{1}{2}U \tag{12.47}$$

The mechanical energy of a satellite is then:

$$E = K + U = -\tfrac{1}{2}U + U = \tfrac{1}{2}U = -\tfrac{1}{2}G\frac{Mm}{r}. \tag{12.48}$$

Consequently, the mechanical energy is exactly the negative of the satellite's kinetic energy:

$$E = -K. \tag{12.49}$$

It is important to note that all of these statements hold true for all orbital radii.

For elliptical orbits with semi-major axis a we obtain the energy of the satellite in a very similar way, but with a little more mathematics. The result is very similar to the one obtained in equation (12.48), replacing the radius r of the circular orbit by the semi-major axis a of the elliptical orbit:

$$E = -\tfrac{1}{2}G\frac{Mm}{a}. \tag{12.50}$$

Geostationary Orbits

For many applications, we would like to have a satellite always at the same point in the sky. For example we need our TV satellite dishes to point at the same place in the sky, where the satellite is located, to be sure that we can get reception of a signal from that location. These satellites that are continuously at the same point in the sky are called geostationary (or geosynchronous).

What are the conditions that a satellite must fulfill so that it can be geostationary? First, it has to move on a circle, because this is the only orbit that has a constant angular velocity. Second, the period of rotation must match that of the Earth's and be exactly one day. And third, the axis of rotation of the satellite's orbit must be exactly aligned with that of the Earth's rotation. Because the center of the Earth must be at the center of each circular orbit for any satellite, the only possible orbit is one exactly above the equator. These considerations leave only the radius of the orbit to be decided.

To find the radius, we return to Kepler's Third Law in the form of equation (12.32) and solve it for r

$$\frac{T^2}{r^3} = \frac{4\pi^2}{GM} \Rightarrow r = \left(\frac{GMT^2}{4\pi^2}\right)^{1/3} \tag{12.51}$$

The mass M that enters now is of course that of the Earth. Inserting the numerical constants, we then find:

$$r = \left(\frac{(6.674 \cdot 10^{-11}\ \text{m}^3\text{kg}^{-1}\text{s}^{-2})(5.9742 \cdot 10^{24}\ \text{kg})(86{,}164\ \text{s})^2}{4\pi^2}\right)^{1/3} = 42{,}168\ \text{km}$$

Note that we used the best available value of the mass of the Earth, and that we used the sidereal day as the correct period of the Earth's rotation (chapter 9). The distance of a geostationary satellite above sea level at the equator is then $42{,}168\ \text{km} - R_E$. Taking into account that the Earth is not a perfect sphere, but slightly oblate, this distance above sea level at the equator is

$$d = r - R_E = 35{,}790 \text{ km}$$

This distance above ground is 5.6 times the radius of the Earth. This is why the geostationary satellites form an almost perfect circle with a radius of $6.6\,R_E$ in Figure 12.21.

Figure 12.23 shows a cross section through Earth and the location of a geostationary satellite, drawn to scale. From the figure you can see what angle ξ relative to the horizontal you should point your satellite dish at for best reception. Since the geostationary satellite will be located in the plane of the equator, your northern hemisphere dish should point in a southerly direction.

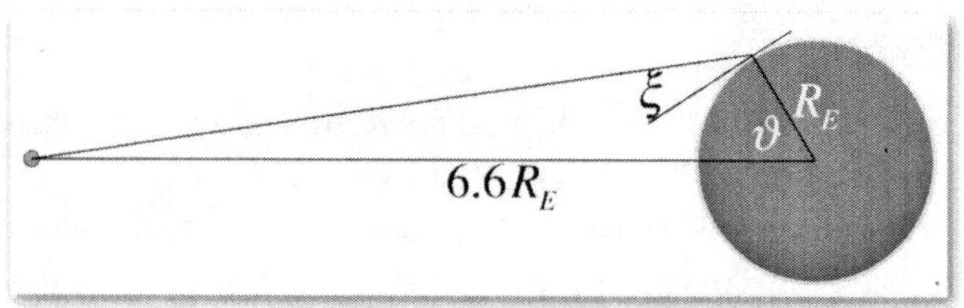

Figure 12.23: Angle of a satellite dish relative to the local horizontal as a function of the angle of latitude.

Solved Problem 12.3: Satellite TV Dish

You just received your new satellite television system, but the company cannot come out and install the dish for you immediately. You want to watch the big game tonight, so you decide to set up the new satellite television system yourself.

Question:

Assuming you live in a location with latitude 42.75° N and that the satellite television company has a satellite aligned with your longitude, in what direction do you point the satellite dish?

Answer:

THINK: Satellite television uses geosynchronous satellites to broadcast the signal. Thus, we know we need to point the satellite dish south, but we need to know the angle of inclination of the satellite dish with respect to the horizontal. Looking at Figure 12.23, we can see that we need to determine the angle ξ, which is angle of the satellite dish relative to the local horizon. To determine ξ, we use the law of cosines incorporating our knowledge of the distance of a satellite in geosynchronous orbit, the radius of the Earth, and the latitude where we want to watch satellite television.

SKETCH: A sketch of the geometry of the geosynchronous satellite and the point on the surface of the Earth where we want to receive the signal is shown in Figure 12.24.

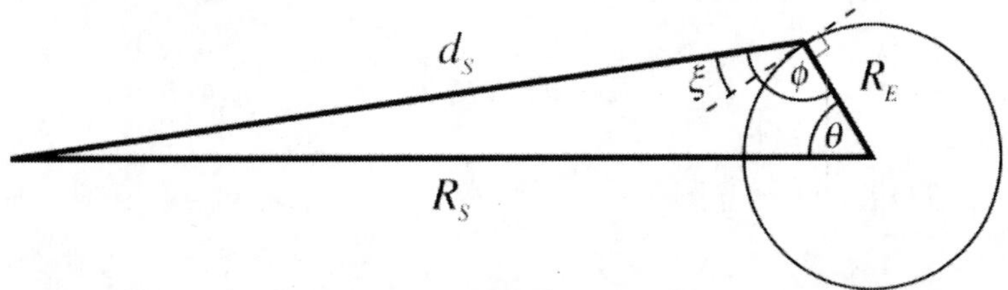

Figure 12.24: Geometry of a geosynchronous satellite in orbit around the Earth.

In this sketch, we define R_E as the radius of the Earth, R_S as the distance of the satellite from the center of the Earth, d_S as the distance from the satellite to the point on the Earth's surface where the signal will be received, θ is the latitude where the signal will be received, and ϕ as the angle between d_S and R_E.

RESEARCH: To determine the angle ξ, we need to determine the angle ϕ. We can see in Figure 12.24 that $\xi = \phi - 90°$ because the dashed line is tangent to the surface of the Earth and thus perpendicular to a line from that point to the center of the Earth. To determine ϕ, we can use the law of cosines applied to the triangle defined by d_S, R_E, and R_S. We will need to apply the law of cosines to this triangle twice to get our result. To use the law of cosines to determine ϕ, we need to know the length of the sides of the triangle d_S and R_E. We know R_E but not d_S. We can determine d_S using the law of cosines, the angle θ, and the two known sides of the triangle R_E and R_S

$$d_S^2 = R_S^2 + R_E^2 - 2R_S R_E \cos\theta . \tag{12.52}$$

We can now get an equation for the angle ϕ from the law of cosines as using the angle ϕ and the two known sides of the triangle d_S and R_E

$$R_s^2 = d_s^2 + R_E^2 - 2d_s R_E \cos\phi . \tag{12.53}$$

SIMPLIFY: We know that $R_s = 6.61 R_E$ for geosynchronous satellites. The angle θ corresponds to the latitude $\theta = 42.75°$. We can substitute these quantities into (12.52) to get

$$d_S^2 = \left(6.61 R_E\right)^2 + R_E^2 - 2\left(6.61 R_E\right) R_E \cos\left(42.75°\right). \tag{12.54}$$

We can now write an expression for d_S in terms of R_E

$$d_S^2 = R_E^2 \left(6.61^2 + 1 - 2\left(6.61\right)\cos\left(42.75°\right)\right) = 34.984 R_E^2 \tag{12.55}$$

or

$$d_S = 5.915R_E. \tag{12.56}$$

We can solve (12.53) for ϕ to get

$$\phi = \cos^{-1}\left(\frac{d_S^2 + R_E^2 - R_S^2}{2d_S R_E}\right). \tag{12.57}$$

CALCULATE: Putting our values for d_S and R_S into (12.57) we get

$$\phi = \cos^{-1}\left(\frac{34.984R_E^2 + R_E^2 - (6.61R_E)^2}{2(5.915R_E)R_E}\right) = 130.66°.$$

The angle at which we need to aim the satellite dish with respect to the horizontal is then

$$\xi = \phi - 90° = 130.66° - 90° = 40.66°.$$

ROUND: Expressing our result with three significant figures gives us

$$\xi = 40.7°.$$

DOUBLE-CHECK: If the satellite were very far away, then the lines d_S and R_S would be parallel to each other and we could redraw our original sketch shown in Figure 12.24. The new sketch is shown in Figure 12.25.

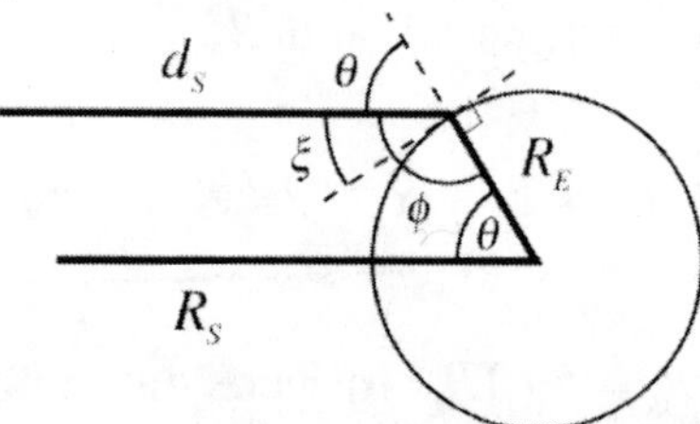

Figure 12.25: Sketch of the geometry of viewing a satellite that is very far away.

We can see from the sketch that $\phi = 180° - \theta$. Remembering that $\xi = \phi - 90°$ we can write

$$\xi = (180° - \theta) - 90° = 90° - \theta.$$

In our case, $\theta = 42.75°$, so our estimated angle is $\xi = 90° - 42.75° = 47.25°$, which is close to our result of $\xi = 40.7°$. Thus, our answer seems reasonable.

Solved Problem

In-class exercise: When a permanent colony is established on Mars, we will want to put martian-stationary satellites in orbit around Mars to facilitate communications. A day on Mars lasts 24 hours, 39 minutes, and 35 seconds. What is the radius of the orbit for a martian-stationary satellite?

a) 12,560 km
b) 15,230 km
c) 20,450 km
d) 29,320 km
e) 43,350 km

12.7. Dark Matter

In our own solar system, almost all of the matter is concentrated in the Sun. The mass of the Sun is approximately 1,000 times greater than the mass of all planets combined (compare Table 12.1). In the Milky Way, our home galaxy, we have found that there are giant clouds of gas and dust, but their combined mass is only on the order of 10% of that contained in the stars of our galaxy.

Extrapolating from these facts, one would be led to believe that the entire universe is almost exclusively composed of luminous matter, i.e. stars. Non-luminous matter in the form of dust, asteroids, moons, and planets should contribute only a small fraction of the mass of the universe.

We know the typical mass of stars and can estimate their number in galaxies. So we can obtain fairly accurate estimates of the mass of galaxies and clusters of galaxies. On the other hand, we can use modern x-ray telescopes like Chandra to take images of the hot interstellar gas trapped within galaxy clusters. Since we can deduce the temperature of this gas from the x-ray emission, we also know how much gravitational force it takes to keep this hot gas from escaping the galaxy clusters.

The surprise that has emerged from this research is that the mass contained in the luminous matter is approximately a factor 3 to 5 too small to provide this gravitational force. This analysis leads us to conclude that there must be other matter, "dark matter", which provides the missing gravitational force.

Other evidence for dark matter has emerged from gravitational lensing observations. We will learn more on this topic in chapter 35 on relativity. There are also observations of rotational velocity spectra of stars within individual galaxies, for which the kinetic energy is larger than one half of the gravitational potential energy, if one only includes the luminous matter in the expression for the gravitational potential energy. New data have also emerged from the WMAP (Wilkinson Microwave Anisotropy Probe) satellite mission that measures the cosmic background radiation left over from the Big Bang. Its best estimate states that 23% of the Universe is composed of dark matter.

Intense speculations and theoretical investigations on the nature of this dark matter have been undertaken during the last couple of decades, and they are still continuing to get modified as new observations emerge. However, all of them require a fundamental rethinking of our standard model of the universe and quite possibly also the fundamental models for the interaction of particles. Whimsical names for classes of candidates for dark matter, such as WIMP (Weakly Interacting Massive Particle) or MACHO (MAssive Compact Halo Object), have emerged. Neither the identity nor the physical properties of these postulated dark matter constituents is known.

During the last few years even stranger puzzles have been unearthed: now it seems that in addition to dark matter there is also "dark energy". This dark energy seems to be responsible for an increasing acceleration in the expansion of the universe. A stunning 73% of the mass/energy of the Universe is estimated to be dark energy. Taken together with the 23% dark matter, this leaves only 4% of the Universe for the stars.

These are very exciting new research developments that are sure to change our picture of the Universe in the coming decades.

Self-Test Opportunity: One of the pieces of evidence for dark matter is the velocity curve of stars in rotating galaxies (see for example Figure 12.26). Astronomers observe that the velocity of the stars in the galaxy first increases and then remains constant as a function of distance from the center of the galaxy. What would one expect for the velocity of stars as a function of distance from the center of the galaxy if the galaxy consists of a disk comprised of stars with equal masses distributed uniformly through the disk and there is no dark matter present?

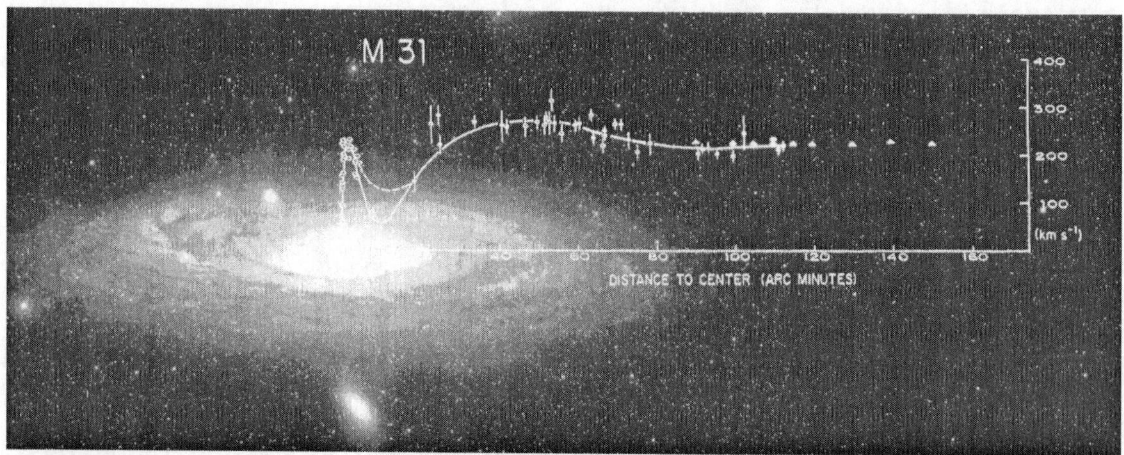

Figure 12.26: Picture of the Andromeda galaxy, with data on orbital speeds of stars superimposed. (Image courtesy of Vera Rubin; the triangles represent radio-telescope data from 1975, and the other symbols show optical wavelengths observations from 1970; the solid and dashed lines were simple fits to guide the eye in the original publication.). The main feature of interest here is that the orbital speeds remain approximately constant well outside the luminous portion of Andromeda, indicating the presence of dark matter.

What we have learned/Exam Study Guide:

- The gravitational force between two point masses is proportional to the product of their masses and inversely proportional to the distance between them, $F(r) = G\frac{m_1 m_2}{r^2}$, with the proportionality constant $G = 6.674 \cdot 10^{-11}\ \text{m}^3\text{kg}^{-1}\text{s}^{-2}$, the universal gravitational constant.
- In vector form, this gravitational force law can be written as: $\vec{F}_{2\to 1} = G\frac{m_1 m_2}{\left|\vec{r}_2 - \vec{r}_1\right|^3}(\vec{r}_2 - \vec{r}_1)$. This is the Newtonian Law of Gravity.
- If more than two objects interact gravitationally, the resulting force on one is given by a vector sum of the forces acting on it.
- Near the surface of the Earth the gravitational acceleration can be approximated by the function $g(h) = g\left(1 - 2\frac{h}{R_E} + \ldots\right)$, i.e. it falls off linearly with height above ground.
- The gravitational acceleration at sea level can be derived from Newton's gravitational force law as $g = \frac{GM_E}{R_E^2}$.
- There is zero gravitational force on an object inside a spherical mass shell. Because of this, the gravitational force inside a uniform spherical body increases linearly with radius, $F(r) = \frac{4}{3}\pi G\rho_E m r$.
- The gravitational potential energy between two objects is given by $U(r) = -G\frac{m_1 m_2}{r}$, with the convention that the potential energy is 0 at infinite separation.
- The escape speed from the surface of the Earth is $v_0 = \sqrt{\frac{2GM_E}{R_E}}$.
- Kepler's Laws for planetary motion:
  - All planets move in elliptical orbits with the Sun at one focal point.
  - A straight line connecting the center of the Sun and the center of any planet sweeps out an equal area in any given time interval, $\frac{dA}{dt} = const.$
  - The square of the period of a planet is proportional to the cube of the semi-major axis of the orbit, $\frac{T^2}{r^3} = \frac{4\pi^2}{GM}$.
- The relationships between kinetic, potential, and total energy of a satellite in a circular orbit are $K = -\frac{1}{2}U$, $E = K + U = -\frac{1}{2}U + U = \frac{1}{2}U = -\frac{1}{2}G\frac{Mm}{r}$, $E = -K$.
- Geostationary orbits are circular, above the equator, and have a radius of 42,168 km.
- Recent research points strongly to the existence of dark matter and dark energy,

two not yet observed components of our universe, which make up the vast majority of the universe.

Additional Solved Problems

Solved Problem

Solved Problem 12.4: Astronaut on a Small Moon

Question:

A small spherical moon has a radius of $6.30 \cdot 10^4$ m and a mass of $8.00 \cdot 10^{18}$ kg. An astronaut standing on the surface of the moon throws a rock straight up. The rock reaches a maximum height of 2.20 km above the surface of the planet before it returns to the surface. What was the initial speed of the rock as it left the hand of the astronaut? (This moon is too small to have an atmosphere.)

Answer:

THINK: We know the mass and radius of the moon, allowing us to computer the gravitational potential. To calculate the height that the rock gains, we can use energy conservation to calculate the initial speed of the rock.

SKETCH: A sketch of the rock at its highest point is shown in Figure 12.27.

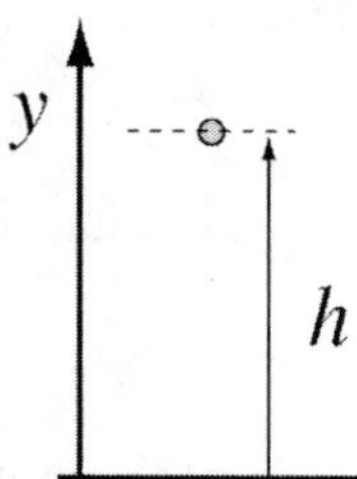

Figure 12.27: Sketch of the rock at its highest point.

RESEARCH: We denote the mass of the rock as m, the mass of the moon as m_{moon}, and the radius of the moon as R_{moon}. The potential energy of the rock on the surface of the planet is then

$$U(R_{\text{moon}}) = -G\frac{m_{\text{moon}}}{R_{\text{moon}}}m. \tag{12.58}$$

The potential energy at the top of the trajectory of the rock is

$$U(R_{\text{moon}} + h) = -G\frac{m_{\text{moon}}}{R_{\text{moon}} + h}m. \tag{12.59}$$

We can equate the kinetic energy of the rock as it leaves the hand of the astronaut with the gravitational potential energy the rock has at its maximum height h

Solved Problem

$$K(R_{\text{moon}}) = \tfrac{1}{2}mv^2 \tag{12.60}$$

and at the top of the trajectory $K(R_{\text{moon}} + h) = 0$. Total energy conservation now helps us to solve the problem:

$$U(R_{\text{moon}}) + K(R_{\text{moon}}) = U(R_{\text{moon}} + h) + \overbrace{K(R_{\text{moon}} + h)}^{=0} \tag{12.61}$$

SIMPLIFY: We insert the energy terms in equations (12.58) through (12.60) into (12.61) and find

$$\begin{aligned}
-G\frac{m_{\text{moon}}}{R_{\text{moon}}}m + \tfrac{1}{2}mv^2 &= -G\frac{m_{\text{moon}}}{R_{\text{moon}} + h}m + 0 \Rightarrow \\
-G\frac{m_{\text{moon}}}{R_{\text{moon}}} + \tfrac{1}{2}v^2 &= -G\frac{m_{\text{moon}}}{R_{\text{moon}} + h} \Rightarrow \\
v &= \sqrt{2Gm_{\text{moon}}\left(\frac{1}{R_{\text{moon}}} - \frac{1}{R_{\text{moon}} + h}\right)}
\end{aligned} \tag{12.62}$$

CALCULATE: Putting in our numerical values we get

$$v = \sqrt{2(6.67 \cdot 10^{-11}\ \text{Nm}^2/\text{kg}^2)(8.00 \cdot 10^{18}\ \text{kg})\left(\frac{1}{6.30 \cdot 10^4\ \text{m}} - \frac{1}{(6.30 \cdot 10^4\ \text{m}) + 2.20 \cdot 10^3\ \text{m})}\right)}$$

$=23.9078$ m/s

ROUND: Rounding to three significant figures we find

$$v = 23.9\ \text{m/s}.$$

DOUBLE-CHECK: If we throw a rock upward on Earth with a speed of 23.9 m/s (54. mph), the rock would attain a height of

$$h = \frac{v^2}{2g} = \frac{(23.9\ \text{m/s})^2}{2 \cdot 9.81\ \text{m/s}^2} = 29.1\ \text{m}.$$

Chapter 13. Solids and Fluids

Figure 13.1: Lone Star Geyser erupts at Yellowstone National Park.

What we will learn

- The atom is the basic building block of macroscopic matter.

- The diameter of an atom is approximately 10^{-10} m.
- Matter can exist as a gas, a liquid, or a solid.
- A gas is a system in which the atoms move freely through space.
- A liquid is a system in which the atoms move freely but form a nearly incompressible state of matter.
- A solid defines its own size and shape.
- Solids are nearly incompressible.
- Solids can be deformed slightly by various forms of pressure including stretching, compression, and shearing. These deformations can be expressed in terms of linear relationship between the applied pressure and the resulting deformation.
- Pressure is force per unit area.
- The pressure of the Earth's atmosphere can be measured using a mercury barometer or similar instrument.
- The pressure of gas can be measured using a mercury manometer.
- Pascal's Principle tells us that pressure applied to a confined fluid is transmitted to all parts of the fluid.
- Archimedes' Principle tells us that the buoyant force on an object in a fluid is equal to the weight of the fluid displaced by the object.
- Bernoulli's Principle tells us that the faster a fluid flows, the less pressure it exerts on its boundary.

13.1. Atoms and the Composition of Matter

During the evolution of physics knowledge, humankind has managed to explore ever-smaller dimensions, looking deeper into matter in order to explore its elementary building blocks. This general way of learning more about a system by finding its subsystems is called "reductionism" and has proven a fruitful guiding principle during the last four or five centuries of modern science.

Here we assume that atoms are the elementary building blocks of matter, but we know that atoms themselves are composite particles. The substructure of atoms, however, can only be resolved with accelerators and other tools of modern nuclear physics. For our purposes it is reasonable to make the assumption that atoms are the elementary matter building blocks. The word "atom" comes from the Greek "atomos", which means indivisible.

The simplest atom is the hydrogen atom, composed of a proton and an electron. The element hydrogen is characterized chemically by having one electron. Hydrogen is the most abundant element in the universe. The next most abundant element is helium. Helium has two protons and two neutrons in its nucleus along with two electrons surrounding the nucleus. Another common atom is oxygen with eight protons and eight electrons as well as usually eight neutrons. The heaviest naturally occurring atom is uranium with 92 protons, 92 electrons and usually 146 neutrons. We now know that there are at least 115 different elements, which are classified in a periodic table of the elements.

The diameter of an atom is about $10^{-10}\ \text{m} = 0.1\ \text{nm}$. This distance is often called an Angstrom, Å.

Consider the number of atoms in 12 grams of ^{12}C, where the 12 in ^{12}C represents the atomic mass number – the total number of protons (6) plus neutrons (6) in the Carbon nucleus. This number has been measured to be $6.022 \cdot 10^{23}$ atoms and is called Avogadro's number, N_A,

$$N_A = 6.022 \cdot 10^{23}. \tag{13.1}$$

To get a feeling for how much carbon corresponds to N_A atoms of carbon, consider two forms of carbon, diamond and graphite. Diamonds are composed of carbon atoms arranged in a crystal lattice while graphite exists in two-dimensional layers.

Figure 13.2: Photograph of diamonds, composed of carbon atoms.

First we have to know the density of carbon in a macroscopic form. The density of diamonds is $3.51\ \text{g}/\text{cm}^3$ and the density of graphite is $2.20\ \text{g}/\text{cm}^3$. Diamonds are often classified in terms of their mass in carat, where $1\ \text{carat} = 200\ \text{mg}$. A 12 g diamond has N_A atoms and 60 carats and has a volume of about 3.5 cubic centimeters, about 1.5 times bigger than the Hope-Diamond. A typical wedding ring might have a 1-carat diamond containing approximately 10^{22} carbon atoms.

One mole of a substance contains $N_A = 6.022 \cdot 10^{23}$ atoms or molecules. Since the mass of the proton and neutron are about equal, and the mass of either is far greater than that of an electron, the mass of one mole of a substance is given by the atomic mass number expressed in grams. Just like one mole of ^{12}C has a mass of 12 grams, one Mole of ^4He has a mass of 4 grams. Listed in the periodic table of the elements is the atomic mass number for each element. This atomic mass number is roughly equal to the number of protons and neutron contained in the nucleus of the atom; it is not an integer because it takes into account the natural isotopic abundances. (Isotopes of an element have varying numbers of neutrons in the nucleus. If a Carbon nucleus has 7 neutrons it is called the ^{13}C isotope.) For molecules, one adds up the relative mass numbers of all atoms in the molecule to obtain the mass number of the molecule. So one mole of water, $^1\text{H}_2\,^{16}\text{O}$, has a mass of 18 grams

Atoms are electrically neutral. They have the same number of positively charged protons as negatively charged electrons. The chemical properties of an atom are determined by the electronic structure of the atoms. This structure can allow bonding of certain atoms with other atoms to form molecules. For example, water is composed of a molecule containing two hydrogen atoms and one oxygen atom. The electronic structure of atoms and molecules determines their macroscopic properties such as whether they exist as a gas, liquid, or solid at a given temperature and pressure.

Self-Test Opportunity: How many molecules of water are in a half liter bottle of water? The relative mass number of water is 18.02.

13.2. States of Matter

A gas is a system in which each atom or molecule moves through space as a free particle. Occasionally the atom or molecule collides with another atom or molecule or with the wall of the container of the gas. A common gas is oxygen, which normally exists as a molecule of two oxygen atoms. If a gas in placed in a container, it will expand to fill the container as illustrated in Figure 13.3 (left). A gas can be treated as a fluid because it can flow and exert pressure on the walls of its container. A gas is compressible, which means that the volume of the container can be changed and the gas will still fill the volume, although the pressure it exerts on the walls of the container will change.

A liquid is similar to a gas in that the atoms or molecules in the liquid can move with respect to the other atoms and molecules. However, in contrast to gases, most liquids are nearly incompressible. Thus when a liquid is placed in a container, it fills only the volume corresponding to the volume of liquid that is present as depicted in Figure 13.3 (center). If the volume of the liquid is less than the volume of the container, the container is only partially filled.

A solid does not require a container but instead defines its own shape as shown in Figure 13.3 (right). Like liquids, solids are nearly incompressible. However, solids are not completely incompressible but can be compressed and deformed slightly.

Figure 13.3: Left: A cubical container filled with a gas; center: the same container partially filled with a liquid; right: a solid, which does not need a container.

Before we leave this overview section, we should point out, however, that the classical separation of matter into solids, liquids and gases does not tell the entire story of composition of matter. Obviously, which state of matter a certain substance is in depends on the temperature. H_2O, for example, can be ice (solid), water (liquid), or steam (gas). And the same truth holds for practically all other substances.

However, there are entirely different states of matter as well that do not fit into the solid/liquid/gas classification. Matter in stars, for example, is strictly speaking not in any of the three states. Instead it forms a plasma, an ionized state of atoms. On Earth, the world's beaches are filled with sand, a prime example of granular media. The grains of granular media are solids, but their macroscopic characteristics can be closer to liquids, as indicated in Figure 13.4. A sand pile can flow like a liquid. Glasses seem to be solids at first glance, because they do not change their shape. However, there is also come justification to the view that glass is a type of liquid with an extremely high viscosity. For the purpose of a classification of matter into states, a glass is neither a solid nor a liquid, but a separate state of matter.

Figure 13.4: Left: Pouring liquid silver (a solid metal at room temperature); right: pouring sand (a granular medium).

During the last few years, so-called Bose-Einstein condensates have been experimentally verified to exist and have made it into the news. We can only gain an understanding of this new state of matter once we grasp some basic concepts of quantum physics. However, for now it is sufficient to point out that at very low temperatures a gas of atoms of certain kinds can assume an ordered state of matter in which all of the atoms prefer to occupy the same energy and momentum state, very similar to the way that light assumes an ordered state in the operation of a laser (see chapter 38).

Finally, the matter in our bodies and in most other biological organisms does not fit into any of the classifications above. Biological tissue consists predominantly of water, but yet is able to keep or change its shape, depending on the environmental boundary conditions.

13.3. Tension, Compression, Shear

After this introductory classification, we turn our attention to solids and study how they respond to external forces.

Elasticity of Solids

Solids are composed of atoms arranged in a three-dimensional lattice in which the atoms have a well-defined equilibrium distance from their neighbors in the lattice. These atoms are held in place by inter-atomic forces that can be modeled as springs. This lattice is very stiff, which implies that the imaginary springs are also very stiff. Macroscopic solid objects such as wrenches and spoons seem to be rigid. These objects are composed of atoms arranged in a rigid lattice. However, there are solid objects such as rubber balls that do not seem to be rigid. These objects are composed of atoms arranged in long chains rather than a well-defined lattice. Depending on their molecular structure, solids can be extremely rigid or more easily deformable.

All rigid objects are somewhat elastic, even though they appear to be very stiff. Compressing it, pulling on it, or twisting it can deform a rigid object. If a rigid object is deformed a small amount, it will return to its original size and shape when the deforming factor is removed. If a rigid object is deformed past a point called its elastic limit, it will not return to its original size and shape, but will remain permanently deformed. If a rigid object is deformed further, it will break.

Stress and Strain

Deformations of solids are usually classified into three classes, stretching or tension, compression, and shear. What these three deformations have in common is that a stress, or deforming force per unit area, produces a strain, or unit deformation. Stretching or tension is associated with tensile stress. Compression is related to hydrostatic stress. Shear is related to shearing stress, sometimes also called deviatory stress. With a shear force, planes of a material parallel to the force and on either side of the force remain parallel when the force is applied but shift relative to each other. Although the stress and strain take different forms for the three types of deformation, stress and strain are related linearly to each through a constant called the modulus of elasticity

$$\text{stress} = \text{modulus} \cdot \text{strain} \tag{13.2}$$

This empirical relationship applies as long as the elastic limit of the material is not exceeded.

In the case of tension, a force F is applied to opposite ends of an object of length L and the object stretches to a new length of $L + \Delta L$ as shown in Figure 13.5.

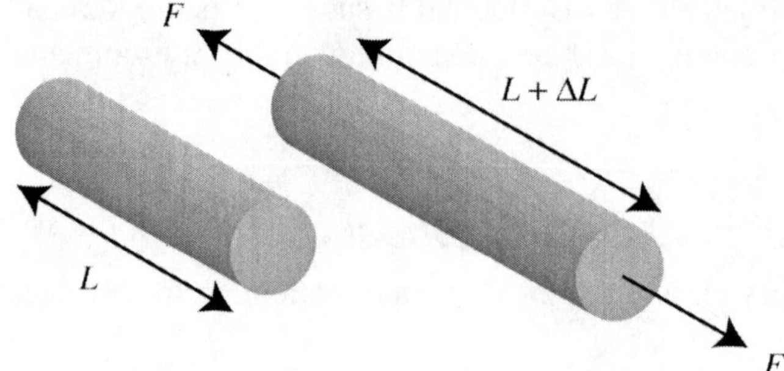

Figure 13.5: Tension applied to an object by pulling with a force on opposite ends of the object. Note: tension can also be applied by pushing, with a resulting negative change in length (not shown).

Table 13.1: Some typical values for Young's Modulus.

Material	Young's Modulus (10^9 N/m^2)
Aluminum	70
Bone	10-20
Concrete	30-60 (compression)
Diamond	1000-1200
Glass	70
Polystyrene	3
Rubber	0.01-0.1
Steel	200
Titanium	100-120
Tungsten	400
Wood	10-15

For stretching, the stress is defined as the force F per unit area A applied to the end of an object. The strain is defined as the fractional change in the length of the object, $\Delta L / L$. The relationship between stress and strain is defined as

$$\frac{F}{A} = Y \frac{\Delta L}{L} \tag{13.3}$$

where Y is called Young's Modulus and depends only on the type of material and not its size or shape . Some typical values for Young's Modulus are shown in Table 13.1.

Linear compression can be treated in a manner similar to stretching for most materials within the elastic limits of the material. However, many materials have different breaking points for stretching and compression. The most notable example is concrete, which resists compression much better than stretching, which is why steel rods are added to it in places where greater tolerance against stretching is required. A steel rod resists stretching much better than compression, because it can buckle under compression stress; so the addition of steel rods to concrete combines the best of both worlds.

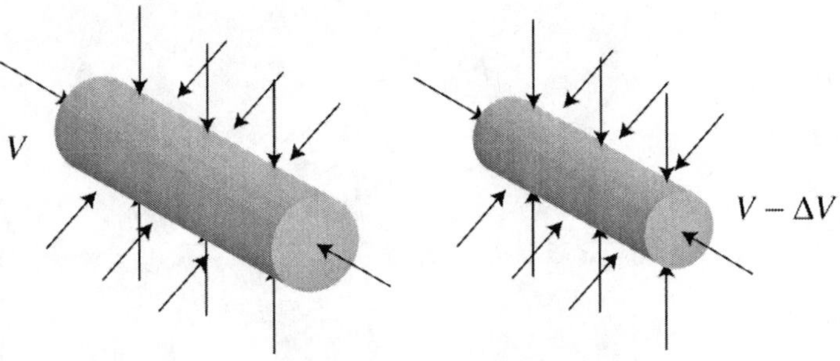

Figure 13.6: Compression of an object by fluid pressure.

The stress related to volume compression is caused by a force per unit area applied to the entire surface area of an object that is submerged in a liquid as in Figure 13.6. Typically this type of compression is caused by fluid pressure p, which is the force exerted by the fluid per unit area of the object being compressed.

The resulting strain is the fractional change in the volume of the object, $\Delta V / V$. The corresponding modulus in this case is the bulk modulus, B. We can then write the equation relating the stress and strain for volume compression as

$$p = B\frac{\Delta V}{V}. \tag{13.4}$$

Some typical values for the bulk modulus are shown in Table 13.2. Note that there is an extremely large jump in bulk modulus between air, which is a gas and can be compressed rather easily, and liquids, which all have values around 10^9 N/m^2 for the bulk modulus. Solids like rocks and metals have a bulk modulus that is higher than that of liquids by a factor between 5 and 100.

Table 13.2: Some typical values for the bulk modulus.

Material	Bulk Modulus (10^9 N/m^2)
Air	0.000142
Aluminum	76
Basalt rock	50-80
Gasoline	1.5
Granite rock	10-50
Mercury	2.85
Steel	160
Water	2.2

In the case of shearing, the stress is again a force per unit area. However, for shearing, the force is parallel to the area rather than perpendicular to it as shown in Figure 13.7.

Here stress is given by the force per unit area, F / A, exerted on the end of the object. The resulting strain is given by the fractional deflection of the object, $\Delta x / L$. The stress is related to the strain through the shear modulus, G, by

$$\frac{F}{A} = G\frac{\Delta x}{L} \tag{13.5}$$

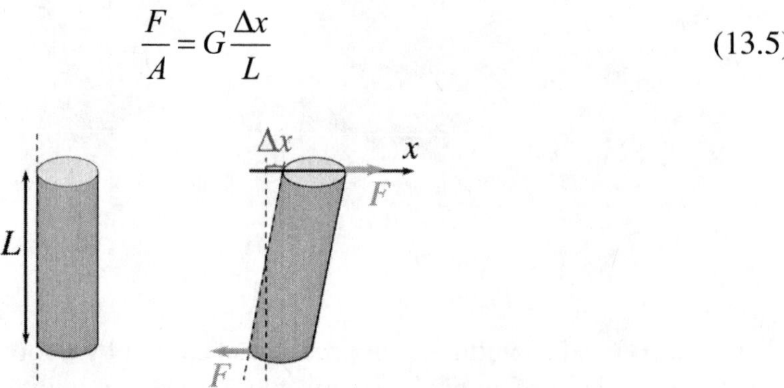

Figure 13.7: Shearing of an object caused by a force parallel to the area of the end of the object.

Some typical values for the shear modulus are shown in Table 13.3.

Table 13.3: Some typical values of the shear modulus.

Material	Shear Modulus (10^9 N/m^2)
Aluminum	25
Copper	63
Glass	26
Polyethylene	0.12
Rubber	0.0003
Titanium	41
Steel	80 to 90

Example

Example 13.1: Plasma-TV Wall Mount

You just bought a new plasma television, as depicted in Figure 13.8, and you are mounting it on the wall with 4 bolts of diameter 0.50 cm. Of course you cannot mount your TV flush against the wall, but you have to leave a gap between wall and TV for air circulation purposes. Let's use 10.0 cm as the width of this gap.

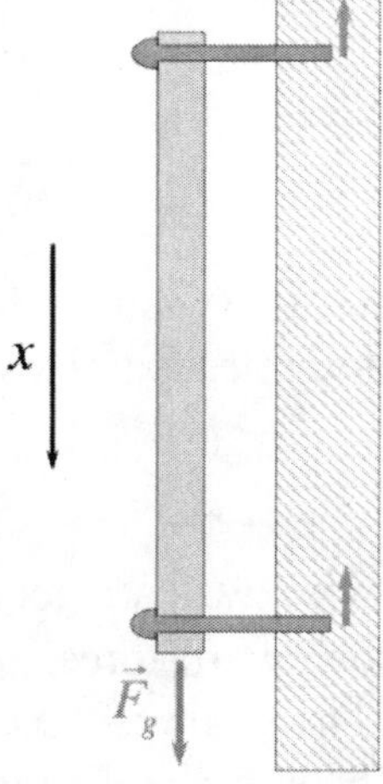

Figure 13.8: Plasma TV wall mount.

Question 1:

If the mass of your new TV is 42.8 kg, what is the shear stress on your bolts?

Answer 1:

The combined cross-sectional area of the bolts is

$$A = 4(\pi d^2 / 4) = \pi (0.005 \text{ m})^2 = 7.85 \cdot 10^{-5} \text{ m}^2$$

One force acting on the bolts is $\vec{F}_g$, the force of gravity on the plasma TV on one end. This is balanced by a force due to the wall on the other end. This wall force holds the TV in place, has exactly the same magnitude as the force of gravity, but points in the opposite direction. Therefore the force entering into our shear stress equation (13.5) is

Example

$$F = mg = (42.8 \text{ kg})(9.81 \text{ m/s}^2) = 420 \text{ N}$$

We thus obtain for the shear stress on the bolts:

$$\frac{F}{A} = \frac{420 \text{ N}}{7.85 \cdot 10^{-5} \text{ m}^2} = 5.35 \cdot 10^6 \text{ N/m}^2$$

Question 2:
The shear modulus of the steel used in the bolts is 90 GN/m^2. What is the resulting vertical deflection of the bolts?

Answer 2:
Solving our result of equation (13.5) for the deflection Δx, we find

$$\Delta x = \frac{F}{A}\frac{L}{G} = (5.35 \cdot 10^6 \text{ N/m}^2)\frac{0.1 \text{ m}}{9.0 \cdot 10^{10} \text{ N/m}^2} = 5.94 \cdot 10^{-6} \text{ m}$$

Even though the shear stress is more than five million N/m^2, the resulting sag of your plasma TV is only six thousandth of a millimeter, which is absolutely invisible to the naked eye.

Solved Problem

Solved Problem 13.1: Stretched Wire

Question:
A 1.50 m long steel wire with diameter 0.100 mm is hanging vertically. A mass $m = 1.50$ kg is attached to the wire and released. How much does the wire stretch?

Answer:

THINK: From the diameter of the wire, we cam get the cross sectional area of the wire. The weight of the mass provides a downward force. The stress on the wire is the weight divided by the cross sectional area. The strain is the change in length of the wire divided by the original length of the wire. The stress and strain are related through Young's Modulus for steel.

SKETCH: A sketch of the wire before and after the mass is attached is shown in Figure 13.9.

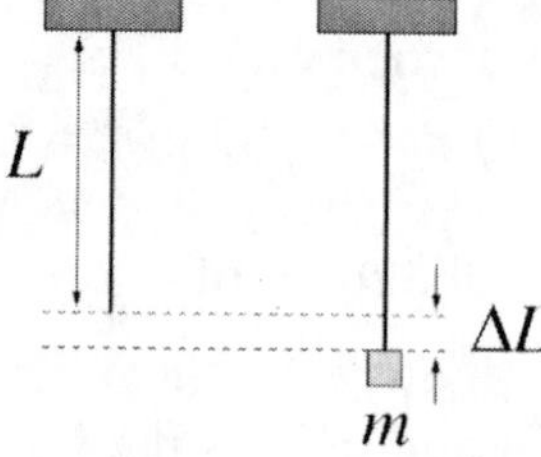

Figure 13.9: A wire before and after having a mass attached to it.

Solved Problem

RESEARCH: The cross sectional area of the wire A can be calculated from the diameter d of the wire

$$A=\pi\left(\frac{d}{2}\right)^2=\frac{\pi d^2}{4}. \tag{13.6}$$

The force on the wire is the weight of the mass

$$F=mg. \tag{13.7}$$

We can relate the stress and the strain on the wire through Young's Modulus Y for steel

$$\frac{F}{A}=Y\frac{\Delta L}{L} \tag{13.8}$$

where ΔL is the change in the length of the wire and L is the original length of the wire.

SIMPLIFY: We can combine (13.6), (13.7), and (13.8) to get

$$\frac{F}{A}=\frac{mg}{\left(\frac{1}{4}\pi d^2\right)}=\frac{4mg}{\pi d^2}=Y\frac{\Delta L}{L}. \tag{13.9}$$

Solving for the change in length of the wire we obtain

$$\Delta L=\frac{4mgL}{Y\pi d^2}. \tag{13.10}$$

CALCULATE: Putting our numerical values into (13.10) gives us the change in length of the wire

$$\Delta L=\frac{4mgL}{Y\pi d^2}=\frac{4\cdot 1.50\text{ kg}\cdot 9.81\text{ m/s}^2\cdot 1.50\text{ m}}{\left(200\cdot 10^9\text{ N/m}^2\right)\cdot\pi\cdot\left(0.100\cdot 10^{-3}\text{ m}\right)^2}=0.0140518\text{ m}.$$

ROUND: We report our result to three significant figures

$$\Delta L=0.0141\text{ m}=1.41\text{ cm}.$$

DOUBLE-CHECK: The wire stretches 1.41 cm compared with its original length of 150 cm, which is less than 1%, which seems reasonable.

13.4. Pressure

For a uniform solid, liquid, or gas we have defined the mass density (or "volume density"), ρ, as the mass per unit volume

$$\rho = \frac{m}{V}. \tag{13.11}$$

Pressure, p, is defined as the force per unit area

$$p = \frac{F}{A}. \tag{13.12}$$

Pressure is a scalar quantity. The SI unit of pressure is $\mathrm{N/m^2}$, which has been given the special name Pascal, abbreviated Pa, given by

$$1\ \mathrm{Pa} = \frac{1\ \mathrm{N}}{1\ \mathrm{m}^2} \tag{13.13}$$

The average pressure of the Earth's atmosphere, $1\ \mathrm{atm}$, is a commonly used non-SI quantity and is often expressed in other units as

$$1\ \mathrm{atm} = 1.01 \cdot 10^5\ \mathrm{Pa} = 760\ \mathrm{torr} = 14.7\ \mathrm{pounds/inch^2}. \tag{13.14}$$

Gauges used to measure how well the air has been removed from a vessel are often calibrated in torr, a unit named after the scientist Italian physicist Evangelista Torricelli (1608-1647). Automobile tire pressures in the United States are often measured in $\mathrm{pounds/inch^2}$ (= psi).

> ***In-class exercise:*** Suppose you pump the air out of a paint can. The paint can is cylindrical in shape, 22.4 cm tall, with a diameter of 16.0 cm. How much force does the atmosphere exert on the lid of the paint can?
> a) 9.81 N
> b) 511 N
> c) 2030 N
> d) 8120 N

Pressure-Depth Relationship

Consider a tank of water open to the Earth's atmosphere as shown in Figure 13.10. In the water we imagine a cube of water (drawn in pink). We assume that the top of the cube is horizontal and at a depth of y_1 and that the bottom of the cube is also horizontal and at a depth of y_2. The other sides of the cube are assumed to be vertical. The water pressure acting on the cube produces forces. By Newton's First Law there must be no net force acting on this stationary cube of water. Thus forces acting on the vertical sides of the cube cancel out. The vertical forces acting on the bottom and top sides of the cube must also sum to zero. The sum of the vertical forces is given by

$$F_2 - F_1 - mg = 0, \tag{13.15}$$

where F_1 is the force downward on the top of the cube, F_2 is the force upward on the bottom of the cube, and mg is the weight of the cube of the water.

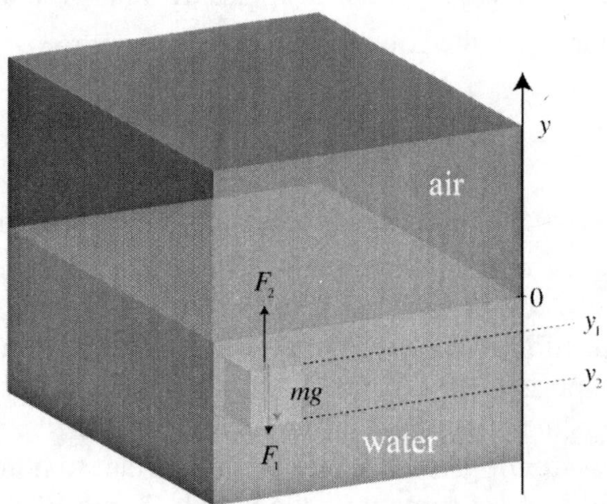

Figure 13.10: Imaginary cube of water in a tank of water.

The pressure at depth y_1 is p_1 and the pressure at depth y_2 is p_2. We can write the forces in terms of the pressure assuming that the area of the top and bottom of the cube is A:

$$\begin{aligned} F_1 &= p_1 A \\ F_2 &= p_2 A \end{aligned} \tag{13.16}$$

We can express the mass, m, of the water in terms of the density of water, ρ, and the volume, V, of the cube

$$m = \rho V \tag{13.17}$$

Substituting into (13.15) we can write

$$p_2 A - p_1 A - \rho V g = 0 \tag{13.18}$$

The volume of the cube is given by

$$V = A(y_1 - y_2) \tag{13.19}$$

Rearranging (13.18) and substituting for the volume we get

$$p_2 A = p_1 A + \rho A(y_1 - y_2)g \tag{13.20}$$

Dividing out the area we get an expression for the pressure as a function of depth in a liquid of density ρ

$$p_2 = p_1 + \rho g(y_1 - y_2) \tag{13.21}$$

A common situation that one wants to describe is the pressure as a function of depth below the surface of a liquid. Starting with (13.21) we can define the pressure at the surface of the liquid ($y_1 = 0$) to be p_o and the pressure at a given depth h ($y_2 = -h$) to be p. These assumptions give the equation

$$p = p_0 + \rho g h \tag{13.22}$$

for the pressure at a given depth of a liquid with density ρ. Note that (13.22) specifies the pressure in a liquid at a vertical depth of h. There is no dependence on any horizontal position. However we have made use of the fact that the density of the fluid does not change as a function of depth in the derivation of equation (13.22). This assumption of an incompressible fluid is essential for obtaining our result. Later in this section we will relax this incompressibility requirement and arrive at a different formula relating height and pressure for gases. Further it is important to note that equation (13.22) holds for any shape of the vessel containing the liquid. Figure 13.11, for example, shows three connected fluid columns. And you can see that the fluid reaches the same height in each one, independent of the shape or cross-sectional area of the container, since the bottoms are interconnected and thus have the same pressure.

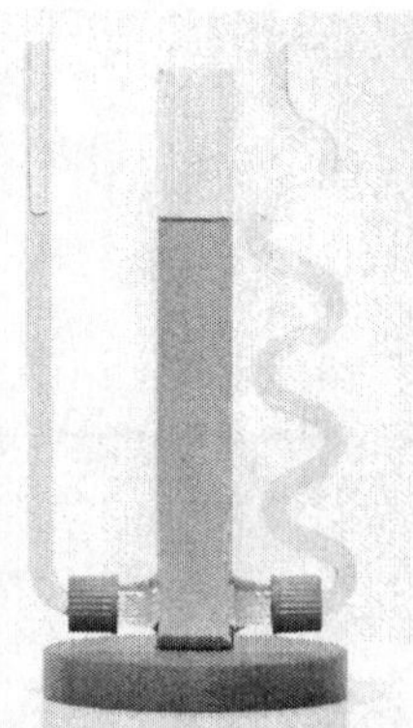

Figure 13.11: Three connected fluid columns.

Example 13.2: Submarine

A U.S. Navy Los Angeles class attack submarine is 110 m long and has a hull diameter of 10 m. For the present exercise, let us assume that it has a flat top with area of $A = 1100 \text{ m}^2$.

Example

Question:
What is the total force acting pushing on the top of this submarine at a diving depth of 250 m?

Answer:
The pressure inside the submarine is normal atmospheric pressure, p_0. According to (13.22) the pressure at a depth of 250 m is given by $p = p_0 + \rho gh$. So the pressure difference between the inside and outside of the submarine is

$$\Delta p = \rho gh = (1024 \text{ kg/m}^3)(9.81 \text{ m/s}^2)(250 \text{ m}) = 2.51 \cdot 10^6 \text{ N/m}^2 = 2.51 \text{ MPa}$$

(this is approximately 25 atm!)

Figure 13.12: Submarine surfacing.

Multiplying the area times the pressure gives the total force, according to (13.12). This way we find a total force of

$$F = \Delta pA = (2.51 \cdot 10^6 \text{ N/m}^2)(1100 \text{ m}^2) = 2.8 \cdot 10^9 \text{ N}$$

This number is astonishingly large and corresponds to a weight of approximately 280,000 tons!

In-class exercise: A steel sphere of diameter 0.250 m is submerged under the ocean at a depth of 500.0 m. What is the fractional change in the volume of the sphere? The bulk modulus of the steel of the sphere is $160 \cdot 10^9$ Pa.

a) 0.0031%
b) 0.045%
c) 0.33%
d) 0.55%
e) 1.5%

Gauge Pressure, Barometer

The pressure p in (13.22) is an absolute pressure. This pressure includes the pressure of the liquid as well as the pressure of the air above it. The difference between an absolute pressure and the atmospheric air pressure is called a gauge pressure. For example, a tire gauge used to measure the air pressure in a tire is calibrated such that the atmospheric pressure reads zero. When connected to the tire's compressed air, the gauge measures the additional pressure present in the tire. In equation (13.22) the gauge pressure is ρgh.

A simple device that is used to measure atmospheric pressure is the mercury barometer, as shown in Figure 13.13. One can construct a mercury barometer by taking a long glass tube filled with mercury and inverting it with the open end in a container of mercury. The space above the mercury is a vacuum and thus has zero pressure. The different in height between the top of the mercury in the tube and the top of the mercury in the container, h, can be related to the atmospheric pressure, p_0, using equation (13.21) with $p_2 = p_1 + \rho g(y_1 - y_2)$, $y_2 = h$, $p_2 = 0$, and $p_1 = p_0$

$$p_0 = \rho gh \tag{13.23}$$

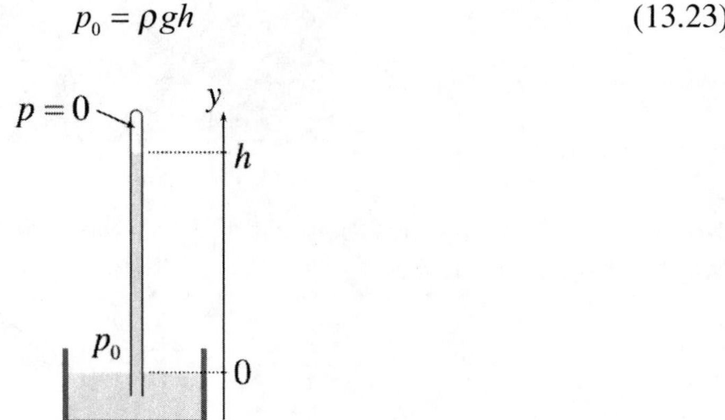

Figure 13.13: Mercury barometer.

Note that the measurement of atmospheric pressure using a mercury barometer depends on the local value of g. Atmospheric pressure is quoted in mm of mercury corresponding to the height difference h. The unit torr stands for mm of mercury and the standard atmospheric pressure is 760 torr or 29.92 inches of mercury (101.3 kPa).

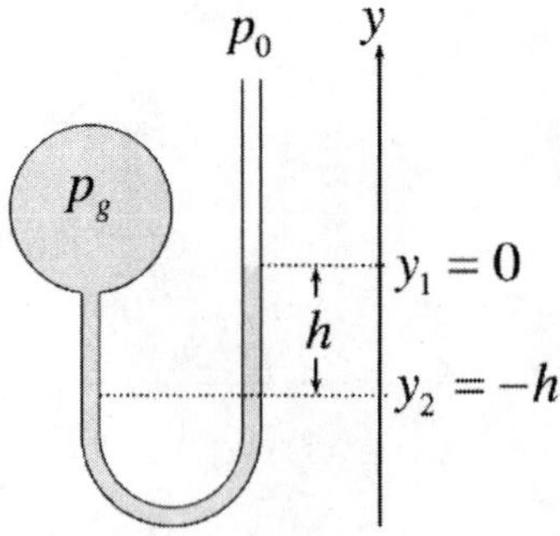

Figure 13.14: Open tube manometer.

An open-tube manometer measures the gauge pressure of a gas. An open-tube manometer consists of a U-shaped tube partially filled with a liquid such as mercury as shown in Figure 13.14. One end of the open tube manometer is connected to a vessel containing to the gas whose gauge pressure, p_g, one wants to measure while the other end is open to atmospheric pressure, p_0.

Using (13.21) with $y_1 = 0$, $p_1 = p_0$, $y_2 = -h$, and $p_2 = p$, where p is the absolute pressure of the gas in the vessel, we obtain

$$p = p_0 + \rho g h \tag{13.24}$$

The gauge pressure of the gas in the vessel is then

$$p_g = p - p_0 = \rho g h \tag{13.25}$$

Note that gauge pressure can be positive or negative. The gauge pressure of the air in an inflated automobile tire is positive. The gauge pressure at the end of a straw of a person drinking a milkshake is negative.

Barometric Altitude Relation for Gases

In the derivation of (13.22) we have made use of the incompressibility of liquids. However, if our fluid is a gas, we cannot make this assumption. We start again with a thin layer of fluid in a fluid column. The pressure difference between the top and bottom surfaces is the negative of the weight of the thin layer of fluid divided by the area,

$$\Delta p = -\frac{F}{A} = -\frac{mg}{A} = -\frac{\rho V g}{A} = -\frac{\rho(\Delta h A)g}{A} = -\rho g \Delta h \tag{13.26}$$

The negative sign comes from the fact that the pressure decreases with increasing altitude, since the weight of the fluid column above is reduced. So far nothing is different from the derivation of the incompressible case. However, for compressible fluids we find that the density is proportional to the pressure.

$$\frac{\rho}{\rho_0} = \frac{p}{p_0} \tag{13.27}$$

Strictly speaking this is only true for ideal gases at constant temperature, as we will see in our chapter 19 on the gas laws. However, if we insert this equation into (13.26), we find

$$\frac{\Delta p}{\Delta h} = -\frac{g\rho_0}{p_0} p \tag{13.28}$$

Taking the limit of $\Delta h \to 0$ we finally find the equation

$$\frac{dp}{dh} = -\frac{g\rho_0}{p_0} p \tag{13.29}$$

This is an example of a differential equation. Here we need to find a function whose derivative is proportional to the function itself, which would be an exponential. Specifically:

$$p(h) = p_0 e^{-h\rho_0 g / p_0} \tag{13.30}$$

It is easy to convince ourselves that (13.30) is indeed a solution to (13.29), simply by taking the derivative with respect to h. Equation (13.30) is sometimes called the barometric pressure formula and relates the altitude to the pressure in gases. It only applies as long as the temperature does not change as a function of altitude, and as long as we can assume that the gravitational acceleration is constant. We will come back to the effect of temperature change when we discuss the ideal gas law in chapter 19.

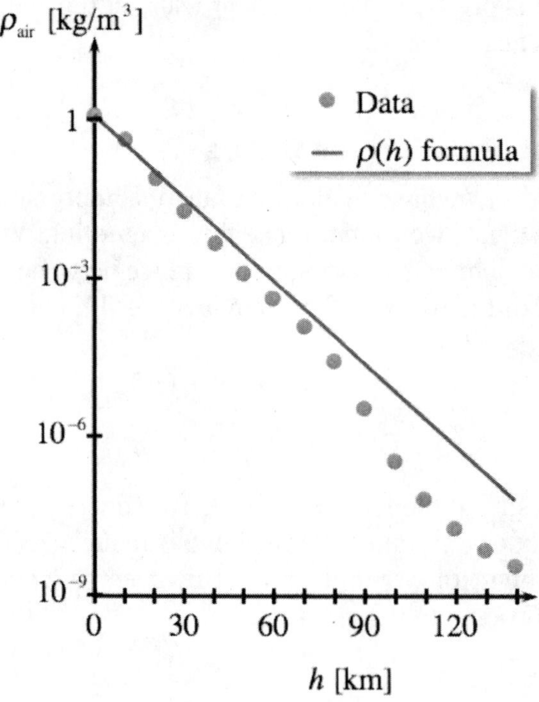

Figure 13.15: Comparison of the barometric altitude formula (13.31) for the air density (blue line) with the data for our atmosphere (red dots).

It is now easy to obtain a formula for the air density ρ as a function of the altitude by combining (13.27) and (13.30), which leads to

$$\rho(h) = \rho_0 e^{-h\rho_0 g / p_0} \tag{13.31}$$

Even though we stated that our results are only an approximation, they compare fairly well to the actual atmospheric data, as shown in, where we used (13.31) with $g = 9.81 \text{ m/s}^2$, $p_0 = 1.01 \cdot 10^5 \text{ Pa}$, the sea level ($h = 0$) air pressure, and $\rho_0 = 1.229 \text{ kg/m}^3$, the air density at sea level. As you can see, the agreement is rather remarkable up to the top of the stratosphere, approximately 50 km above ground.

Example

Example 13.3: Mount Everest Air Pressure

As climbers approach the peak of the Earth's highest mountain, Mount Everest, they usually have to wear breathing equipment. The reason for this is that the air pressure is very low, too low for our lungs that are usually accustomed to near sea-level conditions.

Figure 13.16: Mount Everest.

Question:

What is the air pressure at the top of Mount Everest?

Answer:

This is a case where we can use our barometric pressure formula (13.30). We have to figure out the constants. They are: $p_0 = 1.01 \cdot 10^5 \text{ Pa}$ is the sea level air pressure, and $\rho_0 = 1.229 \text{ kg/m}^3$ is the air density at sea level. So we find for the constants in (13.30)

$$\frac{p_0}{\rho_0 g} = \frac{1.01 \cdot 10^5 \text{ Pa}}{(1.229 \text{ kg/m}^3)(9.81 \text{ m/s}^2)} = 8377 \text{ m} \tag{13.32}$$

We can then rewrite (13.30) for our atmosphere as

$$p(h) = p_0 e^{-h/(8377 \text{ m})} \tag{13.33}$$

The height of Mount Everest is 8850 m. Therefore we find our answer

$$p(8850 \text{ m}) = p_0 e^{-8850/8377} = 0.348 p_0 = 35 \text{ kPa}$$

So the air pressure at the top of Mount Everest is only 35% of the sea level air pressure. (The actual pressure is slightly lower due mainly to temperature effects.)

Pascal's Principle

If we exert pressure on a part of an incompressible fluid, that pressure will be transmitted to all parts of the fluid without loss. This concept is termed Pascal's Principle and can be stated as:

> *When there is a change in pressure at any point in a confined fluid, there is an equal change in pressure at every point in the fluid.*

Pascal's Principle is the basis for many modern hydraulic devices such as automobile brakes and car lifts.

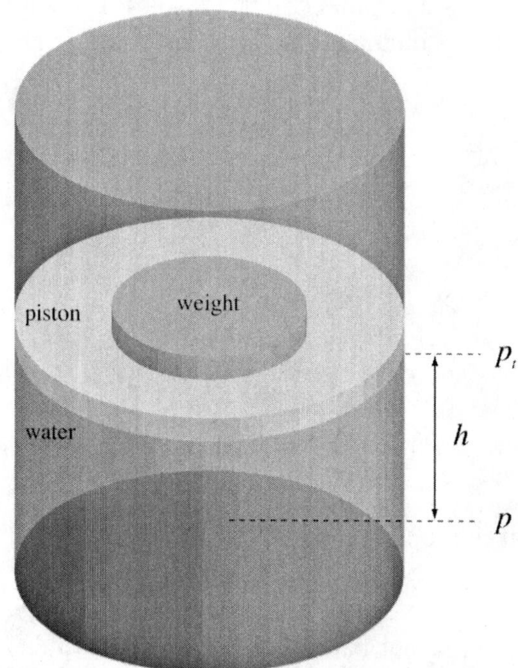

Figure 13.17: Cylinder partially filled with water, with a piston placed on the top of the water. A weight is placed on the piston.

The basic idea of Pascal's Principle can be demonstrated by taking a cylinder partially filled with water, placing a piston on top of the column of water, and placing a weight on top of the piston as shown in Figure 13.17. The weight exerts a pressure, p_t, on the top of the column of water. The pressure p at a depth h is given by

$$p = p_t + \rho g h \qquad (13.34)$$

Because water can be considered incompressible, if we now add a second weight, the change in pressure Δp at depth h is solely due to the change in the pressure Δp_t on the top of the water. The density of the water does not change and the depth does not change, so we can write

$$\Delta p = \Delta p_t \qquad (13.35)$$

This result does not depend on h, so it must hold for all positions in the liquid.

Consider the case of two connected pistons filled with oil as shown in Figure 13.18. One piston has area A_{in} and the other piston has area A_{out} with $A_{in} < A_{out}$. We exert a force F_{in} on the first piston producing a change in pressure in the oil. This change in pressure will be transmitted to all points in the oil including the second piston. We can write

$$\Delta p = \frac{F_{in}}{A_{in}} = \frac{F_{out}}{A_{out}} \tag{13.36}$$

or

$$F_{out} = F_{in} \frac{A_{out}}{A_{in}} \tag{13.37}$$

Because A_{out} is larger than A_{in}, F_{out} is larger than F_{in}, so we have magnified the force applied to the first piston. This concept is the basis of hydraulic devices that can produce large output forces with small input forces.

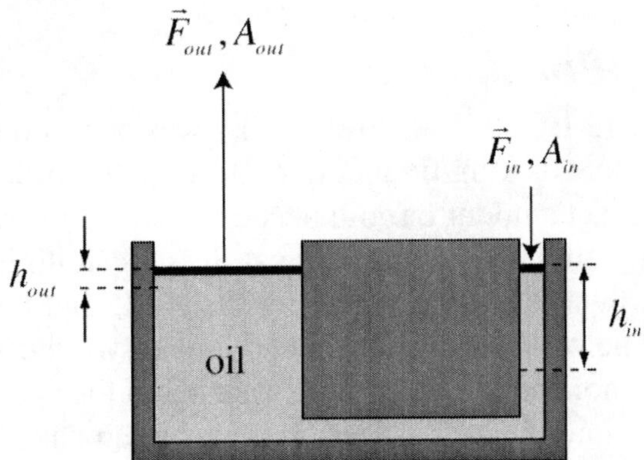

Figure 13.18: Application of Pascal's Principle to produce a hydraulic lift.

The amount of work done on the first piston is the same as the amount of work done by the second piston. To calculate the work done we need to calculate the distance over which the forces act. For both pistons, the volume, V, of incompressible oil that is moved is the same

$$V = h_{in} A_{in} = h_{out} A_{out} \tag{13.38}$$

where h_{in} is the distance the first piston moved and h_{out} is the distance the second piston moved. We can see that

$$h_{out} = h_{in} \frac{A_{in}}{A_{out}} \tag{13.39}$$

which means that the second piston moves a smaller distance than the first piston because $A_{in} < A_{out}$. The work done can be calculated using the fact that work is force times distance and also using equations (13.37) and (13.39) as

$$W = F_{in}h_{in} = \left(F_{out}\frac{A_{in}}{A_{out}}\right)\left(h_{out}\frac{A_{out}}{A_{in}}\right) = F_{out}h_{out} \quad (13.40)$$

Thus, this hydraulic device can transmit a larger force over a smaller distance. However, no additional work is done.

In-class exercise: A car with a mass of 1600 kg is supported by a hydraulic car lift as illustrated in Figure 13.18. The large piston supporting the car has a diameter of 25.0 cm. The small piston has a diameter of 1.25 cm. How much force do you need to exert on the small piston to support the car?
a) 1.43 N
b) 5.22 N
c) 10.2 N
d) 23.1 N
e) 39.2 N

13.5. Archimedes' Principle

Archimedes (287 BC – 212 BC) of Syracuse, Sicily, was one of the greatest mathematicians of all time. His king/tyrant Hiero of Syracuse ordered a new crown and gave the goldsmith the exact amount of gold needed. When the crown was finished, it had the exact weight, but still Hiero suspected that the goldsmith had used some (much cheaper!) silver in the crown as a replacement for the gold. But he could not prove it and went to Archimedes for help. According to legend, the answer occurred to Archimedes when he took a bath and noticed the water level rising and his apparent weight diminishing when he got into the bathtub, whereupon he ran naked through the streets of Syracuse, shouting "eureka!" Using this discovery he was able to demonstrate the silver-for-gold switch and thus the theft committed by the goldsmith. Let us see how to determine density by first learning about buoyant forces and fluid displacement.

Buoyant Force

Consider Figure 13.10, in which we studied an imaginary cube of water in a volume of water. The weight of the cube of water was supported by the force resulting from pressure difference between the top and bottom of the cube given by equation (13.15), which we can re-write as

$$F_2 - F_1 = mg = F_B \quad (13.41)$$

where F_B is defined as the buoyant force acting on the cube of water. For the case of the imaginary cube of water, the buoyant force is equal to the weight of the water. In general the buoyant force acting on a submerged object is given by the weight of the fluid displaced,

$$F_B = m_f g \quad (13.42)$$

We now replace that cube of water with a cube of steel as shown in Figure 13.19. In this case, the steel cube has the same volume and is at the same depth as the cube of water so that the buoyant force is still the same. However, the steel cube weighs more than the cube of water, so that there is a net y – component of force on the steel cube given by

$$F_{net,y} = F_B - mg < 0 \tag{13.43}$$

The net downward force would cause the steel cube to sink.

If we replace the cube of steel with a cube of wood, the weight of the wood would be less that the cube of water that it replaced, and the net force would be upward. The wooden cube would rise toward the surface. If we place an object that is less dense than water in water, it will float. The object of mass m will sink in the water until the weight of the displaced water equals the weight of the object,

$$F_B = m_f g = mg \tag{13.44}$$

A floating body displaces its own weight of fluid.

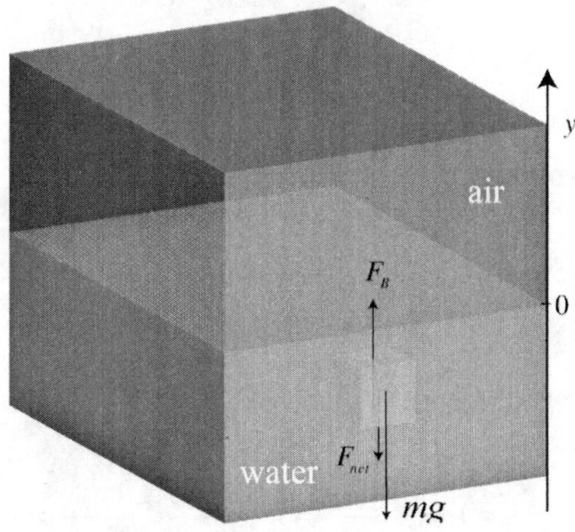

Figure 13.19: Steel cube submerged in water.

If we place an object that has a higher density than water under water, it will experience a buoyant force upward that is less than its weight. Its apparent weight then is given by

$$\text{actual weight} - \text{buoyant force} = \text{apparent weight} \tag{13.45}$$

Example 13.4: Iceberg

Icebergs still pose grave dangers for oceangoing ships. Many ships have sunk after collisions with iceberg. What makes icebergs particularly dangerous is that a large fraction of their volume is hidden below the water line and thus practically invisible to the sailor.

Example

Question:
What fraction of the volume of an iceberg floating in seawater is visible above the surface?

Answer:
Let V_t be the total volume of the iceberg and V_s be the volume of the iceberg that is submerged. The fraction f above water would then be

$$f = \frac{V_t - V_s}{V_t} = 1 - \frac{V_s}{V_t} \tag{13.46}$$

Because the iceberg is floating, the submerged volume must displace a volume of seawater that has the same weight as the entire iceberg. The mass of the iceberg, m_t, can be calculated from the volume of the iceberg and density of ice, $\rho_{ice} = 0.917 \text{ g/cm}^3$. The mass of the displaced seawater can be calculated from the volume submerged and the known density of seawater, $\rho_{seawater} = 1.024 \text{ g/cm}^3$. We can equate these two weights

$$\rho_{ice} V_t g = \rho_{seawater} V_s g$$

or

$$\rho_{ice} V_t = \rho_{seawater} V_s$$

We can rearrange this formula to give

$$\frac{V_s}{V_t} = \frac{\rho_{ice}}{\rho_{seawater}}.$$

We can then state that the fraction above water is

$$f = 1 - \frac{V_s}{V_t} = 1 - \frac{\rho_{ice}}{\rho_{seawater}} = 1 - \frac{0.917 \text{ g/cm}^3}{1.024 \text{ g/cm}^3} = 0.104,$$

or about 10% is above water.

An interesting experiment on buoyancy can be performed as follows (see Figure 13.20). We poured water (with red food coloring) into a container (left panel) and put a swimmer into it (center panel). The swimmer is 90% submerged, and thus its average density is 90% of that of water, as in the previous example.

Next, we pour paint thinner on the top of the water. Paint thinner does not mix with water and has a density of 80% of water. Thus, it will rest on top of the water. If we would put the swimmer into a cup with paint thinner, it would sink to the bottom. So what happens when we pour the paint thinner on top of the water with the swimmer in it? Will the swimmer rise, stay at the same level, or sink?

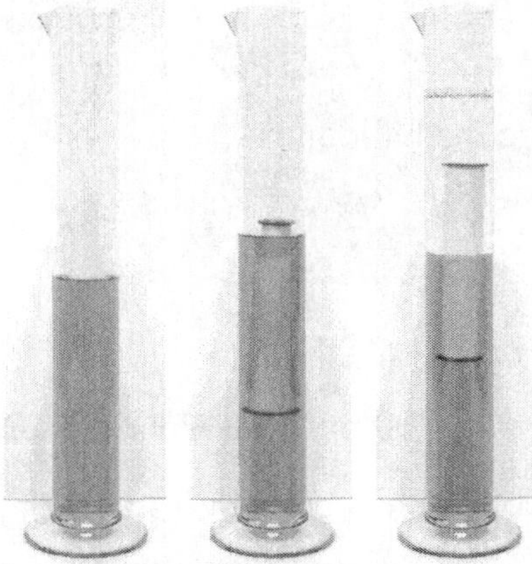

Figure 13.20: Buoyancy experiment with two liquids.

The answer is shown in the right panel of Figure 13.20. The swimmer rises. But why? In two liquids, there are two buoyant forces, one from the fraction of the volume submerged in water, and the other from the fraction of the volume submerged in the pain thinner. So less of the volume of the swimmer needs to be submerged in the water to generate the same buoyant force that balances the weight, as compared to the case where there is air and not paint thinner on top of the water.

Example

Example 13.5: Balloon

A typical hot air balloon has a volume of $2200\ \text{m}^3$. The density of air at a temperature of $20\ ^\circ\text{C}$ is $1.205\ \text{kg/m}^3$. The density of the hot air inside the balloon at a temperature of $100\ ^\circ\text{C}$ is $0.946\ \text{kg/m}^3$.

Figure 13.21: Hot air balloon in flight.

Question:

How much weight can the hot air balloon lift (counting the balloon itself)?

Example

Answer:
The weight of the air at 20 °C the balloon displaces is equal to the buoyant force

$$F_B = \rho_{20} V g$$

The weight of the hot air inside the balloon is

$$W_{balloon} = \rho_{100} V g$$

The weight that can be lifted is

$$\begin{aligned} W &= F_B - W_{balloon} = \rho_{20} V g - \rho_{100} V g \\ &= Vg\left(\rho_{20} - \rho_{100}\right) = \left(2200 \text{ m}^3\right)\left(9.81 \text{ m/s}^2\right)\left(1.205 - 0.946\right)\left(\text{kg/m}^3\right) \\ &= 5590 \text{ N, or } 1260 \text{ pounds} \end{aligned}$$

Note that this weight must include the balloon structure including the balloon envelope, basket, and fuel, as well as any payload such as pilot and passengers.

Self-Test Opportunity: Suppose the balloon in the preceding example were filled with helium instead of hot air. How much weight could the helium filled balloon lift? The density of helium is 0.164 kg/m^3.

Determination of Density

Let us return to Archimedes' problem of figuring out if the crown was pure gold or a mixture of silver and gold. Since the density of gold is 19.3 g/cm^3, and the density of silver is only 10.5 g/cm^3, Archimedes only needed to measure the density of the crown to find out what fraction of it was gold and what was silver. But how can one measure the density?

The answer is to submerge the crown in water and measure its volume from the rise in the water level, resulting in the determination of the volume. Weighing the crown gives us the mass, and dividing the mass by the volume yields the density, our answer that we needed.

Example

Example 13.6: Density
The following experiment, shown in Figure 13.22, determines the density of an object without the need to measure water levels, just by weighing. This is usually the more precise and thus preferred method. We first weigh a beaker with water (with green food coloring added), as done in the upper left corner (a). The mass for the beaker and water is determined to be m_0 = 0.437 kg. In the upper right corner picture a metal ball, suspended by a string is submerged in the water, being careful not to let the ball touch the bottom of the beaker (b). The new total mass of this arrangement is determined in the lower right corner of the figure (c) and is $m_1 = 0.458$ kg. Finally, in the lower right part of the figure (d) we let the ball rest on the bottom of the beaker, without pulling on the

string. Now the mass is determined to be $m_2 = 0.596$ kg.

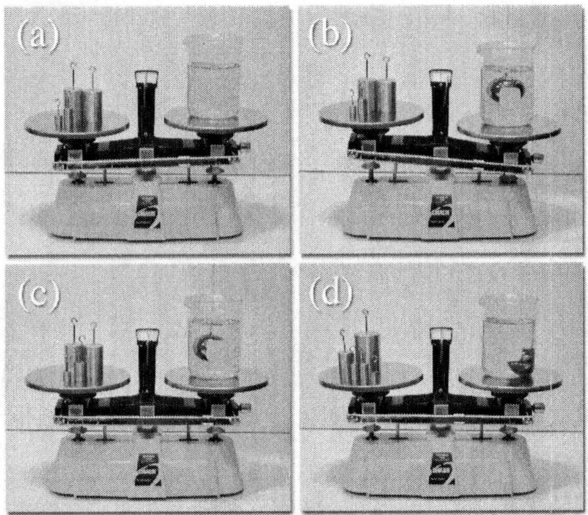

Figure 13.22: Experiment to determine the density of a metal object.

Question:
What is the density of the ball?

Answer:

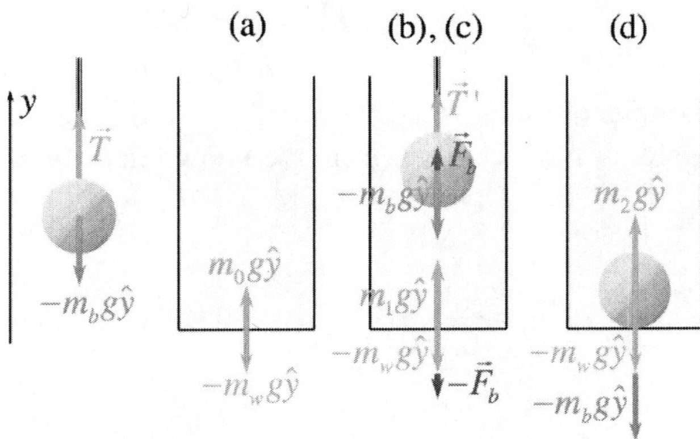

Figure 13.23: Free-body diagrams for the different parts of the experiment.

Let us examine the free-body diagrams in the different parts of this experiment. This is done in Figure 13.23. The left part of the figure shows the ball suspended from the string in equilibrium, with its weight $-m_b g\hat{y}$ balanced by the string tension $\vec{T}$. The second diagram from the left corresponds to the part (a) of the previous figure and shows the only forces acting on the water-filled container, which are its weight $-m_w g\hat{y}$ and the normal force $m_0 g\hat{y}$. The value of m_0 is given in the problem ans is the result of the first measurement. The next panel corresponds to parts (b) and (c) in the previous figure, contains the free-body diagram of the submerged ball as well as the free-body diagram of the container, and shows the effect of the buoyant force $\vec{F}_b$ on the ball and the liquid-filled container. Note that the ball experiences the buoyant force and thus the container must experience a force of equal magnitude and opposite direction, $-\vec{F}_b$, due to Newton's

Third Law. Note the now the normal force required to keep the container in force equilibrium is $m_1 g\hat{y}$. The right-most free-body diagram corresponds to part (d) of the previous figure, and now the normal force is $m_2 g\hat{y}$.

In part (a) we measure m_0, the combined mass of water and beaker. In part (c) we measure in addition the mass of the water displaced by the (yet unknown) volume V of the metal ball. The mass of the displaced water is then $m_{\mathrm{H_2O}} = \rho_{\mathrm{H_2O}} V_{ball}$, and the total mass measured in (c) is

$$m_1 = m_0 + \rho_{\mathrm{H_2O}} V_{ball}.$$

Finally, the mass measured in (d) is the combined mass of the ball plus beaker and water. For the mass of the ball we can again use the product of the density and the volume, but now we use the density of the ball

$$m_2 = m_0 + m_{ball} = m_0 + \rho_{ball} V_{ball}.$$

Combining these equations, we find

$$\frac{m_2 - m_0}{m_1 - m_0} = \frac{\rho_{ball} V_{ball}}{\rho_{\mathrm{H_2O}} V_{ball}} = \frac{\rho_{ball}}{\rho_{\mathrm{H_2O}}}. \qquad (13.47)$$

As you can see, the volume of the ball has cancelled out in this calculation, and we can simply obtain the density of the metal ball from the known density of water and our three measurements m_0, m_1, m_2:

$$\rho_{ball} = \frac{m_2 - m_0}{m_1 - m_0} \rho_{\mathrm{H_2O}} = \frac{0.596 - 0.437}{0.458 - 0.437} 1000 \text{ kg/m}^3 = 7570 \text{ kg/m}^3.$$

13.6. Ideal Fluid Motion

The motion of real-life fluids is complicated and difficult to describe. Numerical techniques are often required to calculate the useful quantities related to the motion of fluids. Here we will consider ideal fluids that can be treated more simply and still lead to important and relevant results. To consider a fluid as ideal we will make the following assumptions related to the flow of ideal fluids: laminar flow, incompressible flow, non-viscous flow, and irrotational flow.

Laminar flow means that the velocity of a moving fluid at a fixed point in space does not change with time. A gently flowing river displays laminar flow as shown in Figure 13.24, left panel. A waterfall is an example of non-laminar, or turbulent flow. Rising smoke is an example of the transition from laminar to turbulent flow as shown in the center of Figure 13.24. The warm smoke initially displays laminar flow as it rises. As the smoke continues to rise, its speed increases until turbulent flow sets in.

Incompressible flow means that the density of the liquid does not change as the liquid flows. A non-viscous fluid flows completely freely. We are familiar with liquids that do not flow freely such as pancake syrup or lava. The viscosity of a fluid is analogous to friction. An object moving in a non-viscous liquid will experience no friction-like forces while the same object moving in a viscous liquid will feel a drag due to viscous forces similar to friction. A flowing viscous fluid will lose kinetic energy of motion to thermal energy. We assume that ideal fluids do not lose energy as they flow.

Figure 13.24: Left: Laminar flow of the Firehole River at Yellowstone; center: transition from laminar to turbulent flow in rising cigarette smoke; right: turbulent flow at the Upper Falls on the Yellowstone River.

Irrotational flow means that no part of the fluid rotates about its own center-of-mass. Rotational motion of a small part of the fluid would mean that the rotating part of the fluid would have rotational energy, which is not treated in ideal fluids.

We can describe laminar flow in terms of streamlines as illustrated in Figure 13.25. A streamline represents the direction that a small element of the fluid takes over time. The velocity $\vec{v}$ of the small element is always tangent to the streamline. Note that streamlines never cross; if they did, the velocity of flow at the crossing point would have two values.

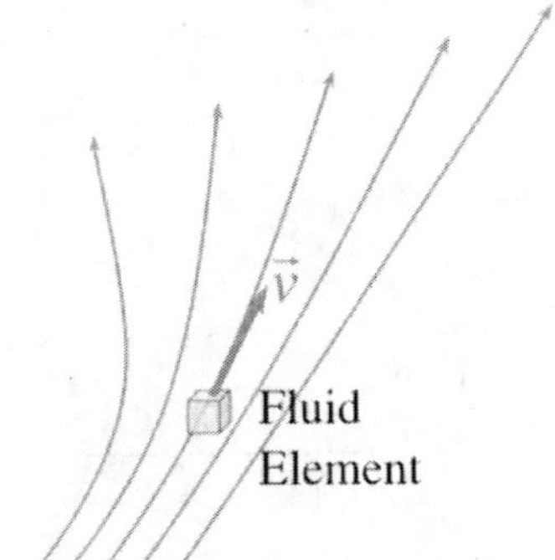

Figure 13.25: Streamlines of a flowing fluid.

Bernoulli's Equation

What provides the lift that allows an airplane to fly through the air? In this section, we will develop the tools to understand the answer. First let us start with a simple demonstration that you can do by using two empty soft drink cans and five drinking straws. Place each empty can on two straws, with a gap of approximately 1 cm between them, as shown in Figure 13.26. In this way, the cans are relatively easily able to make lateral movements. Then blow air through the gap between the cans by using the fifth straw. What happens? We will tell you at the end of this section, but perhaps you might want to do this experiment yourself first.

Figure 13.26: Blowing air through the gap between two soft drink cans.

A similar experiment can be done by holding two sheets of paper parallel to each other at a separation of approximately an inch and blowing air between them. What do you expect the outcome for the motion of the sheets is going to be?

Consider an ideal fluid flowing with speed v in a container with cross sectional area A as shown in Figure 13.27. ΔV is the volume of fluid that flows through the container during time Δt and is given by

$$\Delta V = A\Delta x = Av\Delta t \tag{13.48}$$

so we can write the volume per unit time passing a given point in the container as

$$\frac{\Delta V}{\Delta t} = Av \tag{13.49}$$

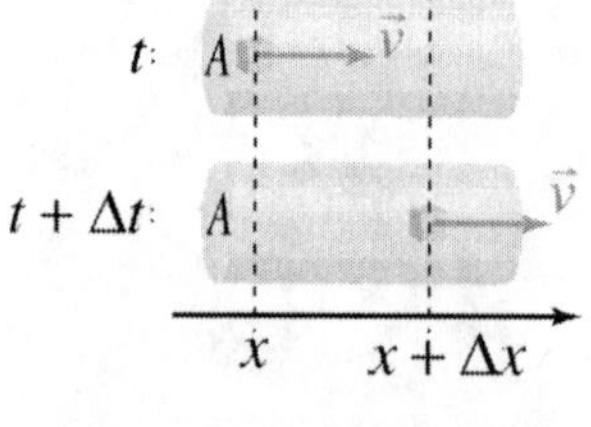

Figure 13.27: Ideal fluid flowing through a pipe with constant cross-sectional area.

Now consider an ideal fluid flowing in a container that changes cross sectional area as shown in Figure 13.28. The fluid is initially flowing with speed v_1 through a part of the container with cross sectional area A_1. Downstream in the container the fluid continues to flow with speed v_2 in a downstream part of the container that has cross sectional area A_2. The volume of ideal fluid that enters this section of the container per unit time must equal the volume of ideal fluid exiting the container per unit time because the fluid is incompressible and there are no leaks.

Figure 13.28: Fluid flowing through a pipe with changing cross-sectional area.

We can express the volume per unit time flowing in the first part of the container as

$$\frac{\Delta V}{\Delta t} = A_1 v_1 \tag{13.50}$$

and the volume per unit time flow in the second part of the container as

$$\frac{\Delta V}{\Delta t} = A_2 v_2 \tag{13.51}$$

The volume per unit time passing any point in time must be the same in all parts of the container, or else we would somehow be creating or destroying fluid. Thus we get

$$A_1 v_1 = A_2 v_2 \tag{13.52}$$

This equation is called the equation of continuity.

We can express (13.52) as a constant volume flow rate, R_V,

$$R_V = Av \tag{13.53}$$

Assuming an ideal fluid whose density does not change we can also express a constant mass flow rate, R_m,

$$R_m = \rho A v \tag{13.54}$$

The SI unit for mass flow rate is kg/s.

We now consider what happens to the pressure in an ideal fluid flowing through a container at a steady rate as shown in Figure 13.29. We start by applying conservation of energy to the flowing ideal fluid between the lower part of the container and the upper part of the container.

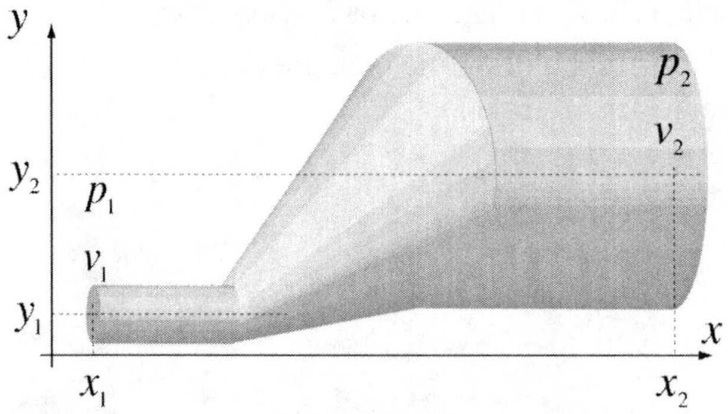

Figure 13.29: Ideal fluid flowing through a container with changing cross-sectional area and elevation.

In the lower left part of the container, the flowing fluid of constant density ρ is characterized by the pressure p_1, speed v_1, and elevation y_1. The same fluid flows through the transition region and flows into the upper right part of the container. Here the fluid is characterized by the pressure p_2, speed v_2, and elevation y_2. The relationship between the pressures and velocities in this situation is given by

$$p_1 + \rho g y_1 + \frac{1}{2}\rho v_1^2 = p_2 + \rho g y_2 + \frac{1}{2}\rho v_2^2 . \tag{13.55}$$

Another way of stating these relationships is

$$p + \rho g y + \frac{1}{2}\rho v^2 = \text{constant} . \tag{13.56}$$

This equation is Bernoulli's equation. If there is no flow, $v = 0$ and this equation is equivalent to (13.22). One major consequence of this equation is realized if we take $y = 0$, which means constant elevation

$$p + \frac{1}{2}\rho v^2 = \text{constant} . \tag{13.57}$$

From this equation, we can see that if the velocity of a flowing fluid is increased, the pressure must decrease. The decrease of the pressure transverse to the fluid flow has practical applications including devices to measure the flow rate of a fluid and the creation of partial vacuum.

Derivation 13.1: Bernoulli's Equation

The net work done of the system, W, is equal to the change in kinetic energy, ΔK, of the flowing fluid between the initial and final parts of the container

$$W = \Delta K \tag{13.58}$$

The change in kinetic energy is given by

$$\Delta K = \frac{1}{2}\Delta m v_2^2 - \frac{1}{2}\Delta m v_1^2 \tag{13.59}$$

where Δm is the amount of mass entering the lower part of the container and exiting the upper part of the container in time Δt. The flow of mass per unit time is the density of the fluid times the change in volume per unit time

$$\frac{\Delta m}{\Delta t} = \rho \frac{\Delta V}{\Delta t}; \tag{13.60}$$

so we can rewrite (13.59) as

$$\Delta K = \frac{1}{2}\rho \Delta V \left(v_2^2 - v_1^2\right) \tag{13.61}$$

The work done by gravity on the flowing fluid is given by the mass per unit time changing elevation

$$W_g = -\Delta m g\left(y_2 - y_1\right) \tag{13.62}$$

where the negative sign arises because negative work is being done by gravity on the fluid when $y_2 > y_1$. We can again restate this result in terms of the volume flow ΔV and the density of the fluid

$$W_g = -\rho \Delta V g\left(y_2 - y_1\right) \tag{13.63}$$

The work done by a force, F, acting over a distance, Δx, is given by $W = F\Delta x$, which we can write as

$$W = F\Delta x = \left(pA\right)\Delta x = p\Delta V \tag{13.64}$$

since in this case the force arises from the pressure in the fluid. We can then write the work done on the fluid by the pressure forcing the fluid to flow into the container as $p_1\Delta V$ and the work done on the exiting fluid as $-p_2\Delta V$, giving the total work done related to pressure,

$$W_p = \left(p_1 - p_2\right)\Delta V \tag{13.65}$$

Using (13.58) and taking $W = W_p + W_g$ in we get

Derivation

$$(p_1 - p_2)\Delta V - \rho\Delta V g(y_2 - y_1) = \frac{1}{2}\rho\Delta V\left(v_2^2 - v_1^2\right) \tag{13.66}$$

Derivation

which we can simplify to

$$p_1 + \rho g y_1 + \frac{1}{2}\rho v_1^2 = p_2 + \rho g y_2 + \frac{1}{2}\rho v_2^2 \tag{13.67}$$

This equation is Bernoulli's Equation.

Applications

Now that we have derived Bernoulli's equation, we can return to the demonstration experiment of Figure 13.26, with which we started this section. If you have performed this experiment of blowing air between the two soft drink cans, you have found that they move closer to each other. This is opposite to what most people expect, that blowing air in the gap would force the cans apart. Bernoulli's equation explains why we obtain this surprising result. Since we have found that $p + \frac{1}{2}\rho v^2 = \text{constant}$, the large speed with which the air is moving between the cans causes the pressure to decrease. So the air pressure on the outsides of the cans is larger than on the insides, causing the cans to be pushed towards each other. This is the so-called Bernoulli effect. Another way to show the same effect is to hold two sheets of paper parallel to each other about an inch apart and then to blow air between them: the sheets get pushed together.

Truck drivers know about this effect as well. When two 18-wheelers with the typical rectangular box trailers drive in two lanes next to each other at high speed, the drivers have to pay attention not to come too close to each other, because then the Bernoulli effect can suck the trailers towards each other.

Figure 13.30: Forces acting on an airplane in flight.

Racecar designers make use of this Bernoulli effect. The biggest limitation to racecar acceleration performance is the maximum friction force between the tires and the road. This friction force, in turn, is proportional to the normal force. One can increase the normal force by increasing the racecar's mass, but this defeats the purpose, because a large mass means smaller acceleration, according to Newton's Second Law. The much more efficient way to increase the normal force is to develop a large pressure difference between the upper and lower surfaces of the racecar. According to Bernoulli's equation this can be accomplished by causing the air to stream faster across the bottom of the car than the top. (Another way to accomplish this would be to use a wing to deflect the air up and thus create a downward force, but these have been ruled out in Formula 1 racing, and so the Bernoulli effect provides the main means to increase the friction there.)

Let us return to the question of what causes an airplane to fly. In Figure 13.30 we show the forces acting on an airplane during flight with constant velocity and at constant altitude. The thrust $\vec{F}_t$ is generated by sucking in air from into front and expelling out the back of the jet engines. This force acts towards the front of the plane. The drag force $\vec{F}_d$ from the air resistance (covered in chapter 4 already) is acting towards the rear of the plane. At constant velocity, these two forces cancel, $\vec{F}_t = \vec{F}_d$. The forces acting in vertical direction are the weight, $\vec{F}_g$, and the lift, $\vec{F}_l$, which is provided almost exclusively by the wings. If the plane flies at constant altitude then these two forces cancel as well, $\vec{F}_l = \vec{F}_g$. Since a typical fully loaded and fueled Boeing 747 has a mass of metric 350 tons, its weight is 3.4 MN. Thus the lift provided by the wings to keep the airplane flying is very large. By comparison, the maximum thrust of the four engines on a 747 combined is 0.9 MN.

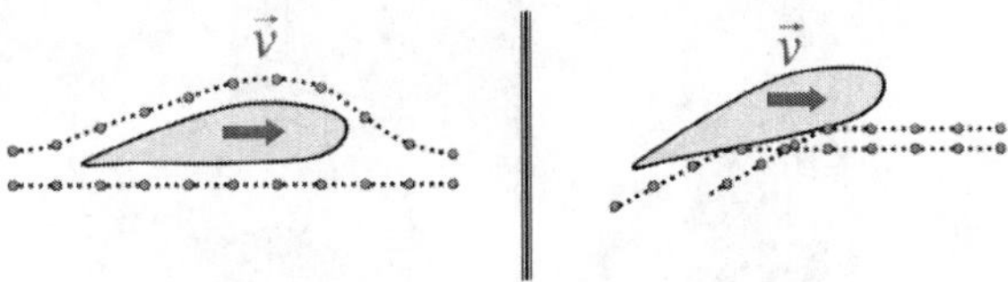

Figure 13.31: Two extreme views of the process that creates lift on the wing of an airplane. Left: Bernoulli; right: Newton.

The most commonly held notion of what generates the lift that allows a plane to stay airborne is shown on the left side of Figure 13.31: The wing moves through the air and forces the air streamlines that move above it onto a longer path and thus higher speed in order to reconnect with the air that moves below the wing. Bernoulli's equation then implies that the pressure on the top side of the wing is lower than on the bottom side. Since the combined area of the two wings of a Boeing 747 is $511.\text{ m}^2$, a pressure difference of $\Delta p = F / A = 3.5 \text{ MN} / 511.\text{ m}^2 = 6.6 \text{ kPa}$ (= 0.66% of the atmospheric pressure at sea level) between the bottom and the top of the wings would be required for this picture to work out quantitatively. An alternative physical picture is shown on the right side of Figure 13.31. In this picture air molecules get deflected downwards by the lower side of the wing, and due to Newton's Third Law the wing then experiences an upward force that provides the lift. In order for this picture to work, the bottom of the wing has to have some non-zero angle (= "angle of attack") relative to the horizontal. (In this position the nose of the aircraft points slightly upwards and the engine thrust also contributes to the lift.)

Both of these two simple pictures contain elements of the truth and contribute to the lift to different degrees, depending on the type of aircraft and the flight phase. The Newton picture is more important during takeoff and landing, and during all flight phases for fighter planes. But as a general statement we can say that air does not act as an ideal incompressible fluid as it streams around the airplane's wing. It is compressed at the front edge of the wing and decompressed at its back edge. This compression-decompression effect is stronger on the top surface than on the bottom surface, creating a higher net pressure at the bottom of the wing and providing the lift. The design of aircraft wings is still under intense study, and research on new wing designs contributing to higher fuel efficiency and stability is ongoing.

We can apply similar considerations to the flight of a curveball in baseball. Curveballs have sideward spin, and if a left-handed pitcher gives it a strong clockwise rotation, then the ball will deviate to the right (as seen by the pitcher, compare Figure 13.32) relative to a straight line. In this figure the relative velocity between the air and a point on the left surface of the ball is larger than the relative velocity between the air and the right side surface. A naïve application of Bernoulli's equation would cause us to expect the pressure to be lower on the left side of the ball than on the right, thus causing the ball to move left.

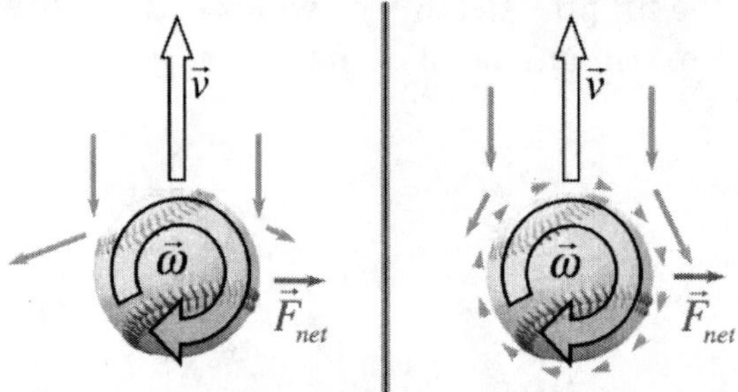

Figure 13.32: Top view of clockwise spinning baseball moving from the bottom of the page to the top of the page; Left: Newton picture; Right: boundary layer picture.

The "Newton" picture comes closer to explaining correctly why a clockwise spinning baseball also experiences a clockwise deflection, see the left side of Figure 13.32. We show the top view of a clockwise spinning baseball, moving from the bottom of the page to the top. We indicate the air molecules that the ball encounters by the red vertical arrows. As the air molecules collide with the surface of the baseball, the ones on the side where the surface rotates towards them (left half of Figure 13.32) receive a stronger sideways kick, i.e. impulse, than those on the right side. The net Newton's Third Law recoil force on the baseball thus deflects the baseball in the same direction as its rotation. While the Newton picture at least gets the sign of the effect right, it is not quite the correct explanation, because the oncoming air molecules do not reach the surface of the baseball undisturbed as required for this picture to work.

But just like the airplane flight, the explanation of the baseball curve is also more complex. A rotating sphere moving through air drags a boundary layer of air along with its surface. The air molecules that this boundary layer encounters then get partially dragged along. This causes the air molecules on the right side of the ball in Figure 13.32 to get accelerated and those on the left side to get slowed down. The differentially higher speed on the right side implies a lower pressure due to Bernoulli's equation and thus causes a deflection to the right. This effect is known as the Magnus effect.

Topspin in tennis causes the ball to dip faster than a ball hit without spin; backspin causes the tennis ball to sail longer. Both work for the same reason we just sketched for the curveball in baseball. Golfers also use backspin for their drives to carry longer. A typical well-hit drive will have backspin of approximately 4000 rpm. Sidespin in golf causes draws/hooks and fades/slices, depending on the severity and direction of the spin. Incidentally, the dimples on a golf ball are essential for the flight characteristics of the ball, causing turbulence around the golf ball and thus reducing the air resistance. Even the best professionals would not be able to hit a golf ball without dimples over a distance of more than 200 m.

Example

Example 13.7: Perfume Atomizer

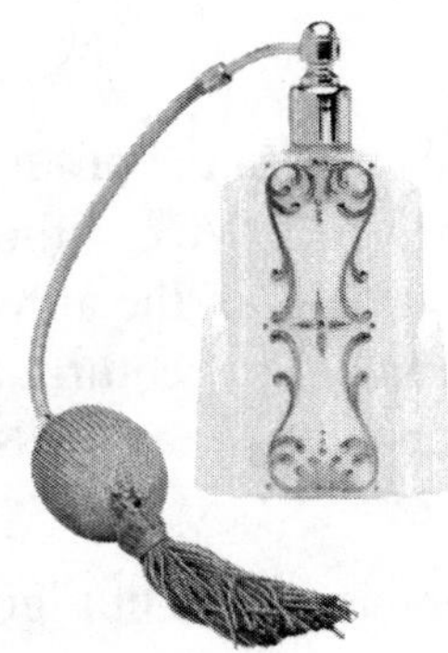

Figure 13.33: Perfume atomizer.

Question:
We squeeze the bulb of a perfume atomizer, causing air to flow horizontally across the opening of a tube that extends down into the perfume. If the air is moving at 50.0 m/s, what is the pressure difference between the top of the tube and the atmosphere?

Answer:
Before we squeeze the bulb, the airflow speed is $v_0 = 0$. Using the Bernoulli equation for 0 height difference (13.57), we find

$$p + \frac{1}{2}\rho v^2 = p_0 + \frac{1}{2}\rho v_0^2 .$$

Solving this for the pressure difference $p - p_0$ under the condition that $v_0 = 0$, we then arrive at

$$p - p_0 = -\frac{1}{2}\rho v^2 = -\frac{1.30 \text{ kg/m}^3 \cdot (50.0 \text{ m/s})^2}{2} = -1630 \text{ Pa} . \quad (13.68)$$

Therefore, we see that the pressure is lowered by 1.63 kPa, causing the perfume to be sucked upward and atomized in the air stream.

Solved Problem

Solved Problem 13.2: Venturi Tube

Question:
On some light aircraft, a device called a venturi tube is used to create a pressure difference that can be used to drive gyroscope-based instruments for navigation. The venturi tube is mounted on the outside of the fuselage of the aircraft in an area of free air flow. We have a venturi tube with a circular opening of 10.0 cm diameter, necking down to a circular opening of 2.50 cm diameter, and then opening back up to the original diameter of 10.0 cm. What is the pressure differential between the opening of the venturi tube and the narrow region of the venturi tube assuming that the aircraft is flying at a constant speed of 38.0 m/s at sea level?

Answer:

THINK: The continuity equation tells us that the product of the area and the velocity of the flow through the venturi tube is constant. We can then relate the area of the opening, the area of the constricted region, the velocity of the air entering the venturi tube, and the velocity of the air in the restricted region of the venturi tube. Using Bernoulli's equation we can then relate the pressure at the opening to the pressure in the restricted region.

SKETCH: A sketch of the venturi tube is shown in Figure 13.34.

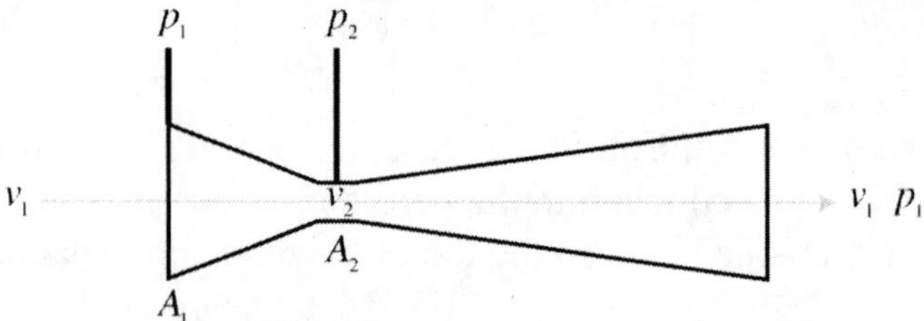

Figure 13.34: A venturi tube with air flowing through it.

RESEARCH: Using the continuity equation we can write

$$A_1v_1 = A_2v_2. \tag{13.69}$$

Bernoulli's equation tells us that

$$p_1 + \frac{1}{2}\rho v_1^2 = p_2 + \frac{1}{2}\rho v_2^2. \tag{13.70}$$

SIMPLIFY: The pressure differential between the opening of the venturi tube and the restricted area is then

Solved Problem

$$p_1 - p_2 = \Delta p = \frac{1}{2}\rho v_2^2 - \frac{1}{2}\rho v_1^2 = \frac{1}{2}\rho\left(v_2^2 - v_1^2\right). \tag{13.71}$$

Solving (13.69) for v_2 and substituting that result into (13.71) gives us the pressure differential between the opening and the restricted area

$$\Delta p = \frac{1}{2}\rho\left(v_2^2 - v_1^2\right) = \frac{1}{2}\rho\left(\left(\frac{A_1}{A_2}v_1\right)^2 - v_1^2\right) = \frac{1}{2}\rho v_1^2\left(\frac{A_1^2}{A_2^2} - 1\right). \tag{13.72}$$

CALCULATE: Putting in our numerical values gives us

$$\Delta p = \frac{1}{2}\rho v_1^2\left(\frac{A_1^2}{A_2^2} - 1\right) = \frac{1}{2}\left(1.30 \text{ kg/m}^3\right)\left(38.0 \text{ m/s}\right)^2\left(\frac{\pi\left(10.0/2\right)^2 \text{ cm}^2}{\pi\left(2.50/2\right)^2 \text{ cm}^2} - 1\right) = 14079 \text{ Pa}$$

where we have use $\rho = 1.30 \text{ kg/m}^3$ as the density of air at sea level.

ROUND: We report our result to three significant figures

$$\Delta p = 14.1 \text{ kPa}.$$

DOUBLE-CHECK: The pressure differential of 14.1 kPa (106 mm of mercury or 4.16 inches of mercury) is small compared with standard atmospheric pressure of 101.3 kPa, and thus seems reasonable.

Self-Test Opportunity: One mole of any gas occupies a volume of 22.4 liter at standard temperature and pressure. What is the density of hydrogen gas? What is the density of helium gas?

Draining a Tank

Let us do another little experiment that you can perform at home. All you need is a large container with a small hole at the bottom. You can fill this container with water and measure how long it takes to drain it. In Figure 13.35 we have performed such an experiment.

t = 0 15 s 30 s 45 s 60 s 75 s 90 s 105 s

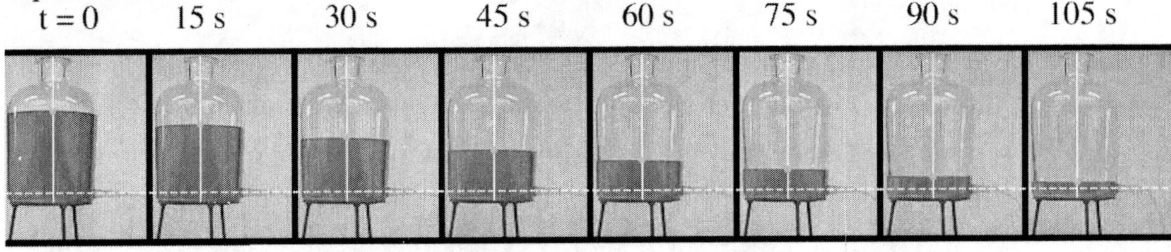

Figure 13.35: Draining a bottle.

Using the tools developed in the previous section, we can analyze this draining process quantitatively and arrive at a description of the height of the fluid column as a function of time. We start out with Bernoulli's equation (13.55). Since the bottle is open at the top, the atmospheric pressure is the same at the upper surface of the fluid column as it is at the drain. We thus obtain from Bernoulli's equation

$$\rho g y_1 + \frac{1}{2}\rho v_1^2 = \rho g y_2 + \frac{1}{2}\rho v_2^2$$

Canceling out the density and reordering the terms we obtain from this

$$v_2^2 - v_1^2 = 2g(y_1 - y_2) = 2gh$$

where $h = y_1 - y_2$ is the height of the fluid column. We had obtained this same result for a particle in free-fall, by the way! This shows that the streaming of an ideal fluid under the influence of gravity proceeds just in the same way as freefalling for a point particle.

The continuity equation (13.52) relates the two speeds v_1 and v_2 to each other via the ratio of their corresponding cross-sectional areas, $A_1 v_1 = A_2 v_2$. So we find for the speed with which the fluid flows from the container as a function of the height of the fluid column above the hole:

$$v_1 = v_2 \frac{A_2}{A_1} \Rightarrow v_2^2 - v_1^2 = v_2^2\left(1 - \frac{A_2^2}{A_1^2}\right) \Rightarrow$$

$$v_2^2 = \frac{2gh}{1 - \dfrac{A_2^2}{A_1^2}} = \frac{2A_1^2 g}{A_1^2 - A_2^2} h \qquad (13.73)$$

If the area A_2 is small compared to A_1, then this result simplifies to

$$v_2 = \sqrt{2gh} \qquad (13.74)$$

The speed with which the fluid streams form the container is sometimes also called speed of efflux.

How does the height of the fluid column change as a function of time? To answer this, we note that the speed v_1 is the negative of the time derivative of the height of the fluid column, h, $v_1 = -dh/dt$, since the height gets reduced in time. From our equation of continuity we then find

$$A_1 v_1 = -A_1 \frac{dh}{dt} = A_2 v_2 = A_2 \sqrt{2gh} \Rightarrow$$

$$\frac{dh}{dt} = -\frac{A_2}{A_1}\sqrt{2gh} \tag{13.75}$$

Since this equation relates the height to its derivative, it is a differential equation. Its solution is

$$h(t) = h_0 - \frac{A_2}{A_1}\sqrt{2gh_0}\,t + \frac{g}{2}\frac{A_2^2}{A_1^2}t^2 . \tag{13.76}$$

You can convince yourself that this is really the solution by taking the derivative of (13.76) and inserting it into (13.75). This derivative is

$$\frac{dh}{dt} = -\frac{A_2}{A_1}\sqrt{2gh_0} + g\frac{A_2^2}{A_1^2}t . \tag{13.77}$$

The point in time where this derivative reaches 0 is the time at which the draining process has finished:

$$\frac{dh}{dt} = 0 \Rightarrow t_f = \frac{A_1}{A_2}\sqrt{\frac{2h_0}{g}} . \tag{13.78}$$

If you insert this result back into (13.76), you see that this is also the time at which the height of the fluid column reaches zero, which is as expected. Since according to (13.75) the time derivative of the height is proportional to the square root of the height, our solution has to arrive at a height zero with a zero derivative.

Equation (13.78) also tells us that the time it takes to drain a cylindrical container is proportional to the cross-sectional area of the container and inversely proportional to the area of the hole you are draining the container through. However, the time is only proportional to the square root of the height of the container! So if you have two containers holding the same volume of liquid and draining through holes of the same size, the one that is higher and with a smaller cross-sectional area will drain faster.

Finally, keep in mind that the solution we have developed holds only in the limit of an ideal fluid in a tank with constant cross-sectional area as a function of height and in the case that the area of the hole is small compared to the area of the tank.

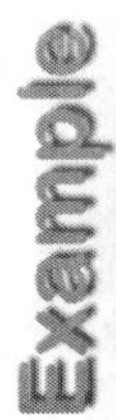

Example 13.8: Draining a Bottle

Figure 13.35 shows a large cylindrical bottle of cross sectional area $A_1 = 0.10\ \text{m}^2$. We drain this bottle through a small hole of radius 7.4 mm, resulting in an area $A_2 = 1.7 \cdot 10^{-4}\ \text{m}^2$. We videotaped this experiment and show one frame each 15 seconds.

Example

The initial height of the fluid column (water with red food coloring) in the bottle above the opening was $h_0 = 0.3\text{ m}$. In Figure 13.35 we have marked the level of the drain with a dashed white horizontal line, and the height of the fluid column in each frame with a green dot.

Question:
How long will it take to drain this bottle?

Answer:
We can simply use equation (13.78) and insert the values given. We arrive at

$$t_f = \frac{A_1}{A_2}\sqrt{\frac{2h_0}{g}} = \frac{0.1\text{ m}^2}{1.7\cdot 10^{-4}\text{ m}^2}\sqrt{\frac{2\cdot 0.3\text{ m}}{9.81\text{ m/s}^2}} = 145\text{ s}$$

While the answer in this case is a simple case of putting in the numbers into an equation that we just derived, it is more instructive to plot the height as a function of time, (13.76). In order to make a quantitative comparison between our solution and the experimental data, we have marked the level of the drain with a dashed white horizontal line, and the height of the fluid column in each frame with a green dot in Figure 13.35.

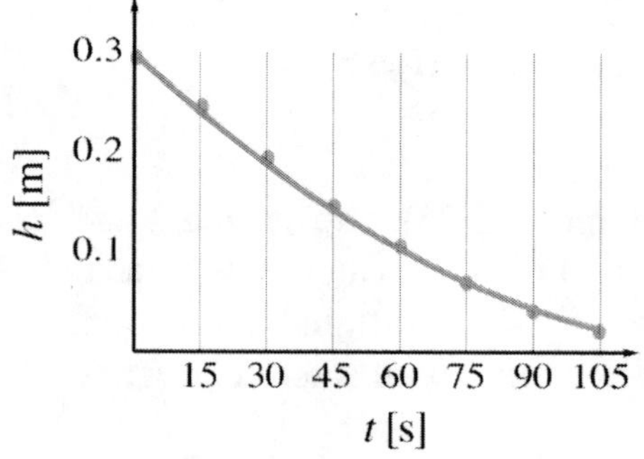

Figure 13.36: Height of fluid column as a function of time. Green dots: data; red line: analytical solution.

In Figure 13.36 we show this comparison between the solution we derived (the red line) and the data we have obtained from our experiment. You can see that the agreement is well within the measurement uncertainties, which are represented by the size of the dots that represent the experimental measurement.

13.7. Viscosity

If you have been drifting on a gentle river in a boat, you may have noticed that you were floating faster with the stream in the middle of the river than very close to the banks. Why could this happen? If water were an ideal fluid in laminar motion in this river, then it should make no difference how far away from shore you are. But it turns out that water is not quite an ideal fluid. Instead it has some "sticky-ness", called viscosity. For water, the viscosity is quite low, but for oil it is significantly higher, and it is even higher yet for substances like honey, which flow very slowly. Viscosity is responsible for causing the fluid streamlines at the surface to partially stick to the boundary, and for neighboring streamlines to partially stick to each other.

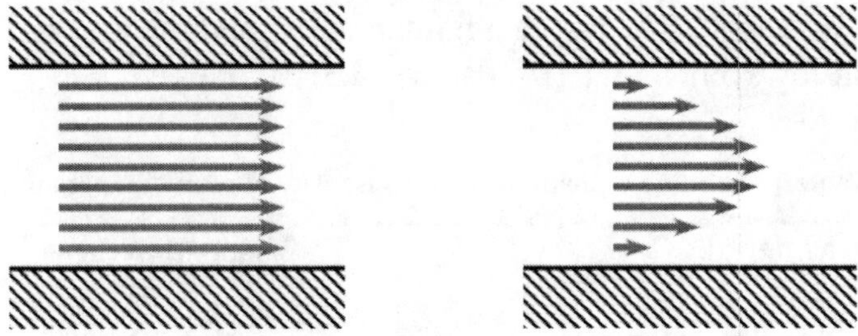

Figure 13.37: Velocity profiles in a cylindrical tube; left: non-viscous ideal fluid flow; right: viscous flow.

The resulting velocity profile for the streamlines is sketched in the right panel of Figure 13.37. It is parabolic, with the velocity approaching 0 at the walls and reaching its maximum value in the center. This flow is still laminar, with the streamlines all flowing parallel to each other.

How does one measure viscosity of a fluid? The standard procedure is to use two parallel plates of area A and fill the gap of width h between them with the fluid. Then one drags one of the plates across the other and measures the force F that is required to do so. The resulting velocity profile between the plates is linear, as shown in Figure 13.38. The viscosity η is then defined as the ratio of the force per unit area divided by the velocity difference between top and bottom plate over the distance between the plates.

$$\eta = \frac{F / A}{\Delta v / h} = \frac{Fh}{A\Delta v} \tag{13.79}$$

The unit of viscosity is then the unit of pressure (force per unit area) multiplied by time, Pa·s. Often this unit is also called a Poiseuille (Pl). (Care must be taken to avoid confusing this SI unit with the cgi-unit of poise (P), because 1 poise = 0.1 Pa·s.

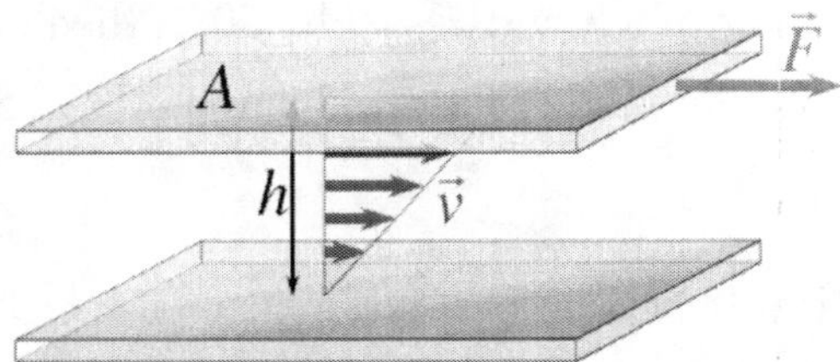

Figure 13.38: Measuring the viscosity.

It is very important to realize that the viscosity of any fluid depends strongly on the temperature. You can see an example for this temperature dependence in the kitchen. If you store olive oil in the fridge and then pour it from the bottle, you can see how slowly it flows. But heat the same olive oil up in a pan, and then it flows almost as easily as water. In the design of motor oils, the temperature dependence is of great concern, and the goal is to have a small temperature dependence. In Table 13.4, we list some typical values of viscosities for different fluids. All values are quoted at room temperature (20 °C = 68 F) except for the viscosity of blood, which we quote at the only physiologically relevant temperature of the human body temperature (37 °C = 98.6 F). Incidentally, the viscosity of blood increases by about 20% during a human's life, and the average value for men is slightly higher than for women ($4.7\cdot10^{-3}$ Pa·s vs. $4.3\cdot10^{-3}$ Pa·s).

Table 13.4: Some typical values for viscosity at room temperature.

Material	Viscosity (Pa·s)
Air	$1.8\cdot10^{-5}$
Alcohol (ethanol)	$1.1\cdot10^{-3}$
Blood (at body temperature!)	$4\cdot10^{-3}$
Honey	10
Mercury	$1.5\cdot10^{-3}$
Motor oil (SAE10 to SAE 40)	0.06 to 0.7
Olive oil	0.08
Water	$1.0\cdot10^{-3}$

The viscosity of a fluid enters if we want to determine how much fluid can flow through a pipe of given radius r and length ℓ. Hagen (1839) and Poiseuille (1840) found independently of each other that R_v, the volume of fluid that can flow per time unit, is

$$R_v = \frac{\pi r^4 \Delta p}{8\eta\ell}. \tag{13.80}$$

Here Δp is the pressure difference between the two ends of the pipe. As expected, the flow is inversely proportional to the viscosity and the length of the pipe. Most significantly, though, it is proportional to the fourth power of the radius of the pipe. In particular, we can consider a blood vessel as such a pipe. This helps us understand the severity of the problem associated with the clogging of arteries. If cholesterol-induced deposits reduce the diameter of a blood vessel by 50%, then the blood flow through this vessel is reduced to $(50\%)^4 = 6.25\%$, i.e. a reduction of 93.75%.

Example

Example 13.9: Hypodermic Needle

One of the scariest parts of a visit to the doctor is an injection. While learning physics cannot enable you to avoid an injection, at least we can understand a little bit of the fluid mechanics behind the hypodermic needle.

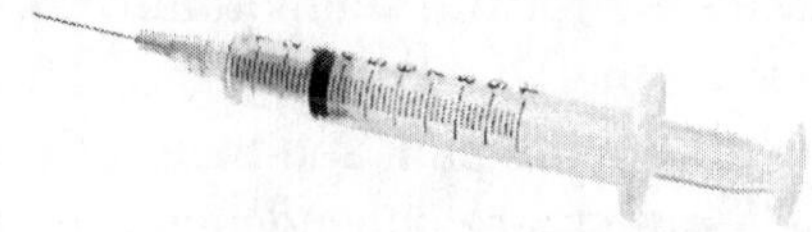

Figure 13.39: Hypodermic needle.

Example

Question 1:
If you want to push 2.0 cubic-centimeter of water out of a 1.0 cm diameter syringe through a 3.5 cm long 15-gauge needle (interior needle diameter = 1.37 mm) in 0.4 seconds, what force is required to push on the piston of this syringe?

Answer 1:
The Hagen-Poiseuille law (13.80) relates the fluid flow to the pressure difference. Thus, we can solve this equation for the pressure difference Δp between the tip of the needle and the end that is connected to the syringe. We find

$$\Delta p = \frac{8\eta \ell R_v}{\pi r^4}$$

The viscosity of water can be obtained form Table 13.2 and is $\eta = 1.0 \cdot 10^{-3}\ \text{Pa} \cdot \text{s}$. The flow is just the ratio of volume and time,

$$R_v = \Delta V / \Delta t = 2.0 \cdot 10^{-6}\ \text{m}^3 / 0.4\ \text{s} = 5.0 \cdot 10^{-6}\ \text{m}^3/\text{s}.$$

All other geometric quantities are specified in the problem, and so we obtain

$$\Delta p = \frac{8\left(1.0 \cdot 10^{-3}\ \text{Pa} \cdot \text{s}\right)\left(0.035\ \text{m}\right)\left(5.0 \cdot 10^{-6}\ \text{m}^3/\text{s}\right)}{\pi\left(0.5 \cdot 1.37 \cdot 10^{-3}\ \text{m}\right)^4} = 2020\ \text{Pa}$$

Since the pressure is force per unit area, we can obtain our force by multiplication of the pressure difference we just calculated with the appropriate area. But what is this area? The proper answer is to use the area of the plunger,

$$A = \pi R^2 = \pi (0.5 \cdot 0.01\ \text{m})^2 = 7.8 \cdot 10^{-5}\ \text{m}^2.$$

So the force required to push out the 2.0 cubic-centimeter of water in 0.4 seconds is only

$$F = A\Delta p = (8.8 \cdot 10^{-5}\ \text{m}^2)(2020\ \text{Pa}) = 0.16\ \text{N}$$

Question 2:
What is the speed with which the water emerges from the needle?

Answer 2:
We had seen that the speed of fluid flow is related to the flow by $R_v = Av$, see (13.50), where A is the cross-sectional area, in this case the area of the needle tip with the diameter of 1.37 mm. Solving this equation for the speed, we find

$$v = \frac{R_v}{A} = \frac{5.0 \cdot 10^{-6}\ \text{m}^3/\text{s}}{\pi\left(0.5 \cdot 1.37 \cdot 10^{-3}\ \text{m}\right)^2} = 3.4\ \text{m/s}$$

Discussion:
If you have ever pushed on the plunger of a syringe, you know that it takes more force than 0.16 N to push it. (0.16 N is the equivalent to the weight of a cheap ballpoint pen.) Where does this extra force requirement come from? Remember that the plunger has to

provide a tight seal with the wall of the syringe. And the main effort to push in the plunger results from overcoming the friction force between the syringe wall and the plunger. It would be an altogether different story, though, if you would fill your syringe with honey…

13.8. Turbulence and Research Frontiers in Fluid Flow

In laminar flow, the streamlines of a fluid follow smooth paths. In contrast, for a fluid in turbulent flow vortices form, detach, and propagate. We have already mentioned that the laminar ideal fluid flow or laminar viscous fluid flow transitions into turbulent flow when flow velocities exceed a certain value. This is impressively visible in the middle panel of Figure 13.24, in which rising cigarette smoke undergoes a transition from laminar flow to turbulent flow. But what is the criterion that decides if flow is laminar or turbulent?

Figure 13.40: Extreme turbulent flow – a tornado.

The answer lies in the so-called Reynolds number. It is defined as the ratio of typical inertial forces to viscous forces and thus is a pure dimensionless number. The inertial force has to be proportional to the density ρ and the typical velocity of the fluid $\bar{v}$, because $F = dp/dt$ according to Newton's Second Law. Thus, the viscous force is proportional to the viscosity η and inversely proportional to the characteristic length scale L over which the flow varies. Without diving any deeper into the motivation for this ratio, here it is

$$\mathrm{Re} = \frac{\rho \bar{v} L}{\eta}. \tag{13.81}$$

For flow through a pipe with circular cross section, this length scale is the diameter of the pipe, $L = 2r$. As a rule of thumb, a Reynolds number less than 2,000 leads to laminar flow, and one higher than 4,000 to turbulent flow. For Reynolds numbers inside the interval from 2,000 to 4,000 the flow character depends on many fine details of the exact configuration, and engineers try hard to avoid this region in their designs because of its essential unpredictability.

Figure 13.41: Wind tunnel testing of a scale model of a wing.

The true power of the Reynolds number lies in the fact that flows in systems which have the same geometry and the same Reynolds number behave similarly to each other. This allows one to reduce the typical length scales or velocity scales, build scale models of boats or airplanes, and test their performance in relatively modest scale water tanks or wind tunnels.

Beyond scale models, modern research on fluid flow and turbulence relies heavily on computer models such as in Figure 13.42. Hydrodynamics modeling is employed in an incredible variety of physical systems. Of course, there are the applications that come to mind right away, such as the performance and aerodynamics of cars, airplanes, rockets, and boats. But hydrodynamic modeling is also utilized in the collision of atomic nuclei at the highest energies available with modern accelerators, or in the modeling of supernova explosions. Just in the year 2005, the experimental groups working at the Relativistic Heavy Ion Collider in Brookhaven, NY, proclaimed that they have discovered that gold nuclei show the characteristics of a perfect non-viscous fluid when smashed into each other at the highest available energies. One of the authors (Westfall) had the privilege to announce this discovery at the 2006 annual meeting of the American Physical Society. Exciting new research results on fluid motion can be predicted to continue to emerge for the next decades, as this is one of the most interesting areas of interdisciplinary relevance in the physical sciences.

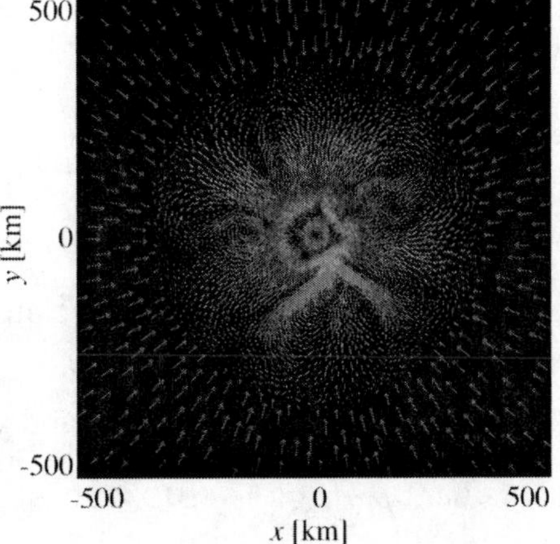

Figure 13.42: Fluid-dynamical modeling of a supernova core collapse. (The Astrophysical Journal, Fryer & Warren 2002 (ApJ, 574, L65). Reproduced by permission of the AAS.).The arrows indicate flow direction of the fluid elements, and the color indicates the temperature.

What we have learned/Exam Study Guide:

- 1 Mole of a material has $N_A = 6.022 \cdot 10^{23}$ atoms or molecules. The mass of one Mole of a material is given by the sum of the atomic mass numbers of the material times one gram.
- For a solid, stress = modulus · strain, where stress is force per unit area and strain is a unit deformation. We define three types of stress and strain each with its own modulus
    - Tension or linear compression leading to a positive or negative change in length $\frac{F}{A} = Y\frac{\Delta L}{L}$; Y is Young's Modulus
    - Volume compression leading to a change in volume $p = B\frac{\Delta V}{V}$; B is the bulk modulus
    - Shear leading to bending $\frac{F}{A} = G\frac{\Delta x}{L}$; G is the shear modulus
- Pressure is defined as force per unit area, $p = \frac{F}{A}$.
- The absolute pressure p at a depth h in a liquid with density ρ with pressure p_0 on the surface of the liquid is $p = p_0 + \rho gh$.
- The pressure of the Earth's atmosphere p_0 can be measured using a mercury barometer to be $p_0 = \rho gh$ where ρ is the density of mercury and h is the height difference between the two vertical parts of the column of mercury.
- Gauge pressure is the difference in pressure between the gas in a container and the pressure of the Earth's atmosphere.
- Pascal's Principle: When there is a change in pressure at any point in a confined incompressible fluid, there is an equal change in pressure at every point in the fluid.
- The buoyant force on an object immersed in a fluid is equal to the weight of the fluid displaced, $F_B = m_f g$.
- To consider a fluid as ideal, we assume laminar flow, incompressible flow, non-viscous flow, and irrotational flow.
- The flow of an ideal gas follows streamlines.
- The continuity equation for a flowing ideal fluid relates the velocity and area of the fluid flowing through a container, $A_1 v_1 = A_2 v_2$.
- Bernoulli's Equation relates the pressure, height, and velocity of an ideal fluid flowing through a container, $p + \rho gy + \frac{1}{2}\rho v^2 = \text{constant}$.
- For viscous fluids, the viscosity η is defined as the ratio of the force per unit area divided by the velocity difference per unit length, $\eta = \frac{F/A}{\Delta v/h} = \frac{Fh}{A\Delta v}$.
- For viscous fluids, the volume fluid flow rate through a cylindrical pipe of radius

r and length ℓ is given by $R_v = \dfrac{\pi r^4 \Delta p}{8\eta\ell}$, where Δp is the pressure difference between the two ends of the pipe.

- The Reynolds number determines the ratio of inertial to viscous forces and is defined as $\mathrm{Re} = \dfrac{\rho\bar{v}L}{\eta}$. $\mathrm{Re} < 2{,}000$ leads to laminar flow, and $\mathrm{Re} > 4{,}000$ to turbulent flow. $\bar{v}$ is the average fluid velocity, and L the characteristic length scale over which the flow changes.

Additional Solved Problems

Solved Problem 13.3: Unknown Liquid

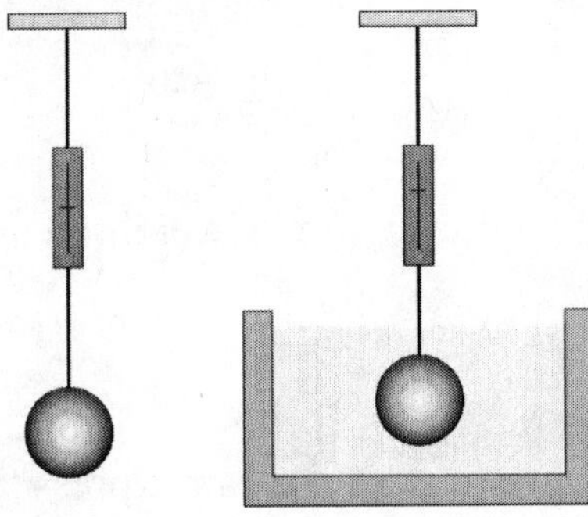

Figure 13.43: The left panel shows the aluminum sphere in air and the right panel shows the aluminum sphere submerged in the unknown liquid.

Question:
A solid aluminum sphere (density 2700. kg/m^3) is suspended from a scale in air. The scale reads 13.06 N. The sphere is then submerged in a liquid with unknown density. The scale now reads 8.706 N. What is the density of the liquid?

Answer:

THINK: From Newton's Third Law the buoyant force exerted by the unknown liquid on the aluminum sphere is the difference between the scale reading in when the sphere is in air and the scale reading when sphere is submerged in the unknown liquid.

SKETCH: A sketch of aluminum sphere in air and in the unknown liquid is shown in Figure 13.43. A Free-body diagram of the sphere is shown in Figure 13.44.

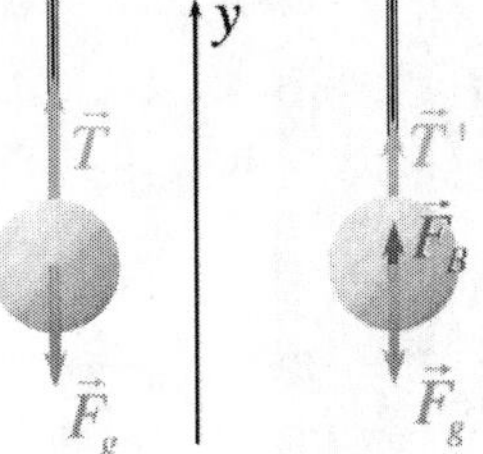

Figure 13.44: Free-body diagram for the sphere in air (left) and submerged in the liquid (right).

Solved Problem

RESEARCH: The buoyant force F_B exerted by the unknown liquid is

$$F_B = m_l g \tag{13.82}$$

where the mass of the displaced liquid m_l can be expressed in terms of the volume of the sphere V and the density of the liquid

$$m_l = \rho_l V \,. \tag{13.83}$$

The buoyant force exerted by the unknown liquid can be obtained by subtracting the measured weight of the sphere while submerged under the unknown liquid F_{sub} from the measured weight in air F_{air}

$$F_B = F_{air} - F_{sub} \,. \tag{13.84}$$

The mass of the sphere can be obtained from its weight in air

$$F_{air} = m_s g \,. \tag{13.85}$$

Using the known density of aluminum ρ_{Al} we can express the volume of the aluminum sphere as

$$V = \frac{m_s}{\rho_{Al}} \,. \tag{13.86}$$

SIMPLIFY: We can combine (13.82), (13.83), and (13.84) to get

$$F_B = m_l g = \rho_l V g = F_{air} - F_{sub} \,. \tag{13.87}$$

We can use (13.85) and (13.86) to get an expression for the volume of the sphere in terms of known quantities

$$V = \frac{m_s}{\rho_{Al}} = \frac{\left(\dfrac{F_{air}}{g}\right)}{\rho_{Al}} = \frac{F_{air}}{\rho_{Al} g} \tag{13.88}$$

Substituting this equation into (13.87) gives us

$$\rho_l V g = \rho_l \left(\frac{F_{air}}{\rho_{Al} g}\right) g = F_{air} \frac{\rho_l}{\rho_{Al}} = F_{air} - F_{sub} \,. \tag{13.89}$$

Solving this equation for the density of the unknown liquid gives us

Solved Problem

$$\rho_l = \rho_{Al} \frac{(F_{air} - F_{sub})}{F_{air}}. \tag{13.90}$$

CALCULATE: Putting our numerical values into (13.90) gives us the density of the unknown liquid

$$\rho_l = \rho_{Al} \frac{(F_{air} - F_{sub})}{F_{air}} = (2700.\ \text{kg/m}^3) \frac{13.06\ \text{N} - 8.706\ \text{N}}{13.06\ \text{N}} = 900.138\ \text{kg/m}^3.$$

ROUND: We report our result to four significant figures

$$\rho_l = 900.1\ \text{kg/m}^3.$$

DOUBLE-CHECK: The density of the unknown liquid is 90% the density of water. There are many liquids with such densities so our answer seems reasonable.

Solved Problem

Solved Problem 13.4: Diving Bell

Question:

A diving bell with atmospheric pressure inside is in Lake Michigan at a depth of 185 m. The diving bell has a flat, transparent, circular viewing port with a diameter of 20.0 cm. What is the magnitude of the net force on the viewing port?

Answer:

THINK: The pressure on the viewing port depends on the depth of the diving bell. The pressure on the port is the total force divided by the area of the port.

SKETCH: A sketch of the diving bell submerged in Lake Michigan is shown in Figure 13.45.

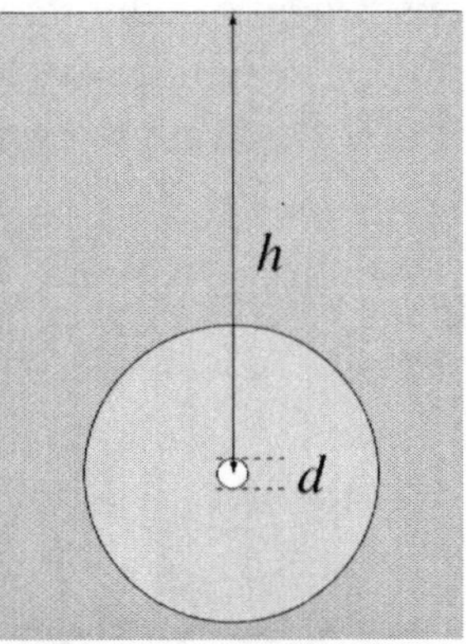

Figure 13.45: Diving bell submerged in Lake Michigan.

RESEARCH: The pressure p at a depth h is given by (13.24) $p = p_0 + \rho g h$, where ρ

Solved Problem

is the density of water and p_0 is the atmospheric pressure at the surface of Lake Michigan. The pressure inside the diving bell is atmospheric pressure. Therefore, the pressure difference between the outside and the inside of the viewing port is

$$p = \rho g h. \tag{13.91}$$

We can then obtain the net force F on the viewing port (A is the area of the viewing port) using the definition of pressure

$$p = \frac{F}{A} \tag{13.92}$$

SIMPLIFY: We can combine (13.91) and (13.92) to get

$$p = \rho g h = \frac{F}{A}.$$

which we can solve for the net force on the viewing port

$$F = \rho g h A.$$

CALCULATE: Putting in our numerical values gives us the net force on the viewing port

$$F = \rho g h A = \left(1000 \text{ kg/m}^3\right)\left(9.81 \text{ m/s}^2\right)\left(185 \text{ m}\right)\left(\pi\left(0.200/2\right)^2 \text{ m}^2\right) = 57015.2 \text{ N}.$$

ROUND: We report our result to three significant figures

$$F = 5.70 \cdot 10^4 \text{ N}.$$

DOUBLE-CHECK: The net force of $5.70 \cdot 10^4$ N corresponds to 12,800 pounds. The viewing point would need to be constructed of very thick glass or quartz. In addition, the size of the viewing port must be limited, which is why the problem specifies a relatively small viewing port with a diameter of 20 cm (approximately 8 inches).

Chapter 14. Oscillations

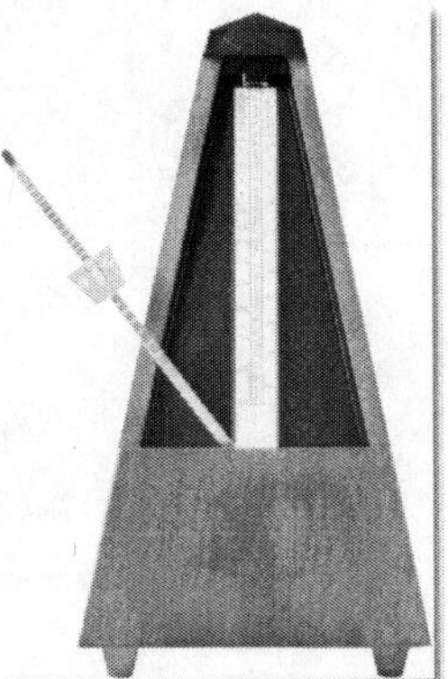

Figure 14.1: Metronome performing harmonic oscillations.

What we will learn:

- The spring force leads to a sinusoidal oscillation in time referred to as simple harmonic motion.
- A similar force law and time oscillation can be found for the pendulum swinging

through small angles.

- Oscillations can be represented as a projection of circular motion onto one of the two Cartesian coordinate axes.
- In the presence of damping, the oscillations slow down exponentially in time. Depending on the strength of the damping, it is possible that there are no more oscillations.
- Periodic external driving of an oscillator leads to sinusoidal motion at the driving frequency, but now with a maximum amplitude at a driving frequency called the resonant frequency.
- We can study oscillators by plotting their motion in terms of the velocity and position, where un-damped oscillators move on ellipses and damped oscillators spiral in.
- We can observe chaotic motion for damped driven oscillators or for the double pendulum. In this case, the trajectory in time depends sensitively on the initial conditions.

14.1. Simple Harmonic Motion

Simple harmonic motion is a particular type of repetitive motion, such as is displayed by the metronome (Figure 14.1) or by a mass on a spring. We have already introduced the spring force and found that we can describe it by Hooke's Law, which states that the spring force is proportional to the displacement from equilibrium. The spring force is a restoring force, always pointing towards the equilibrium position and is thus opposite in direction to the displacement vector,

$$F_x = -kx \tag{14.1}$$

The proportionality constant k is simply called the spring constant.

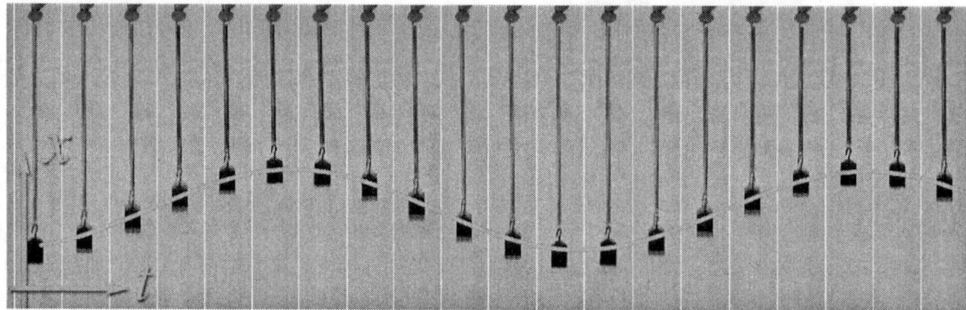

Figure 14.2: Time-lapse photographs of a mass hanging from a spring undergoing simple harmonic motion. A coordinate system and graph of the position as a function of time are overlaid on the photographs

Now we consider the situation in which we attach a mass, m, to a spring and stretch or compress the spring out of the equilibrium position. When we release the mass, the mass oscillates back and forth. This motion is called "simple harmonic motion" and it occurs whenever the restoring force is proportional to the displacement. In Figure 14.2 we demonstrate these oscillations by videotaping the vertical oscillation of a mass on a spring, with a vertical x axis. Then we put the individual frames of the video next to each other so that the horizontal axis of this composite picture represents the time axis, with each frame 0.06 s apart from the neighboring ones. Overlaid on this sequence is a sine function, the red curve.

With the insight gained from Figure 14.2, we now derive the mathematical description of this type of motion. We start with our force law for the spring force (14.1) and use Newton's Second Law, $F = ma$, to obtain:

$$ma = -kx \tag{14.2}$$

We know that the acceleration is the second time derivative of the position: $a = d^2x/dt^2$. Inserting this result into equation (14.2) gives us:

$$m\frac{d^2x}{dt^2} = -kx$$

$$\frac{d^2x}{dt^2} + \frac{k}{m}x = 0 \tag{14.3}$$

Equation (14.3) shows that the position x and its second derivative with respect to time appear in the same equation. Both are a function of the time t. This type of equation is called a "differential equation". We will find solutions to these types of equations and will call them simple harmonic motion.

From Figure 14.2 you see that the solution to our mathematics problem should be a sine or a cosine function. So let us try

$$x = A\sin(\omega_0 t) \tag{14.4}$$

The constants A and ω_0 are called the amplitude of the oscillation and its angular frequency, respectively. The amplitude is the maximum displacement away from the equilibrium position. This solution works for any value of the amplitude A. However we cannot make the amplitude arbitrarily big or else we would overstretch the spring. On the other hand, we will see that *not* all values of ω_0 will produce a solution.

Taking the second derivative of our trial function results in

$$x = A\sin(\omega_0 t) \Rightarrow$$

$$\frac{dx}{dt} = \omega_0 A\cos(\omega_0 t) \Rightarrow$$

$$\frac{d^2x}{dt^2} = -\omega_0^2 A\sin(\omega_0 t) \tag{14.5}$$

And inserting this result into our differential equation (14.3) yields

$$\frac{d^2x}{dt^2}+\frac{k}{m}x=-\omega_0^2 A\sin(\omega_0 t)+\frac{k}{m}A\sin(\omega_0 t)=0 \tag{14.6}$$

This condition is fulfilled if $\omega_0^2 = k/m$, or

$$\omega_0=\sqrt{\frac{k}{m}}. \tag{14.7}$$

We have thus found a valid solution to our differential equation for simple harmonic motion. In the same way we can show that the cosine is a solution as well, also with arbitrary amplitude, but with the same angular frequency. So our complete solution is

$$x(t)=A\sin(\omega_0 t)+B\cos(\omega_0 t) \text{ with } \omega_0=\sqrt{\frac{k}{m}} \tag{14.8}$$

The units of ω_0 are radians/s or simply Hz, since a radian is not a unit but a unit-less label. In applying (14.8) the argument of the trigonometric functions, $\omega_0 t$, will have units of radians and not degrees. With more advanced mathematical theory outside the scope of this book, one can show that this result is indeed the complete solution to the above differential equation, i.e. there are no other solutions besides the sine and cosine functions. Before we demonstrate the physical implications of this formulation, we will write down one more useful form of the same solution:

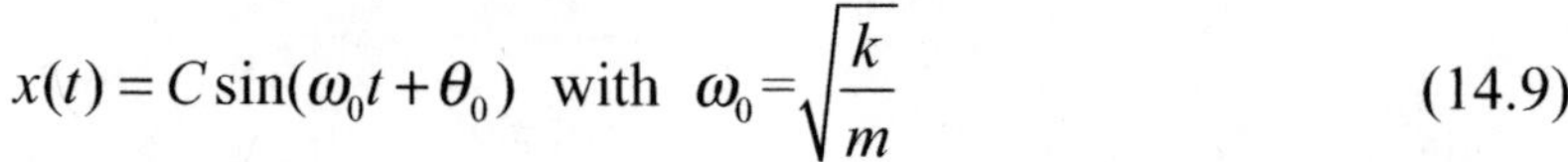

$$x(t)=C\sin(\omega_0 t+\theta_0) \text{ with } \omega_0=\sqrt{\frac{k}{m}} \tag{14.9}$$

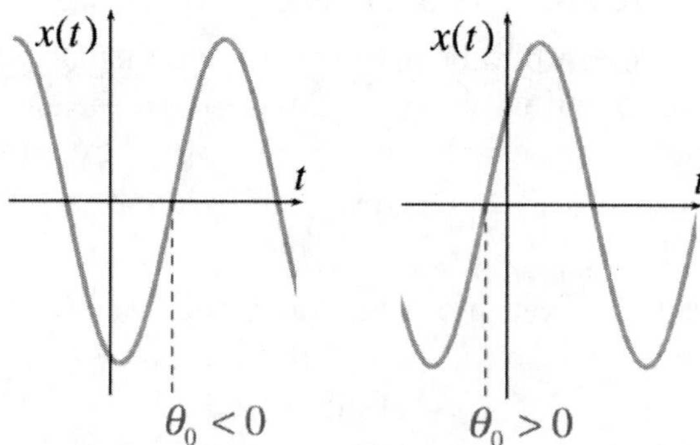

Figure 14.3: Graphical illustration of the phase angle.
Left: an example case where the phase angle is smaller than 0;
right: here the phase angle is bigger than 0.

In this form one can see more easily that we do have sinusoidal motion. Instead of having two amplitudes for the sine and cosine functions, we now have one amplitude, C, and a phase angle, θ_0, with these two constants yet to be determined. They are related to the above constants A and B via

$$C = \sqrt{A^2 + B^2} \tag{14.10}$$

$$\theta_0 = \arctan\left(\frac{B}{A}\right) \tag{14.11}$$

Self-Test Opportunity: Show that $x(t) = C\sin(\omega_0 t + \theta_0)$ is a solution for the differential equation given in equation (14.3).

Initial Conditions

How does one determine what values to use for the constants A and B for the amplitudes of the sine and cosine functions in our solution? The answer is that one needs to know two pieces of information, often given in the form of the initial position, $x_0 = x(t=0)$, and velocity, $v_0 = v(t=0) = (dx/dt)\big|_{t=0}$, as the following example will illustrate.

Example

Example 14.1: Initial Conditions

Question 1:
A spring shown in Figure 14.4 with spring constant 56.0 N/m has a mass of 1.00 kg attached to its end. The mass is pulled +5.5 cm from its equilibrium position and pushed so that it receives an initial velocity of –0.32 m/s. What is the equation of motion for this oscillation?

Answer 1:
The solution to the equation of motion gives the dependence of the position on time. We already have the general equation of motion for this problem. Its solution is that of simple harmonic motion:

$$x(t) = A\sin(\omega_0 t) + B\cos(\omega_0 t) \text{ with } \omega_0 = \sqrt{k/m}$$

From the data given in the question, we can calculate the angular frequency. It has the value $\omega_0 = \sqrt{k/m} = \sqrt{(56.0 \text{ N/m})/(1.00 \text{ kg})} = 7.48 \text{ s}^{-1}$. Now we must determine the constants A and B.

We were given the initial conditions for the position, $x_0 = 0.055$ m, and velocity, $v_0 = -0.32$ m/s. We can insert this into the equation of motion and its first derivative evaluated at time 0:

$$\begin{aligned} x(t) &= A\sin(\omega_0 t) + B\cos(\omega_0 t) \\ \Rightarrow v(t) &= \omega_0 A\cos(\omega_0 t) - \omega_0 B\sin(\omega_0 t) \end{aligned} \tag{14.12}$$

At time 0 these equations reduce to:

$$\begin{aligned} x_0 &= x(t=0) = B \\ v_0 &= v(t=0) = \omega_0 A \end{aligned} \tag{14.13}$$

because $\sin(0) = 0$ and $\cos(0) = 1$. So we find that $B = x_0 = 0.055 \text{ m}$ and $A = -0.043 \text{ m}$.

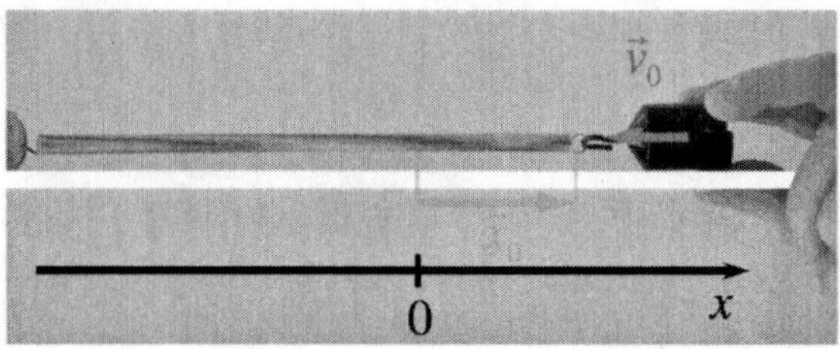

Figure 14.4: Mass on a spring with the initial position and velocity vectors shown

Example

Question 2:
What is the amplitude of this oscillation? What is the phase angle?

Answer 2:
Although we have found the constants A and B, it is not obvious what the amplitude will be. We can use the trigonometric relations above to get the amplitude and phase shift:

$$C = \sqrt{A^2 + B^2} = \sqrt{0.043^2 + 0.055^2} \text{ m} = 0.070 \text{ m}$$

So the amplitude of this oscillation is 7.0 cm. Note that as a consequence of the nonzero initial velocity, the amplitude is *not* 5.5 cm, the value of the initial elongation of the spring!

The phase angle is the result of a straightforward application of (14.11):

$$\theta_0 = \arctan\left(\frac{B}{A}\right) = \arctan\left(-\frac{0.055}{0.043}\right) = -0.907$$

Expressed in degrees this phase angle is thus $\theta_0 = -52.0 \text{ degrees}$.

Position, Velocity, and Acceleration

Let us look again at the relationship between position, velocity, and acceleration. In the form of our solution that describes the motion in terms of amplitude C and a phase shift θ_0, they are:

$$\begin{aligned} x(t) &= C\sin(\omega_0 t + \theta_0) \\ v(t) &= \omega_0 C\cos(\omega_0 t + \theta_0) \\ a(t) &= -\omega_0^2 C\sin(\omega_0 t + \theta_0) \end{aligned} \quad (14.14)$$

where the velocity and acceleration are obtained from the position vector by taking successive time derivatives. These equations suggest that the velocity and acceleration vectors have the same phase shifts θ_0 as the position vector, but they have additional phase shifts of $\pi/2$ (for the velocity) and π (for the acceleration), which are the phase differences between the sine and cosine, and between the sine and the negative sine function respectively.

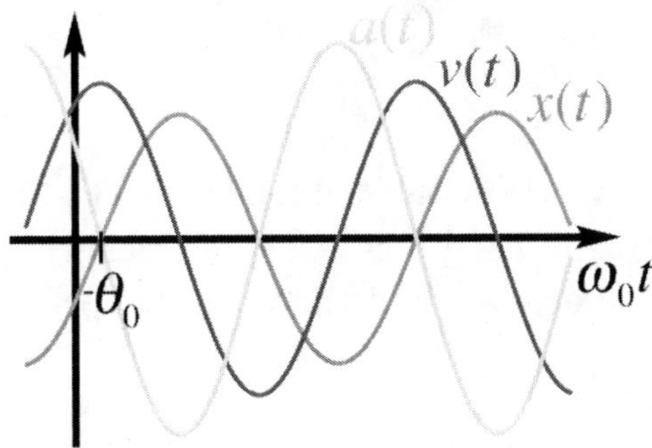

Figure 14.5: Graphs of the position, velocity, and acceleration for simple harmonic motion as a function of time.

We plot these three functions together in Figure 14.5. There we show as an example the resulting curves for a choice of constants $\omega_0 = 1.25\ \text{s}^{-1}$ and $\theta_0 = -0.5$ rad. Indicated in Figure 14.5 is the phase shift, as well as the three amplitudes of the oscillations: C is the amplitude of the oscillation of the position vector, $\omega_0 C$ (=1.25 C in this case) the amplitude of the oscillation of the velocity vector, and $\omega_0^2 C$ (=1.25^2 C here) that of the acceleration vector. One can see that wherever the position vector passes through 0, the value of the velocity vector is at a maximum or a minimum, and vice versa. One can also observe that the acceleration (just like the force) is always in opposite direction to the position vector. When the position passes through 0, so does the acceleration.

In-class exercise: A spring with spring constant 12.0 N/m has a mass of 3.00 kg attached to its end. The mass is pulled +10.0 cm from its equilibrium position and released from rest. What is the velocity of the mass as it passes the equilibrium point?

a) –0.125 m/s
b) +0.750 m/s
c) –0.200 m/s
d) +0.500 m/s
e) –0.633 m/s

Period and Frequency

As you know, the sine and cosine functions are periodic with period 2π. Since the position, velocity, and acceleration for our oscillations are all given by a sine or cosine function, adding a multiple of 2π to their arguments does thus not change their values,

$$\sin(\omega t) = \sin(2\pi + \omega t) = \sin\left(\omega\left(\frac{2\pi}{\omega} + t\right)\right) \tag{14.15}$$

Here we have dropped the index 0 for ω, because the result we are deriving here is a universal one that is valid for all angular frequencies, not just the one that we have derived for this particular situation for a mass on a spring. The time interval over which a sinusoidal function repeats itself is the "period", and we abbreviate the period with the symbol T. From equation (14.15) we can see that

$$T = \frac{2\pi}{\omega} \tag{14.16}$$

because $\sin(\omega t) = \sin(\omega(T + t))$. The same argument works for the cosine function. In other words, if you replace t by $t + T$ you obtain the identical position, velocity, and acceleration vector, as demanded by our definition of the period.

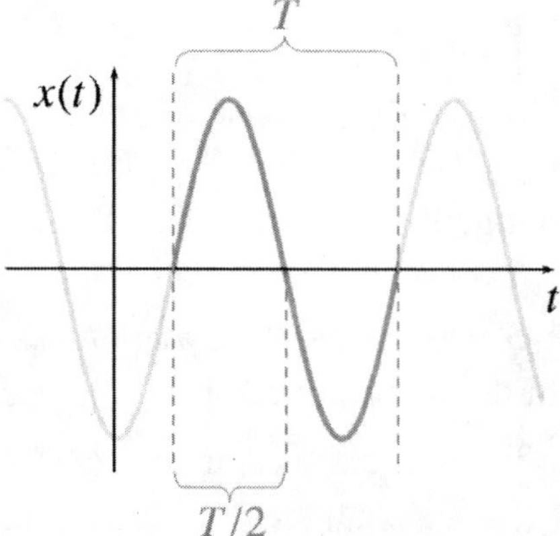

Figure 14.6: Graphical illustration of the period, *T*, of a sine or cosine function.

Graphically, one can determine the period of a periodic function (sine or cosine) as the horizontal separation between any two consecutive points where the horizontal axis intersects the function "on the way up". (Two consecutive crossings of the horizontal axis are exactly half of a period apart; see Figure 14.6).

One more definition: We call the inverse of the period the "frequency", f:

$$f = \frac{1}{T} \tag{14.17}$$

where f is the number of complete oscillations per unit time. For example, if $T = 0.2s$

there will be 5 oscillations in one second and $f = \frac{1}{T} = \frac{1}{0.2s} = 5.0s^{-1} = 5.0Hz$

One more relationship that you obtain when you plug in what we have just obtained for the period into the definition of the frequency is:

$$f = \frac{1}{T} = \frac{1}{2\pi / \omega} = \frac{\omega}{2\pi} \quad \text{or} \quad \omega = 2\pi f \tag{14.18}$$

For our particular example of the mass on a spring, we obtain for the period and frequency:

$$T = \frac{2\pi}{\omega_0} = \frac{2\pi}{\sqrt{k/m}} = 2\pi\sqrt{\frac{m}{k}} \tag{14.19}$$

$$f = \frac{\omega_0}{2\pi} = \frac{1}{2\pi}\sqrt{\frac{k}{m}} \tag{14.20}$$

Interestingly, the period does not depend on the amplitude of the motion.

Example

Example 14.2: Tunnel through the moon

Suppose we drill a tunnel straight through the center of the Moon, from one surface of the Moon to the other. The fact that the Moon has no atmosphere and the fact that the Moon is composed of solid rock make this scenario slightly more realistic than drilling a tunnel through the center of Earth.

Question:
If we go to one end of this tunnel and release a steel ball of mass 5.0 kg from rest, what can we say about the motion of this ball?

Answer:
In our chapter 12 on gravity, we have found that the magnitude of the gravitational force inside a spherical mass distribution of constant density is $F_g(r < R) = mgr / R$, and that this force points towards the center, i.e. in opposite direction of the displacement. So we see that the gravitational force inside a homogeneous spherical mass distribution follows Hooke's Law, $F(x) = -kx$, with a "spring constant" $k = mg / R$. Here g is the gravitational acceleration experienced at the surface.

We start by calculating the surface gravity on moon. Since the mass of the moon is $7.35 \cdot 10^{22}$ kg (1.2% of the mass of Earth) and its radius is $1.735 \cdot 10^{6}$ m (one quarter of the radius of Earth, we find for the surface gravity of the moon (see chapter 12):

Example

$$g_M = \frac{GM_M}{R_M^2} = \frac{\left(6.67\cdot 10^{-11}\ \text{m}^3\text{kg}^{-1}\text{s}^{-2}\right)\left(7.35\cdot 10^{22}\ \text{kg}\right)}{\left(1.735\cdot 10^6\ \text{m}\right)^2} = 1.63\ \text{m/s}^2$$

So the surface gravitational acceleration on the moon is approximately 1/6 of the value of that on the surface of the Earth.

We have found that the solution to the equation of motion with a spring force is the oscillatory motion:

$$x(t) = A\sin(\omega_0 t) + B\cos(\omega_0 t)$$

Releasing the ball from the surface of the moon at time = 0 implies that $x(0) = R_M = A\sin(0) + B\cos(0)$ or $B = R_M$. For the other initial condition we use the velocity equation from (14.12). The ball was released from rest so $v(0) = 0 = \omega_0 A\cos(0) - \omega_0 B\sin(0) = \omega_0 A$ so that $A = 0$. Thus our equation of motion is in this case:

$$x(t) = R_M \cos(\omega_0 t)$$

The angular frequency of the oscillation is:

$$\omega_0 = \sqrt{\frac{k}{m}} = \sqrt{\frac{g_M}{R_M}} = \sqrt{\frac{1.63\ \text{m/s}^2}{1.735\cdot 10^6\ \text{m}}} = 9.69\cdot 10^{-4}\ \text{Hz}$$

Note that the mass of the steel ball turned out to be irrelevant. The period of this oscillation is

$$T = \frac{2\pi}{\omega_0} = 6485\ \text{s}$$

Our steel ball will come to the surface at the other side of the moon 3242 s after release, and then oscillate back. To transit through the entire moon in a little less than an hour would make this mode of transportation extremely efficient, in particular since no power supply would be needed.

The velocity of the steel ball during this oscillation would be:

$$v(t) = \frac{dx}{dt} = -\omega_0 R_M \sin(\omega_0 t)$$

The maximum velocity would be reached as the ball crosses the center of the moon and would have the numerical value of:

$$v_{\max} = \omega_0 R_M = (9.69\cdot 10^{-4}\ \text{s}^{-1})(1.735\cdot 10^6\ \text{m}) = 1680\ \text{m/s} = 3760\ \text{mph}$$

Example

If the tunnel would be big enough, the same motion could be obtained for a vehicle holding one or more people, providing for very efficient transportation to the other side of the moon without the need for propulsion. During the entire journey the people inside the vehicle would feel absolute weightlessness, since they would have no supporting force from the vehicle! In fact, it would not be necessary to even have a vehicle to make this trip as one could just jump into the tunnel.

Solved Problem

Solved Problem 14.1: Mass on a Spring

Question:
A 1.55 kg mass sliding on a frictionless horizontal plane is connected to a horizontal spring with spring constant $k = 2.55$ N/m. The mass is pulled to the right a distance $d = 5.75$ cm and released from rest. What is the velocity of the mass 1.50 s after the mass is released?

Answer:

THINK:

The mass will undergo simple harmonic motion. We can use the initial conditions to determine the parameters of the motion. Having the parameters of the motion we can calculate the velocity of the mass at the specified time.

SKETCH:

A sketch of mass attached to a spring displaced a distance d from equilibrium is shown in Figure 14.7.

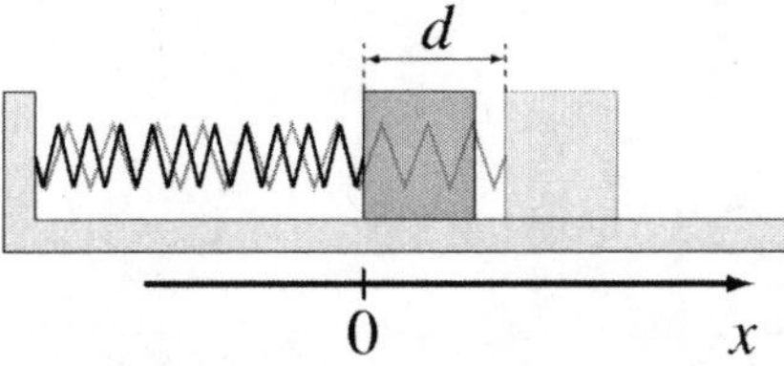

Figure 14.7: A sketch of a mass attached to s spring displaced a distance *d* from the equilibrium point.

RESEARCH:

We use the first initial condition that states that at $t = 0$, the position is $x = d$. Thus, we can write

$$x(t=0) = d = C\sin(\omega_0 \cdot 0 + \theta_0) = C\sin(\theta_0). \qquad (14.21)$$

Here we have one equation and two unknowns. To get a second equation, we use the second initial condition, which states that at $t = 0$, the velocity is

$$v(t=0) = 0 = \omega_0 C\cos(\omega_0 \cdot 0 + \theta_0) = \omega_0 C\cos(\theta_0). \qquad (14.22)$$

We now have two equations and two unknowns.

Solved Problem

SIMPLIFY:
We can simplify (14.22) to obtain

$$\cos(\theta_0) = 0 \tag{14.23}$$

from which we get the phase

$$\theta_0 = \pi / 2 . \tag{14.24}$$

Substituting this result into (14.21) gives us

$$d = C\sin(\theta_0) = C\sin(\pi/2) = C . \tag{14.25}$$

Thus, we can write the velocity as a function of time as

$$v(t) = \omega_0 d\cos(\omega_0 t + (\pi/2)) = -\omega_0 d\sin(\omega_0 t) . \tag{14.26}$$

The angular frequency is given by

$$\omega_0 = \sqrt{\frac{k}{m}} . \tag{14.27}$$

Our final expression for the velocity of the mass as a function of time is then

$$v(t) = -\sqrt{\frac{k}{m}} d\sin(\sqrt{\frac{k}{m}} t) . \tag{14.28}$$

CALCULATE:
Putting in our numerical values gives us

$$v(t = 1.50 \text{ s}) = -\sqrt{\frac{2.55 \text{ N/m}}{1.55 \text{ kg}}} \cdot (0.0575 \text{ m}) \cdot \sin\left(\sqrt{\frac{2.55 \text{ N/m}}{1.55 \text{ kg}}} \cdot 1.50 \text{ s}\right) = \text{-0.06920005 m/s} .$$

ROUND:
We report our result to three significant figures

$$v = -0.0692 \text{ m/s} = -6.92 \text{ cm/s} .$$

DOUBLE-CHECK: The maximum speed that the mass can attain is $v = \omega_0 d = 7.38$ cm/s. The magnitude of our result is less than the maximum speed so it seems reasonable.

Relationship to Circular Motion

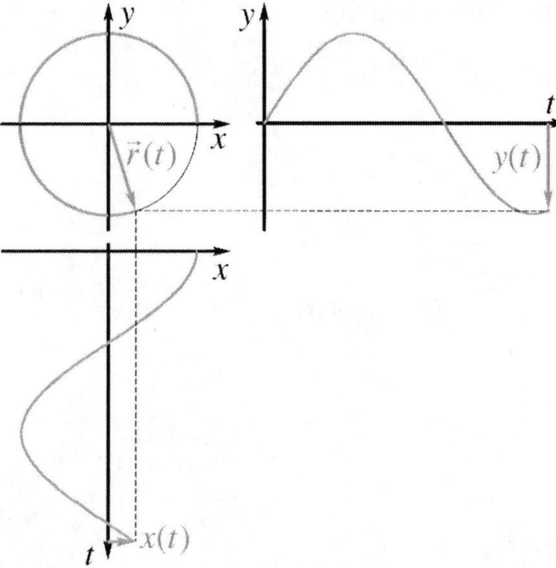

Figure 14.8: *x*- and *y*-coordinates as a function of time for a position vector with constant length, rotating with constant angular velocity.

In chapter 8 on circular motion, we studied motion with a constant angular velocity ω on a path with constant radius r. We found that the x- and y-coordinates follow the equations $x(t)=r\cos(\omega t+\theta_0)$ and $y(t)=r\sin(\omega t+\theta_0)$. This result is shown in Figure 14.8 for an initial angle of $\theta_0=0$. In the upper left corner we show how the vector $\vec{r}(t)$ performs a circular motion with constant angular velocity as a function of time. The red arc segment shows the path that the tip of the radius vector has traveled. In the upper right panel of Figure 14.8, we show the projection of the radius vector on the y-direction. We can clearly see that the motion of the y-component of the radius vector traces out a sine function. In the same way we show the motion of the x component as a function of time in the lower left panel, finding that it traces out a cosine function. We see that these two projections of the circular motion with constant angular velocity perform simple harmonic oscillations.

Thus it is now obvious that the definitions for the frequency, angular velocity, and period are referring to the identical quantities of the same name introduced in chapter 8.

14.2. Pendulum Motion

There is a second important system that oscillates with which we are all familiar: the pendulum. In its ideal manifestation, it consists of a thin string attached to a massive object that swings back and forth. The string is assumed to be massless, i.e. of such small mass that we can neglect it. This assumption is, by the way, a very good approximation to the situation of a person on a swing. Let us look at this person, or any object, on the swing and determine the equation of motion. Shown in Figure 14.9 is a ball on a rope of length ℓ at an angle θ relative to the vertical. For small angles θ, we will derive below the differential equation for the pendulum:

$$\frac{d^2\theta}{dt^2}+\frac{g}{\ell}\theta=0 \tag{14.29}$$

Equation (14.29) has the solution:

$$\theta(t)=A\sin(\omega_0 t)+B\cos(\omega_0 t) \text{ with } \omega_0=\sqrt{\frac{g}{\ell}} \tag{14.30}$$

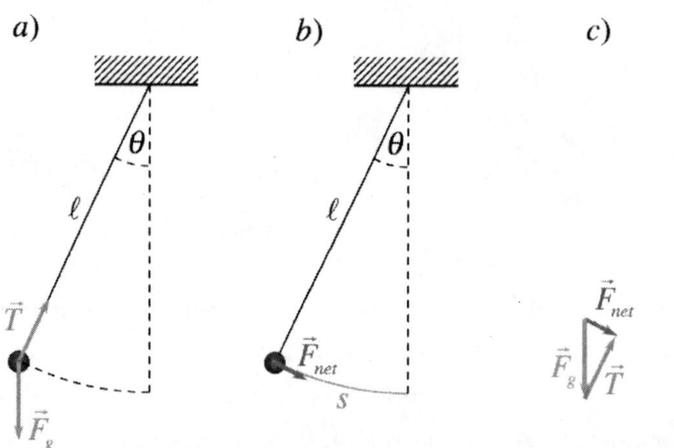

Figure 14.9: a) Sketch of a pendulum with the force vectors due to gravity and string tension indicated. b) the net force points in tangential direction; c) geometrical construction of the net force as the vector sum of the string tension and gravity force vectors.

Derivation 14.1:
Our displacement, s, is given along the perimeter of a circle with radius ℓ. This displacement can be obtained from the length of the string and the angle as $s=\ell\,\theta$. Because the length does not change with time, we can calculate the second derivative as:

$$\frac{d^2s}{dt^2}=\frac{d^2(\ell\theta)}{dt^2}=\ell\frac{d^2\theta}{dt^2} \tag{14.31}$$

The task is now to calculate the angular acceleration, $d^2\theta/dt^2$, as a function of time. To do this calculation, we need to determine the force that causes the acceleration. There are two forces acting on the ball, the force of gravity, $\vec{F}_g$, acting in the downward direction, and the force of the string tension, $\vec{T}$, acting along the direction of the rope. Since the string stays taut and does not stretch, the string tension must equal the component of the gravitational force along the string, $T=mg\cos\theta$. The vector sum of the forces gives a net force of magnitude $F_{\text{net}}=mg\sin\theta$, directed as shown in Figure 14.9. The net force is always in the opposite direction to the displacement s.

Derivation

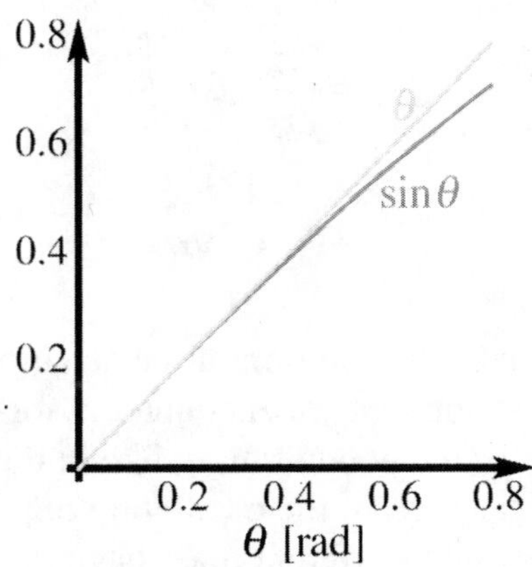

Figure 14.10: Graph indicating the error incurred using the small angle approximation $\sin\theta \approx \theta$, where θ is measured in radians.

Using $F_{net} = ma$, we then obtain:

$$m\frac{d^2 s}{dt^2} = -mg\sin\theta \Rightarrow$$
$$\frac{d^2 s}{dt^2} = -g\sin\theta \Rightarrow$$
$$\ell\frac{d^2\theta}{dt^2} + g\sin\theta = 0 \Rightarrow$$
$$\frac{d^2\theta}{dt^2} + \frac{g}{\ell}\sin\theta = 0$$

This equation is difficult to solve without making the "small-angle approximation", where we approximate $\sin\theta \approx \theta$ (radians). Doing so we obtain our desired differential equation. In Figure 14.10 you can see that this approximation is very good for $\theta < 0.5$ radians (approximately 30 degrees). For these small angles, the motion of a pendulum is approximately simple harmonic motion since the restoring force is approximately proportional to θ.

We could now go through exactly the same steps that lead to the solution of the differential equation for the spring problem. However since the equations (14.3) and (14.29) are identical except for constants, we simply take the solution for the spring problem and perform the appropriate substitutions. The angle θ now takes the place of x, and g/ℓ takes the place of k/m. In this manner we arrive at our solution without deriving our previous result a second time.

Derivation

Pendulum Period and Frequency

The period and frequency are simply related to the angular frequency as before, but with the angular frequency given now by (14.30):

$$T = \frac{2\pi}{\omega_0} = 2\pi\sqrt{\frac{\ell}{g}} \tag{14.32}$$

$$f = \frac{1}{2\pi}\sqrt{\frac{g}{\ell}} \tag{14.33}$$

We see that the time evolution of the solution of the equation of motion for the pendulum leads to the same harmonic motion that we encountered for the case of a mass on a spring. We also observe that for the pendulum, unlike in the case for the spring, the frequency is independent of the mass of the oscillating object. This result means that two otherwise identical pendulums with different mass have the same period. The only way one can adjust the period of a pendulum, other than going to another planet or the moon where the gravitational acceleration is different, is by varying its length.

Figure 14.11: Video Sequence of the oscillation of two pendulums with ratio of length of 4:1.

If you want to shorten the period of a pendulum by a factor of 2, you have to shorten the length of the string by a factor of 4. This is shown in Figure 14.11, where we present two pendulums with lengths of the longer a factor 4 greater than the other. In this sequence the shorter pendulum completes two oscillations in the time that the longer one performs one.

Self-Test Opportunity: You have a pendulum with a period T on Earth. You take this pendulum to the Moon. What is the period of this pendulum in terms of the period on Earth?

Example

Example 14.3: Restricted Pendulum

Question:

A pendulum of length 45.3 cm is hanging from the ceiling and is restricted in its motion by a peg that is sticking out of the wall 26.6 cm directly below its pivot point as shown in Figure 14.12. What is its period of oscillation? (Note that specifying the mass is not necessary.)

Answer:

We must solve this problem separately for the left side and for the right side of the peg. On the left side, the pendulum can oscillate with its full length, $\ell_1 = 45.3 \text{ cm}$, and on the

Example

right side the pendulum oscillates with a reduced length $\ell_2 = 45.3\text{ cm} - 26.6\text{ cm} = 18.7\text{ cm}$. For each side, it performs exactly 1/2 of a full oscillation. So the period of the pendulum will be the ½ of the sum of the two periods calculated with the different lengths.

$$T = \frac{1}{2}(T_1 + T_2) = \frac{2\pi}{2}\left(\sqrt{\frac{\ell_1}{g}} + \sqrt{\frac{\ell_2}{g}}\right) = \frac{\pi}{\sqrt{g}}\left(\sqrt{\ell_1} + \sqrt{\ell_2}\right)$$

$$= \frac{\pi}{\sqrt{9.81\text{ m/s}^2}}\left(\sqrt{0.453\text{ m}} + \sqrt{0.187\text{ m}}\right)$$

$$= 1.11\text{ s}$$

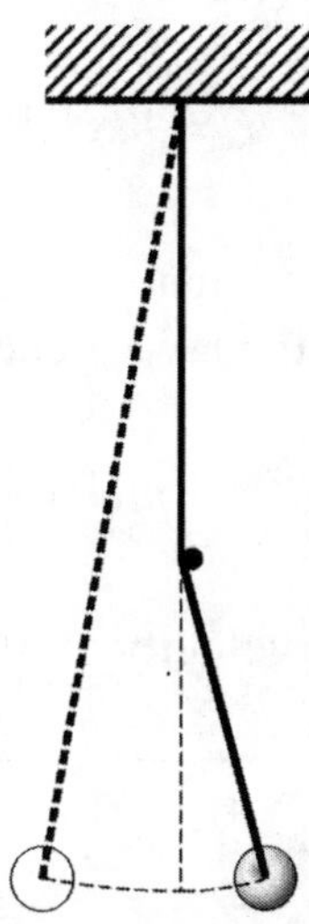

Figure 14.12: Restricted pendulum.

In-class exercise:

A grandfather clock keeps time using a pendulum. Assume that this pendulum consists of a light rod connected to a small heavy mass. What should be length of the rod be if the period of the oscillation were 1.00 s?

a) 0.0150 m
b) 0.145 m
c) 0.248 m
d) 0.439 m
e) 0.750 m

14.3. Work and Energy in Harmonic Oscillations

We have already introduced the concepts of work and kinetic energy in chapter 5. In chapter 6 we calculated the potential energy of the spring force. In this section we start again with the mass on the spring. For the pendulum, we will find out that almost all results are applicable as well, but that we need to correct for the small angle approximation that we made in solving the differential equation.

Mass on a Spring

In chapter 6 we did not yet have the solution of the displacement as a function of time at our disposal. However, we already derived that the potential energy stored in a spring is

$$U_s = \tfrac{1}{2}kx^2 \tag{14.34}$$

where k is the spring constant, and x is the displacement from the equilibrium position. We also found that the total mechanical energy of a mass on a spring undergoing simple harmonic motion of amplitude C is given by

$$E = \tfrac{1}{2}kC^2 \tag{14.35}$$

Conservation of total mechanical energy then means that this is the value of the energy for any point in the oscillation. Using the law of energy conservation, we are able to write

$$\tfrac{1}{2}kC^2 = \tfrac{1}{2}mv^2 + \tfrac{1}{2}kx^2 \tag{14.36}$$

Then we can get an expression for the velocity as a function of the position:

$$v = \sqrt{(C^2 - x^2)\frac{k}{m}} \tag{14.37}$$

.

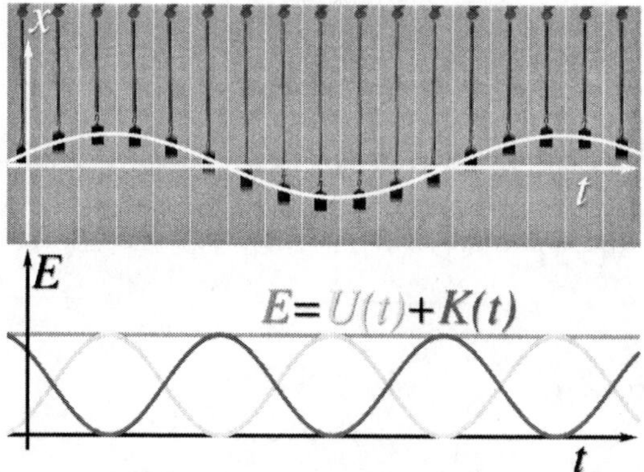

Figure 14.13: Harmonic oscillation of a mass on a spring as a function of time. Upper part: displacement; lower part: potential and kinetic energies as a function of time on the same time scale.

Now we have calculated the functions $v(t)$ and $x(t)$ that describe the oscillation of a mass on a spring in time, see (14.14). We can use these functions to verify that our solutions indeed fulfill the relationship between position and speed expressed in (14.37) and obtained from energy conservation. So we can directly test if our new results are consistent with what we had found previously. First we compute

$$\begin{aligned} C^2 - x^2 &= C^2 - C^2 \sin^2(\omega_0 t + \theta_0) \\ &= C^2(1 - \sin^2(\omega_0 t + \theta_0)) \\ &= C^2 \cos^2(\omega_0 t + \theta_0) \end{aligned} \tag{14.38}$$

Multiply both sides by $\omega_0^2 = k/m$ and obtain:

$$\frac{k}{m}(C^2 - x^2) = \frac{k}{m} C^2 \cos^2(\omega_0 t + \theta_0) = v^2 . \tag{14.39}$$

By taking the square root on both sides of this equation, we obtain exactly the result for the velocity that we have reached applying our energy considerations in (14.37).

Figure 14.13 illustrates the oscillations of the kinetic and potential energies as a function of time for the case of a mass oscillating on a spring. As you can see, even though the potential and kinetic energies oscillate in time, their sum, the total mechanical energy, is constant. The kinetic energy always reaches its maximum wherever the displacement passes through 0, and that the potential energy reaches its maximum for maximum elongation from the equilibrium position.

Pendulum

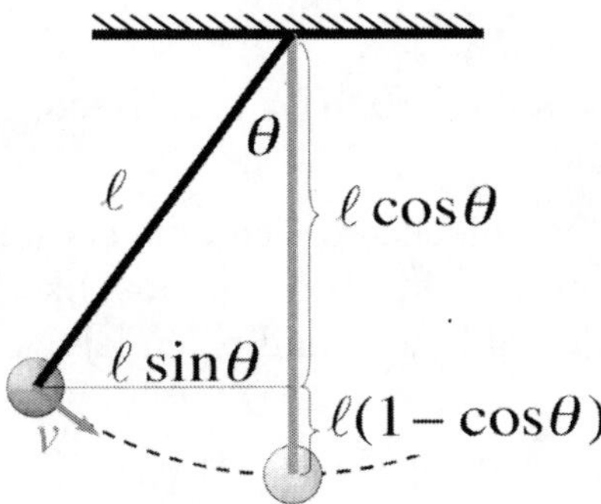

Figure 14.14: Pendulum

In section 14.2 we found that the solution for the time-dependence of the deflection angle of the pendulum is

$$\theta(t) = \theta_0 \cos\left(\sqrt{\frac{g}{\ell}}t\right), \tag{14.40}$$

provided that we give the initial conditions of maximum deflection and zero speed at time zero, $\theta(t=0) = \theta_0$. We can then calculate the orbital velocity at each point in time by taking the derivative, $d\theta / dt = \omega$, and multiplying this angular velocity with the radius of the circle, ℓ. This yields

$$v = \ell \frac{d\theta(t)}{dt} = -\theta_0 \sqrt{g\ell} \sin\left(\sqrt{\frac{g}{\ell}} t\right). \tag{14.41}$$

Since $\sin\alpha = \sqrt{1-\cos^2\alpha}$, we then obtain by inserting (14.40) into (14.41) the speed as a function of the angle for the pendulum,

$$\begin{aligned} |v| &= |\theta_0| \sqrt{g\ell} \left| \sin\left(\sqrt{\frac{g}{\ell}} t\right) \right| \\ &= |\theta_0| \sqrt{g\ell} \sqrt{1-\cos^2\left(\sqrt{\frac{g}{\ell}} t\right)} \\ &= |\theta_0| \sqrt{g\ell} \sqrt{1-\frac{\theta^2}{\theta_0^2}} \Rightarrow \\ |v| &= \sqrt{gl(\theta_0^2 - \theta^2)} \end{aligned} \tag{14.42}$$

What is the result of our energy calculations? At time zero, we have only potential energy, which is of the gravitational kind. We normalize this potential energy so that it is zero at the lowest point of the arc. According to the drawing in Figure 14.14, the potential energy at maximum deflection θ_0 is:

$$E = K + U = 0 + U = mg\ell(1-\cos\theta_0). \tag{14.43}$$

This is also the value for the total mechanical energy, because by definition we have zero kinetic energy at the point of maximum deflection, just like for the spring. For any other deflection, the energy is the sum of kinetic and potential energy:

$$E = mg\ell(1-\cos\theta) + \tfrac{1}{2}mv^2. \tag{14.44}$$

Combining the last two equations (because the total energy is conserved), we then find

$$\begin{aligned} mg\ell(1-\cos\theta_0) &= mg\ell(1-\cos\theta) + \tfrac{1}{2}mv^2 \Rightarrow \\ mg\ell(\cos\theta - \cos\theta_0) &= \tfrac{1}{2}mv^2 \end{aligned} \tag{14.45}$$

Solving this expression for the speed (=absolute value of the velocity), we obtain:

$$|v| = \sqrt{2g\ell(\cos\theta - \cos\theta_0)}. \tag{14.46}$$

This is the exact expression for the speed at any angle θ, obtained quite straightforwardly and without the need to solve a differential equation. This expression, however, does not look quite like what we have obtained from the solution of the differential equation, (14.42). However, remember that we relied on the small-angle approximation when finding the solution of the differential equation, and for small angles one can approximate $\cos\theta \approx 1-\frac{1}{2}\theta^2+...$, so that (14.42) is recovered as a special case of (14.46). The expression (14.46) that we derived now by using energy considerations does not make use of the small angle approximation and is valid for all deflection angles. However, the differences between the two solutions are quite small, as you can see from Figure 14.15.

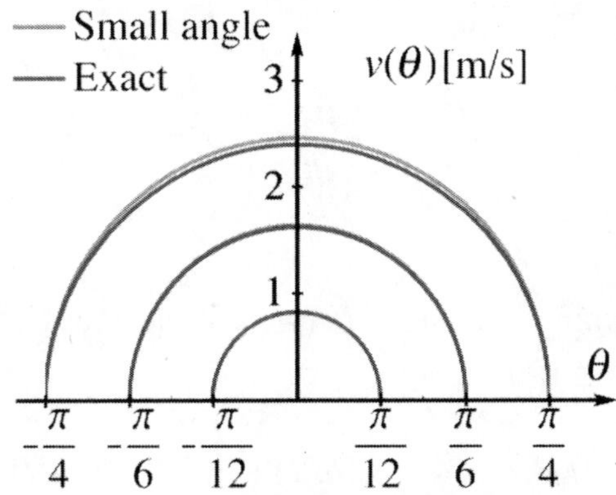

Figure 14.15: Comparison of the speeds as a function of the deflection angle, calculated with the small angle approximation (red curves) and the exact formula based on conservation of energy (blue curves). The three sets of curves represent initial angles of 15, 30, and 45 degrees (from inside to outside), and the pendulum length was chosen as 1 m.

Example

Example 14.4: Pendulum

Question:

A trapeze artist in the circus starts her motion on the trapeze at rest with angle of 45 degrees relative to the vertical. Her swing has a length of 5.00 m. What is her speed at the lowest point in her trajectory?

Answer:

Per our initial condition, $\theta_0 = 45° = \pi/4$ rad. We are interested in $v(\theta=0)$. Applying our energy conservation techniques, we have obtained (14.46)

$$v(\theta) = \sqrt{2g\ell(\cos\theta - \cos\theta_0)}$$

Inserting the numbers, we find:

$$v(\pi/4) = \sqrt{2\cdot(9.81 \text{ m/s}^2)\cdot(5.00 \text{ m})\cdot(1-\sqrt{1/2})} = 5.36 \text{ m/s}$$

Using the small angle approximation, for comparison, we would have found $v(\pi/4) = \theta_0\sqrt{g\ell} = 5.50$ m/s. This is close, but for many applications not quite sufficient.

14.4. Damped Harmonic Motion

Springs and pendulums do not go on oscillating forever. At some point, they come to rest. So there must be a force that slows them down. This effect goes under the name of "damping". As we have just seen, a force that depends linearly on position does not accomplish this damping. However, a force that depends on the velocity does. For speeds that are not too large, the damping is given by a drag force of the form $-bv$, where b is a constant and $v = dx/dt$ is the velocity. With this additional force our differential equation to solve now becomes:

$$m\frac{d^2x}{dt^2} = -b\frac{dx}{dt} - kx \Rightarrow$$

$$\frac{d^2x}{dt^2} + \frac{b}{m}\frac{dx}{dt} + \frac{k}{m}x = 0 \tag{14.47}$$

Small Damping

For small values of the damping constant b (we will define what "small" means), the solution of this equation is given as:

$$x(t) = Ae^{-\omega_\gamma t}\cos(\omega' t) + Be^{-\omega_\gamma t}\sin(\omega' t) \tag{14.48}$$

The coefficients A and B are determined by the initial conditions, i.e. the position x_0 and velocity v_0 at time $t = 0$,

$$A = x_0 \text{ and } B = \frac{v_0 + x_0\omega_\gamma}{\omega'} \tag{14.49}$$

The angular frequencies appearing in this solution are given by:

$$\omega_\gamma = \frac{b}{2m}$$

$$\omega' = \sqrt{\omega_0^2 - \omega_\gamma^2} = \sqrt{\frac{k}{m} - \left(\frac{b}{2m}\right)^2} \tag{14.50}$$

$$\omega_0 = \sqrt{\frac{k}{m}}$$

This solution is valid for all values of the damping constant b for which the argument of the square root for ω' remains positive:

$$b < 2\sqrt{mk} \tag{14.51}$$

This is the condition for "small" damping.

Derivation 14.2:
We will show that equation (14.48) satisfies the differential equation for damped harmonic motion (14.47) in the limit of small damping. In mathematics, we call this assumed solution an *Ansatz* (the German word for *attempt*).
Ansatz:

$$x(t) = Ae^{-\omega_\gamma t}\cos(\omega' t)$$

$$\Rightarrow \frac{dx}{dt} = -\omega_\gamma Ae^{-\omega_\gamma t}\cos(\omega' t) - \omega' Ae^{-\omega_\gamma t}\sin(\omega' t)$$

$$\Rightarrow \frac{d^2x}{dt^2} = (\omega_\gamma^2 - \omega'^2)Ae^{-\omega_\gamma t}\cos(\omega' t) + 2\omega_\gamma\omega' Ae^{-\omega_\gamma t}\sin(\omega' t)$$

Insert this result into the above differential equation that we want to solve:

$$\begin{aligned}&(\omega_\gamma^2 - \omega'^2)Ae^{-\omega_\gamma t}\cos(\omega' t) + 2\omega_\gamma\omega' Ae^{-\omega_\gamma t}\sin(\omega' t)\\ &+\frac{b}{m}\left(-\omega_\gamma Ae^{-\omega_\gamma t}\cos(\omega' t) - \omega' Ae^{-\omega_\gamma t}\sin(\omega' t)\right)\\ &+\frac{k}{m}\left(Ae^{-\omega_\gamma t}\cos(\omega' t)\right) = 0\end{aligned}$$

Re-sort terms:

$$\begin{aligned}&\left(\omega_\gamma^2 - \omega'^2 - \frac{b}{m}\omega_\gamma + \frac{k}{m}\right)Ae^{-\omega_\gamma t}\cos(\omega' t) +\\ &\left(2\omega_\gamma\omega' - \frac{b}{m}\omega'\right)Ae^{-\omega_\gamma t}\sin(\omega' t) = 0\end{aligned}$$

This equation can only work for all times t if the coefficients in front of the sine and the cosine functions are each zero. We then get two conditions:

$$2\omega_\gamma\omega' - \frac{b}{m}\omega' = 0 \Rightarrow \omega_\gamma = \frac{b}{2m}$$

and

$$\omega_\gamma^2 - \omega'^2 - \frac{b}{m}\omega_\gamma + \frac{k}{m} = 0$$

To simplify the latter, we use the expression we just obtained for ω_γ and introduce the abbreviation $\omega_0 = \sqrt{k/m}$ for the angular frequency we obtained from the case without damping. We then obtain from this second condition:

$$\left(-\omega'^2 - \omega_\gamma^2 + \omega_0^2\right) = 0 \Rightarrow \omega' = \sqrt{\omega_0^2 - \omega_\gamma^2}$$

You can go through exactly the same steps to show that $Be^{-\omega_\gamma t}\sin(\omega' t)$ is also a valid solution. One can further show that these two solutions are the only possible solutions. (But we will skip this.)

Derivation

In all of the derivations in this chapter that involve differential equations we have proceeded in the same manner. This method is a general approach to the solution of problems involving differential equations: One chooses a trial solution and adjusts parameters and makes changes based on the results obtained by inserting the trial solution into the differential equation.

Now that we have solved this differential equation, let us take a look at the features of our solution, as shown in Figure 14.16. The sine and cosine functions take care of the oscillating behavior. Their combination results in another sine function, with a phase shift. The exponential function that multiplies them can be thought of as reducing the amplitude in time. So we find an oscillation with an amplitude which is exponentially decaying as our result. The frequency ω' of our oscillation is reduced relative to the frequency of oscillation in the case without damping, ω_0. The drawing in Figure 14.16 was generated for $k = 11$ N/m, $m = 1.8$ kg, and $b = 0.5$ kg/s. These parameters result in a frequency of $\omega' = 2.468/\text{s}$, as compared to a frequency of $\omega_0 = 2.472/\text{s}$ for the case without damping. We used an amplitude of $C = 5$ cm, and a phase shift of $\theta_0 = 1.6$. The dark blue curve is the result of plotting the complete function, and the two light blue curves show only the exponential envelope, by which the amplitude is reduced as a function of time.

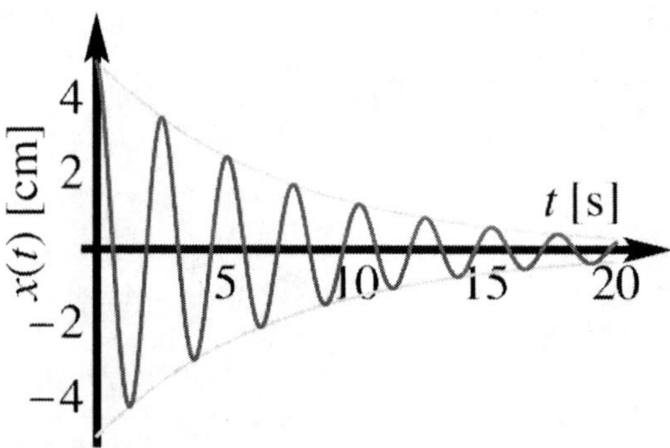

Figure 14.16: Graph of position versus time for a weakly damped harmonic oscillator.

Example

Example 14.5: Bungee Jumping

A bridge over a deep valley is ideal for bungee jumping, the thrill ride where you attach an elastic rope to your legs and jump off. The first part of your bungee jump consists of a free-fall for the length of the rope

Suppose the height of the bridge is 50 m. We use a 30 m long bungee rope that gets stretched by 5 m by the weight of a 70 kg person. From empirical data we have found that this bungee rope has a damping angular frequency of 0.3 Hz.

Question:
What is the trajectory of the bungee jump?

Answer:
From the top of the bridge the jumper experiences free-fall for the first 30 m of her descent, the red part of the trajectory in Figure 14.17. Once she has fallen the length of the rope, 30 m, she has reached a velocity of $v_0 = -\sqrt{2g\ell} = -24.26 \text{ m/s}$. This part of the trajectory takes a time of $t = \sqrt{2\ell / g} = 2.47$ s.

Then she enters a damped oscillation about the equilibrium position of $y = 50 \text{ m} - 35 \text{ m} = 15 \text{ m}$, with the initial displacement of $x_0 = \ell_0 - \ell = 5 \text{ m}$. We can calculate the oscillation angular frequency from knowing that the rope was stretched by 5 m due to the 70 kg weight:

$$\omega_0 = \sqrt{\frac{k}{m}} = \sqrt{\frac{g}{\ell_0 - \ell}} = \sqrt{\frac{9.8 \text{ m/s}^2}{5 \text{ m}}} = 1.4 \text{ s}^{-1}$$

Since $\omega_\gamma = 0.3 \text{ s}^{-1}$, as specified, and thus $\omega' = \sqrt{\omega_0^2 - \omega_\gamma^2} = 1.367 \text{ s}^{-1}$, our bungee jumper then will oscillate according to equation (14.48), with coefficients $A = x_0 = 5$ m and $B = (v_0 + x_0\omega_\gamma)/\omega' = -17.65 \text{ m/s}$, as specified by equation (14.49). This is indicated by the green part of the trajectory in Figure 14.17.

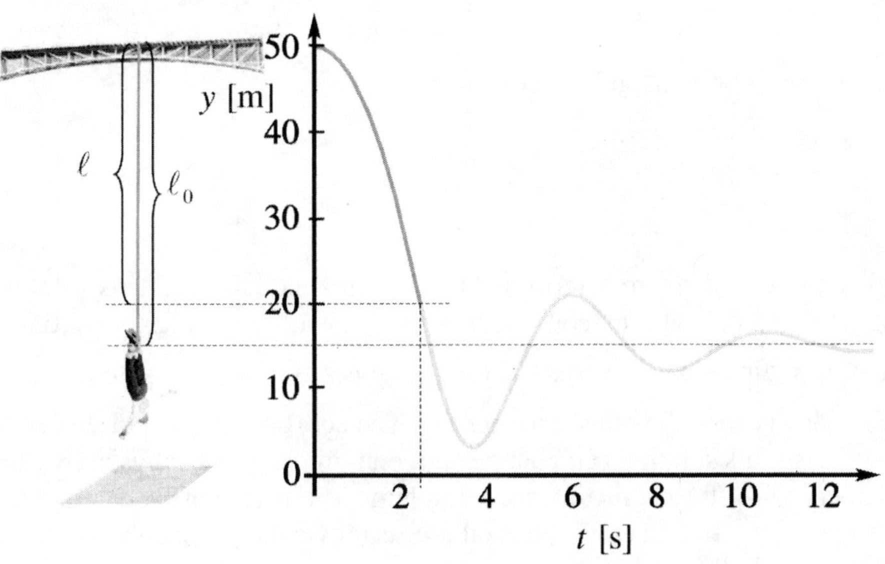

Figure 14.17: Idealized trajectory of a bungee jump.

Discussion:
A final remark / reality check for this example: The approximation of a damped harmonic motion for the final part of the jump is not quite accurate. If you examine Figure 14.17 carefully, you see that the trajectory rises above 20 m for approximately 1 s, starting at approximately 5.5 s. During this interval the bungee cord would not be

Example

Example

stretched and thus this part of the sinusoidal motion would have to be replaced with a parabola during this time in which the bungee jumper is again in free-fall motion. However, for the present qualitative discussion, our damped harmonic motion approximation is sufficient. If you plan to actually jump (for legal reasons strongly discouraged by the authors), you should always test the setup first with an object of equal or greater weight than yours.

Large Damping

Now you may ask what happens when the condition $b < 2\sqrt{mk}$ is no longer fulfilled. Then the argument of the square root that determined ω' would actually be smaller than 0. So the *Ansatz* we made for small damping does not work any more. The solution of the differential equation for damped harmonic oscillations (14.47) for the case that $b > 2\sqrt{mk}$ is:

$$x(t) = Ae^{-\omega_\gamma t + \sqrt{\omega_\gamma^2 - \omega_0^2}\,t} + Be^{-\omega_\gamma t - \sqrt{\omega_\gamma^2 - \omega_0^2}\,t} \tag{14.52}$$

(for $b > 2\sqrt{mk}$), with the amplitudes now given by:

$$A = \tfrac{1}{2}x_0 + \frac{x_0\omega_\gamma + v_0}{2\sqrt{\omega_\gamma^2 - \omega_0^2}}, \quad B = \tfrac{1}{2}x_0 - \frac{x_0\omega_\gamma + v_0}{2\sqrt{\omega_\gamma^2 - \omega_0^2}} \tag{14.53}$$

And again we have for the angular frequencies:

$$\omega_\gamma = \frac{b}{2m}, \quad \omega_0 = \sqrt{\frac{k}{m}} \tag{14.54}$$

The coefficients A and B are determined by the initial conditions. This solution has no oscillations. Instead the solution consists of two exponentials. The exponential with the argument $-\omega_\gamma t + \sqrt{\omega_\gamma^2 - \omega_0^2}\,t$ governs the long-time behavior of the system because it decays more slowly than the other exponential. The coefficients A and B can have opposite signs; so this solution can change sign one time at most. Physically, this sign change happens when the oscillator receives a large initial velocity towards the equilibrium position. In that case, the oscillator can overshoot the equilibrium location and approach it from the other side.

Critical Damping

Because we have already covered the cases for $b < 2\sqrt{mk}$ and $b > 2\sqrt{mk}$, one might be tempted to think that one can obtain the solution for $b = 2\sqrt{mk}$ in some limit or via some interpolation between the two solutions. This case, however, is not quite this straightforward. To obtain the answer, one has to employ a slightly different ansatz. The solution for the critical damping case is given by:

$$x(t) = A\mathrm{e}^{-\omega_\gamma t} + tBe^{-\omega_\gamma t} \qquad (14.55)$$

(for $b = 2\sqrt{mk}$), where the amplitude coefficients now have the values of

$$A = x_0, \; B = v_0 + x_0\omega_\gamma \qquad (14.56)$$

We still have $\omega_\gamma = b/2m$ as the angular frequency that appears in this solution.

Let us look at an example for damped harmonic motion in which we determine the coefficients A and B from the initial conditions.

Example

Example 14.6: Damped Motion

Question:
A spring with a spring constant of $k = 1.00$ N/m , has a mass $m = 1.00$ kg attached to it, and moves in a medium with damping constant $b = 2.00$ kg/s . The mass is released from rest at a position of +5 cm from equilibrium. Where will it be after a time of 1.75 s?

Answer:
First we have to find out which of our three cases applies here. To find out, we have to calculate $2\sqrt{mk} = 2\sqrt{(1 \text{ kg})\cdot(1 \text{ N/m})} = 2$ kg/s which happens to be exactly equal to the value that was given for the damping constant b . So this system, like the shock absorber on your car, is critically damped. We can also calculate the damping frequency, $\omega_\gamma = b/2m = 1.00/\text{s}$.

The question posed gives us the initial conditions as $x_0 = x(t=0) = +5$ cm and $(dx/dt)\big|_{t=0} = v(t=0) = v_0 = 0$. Now we determine the constants A and B from these initial conditions. (They are already given explicitly in (14.56), but it is good to see how one arrives at this result). We use our solution for the case of critical damping:

$$x(t) = Ae^{-\omega_\gamma t} + tBe^{-\omega_\gamma t}$$
$$\Rightarrow x(0) = Ae^{-\omega_\gamma 0} + 0Be^{-\omega_\gamma 0} = A$$

and take the time derivative:

$$v = \frac{dx}{dt} = -\omega_\gamma Ae^{-\omega_\gamma t} + B(1 - \omega_\gamma t)e^{-\omega_\gamma t}$$
$$\Rightarrow v(0) = -\omega_\gamma Ae^{-\omega_\gamma 0} + B(1 - \omega_\gamma 0)e^{-\omega_\gamma 0} = -\omega_\gamma A + B$$

Example

According to the way the problem was posed, $v_0 = 0$, which results in $B = \omega_\gamma A$ from equation (14.56), and $x_0 = +5\text{ cm}$, which determines A. Thus, our complete solution is given by:

$$x(t) = (5\text{ cm})(1+\omega_\gamma t)e^{-\omega_\gamma t}$$
$$= (5\text{ cm})(1+(1.00/\text{s})t)e^{-(1.00/\text{s})t}$$

because we have already calculated $\omega_\gamma = 1.00/\text{s}$. We then get for the position of the mass after 1.75 s:

$$x(1.75\text{ s}) = (5\text{ cm})(1+1.75)e^{-1.75} = 2.39\text{ cm}$$

Finally, we compare under-damped, over-damped, and critically damped motion. In Figure 14.18 we show the three cases. All three cases shown are started from rest at time 0. The green line represents the under-damped case. One can see that there are still oscillations present. The red line is the result of large damping above the critical value, and the blue line is the time evolution for the case of critical damping.

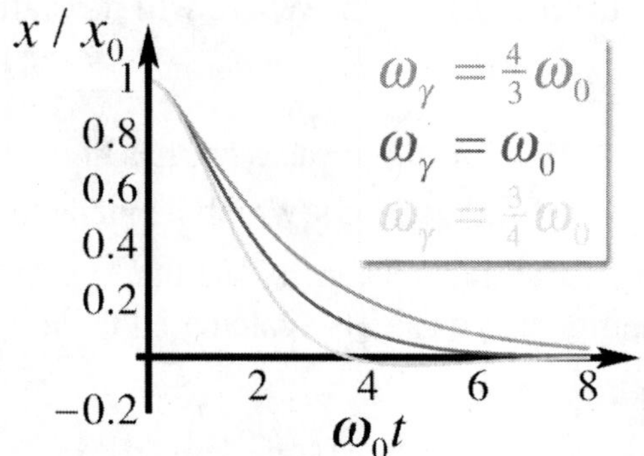

Figure 14.18: Graph of position versus time for under-damped motion (green line), over-damped motion (red line), and critically damped motion (blue line).

If we need to have an engineering solution for a damped oscillation that returns as fast as possible to the equilibrium position and has no oscillations, then we need to use the condition of critical damping. Examples are the shock absorbers in our cars, motorcycles (as in Figure 14.19) or bicycles. For maximum performance, they need to work at the critical damping limit or just slightly under-damped. As they get worn, the damping becomes weaker, and the shock absorbers follow the small damping motion case. This results in the "bouncing" sensation when you ride in your vehicle and indicates that it is time to change the shock absorbers.

Figure 14.19: Shock absorbers on front wheel of motorcycle.

Self-Test Opportunity: Consider a pendulum whose motion is lightly damped by a term given by the product of a damping constant α times the speed of the moving mass. Making the small angle approximation we can write differential equation

$$\frac{d^2\theta}{dt^2}+\alpha\frac{d\theta}{dt}+\frac{g}{\ell}\theta=0$$

By analogy with the case of a mass on a spring, give expressions for the angular frequencies characterizing the angular motion, ω_γ, ω', and ω_0.

In-class exercise: An automobile with a mass 1640 kg is lifted into the air. When the car is lifted, the suspension spring on each wheel lengthens by 30.0 cm. What is the damping constant required for the shock absorber on each wheel to produce critical damping on each wheel?

a) 101 kg/s
b) 234 kg/s
c) 1230 kg/s
d) 2310 kg/s
e) 4690 kg/s

Energy-Loss in Damped Oscillations

When we just discussed damped oscillations, we introduced the velocity dependent (and thus non-conservative!) damping force $F_\gamma = -bv$, resulting in the differential equation (compare (14.47))

$$\frac{d^2x}{dt^2}+2\omega_\gamma\frac{dx}{dt}+\omega_0^2x=0 \qquad (14.57)$$

where $\omega_0=\sqrt{k/m}$ (k = spring constant, m = mass) is the angular frequency of the harmonic oscillation without damping, and $\omega_\gamma = b/2m$ is the damping angular frequency. The non-conservative damping force must result in a loss of total mechanical energy. Here we will only examine the energy in the small damping case, because this is overwhelmingly the case of technological importance. But large and critical damping can be treated in an analogous manner. For the small damping case we found that a solution for the displacement as a function of time can be written as (14.48) or in terms of a single sinusoidal function with a phase shift as

$$x(t) = Ce^{-\omega_\gamma t}\sin(\omega' t - \theta_0) \qquad (14.58)$$

This solution can be understood as a sinusoidal oscillation in time with angular frequency $\omega' = \sqrt{\omega_0^2 - \omega_\gamma^2}$, with exponentially decreasing amplitude.

We already know that the damping force is non-conservative, and so we can be sure that mechanical energy is lost as a function of time. Since we had seen in equation (14.35) that the energy for the harmonic oscillation is proportional to the square of the amplitude, we might be led to conclude that the energy decreases smoothly and exponentially for the damped oscillation. However, as we will show in the following, this is not quite the case.

First we can calculate the velocity as a function of time by taking the time derivative of (14.58), resulting in

$$v(t) = \omega' Ce^{-\omega_\gamma t}\cos(\omega' t - \theta_0) - \omega_\gamma Ce^{-\omega_\gamma t}\sin(\omega' t - \theta_0) \qquad (14.59)$$

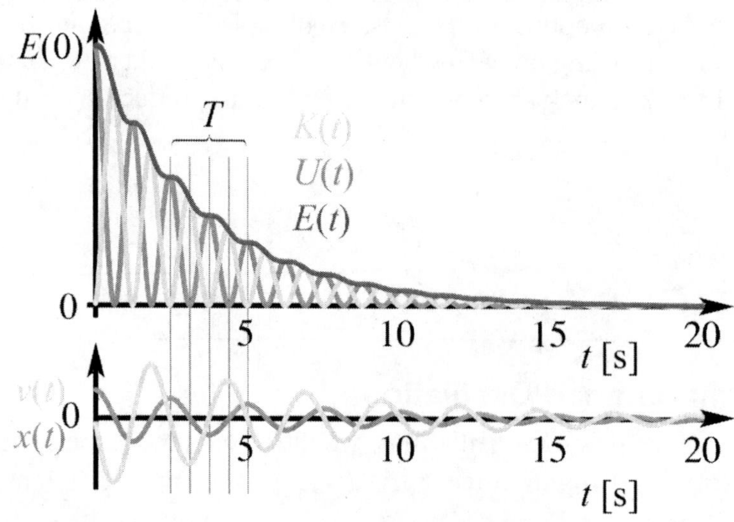

Figure 14.20: Bottom part: coordinate (red) and velocity (green for a weakly damped harmonic oscillator. Top part: Potential (red), kinetic (green), and total energy (blue). The 5 thin vertical lines mark one complete oscillation period, *T*.

Then we can calculate the potential energy stored in the spring as a function time, $\frac{1}{2}kx^2(t)$, as well as the kinetic energy due to the motion of the mass, $\frac{1}{2}mv^2(t)$. This was done in Figure 14.20 for a choice of parameters of $k = 11\text{ N/m}$, $m = 1.8\text{ kg}$, and $b = 0.5\text{ kg/s}$. These parameters result in a frequency of $\omega' = 2.468/\text{s}$, as compared to a frequency of $\omega_0 = 2.472/\text{s}$ for the case without damping, and a damping frequency of $\omega_\gamma = 0.139/\text{s}$. We used the amplitude of $C = 5\text{ cm}$, and a phase shift of $\theta_0 = 1.6$.

We can see in Figure 14.20 that the total energy does not decrease as a smooth exponential, but instead more in a stepwise fashion. This can be understood quite straightforwardly. In order to do this, we can calculate the power, i.e. the rate of energy loss. It is

$$\frac{dE}{dt} = -bv^2 = vF_\gamma \tag{14.60}$$

Thus we see that the energy loss is largest wherever the velocity has the largest absolute value, which happens as the mass passes through the equilibrium position. When the mass reaches the points where the velocity is zero and the masses turns around, all energy is in potential energy and thus there is 0 energy loss at these points in time.

Derivation 14.3:
We can derive the formula for the energy loss by taking the time derivatives of kinetic and potential energies,

$$\frac{dE}{dt} = \frac{dK}{dt} + \frac{dU}{dt} = \frac{d}{dt}\left(\tfrac{1}{2}mv^2\right) + \frac{d}{dt}\left(\tfrac{1}{2}kx^2\right) = mv\frac{dv}{dt} + kx\frac{dx}{dt}$$

Now we use $v = dx/dt$, and factor out a common factor of mdx/dt. This results in

$$\frac{dE}{dt} = m\frac{dx}{dt}\frac{d^2x}{dt^2} + kx\frac{dx}{dt} = m\frac{dx}{dt}\left(\frac{d^2x}{dt^2} + \frac{k}{m}x\right)$$

Now we can use $\omega_0^2 = k/m$ and find

$$\frac{dE}{dt} = m\frac{dx}{dt}\left(\frac{d^2x}{dt^2} + \omega_0^2 x\right)$$

We can reorder our differential equation (14.57) by moving the damping term to the right hand side, resulting in:

$$\frac{d^2x}{dt^2} + \omega_0^2 x = -2\omega_\gamma\frac{dx}{dt} = -\frac{b}{m}\frac{dx}{dt}$$

Since the left hand side of this differential equation is now exactly equal to the term inside the bracket in the previous equation for the rate of energy loss, we then obtain finally

Derivation

$$\frac{dE}{dt} = m\frac{dx}{dt}\left(-\frac{b}{m}\frac{dx}{dt}\right) = -b\left(\frac{dx}{dt}\right)^2 = -bv^2$$

Our damping force is $F_\gamma = -bv$, and so we find that the rate of energy loss is indeed $dE/dt = vF_\gamma$.

In practical applications, one introduces the quality of the oscillator, Q, which specifies the ratio of total energy E to the energy loss over one complete oscillation period T, ΔE:

$$Q = 2\pi\frac{E}{|\Delta E|} \tag{14.61}$$

In the limit of zero damping the oscillator experiences no energy loss, and $Q \to \infty$. In the limit of weak damping, one can show that the quality of the oscillator can be approximated by

$$Q \cong \frac{\omega_0}{2\omega_\gamma} \tag{14.62}$$

Combining these two results for the weakly damped case then provides us with a handy formula for the energy loss for a complete oscillation period:

$$|\Delta E| = E\frac{2\pi}{Q} = E\frac{4\pi\omega_\gamma}{\omega_0} \tag{14.63}$$

For the example of the oscillator shown in Figure 14.20, this results in $Q = 2.472/0.139 = 17.8$. Inserting this result into (14.63) leads us to an energy loss of $|\Delta E| = 0.71E$ during each oscillation period. We can compare this to the exact result in for Figure 14.20 by measuring the energy at the beginning and end of the interval indicated in the figure. We then find for the energy difference divided by the average energy a value of 0.68, in fairly good agreement with the value of 0.71 obtained by using the approximation of (14.62).

14.5. Forced Harmonic Motion and Resonance

If you are pushing someone sitting on a swing, you give that person periodic pushes, in general with the goal to make him/her swing higher, i.e. to increase the amplitude of the oscillation. This situation is an example of a forced harmonic motion. Periodically forced or driven oscillations represent a very important class of problems that we will encounter in many areas: mechanics, acoustics, optics, electromagnetism, and all areas of modern physics. To represent the periodic driving force, we use

$$F(t) = F_d \cos(\omega_d t) \tag{14.64}$$

where F_d and ω_d are constants. We start by considering the case with no damping. Using the driving force we just introduced, our differential equation for this problem becomes:

$$m\frac{d^2x}{dt^2} = -kx + F_d \cos(\omega_d t) \Rightarrow$$
$$\frac{d^2x}{dt^2} + \frac{k}{m}x - \frac{F_d}{m}\cos(\omega_d t) = 0 \tag{14.65}$$

The solution to this problem is:

$$x(t) = A\sin(\omega_0 t) + B\cos(\omega_0 t) + C_d \cos(\omega_d t) \tag{14.66}$$

The coefficients A and B for the part of the solution that oscillates with the intrinsic angular frequency $\omega_0 = \sqrt{k/m}$ can be determined from the initial conditions. But much more interesting is the part of the solution that oscillates with the driving angular frequency. The amplitude of this forced oscillation is given by:

$$C_d = \frac{F_d}{m(\omega_0^2 - \omega_d^2)} \tag{14.67}$$

This result means that the closer the driving frequency ω_d is to the intrinsic angular frequency ω_0, the bigger the amplitude becomes. If we return to the example of pushing a person on a swing, this amplification is apparent. You can only increase the amplitude when you push at approximately the same frequency with which the person on the swing is oscillating. If you push with that frequency, the person on the swing will go higher and higher.

Of course, if the driving frequency is exactly equal to the intrinsic frequency of the oscillator, our formula (14.67) above predicts that the amplitude will grow infinitely big. In real life this infinite growth does not occur. There is always some damping in the system. In the presence of damping, the differential equation to solve instead becomes:

$$\frac{d^2x}{dt^2} + \frac{b}{m}\frac{dx}{dt} + \frac{k}{m}x - \frac{F_d}{m}\cos(\omega_d t) = 0 \tag{14.68}$$

and has the steady-state solution

$$x(t) = C_\gamma \cos(\omega_d t - \theta_\gamma) \tag{14.69}$$

where x oscillates at the driving frequency and the amplitude is now:

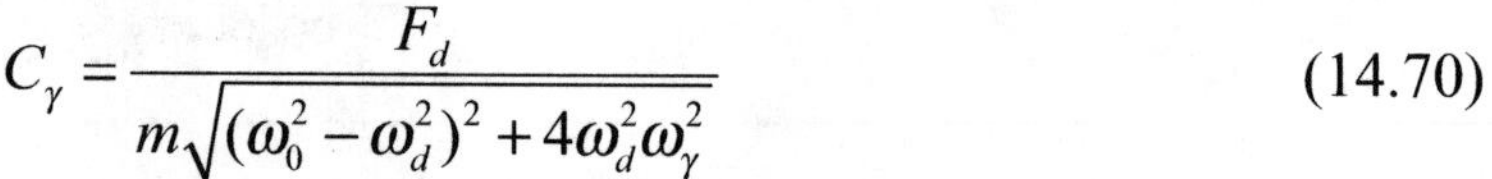

$$C_\gamma = \frac{F_d}{m\sqrt{(\omega_0^2-\omega_d^2)^2+4\omega_d^2\omega_\gamma^2}} \tag{14.70}$$

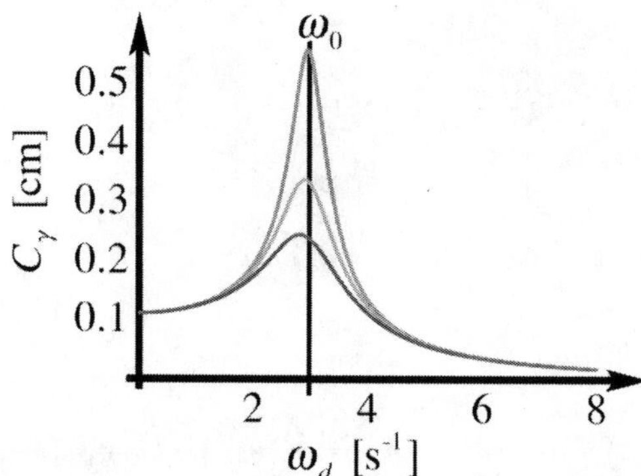

Figure 14.21: Graph of the amplitude of forced oscillation as a function of the angular frequency of the driving force. The three curves represent different damping angular frequencies of 0.3, 0.5, and 0.7 Hz, from top to bottom.

As you can see, this amplitude cannot be infinite, because even at $\omega_d = \omega_0$, it still has a finite value, $F_d/(2m\omega_d\omega_\gamma)$, which is also *approximately* its maximum. The shape of the curve of the amplitude C_γ as a function of the driving frequency ω_d is called a resonance shape and is characteristic for all resonance phenomena. When $\omega_d = \omega_0$ the driving frequency is called the resonant frequency; C_γ is a maximum at this frequency. In Figure 14.21 we show the case for $\omega_0 = 3$ s^{-1} and three values of the damping angular frequency $\omega_\gamma = (0.3, 0.5, 0.7)$ s^{-1} (from top to bottom). As the damping gets weaker, the resonance becomes sharper. Also marked in the drawing is the location of the natural angular frequency of the harmonic oscillator in the absence of damping, ω_0, chosen as 3 Hz here. You can see that the resonance curve reaches its maximum slightly below ω_0 in every case.

The phase shift θ_γ appearing in (14.69) is dependent on the driving angular frequency as well as on the damping and intrinsic angular frequencies,

$$\theta_\gamma = \tfrac{1}{2}\pi - \arctan\left(\frac{\omega_0^2-\omega_d^2}{2\omega_d\omega_\gamma}\right) \tag{14.71}$$

The phase shift as a function of driving frequency is graphed in Figure 14.22 for the same three sets of parameters used in Figure 14.21. You can see that for small driving frequencies the forced oscillation follows the driving in phase. As we approach the resonance, the phase difference begins to grow and reaches $\frac{1}{2}\pi$ at $\omega_d = \omega_0$. For driving frequencies much larger than the resonance frequency the phase shift approaches π. The lower the damping frequency ω_γ is, the steeper the transition from 0 to π phase shift becomes.

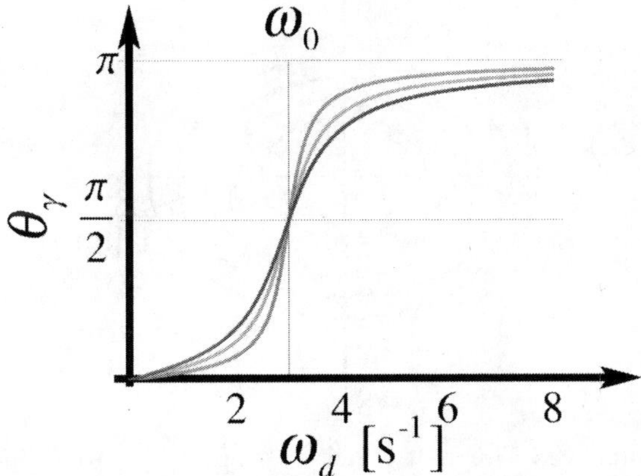

Figure 14.22: Phase shift as a function of driving frequency for the same parameters as used in the previous figure. The three curves represent different damping angular frequencies of 0.3 (shallowest curve), 0.5, and 0.7 Hz (steepest curve).

A final practical note is in order at this point: The solution contained in equation (14.69) is usually only reached after some time. The full solution for the differential equation for the damped driven oscillation (14.68) is the solution given in (14.69), plus the solution to the damped oscillation problem without driving that we had solved before. During this transition time the effect of the particular initial conditions given to the system initially are damped out, and (14.69) is approached asymptotically.

Driving mechanical systems at resonance has important technical applications, not all of them desired. Most worrisome are resonance frequencies in architectural structures. One has to be very careful, for example, not to construct high-rises in such a way that they can pick up resonance in earthquakes. Perhaps the most infamous example of a structure that was destroyed by resonance phenomena was the Tacoma Narrows Bridge, "Galloping Gertie", in the State of Washington. It collapsed on November 7, 1940, only a few months after construction was finished. During the collapse, a 40 mph wind was able to excite the bridge at resonance until catastrophic mechanical failure occurred.

Columns of soldiers marching across a bridge are told to fall out of lockstep to avoid exciting a resonance due to the periodic stomping of the soldiers' feet. But it is possible that a large group of people can get locked into phase through feedback mechanisms. Such a case of driving a bridge at resonance with feedback coupling occurred on June 13, 2000. On this day, the London Millennium Bridge of the Thames River had to be closed after only three days of operation, because the 2000 pedestrians walking over the bridge drove the bridge into resonance and earned it the nickname "wobbly bridge". The lateral swaying of the bridge was such that it provided feedback and locked the pedestrians into a rhythm that amplified the oscillations.

14.6. Phase Space

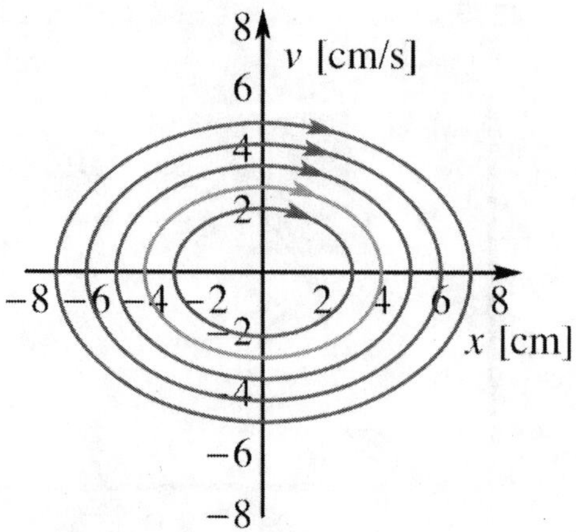

Figure 14.23: Graph of velocity versus position for different amplitudes of simple harmonic motion

We will return repeatedly to the physics of oscillations during the course of this book. The reason for this emphasis is that many systems have restoring forces that drive them back to equilibrium, if they are dislocated only a small distance from equilibrium. Many problems in physics can be mapped to that of a pendulum or spring. Before we leave the topic of oscillations, we will cover one more interesting way of displaying the trajectories that oscillating systems take. Instead of plotting displacement, velocity, or acceleration as a function of time, we plot velocity versus displacement. This display of velocity versus displacement is called "phase space". By looking at physical motion in this way, one can gain interesting insights.

Let's start by looking at the oscillator without damping. If we use an oscillation with the time dependence given by $x(t) = A\sin(\omega t)$ with an amplitude of $A = 3$ cm and an angular frequency of $\omega = 0.7$ s^{-1}, and plot this motion in phase space, we obtain an ellipse, as indicated by the red curve in Figure 14.23. For other values of the amplitude, we get different curves, as indicated by the blue lines, for which the amplitude was varied between values of 2 and 7 in steps of 1.

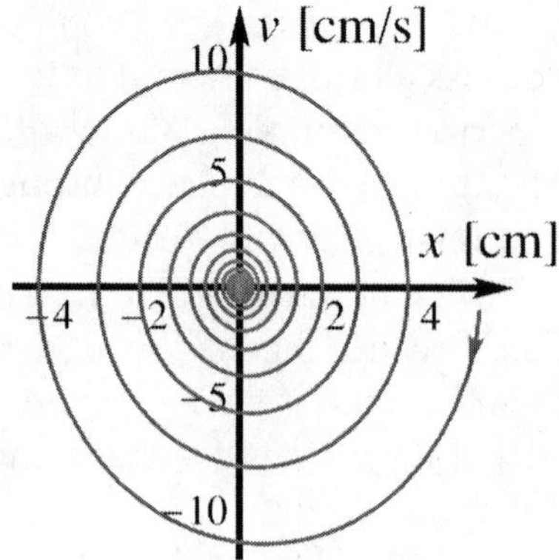

Figure 14.24: Graph of velocity versus position for a damped oscillator.

Here is another example: In Figure 14.24 we plot the damped oscillator ($k = 11$ N/m, $m = 1.8$ kg, and $b = 0.5$ kg/s, $C = 5$ cm, and $\theta_0 = 1.6$) motion that we already had displayed above as a function of time in our phase space. Now you can see the starting point of the oscillation motion. It starts at the point $x(t = 0) = 5$ cm, $v(t = 0) = -1.05$ cm/s. One can see that the trajectory in phase space spirals inward towards the point $(0,0)$. It looks as if the trajectory were attracted to that point. If we had started the oscillation with different initial conditions, we would also have spiraled in on a different trajectory. A point to which all trajectories will eventually converge is called a "point attractor".

14.7. Chaos

There is a field of current research that has opened up only recently with the arrival of computers. This field deals with non-linear dynamics and chaos and has yielded interesting and relevant results during the last decade. If we look hard enough and under certain conditions, we can discover signatures of chaotic motion even in the oscillators that we have been dealing with in this chapter. In chapter 7 we already took at look at chaos and sensitivity to initial conditions, and here we continue this thread in greater detail.

When we looked at the pendulum, we made the "small-angle" approximation. But suppose we want to use large deflection angles. We can do this by using a pendulum that replaces the string with a thin solid rod. This pendulum can then even go over the top. In that case our approximation $\sin\theta \approx \theta$ does not work, and we have to use the sine function in our differential equation. In the case that we have a periodic external driving force as well as damping present for this pendulum, we cannot solve the equation of motion in an analytic fashion.

However, we can still use the computer and numerical integration procedures to obtain our desired solution. The solution, of course, depends on the initial conditions given. Based on what we have learned so far about oscillators, we would expect that similar initial conditions give similar trajectories in time. However, for some combinations of driving frequency and amplitude, damping constant, and pendulum length this is not true.

If you look at Figure 14.25, you find that we have plotted the trajectory of the pendulum angle as a function of time for three initial conditions of the same equation of motion. In all cases we used the identical value for the initial velocity. For the red curve, we used an initial angle of exactly 0 radians. For the green curve, we made a small change and started our pendulum with an initial angle of 10^{-3} radians. We can see that the two curves stay close for a few oscillations, but then rapidly diverge from each other. Even if we change the initial angle to 10^{-5} radians (blue line), the trajectories do not stay close for much longer. Since the blue curve started a factor 100 times closer to the red curve, we might have expected that it would also stay close a factor of 100 longer in time. This is not the case. This behavior is called sensitive dependence on initial conditions. If a system turns out to be sensitively dependent on its initial conditions, then a long-time prediction of its motion is impossible. This behavior is one of the hallmarks of chaotic motion.

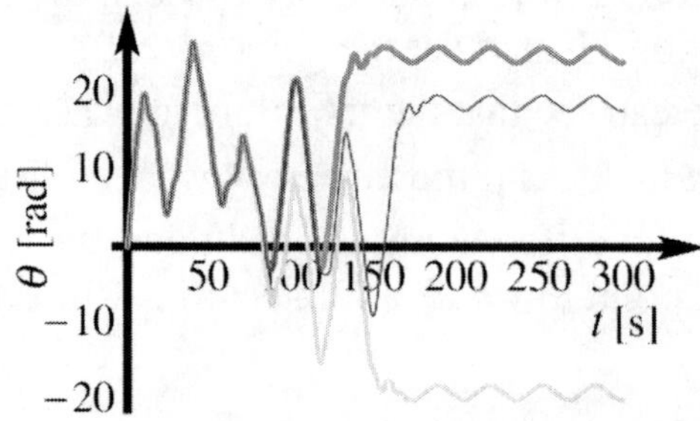

Figure 14.25: Graph of deflection angle as a function of time for a driven pendulum for three different initial conditions. The red line shows an initial angle of zero. The green line represents an initial angle of 10^{-3} rad. The blue line is for an initial angle of 10^{-5} rad.

Precise long-range weather forecasts are impossible for similar reasons of sensitive dependence on initial conditions. With the advent of computers in the 1950s, meteorologists became convinced that they could calculate the weather accurately into the future, if they only generated enough measurements of all the relevant variables such as temperature and wind direction at as many points as possible across the country. But in the 1960s, it became obvious that the basic differential equations for the atmosphere also show similar sensitive dependence on initial conditions as exhibited in Figure 14.25. Thus, the dream of long-range precise weather forecasting has come to a halt.

What we have learned/Exam Study Guide:

- Hooke's Law: $F = -kx$
- Equation of motion for a mass on a spring (no damping): $\frac{d^2x}{dt^2} = -\frac{k}{m}x$ with solution $x(t) = A\sin(\omega_0 t) + B\cos(\omega_0 t)$ with $\omega_0 = \sqrt{k/m}$ or, alternatively, $x(t) = C\sin(\omega_0 t + \theta_0)$
- Equation of motion for a pendulum (no damping): $\theta(t) = A\sin(\omega_0 t) + B\cos(\omega_0 t)$ with $\omega_0 = \sqrt{g/\ell}$
- Velocity and acceleration in simple oscillations: $x(t) = C\sin(\omega_0 t + \theta_0)$ $\Rightarrow v(t) = \omega_0 C\cos(\omega_0 t + \theta_0)$ $\Rightarrow a(t) = -\omega_0^2 C\sin(\omega_0 t + \theta_0)$
- Period of the oscillation: $T = 2\pi / \omega$
- Frequency: $f = 1/T = \omega / 2\pi$ or $\omega = 2\pi f$
- Equation of motion for mass on a spring with small damping ($b < 2\sqrt{mk}$): $x(t) = Ae^{-\omega_\gamma t}\cos(\omega' t) + Be^{-\omega_\gamma t}\sin(\omega' t)$ with

$$\omega_\gamma = b/2m,\ \omega' = \sqrt{k/m-(b/2m)^2} = \sqrt{\omega_0{}^2-\omega_\gamma{}^2},\ \omega_0 = \sqrt{k/m}$$

- Equation of motion for mass on a spring with large damping ($b > 2\sqrt{mk}$):
  $x(t) = Ae^{-(\omega_\gamma+\sqrt{\omega_\gamma^2-\omega_0^2})t} + Be^{-(\omega_\gamma-\sqrt{\omega_\gamma^2-\omega_0^2})t}$
- Equation of motion for mass on a spring with critical damping ($b = 2\sqrt{mk}$): $x(t) = (A+tB)e^{-\omega_\gamma t}$
- For a damped harmonic oscillator, the rate of energy loss is $\dfrac{dE}{dt} = -bv^2 = vF_\gamma$
- The quality of the oscillator is related to the energy loss during one complete oscillation period, $Q = 2\pi\dfrac{E}{|\Delta E|}$
- Resonance: if a periodic external driving force $F(t) = F_d\cos(\omega_d t)$ is applied, then the equation of motion becomes (after some transient time):
  $x(t) = C_\gamma\cos(\omega_d t-\theta_\gamma)$, with the amplitude $C_\gamma = \dfrac{F_d}{m\sqrt{(\omega_0^2-\omega_d^2)^2+4\omega_d^2\omega_\gamma^2}}$
  displaying a resonance shape in which the amplitude is a maximum when the driving frequency equals the natural frequency ($\omega_d = \omega_0$).
- In phase space, we plot the velocity versus the position. Simple harmonic motion follows an ellipse in this phase space, passing through the ellipse exactly once each period. Damped harmonic motion spirals in towards the point attractor at (0,0).
- For the right choice of parameters, a damped driven rod pendulum can show chaotic motion in which its motion is sensitively dependent on its initial conditions. Then its long-time behavior is not predictable.

Additional Solved Problems

Solved Problem

Solved Problem 14.2: Damped Motion

Question:

A 1.75 kg mass sliding on a frictionless horizontal plane is connected to a horizontal spring with spring constant $k = 3.50$ N/m. The mass is pulled to the right a distance $d = 7.50$ cm and released from rest. After 113 complete oscillations, the amplitude of oscillation is one half the original amplitude of oscillation. The damping of the motion of the mass is proportional to the speed of moving mass. What is the damping coefficient b?

Answer:

THINK: Because the mass executes 113 oscillations and the amplitude decreases by a factor of two, we know we are dealing with small damping. After an integer number of oscillations, the cosine term will be one and the sine term will be zero. Knowing that the amplitude decreases by a factor of two after 113 oscillations, we can get an expression for

ω_γ in terms of the time required to complete 113 oscillations from which we can obtain the damping constant.

SKETCH: A sketch of the position of the mass at $t=0$ and at $t=113T$, where T is the period of oscillation is shown in Figure 14.26.

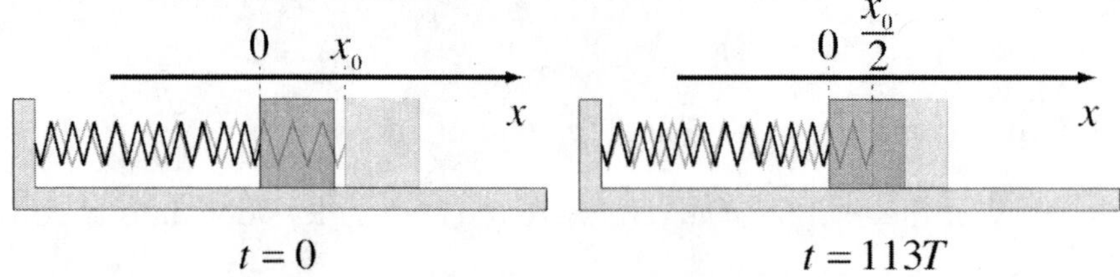

Figure 14.26: Position of the mass at $t = 0$ (right panel) and at $t = 113T$ (right panel).

RESEARCH:

Because we know that we are dealing with small damping we can apply (14.48)

$$x(t)=Ae^{-\omega_\gamma t}\cos(\omega' t)+Be^{-\omega_\gamma t}\sin(\omega' t). \tag{14.72}$$

At $t=0$, we know that $x=x_0$ so that $A=x_0$. After 113 complete oscillations, the cosine term will be one, the sine term will be zero, and $x=x_0/2$. Thus we can write

$$x_0/2=x_0e^{-\omega_\gamma(113T)}\cdot 1+0. \tag{14.73}$$

where $T=2\pi/\omega'$ is the period of oscillation. We can now express the previous equation as

$$0.5=e^{-\omega_\gamma(113\cdot 2\pi/\omega')}. \tag{14.74}$$

Taking the natural logarithm of both sides of this equation gives us

$$\ln(0.5)=-\omega_\gamma(113\cdot 2\pi/\omega'). \tag{14.75}$$

Remembering that $\omega'=\sqrt{\omega_0^2-\omega_\gamma^2}$ where $\omega_0=\sqrt{k/m}$ where k is the spring constant and m is the mass, we can write

$$-\frac{\ln(0.5)}{113\cdot 2\pi}=\frac{\omega_\gamma}{\omega'}=\frac{\omega_\gamma}{\sqrt{\omega_0^2-\omega_\gamma^2}}. \tag{14.76}$$

We can square this equation to obtain

$$\frac{\omega_\gamma^2}{\omega_0^2-\omega_\gamma^2}=\left(-\frac{\ln(0.5)}{113\cdot 2\pi}\right)^2. \tag{14.77}$$

Solved Problem

SIMPLIFY:

Taking

$$c^2 = \left(-\frac{\ln(0.5)}{113 \cdot 2\pi} \right)^2 \tag{14.78}$$

we can write

$$\omega_\gamma^2 = \left(\omega_0^2 - \omega_\gamma^2\right)c^2 = \omega_0^2 c^2 - \omega_\gamma^2 c^2 . \tag{14.79}$$

We can then solve for ω_γ

$$\omega_\gamma = \sqrt{\frac{\omega_0^2 c^2}{1+c^2}} . \tag{14.80}$$

Remembering that $\omega_\gamma = b/2m$, we can write an expression for the damping constant b

$$b = 2m\sqrt{\frac{\omega_0^2 c^2}{1+c^2}} . \tag{14.81}$$

Substituting $\omega_0 = \sqrt{k/m}$ we obtain

$$b = 2m\sqrt{\frac{(k/m)c^2}{1+c^2}} = 2\sqrt{\frac{mkc^2}{1+c^2}} . \tag{14.82}$$

CALCULATE:

We first put in the numerical values to get c^2

$$c^2 = \left(-\frac{\ln(0.5)}{113 \cdot 2\pi} \right)^2 = 9.53091 \cdot 10^{-7} .$$

We can now calculate the damping constant

$$b = 2\sqrt{\frac{(1.75 \text{ kg})(3.50 \text{ N/m})\left(9.53091 \cdot 10^{-7}\right)}{1 + 9.53091 \cdot 10^{-7}}} = 0.00483226 \text{ kg/s} \tag{14.83}$$

ROUND:

We report our result to three significant figures

$$b = 4.83 \cdot 10^{-3} \text{ kg/s} .$$

DOUBLE-CHECK:

We can check that the extracted damping constant is consistent with small damping by checking that $b < \sqrt{mk}$

Solved Problem

$$4.83 \cdot 10^{-3} \text{ kg/s} < \sqrt{(1.75 \text{ kg})(3.50 \text{ N/m})} = 2.47 \text{ kg/s}$$

Thus, the damping constant is consistent with our insight that the system undergoes small damping.

Solved Problem 14.3: Oscillation of a Thin Rod

Question:
A long, thin rod hangs from one end. The rod has a mass of 2.50 kg and a length of 1.25 m. The bottom of the rod is pulled to the right such that the rod makes an angle of $\theta = 20.0°$ with respect to the vertical. The rod is released from rest and oscillates in simple harmonic motion. What is the period of this motion?

Answer:

THINK:
We cannot apply our standard pendulum analysis to this situation. Here we must take into account the moment of inertia of the thin rod. This type of pendulum is called a physical pendulum. We can relate the torque exerted by the weight of the rod acting at the center of gravity of the rod to the angular acceleration. From this relation we can get a differential equation that has a form similar to the equation we derived for a simple pendulum. From the analogy with the simple pendulum we can get the period of the oscillating thin rod.

SKETCH: A sketch of the oscillating thin rod is shown in Figure 14.27.

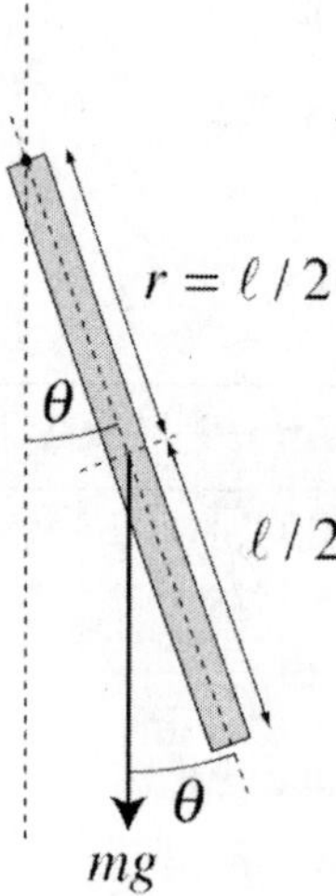

Figure 14.27: A physical pendulum consisting of a thin rod swinging from one end.

RESEARCH:
Looking at Figure 14.27 we can see that the weight mg of the thin rod acts as a force producing a torque τ on the thin rod given by

Solved Problem

$$\tau = I\alpha = -mgr\sin\theta . \tag{14.84}$$

where α is the resulting angular acceleration, r is the moment arm, and θ is the angle between the force and the moment arm. The problem states that the initial angular displacement is $20°$, so we can make the small angle approximation and use $\sin\theta \approx \theta$. We can the rewrite (14.84) as

$$I\alpha + mgr\theta = 0 . \tag{14.85}$$

We now replace the angular acceleration with the second derivative of the angular displacement and divide through by the moment of inertia, which gives us

$$\frac{d^2\theta}{dt^2} + \frac{mgr}{I}\theta = 0 . \tag{14.86}$$

This equation has the same form as (14.29), therefore we can write the solution as

$$\theta(t) = A\sin(\omega_0 t) + B\cos(\omega_0 t) \text{ with } \omega_0 = \sqrt{\frac{mgr}{I}} . \tag{14.87}$$

Solved Problem

SIMPLIFY:

We can obtain the period of oscillation of the thin rod from

$$T = \frac{2\pi}{\omega_0} = 2\pi\sqrt{\frac{I}{mgr}} . \tag{14.88}$$

This result is general for the period of a physical pendulum with moment of inertia I whose center of gravity is a distance r from the pivot point. In this case, $r = \ell/2$ and $I = (1/3)m\ell^2$ so we can write

$$T = 2\pi\sqrt{\frac{(1/3)m\ell^2}{mg(\ell/2)}} = 2\pi\sqrt{\frac{2\ell}{3g}} . \tag{14.89}$$

CALCULATE:

Putting in our numerical values gives us

$$T = 2\pi\sqrt{\frac{2\cdot 1.25 \text{ m}}{3\cdot 9.81 \text{ m/s}^2}} = 1.83128 \text{ s} .$$

ROUND:

We report our result to three significant figures

$$T = 1.83 \text{ s} .$$

DOUBLE-CHECK: If the mass m of the rod were concentrated at a point a distance ℓ from the pivot point, we would have a simple pendulum and the period would be

$$T = 2\pi\sqrt{\frac{\ell}{g}} = 2.24 \text{ s}.$$

The period of the thin rod is less than this value, which is reasonable because the mass of the thin rod is spread out over the length of the rod rather than being concentrated at the end.

As a second double-check, we start with (14.88) and we insert the moment of inertia of a point mass pivoting around a point a distance r away, $I = mr^2$, and take $r = \ell$ we get

$$T = 2\pi\sqrt{\frac{m\ell^2}{mg\ell}} = 2\pi\sqrt{\frac{\ell}{g}}$$

which is the result for the period of a simple pendulum.

Chapter 15. Waves

What We Will Learn

- Waves are disturbances (or excitations) that propagate through space as a function of time. They can be understood as a series of individual oscillators coupled to their nearest neighbors.
- Waves can be either longitudinal or transverse
- There is a general equation that governs wave motion
- Waves transport energy across spatial distances. But even though a wave involves vibrating atoms in a medium, usually waves do not transport matter with them.
- Of central importance is the superposition principle, which states that two waveforms can be added to form another one.
- Waves can interfere with each other, and under certain conditions interference patterns form, which we can analyze.
- Standing waves can be formed by superposition of two traveling waves.
- Boundary conditions on strings determine the possible wavelengths and frequencies of standing waves.

15.1. Wave Motion

If you throw a stone in a pond, it creates circular ripples that travel along the surface of the pond, in radial outward direction as in Figure 15.1. If there are objects floating on the surface of the pond (a stick, dead leaves, a rubber duck), you can observe that these objects move up and down as the ripples move outward underneath them, but they do not move noticeably outward with the wave.

Figure 15.1: Circular wave fronts on the surface of water.

If you tie a rope to the wall, hold it so that it is stretched out, and then rapidly move your arm up and down, this arm motion will create a wave crest that travels down the rope, then gets reflected at the wall and travels back to you. Again this wave moves, but the material that the waves travel through moves up and down but remains in place otherwise.

These two examples illustrate a major characteristic of waves: a wave is an excitation that propagates though space (with or without a propagation medium) as a function of time, but this excitation does not generally transport a medium along with it. In this fundamental way, wave motion is completely different from the motion of objects that we studied so far. Waves are oscillations that are moving through space. Electromagnetic and gravitational waves do not need a medium in which to propagate. Other waves propagate in a medium; for example sound waves travel through air or a liquid or a solid but not through a vacuum.

There are many other examples of waves around us in our everyday lives, most of them with oscillations that are too small for us to observe. Light itself is an electromagnetic wave, as are the radio waves that our FM and AM radios receive, or the waves that carry our TV signals into our houses, either through co-axial cables, or through the air via broadcasts from surface antenna towers or geostationary satellites. As mentioned in the previous paragraph light waves and electromagnetic waves are special in the sense that they do not even need a medium through which they propagate, and we will devote a separate chapter, chapter 31, to them after we have studied electricity in chapters 21 through 30.

In this chapter we begin to study wave motion through media. Mechanical vibrations fall under this category, as do sound waves, earthquake waves, and water waves. Since sound is such an important part of our communications, we will devote the following chapter exclusively to the study of it.

The stadium wave or simply "the wave" is now a part of most major sports events: spectators stand up and raise their arms as soon as they see their neighbor doing the same, and then they sit down again. Thus the wave travels around the stadium, but of course each spectator stays in place. How fast does this wave travel? Let us suppose that each person has a time delay comparable to his reaction time, 0.1 s, before imitating his neighbor getting up from her seat. The seats are typically approximately 2 feet (~0.6 m) wide. This means that the wave travels 0.6 m in 0.1 s. From our study of simple kinematics, we know that this corresponds to a velocity of $v = \Delta x / dt = (0.6\text{ m})/(0.1\text{ s}) = 6\text{ m/s}$. Since a typical football stadium is an oval with a perimeter length of approximately 400 m, one would conclude that it takes about one minute for "the wave" to make it around the stadium once. This rather crude estimate is approximately right, within a factor of two, as everybody knows who has taken part in this spectator entertainment. Empirically one finds that "the wave" moves with a speed of approximately 12 m/s. The reason for this higher speed is that people anticipate the arrival of the wave and jump up when they see the person two or three seats ahead of them jump up.

15.2. Coupled Oscillators

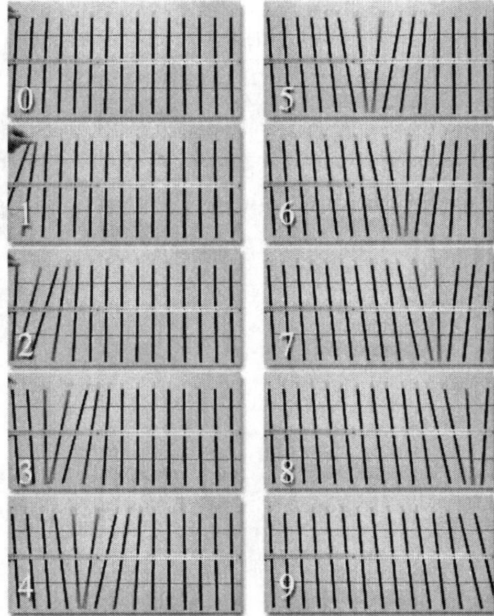

Figure 15.2: Series of identical rods coupled to their nearest neighbors by springs. The time sequence is indicated by the numbers on the frames. Each pair of frames is separated by a time interval of 0.133 s.

Let us start our quantitative discussion of waves by examining a series of coupled oscillators, for example a string of identical masses coupled by identical springs. One physical realization is shown in Figure 15.2. A series of identical metal rods is held in place by a central horizontal bar. The rods can pivot freely about their center and are connected to their nearest neighbors by identical springs. When we push the first rod, we see that this excitation is transmitted from each rod to its neighbor, and the pulse that we generated in this way travels down the row of rods.

Each rod is an oscillator and moves back and forth in the plane of the paper. This represents a longitudinal coupling between the oscillators in the sense that the direction of motion and the direction of coupling to the nearest neighbors are the same. We can also physically realize a transverse coupling, see Figure 15.3. On the left side of this figure all rods are shown attached to a tension strip in their horizontal equilibrium position, and on the right side rod i is deflected by an angle θ_i.

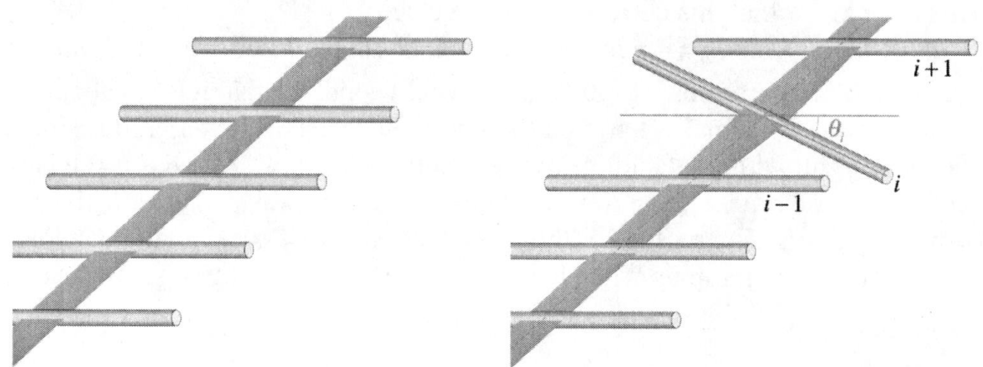

Figure 15.3: Parallel rods supported by a tension strip as a model for transversely coupled oscillators.

A deflection of this kind has two effects. First, the tension strip creates a restoring force that tries to pull rod i back to the equilibrium position. Second, since the tension strip is now twisted on both sides of rod i, the deflection of that rod also creates a force that tries to deflect rods $i-1$ and $i+1$ towards the angle θ_i that rod i is at. If we allow the rods to move freely, they will follow the forces generated in the way just described and in turn each generate forces on their two nearest neighbors.

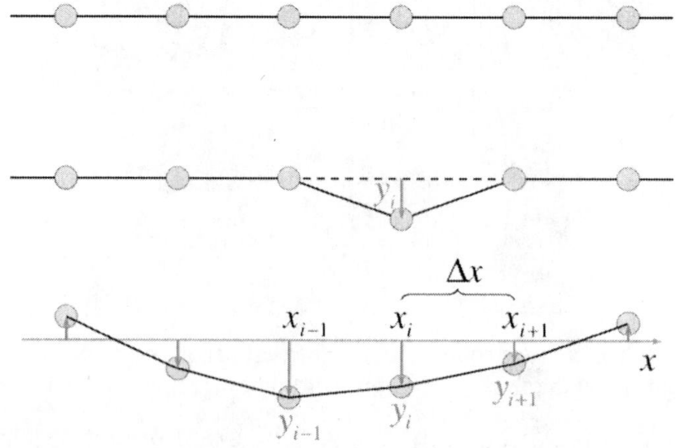

Figure 15.4: Side-view of coupled rods of previous figure. Top: equilibrium position; center: one rod is deflected; bottom all rods are allowed to become deflected.

In Figure 15.4 we show a side view of the arrangement of our parallel rods. Each circle represents the end of a rod, and we can characterize the motion of this circle by a coordinate y_i, which is related to the deflection angle θ_i via $y_i = \frac{1}{2} l \sin\theta_i$, where l is the length of each rod. The line connecting the circles is the tension strip. In the upper part of Figure 15.4 all rods are in equilibrium position, which implies that all deflections are 0. In the middle part of Figure 15.4 we show the case of rod i experiencing a deflection, the same case as depicted in the right part of Figure 15.3. One finds that the force acting on rod i due to the tension in the tension strip is of the spring force type, $F_i = -ky_i$, where the effective spring constant is determined from the properties of the tension strip.

Finally, in the lower part of Figure 15.4 we allow all rods to move. The net force acting on rod i is then the sum of the forces exerted by rods $i+1$ and $i-1$ on it, as mediated by the tension strip that connects the rods. These forces now depend on the difference of the y-coordinates at the beginning and the end of the section of tension strip that connects the rods and are thus given by:

$$F_+ = -k(y_i - y_{i+1})$$
$$F_- = -k(y_i - y_{i-1})$$

Thus the net force acting of rod i, the sum of these two forces, is:

$$F_i = F_+ + F_- = -k(y_i - y_{i+1}) - k(y_i - y_{i-1}) = k(y_{i+1} - 2y_i + y_{i-1}). \qquad (15.1)$$

From Newton's Second Law, $F = ma$, we then find for the acceleration a_i of rod i

$$ma_i = k(y_{i+1} - 2y_i + y_{i-1}). \qquad (15.2)$$

Once we provide initial conditions for the position and velocity of each oscillator, then we can solve the resulting set of equations on a computer. But we can go further and actually derive a wave equation by starting from (15.2). This will be done in the following section.

Transverse and Longitudinal Waves

Before we leave this section of coupled oscillators, we want to point out an essential difference between the two systems of oscillators shown in Figure 15.2 and Figure 15.3. In the first case the oscillators are only allowed to move in the direction of their nearest neighbors, whereas in the second case the oscillators are restricted to moving in a direction perpendicular to direction to their nearest neighbor. In general, if a wave propagates along the direction in which the oscillators move, this wave is called a longitudinal wave. In the next chapter we will see that sound waves are prototypical longitudinal waves. If a wave moves in a direction perpendicular to the direction in which the individual oscillators move, this wave is called a transverse wave. Light waves are transverse waves, as we will discuss in our chapter 31 on electromagnetic waves.

Longitudinal and transverse waves are illustrated in Figure 15.5.

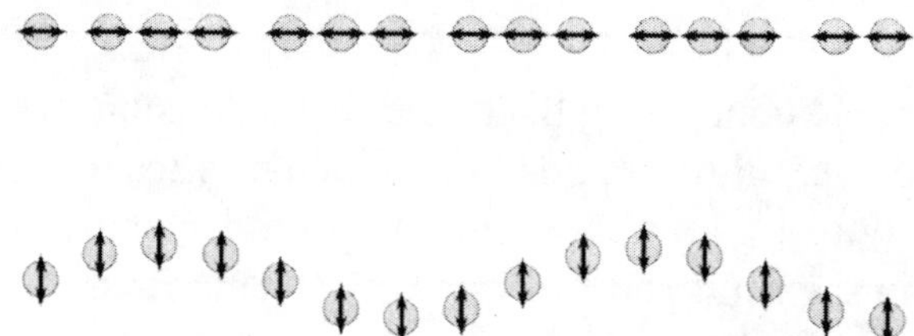

Figure 15.5: Snapshots of longitudinal (upper part) and transverse (lower part) waves propagating horizontally to the right.

15.3. Mathematical Description of Waves

So far we have only examined a single wave pulse. The stadium wave is such a pulse. Pushing once on the chain of coupled oscillators also constitutes a single pulse. But a much more common class of wave phenomena is obtained by considering a periodic excitation, and in particular a sinusoidal excitation. In our chain of oscillators of Figure 15.2 or Figure 15.3 we can accomplish this by moving the first rod back and forth periodically. This sinusoidal oscillation also travels down the chain of oscillators, just like a single wave pulse.

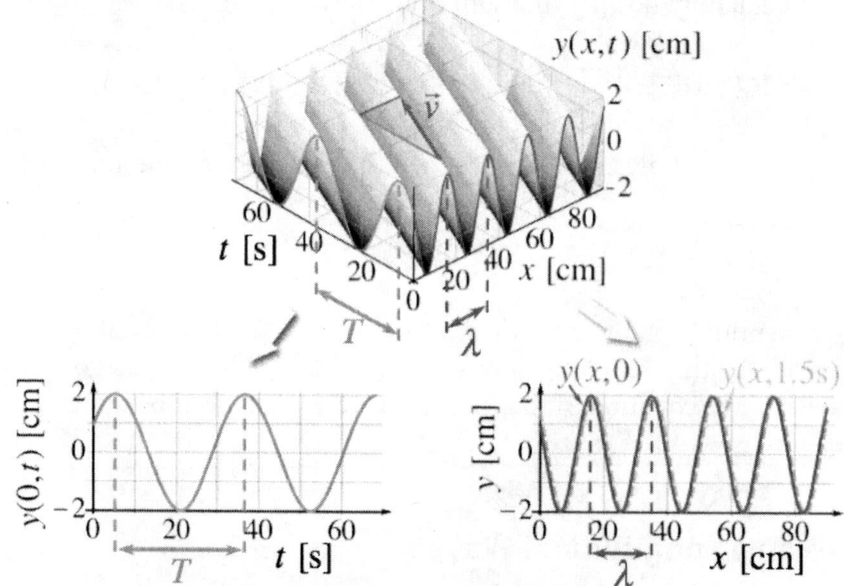

Figure 15.6: Sinusoidal wave; Center top: the wave as a function of space and time coordinate; Lower left: dependence of the wave on time at the position $x = 0$; Lower right: dependence of the wave on the position for time $t = 0$ (blue curve) and at a later time $t = 1.5$ s (gray dashed curve).

Period, Wavelength, and Wave Velocity

At the top of Figure 15.6 we display the result of a sinusoidal excitation in time as a function of the time and horizontal coordinate, in the limit that there are a very large number of coupled oscillators that are very close to each other, that is to say in the continuum limit. First let's examine this figure along the time axis for $x = 0$. This projection is shown in the lower left panel of Figure 15.6. It shows the harmonic oscillation of the first oscillator in our chain,

$$y(x=0,t) = A\sin(\omega t + \theta_0) = A\sin(2\pi ft + \theta_0) \tag{15.3}$$

where ω is the angular frequency (or angular velocity), f is the frequency, A is the amplitude of the oscillation, and θ_0 is the phase shift. For the example in Figure 15.6 we used values of $A = 2.0$ cm, $\omega = 0.2$ s^{-1}, and $\theta_0 = 0.5$. Just like for all oscillators, the period T is defined as the time interval between two subsequent maxima and is related to the frequency as

$$T = \frac{1}{f}. \tag{15.4}$$

In the same figure you can also see that for any given time the dependence on the horizontal coordinate x of the oscillations is sinusoidal as well. This is shown for the time $t = 0$ (blue curve) and time $t = 1.5$ s (gray dashed curve) in the right lower panel of Figure 15.6. The distance in space between two consecutive maxima is defined as the wavelength, λ.

As you can see in the top part of Figure 15.6, there are diagonal lines of equal height of the wave motion in the xt-plane. These are called wave fronts. What is most important to realize about Figure 15.6 and about wave motion in general is that during one period any given wave front advances by one wavelength.

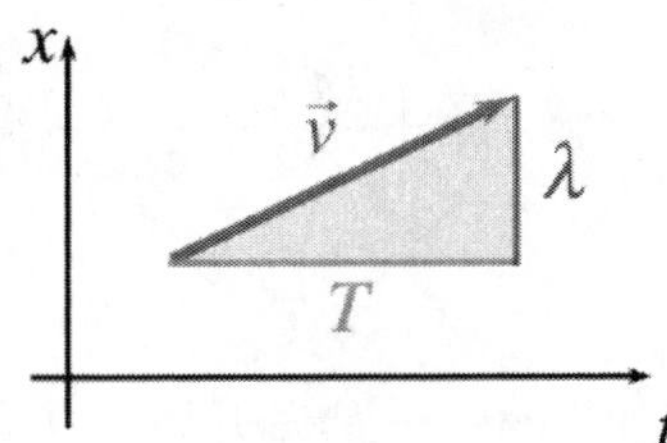

Figure 15.7: *xt*-plane of Figure 15.6; relation of the wave velocity to the period and wavelength.

In Figure 15.7 we redraw the light purple triangle on the top surface of Figure 15.6 in the xt-plane to further illustrate the relationship between the wave velocity and the period and wavelength. Now you can easily see that the speed of propagation of the waves is in general given as

$$v = \frac{\lambda}{T} \tag{15.5}$$

or, using the relationship between period and frequency of (15.4),

$$v = \lambda f. \tag{15.6}$$

This relationship between wavelength, frequency and wave velocity holds for all types of waves and is one of the most important results of the present chapter.

Self-Test Opportunity: We are sitting in a boat in the middle of Lake Michigan. The water waves hitting the boat are traveling at 3.0 m/s and the crests are 7.5 m apart. What is the frequency at which the wave crests strike the boat?

Sinusoidal Waveform, Wave Number, Phase

How do we obtain a functional form of a sinusoidal wave as a function of space and time? We start again with the oscillation of the oscillator at $x = 0$, see equation (15.3), and realize that it takes a time $t = x / v$ for the excitation to move a displacement x. Thus we can simply replace t in (15.3) by $t - \frac{x}{v}$ to find the elongation $y(x,t)$ away from equilibrium as a function of space and time

$$y(x,t) = A\sin\left(\omega\left(t - \frac{x}{v}\right) + \theta_0\right).$$

We can then use the result (15.6) that we just obtained for the wave velocity, $v = \lambda f$, and find

$$\begin{aligned} y(x,t) &= A\sin\left(2\pi f\left(t - \frac{x}{v}\right) + \theta_0\right) \\ &= A\sin\left(2\pi ft - \frac{2\pi fx}{\lambda f} + \theta_0\right) \\ &= A\sin\left(\frac{2\pi}{T}t - \frac{2\pi}{\lambda}x + \theta_0\right). \end{aligned} \tag{15.7}$$

In a similar way that $\omega = 2\pi / T$, we can introduce the wave number κ as

$$\kappa = \frac{2\pi}{\lambda} \tag{15.8}$$

and obtain from (15.7) the final functional form of our wave motion

$$y(x,t) = A\sin\left(\omega t - \kappa x + \theta_0\right). \tag{15.9}$$

A sinusoidal waveform of this kind is almost universally applicable to waves of all kinds in the case that there is only one spatial dimension in which the wave can propagate. We can also generalize this waveform to more than one spatial coordinate and will return to this point later in this chapter.

One can also start with a given sinusoidal wave form in space and ask where this waveform will be at a later time. In this way of looking at waves, one would write the expression for the waveform as a function of space and time as

$$y(x,t) = A\sin\left(\kappa x - \omega t + \phi_0\right). \tag{15.10}$$

The two expressions (15.9) and (15.10) are equivalent to each other, because $\sin(-x) = -\sin(x)$. The phase shift ϕ_0 of (15.10) is related to the phase shift θ_0 of (15.9) via $\phi_0 = \pi - \theta_0$. Since the expression (15.10) is more commonly used, we will also use it from now on.

The argument of the sine function in (15.10) is called the phase ϕ of the wave,

$$\phi = \kappa x - \omega t + \phi_0. \tag{15.11}$$

When we consider more than one wave simultaneously, the relationship of the phases of the waves will play an essential role. Later in this chapter we will return to this point.

Just like the angular frequency ω counts the number of oscillations per time interval of 2π seconds, $\omega = \frac{2\pi}{T}$ where T is the period, the wave number κ counts the number of wavelengths λ that fit into a distance of 2π meters, $\kappa = \frac{2\pi}{\lambda}$. For example, we used $\kappa = 0.33\ \text{cm}^{-1}$ in the example plot of Figure 15.6.

Finally, we note that with the introduction of the wave number, we can rewrite the equation for the speed of the wave front (15.6) in terms of the wave number and the angular frequency as

$$v = \frac{\omega}{\kappa}. \tag{15.12}$$

Self-Test Opportunity: In the figure we show a snapshot at $t = 0$ of a traveling wave of the form $y(x,t) = A\sin\left(\kappa x - \omega t + \phi_0\right)$. From the graph, determine the amplitude A, the wave number κ, and the phase shift ϕ_0.

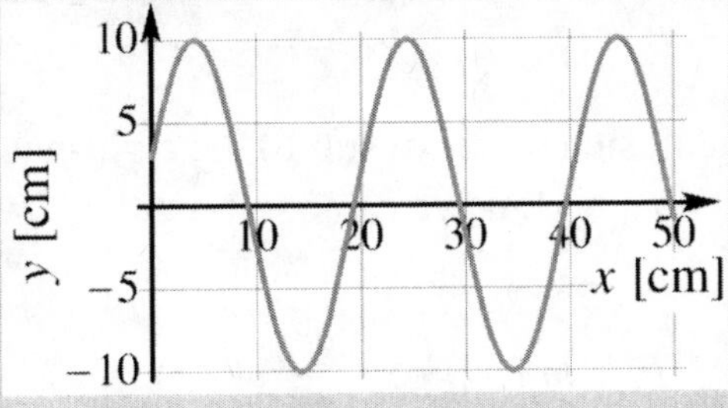

Snapshot of a traveling wave at $t = 0$.

15.4. Derivation of the Wave Equation

In this section we derive a general equation of motion for waves, the wave equation. This equation is

$$\frac{\partial^2}{\partial t^2}y(x,t)-v^2\frac{\partial^2}{\partial x^2}y(x,t)=0. \tag{15.13}$$

Here $y(x,t)$ is the displacement from the equilibrium position as a function of a single space coordinate x and a time coordinate t. v is the speed of propagation of the wave. This wave equation describes all un-damped wave motion in one dimension.

Derivation 15.1: Wave Equation

Let us return to Figure 15.4, where we have also indicated an x-axis, pointing in the conventional horizontal direction and to the right. This axis is perpendicular to the y-axis, along which the motion of each individual oscillator occurs. Let us call the horizontal distance between neighboring oscillators Δx. The displacements of the oscillators are then a function of time and of position along the x-axis, $y(x,t)$, with $y_i = y(x_i,t)$. The acceleration is defined as the second derivative of the position vector $y(x,t)$ with respect to time. Since now the position vector depends on more than one variable, in this case time as well as the horizontal coordinate, we need to use partial derivatives (which treat the variables that are not being differentiated as constants) to express this relationship,

$$a=\frac{\partial^2}{\partial t^2}y(x,t) \tag{15.14}$$

And in the same way we can also introduce a derivative with respect to the x-coordinate, $\partial y/\partial x$. If we go back to the original definition of the derivative as the limit of the ratio of differences, we can approximate this partial derivative as

$$\frac{\partial}{\partial x}y(x,t)=\frac{\Delta y}{\Delta x}=\frac{y_{i+1}-y_i}{\Delta x} \tag{15.15}$$

In the same way we can approximate the second derivative as

$$\frac{\partial^2}{\partial x^2}y(x,t)=\frac{\Delta\left(\frac{\Delta y}{\Delta x}\right)}{\Delta x}=\frac{\frac{(y_{i+1}-y_i)}{\Delta x}-\frac{(y_i-y_{i-1})}{\Delta x}}{\Delta x}=\frac{y_{i+1}-2y_i+y_{i-1}}{\Delta x^2} \tag{15.16}$$

If you compare the right-hand side of this result to the right-hand side of (15.2), you see that both contain $y_{i+1}-2y_i+y_{i-1}$. Thus we can combine these two equations and find

$$ma_i=k\Delta x^2\frac{\partial^2}{\partial x^2}y(x,t)$$

Derivation

Inserting our second partial derivative for the acceleration, we see

$$m\frac{\partial^2}{\partial t^2}y(x,t)=k\Delta x^2\frac{\partial^2}{\partial x^2}y(x,t) \tag{15.17}$$

Finally, we divide by the mass of the oscillator and obtain

$$\frac{\partial^2}{\partial t^2}y(x,t)-\frac{k}{m}\Delta x^2\frac{\partial^2}{\partial x^2}y(x,t)=0\,. \tag{15.18}$$

This equation that relates the second partial derivative in time and position to each other is called a wave equation. The ratio of the spring constant over the mass of the oscillator is equal to the square of the angular frequency, as we have found in the previous chapter. This is also the angular frequency of the traveling wave. Thus the product of the angular frequency ω times the horizontal displacement Δx is the velocity of the wave (how fast the wave moves in space),

$$\frac{k}{m}\Delta x^2=\omega^2\Delta x^2=v^2\,. \tag{15.19}$$

So our wave equation finally becomes

$$\frac{\partial^2}{\partial t^2}y(x,t)-v^2\frac{\partial^2}{\partial x^2}y(x,t)=0\,. \tag{15.20}$$

Derivation

In the limit that the oscillators get very close to each other, i.e. that $\Delta x\to 0$, the solution to the wave equation (15.20) will provide the exact solution to the difference equation (15.2). The wave equation (15.20) is of general importance, and its applicability far exceeds the problem of coupled oscillators, for which we have derived it. The same wave equation in the basic form (15.20) holds for the propagation of sound, light, or waves on a string, as it holds for a system of coupled oscillators. The difference in physical systems exhibiting wave motion only manifests itself in the way we have to calculate v, the speed of propagation of the wave.

In mathematical terms, this wave equation (15.20) is the first example of a partial differential equation that we have encountered. As you may know, there are entire semester-long courses devoted to partial differential equations, and you will encounter many more if you elect a major in the physical sciences or engineering. But for the introductory curriculum this wave equation will remain almost the only partial differential equation that we will have to study in a bit more detail. For the level of depth that we are interested in, it will be sufficient to treat the partial derivatives just like conventional derivatives of functions in one variable.

Solutions of the Wave Equation

In the previous section, we had developed a sinusoidal waveform, (15.9). Let us first see now if this solution indeed fulfills the general wave equation (15.20), which we just obtained. To do this we have to take the partial derivatives with respect to the x-coordinate and with respect to time. They are

$$\frac{\partial}{\partial t}y(x,t)=\frac{\partial}{\partial t}\left(A\sin\left(\kappa x-\omega t+\phi_0\right)\right)=-A\omega\cos\left(\kappa x-\omega t+\phi_0\right)$$
$$\frac{\partial^2}{\partial t^2}y(x,t)=\frac{\partial}{\partial t}\left(-A\omega\cos\left(\kappa x-\omega t+\phi_0\right)\right)=-A\omega^2\sin\left(\kappa x-\omega t+\phi_0\right)$$
$$\frac{\partial}{\partial x}y(x,t)=\frac{\partial}{\partial x}\left(A\sin\left(\kappa x-\omega t+\phi_0\right)\right)=A\kappa\cos\left(\kappa x-\omega t+\phi_0\right)$$
$$\frac{\partial^2}{\partial x^2}y(x,t)=\frac{\partial}{\partial x}\left(A\kappa\cos\left(\kappa x-\omega t+\phi_0\right)\right)=-A\kappa^2\sin\left(\kappa x-\omega t+\phi_0\right).$$

By inserting these partial derivatives into our wave equation (15.20) we find

$$\begin{gathered}\frac{\partial^2}{\partial t^2}y(x,t)-v^2\frac{\partial^2}{\partial x^2}y(x,t)=\\ \left(-A\omega^2\sin\left(\kappa x-\omega t+\phi_0\right)\right)-v^2\left(-A\kappa^2\sin\left(\kappa x-\omega t+\phi_0\right)\right)=\\ -A\sin\left(\kappa x-\omega t+\phi_0\right)\cdot\left(\omega^2-v^2\kappa^2\right)=0.\end{gathered} \tag{15.21}$$

So we see that our function (15.9) is indeed a solution of the wave equation (15.20), provided that $(\omega^2-v^2\kappa^2)=0$. However, we already know from equation (15.12) that this is indeed the case, and so we have established that (15.9) is truly a solution of the wave equation.

Is there a larger class of solutions than the one that we have already found? Yes, this is indeed the case. Any arbitrary (continuously differentiable) function Y with arguments in the same linear combination of the x-coordinate and the time as (15.9), $\kappa x-\omega t$, is a solution to the wave equation. The constants ω, κ, and ϕ_0 can have arbitrary values. However, one usually uses the convention that the angular frequency and the wave number are both quoted as positive numbers. Then we can differentiate two different solutions to the wave equation,

$$Y(\kappa x-\omega t+\phi_0) \text{ for a wave moving in positive } x\text{-direction} \tag{15.22}$$
$$Y(\kappa x+\omega t+\phi_0) \text{ for a wave moving in negative } x\text{-direction.} \tag{15.23}$$

This is perhaps more obvious when we write these functions in terms of arguments that involve the wave speed, $v=\omega/\kappa$. We then find $Y(x-vt+\phi_0)$ is a solution of an arbitrary waveform moving in positive x-direction and $Y(x+vt+\phi_0)$ is a solution for one moving in negative x -direction.

As previously stated, the functional form of Y does not matter at all. We can see this by looking at the chain rule of differentiation, $df(g(x))/dx = (df/dg)(dg/dx)$. The partial derivatives in space and time contain the common factor df/dg, which cancels out in the same way that the sine function cancelled out in (15.21). And the derivatives of the function $g = \kappa x \pm \omega t + \phi_0$ always lead to the same condition $(\omega^2 - v^2\kappa^2) = 0$ that we have encountered above for our particular sinusoidal solution.

Waves on a String

A large class of musical instruments is string instruments. Guitars (as in Figure 15.8), cellos, violins, mandolins, harps, and others fall in this category. These string instruments produce musical sounds by inducing vibrations on strings.

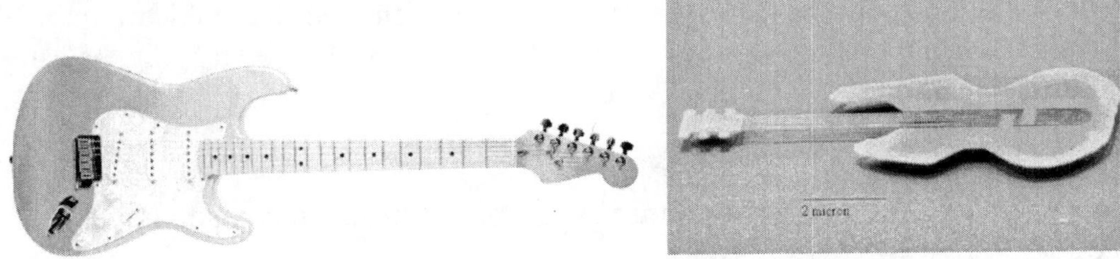

Figure 15.8: Left: Typical electric guitar used by a rock band; right: world's smallest guitar, produced in 2004 in the Cornell Nanofabrication facility. It is a factor of 100,000 smaller than the guitar on the left and has a length of 10 μm, approximately 1/20th of the width of a human hair.

Suppose our string has a mass M and a length L. In order to find the wave speed v on strings, we can think of the string as composed of many small individual segments of length Δx and mass m, where

$$m = M\Delta x / L = \mu \Delta x . \tag{15.24}$$

Here we have introduced the mass density of the string as the mass per unit length of the string

$$\mu = \frac{M}{L} . \tag{15.25}$$

We can then treat the problem of waves on a string as that of coupled oscillators. The restoring force is provided by the string tension, $T = k\Delta x$. Inserting this result into our equation for the wave velocity for coupled oscillator systems (15.19), we find for the wave velocity on a string

$$v = \sqrt{\frac{k}{m}}\Delta x = \sqrt{\frac{k}{\mu \Delta x}}\Delta x = \sqrt{\frac{k\Delta x}{\mu}} = \sqrt{\frac{T}{\mu}} . \tag{15.26}$$

We could have also obtained this result (except for a possible numerical factor) from a dimensional analysis, realizing that the dimension of the string tension is that of a force, $[T] = \text{m kg/s}^2$, and the dimension of the mass density is $[\mu] = \text{kg/m}$. So the ratio of string tension to mass density has the dimension of $[T/\mu] = (\text{m kg/s}^2)/(\text{kg/m}) = (\text{m/s})^2$, the dimension of the square of a velocity.

What does this result imply? There are two immediate consequences. First, if you increase the mass density of the string, i.e. you use a heavier string, you reduce the wave velocity on the string. Second, if you increase the string tension (by tightening the tuning knobs shown, for example, at the top of the electric guitar in Figure 15.8), you increase the wave velocity. If you play a string instrument, then you know that tightening the tension increases the pitch of sound produced by that string. We will return to this later in this chapter.

Example

Example 15.1: Elevator Cable

An elevator repairman (mass 73 kg) sits on top of an elevator cabin of mass 655 kg inside a shaft of a skyscraper. The cabin is suspended by a 61 m long steel cable of mass 38 kg. He sends a signal to his colleague at the top of the elevator shaft by tapping the cable with his hammer.

Question:

How long will it take for the wave pulse generated by the hammer tap to travel up the cable?

Answer:

The cable is under tension from the weight of the elevator cabin and that of the repairman,

$$T = mg = (73\text{ kg} + 655\text{ kg})(9.81\text{ m/s}^2) = 7142\text{ N}$$

The mass density of the steel cable is

$$\mu = \frac{M}{L} = \frac{38\text{ kg}}{61\text{ m}} = 0.623\text{ kg/m}$$

So the wave speed on this cable is according to (15.26):

$$v = \sqrt{\frac{T}{\mu}} = 107\text{ m/s}$$

In order to travel up the 61 m long cable, the pulse then needs a time of

$$t = \frac{L}{v} = \frac{61\text{ m}}{107\text{ m/s}} = 0.57\text{ s}$$

Discussion:
In our solution we implied that the string tension is the same everywhere in the cable. But is this really true? Not quite! We cannot really neglect the weight of the cable itself in determining the tension. Our answer is correct for the lowest point of the cable, where it attaches to the cabin. However, the tension also has to include the complete weight at the upper end of the cable. There it has the value of

$$T = mg = (73 \text{ kg} + 655 \text{ kg} + 38 \text{ kg})(9.81 \text{ m/s}^2) = 7514 \text{ N},$$

resulting in a wave speed of 110 m/s, 3% greater than what we calculated. If we had to worry about this correction, then we would have to calculate how the wave speed depends on the height and then perform the proper integration. But since the maximum correction is 3%, we can assume that the average correction will be about 1.5%, use an average wave speed of 108.5 m/s, and obtain a signal propagation time of 0.56 s. So we see that taking the mass of the rope into account amounts to a correction of one hundredth of a second.

15.5. Waves in 2- and 3-Dimensional Spaces

So far we have only considered one-dimensional cases. For waves on a string or a linear chain of coupled oscillators this is completely sufficient. However, for the water surface waves of Figure 15.1 this is obviously insufficient, because the waves spread in a two-dimensional space, the plane of the surface of the water. A light bulb and a loudspeaker also emit waves and these waves spread in a three-dimensional space. So it is legitimate to ask for a mathematical description. The general answer to this question exceeds the scope of this text, but fortunately we can give the answer for two special cases that cover most of the important wave phenomena that occur in nature.

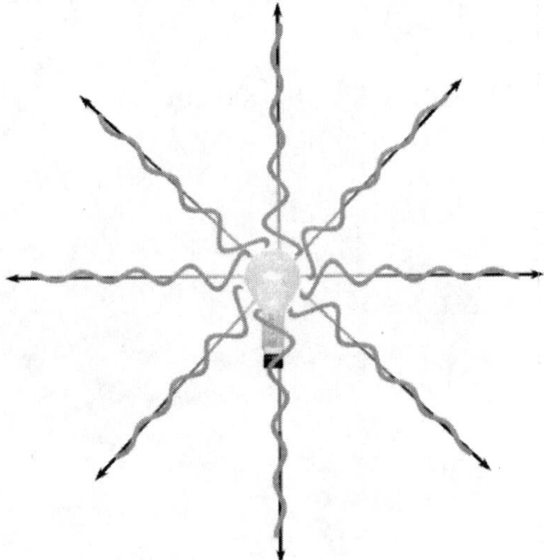

Figure 15.9: Waves spreading spherically from a point source (a light bulb in this case). The inner and outer surfaces of each yellow band are one wavelength apart.

Spherical Waves

If you examine Figure 15.1 and Figure 15.9, you see waves generated from one point, which spread as concentric circles. In the mathematical idealization of waves that are emitted from point sources, we can describe all waves as moving outward in concentric circles in 2 spatial dimensions or concentric spheres in 3 spatial dimensions. Mathematically, we can write sinusoidal waveforms that spread in this way as

$$y(\vec{r},t) = A(r)\sin\left(\kappa r - \omega t + \phi_0\right). \tag{15.27}$$

Here $\vec{r}$ is the position vector (in 2 or 3 dimensions), and $r = |\vec{r}|$ is its absolute value. We can convince ourselves that this function indeed describes concentric waveform circles (in 2 dimensions) or spheres (in 3 dimensions) when we realize that the perimeter of a circle or surface of a sphere has a constant distance to the origin and thus a constant value of r. A constant value of r at some given time t implies a constant phase $\phi = \kappa r - \omega t + \phi_0$. Since all of the points on a given circle or surface of a sphere have the same phase, they have the same state of their oscillation. Therefore (15.27) indeed describes spherical waves.

In (15.27) we are not using a constant amplitude A, but one that depends on the radial distance to the origin of the wave such as in Figure 15.10. When we talk about energy transport of waves, it will become clear that a radial dependence of the amplitude is needed for 2- and 3-dimensional waves, and that this amplitude has to be a monotonically decreasing function of the distance. When we will talk about the energy of traveling waves, we will employ energy conservation arguments to find out how the amplitude varies with distance. For now we simply state the result that $A(r) = C/r$ (where C is a constant) for a 3-dimensional spherical wave, and so our waveform solution (15.27) in 3 dimensions becomes

$$y(\vec{r},t) = \frac{C}{r}\sin\left(\kappa r - \omega t + \phi_0\right). \tag{15.28}$$

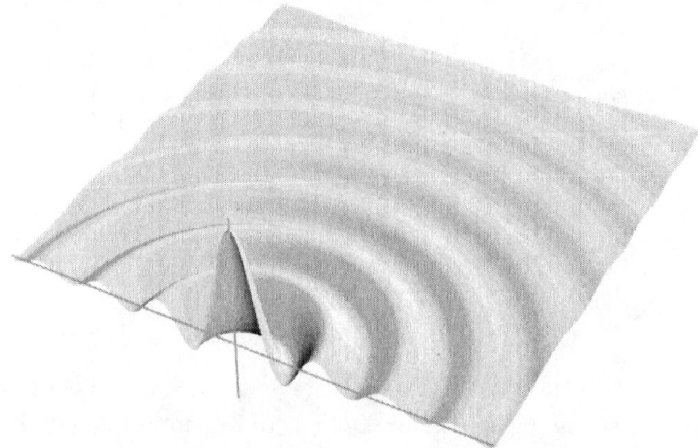

Figure 15.10: Snapshot of a spherical wave as a function of two spatial coordinates.

Plane Waves

While we may think of all waves in 3 dimensions originating from a point source as spherical waves, we can approximate these same spherical waves as plane waves if we are very far away from the source. As shown in Figure 15.11, plane waves are waves for which the surfaces of constant phase are planes. The light coming to us from the Sun is in the form of plane waves when it hits the Earth, for example. Why can we use the plane-wave approximation? If we calculate the curvature of a sphere as a function of its radius and let that radius approach infinity, this curvature approaches 0. This means that any surface segment of this sphere locally looks like a plane. For example consider the surface of Earth. We all know, of course, that the Earth is a sphere. But since this sphere is so big, the surface of Earth still locally looks like a plane to us.

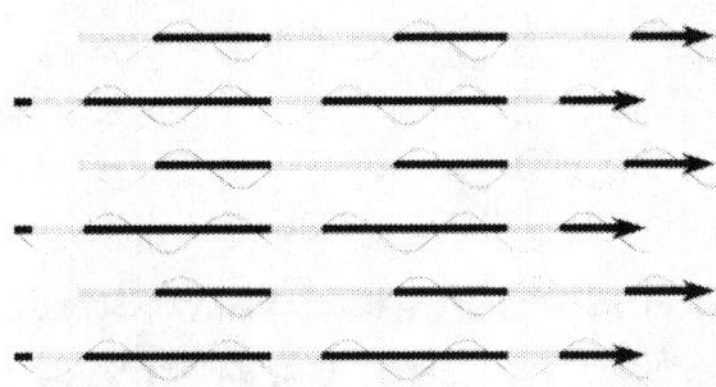

Figure 15.11: Plane waves. Each plane represents a surface of constant phase, and each two neighboring parallel planes shown are two wavelengths apart.

For a mathematical description of a plane wave we can use the same functional form as that of a one-dimensional wave,

$$y(\vec{r},t) = A\sin\left(\kappa x - \omega t + \phi_0\right) \tag{15.29}$$

where we have now defined the x-axis locally as the axis perpendicular to the plane of the wave. You may wonder why we have now used a constant amplitude again. The answer is that very far away from the origin A/r varies only very slowly as a function of r, and so we can use a constant amplitude to the same degree of approximation that we can approximate the curvature of the sphere as 0. For a perfectly flat planar wave the amplitude is indeed constant.

Surface Waves

On December 26, 2004, and Earthquake of magnitude 9.0 under the Indian Ocean off the coast of Sumatra triggered a tsunami (Japanese: harbor wave). This tsunami created incredible destruction in the Aceh province of Indonesia, but it also raced across the Indian Ocean with the speed of an airliner and caused many casualties in India and Sri Lanka. So the question arises as to what the physical basis of the motion of a tsunami is.

When an underwater earthquake occurs, the seafloor is often displaced and locally shifted up as two tectonic plates of the Earth's crust shift over each other. Thus the water in the ocean is displaced, causing a pressure wave. This is one of the rare instances where waves actually carry matter (in this case water) along with them in the sense that water does crash upon the shore. However this water reaching shore did not originate at the site of the earthquake so there is no long-distance transportation of water in this tsunami water wave. We will return to pressure waves in much more detail in the next chapter. However, for now all we need to know about the resulting pressure waves in the ocean is that they have very long wavelengths, up to 100 km or even more. Since this wavelength is much larger than the typical depth of the ocean, approximately 4 km, the resulting pressure waves cannot spread spherically, but only as surface waves. For these surface waves the local wave speed is not constant any more, but depends on the depth of the ocean. One finds that the speed is

$$v_{surface} = \sqrt{gd} \ . \tag{15.30}$$

Here $g = 9.81 \text{ m/s}^2$ is the gravitational acceleration, and d is the depth of the ocean, in meters. For a depth of 4,000 m, this results in a wave speed of 200 m/s, approximately 450 miles/hour. This explains why a tsunami wave races across an ocean with the speed of a jetliner. But when the leading edge of a tsunami reaches the shallow coastal waters, then according to (15.30) the wave speed decreases. This causes a pile-up, as water further out in the ocean still has a larger speed and catches up with the water that forms the leading edge of the tsunami. The exact details of the pile-up depend strongly on the shape of the ocean floor just off the coast. This explains why a tsunami wave crest only has a height of on the order of a foot in the open ocean and can pass unnoticed under ships, while near shore it creates a wall of water of height of up to 100 feet that sweeps away everything in its path.

In-class exercise: On the golf course you stand at the edge of a 120.0 m diameter circular water hazard that is 1.00 m deep. Instead of hitting over the hazard as planned, you hit your ball into the middle of the lake. How long does it take for the water wave created by your golf ball to arrive at your feet?

a) 19.2 s
b) 34.7 s
c) 56.1 s
d) 67.1 s
e) 89.3 s

15.6. Energy, Power, Intensity

In the introductory remarks to this chapter we pointed out that waves generally do not transport matter. However, they do transport energy that is radiated out with them, and in this section we will calculate how much.

Energy

In the previous chapter on oscillations, we found that the energy of a mass oscillating on a spring is proportional to the square of the oscillation amplitude, and is also proportional to the spring constant, $E = \frac{1}{2}kA^2$. Since we can envision our wave as the oscillation of many coupled oscillators, each small volume of the medium that the wave passes through has this energy per oscillator. Using (again) $k/m = \omega^2$, and thus $k = m\omega^2$, the energy of the wave is

$$E = \tfrac{1}{2}m\omega^2 A(r)^2. \tag{15.31}$$

Here we have allowed the amplitude of the wave to have a radial dependence, as explained above in the general discussion of waves in 2 and 3 dimensions. We see that the energy of a wave is proportional to the square of the amplitude and the square of the frequency.

If the wave moves through an elastic medium, then the mass that appears in (15.31) can be calculated as $m = \rho V$, where ρ is the density and V is the volume that the wave passes through. This volume is the product of the cross-sectional area $A_\perp$ (the area perpendicular to the velocity vector of the wave) that the wave passes through times the distance that the wave travels through per time t, $l = vt$. So we find for the energy in this case

$$E = \tfrac{1}{2}\rho V\omega^2 A(r)^2 = \tfrac{1}{2}\rho A_\perp l\omega^2 A(r)^2 = \tfrac{1}{2}\rho A_\perp vt\omega^2 A(r)^2. \tag{15.32}$$

If the wave is a spherical wave radiating outward from a point source, and if no energy is lost to damping, then we can calculate the radial dependence of the amplitude from (15.32). In this case the energy is a constant at a fixed value of r, as are the density of the medium, the angular frequency, and the wave velocity. So we obtain from (15.32) the condition $A_\perp A(r)^2 = \text{constant}$. For a spherical wave in three dimensions the area that the wave passes through is a surface of a sphere, as in Figure 15.9. Thus in this case $A_\perp = 4\pi r^2$, and we then obtain $r^2 A(r)^2 = \text{constant} \Rightarrow A(r) \propto 1/r$. This is exactly the result for the radial dependence of the amplitude that we stated in (15.28).

If the wave is strictly spreading in a 2-dimensional space, as is the case for surface waves on water, then the cross-sectional area is proportional to the perimeter of a circle and thus proportional to r, and not r^2. In this case we obtain for the radial dependence of the wave amplitude $rA(r)^2 = \text{constant} \Rightarrow A(r) \propto 1/\sqrt{r}$.

Power and Intensity

In chapter 5 we have learned that the average power is the rate of energy transfer per time. For the energy contained in the wave as calculated in (15.32), we then simply find

$$\overline{P} = \frac{E}{t} = \tfrac{1}{2}\rho A_\perp v\omega^2 A(r)^2. \tag{15.33}$$

As always, the power measures the rate of energy transfer. Since all quantities on the right hand-side of (15.33) are independent of time, we find that the power radiated by a wave is constant in time.

We define the intensity I as the power radiated per unit cross-sectional area,

$$I = \frac{\bar{P}}{A_\perp}. \tag{15.34}$$

Inserting the result of (15.33) into this definition leads us to

$$I = \tfrac{1}{2}\rho v \omega^2 A(r)^2. \tag{15.35}$$

As you can see from this result, the intensity depends on the square of the amplitude, and so the entire radial dependence of the intensity comes from the dependence of the amplitude on the radial distance. For a spherical wave in 3 dimensions, $A(r) \propto 1/r$, and so we find

$$I \propto \frac{1}{r^2} \tag{15.36}$$

Thus, if we consider two points that are at distances of r_1 and r_2 from the center of a spherical wave, then the intensities $I_1 = I(r_1)$, $I_2 = I(r_2)$ measured at these two locations are related via

$$\frac{I_1}{I_2} = \left(\frac{r_2}{r_1}\right)^2 \tag{15.37}$$

as shown in Figure 15.12. If you, for example, double the distance, you reduce the intensity by a factor of 4.

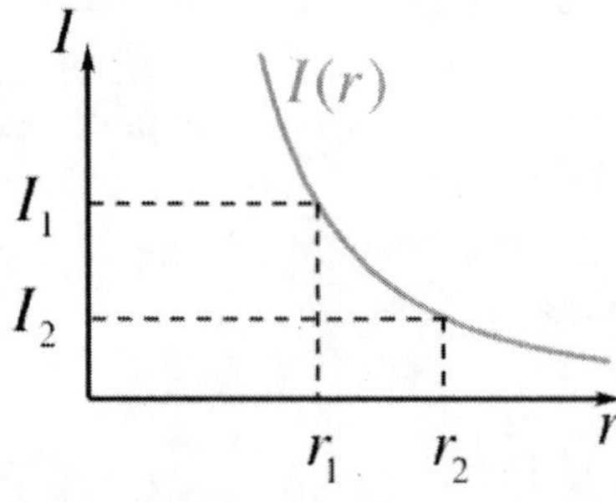

Figure 15.12: Inverse square law for the intensities.

Self-Test Opportunity: The intensity of electromagnetic waves from the Sun on the Earth is approximately 1400 W/m^2. What is the intensity of electromagnetic waves from the Sun on Mars? The distance of the Earth from the Sun is $149.6 \cdot 10^6$ km and the distance from Mars to the Sun is $227.9 \cdot 10^6$ km.

In-class exercise: The intensity of electromagnetic waves from the Sun on the Earth is 1400 W/m^2. How much total power does the Sun generate? The distance from the Earth to the Sun is $149.6 \cdot 10^6$ km.

a) $1.21 \cdot 10^{20}$ W
b) $2.43 \cdot 10^{24}$ W
c) $3.94 \cdot 10^{26}$ W
d) $2.11 \cdot 10^{28}$ W
e) $9.11 \cdot 10^{30}$ W

Solved Problem

Solved Problem 15.1: Power Transmitted by a Wave on a String

Question:
The transverse displacement from equilibrium of a stretched string as a function of position and time is given by $y(x,t) = (0.130 \text{ m})\cos\left((9.00 \text{ m}^{-1})x + (72.0 \text{ s}^{-1})t\right)$. The linear mass density of the string is 0.00677 kg/m. What is the average power transmitted by the string?

Answer:

THINK:

We start with (15.33), which represents the average power transmitted by a general wave. We can extract the required amplitude $A(r)$, the wave number κ, the angular frequency ω, and the wave velocity v from the form of $y(x,t)$ by comparing with our solution to the wave equation for a wave traveling in the negative x direction. The product $\rho A_\perp$ is given by the linear mass density μ.

SKETCH:

A sketch of the wave function isolating the relevant factors of the function is shown in Figure 15.13.

$$y(x,t) = \overbrace{(0.130 \text{ m})}^{A}\cos\left(\overbrace{(9.00 \text{ m}^{-1})}^{\kappa}x + \overbrace{(72.0 \text{ s}^{-1})}^{\omega}t\right)$$

Figure 15.13: The wave function with the relevant factors isolated.

RESEARCH:

The power transmitted by a traveling wave is given by (15.33)

$$\bar{P} = \tfrac{1}{2}\rho A_{\perp} v\omega^2 A(r)^2$$

For a wave moving on an elastic string, the product of the density ρ and the cross sectional area $A_{\perp}$ can be written as

$$\rho A_{\perp} = \frac{m}{V}A_{\perp} = \frac{m}{l \cdot A_{\perp}}A_{\perp} = \frac{m}{l} = \mu \qquad (15.38)$$

where $\mu = m/l$ is the linear mass density of the string. For a wave moving on an elastic string, $A(r)$ is constant, so we can write the transmitted power as

$$\bar{P} = \tfrac{1}{2}\mu v\omega^2 A(r)^2. \qquad (15.39)$$

We can use (15.12) to obtain the speed of the wave

$$v = \frac{\omega}{\kappa}.$$

Solved Problem

SIMPLIFY:

From the form of the wave function specified in this problem, we can extract $A(r)$, κ, and ω. We can see that $A(r) = 0.130$ m, $\kappa = 9.00$ m^{-1}, and $\omega = 72.0$ s^{-1}. Here we have followed the convention that ω is a positive number and that the specified wave function represents a wave traveling in the negative x direction. We can then calculate v as

$$v = \frac{\omega}{\kappa} = \frac{72.0 \text{ s}^{-1}}{9.00 \text{ m}^{-1}} = 8.00 \text{ m/s}.$$

CALCULATE:

Putting our numerical values together we get

$$\bar{P} = \tfrac{1}{2}\mu v\omega^2 A(r)^2 = \tfrac{1}{2}(0.00677 \text{ kg/m})(8.00 \text{ m/s})(72.0 \text{ s}^{-1})^2 (0.130 \text{ m})^2 = 2.37247 \text{ W}.$$

ROUND:

We report our result to three significant digits

$$\bar{P} = 2.37 \text{ W}.$$

DOUBLE-CHECK:

To double-check our answer, let's assume that the wave is an object with the mass of string corresponding to one wavelength moving in the negative x direction at the speed of the traveling wave. The power would then be the energy transmitted in one period. From the form of the wave equation we get the wavelength

Solved Problem

$$\lambda = 2\pi / \kappa = 0.698 \text{ m}$$

and the period

$$T = 2\pi / \omega = 0.0873 \text{ s}.$$

We can write the kinetic energy as

$$K = \frac{1}{2}(\mu\lambda)v^2 = 0.151 \text{ J}.$$

The power then be

$$P = K / T = 0.151 \text{ J} / 0.0873 \text{ s} = 1.73 \text{ W}.$$

This result is similar to but not equal to our result for the power transmitted along the string. Thus our result for the power transmitted seems to be a reasonable result.

15.7. Superposition Principle and Interference

Wave equations of the kind we have derived in (15.13) have a very important property: they are linear. What does this mean? If you find two different solutions $y_1(x,t)$ and $y_2(x,t)$ to a linear differential equation, then any linear combination

$$y(x,t) = ay_1(x,t) + by_2(x,t) \tag{15.40}$$

of these two solutions is also a solution to the same linear differential equation, where a and b are arbitrary constants. One can see this linear property directly from the differential equation, because it contains the function $y(x,t)$ only to the first power (there is no $y(x,t)^2$ or $\sqrt{y(x,t)}$ or any other power of the function).

In physical terms this means that wave solutions can be added or subtracted or combined in any other linear combination, and the result is again a wave solution. This is the mathematical basis of the physical superposition principle:

Two or more wave solutions can be added to result in another wave solution.

$$y(x,t) = y_1(x,t) + y_2(x,t) \tag{15.41}$$

Equation (15.41) is a special case of (15.40) with $a = b = 1$. Let us look at an example in which we have calculated the superposition of two wave pulses with different amplitudes and different velocities.

Example

Example 15.2: Superposition

We start two wave packets $y_1(x,t) = A_1e^{-(x-v_1t)^2}$ and $y_2(x,t) = A_2e^{-(x+v_2t)^2}$ with $A_2 = 1.7A_1$ and $v_1 = 1.6v_2$ off at some distance from each other. Because of their mathematical form these are called Gaussian wave packets. We assume that these two waves are the same

Example

types of waves, such as waves on a rope.

Question:
What is the amplitude of the resulting wave at maximum overlap, and at what time does this occur?

Answer:
Both of these Gaussians are of the functional form $y(x,t) = Y(x \pm vt)$ and are therefore guaranteed to be valid solutions of the one-dimensional wave equation (15.13). According to what we just learned, the superposition principle (15.40) holds and we can simply add the two wave functions to obtain their superposition. The two Gaussian wave packets have maximum overlap when their centers are at the same position in coordinate space. The center of a Gaussian wave packet is at the location where the exponent has a value of 0. As you can see from the Gaussians, both Gaussians will be centered at $x = 0$ at the time $t = 0$, which is the answer to the question as to when and where the maximum overlap occurs.

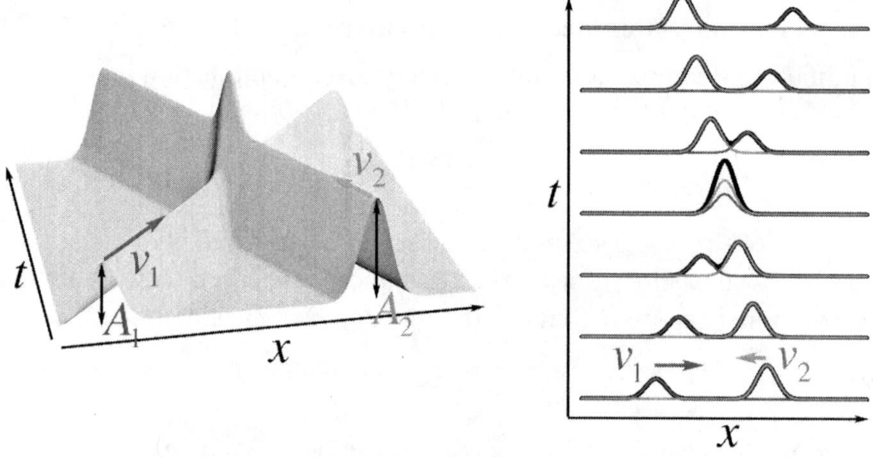

Figure 15.14: Superposition of two Gaussian wave packets.
Left 3d-representation; right: coordinate space plots for different times.

The amplitude at maximum overlap is then simply $A = A_1 + A_2 = 2.7A_1$ (because $A_2 = 1.7A_1$, as specified in the setup of the problem).

Discussion:
It is instructive to make a plot for this case. We have started the two Gaussians out at a time $t = -3$, in units of the width of a Gaussian divided by the speed v_1 and let them propagate. In Figure 15.14 we show the resulting plot. The left side of the plot contains a 3d-plot of the wave function $y(x,t) = y_1(x,t) + y_2(x,t)$ as a function of the coordinate x and time t. The velocity vectors v_1 and v_2 are marked by the arrows. On the right side we show coordinate space plots of the waves at different points in time. The blue curve represent $y_1(x,t)$, the red curve $y_2(x,t)$, and the black curve is their sum. In the middle of the seven time slices the two wave packets have achieved maximum overlap.

Again, what is essential in the superposition principle is that waves can penetrate through each other without changing each other's frequency, amplitude, speed, or direction. Our modern communication technology is absolutely dependent on this fact. In any city there are several TV and radio stations that broadcast their signals at different frequencies. Add to this cell phone communication, satellite television transmissions, as well as the light waves and sound waves. All of these waves have to be able to penetrate each other without changing each other. Thus it is clear that without the superposition principle these methods of everyday communication would be impossible.

Interference

Interference is one aspect of the superposition principle. If waves pass through each other, their displacements simply add, according to (15.41). Interesting cases arise when the wavelengths and frequencies of the two waves are the same or at least close to each other. For now we look at the case of two waves with identical wavelengths and frequencies. The case where the frequencies are close to each other will be postponed until the next chapter on sound, when we discuss beats.

First, let us have a look at the one-dimensional case and set up to waves with identical amplitude A, wave number κ, and angular frequency ω. We allow for different phase shifts by setting the phase shift to 0 for wave 1 and varying ϕ_0 for wave two. The sum of the waveforms is then

$$y(x,t) = A\sin(\kappa x - \omega t) + A\sin(\kappa x - \omega t + \phi_0). \tag{15.42}$$

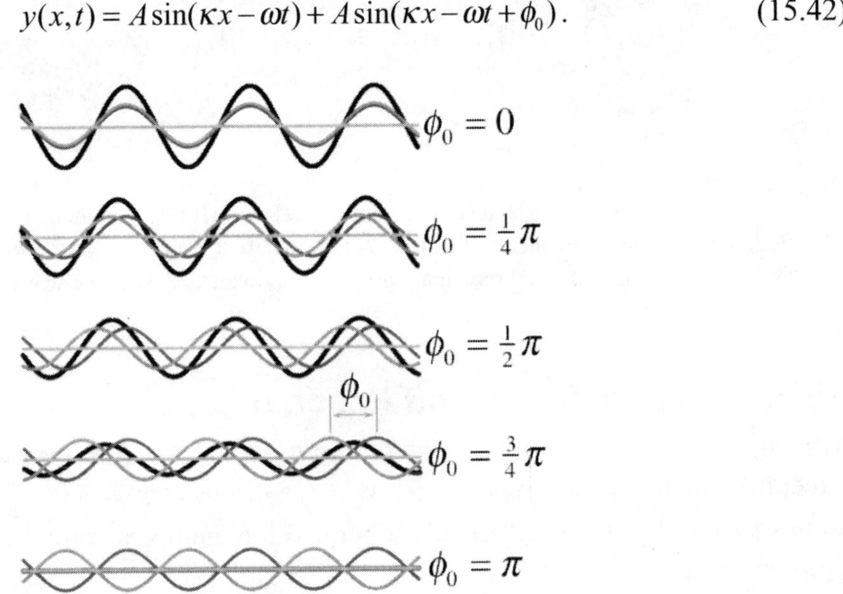

Figure 15.15: Interference of 1-dimensional waves as a function of their relative phase at $t = 0$. At later times the patterns shown move rigidly to the right.

The case for $\phi_0 = 0$ is easy. In this case the two sine functions have identical arguments, and so the sum in (15.42) is simply $y(x,t) = 2A\sin(\kappa x - \omega t)$. In this case the two waves add to the maximum extent possible, and we have *constructive* interference.

We find another special case for $\phi_0 = \pi$. If we shift the argument of a sine or cosine function by π, we obtain the negative of that function: $\sin(\theta + \pi) = -\sin\theta$. For this reason the two terms in (15.42) exactly add up to 0 in the case of $\phi_0 = \pi$. These cases, along with three others, are shown in Figure 15.15 for $t = 0$.For wave functions in more than one spatial dimension we can obtain appealing interference patterns by using two identical spherical waves and displacing their centers some distance from each other. In Figure 15.16 we show the interference pattern for two identical waves with wave number $\kappa = 1\ m^{-1}$ and the same value of ω and amplitude A. One of the waves was shifted by Δx to the right and the other by $-\Delta x$ to the left. We show ten different values of Δx in this figure, and you can get a good idea on how the interference pattern develops as a function of the separation of the centers of the waves. Anybody who has ever dropped more than one stone at a time into a pond will recognize these interference patterns as the same that the surface ripples produced by the stones.

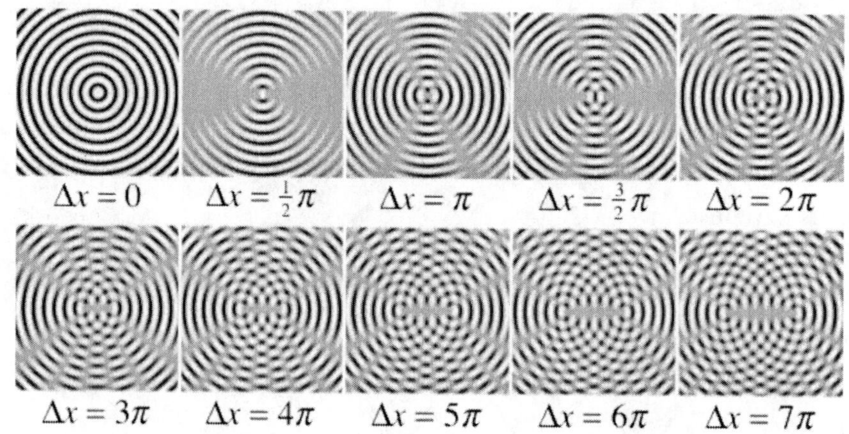

Figure 15.16: Interference pattern of two identical 2-dimensional waves shifted a distance of Δx to either side of the origin, where the units of Δx are m . White and black mark minima and maxima, while gray indicates zeros in the wave form.

15.8. Standing Waves and Resonance

We can obtain special superposition of two traveling waves if they are identical with the exception of an opposite sign for ω: $y_1(x,t) = A\sin(\kappa x + \omega t)$, $y_2(x,t) = A\sin(\kappa x - \omega t)$ Let us first look at the result of this superposition mathematically and then discuss it to gain physical insight.

$$\begin{aligned} y(x,t) &= y_1(x,t) + y_2(x,t) \\ &= A\sin(\kappa x + \omega t) + A\sin(\kappa x - \omega t) \Rightarrow \\ y(x,t) &= 2A\sin(\kappa x)\cos(\omega t). \end{aligned} \tag{15.43}$$

In the last step of this equation we have used the trigonometric addition formula

$\sin(\alpha \pm \beta) = \sin\alpha\cos\beta \pm \cos\alpha\sin\beta$. So we find that for this superposition of two traveling waves with the same amplitude, same wave number, same speed, but opposite propagation direction the dependence on the spatial coordinate and the dependence on the time separate (or factorize) into a function of just x times a function of just t. The result of this superposition is a wave that has nodes (where $y = 0$) and antinodes (where y can reach its maximum value) at particular points along the x-axis. The antinodes are located midway between neighboring nodes. Thus the superposition of two otherwise identical waves traveling in opposite direction yields a solution for which the dependence on time and the dependence on space factorize.

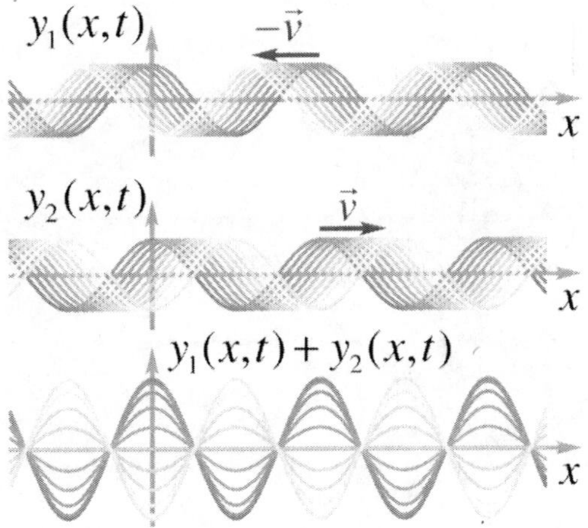

Figure 15.17: Superposition of two traveling waves with opposite velocity vectors, resulting in a standing wave.

This is much easier to visualize in graphical form. Figure 15.17 shows in the upper panel a wave $y_1(x,t) = A\sin(\kappa x + \omega t)$ and in the middle panel a wave $y_2(x,t) = A\sin(\kappa x - \omega t)$. The lower panel contains the addition of the two waves. In all panels, the waveform is shown as a function of the x-coordinate. In each panel show the waves at 11 different instants in time, with a time difference of $\pi/10$ between each two times. In order to be able to compare the same time instances in each panel we have color-coded the time in terms of the hue of the curves, starting from red and progressing through orange to yellow. You can see that the individual waves travel to the left and right, respectively, and that their addition oscillates in place, with the nodes and antinodes remaining at fixed locations on the x-axis. This is the result of the factorization of the time dependence and space dependence that we found in (15.43). The two traveling waves are always out of phase at the nodes.

The nodes of a standing wave always have amplitude 0. According to (15.31) the energy contained in a wave is proportional to the square of the amplitude. And so we find that no energy is transported across a node by a standing wave. Wave energy gets trapped between the nodes of a standing wave and remains localized there.

Also, note that while the standing wave is not moving, the relationship between wavelength, frequency, and wave speed, $v = \lambda f$ still holds. v is still the speed with which each of the two traveling waves, which make up the standing wave, moves.

Standing Waves on a String

The basis for the creation of musical sounds for all string instruments is the generation of standing waves on strings that are put under tension. Earlier in this chapter (15.26) we have discussed how the velocity of a wave on a string depends on the string tension and the mass density of the string. And in this section we discuss the basic physics of one-dimensional standing waves. So we are ready to treat standing waves on strings in quantitative detail.

Figure 15.18: Experimental generation of standing waves on a string.

Let us start our discussion with a little demonstration experiment, as shown in Figure 15.18. Shown is a string that is tied to an anchor on the left side and to a piston on the right. The piston oscillates up and down, in sinusoidal fashion, with a variable frequency f. The up-and-down motion of the piston has only a very small amplitude so that we can consider the string to be fixed at both ends. As we vary the frequency of the piston's oscillation, we find a certain frequency f_0 for which the string develops a large amplitude motion with a central anti-node, as shown in the upper panel of Figure 15.18. After what we have learned about standing waves, we clearly recognize this excitation of the string as such. This is a resonant excitation of the string in the sense that the amplitude gets large only at a well-defined resonance frequency. If we increase the frequency by 10%, as shown in the 2nd panel from the top, this resonant oscillation of the string vanishes. Lowering the piston's frequency by 10% has the same effect. Increasing the frequency to twice the value of f_0 results in another resonant excitation, this time one that has a single node in the center, and antinodes at ¼ and ¾ of the length of the string. Increasing the frequency to triple the value of f_0 again gives us a resonant frequency, now resulting in a standing wave with two nodes and three antinodes. The continuation of this series is obvious: a frequency of $n f_0$ will result in a standing resonant wave with n antinodes and $n-1$ nodes (plus the two nodes at both ands of the string) that are equally spaced along the length of the string.

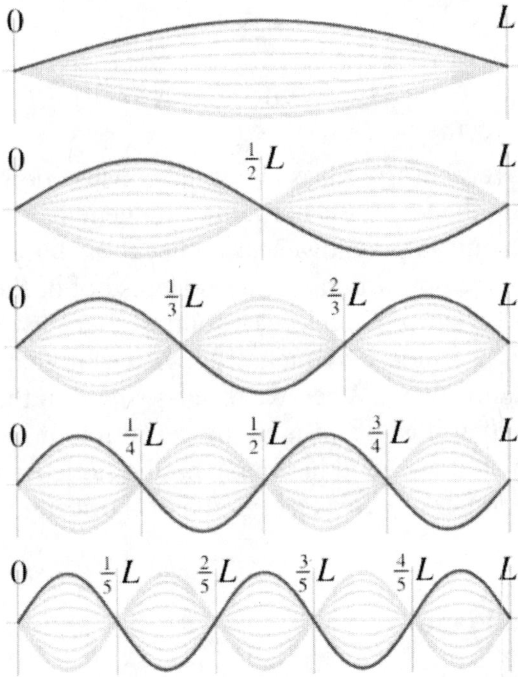

Figure 15.19: Lowest five standing wave excitations of a string.

Examining Figure 15.19 we can see that the condition for a standing wave is that an integer multiple n of half wavelengths fits exactly into the length of the string L. We give these special wavelengths the index n and write

$$n\frac{\lambda_n}{2}=L\,,\ n=1,2,3,... \tag{15.44}$$

Solving this for the wavelengths we obtain

$$\lambda_n=\frac{2L}{n},\ n=1,2,3,... \tag{15.45}$$

The index n labels the harmonic. $n=1$ labels the first harmonic, also called fundamental. $n=2$ labels the second harmonic, $n=3$ the third, and so on.

As discussed before, $v=\lambda f$ still holds, even for a standing wave. Using this relationship, we can then find the harmonic resonance frequencies of a string from (15.45),

$$f_n=\frac{v}{\lambda_n}=n\frac{v}{2L},\ n=1,2,3,... \tag{15.46}$$

Finally, using the expression (15.26) for the wave velocity on a string with mass density

μ under tension T, $v=\sqrt{T/\mu}$, we see that

$$f_n = \frac{v}{\lambda_n} = n\frac{\sqrt{T}}{2L\sqrt{\mu}} = n\sqrt{\frac{T}{4L^2\mu}} . \qquad (15.47)$$

This equation gives as several useful ideas about the construction of string instruments. First, the longer the string, the lower the harmonic frequencies. This is the basic reason why a cello, with which you can play lower notes, has to be longer than a violin. Second, the harmonic frequencies are proportional to the square root of the tension on the string. So if your instrument's frequency is too low (it sounds "flat"), you need to increase the tension. And third, the 2nd harmonic frequency is twice as high as the fundamental, the third three times higher, and so on. When we discuss sound in the next chapter, we will return to this fact and see that it is the basis of the definition of the octave. But for now we can see that we can play the second harmonic on the same string that we use for the fundamental, if we put a finger on the exact middle of the string and thus force a node to be located there.

Example

Example 15.3: Tuning a Piano

A piano tuner's job is make sure that all keys produce the proper tones. On one piano the string for the middle-A key is under a tension of 2900 N, has a mass 0f 0.0060 kg, and a length of 0.63 m.

Question:
By what fraction does the tuner have to change the tension on this string in order to obtain the proper frequency of 440 Hz?

Answer:
First we calculate the fundamental frequency that this string produces. This fundamental (or first harmonic) frequency is the frequency with $n=1$ in equation (15.47). So the frequency produced by this string under the tension given is

$$f_1 = \sqrt{\frac{2900 \text{ N}}{4(0.63 \text{ m})(0.0060 \text{ kg})}} = 438 \text{ Hz}$$

This is off by 2 Hz. So this frequency is too low by 0.5%, and so the tension has to be increased. The proper tension needed can also be found by solving (15.47) for the tension and then using the fundamental frequency of 440 Hz, the proper frequency for middle-A:

$$f_n = n\sqrt{\frac{T}{4Lm}} \Rightarrow T = 4Lm\left(\frac{f_n}{n}\right)^2 \qquad (15.48)$$

Example

Inserting the numbers, we find for the tension needed:

$$T = 4(0.63\ \text{m})(0.0060\ \text{kg})(440\ \text{Hz})^2 = 2927\ \text{N}$$

So the tension needs to be increased by 27 N, which is 0.94% of 2900 N. Therefore the piano tuner needs to increase the tension by 0.94% to produce the proper middle-A frequency for this particular string.

Discussion:
We could also have seen what change in the tension needs to be made by arguing in the following way: The frequency is proportional to the square root of the tension, and $\sqrt{1-x} \approx 1 - \frac{1}{2}x$ for small x. Since we need a 0.5% change in the frequency, the tension thus needs to be changed by twice that amount, 1%.

By the way, a piano tuner can detect a frequency which is off by 2 Hz easily, by using beats. Let us postpone discussing beats until the next chapter on sound.

Self-test opportunity: The researchers at the Cornell Nanofabrication Facility, where the guitar on the right of Figure 15.8 was built, have succeeded to build an even smaller guitar string made from a single carbon nanotube of only 1 to 4 nm diameter. It is suspended over a trench of width $W = 1.5\ \mu\text{m}$. In their 2004 paper in Nature, the Cornell group report a resonance of the carbon nanotube at a frequency of 55 MHz. What then is the speed of sound on this carbon nanotube that one would estimate with the concepts provided in the present chapter?

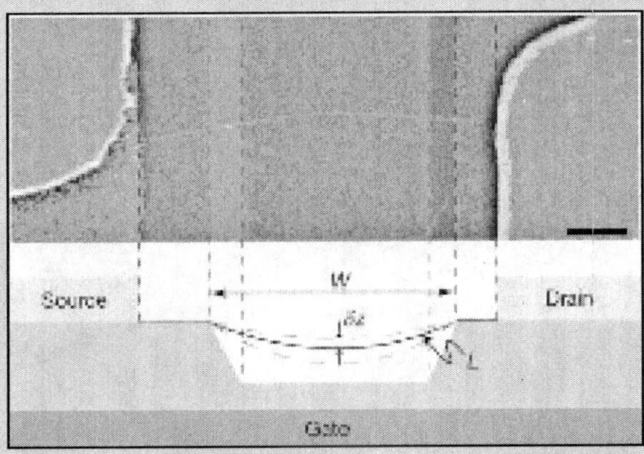

In-class exercise: A guitar string is 0.750 m long and has a mass of 5.00 g. The string is tuned to E (660 Hz). The string vibrates in its fundamental mode. What is the required tension on the string?

a) $2.90 \cdot 10^3$ N b) $4.84 \cdot 10^3$ N c) $6.53 \cdot 10^3$ N d) $8.11 \cdot 10^3$ N e) $1.23 \cdot 10^4$ N

15.9. Research on Waves

The present chapter gives only a very brief overview of wave phenomena. All physics majors and most engineering majors will take another complete course on waves that goes into much more detail. Within this book we will also return to waves several times. The following chapter is devoted to special longitudinal pressure waves called sound waves. After we have had a chance to introduce electricity and magnetism, we will return to waves and devote a chapter to electromagnetic waves. When we talk about optics, there will be an entire chapter on wave optics, in which we describe reflection, refraction, dispersion, and other wave phenomena. And finally, when we talk about quantum physics, we will get exposed to a wave description of matter. This wave character of matter directly leads to the development of quantum mechanics, the basis for most of our modern physics, nanoscience and nanotechnology.

The subject of waves is by no means closed. Scientists and engineers continue to discover new aspects of wave physics. These investigations cover the entire spectrum, from the most applied to the most fundamental.

On the applied side engineers are studying ways to guide microwaves through different geometries with the aid of finite element methods (which break a large object into a large number of small objects) and very CPU-time intensive computer programs. If these geometries break spatial symmetries, i.e. if they are not exactly round or exactly rectangular, then one can find surprising results. For example, physicists study quantum chaos with the aid of microwaves that are sent into metal cavities in the shape of a stadium, i.e. a shape that has semicircles at both ends that are connected by straight sections.

Figure 15.20: Iron atoms on a copper surface form a stadium-shaped cavity in which one can study the electron waves.

Figure 15.20 shows such a stadium-geometry, but for an entirely different physical system, a collection of individual iron atoms arranged by using a scanning tunneling microscope on a copper surface. The wave ripples in the interior of the stadium are standing electron matter waves.

On the most microscopic level of investigations into matter, particle theorists and mathematicians have come up with new classes of theories, so-called string theories. The mathematics of string theory exceeds the scope of this book. However it is still interesting to note that string theorists obtain their physical insights from considering systems like the ones we have considered in this chapter, in particular of standing waves on a string. We will touch on this subject again in chapter 39 on particle physics.

Perhaps one of the most interesting experimental investigations into wave physics is the search for gravitational waves. Gravitational waves were already predicted by Albert Einstein's theory of general relativity (see chapter 35). Astrophysicists have postulated that some astronomical objects emit gravitational waves of such intensity that they should be observable on Earth. We have indirect evidence of the existence of gravitational waves from the study of orbital frequencies of neutron star pairs, where the decrease of the measured rotation energy in the pair can be explained by the radiation of gravitational waves. However, no direct observation has yet been successful. To this end, US and international groups of physicists have constructed or are still in the process of constructing gravitational wave detectors, such as LIGO (Laser Interferometer Gravitational-Wave Observatory).

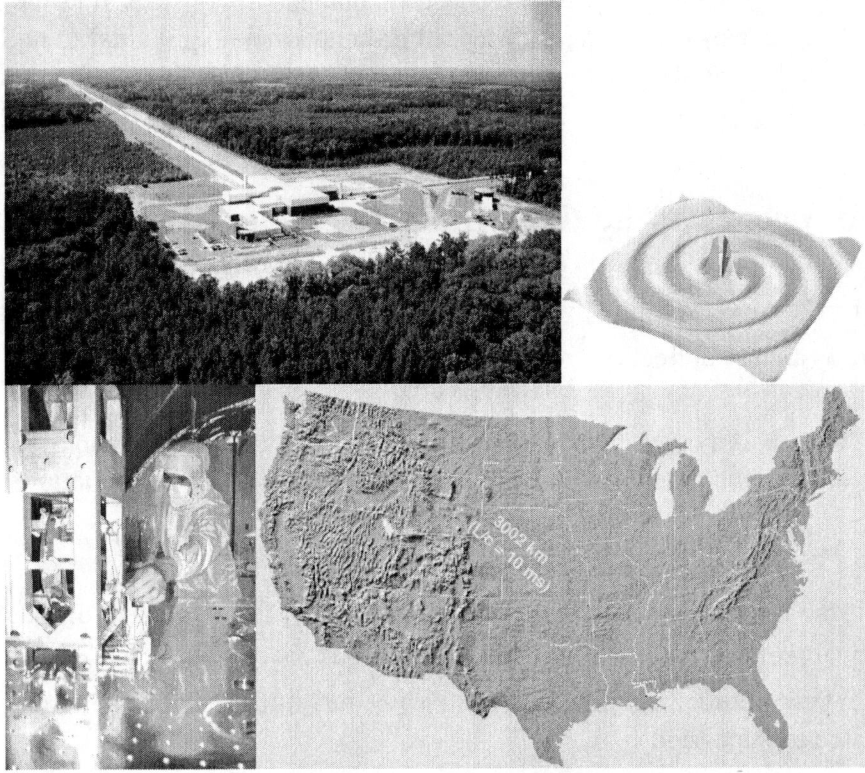

Figure 15.21: Upper left: Aerial view of the Livingston site of LIGO (Laser Interferometer Gravitational-Wave Observatory); upper right: visualization of a gravitational wave; lower left: a scientist adjusts the interferometer; lower right: map of LIGO. (Images courtesy of LIGO Laboratory)

These gravitational wave detectors all work by using the principle of light wave interference, which we will cover in more detail in chapter 34 on wave optics. The basic idea is to suspend very heavy test masses with mirrored sides in vacuum by very thin wires. As a gravitational wave passes by, it should cause alternating stretching and compressing of the fabric of space-time, out of phase for the two arms, which should be observable as minute movements of these mirrors, which can, in principle, be detected by bouncing a laser light off of the mirrors and using laser light interference (interference of light will be covered in detail in chapter 34 on wave optics. These gravitational wave detectors require very long tunnels for the lasers. LIGO consists of two observatories, one in Hanford, WA, and the other in Livingston, LA, with a distance of 3,002 km between them. Each observatory consists of two tunnels of 4 km length each, arranged in L-shape. These experiments push the envelope of what is currently technically possible and what is measurable on many fronts. For example, the expected movement of these test masses due to a gravitational wave hitting it is only on the order of $10^{-18}\,\text{m}$, which is a factor of 100 million smaller than the diameter of a single hydrogen atom. Measuring a deflection that small is a huge technological challenge.

Other gravitational wave laboratories in Europe (Virgo and GEO-600) and Japan (TAMA) are also trying to measure the effect of gravitational waves. And there are plans for a space-based gravitational wave observatory, named LISA (Laser Interferometer Space Antenna), consisting of three spacecraft arranged in an equilateral triangle of side length 5 million km. So the future of research on gravitational waves looks very interesting.

What We Have Learned / Exam Study Guide

- The equation of motion for a linear chain of coupled oscillators is $ma_i = k(y_{i+1} - 2y_i + y_{i-1})$, where m is the mass, k is the spring constant, and y_i and a_i are the deflection from equilibrium and acceleration of oscillator i in the chain.
- In the case of a continuous distribution of oscillators, the equation of motion for the displacement $y(x,t)$ from equilibrium becomes the wave equation, $\frac{\partial^2}{\partial t^2} y(x,t) - v^2 \frac{\partial^2}{\partial x^2} y(x,t) = 0$.
- v is the wave velocity, λ the wavelength, and f the frequency of the wave, and they are related via $v = \lambda f$.
- The wave number is defined as $\kappa = 2\pi / \lambda$, just like the angular frequency is related to the period $\omega = 2\pi / T$.
- Any function of the form $Y(\kappa x - \omega t + \phi_0)$ or $Y(\kappa x + \omega t + \phi_0)$ is a solution to the wave equation. The first one is a wave traveling to the right, and the second is one traveling to the left.
- The wave speed on a string is $v = \sqrt{T / \mu}$, where $\mu = m / l$ is the mass per unit length of the string, and T is the string tension. (Note that we use the same letter

for the string tension and the oscillation period, in accordance with common convention. Make sure you understand which use applies to which situation.)

- A one-dimensional sinusoidal solution of the wave equation is $y(x,t) = A\sin(\kappa x - \omega t + \phi_0)$, where the argument of the sine function is called the phase of the wave, and where A denotes the wave amplitude.
- A three-dimensional spherical wave solution is $y(\vec{r},t) = \frac{A}{r}\sin(\kappa r - \omega t + \phi_0)$, and a plane wave is $y(\vec{r},t) = A\sin(\kappa x - \omega t + \phi_0)$.
- The energy contained in a wave is $E = \frac{1}{2}\rho V\omega^2 A(r)^2 = \frac{1}{2}\rho(A_\perp l)\omega^2 A(r)^2 = \frac{1}{2}\rho(A_\perp vt)\omega^2 A(r)^2$, where $A_\perp$ is the perpendicular cross sectional area that the wave passes through.
- The power transmitted by the wave is $\bar{P} = \frac{E}{t} = \frac{1}{2}\rho A_\perp v\omega^2 A(r)^2$, and the intensity is $I = \frac{1}{2}\rho v\omega^2 A(r)^2$
- For a spherical three-dimensional wave the intensity is inversely proportional to the square of the distance to the source.
- The superposition principle holds for waves: If you add two solutions of the wave equations to each other, you find another valid solution.
- Waves can interfere in space and time, constructively and destructively, depending on their relative phase.
- Adding two traveling waves that are identical, except for velocity vectors that point in opposite directions, yields a standing wave such as $y(x,t) = 2A\sin(\kappa x)\cos(\omega t)$, for which the dependence on space and time factorizes.
- The harmonic frequencies for waves on a string are given by $f_n = \frac{v}{\lambda_n} = n\frac{\sqrt{T}}{2L\sqrt{\mu}}$, for $n = 1,2,3,...$ Here n labels the harmonic, so $n = 4$ would correspond to the fourth harmonic.

Additional Solved Problems

Solved Problem

Solved Problem 15.2: Traveling Wave

Question:

The wave function of a wave on a string is given by

$$y(x,t) = (0.00200 \text{ m})\sin\left((78.8 \text{ m}^{-1})x + (346 \text{ s}^{-1})t\right).$$

What is the wavelength of this wave? What is the period of this wave? What is the velocity of this wave?

Answer:

THINK:

We can answer this question by referring to the form of the solution to the wave equation. We can identify the wave number and the angular frequency from which we can extract the wavelength and period. We can then calculate the velocity of the traveling wave from the ratio of the angular frequency to the wave number.

SKETCH: A sketch of the wave function is shown in Figure 15.22. The top panel shows a snapshot at $t = 0$ and the bottom panel shows the behavior of the wave function at $x = 0$.

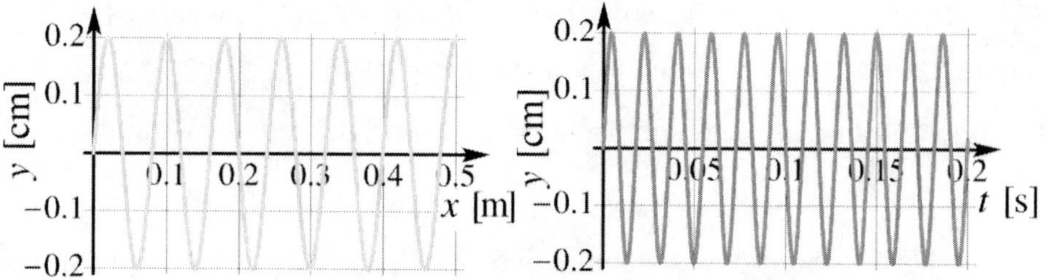

Figure 15.22: Left panel shows a snapshot of the wave function at $t = 0$. Right panel shows the wave function as a function of time at $x = 0$.

RESEARCH:

Looking at the wave function in this problem $y(x,t) = (0.00200 \text{ m})\sin\left((78.8 \text{ m}^{-1})x + (346 \text{ s}^{-1})t\right)$ and comparing that wave function with the solution to the wave equation for a wave traveling in the negative x direction

$$y(x,t) = A\sin(\kappa x + \omega t + \phi_0)$$

we can identify $\kappa = 78.8 \text{ m}^{-1}$ and $\omega = 346 \text{ s}^{-1}$.

SIMPLIFY:

We can obtain the wavelength from the wave number

$$\lambda = 2\pi / \kappa$$

and the period from the angular frequency

$$T = 2\pi / \omega.$$

We can then calculate the velocity of the wave as

$$v = \omega / \kappa.$$

CALCULATE:

Putting in our numerical values we get the wavelength

Solved Problem

$$\lambda = 2\pi / 78.8 \text{ m}^{-1} = 0.079736 \text{ m}$$

and the period

$$T = 2\pi / 346 \text{ s}^{-1} = 0.018159 \text{ s}.$$

We can calculate the velocity of the traveling wave as

$$v = 346 \text{ s}^{-1} / 78.8 \text{ m}^{-1} = 4.39086 \text{ m/s}.$$

ROUND:

We report our result to three significant figures

$$\lambda = 0.0797 \text{ m}$$
$$T = 0.0182 \text{ s} \quad .$$
$$v = 4.39 \text{ m/s}$$

DOUBLE-CHECK: To double-check our results for the wavelength, we look at the top panel of Figure 15.22. We can see in that plot that the wavelength (the distance required to complete one oscillation) is approximately 0.08 m, in agreement with our result. Looking at the bottom panel of Figure 15.22, we can see that the period (the time required to complete one oscillation) is approximately 0.018 s, in agreement with our result.

Solved Problem

Solved Problem 15.3: Standing Wave on a String

Question:

A wave driver is used to set up a standing wave on an elastic string as shown in Figure 15.23.

Figure 15.23: A standing wave on an elastic string driven by a mechanical wave driver.

Tension is put on the string by running the string over a frictionless pulley and hanging a metal block from the string. The length of the string from the top of the pulley to the wave driver is 1.25 m and the linear mass density of the string is 5.00 g/m. The frequency of the wave driver is 45.0 Hz. What is the mass of the metal block?

Answer:

THINK:

The weight of the metal block is equal to the tension placed on the elastic string. We can see from Figure 15.23 that the string is vibrating in its third harmonic because three antinodes are visible. We can then use (15.47) to relate the tension on the string, the

Solved Problem

harmonic, the linear mass density of the string, and frequency. Once we have determined the tension on the string, we can calculate the mass of the metal block.

SKETCH: In the left panel of Figure 15.24, a sketch is shown of an elastic string being held at tension by running the string over a pulley and hanging a metal block from the string. A mechanical wave driver sets up a standing wave on the string. L is the length of the string from the pulley to the wave driver, μ is the linear mass density of the string, and m is the mass of the metal block. In the right panel of Figure 15.24, the free body diagram of the hanging metal block is shown where T is the tension on the string and mg is the weight of the metal block.

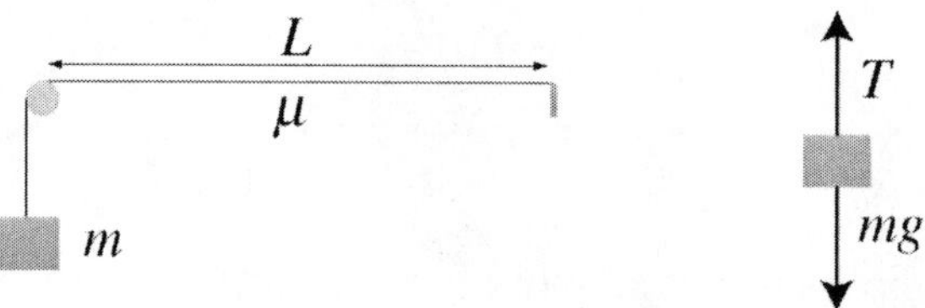

Figure 15.24: The left panel shows a vibrating string driven by a mechanical wave driver and held at tension with a hanging mass. The right panel shows the free body diagram for the hanging mass.

RESEARCH:

For a standing wave of harmonic n and frequency f_n on an elastic string of length L and linear mass density μ, (15.47) tells us

$$f_n = n\sqrt{\frac{T}{4L^2\mu}}.$$

We can see in Figure 15.23 that the string is vibrating in its third harmonic (three antinodes are visible) so that $n = 3$. From the free body diagram shown in the right panel of Figure 15.24 we can write

$$T - mg = 0 \tag{15.49}$$

because the metal block does not move. Therefore the tension of the string is $T = mg$.

SIMPLIFY:

We can solve (15.47) for the tension on the string

$$T = 4L^2\mu\frac{f_n^2}{n^2}.$$

Relating the tension to the mass and rearranging terms we get

$$m = \frac{\mu}{g}\left(\frac{2Lf_n}{n}\right)^2.$$

CALCULATE:
Putting in our numerical values we get

$$m = \frac{\mu}{g}\left(\frac{2Lf_n}{n}\right)^2 = \frac{0.00500 \text{ kg/m}}{9.81 \text{ m/s}^2}\left(\frac{2 \cdot 1.25 \text{ m} \cdot 45.0 \text{ Hz}}{3}\right)^2.$$

$$m = 0.716743 \text{ kg}$$

ROUND:
We report our result to three significant figures

$$m = 0.717 \text{ kg}.$$

DOUBLE-CHECK: To double-check our result, we realize that a half liter bottle of water has a mass of about 0.5 kg. Even a light string could support this mass without breaking. Thus, our answer seems reasonable.

Chapter 16. Sound

What We Will Learn

- Sound is a longitudinal pressure wave and needs a medium in which to propagate.
- The speed of sound in solids is usually larger than in liquids and larger still than in gases.
- The speed of sound in air is approximately 343 m/s at normal atmospheric pressure and a temperature of $20\ ^\circ\text{C}$, and depends on the temperature.
- Sound waves can interfere in space and time, and we will find the conditions for destructive and constructive interference.
- Interference in the time domain is called beats, and we will learn how to calculate the beat frequency.
- If the sound source moves with a speed greater than that of sound, a Mach cone develops.
- The Doppler effect is the shift in frequency due to a sound source that moves (approaching or receding) relative to an observer.
- Standing waves in open or closed pipes can only be generated at discrete wavelengths.

16.1. Longitudinal Pressure Waves

Sound is a pressure variation or fluctuation, which propagates through space. In air the pressure variations cause abnormal motion of air molecules in the direction of propagation, hence the wave is longitudinal. When we hear a sound, our eardrums are set in vibration by the air that rests against them. If this air has a repetitive pressure variation with a certain frequency, the eardrums vibrate at this frequency. The pressure of this air was set into vibration by a pressure wave that originated from the source of sound and traveled through the air. Sound needs a medium for propagation. One can show this by pumping out the air around a sound source, for example a ringing bell inside a glass jar. One then finds that the sound ceases as the air is evacuated from the glass jar, even though the hammer clearly still hits the bell. Thus, sound waves need an emitter and a medium to travel through.

Figure 16.1 shows a continuous pressure wave composed of alternating fluctuations (or variations) of air pressure - a pressure excess (compression) followed by a reduced pressure (rarefaction). By plotting these fluctuations along an $x-$axis for various times, as in Figure 16.1, on can deduce the wave speed.

Sound does not necessarily need air for propagation. Other media work just as well, perhaps even better. When you are diving under water, you can still hear sounds. So we know that sound also propagates through liquids. In addition, you know about putting your ear to the train track to obtain advance information on approaching trains. So we also know that sound propagates through solids. In fact, it propagates faster and with less loss through metals than through air. Otherwise putting your ear to the train track would be pointless.

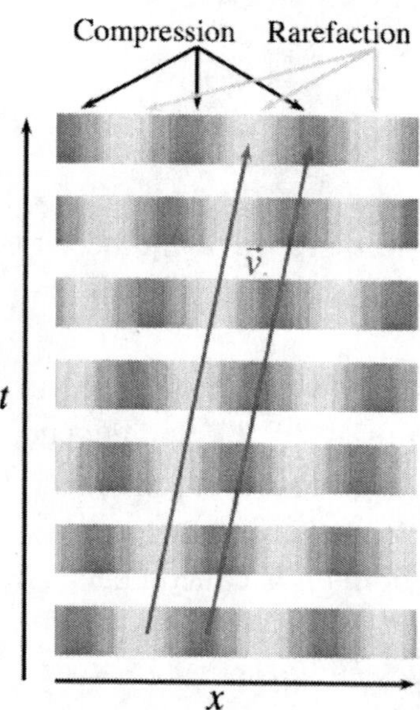

Figure 16.1: Propagation of longitudinal pressure wave along x-axis as a function of time.

Sound Velocity

If you watch the fireworks like those in Figure 16.2 on the 4th of July, you notice that you see the explosions of the rockets quite noticeably before you hear the sound of this explosion. The reason, of course, is that the light emitted from the explosions reaches your eyes almost instantaneously, because the speed of light is 300,000 km/s. However, the speed of sound is very much lower, and so it takes some time for the sound waves from the explosion of the fireworks to reach you after the light has already arrived.

Figure 16.2: Fireworks.

The question is now: how fast does sound propagate, what is the speed of sound? For waves on a string or wire, we had found in the previous chapter that the wave speed is

$$v = \sqrt{\frac{T}{\mu}} \text{ , for a string,}$$

where T is the string tension, a force, and μ is the linear mass density of the string. In this equation v is the square root of the ratio of the restoring force divided by the inertial response. If the wave propagates through a three-dimensional bulk medium instead of a one-dimensional string, the inertial response originates from the bulk density of the medium, ρ. In chapter 13 we talked about fluids, solids, and their elastic response, and we introduced the elastic modulus, Young's modulus E. This modulus determines the fractional length change of a thin rod as a function of the force per unit area. A dimensional analysis reveals that this modulus then is the appropriate force term for the case of a wave propagating along a thin solid rod, and we obtain

$$v = \sqrt{\frac{E}{\rho}} \tag{16.1}$$

for the speed of sound in a thin solid rod.

There is also a connection between bulk modulus B as the restoring force term and the speed of sound in fluids, both liquids and gases. In chapter 13 we defined the bulk modulus as the elastic response to external pressure in terms of a fractional volume change. Thus, the same dimensional analysis that we have just employed to find the speed of sounds in a thin solid rod now yields the speed of sound in a gas or liquid

$$v = \sqrt{\frac{B}{\rho}}. \tag{16.2}$$

For the experienced physicist these dimensional arguments are persuasive. However this approach does not determine numerical factors; one must do a more fundamental analysis to determine that these constants are 1.0 in (16.1) and (16.2). We do such an analysis to determine the speed of sound in liquids in the following derivation.

Derivation 16.1: Speed of Sound

Suppose we have a fluid contained in a thin long cylinder, with a moveable piston on one end, as in Figure 16.3. If we move this piston with speed v_p into the fluid, it will compress the fluid element in front of it. This fluid element in turn will move due to the pressure change and its leading edge will move with the speed of sound v in the fluid, which, by our definition of sound, is the speed of pressure waves in the medium.

Pushing the piston with a force F into the fluid will cause a pressure change $p = F/A$ in the fluid (see chapter 13), where A is the cross sectional area of our cylinder, which is also the area of our piston. The force exerted on the fluid element causes an acceleration

$$F = m\frac{\Delta v}{\Delta t} = m\frac{v_p}{\Delta t} \Rightarrow p = \frac{F}{A} = \frac{m\,v_p}{A\,\Delta t}$$

where m is the mass of the fluid element. Since the mass is the density of the fluid times its volume, $m = \rho V$, and the volume is the volume of the cylinder of base area A and length l, we can write for the mass of the fluid element

$$m = \rho V = \rho A l \Rightarrow p = \frac{m\,v_p}{A\,\Delta t} = \frac{\rho A l\,v_p}{A\;\Delta t} = \frac{\rho l v_p}{\Delta t}$$

Since this fluid element responds to compression by moving with a speed v during the time interval Δt, the length of the fluid element that has experienced the pressure wave is $l = v\Delta t$, which finally yields for the pressure difference:

$$p = \frac{\rho l v_p}{\Delta t} = \frac{\rho(v\Delta t)v_p}{\Delta t} = \rho v v_p.$$

Since by the definition of the bulk modulus (see chapter 13) $p = B\Delta V/V$, we can combine this definition with the result of the pressure that we have just obtained and find

$$p = \rho v v_p = B\frac{\Delta V}{V}.$$

Derivation

Again, the volume of the fluid moving that has experienced the pressure wave, V, is proportional to v since $V = Al = Av\Delta t$. In addition, the volume change in the cylinder caused by pushing the piston into it is $\Delta V = Av_p\Delta t$. So, we obtain for the ratio $\Delta V / V = v_p / v$, the ratio of the piston's speed to the sound speed. Inserting this result into our previous equation yields then

$$\rho v v_p = B\frac{\Delta V}{V} = B\frac{v_p}{v} \Rightarrow$$
$$\rho v^2 = B \Rightarrow$$
$$v = \sqrt{\frac{B}{\rho}}$$

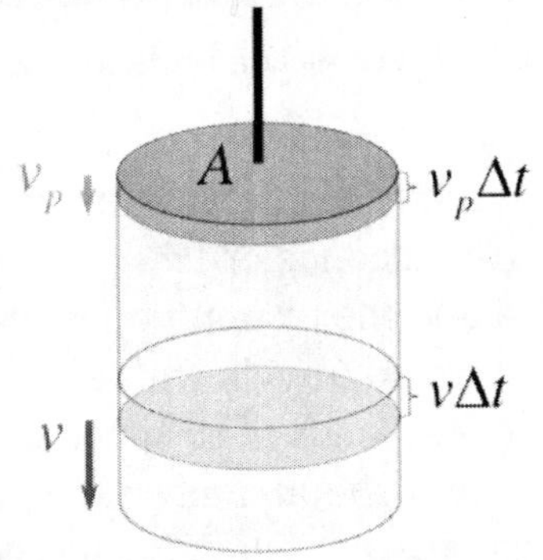

Figure 16.3: Piston compressing a fluid.

As you can see, the speed with which the piston is pushed into the fluid cancels out. So it does not matter what the speed of the excitation is; the sound always propagates with the same speed in the medium.

Derivation

In general, the bulk modulus for solids is larger than that for liquids, and the bulk modulus for liquids is higher than that for gases. From (16.2) it then follows that for the speeds of sound in solids, liquids and gases

$$v(\text{solid}) > v(\text{liquid}) > v(\text{gas}). \tag{16.3}$$

The speed of sound we are most interested in is of course the speed of sound in air. At normal atmospheric pressure and at 20 °C temperature, this speed of sound is

$$v(\text{air}) = 343 \text{ m/s}. \tag{16.4}$$

Other gases have similar values of the speed of sound. Carbon dioxide has one of the lower values of 260 m/s, while helium (960 m/s) and hydrogen (1280 m/s) have the highest values for gases. The speed of sound in water is 1500 m/s, more than 4 times higher than in air. The speed of sound in steel is 5800 m/s. Concrete has a speed of sound of approximately 3200 m/s, and diamond 12,000 m/s. Hardwoods have speeds of sound in the range of 4000 m/s, and aluminum's is 6400 m/s.

Figure 16.4: Five-second-rule for lightning.

Now that we know the speed of sound, it is easy to understand the five-second-rule for lightning. This rule says that if five seconds or less pass between the instant you see the lightning strike (as in Figure 16.4 and the instant you hear the thunder, the thunderstorm is one 1 mile or less away. Since sound travels with approximately 340 m/s, it travels 1700 m, approximately 1 mile, in 5 seconds. The speed of light is approximately 1 million times higher than the speed of sound, and so the visual information on the lightning strike arrives with essentially no delay. Each second delay between lightning and thunder corresponds to approximately 1/5th of a mile distance between the lightning strike and the observer. In countries that use the metric system, there is a three-second rule: there are three seconds of delay for each kilometer distance to the lightning strike as indicated in Figure 16.5.

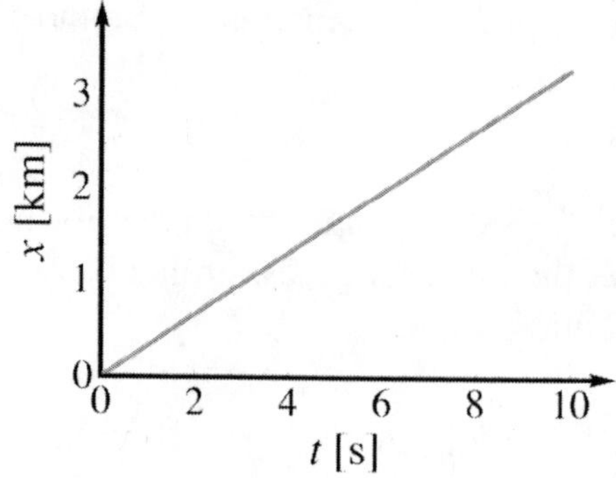

Figure 16.5: Distance to the source of the sound as a function of the time delay in hearing the sound.

Sound speed in air is (weakly) dependent on the air temperature. Experimentally, one finds an approximately linear dependence

$$v(T) = \left(331 + 0.6(T\,/\,°\mathrm{C})\right)\ \mathrm{m/s}\,. \tag{16.5}$$

Example

Example 16.1: Football Cheers

A student's apartment is located exactly 3.75 km from the university's football stadium. He is watching the game live on TV and sees his home team score a touchdown 11.2 seconds after he hears the roar of the crowd on TV, he hears it again from outside, as the sound wave has finally made it to his house.

Question:
What is the temperature at game time?

Answer:
The TV signal moves with the speed of light and thus arrives at the students TV essentially at the same instant as the action is happening in the stadium. So the delay in the arrival of the roar can be entirely attributed to the finite speed of sound. We find for this speed of sound from the data given:

$$v = \frac{\Delta x}{\Delta t} = \frac{3750 \text{ m}}{11.2 \text{ s}} = 334.8 \text{ m/s}$$

Using the temperature dependence given in (16.5), we find for the game time temperature

$$T = \frac{v(T)/(\text{m/s}) - 331}{0.6} \text{ °C} = \frac{3.8}{0.6} \text{ °C} = 6.4 \text{ °C}$$

Discussion:
Before you do this experiment at home and use it to re-calibrate your thermometer, a word of caution is in order. We need to discuss the uncertainties inherent in this measurement. First, we could redo the entire calculation for a time delay of 11.1 seconds, instead of 11.2. You would find that then the temperature would compute to 11.4 degrees Celsius, five degrees higher than what we found from using 11.2 seconds as the delay. Therefore, one tenth of a second makes a big difference in the determined temperature. If one tenth of a second plays such a big role, then we need to ask if the TV signal really gets to the house of the student instantaneously. On the level of a tenth of a second, the answer is no. If the student watches satellite TV, it takes about two tenths of a second for the signal to make it up to the geostationary satellite and down to the student's dish.

In-class exercise: You are in the middle of a concert hall. The hall is 120.0 m deep. What is the time difference between the arrival of the sound directly from the orchestra and the sound reflected from the back of the concert hall?
a) 0.010 s
b) 0.056 s
c) 0.11 s
d) 0.35 s
e) 0.77 s

16.2. Sound Intensity

In the previous chapter, we have discussed intensity of waves and defined it as the power per unit area. We found that for spherical waves the intensity falls as the second power of the distance to the source, $I \propto r^{-2}$, and so we have for the ratio of the intensities

$$\frac{I(r_1)}{I(r_2)} = \left(\frac{r_2}{r_1}\right)^2 . \tag{16.6}$$

This relationship also holds for sound waves. Since the intensity is power per unit area, its physical units are W/m^2. Intensities of sound waves that can be detected by the human ear have a very large range, from whispers as low as 10^{-12} W/m^2 to the output of a jet engine or a rock band at close distance, which can reach 1 W/m^2.

By the way, the oscillations in pressure due to even the loudest sounds at the pain threshold of 10 W/m^2 are only on the order of tens of milli-Pascal. The normal atmospheric air pressure on the other hand is 10^5 Pa. So you see that the relative pressure oscillations are one part in ten billion, even for the loudest sounds. In addition, the oscillations are several orders of magnitude less for the quietest sounds that we can still hear. This should give you a completely new appreciation for the capabilities of your ears.

Since there are many orders of magnitude of intensities that our ears can register, a logarithmic scale is introduced to measure sound intensities. The unit of this scale is the bel (B, after Alexander Graham Bell), but much more commonly the decibel (dB) = 1/10 bel is used. One usually uses the Greek letter β to specify the sound level in this decibel scale, and it is defined as

$$\beta = 10 \log \frac{I}{I_0} \tag{16.7}$$

where $I_0 = 10^{-12}$ W/m^2, which corresponds approximately to the minimum intensity that a human ear can hear. The notation log refers to the logarithm of base 10. (See the math appendix for a refresher on logs, if you need one). So a sound intensity of 1000 times the reference intensity I_0 results in $\beta = 10 \log 1000 \text{ dB} = 10 \cdot 3 \text{ dB} = 30 \text{ dB}$. This sound level corresponds to a whisper not very far from your ear.

Typical sound levels are 30 dB in a quiet home, 40 to 50 dB on a golf course, 60 to 70 dB for street traffic, 90 dB at a railroad crossing, 110 dB in a dance club, 120 dB when operating a jackhammer, and 130 to 150 dB is the noise level on the deck of an aircraft carrier when a fighter jet starts.

Self-Test Opportunity: You hear a sound with level 80.0 dB and you are located 10.0 m from the sound source. What is the power being emitted by the sound source?

Relative Intensity, Dynamic Range

We can also compare two arbitrary intensities to each other and obtain their relative sound level, $\Delta\beta$,

$$\begin{aligned}\Delta\beta &= \beta_2 - \beta_1 \\ &= 10\log\frac{I_2}{I_0} - 10\log\frac{I_1}{I_0} \\ &= 10(\log I_2 - \log I_0) - 10(\log I_1 - \log I_0) \\ &= 10\log I_2 - 10\log I_1\end{aligned}$$

$$\Delta\beta = 10\log\frac{I_2}{I_1} \tag{16.8}$$

The dynamic range is measured in terms of the relative sound level of the loudest to the quietest sound. The dynamic range of a compact disk is approximately 90 dB, whereas it was only about 70 dB for old-fashioned LPs. For all of the high-end loudspeakers and headphones the manufacturers list the dynamic range as well. In general, the rule is the higher the dynamic range, the better. However, the price also increases with the dynamic range as well.

Solved Problem

Solved Problem 16.1: Relative Intensity at the Rock Concert

Two friends attend a rock concert and have brought along a sound level meter. With this device, one of the two friends measures an average intensity of $I_1 = 105.0\text{ dB}$, whereas her friend, who sits 4 rows (= 2.8 m) closer, measures $I_2 = 108.0\text{ dB}$.

Question:
How far away are the two friends from the loudspeakers on the stage?

Answer:

THINK:

We express the relative intensities at the two seats using (16.6) and the relative sound levels at the two seats using (16.8). We can combine these two equations to obtain an expression for relative sound levels at the two seats. Knowing the distance between the two seats, we can then calculate the distance of the seats to the loudspeakers on the stage.

SKETCH:

A sketch of the relative positions of the two friends is shown in Figure 16.6.

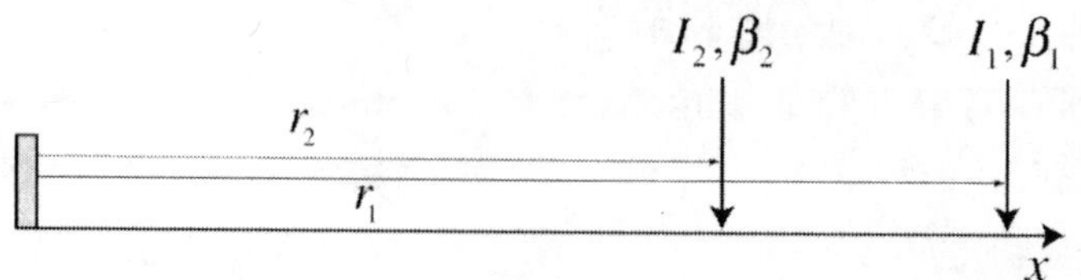

Figure 16.6: Sketch of the relative distances of the two friends from the loudspeakers at a concert.

Solved Problem

RESEARCH:

We call the distance of the first friend from the loudspeakers to be r_1 and the distance of the second friend to the loudspeakers to be r_2. The intensity of the sound at r_1 is I_1 and the intensity of the sound at r_2 is I_2. The sound level at r_1 is β_1 and the sound level at r_2 is β_2. We can express the two intensities in terms of the two distances using (16.6)

$$\frac{I_1}{I_2} = \left(\frac{r_2}{r_1}\right)^2 \qquad (16.9)$$

We can then relate the sound levels at r_1 and r_2 to the sound intensities using (16.8)

$$\beta_2 - \beta_1 = 10\log\frac{I_2}{I_1} \qquad (16.10)$$

Combining (16.9) and (16.10) we get

$$\beta_2 - \beta_1 = \Delta\beta = 10\log\left(\left(\frac{r_1}{r_2}\right)^2\right) = 20\log\left(\frac{r_1}{r_2}\right) \qquad (16.11)$$

The relative sound level $\Delta\beta$ is specified in the problem and we know that

$$r_2 = r_1 - 2.8 \text{ m} \qquad (16.12)$$

so we can solve for the distance r_1 and then obtain r_2.

SIMPLIFY:

Substituting (16.12) into (16.11) gives us

$$\Delta\beta = 20\log\left(\frac{r_1}{r_1 - 2.8 \text{ m}}\right). \qquad (16.13)$$

Rearranging (16.13) gives us

$$10^{\frac{\Delta\beta}{20}} = \frac{r_1}{r_1 - 2.8\text{ m}}. \tag{16.14}$$

We can rewrite (16.14) as

$$(r_1 - 2.8\text{ m})10^{\frac{\Delta\beta}{20}} = r_1 10^{\frac{\Delta\beta}{20}} - (2.8\text{ m})10^{\frac{\Delta\beta}{20}} = r_1. \tag{16.15}$$

We can solve (16.15) for r_1

$$r_1 = \frac{(2.8\text{ m})10^{\frac{\Delta\beta}{20}}}{10^{\frac{\Delta\beta}{20}} - 1}. \tag{16.16}$$

CALCULATE:

Putting in our numerical values, we obtain the distance of the first friend from the loudspeakers

$$r_1 = \frac{(2.8\text{ m})10^{\frac{108.0\text{ dB}-105.0\text{ dB}}{20}}}{10^{\frac{108.0\text{ dB}-105.0\text{ dB}}{20}} - 1} = 9.58726\text{ m}. \tag{16.17}$$

The distance of the second friend is

$$r_2 = 9.58726 - 2.8\text{ m} = 6.78726\text{ m}. \tag{16.18}$$

ROUND:

We report our results to two significant figures

$$\begin{aligned} r_1 &= 9.6\text{ m} \\ r_2 &= 6.8\text{ m} \end{aligned}. \tag{16.19}$$

DOUBLE-CHECK:

To double-check our we put our results for the distances back into (16.11) and check to see that we get our specified sound level difference

$$\Delta\beta = 108.0\text{ dB} - 105.0\text{ dB} = 3.0\text{ dB} = 20\log\left(\frac{9.6\text{ m}}{6.8\text{ m}}\right) = 3.0\text{ dB}. \tag{16.20}$$

Therefore, our answer seems reasonable.

Solved Problem

Limits of Human Hearing

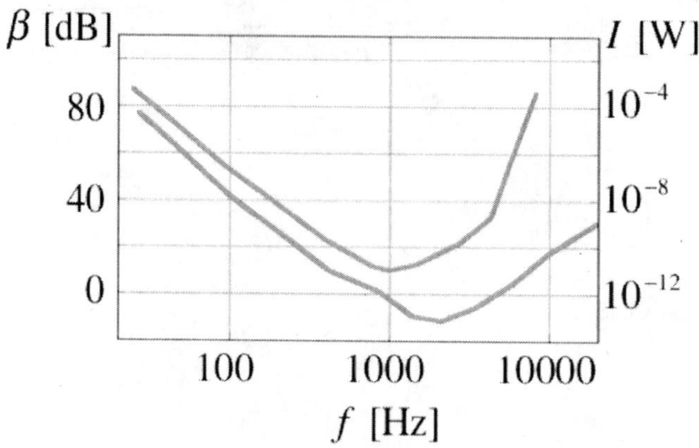

Figure 16.7: Frequency response of human hearing threshold.
Lower curve: teenager; upper curve: retirement age.

Human ears can detect sound waves with frequencies between approximately 20 and 20,000 Hz. Dogs, by the way, can detect even higher frequency sound. We have already stated that the human hearing threshold was used as the anchor for the decibel scale. However, there is strong frequency dependence in the ability of the human ear to detect sound. This frequency dependence of the human hearing threshold is sketched in Figure 16.7. In addition to a dependence on the frequency, there is also a strong dependence of the hearing threshold on the age of the person. The lower curve in Figure 16.7 represents the values for a typical teenager, and the upper curve that of a person at retirement age. While teenagers have no trouble hearing frequencies of 10,000 Hz, retirees cannot hear them at all any more.

The frequencies that we can hear best are around 1,000 Hz. If you hear music, the sound spectrum of this music typically extends over the entire range of human hearing, because all instruments have a characteristic mixture of their base frequencies of the notes played together with several overtones at higher frequencies. If you play this music on your stereo system, and then turn down the volume, you reduce the sound intensity in all frequency ranges approximately uniformly. Depending on how far you turn the volume down, you can then approach sound intensities in the very high and very low frequencies that slip close to or below the threshold of your hearing ability. Then the music sounds flat. In order to correct for this perceived narrowing of the frequency spectrum of the sound, there is a "Loudness" switch on many stereo systems, which enhances the power output in the very low and very high frequencies artificially relative to the rest of the spectrum, giving the music a fuller sound at low volume settings.

A sound level of above 130 dB will cause pain, and above 150 dB, there is significant risk of rupture of the eardrum. In addition, long-term exposure to sound levels of above 120 dB will cause loss of sensitivity of the hearing apparatus in the human ear. Very loud music played over long times should thus be avoided. In addition, where loud noises are part of the work environment, it is necessary to wear ear protection to avoid ear damage.

Example

Example 16.2: Wavelength Range

Now that we know the range of frequencies that the human ear can receive, let us think about the length scales involved.

Question:
What is the range of wavelengths that the human ear is sensitive to?

Answer:
The frequency range of the ear is between 20 and 20,000 Hz. At room temperature the speed of sound is 343 m/s. Wavelength, speed, and frequency are related by

$$v = \lambda f \Rightarrow \lambda = \frac{v}{f}$$

For the lowest frequency we then obtain;

$$\lambda_{\max} = \frac{v}{f_{\min}} = \frac{343\text{ m/s}}{20\text{ Hz}} = 17\text{ m}$$

Since the highest frequency is 1,000 times bigger than the smallest frequency, the smallest wavelength of audible sound is 1,000 times smaller than the value we just calculated. $\lambda_{\min} = 17\text{ mm} = 0.017\text{ m}$.

In-class exercise: A new cell phone ring tone is being used by teenagers. The ring tone is a sound with a frequency of 17 kHz. The hearing threshold for a typical teenager at this frequency is 30 dB while the hearing threshold for an adult at this frequency might be 100 dB (if he/she can hear it at all). Thus, a teenager's cell phone ring is audible only to teenagers and not to adults. How close would this adult need to be to the phone to hear it ring if the teenager can hear it at a distance of 10.0 m?

a) 0.32 cm
b) 4.5 cm
c) 8.9 cm
d) 25 cm
e) 3.0 m

16.3. Sound Interference

Sound waves from two or more sources can interfere in space and time. Let us first address spatial interference. For this we assume two coherent sources of sound, i.e. two sound sources that have the same frequency and are in phase.

In Figure 16.8, we show two loudspeakers emitting identical pure sinusoidal pressure fluctuations in phase. The semicircular rings represent the maxima of the sound waves at some given instant in time. On a horizontal line in front of each loudspeaker, we have drawn the sine curve to show that there is a semicircle wherever the sine has a maximum. The distance between neighboring semicircles emanating form one source is exactly one wavelength, λ. We can clearly see that the semicircles from the different loudspeakers intersect each other. Examples for such intersections are points *A* and *C*. If you count the maxima, you see that both points *A* and *C* are exactly 8λ away from the lower loudspeaker, and *A* is 5λ away from the upper speaker, while *C* is 6λ away. So the path length difference $\Delta r = r_2 - r_1$ is an integer multiple of the wavelength. We can write this down as a general condition for constructive interference at a given spatial point:

$$\Delta r = n\lambda; \text{ for all } n = 0,1,2,3,... \Rightarrow \text{constructive interference} \qquad (16.21)$$

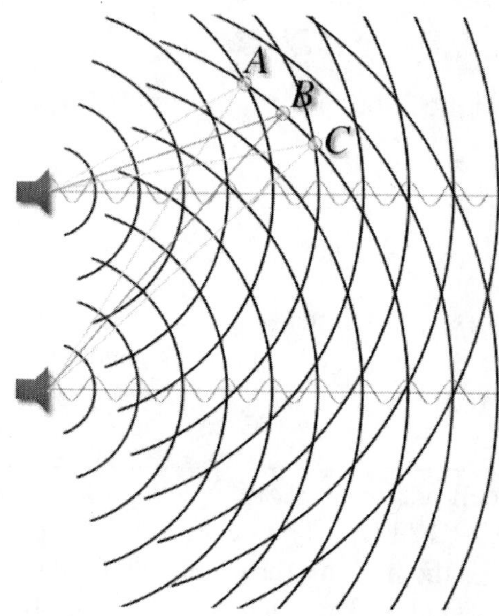

Figure 16.8: Interference of two identical pure sine tones.

Approximately halfway between points *A* and *C* we have marked point *B*. Just like for the other two points, the distance between *B* and the lower speaker is 8λ. But now this point is 5.5λ away from the upper speaker; so the maximum of the sound wave from the lower speaker falls on a minimum of the sound wave from the upper speaker, and they cancel out. This means that at this point we have destructive interference. Of course you have noticed now that the path length difference is a half-integer. And this is also the general condition for destructive interference:

$$\Delta r = (n+\tfrac{1}{2})\lambda; \text{ for all } n = 0,1,2,3,... \Rightarrow \text{destructive interference} \qquad (16.22)$$

In fact, all points of constructive interference fall on lines that are shown in green color in Figure 16.9. These lines are approximately straight lines, and are actually hyperbolas. Lines of destructive interference are shown in red. As the sound waves move away from the speakers, at a fixed point the path length difference still remains, and these lines of constructive and destructive interference remain constant in time. If your ear is positioned on any of the red lines, you hear nothing of this sine tone. The sound is still emitted from both speakers, but the two sound sources cancel each other out. (In this section we just consider an ideal situation where there are no sound reflections.) So why do we not detect these dead zones in our home in front of our stereo speakers when we listen to music?

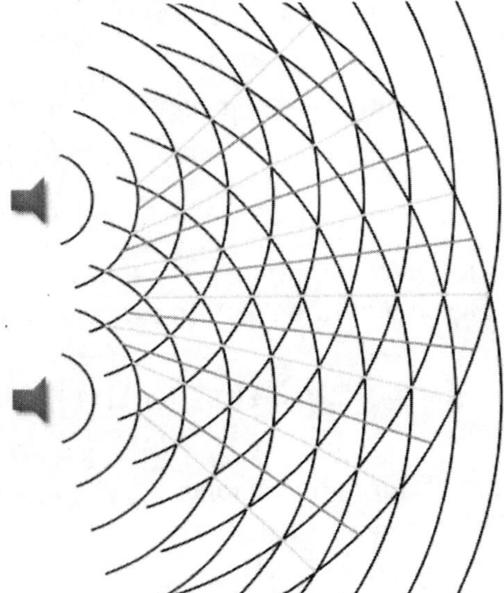

Figure 16.9: Same as previous figure, but now the lines of constructive interference are indicated in green, and the lines of destructive interference in red.

Here is the answer. Of course these lines of interference depend on the wavelength and thus on the frequency. So for different frequencies there are different areas where the sounds cancel each other out, and where they add up maximally. And any note played by any instrument has a rich mixture of different frequencies. So even if one particular frequency cancels, we can still hear all or most of the rest, and so we do not detect what is missing. In addition, all objects in the room scatter and reflect the sound emitted from the loudspeakers to some degree, which makes a possible detection of a dead zone even less likely.

Beats

We can also have interference of two waves in time. To observe this effect, we keep the location of the observer fixed at some arbitrary point x_0 in space and emit two sound waves with slightly different frequencies and the same amplitude,

$$y_1(x_0,t) = A\sin(\kappa_1 x_0 + \omega_1 t + \phi_1) = A\sin(\omega_1 t + \tilde{\phi}_1)$$
$$y_2(x_0,t) = A\sin(\kappa_2 x_0 + \omega_2 t + \phi_2) = A\sin(\omega_2 t + \tilde{\phi}_2)$$

In the second step of each equation, we have used that the product of the wave number and the position is a constant for a given point in space and thus just added it to the phase. We wrote these wave functions down as one-dimensional waves, but we could have done the same in three dimensions. The outcome is the same. For the next step, we will simply set the two phase constants $\tilde{\phi}_1, \tilde{\phi}_2$ to zero. They will only cause a phase shift in our result, but have otherwise no essential role. Therefore, the two time dependent oscillations that form our starting point are

$$\begin{aligned} y_1(x_0,t) &= A\sin(\omega_1 t) \\ y_2(x_0,t) &= A\sin(\omega_2 t) \end{aligned} \tag{16.23}$$

If we do this experiment with two angular frequencies ω_1, ω_2 that are close to each other, we can hear a sound that oscillates in volume as a function of time. Why does this happen?

In order to answer this question, we add the two sine tones of (16.23). If we want to add two sine functions, we can use an addition theorem for trigonometric functions,

$$\sin(\alpha)+\sin(\beta) = 2\cos\left(\tfrac{1}{2}(\alpha-\beta)\right)\sin\left(\tfrac{1}{2}(\alpha+\beta)\right). \tag{16.24}$$

So, we obtain for the addition of our two sine tones

$$\begin{aligned} y(x_0,t) &= y_1(x_0,t) + y_2(x_0,t) \\ &= \sin(\omega_1 t) + \sin(\omega_2 t) \\ &= 2\cos\left(\tfrac{1}{2}(\omega_1-\omega_2)t\right)\sin\left(\tfrac{1}{2}(\omega_1+\omega_2)t\right) \end{aligned} \quad . \tag{16.25}$$

It is more common to write this result in terms of frequencies instead of angular frequencies. Then our result becomes

$$y(x_0,t) = 2\cos\left(2\pi\tfrac{1}{2}(f_1-f_2)t\right)\sin\left(2\pi\tfrac{1}{2}(f_1+f_2)t\right). \tag{16.26}$$

The term $\tfrac{1}{2}(f_1+f_2)$ is simply the average frequency of the two individual frequencies,

$$\bar{f} = \tfrac{1}{2}(f_1+f_2). \tag{16.27}$$

When the cosine has a maximum or minimum value (plus one or minus one) we say that there is a beat; $f_1 - f_2$ is the beat frequency,

$$f_b = |f_1 - f_2|. \tag{16.28}$$

Two questions may arise now: First, what happened to the factor ½ in the cosine function of (16.26), and second, why is the beat frequency defined in terms of an absolute value?

First, we have introduced the absolute value because this ensures that the beat frequency is positive, independent of which of the two frequencies of the two sine tones is larger. For the cosine function, this does not matter at all, because $\cos|\alpha| = \cos\alpha = \cos(-\alpha)$. For the answer to why there is no factor ½, we take a look at Figure 16.10. There we plot two sine tones as a function of time in the upper part. In the middle part, we show the addition of the two functions in magenta. The dashed envelope is given by $\pm 2A\cos\left(2\pi \frac{1}{2}(f_1 - f_2)t\right)$. We can see in Figure 16.10, middle panel, that the amplitude of the addition of the two sine tones reaches a maximum twice for a given complete oscillation of the cosine function. This is perhaps more apparent when we plot the square of the function (16.26), which is after all proportional to the sound intensity, in the lower part of the figure. Hence we define the beat frequency, the frequency at which the volume oscillates up and down, as done in (16.28), properly omitting the factor ½.

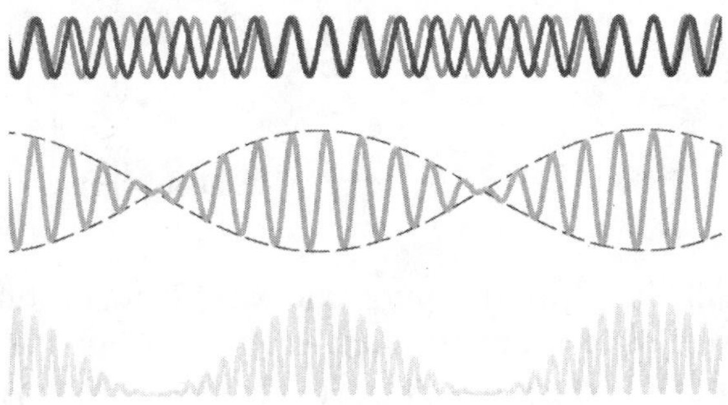

Figure 16.10: Beats of two sine tones. Upper part: the blue and red sine curves have frequencies that are 10% different from each other; middle part: addition of the two sine tones; lower part: square of the sum

For example if we strike two bars on a xylophone, where one bar emits at the proper frequency for the middle-A, 440 Hz, and another one emits a frequency of 438 Hz, we hear two sound volume oscillations per second. This is because the beat frequency is $f_b = |440 - 438|\ \text{Hz} = 2\ \text{Hz}$, and the period of oscillation of the volume is therefore $T_b = 1/f_b = \frac{1}{2}\ \text{s}$. From this example one can understand how useful beats can be in tuning one musical instrument relative to another.

Active Noise Cancellation

We all know that noise is muffled and attenuated, in some materials better than others. For example, if noise bothers you at night, then you can use your pillow to cover your ears. Construction workers and other workers who have to spend extended periods in very loud environments use headphone-like ear protection for this purpose. Of course, this reduces the amplitude of all sounds that you can hear.

If you want to reduce background noise while listening to music, an advanced way to accomplish this is the principle of active noise cancellation. This technique relies also on sound interference and is sketched in Figure 16.11. An external sinusoidal sound wave arrives at the headphone and is recorded by a microphone. A processor inverts the phase of this sound wave and sends out the sound wave with the same frequency and amplitude, but opposite phase. The two sine waves add up (superposition principle!), interfere destructively, and cancel out completely. What is left? Silence. At the same time, the loudspeaker inside the headphones sends out the music you want to hear, and the result is a listening experience that is free of background noise.

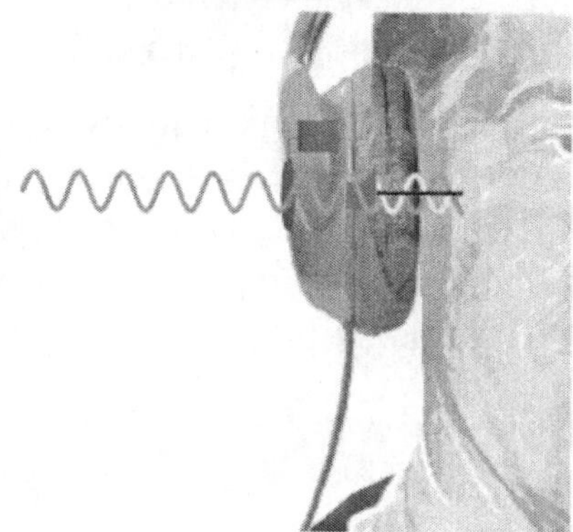

Figure 16.11: Active noise cancellation scheme.

In practice, we never only have just one pure sine wave that constitutes background noise. Instead, many sounds of many different frequencies are mixed. In particular, the high-frequency sounds then constitute a problem for the active noise cancellation scheme. However, this method works very well for periodic low frequency sounds, such as the engine noise from airliners. Another application is inside cars, where some luxury automobiles rely on active noise cancellation techniques to reduce wind and tire noise.

16.4. Doppler Effect

We've all had an experience at a railroad crossing or while watching a car race, whereby an approaching train sounds its warning horn or a race car engine emits a roar, and as the train or car moves past our position the sound pitch changes from a higher frequency to a lower one. This is called the Doppler effect, which we now discuss.

In order to gain a qualitative understanding of the Doppler effect, consult **Error! Reference source not found.**. First let's look at the left column. A stationary sound source emits spherical waves that travel outward. In this figure, we have sketched the time evolution of these radial waves at six equally spaced points in time, from top to bottom. The left column of this figure shows the situation for a stationary source: the maxima of the sine wave radiate outward as circles, where we have color coded the corresponding wave maxima in each frame, from yellow to red.

As soon as the source moves, different maxima of the same sound waves are emitted from different points in space. However, from these points in space these maxima again travel outward as circles. This is shown in the center-left and center-right columns of **Error! Reference source not found.**. The difference between these two columns is only the speed with which the source of the sound waves moves from left to right. In each case, you can see a bunching-up of the sound waves in front of the emitter, on the right side in this case. This bunching-up effect is stronger with higher source velocity and is the entire key to understanding the Doppler effect. An observer located to the right of the source, that is to say with the source moving towards her, experiences more wave fronts per time unit passing her ear and thus a higher frequency. An observer located to the left of the moving source, with the source moving away from her, experiences fewer wave fronts per time unit an thus a reduced frequency.

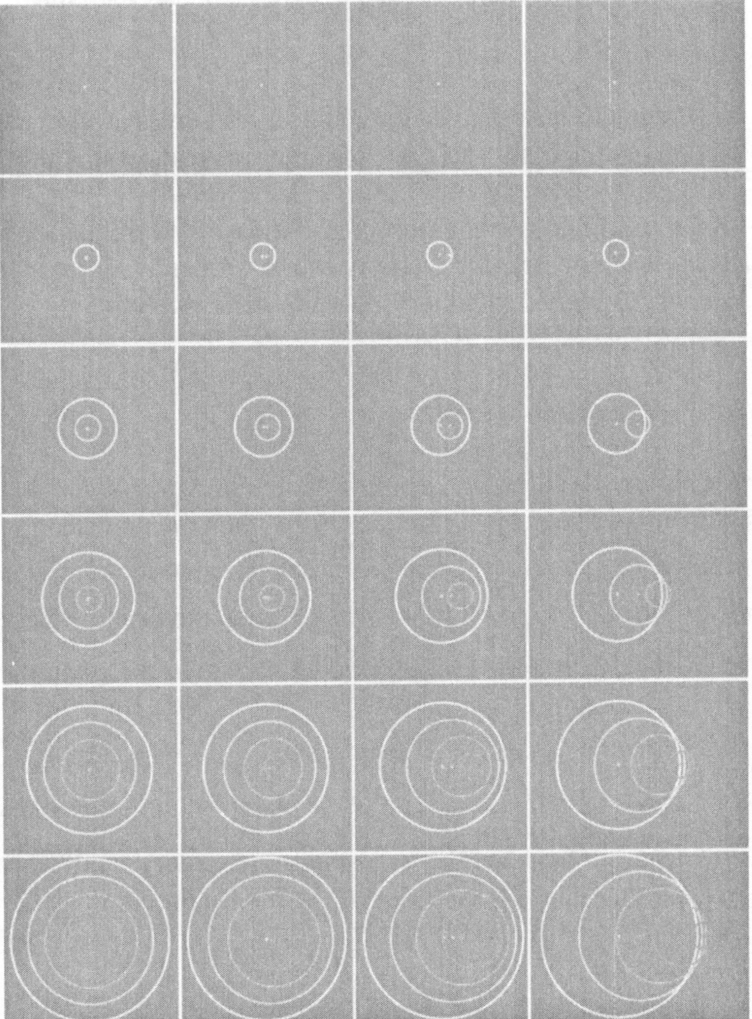

Figure 16.12: Doppler effect.

Quantitatively, the observed frequency, f_o, is given as

$$f_o = f \frac{v_{\text{sound}}}{v_{\text{sound}} \pm v_{\text{source}}}, \qquad (16.29)$$

where f is the frequency of the sound as emitted in the frame of the source, and v_{sound} and v_{source} are the speeds of sound and the sound source, respectively. The upper sign $(+)$ refers to the case where the source moves away from the observer, and the lower sign $(-)$ to the case where the source moves towards the observer.

The source can also be stationary and the observer can move. In this case, the observed frequency is given by

$$f_o = f\frac{v_{\text{sound}} \mp v_{\text{observer}}}{v_{\text{sound}}} = f\left(1 \mp \frac{v_{\text{observer}}}{v_{\text{sound}}}\right) \tag{16.30}$$

The upper sign ($-$) refers to the case where the observer moves away from the source, and the lower sign ($+$) to the case where the observer moves towards the source.

In each case, moving source or moving observer, the observed frequency is lower than the source frequency when observer and source move further away from each other, and the observed frequency is higher when they move toward each other.

Derivation 16.2: Doppler Shift

Let's begin with an observer at rest and a sound source moving toward it. If the sound source is at rest and emits a sound with frequency f, then the wavelength is $\lambda = v_{\text{sound}} / f$, which is also the distance between two successive wave crests. If the sound source moves toward the observer with speed v_{source}, then the distance between two successive crests as seen by the observer is reduced to

$$\lambda_o = \frac{v_{\text{sound}} - v_{\text{source}}}{f}$$

Using again the relationship between the wavelength, frequency, and (fixed!) speed of sound, $v_{\text{sound}} = \lambda f$, we then find for the frequency of the sound as detected by the observer:

$$f_o = \frac{v_{\text{sound}}}{\lambda_o} = f\frac{v_{\text{sound}}}{v_{\text{sound}} - v_{\text{source}}}.$$

This result proves one case of (16.29). The other sign is obtained by reversing the sign of the source velocity vector.

We leave the derivation of the case of the moving observer as an exercise.

Derivation

The Doppler radar that we all know from the evening news weather report utilizes the Doppler effect. Moving raindrops change the reflected the radar waves to different frequencies and thus are visible to the Doppler radar. (However the Doppler shift for electromagnetic waves such as radar are governed by a different formula than those given for sound.) Doppler radar is also used to detect rotation (and possible tornados) in a thunderstorm by finding regions with motion both towards and away from the observer. Another common utilization of the velocity dependence of the Doppler effect are radar speed detectors employed by police forces around the world.

Self-Test Opportunity: You are waiting at a train crossing. A train traveling at 80.0 mph crosses in front you. The train when at rest has a horn that operates with a frequency of 440.0 Hz. What is the shift in frequency from the approaching train to the departing train?

Mach Cone

We have still left to cover the right-most column of **Error! Reference source not found.**. In this column the source speed exceeds the speed of sound. As you can see from the figure, in this case the origin of the next wave crest lies outside the circle formed by the previous wave crest at the time of emission of the next one.

In the left part of Figure 16.13 we show a supersonic (= speed greater than speed of sound) sound source and the successive wave crests it emitted. You can see that all of these circles form tangent lines that have an angle θ_M with the direction of the velocity vector (in this case the horizontal). This particular accumulation of wave fronts produces a large, abrupt, conical-shaped wave called a shock wave. The so-called Mach-angle of the cone is given by

$$\theta_M = \arcsin\left(\frac{v_{\text{sound}}}{v_{\text{source}}}\right) \tag{16.31}$$

This formula is only valid for source speeds that exceed the sound speed; and in the limit that the source speed is equal to the sound speed, θ_M approaches 90 degrees. The bigger the source speed, the smaller is the Mach angle.

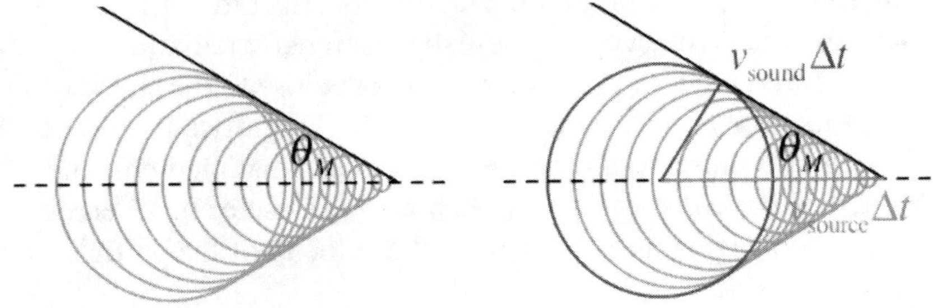

Figure 16.13: Mach cone.

Derivation 16.3: Mach Angle

The derivation of (16.31) is quite straightforward if we examine the right part of Figure 16.13. There we show the circle of the wave crest that was formed at some initial time $t = 0$, but now at a later time Δt. The radius of this circle at time Δt is $v_{\text{sound}}\Delta t$ and is shown by the blue straight line. Note that the radius makes a 90-degree angle with the tangent line, indicated in black. However, during the same time Δt, the source has moved a distance of $v_{\text{source}}\Delta t$, which is indicated by the red line in the figure.

Consequently, the red, blue, and black lines in the figure form a right triangle. Then the sine of the Mach angle θ_M is by definition of the sine function:

$$\sin\theta_M = (v_{\text{sound}}\Delta t)/(v_{\text{source}}\Delta t) .$$

Canceling out the common factor Δt and taking the inverse sine on both sides of this equation then yields the result of (16.31).

Derivation

Interestingly, Mach cones and shock waves can be detected in all kinds of physical systems for all kinds of waves. Surface waves on shallow water have relatively low wave speeds, as discussed in the previous chapter. So motorboats can relatively easily create shock waves by moving across the water surface at high speeds. From these triangular bow waves you can determine the speed of sound of the surface waves on a lake, if you know the speed of the boat.

The speed of sound in atomic nuclei is approximately 1/3 of the speed of light. Since we can collide nuclei at speeds of very close to the speed of light, one can expect that shock waves are even created in this environment. Some computer simulations have shown that this effect is present in nuclear collisions, but definite experimental proof has been difficult to obtain.

Finally, it would seem even more unlikely that one could observe shock waves and Mach cones with light, since the speed of light in vacuum is the maximum speed possible in nature, and thus the source velocity cannot exceed the speed of light in vacuum. When the Russian physicist Cerenkov proposed exactly this effect in the 1960s, it was dismissed as impossible. However, this so-called Cerenkov radiation can be emitted when a source such as a high-energy proton moves at close to the speed of light and enters a medium, like water, where the speed of light is significantly lower. Then this emitter can indeed move faster than the speed of light in that medium, and a "Mach cone" can form. Modern particle detectors actually now make use of this Cerenkov radiation, and from the emission angle one can calculate the velocity of the particle that emitted the radiation.

Example

Example 16.3: The Concorde

The speed of a supersonic aircraft is often given in Mach number, M. A speed of Mach 1 ($M = 1$) means that the aircraft is traveling at the speed of sound. A speed of Mach 2 ($M = 2$) means that the aircraft is traveling at twice the speed of sound. The now retired Concorde supersonic airliner, shown in Figure 16.14, cruised at 60,000 feet, where the speed of sound is 295 m/s (661 miles per hour). The maximum cruise speed of the Concorde was Mach 2.04 ($M = 2.04$). At this speed, what was the angle of the resulting Mach cone produced by the Concorde?

Example

Figure 16.14: The supersonic jetliner Concorde takes off.

The angle of Mach cone is given by (16.31)

$$\theta_M = \arcsin\left(\frac{v_{\text{sound}}}{v_{\text{source}}}\right).$$

The speed of the source in this case is the Concorde, which is traveling at a speed of

$$v_{\text{source}} = Mv_{\text{sound}} = 2.04v_{\text{sound}}.$$

Thus, we can write the angle of the Mach cone as

$$\theta_M = \arcsin\left(\frac{v_{\text{sound}}}{Mv_{\text{sound}}}\right) = \arcsin\left(\frac{1}{M}\right).$$

For the Concorde we then have

$$\theta_M = \arcsin\left(\frac{1}{2.04}\right) = 0.512 \text{ rad} = 29.4°.$$

In-class exercise: What is the maximum cruise speed of the Concorde when it is cruising at 60,000 ft?
a) 665 mph
b) 834 mph
c) 1350 mph
d) 2130 mph
e) 3450 mph

16.5. Resonance

Basically all musical instruments rely on the excitation of resonances in the instrument or parts of the instrument to generate sound waves of discrete, reproducible, and pre-determined frequencies. Of course, no discussion of sound could possibly be complete without a discussion of musical tones. Which frequencies make which tones?

Tones

Which frequencies make which tones? The answer to this simple question is not so simple and has changed over time. The current tonal scale dates back to 1722, to Johann Sebastian Bach, with the publication of his work "Das wohltemperierte Klavier". We will not give you a historical discussion at this point, but just state the currently accepted values.

The names of the tones associated with the white keys of the piano are: A, B, C, D, E, F, G. The first C from the left side gets the name C1. And, strangely perhaps, the note below it is B0. So the sequence of tones for the white keys from left to right on the piano is: A0, B0, C1, D1, E1, F1, G1, A1, B1, C2, D2, ..., A7, B7, C8. The scale is anchored with the middle-A (A4) at precisely 440 Hz. The next higher A (A5) is an octave higher, which means that it has exactly twice the frequency, 880 Hz. Between these two A's are 11 halftones: A-sharp/B-flat, B, C, C-sharp/D-flat, D, D-sharp/E-flat, E, F, F-sharp/G-flat, G, G-sharp/A-flat. Ever since the work of J.S. Bach we thus use these 11 halftones to divide the octave into exactly 12 equal intervals, all of which are different by the same factor. This means that we have to find a factor that will give the number of 2 when multiplied with itself 12 times. This factor is: $2^{1/12} = 1.0595$. Now we can generate all frequencies by successive multiplication with this factor. Example: D (D5) is 5 steps up, $1.0595^5 \cdot 440$ Hz = 587.4 Hz. We can always obtain notes in other octaves by multiplication or division of the frequencies by factors of 2. Example: the next higher note D (D6) can be found at a frequency of $2 \cdot 587.4 \text{ Hz} = 1174.8 \text{ Hz}$.

Human voices have average ranges as follows:

- Bass: E2 (82 Hz) to G4 (392 Hz)
- Baritone: A2 (110 Hz) to A4 (440 Hz)
- Tenor: D3 (147 Hz) to B4 (494 Hz)
- Alto: G3 (196 Hz) to F5 (698 Hz)
- Soprano: C4 (262 Hz) to C6 (1046 Hz)

Thus basically all songs sung by humans exist in a range of one order of magnitude in frequency, between 100 and 1000 Hz.

Of course, no human voice and practically no musical instrument generate a pure single-frequency sine tone. Instead, what makes musical tones interesting is a rich admixture of overtones that gives each instrument and each human voice its own characteristics. For string instruments this admixture is influenced by the wooden shell surrounding the strings.

Touch-tone phones have almost completely replaced dial phones in the United States and rely on sounds of pre-assigned frequencies. For each key that you press on the phone, two relatively pure sine-tones are generated. Figure 16.15 shows you the arrangement of the matrix that determines the tone. Each row of keys has the same tone that is displayed to its right, and each column of keys has the tone that is displayed under it. So if you press the "2"-key, for example, you get the frequencies 697 Hz and 1336 Hz played for you.

Figure 16.15: Touch-tone phone.

Half-Open and Open Pipes

We have already covered waves on strings in the last chapter. These form the basis for a all string instruments. What is essential in this context is that standing waves can only be excited on strings at discrete resonance frequencies. Most percussion instruments, like drums, also work on the principle of exciting discrete resonances. However, the wave forms are typically two-dimensional and are much more complicated.

Wind instruments use half-open or open pipes to generate sounds. A half-open pipe is a pipe that is open at only one end and closed on the other; an open pipe is open on both ends. Which resonance frequencies can be generated this way? Let us start with an experiment that you can do at home. You can generate a sound by blowing air over the opening of a bottle, as shown in Figure 16.16. (This example is a qualitative one because of the non-cylindrical exotic shape of the container.) If you have ever done this, you will remember that the sound pitch is higher if the bottle is fuller. And an empty liter bottle produces a lower sound than an empty half-liter bottle, like the one used in Figure 16.16.

Figure 16.16: Exciting a resonant sound.

This system is a (rather poor, but readily available!) approximation for a half-open pipe.

The air molecules at the bottom of the pipe are in contact with the wall and thus do not vibrate. Therefore the closed end of the pipe constitutes a node in the sound wave. The other end is open and the air molecules can vibrate freely. By blowing air over the end of the pipe, a resonant sound wave is excited which has an anti-node at the open end of the pipe and a node at the close end.

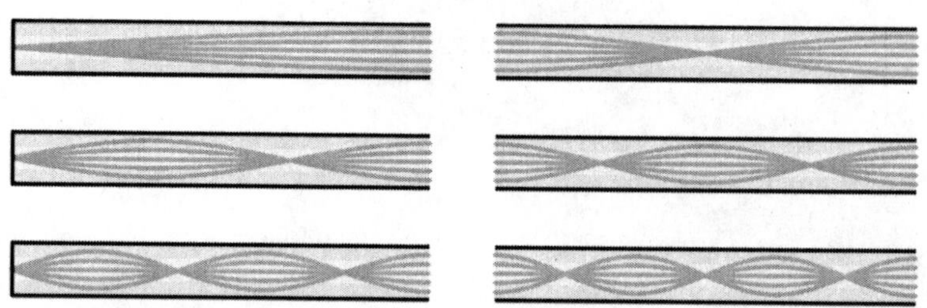

Figure 16.17: Left: standing waves in half-open pipes; right: standing waves in open pipes. The red lines represent the sound amplitude at various times.

Figure 16.17 shows on the left some of the possible standing waves in a half-open pipe. In the top pipe, we show the standing wave with the largest wavelength, where the first anti-node coincides with the length of the pipe. Since the distance between a node and the first anti-node is ¼ of a wavelength, this resonance condition corresponds to $L = \frac{1}{4}\lambda$, where L is the length of the pipe. Below this case we show the next smaller possible wavelengths, where the second or third anti-nodes fall on the pipe opening, and $L = \frac{3}{4}\lambda$ and $L = \frac{5}{4}\lambda$, respectively. In general, the condition for a resonant standing wave in a half-open pipe is thus

$$L = \frac{2n-1}{4}\lambda \text{ for } n = 1,2,3,... \tag{16.32}$$

Solving this equation for the possible wavelengths results in

$$\lambda_n = \frac{4L}{2n-1} \text{ for } n = 1,2,3,... \tag{16.33}$$

and by using $v = \lambda f$ we obtain the possible frequencies

$$f_n = (2n-1)\frac{v}{4L} \text{ for } n = 1,2,3,.... \tag{16.34}$$

On the right side of Figure 16.17, we display the longest wavelength solutions for standing waves in open pipes. In this case we have anti-nodes at both ends of the pipe, and the condition for a resonant standing wave is

$$L = \frac{n}{2}\lambda \text{ for } n = 1, 2, 3, \ldots \tag{16.35}$$

This relation results in wavelengths and frequencies of

$$\lambda_n = \frac{2L}{n} \text{ for } n = 1, 2, 3, \ldots \tag{16.36}$$

$$f_n = n\frac{v}{2L} \text{ for } n = 1, 2, 3, \ldots \tag{16.37}$$

For both half-open and open pipes, the fundamental frequency is obtained for $n = 1$. For a half-open pipe the first harmonic ($n = 2$) is three times as high as the fundamental frequency. However, for an open pipe the first harmonic ($n = 2$) is twice as high as the fundamental frequency, or one octave higher.

Self-Test Opportunity: Estimate the fundamental frequency of the resonant sound induced by blowing on the open end of a ½ liter bottle as illustrated in Figure 16.16.

Example 16.4: Organ

Church-organs are built on the principle of creating standing waves in pipes. If you have ever looked around in an old cathedral, it is very likely that you have seen an impressive collection of organ pipes, like that in Figure 16.18.

Figure 16.18: Pipes of a church organ.

Question:
If you need to build an organ whose fundamental frequencies cover the frequency range of a piano, from A0 to C8, what is the range of the lengths of the pipes that you need to use?

Answer:
The frequencies for A0 and C8 are: $f(\text{A0}) = 27.5 \text{ Hz}, f(\text{C8}) = 7902 \text{ Hz}$. The fundamental frequency for a half-open pipe and an open pipe are according to (16.34) and (16.37):

Example

$$f_{1,\text{half-open}} = \frac{v}{4L},\ f_{1,\text{open}} = \frac{v}{2L}$$

This means that the pipes for the open case have to be twice as long as the corresponding half-open ones for the same frequency. The lengths of pipes needed for the highest and lowest frequencies in the case of half-open pipes are

$$L_{\text{half-open}}(\text{C8}) = \frac{v}{4f(\text{C8})} = \frac{343 \text{ m/s}}{31608 \text{ Hz}} = 0.0108 \text{ m}$$

$$L_{\text{half-open}}(\text{A0}) = \frac{v}{4f(\text{A0})} = \frac{343 \text{ m/s}}{110 \text{ Hz}} = 3.118 \text{ m}$$

Note: Real organ pipes indeed can be up to 10 feet long. For the shortest organ pipes the part that produces the standing wave can be as short as half of an inch. However, the base of the pipe alone is approximately one half of a foot in length, and so the shortest pipes that one typically observes in a church organ are at least that long.

What We Have Learned / Exam Study Guide

- Sound is a longitudinal pressure wave.
- The speed of sound in air at normal pressure and temperature is 343 m/s.
- In general, the speed of sound in a solid is given by $v = \sqrt{E/\rho}$ and in a liquid or gas is given by $v = \sqrt{B/\rho}$.
- If two sine waves with equal amplitudes and slightly different frequencies are present at the same time, the results are beats with a beat frequency of $f_b = |f_1 - f_2|$.
- The frequency observed by a stationary observer is $f_o = f\dfrac{v_{\text{sound}}}{v_{\text{sound}} \pm v_{\text{source}}}$, where f is the frequency of the sound as emitted in the frame of the source, and v_{sound} and v_{source} are the speeds of sound and the sound source, respectively. The upper sign $(+)$ refers to the case where the source moves away from the observer, and the lower sign $(-)$ to the case where the source moves towards the observer.
- The source can also be stationary and the observer can move. In this case, the observed frequency is given by $f_o = f\dfrac{v_{\text{sound}} \mp v_{\text{observer}}}{v_{\text{sound}}} = f\left(1 \mp \dfrac{v_{\text{observer}}}{v_{\text{sound}}}\right)$. Now the upper sign $(-)$ refers to the case where the observer moves away from the source, and the lower sign $(+)$ to the case where the observer moves towards the source.
- The Mach angle of the shockwave formed by sources moving at supersonic

speeds is $\theta_M = \arcsin\left(\frac{v_{\text{sound}}}{v_{\text{source}}}\right)$.

- The relationship between the length of an half-open pipe and the wavelengths of possible standing waves is $L = \frac{2n-1}{4}\lambda$ for $n = 1, 2, \ldots$; for open pipes we find $L = \frac{n}{2}\lambda$ for $n = 1, 2, \ldots$.

Additional Solved Problems

Solved Problem 16.2: Doppler Shift

Question:
A person in a parked car sounds his horn. The frequency of the sound from his horn is 290.0 Hz. A driver in an approaching car measures the frequency of the sound coming from the parked to be 316.0 Hz. What is the speed of the approaching car?

Answer:

THINK:

The frequency of the measured sound in the approaching car will be Doppler shifted. Knowing the emitted frequency f, the observed frequency f_o, and speed of sound v_{sound} we can calculate the speed of the approaching car.

SKETCH:

A sketch of the observing vehicle moving toward the stationary sound-emitting vehicle is shown in Figure 16.19.

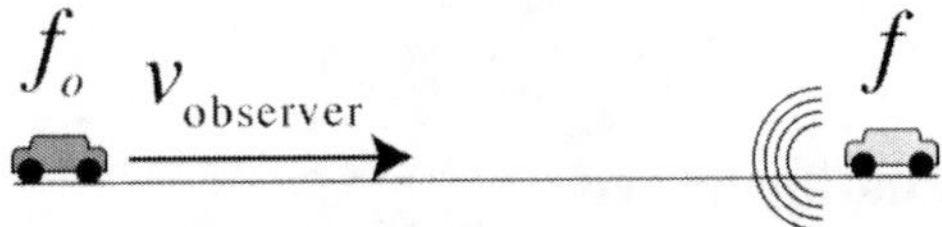

Figure 16.19: An observing vehicle approaching a vehicle sounding its horn.

RESEARCH:

The frequency of sound measured by a moving observer f_o resulting from a sound with frequency f emitted by a stationary observer is given by

$$f_o = f\left(1 + \frac{v_{\text{observer}}}{v_{\text{sound}}}\right) \tag{16.38}$$

where v_{observer} is the speed that the observer approaches emitting vehicle and v_{sound} is the speed of sound in air.

Solved Problem

Solved Problem

SIMPLIFY:

We can rearrange (16.38) to obtain

$$\frac{f_o}{f} - 1 = \frac{v_{\text{observer}}}{v_{\text{sound}}}. \tag{16.39}$$

From this equation we can solve for the speed of the moving observer

$$v_{\text{observer}} = v_{\text{sound}}\left(\frac{f_o}{f} - 1\right). \tag{16.40}$$

CALCULATE:

Putting in our numerical values we get

$$v_{\text{observer}} = (343 \text{ m/s})\left(\frac{316.0 \text{ Hz}}{290.0 \text{ Hz}} - 1\right) = 30.7517 \text{ m/s}. \tag{16.41}$$

ROUND:

We report our result to three significant figures

$$v_{\text{observer}} = 30.8 \text{ m/s}.$$

DOUBLE-CHECK:

A speed of 30.8 m/s (= 68.9 mph) is reasonable for a car.

Solved Problem

Solved Problem 16.3: Standing Wave

Question:

A standing sound wave is set up in a closed pipe of length 0.410 m as shown in Figure 16.20. What is the frequency of this sound?

Figure 16.20: A standing sound wave in a pipe.

Answer:

THINK:

First we recognize that the standing sound wave shown in Figure 16.20 corresponds to a standing sound wave in a pipe that is closed on the left end and open on the right end. Thus, we are dealing with a standing sound wave in a half-open pipe. Four nodes are visible. Combining these observations with the speed of sound we can calculate the frequency of the standing wave.

SKETCH:

A sketch of the standing wave with the pipe drawn in and the nodes marked is shown in Figure 16.21.

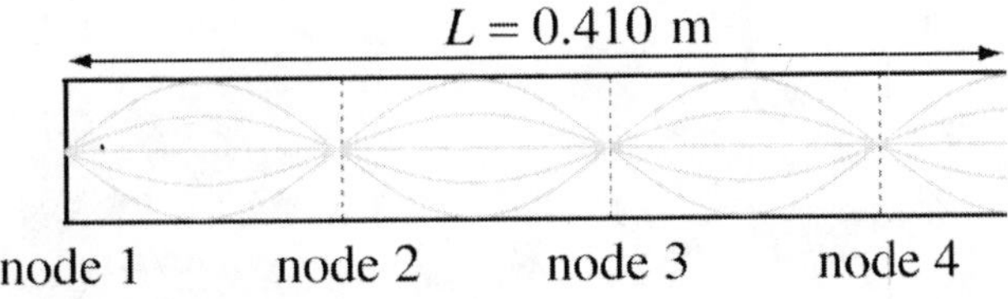

Figure 16.21: A standing sound wave in a half-open pipe with four nodes.

RESEARCH:

The frequency of this standing sound wave in a half-open pipe is given by

$$f_n = (2n-1)\frac{v}{4L} \tag{16.42}$$

where $n = 4$ is the number of nodes. The speed of sound is $v = 343$ m/s and the length of the pipe is $L = 0.410$ m.

SIMPLIFY:

We can write (16.42) as

$$f_{n=4} = \left((4\cdot 2)-1\right)\frac{v}{4L} = \frac{7v}{4L}. \tag{16.43}$$

CALCULATE:

Putting in our numerical values we get

$$f = \frac{7\cdot 343 \text{ m/s}}{4\cdot 0.410 \text{ m}} = 1464.02 \text{ Hz}$$

ROUND:

We report our result to three significant figures

$$f = 1460 \text{ Hz}.$$

Solved Problem

DOUBLE-CHECK:

This frequency is well within the range of human hearing and just above the range of frequencies produced by the human voice. Therefore our answer seems reasonable.

Mathematics Primer

Notation:
The letters a, b, c, x, y, and z are symbols used for real numbers.
The letters i, j, m, and n are used for integer numbers.
The Greek letters α, β, and γ are used for angles and are measured in radians.

1. Algebra

1.1 Basics

Factors:

$$ax + bx + cx = (a + b + c)x \tag{A.1}$$

$$(a + b)^2 = a^2 + 2ab + b^2 \tag{A.2}$$

$$(a - b)^2 = a^2 - 2ab + b^2 \tag{A.3}$$

$$(a + b)(a - b) = a^2 - b^2 \tag{A.4}$$

Quadratic equation:
An equation of the form

$$ax^2 + bx + c = 0 \tag{A.5}$$

for given values of a, b, and c has the two solutions:

$$x = \frac{-b + \sqrt{b^2 - 4ac}}{2a} \quad \text{and} \quad x = \frac{-b - \sqrt{b^2 - 4ac}}{2a} \tag{A.6}$$

The solutions of this quadratic equation are called "roots". The roots will be real numbers, if $b^2 \geq 4ac$.

1.2 Exponents

If a is a number, then a^n means taking the product of a with itself n times:

$$a^n = \underbrace{a \times a \times a \times \ldots \times a}_{n \text{ factors}} \quad \text{(A.7)}$$

The number n is called the exponent. However, an exponent does not necessarily need to be a positive number or an integer. Any real number x can be used as an exponent.

$$a^{-x} = \frac{1}{a^x} \quad \text{(A.8)}$$

$$a^0 = 1 \quad \text{(A.9)}$$

$$a^1 = a \quad \text{(A.10)}$$

Roots:

$$a^{\frac{1}{2}} = \sqrt{a} \quad \text{(A.11)}$$

$$a^{\frac{1}{n}} = \sqrt[n]{a} \quad \text{(A.12)}$$

Multiplication and division:

$$a^x a^y = a^{x+y} \quad \text{(A.13)}$$

$$\frac{a^x}{a^y} = a^{x-y} \quad \text{(A.14)}$$

$$\left(a^x\right)^y = a^{xy} \quad \text{(A.15)}$$

1.3 Logarithms

The logarithm is the inverse function of the exponentiation function of the previous section.

$$y = a^x \Leftrightarrow x = \log_a y \quad \text{(A.16)}$$

The notation $\log_a y$ indicates the logarithm of y with respect to the base a. Since exponentiation and logarithm are inverse functions of each other, we can also write the identity:

$$x = \log_a(a^x) = a^{\log_a x} \text{ for any base } a \quad \text{(A.17)}$$

The two bases most commonly used are base 10, "common logarithm base", and base e, "natural logarithm base". The numerical value of e is:

$$e = 2.718281828\ldots \quad \text{(A.18)}$$

Base 10:

$$y = 10^x \Leftrightarrow x = \log_{10} y \quad \text{(A.19)}$$

Base e:

$$y = e^x \Leftrightarrow x = \ln y \tag{A.20}$$

Please note that we follow the common notation convention of using $\ln$ for the logarithm with respect to the base e.

The rules for calculating with logarithms follow from the rules of calculating with exponents:

$$\log(ab) = \log a + \log b \tag{A.21}$$

$$\log\left(\frac{a}{b}\right) = \log a - \log b \tag{A.22}$$

$$\log(a^x) = x \log a \tag{A.23}$$

$$\log 1 = 0 \tag{A.24}$$

These rules are valid for any base, and thus we have omitted the subscript indicating the base.

1.4 Linear Equations

The general form of a linear equation is

$$y = ax + b \tag{A.25}$$

with a and b constant numbers. The graph of y versus x is a straight line, a is the slope of this line, and b is the offset; see Figure A.1.

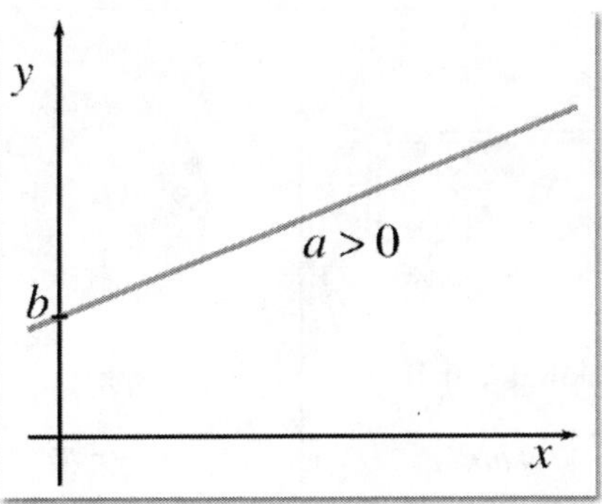

Figure A.1: Graphical representation of a linear equation.

The slope of the line can be calculated by inserting two different values x_1 and x_2 into the linear equation and calculating the resulting values y_1 and y_2:

$$a = \frac{y_2 - y_1}{x_2 - x_1} = \frac{\Delta y}{\Delta x} \tag{A.26}$$

If $a = 0$, then the line will be horizontal; if $a > 0$, then the line will rise as shown in the example of Figure A.1; if $a < 0$, then the line will fall.

2. Geometry

2.1 Geometrical Shapes in Two Dimensions

In this section we list the area, A, and perimeter length or circumference, C, of common two-dimensional geometrical objects.

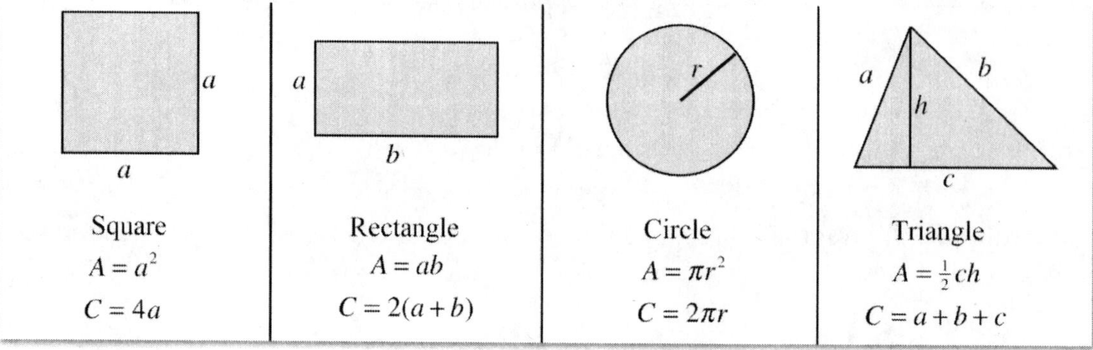

Figure A.2: Area, A, and perimeter length, C, for a square, rectangle, circle, and triangle.

2.2 Geometrical Shapes in Three Dimensions

In this section we list the volume, V, and surface area, A, of common three-dimensional geometrical objects.

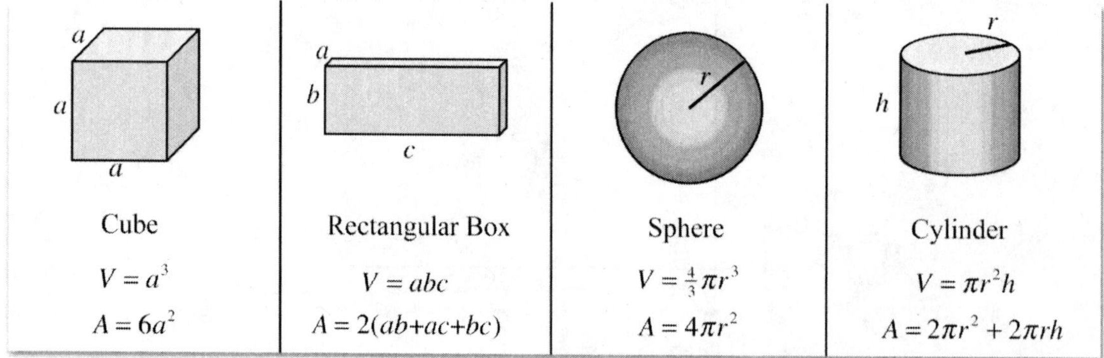

Figure A.3: Volume, V, and surface area, A, for a cube, rectangular box, sphere, and cylinder.

3. Trigonometry

It is important to note that for the following all angles need to be measured in radians!

3.1 Right Triangles

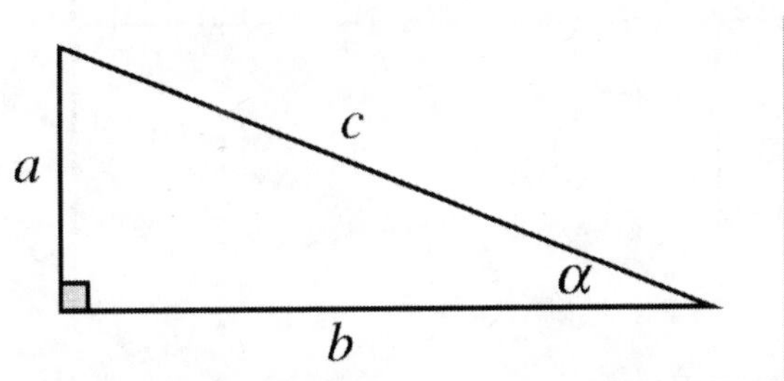

Figure A.4: Definition of the side lengths *a*, *b*, *c*, and angles for the right triangle.

A right triangle is a triangle for which one of the three angles is a right angle, i.e. an angle of exactly 90 degrees ($=\pi/2$). The hypotenuse is the side opposite to the 90-degree angle (indicated by the small blue square in the figure). Conventionally, one uses the letter c to mark the hypotenuse.

Pythagoras' Theorem:

$$a^2 + b^2 = c^2 \tag{A.27}$$

Definition of trigonometric functions:

$$\sin\alpha = \frac{a}{c} = \frac{\text{opposite side}}{\text{hypotenuse}} \tag{A.28}$$

$$\cos\alpha = \frac{b}{c} = \frac{\text{adjacent side}}{\text{hypotenuse}} \tag{A.29}$$

$$\tan\alpha = \frac{\sin\alpha}{\cos\alpha} = \frac{a}{b} \tag{A.30}$$

$$\cot\alpha = \frac{\cos\alpha}{\sin\alpha} = \frac{1}{\tan\alpha} = \frac{b}{a} \tag{A.31}$$

Inverse trigonometric functions:

$$\sin^{-1}\frac{a}{c} \equiv \arcsin\frac{a}{c} = \alpha \tag{A.32}$$

$$\cos^{-1}\frac{b}{c} \equiv \arccos\frac{b}{c} = \alpha \tag{A.33}$$

$$\tan^{-1}\frac{a}{b} \equiv \arctan\frac{a}{b} = \alpha \tag{A.34}$$

$$\cot^{-1}\frac{b}{a} \equiv \text{arccot}\frac{b}{a} = \alpha \tag{A.35}$$

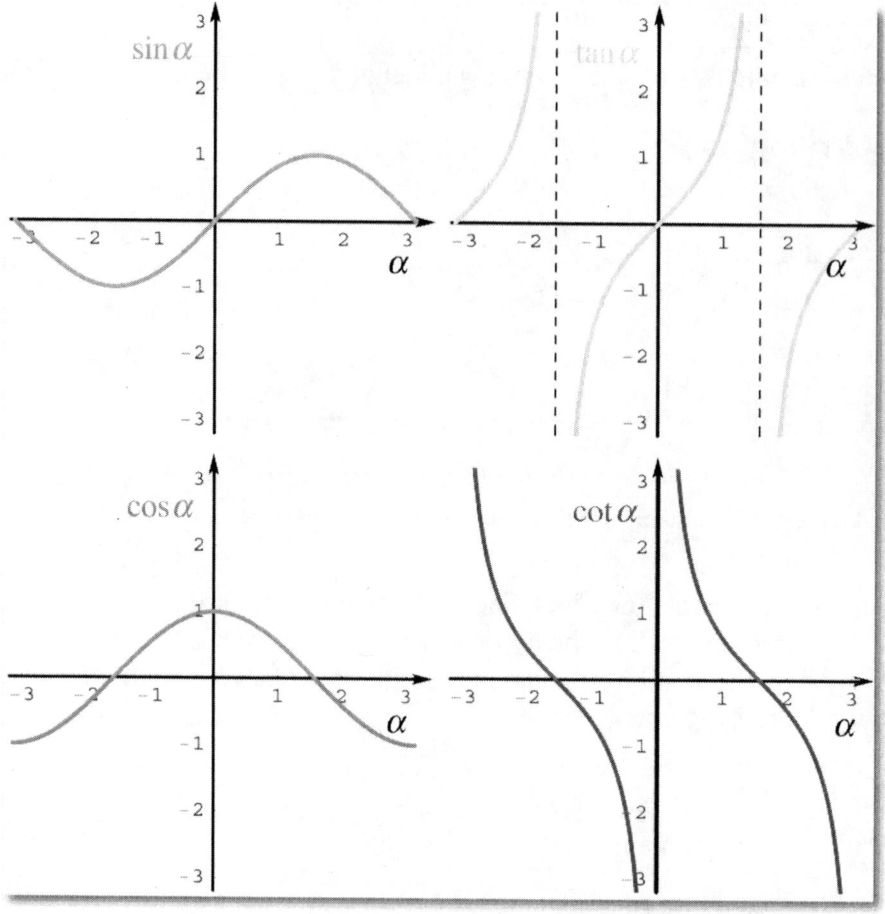

Figure A.5: The trigonometric functions.

All trigonometric functions are periodic:

$$\sin(\alpha + 2\pi) = \sin\alpha \quad \text{(A.36)}$$

$$\cos(\alpha + 2\pi) = \cos\alpha \quad \text{(A.37)}$$

$$\tan(\alpha + \pi) = \tan\alpha \quad \text{(A.38)}$$

$$\cot(\alpha + \pi) = \cot\alpha \quad \text{(A.39)}$$

Other relations between the trigonometric functions:

$$\sin^2\alpha + \cos^2\alpha = 1 \quad \text{(A.40)}$$

$$\sin(-\alpha) = -\sin\alpha \quad \text{(A.41)}$$

$$\cos(-\alpha) = \cos\alpha \quad \text{(A.42)}$$

$$\sin(\alpha \pm \pi/2) = \pm\cos\alpha \quad \text{(A.43)}$$

$$\sin(\alpha \pm \pi) = -\sin\alpha \quad \text{(A.44)}$$

$$\cos(\alpha \pm \pi/2) = \mp\sin\alpha \quad \text{(A.45)}$$

$$\cos(\alpha \pm \pi) = -\cos\alpha \quad \text{(A.46)}$$

Addition formulas:

$$\sin(\alpha \pm \beta) = \sin\alpha\cos\beta \pm \cos\alpha\sin\beta \tag{A.47}$$

$$\cos(\alpha \pm \beta) = \cos\alpha\cos\beta \mp \sin\alpha\sin\beta \tag{A.48}$$

Small angle approximations:

$$\sin\alpha \approx \alpha - \tfrac{1}{6}\alpha^3 + \ldots \text{ for } \alpha \ll 1 \tag{A.49}$$

$$\cos\alpha \approx 1 - \tfrac{1}{2}\alpha^2 + \ldots \text{ for } \alpha \ll 1 \tag{A.50}$$

For small angles $\alpha \ll 1$, it is often sufficient to approximate $\cos\alpha = 1$ and $\sin\alpha = \tan\alpha = \alpha$.

3.2 General Triangles

The three angles of any triangle add up to π:

$$\alpha + \beta + \gamma = \pi \tag{A.51}$$

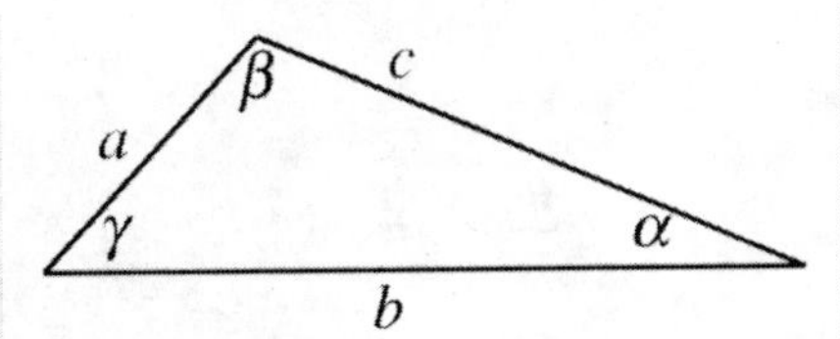

Figure A.6: Definition of the sides and angles for a general triangle.

Law of cosines:

$$c^2 = a^2 + b^2 - 2ab\cos\gamma \tag{A.52}$$

(= Generalization for Pythagoras' Theorem for the case that the angle γ has a value that it not 90 degrees, $\pi / 4$)

4. Calculus

4.1 Derivatives

Polynomials:

$$\frac{d}{dx}x^n = nx^{n-1} \tag{A.53}$$

Trigonometric functions:

$$\frac{d}{dx}\sin(ax) = a\cos(ax) \tag{A.54}$$

$$\frac{d}{dx}\cos(ax) = -a\sin(ax) \tag{A.55}$$

$$\frac{d}{dx}\tan(ax) = \frac{a}{\cos^2 ax} \tag{A.56}$$

$$\frac{d}{dx}\cot(ax) = -\frac{a}{\sin^2(ax)} \tag{A.57}$$

Exponentials and logarithms:

$$\frac{d}{dx}e^{ax} = ae^{ax} \tag{A.58}$$

$$\frac{d}{dx}\ln(ax) = \frac{1}{x} \tag{A.59}$$

$$\frac{d}{dx}a^x = a^x \ln a \tag{A.60}$$

Product rule:

$$\frac{d}{dx}(f(x)g(x)) = \left(\frac{df(x)}{dx}\right)g(x) + f(x)\left(\frac{dg(x)}{dx}\right) \tag{A.61}$$

Chain rule:

$$\frac{dy}{dx} = \frac{dy}{du}\frac{du}{dx} \tag{A.62}$$

4.2 Integrals

All indefinite integrals have an additive integration constant, c.

Polynomials:

$$\int x^n dx = \frac{1}{n+1}x^{n+1} + c \text{ for } n \neq -1 \tag{A.63}$$

$$\int x^{-1}dx = \ln x + c \tag{A.64}$$

$$\int \frac{1}{a^2 + x^2}dx = \frac{1}{a}\arctan\frac{x}{a} + c \tag{A.65}$$

$$\int \frac{1}{\sqrt{a^2 + x^2}}dx = \ln\left(x + \sqrt{a^2 + x^2}\right) + c \tag{A.66}$$

$$\int \frac{1}{\sqrt{a^2 - x^2}}dx = \arcsin\frac{x}{|a|} + c \equiv \arctan\frac{x}{\sqrt{a^2 - x^2}} + c \tag{A.67}$$

$$\int \frac{1}{\left(a^2 + x^2\right)^{3/2}}dx = \frac{1}{a^2}\frac{x}{\sqrt{a^2 + x^2}} + c \tag{A.68}$$

$$\int \frac{x}{\left(a^2 + x^2\right)^{3/2}}dx = -\frac{1}{\sqrt{a^2 + x^2}} + c \tag{A.69}$$

Trigonometric functions:

$$\int \sin(ax)dx = -\frac{1}{a}\cos(ax) + c \tag{A.70}$$

$$\int \cos(ax)dx = \frac{1}{a}\sin(ax) + c \tag{A.71}$$

Exponentials:

$$\int e^{ax}dx = \frac{1}{a}e^{ax} + c \tag{A.72}$$

Unit Conversion Factors

Length

Metric		British
1 cm	=	0.39370079 in
1 cm	=	0.0328084 ft
1 m	=	3.28084 ft
1 km	=	0.621371 mile

British		Metric
1 in	=	2.54 cm
1 ft	=	30.48 cm
1 ft	=	0.3048 m
1 mile	=	1.609344 km

Area

Metric		British
1 m^2	=	10.76391 sqft
1 km^2	=	0.386102 $mile^2$
1 km^2	=	247.10538 acre

British		Metric
1 sqft		0.092903 m^2
1 $mile^2$	=	2.589988 km^2
1 acre	=	2147.483647 m^2

Volume

Metric		British
1 cm^3	=	0.061024 in^3
1 m^3	=	35.314667 ft^3
1 liter	=	0.264172 gallon

British		Metric
1 in^3		16.387064 cm^3
1 ft^3	=	0.028317 m^3
1 gallon	=	3.785412 liter

Mass

Metric		British
1 g	=	0.035274 oz
1 kg	=	2.204623 lb
1 kg	=	0.001102 ton

British		Metric
1 oz		28.349523 g
1 lb	=	0.453592 kg
1 ton	=	907.18474 kg

Artwork and Photography Credits

The Big Picture

Figure 1: M. F. Crommie, C. P. Lutz, and D. M. Eigler, IBM Almaden Research Center Visualization Lab, http://www.almaden.ibm.com/vis/stm/images/stm15.jpg. Image reproduced by permission of IBM Research, Almaden Research Center. Unauthorized use not permitted; Figure 2: M. Feig, Michigan State University; Figure 3: STAR collaboration, Brookhaven National Laboratory; Figure 4: CERN; Figure 5: Kim Steele/Getty Images; Figure 6: Andrew Fruchter (STScI) et al., WFPC2, HST, NASA

Chapter 1

Figure 1.1: PhotoLink/Getty Images; Figure 1.2: Source: National Institute of Standards and Technology; Figure 1.3: Courtesy NASA/JPL-Caltech; Figure 1.4: Source: National Institute of Standards and Technology

Chapter 2

Figure 2.8: Ryan McVay/Getty Images; Figure 2.15: NHRA

Chapter 3

Figure 3.10: Rim Light/PhotoLink/Getty Images; Figure 3.18: Edmond Van Hoorick/Getty Images

Chapter 4

Figure 4.10/11: Ryan McVay/Getty Image; Figure 4.28: PhotoLink/Getty Images; Figure 4.29: Used with permission by D. J. Spaanderman, precision engineer. FOM Institute for Atomic and Molecular Physics, Kruislaan 407, 1098 SJ Amsterdam, the Netherlands

Chapter 5

Figure 5.1: Malcolm Fife/Getty Images; Figure 5.3: left: Royalty-Free/CORBIS, right: Geostock/Getty Images

Chapter 7

Figure 7.1: Sandia National Laboratories/Getty Images; Self-test opportunity: Photron; Figure 7.15: DØ collaboration and Fermi National Accelerator Laboratory, education office.

Chapter 8

Figure 8.16: NASA/Getty Images

Chapter 9

Figure 9.1: Royalty-Free/CORBIS; Figure 9.5&9.6: B. Bi, Michigan State University; Figure 9.12: Royalty-Free/CORBIS

Chapter 10

Figure 10.1: Left: StockTrek/Getty Images; Right: Gemini Observatory-GMOS Team; Figure 10.23: left: Don Farrall/Getty Images, right: Jules Frazier/Getty Images; Figure 10.24: Computer calculations by Tobias Bollenbach, MSU graduate student.

Chapter 11

Figure 11.12: University of Washington Libraries, Special Collections, UW 21422.

Chapter 12

Figure 12.1: NASA/Johnson Space Center; Figure 12.6: D. Crisp and WFPC2 Team/JPL/Caltech, HST, STSI, NASA; Figure 12.14: U.S. Geological Survey; Figure 12.26: Vera Rubin.

Chapter 13

Figure 13.2: Corbis Royalty Free; Figure 13.4: Left: PhotoLink/Getty Images; right: Don Farrall/Getty Images; Figure 13.12: Royalty-Free/CORBIS; Figure 13.16: Royalty-Free/CORBIS; Figure 13.21: PhotoLink/Getty Images; Figure 13.24: center: Don Farrall/Getty Image; Figure 13.33: C Squared Studios/Getty Images; Figure 13.39: Siede Preis/Getty Images; Figure 13.40: Royalty-Free/CORBIS; Figure 13.41: Kim Steele/Getty Images; Figure 13.42: The Astrophysical Journal, Fryer & Warren 2002 (ApJ, 574, L65). Reproduced by permission of the AAS.

Chapter 14

Figure 14.1: C Squared Studios/Getty Images.

Chapter 15

Figure 15.1: Don Farrall/Getty Images; Figure 15.8: left: (c) Brand X Pictures/PunchStock, right: Cornell Nanofabrication Facility; Self-test opportunity: Cornell Nanofabrication Facility; Figure 15.20: M. F. Crommie, C. P. Lutz, and D. M. Eigler, IBM Almaden Research Center Visualization Lab, http://www.almaden.ibm.com/vis/stm/images/stm15.jpg. Image reproduced by permission of IBM Research, Almaden Research Center. Unauthorized use not permitted; Figure 15.21: LIGO Laboratory.

Chapter 16

Figure 16.2: Royalty-Free/CORBIS; Figure 16.4: R. Morley/PhotoLink/Getty Images.